Rational Expectations
and Econometric Practice

Rational Expectations

and Econometric Practice

Edited by
Robert E. Lucas, Jr.
University of Chicago
and
Thomas J. Sargent
*University of Minnesota
and Federal Reserve Bank
of Minneapolis*

The University of Minnesota Press
Minneapolis

Published by the University of Minnesota Press,
2037 University Avenue Southeast, Minneapolis MN 55414
Printed in the United States of America

Library of Congress Cataloging in Publication Data

Main entry under title:
Rational expectations and econometric practice.
Bibliography: p.
   1. Econometrics—Addresses, essays, lectures.
2. Time-series analysis—Addresses, essays, lectures.
3. Monetary policy—Mathematical models—Addresses,
essays, lectures.   4. Economic policy—Mathematical
models—Addresses, essays, lectures.   I. Lucas,
Robert E.   II. Sargent, Thomas J.
HB139.R37   330′.028   80-24602
ISBN 0-8166-0916-0
ISBN 0-8166-0917-9 v. I (pbk.)
ISBN 0-8166-1071-1 v. II (pbk.)
ISBN 0-8166-1098-3 Set (pbk.)

To our parents

Contents

6. Macroeconomic Control Problems

Introduction

I

After a remarkably quiet first decade John Muth's idea of "rational expectations" has taken hold, or taken off, in an equally remarkable way. The term now enjoys popularity as a slogan or incantation with a variety of uses. It may also suffer some notoriety due to presumed links with conservative political views or with excessive concern over the consequences of money supply changes. The term "rational expectations" carries, it seems, a *charge* of some magnitude.

In our view, this charge is not incidental or uninteresting: Muth's hypothesis *is* a contribution of the most fundamental kind, an idea that compels rethinking on many dimensions, with consequent enthusiasm and resistance. One of the purposes of this volume is to collect in a convenient place some of the papers which conveyed this fact most forcefully to economists concerned with the connections between observed behavior and the evaluation of economic policies.

Yet how, exactly, does the economist who is persuaded of the usefulness of this idea, or is at least interested enough to give it an honest test, alter the way he practices his trade? A full answer to this question is, we believe, a central issue on the current research agenda of time-series econometrics and dynamic economic theory. We do not presume to answer it in this volume. At the same time, progress on this question has been rapid in recent years, scattered in articles in many journals and conference volumes. In the main, these articles are motivated by a variety of specific substantive concerns, but they also contain many operational ideas and methods of much wider applicability. The function, we hope, of the present collection will be to increase the accessibility to these ideas and to display their methodological contributions as clearly as possible.

The papers in this collection deal with various aspects of the general problem of drawing inferences about behavior from observed economic time series: we observe an agent, or collection of agents, behaving through time; we wish to use these observations to infer how this behavior *would have* differed had the agent's environment been altered in some specified

We would like to thank John Taylor, Gregory Chow, Finn Kydland, Edward Prescott, and Christopher Sims for thoughtful comments on earlier versions of this introduction.

way. Stated so generally, it is clear that some inferences of this type will be impossible to draw. (How would one's life have been different had one married someone else?) The belief in the possibility of a nonexperimental empirical economics is, however, equivalent to the belief that inferences of this kind *can* be made, under *some* circumstances.

The dimensions of this generally stated problem can be clarified by reference to an example, which we will use as a device for clarifying the relationships among the various papers. Consider a single decision maker, whose situation or state at time t is completely described by two variables x_t and z_t. Here $z_t \epsilon S_1$ is thought of as selected by "nature," and evolves through time according to

$$z_{t+1} = f(z_t, \epsilon_t), \tag{1}$$

where the "innovations" $\epsilon_t \epsilon \mathcal{E}$ are independent drawings from a fixed cumulative probability distribution function $\Phi(\cdot): \mathcal{E} \to [0, 1]$. (At the formal level at which this discussion will be conducted, the set S_1 can be conceived very generally; for example, one may think of z_t as the entire history of a process from $-\infty$ through t.) We will refer to the function $f: S_1 x \mathcal{E} \to S_1$ as the decision maker's environment.

Think of $x_t \epsilon S_2$ as a state variable under partial control of the decision maker. Each period, he selects an action $u_t \epsilon U$. There is a fixed technology $g: S_1 x S_2 x U \to S_2$ describing the motion of x_t given actions u_t by the agent and actions z_t by "nature":

$$x_{t+1} = g(z_t, x_t, u_t). \tag{2}$$

The agent is viewed as purposively selecting his action u_t as some fixed function $h: S_1 x S_2 \to U$ of his situation:

$$u_t = h(z_t, x_t). \tag{3}$$

As econometricians, we observe some or all of the process $\{z_t, x_t, u_t\}$, the motion of which is given by (1), (2), and (3). With the model suitably specialized, the estimation of the functions f, g, and h from such observations is a well-posed statistical problem, and given long enough time series we can speak of observing f, g, and h. Under what circumstances, then, do these observations amount to an answer to our original question: how would the agent's behavior have differed had his environment been different in some particular way?

To answer this, we need to be somewhat more specific about what we mean by a "change in the environment." One form of change, or intervention, one can imagine is the alteration of one, or a "few," realizations of the shocks ϵ_t which enter into (1). If carried out in such a way as not to lead the agent to perceive that either f or Φ has changed, it is reasonable to suppose that such an intervention would not induce any change in the decision rule h and hence that knowledge of f, g, and h amounts to having the ability accurately to evaluate the consequences of the intervention.

In typical economic applications, however, and certainly in macroeconomic applications, the policy interventions we are interested in are not one-time interventions but rather systematic changes in the way policy variables react to the situation: changes in the function f. Thus a change from balanced-budget peacetime fiscal policy to Keynesian countercyclical policy affects not just one year's deficit, but *how* fiscal policy is formulated, year in and year out. In general, one would imagine that nontrivial changes in f, of this or other sorts, would involve nontrivial changes in agents' decision rules h. If so, the ability to evaluate the consequences of changes in the environment requires knowledge of some function T relating decision rules to environments: $h = T(f)$. If time-series observations arise under a given environment f_0, say, then we estimate only $h_0 = T(f_0)$. This estimate, no matter how accurate, tells us *nothing* about the way $T(f)$ varies with f.

Experimentally, one can think of varying f and tracing out the observed responses in behavior, $h = T(f)$. This is the form, for example, of the classical Skinnerian animal experiments, and of much successful empirical research in psychology and education. Occasionally, economic experience (e.g., international comparisons) provides "natural" experimental information on $T(f)$ for many different environments f, but such good fortune cannot be relied on in general.

A nonexperimental solution to this problem requires a more detailed theoretical analysis of the decision problem underlying the agent's choice of a decision rule h, typically based on the hypothesis that he is solving some well-posed maximum problem. Thus let $V: S_1 x S_2 x U \to R$ be a current period return function and take the agent's objective to be to select the decision rule h so as to maximize

$$E_0 \left\{ \sum_{t=0}^{\infty} \beta^t V(z_t, x_t, u_t) \right\}, \qquad 0 < \beta < 1, \tag{4}$$

given (z_0, x_0) and given f and g, where the mathematical expectation $E_0\{\cdot\}$ is taken with respect to the distribution of $z_1, z_2, \ldots$, conditional on (x_0, z_0). Provided this maximum problem is theoretically soluble, knowledge of the return function V enables one to infer the decision rule h for a given technology g and environment f, or, in other words, to calculate $h = T(f)$ theoretically. In an empirical context, the issue is whether, or under which conditions, one can infer a return function V from observations on f, g, and h. If so, we can then construct a robot decision maker (4), or model, confront it theoretically with various environments f, and trace out its responses $T(f)$.[1]

---

[1] In general, the decision function h is a functional of the functions f, g, and V, so that maybe we should write $h = T(f, g, V)$. At this point, we suppress the explicit dependence of h on g and V, although it should be understood. Below, we shall find it useful to make this dependence explicit.

On a little reflection, it is difficult to feel any general optimism as to the solubility of this problem, or as to our ability to reconstruct V from knowledge of f, g, and h. One would need to know a great deal about pigeons in order to construct a robot which would serve as a good imitator of an actual pigeon in Skinner's tests. As time-series econometricians, we are in the position of attempting to do exactly this, using observations only on pigeons in their natural environment. If any success is to be possible, it will clearly involve some boldness in the use of economic theory.

Evidently no progress can be made on this difficult problem at the level of generality at which this discussion has so far been set. It will be necessary to restrict the sets S_1, S_2, and U and the functions V, f, Φ, and g in order to bring available mathematical and computational technology to bear on the various aspects of this general problem. In practice, some success has been achieved with two quite different strategies. One strategy is to impose severe restrictions on the dimensionality of S_1, S_2, and U, and seek qualitative information on $h = T(f)$. In this collection, Chapter 6 is an example of this approach; many others exist in the literature. A second strategy, followed in the remaining contributions to this volume, is so to restrict V, f, g, and Φ that the function h is *linear*. A primary advantage of this second strategy is that it permits wide latitude as to the dimensions of S_1, S_2, and U. A second is that it permits one to exploit the property which Simon (1956) and Theil (1964) termed "certainty equivalence."

With the return function V restricted to be quadratic in a particular way, and g restricted to be linear, Simon and Theil found that the optimal decision $u_t = h(z_t, x_t)$ can be expressed in composite form, in the following, very useful, way. Let $\tilde{z}_t = (z_t, {}_{t+1}z_t^e, {}_{t+2}z_t^e, \ldots)\epsilon S_1^\infty = S_1 x S_1 x S_1 x \ldots$ be an optimal (in the least-mean-squared error sense) sequence of point forecasts of all current and future states z. Here ${}_{t+j}z_t^e$ denotes the optimal point forecast of z_{t+j} formed using information available at time t. The optimal forecast $\tilde{z}_t$ can be expressed as a function, in general a nonlinear one, $h_2: S_1 \to S_1^\infty$ of the current state z_t (which may, as remarked earlier, consist of the entire history of the system):

$$\tilde{z}_t = h_2(z_t). \tag{5}$$

The function h_2 itself in general depends in a complicated way on the functions f and Φ.

Next, given a quadratic V and linear g, the optimal decision u_t can be expressed as a linear function $h_1: S_1^\infty x S_2 \to U$ of $\tilde{z}_t$ and x_t:

$$u_t = h_1(\tilde{z}_t, x_t). \tag{6}$$

In other words, h can be written as the composite function

$$h(z_t, x_t) = h_1[h_2(z_t), x_t]. \tag{7}$$

The convenience of these consequences of certainty equivalence (and not, of course, a convenience that will obtain in general) is that they permit a very clear separation of the dependence of the decision rule h on tastes V and technology g from the dependence of h on the environment f. In particular, the function h_1 will depend *only* on V and g, while the function h_2 depends *only* on the environment through f and Φ. Since it is consequences of changes in f which concern us, this simplification is important. In particular, one can relate optimal functions h_2 to f, as, say, $h_2 = S(f)$ on the basis of forecasting considerations only. The forecasting problem of determining h_2 as a function of f and Φ can be simplified considerably by restricting f to be linear, which implies that h_2 is also linear. Alternatively, one can permit f to be nonlinear, but restrict h to belong to the class of decision rules that are linear in z_t and x_t. Either of these devices implies computing h_2 as a linear least-squares predictor, which is immensely easier to compute than are nonlinear predictors in most contexts. Once $h_2 = S(f)$ has been computed, the relationship $h = T(f)$ of original interest can be obtained directly from (7).

A second convenience of certainty equivalence is that it permits the theoretical derivation of the decision rule h_1 from tastes V and technology g under the hypothesis that the decision maker knows the future z_t with certainty (this, of course, is the origin of the term "certainty equivalence") even if his environment is in fact stochastic. To study the relationship of V and g to h_1, then, one can study a much simpler problem than the one originally posed.

While it was this feature of the approximate linear formulation which first caught the attention of Simon and Theil, the separation of the maximum problem facing an agent into two parts, an "optimization" part and a "forecasting" part, which it permitted was rather badly misinterpreted by much of the profession. Implicitly, many economists took the postulate, standard to economic theory, that agents act in their own interests as a stimulus to the careful theoretical derivation of h_1 from hypotheses about V and g. Many good examples of such derivations of h appeared in the 1960s, especially in the study of investment theory. The same type of economic reasoning, namely, the appeal to agents' pursuit of self interest, should also have led researchers to derive specifications for h_2 by using the mapping $h_2 = S(f)$ that describes how h_2 optimally varies with changes in the environment f. Inexplicably, on logical grounds, for a long time this step was not taken. Instead, in typical econometric applications a particular function h_2 was directly postulated, with a set of free parameters designed to characterize expectations formation directly. The "adaptive expectations" formulation of Friedman (1956) and Cagan (1956) is one of several such formulations that were motivated by plausibility and perhaps tractability. The idea was that the free parameters of h_2 would be estimated directly, and without any reference to the nature of the function f, by estimating the decision rule $u_t = h_1[h_2(z_t), x_t]$ econometrically.

What is "wrong" with simply postulating a particular h_2 is *not* that an h_2 so postulated expresses forecasts of future variables as distributed lags of current and lagged variables. The future must be forecast on the basis of the past, and it is surely acceptable to simplify things by modeling agents as using linear forecasting rules. (These points are obvious enough, but are so widely misunderstood as to warrant emphasis here.) The difficulty lies not in postulating forecasts which are linear functions of history but rather in introducing the coefficients in these linear functions as so many additional "free parameters," unrestricted by theory. That this practice is unnecessary, and in an important way fatal to the purposes of the empirical study of economic time series, is the message of Muth's classic paper, Chapter 1.

The terminology "rational expectations" has not so far been used in this introduction, but the idea has been applied. Perhaps we should review the above, and point out where and why. In postulating the objective function (4) for our exemplary decision maker we used the expectation operator $E\{\cdot\}$, adding that it is "taken with respect to *the* distribution of $z_1, z_2, \ldots$" (italics added). From the point of view of normative decision theory, "*the* distribution of $z_1, z_2, \ldots$" means just whatever distribution (i.e., environment f) the decision maker *thinks* is appropriate. From the point of view of an outside observer who wishes to predict the agent's responses to changes in f, or to calculate $T(f)$, we are using "f" to denote the *actual* environment, as observed in the data and as altered by the hypothetical policy changes we wish to assess. If the decision problem (4) is to be helpful in calculating $T(f)$, then it is essential to view the subjective z-distribution f used by decision makers and the actual distribution f assumed to generate our data as being, if not identical, as least theoretically linked in an explicit way. The hypothesis of rational expectations amounts to equating the subjective z-distribution to the objective distribution f.

II

The papers collected herein treat various specific aspects of this general issue of constructing $T(f)$, or of extrapolating from observed behavior in actual, past environments to the prediction of behavior in environments which are without exact precedent. At the risk of some arbitrariness, we have grouped them into sections. Section 1 contains an introduction to the subject, with emphasis on time-series implications. Section 2 contains papers on macroeconomic policy, early demonstrations of the importance of the treatment of expectations in drawing policy inferences from econometric models. Some general methods for utilizing the restrictions implied by rationality are presented in Section 3. Sections 4 and 5 are continuations, Section 4 containing a variety of applications, while Section 5 contains papers using rational expectations to model and test for "neutrality." Section 6 illustrates some approaches to problems of optimal control in models with rational expectations.

Muth's Chapter 1 needs no introduction, except perhaps a reminder that it is one of the most carefully and compactly written papers of recent vintage: every sentence in the introduction counts, and many have since been expanded into entire articles. Muth introduces the hypothesis at a general, verbal level, motivating it as a corollary of the general principles of economic equilibrium, and then turns to specific, certainty-equivalent examples. The latter illustrate the explicit construction of $h_2 = S(f)$, in our notation, and hence of $h = T(f)$.

In several interesting contexts, Muth's Chapter 2 characterizes the mapping $\tilde{z}_t = h_2(z_t)$, using the hypothesis of rational expectations and the theory of linear least-squares prediction to show how h_2 depends on the functions f and Φ. Muth was partly motivated by a desire to discover *economic* arguments which could be used to rationalize the "adaptive expectations" mechanism advanced by Milton Friedman (1956) and Phillip Cagan (1956). As formulated by Friedman and Cagan, the adaptive expectations hypothesis was

$$\theta_t^e - \theta_{t-1}^e = \lambda(\theta_t - \theta_{t-1}^e), \qquad 0 < \lambda < 1$$

or

$$\theta_t^e = \lambda \sum_{i=0}^{\infty} (1 - \lambda)^i \theta_{t-i}, \tag{8}$$

where θ_t is the actual value of a variable of interest to an agent, and θ_t^e is the agent's expectation (about future values?) of that variable.

In effect, Muth works backwards from the particular specification of h_2 given in (8) to restrictions on the f and Φ actually describing θ_t that are needed to reconcile the adaptive expectations mechanism with the hypothesis that agents are optimally forecasting θ in light of f and Φ. One feature of this procedure was that Muth was forced to be much more explicit about the nature of θ_t^e than either Friedman or Cagan was: Muth had to specify precisely the *horizon* over which θ_t^e is supposed to apply (in our notation, whether it corresponds to $_{t+j}z_t^e$ for some particular $j \geq 1$ or an average of $_{t+j}z_t^e$ for several j's ≥ 1, or something else). Notice how one outcome of Muth's calculations was to characterize the way the function h_2 depends on the function f. In effect, Muth found a set of cross-equation restrictions which could be expressed in terms of our notation

$$\tilde{z}_t = h_2(z_t) = S(f)(z_t). \tag{9}$$

Equation (9) displays one hallmark of using rational expectations models to think about economic time series: they usually give rise to restrictions *across* distributed lags in different equations, rather than to any simply stated conditions on the distributed lag in a *single* equation. The note by Sargent (Chap. 3) is an application of this general point to criticizing a restriction on lag distributions that has often been used to identify the effects of expectations in particular equations. This common restriction is that $\Sigma_{j=0}^{\infty} h_{2j} = 1$ in "generalized adaptive expectations" equations of the form

$$\theta_t^e = \sum_{j=0}^{\infty} h_{2j} \theta_{t-j}.$$

(Notice that the condition $\Sigma_{j=0}^{\infty} h_{2j} = 1$ is imposed in [8].) This restriction is still commonly used to identify important parameters, and is justified by mistaken arguments purporting to establish that $\Sigma h_{2j} = 1$ is an implication of rationality.

Lucas's paper, Chapter 4, written in October 1965 but unpublished until now, studies how the functions V and g influence the function $h_1(\tilde{z}_t, x_t)$ in the context of a firm planning its investment under certainty. Lucas studies how variations in the form of gestation lags and depreciation hypotheses influence the form of "optimal" distributed lags of u_t on x_t. Lucas restricts the analysis to situations in which the firm faces extremely simple forcing functions, in particular z-sequences (really, z-functions, since he assumes continuous time) that are known with certainty to be constant over time. As a consequence, Lucas fully analyzes only the dependence of the function h_1 on x_t. However, in the linear quadratic context of Lucas's analysis, there is a sort of symmetry between the "feedback part" of h_1 (the dependence on x_t) and the "feedforward part" (the dependence on $\tilde{z}_t$). It turns out that the feedforward part can be computed from what Lucas reports. Further, by appealing to certainty equivalence and using linear prediction theory in continuous time, it is possible to use Lucas's results to compute $h(z_t, x_t)$ itself. This involves using continuous-time versions of the formulas reported by Hansen and Sargent, Chapters 7 and 8.

Lucas's analysis is done in continuous time, so that he has to make approximations to convert to the discrete-time formulations resembling those used in empirical work. This step of Lucas's paper should be redone in light of what we have since learned about moving from continuous-time to discrete-time models (see Sims 1971 and Phillips 1973). There is a need to study aggregation over time in the context of rational expectations models, in particular the question of whether the rational expectations cross-equation restrictions can substitute for the exclusion restrictions of Phillips as a device for identifying continuous-time models (i.e., continuous-time analogues of V, f, and g) from discrete data.

Lucas, in Chapter 4, takes prices as given to the firm, even though in the aggregate the investment plans of firms will influence the market price. In another previously unpublished paper, Lucas (Chap. 5) indicates how this influence can be taken into account, in the context of a model where each firm behaves competitively. Lucas's Chapter 5 is again in continuous time and under certainty. Lucas and Prescott, in Chapter 6, extend the analysis to the case in which there is uncertainty due to a randomly shifting demand schedule.

Lucas and Prescott's study of investment behavior essentially parallels Muth's examples, but in a context in which certainty equivalence cannot be invoked, so that other methods are needed to trace out T theoretically. Their treatment emphasizes the intimate connection between the idea of rational expectations and the modern "Arrow-Debreu" definition of competitive equilibrium for situations in which all agents possess common, up-to-date information. Hansen and Sargent analyze the mapping T more fully, sometimes utilizing the connection between equilibrium and optimality as do Lucas and Prescott, but in a linear-quadratic setting. In this context, the restrictions implied by equilibrium behavior (expectations rationality included) can be obtained in an econometrically useable (as opposed to purely qualitative) way for lag structures much more complex from those treated by Muth. All papers in this section, then, deal in various contexts with the theoretical problem: given V, g, and f (or given h_1 and f), how can $h = T(f)$ (or $h_2 = S[f]$) be constructed?

The papers in Section 2 illustrate, in various ways, why we *care* about this question for purposes of applied economics. All are focused on a common substantive question: the effects on real output and employment of changes in monetary policy. Robert Barro, Chapter 12, develops a labor (and goods) supply theory based on the idea that money supply movements induce output movements in the same direction due to suppliers' inability to distinguish between relative demand shifts and money-induced shifts. In this model expectations are rational, but agents have different, incomplete information sets. This model illustrates the importance of a distinction between *anticipated* inflations (or deflations) which have no real output effects, and "surprise" inflations, which do.

The two papers by Thomas Sargent and Neil Wallace (Chaps. 10 and 11) and the paper by Sargent (Chap. 9) combined the goods supply hypothesis used in Chapter 12 with a then-conventional IS-LM description of aggregate demand determination. In this setting, they contrast the evaluations of alternative monetary policies under the assumption that forecast rules h_2 are invariant with respect to policy changes to the evaluations under the alternative assumption that $h_2 = S(f)$, with S implied by expectations rationality. They show that the *same* model which implies the ability to fine-tune the economy by means of monetary policy under one expectations hypothesis (h_2 fixed) implies *no* ability whatever to improve real performance when $h_2 = S(f)$ is rationally formed.

The striking examples in Chapters 10–12 rest *jointly* on their treatment of expectations and their assumption that employment and wage rates are competitively determined. Stanley Fischer, Chapter 13, reworks the Sargent-Wallace examples, retaining expectations rationality but replacing the second of these assumptions with the hypothesis that nominal wages are prevented, in part, from responding to demand changes by previous contractual arrangements. This variation, perhaps implicitly viewed as a variation in the assumed technology g, alters the calculation of $h = T(f)$ in such a way as to permit output-improving monetary policy. Of course, Fischer's argument is not a defense of the view that h is invariant to f changes. In Chapter 14 Bennett McCallum shows that Sargent and Wallace's "extreme" conclusion still holds under certain forms of "price stickiness." His Chapter 15 provides an up-to-date summary of where the substantive question of monetary policy's effectiveness now stands.

The substantive issue treated by all of these papers is, obviously, very much an open question. Yet it is instructive to review the change in the terms of the discussion between the first Sargent-Wallace paper (Chap. 11, 1975) and McCallum's recent assessment (Chap. 15, 1979). Sargent and Wallace used a conventional Keynesian structure to demonstrate the serious unreliability of policy evaluations it is capable of producing: logically it, together with Chapter 10, served as a counter-example to some then widely accepted propositions on the effects of monetary policy. By 1979, it was clear that any emerging rationale in favor of activist monetary policy will bear little resemblance to that originally criticized in Chapters 10 and 11.

The papers in Section 3 deal with some general econometric implications of rational expectations models. Each of the papers takes as a point of departure the observation that the style of econometric identification in rational expectations models is characterized by heavy emphasis on cross-equation restrictions, with a deemphasis of the exclusion restrictions that are the mainstay of Cowles Commission methods. Lucas and Sargent (Chap. 16) criticize dynamic econometric models which are identified mainly through imposition of exclusion restrictions as being inconsistent with the body of dynamic economic theory summarized above. They suggest that existing econometric models can be improved by building dynamic models that are motivated by reference to dynamic economic theory, and which impose the cross-equation restrictions characteristic of that theory. Muth (Chap. 17), Wallis (Chap. 18), and Chow (Chap. 19) describe econometric methods for estimating models of this type. Muth's paper, written in July 1960 but not published until now, points the way to literally all of the estimation techniques for rational expectations models that subsequent researchers have used or proposed. He points out that, provided suitable care is taken, rational expectations models can be estimated by replacing agents' expectations about random variables with the actual values of those variables, and then using an estimator appropriate for a situation where there are errors in variables. He suggests both full information and limited information methods. Although his treatment is restricted to a simple static context, his remarks in section III of his paper indicate how the estimators he suggests might be applied in dynamic situations, provided that the assumption (necessary for his method) of no serial correlation on the disturbances is met. Finally, attention should be directed to Muth's suggestion (sec. III of his paper) for handling advance information with dummy variables, a procedure applied with some success by Stanley Black (1972).

The paper by Wallis in effect develops many of Muth's suggestions in more detail and in the context of richer dynamic models. Wallis sets out several systems of stochastic difference equations in which there appear expectations of random variables, variously dated. How might those equations be interpreted in light of the dynamic economic theory sketched above? Some of these equations might be interpreted as versions of our equations (6), $u_t = h_1(\tilde{z}_t, x_t)$ or (2), $x_{t+1} = g(z_t, x_t, u_t)$. Those equations involving expectations of future values of endogenous variables should probably be viewed as versions of the system of stochastic Euler equations in x_t that are among the first-order necessary conditions for sufficiently smooth versions of our optimum problems.[2] Since the equations studied by Wallis are linear, if they are to have exactly these interpretations, rather than being interpreted merely as linear approximations to appropriate Euler equations or h_1 or g functions, they must correspond to optimum problems with quadratic V and linear g functions. In papers reproduced in Section 2 of this volume, Hansen and Sargent (Chaps. 7, 8) characterize restrictions that linear stochastic difference equations should satisfy if they are to be Euler equations for linear quadratic optimum problems. In any event, both in Wallis (Chap. 18) and the applied papers in the next section by Hall (Chap. 26), Sargent and Wallace (Chap. 22), and Sargent (Chap. 23), the econometric model is parameterized at the level of what can at best be interpreted as approximations to stochastic Euler equations or else h or g functions.

The paper by Chow (Chap. 19) describes in a general way how a researcher can go about estimating a model specified at the level of the functions V, f, and g that, in our notation, characterize preferences and constraints. Chow considers the case in which V is quadratic and f, g, and h are linear, and describes how the recursive techniques of dynamic programming can in practice be used to evaluate the likelihood function. Chow's procedure is usefully to be compared to the mixture of recursive and classical procedures recommended by Hansen and Sargent (Chap. 8) for a similar class of problems. Which method is computationally superior may depend on particular features of the problem at hand. In common with many other papers in this volume, Chow emphasizes the feature that

---

[2] For descriptions of stochastic Euler equations, see Sargent (1979). For particular versions, see the papers (Chapters) by Sargent (25) Hansen and Sargent (7, 8) and Hall (26).

the maximization of the likelihood function or "fit" of the model is to occur over the free parameters of $V, f,$ and g; the parameters of the decision rule h are not themselves among the free parameters of the model.

Notice that Muth and Wallis require that the stochastic errors in their equations be serially uncorrelated, and that this assumption is important in delivering the good statistical properties that they claim for estimators they propose. What reason can be advanced for supposing the errors in the equation are serially uncorrelated? The answer to this question must depend on how the researcher intends to interpret these stochastic error processes. Several possible interpretations of these error processes are possible if one views the stochastic difference equations, as written down by Wallis and others, as being Euler equations corresponding to optimum problems of the class described in our introduction. Two of these interpretations are explored by Hansen and Sargent (Chap. 7). The decision theory summarized above virtually forces the econometrician to think of the error term along lines like those developed by Hansen and Sargent (Chap. 7), since the theory predicts that both the Euler equation and the solution $x_{t+1} = g[z_t, x_t, h(z_t, x_t)]$ are *exact* functions of the agent's information set that contains no random "errors." Errors in the estimated equations crop up perhaps because the econometrician has less information than the agent, in some sense, or else because the model is misspecified in some way. Hansen and Sargent investigate only the former possibility for interpreting the errors. The model misspecification route seems less likely to deliver error terms with the good statistical properties—namely, certain orthogonality properties—delivered by the Hansen-Sargent interpretation. In any event, developments along either of these lines do not seem to provide any presumption that the errors in the difference equations associated with rational expectations models can safely be assumed to be serially uncorrelated. Taking this into account involves modifying some of the procedures of Muth and Wallis. Some of these modifications are indicated in Chapter 7 by Hansen and Sargent.

Section 4 contains examples that in several diverse contexts use the hypothesis of rational expectations to interpret economic time series.

The paper by Christopher Sims (Chap. 21) never mentions the hypothesis of rational expectations, yet it and the important paper by C. W. J. Granger (Chap. 20) have helped to shape the thoughts of other researchers who use the rational expectations hypothesis in interpreting economic time series. The concept of "causality" that Granger describes is useful in two contexts associated with rational expectations modeling. First, in any particular application of the decision theory summarized by equations (1)–(6), the researcher has to specify a concrete z_t and S_1. Recall that the agent is assumed to maximize

$$E_0 \sum_{t=0}^{\infty} \beta^t V(z_t, x_t, u_t), \qquad 0 < \beta < 1 \qquad (4)$$

subject to (z_0, x_0) given and the laws of motion

$$z_{t+1} = f(z_t, \epsilon_t) \tag{1}$$

$$x_{t+1} = g(z_t, x_t, u_t). \tag{2}$$

In most economic applications, many of the components of z_t that appear in f are excluded from the functions g and V. The reason for this is as follows. In particular applications of this framework, the analyst would first "make up" functions V and g, together with a list of the arguments that appear in them. The return function V and the technology g will contain a list of z variables, say, z_{1t}. For example, in modeling a price-taking firm's decisions, z_{1t} might include factor rentals, output prices, and random disturbances to productivity. So z_{1t} is the list of uncontrollable state variables that the decision maker cares directly about because they enter V or g. Given z_{1t}, the analyst must specify the function f and its arguments. In general, to form z_t, z_{1t} should be augmented by a list of additional variables z_{2t} which interact dynamically with z_{1t}. Any variables z_{2t} that the decision maker observes and that dynamically interact with the z_{1t} variables that he directly cares about belong in the function f. They belong there in the sense that if the decision maker ignores them, he will attain a lower value of the objective function (4).

In particular applications, specifying the instantaneous return function V, the technology g, and their arguments is usually the result of a straight-forward, if arbitrary, process involving thinking about the economics of the phenomenon to be studied. But *economic* reasoning typically provides no precise a priori guidance on how z_{1t} ought to be augmented with z_{2t} to form the z_t that appears in f, and that is in effect used to forecast future z_{1t}'s. For recall that the function f is taken as given in this setup and is not itself the outcome of the economic analysis. But economic considerations do establish a presumption that agents will augment z_{1t} with any z_{2t}'s that they see and that marginally help predict future z_{1t}'s, given that current and past z_{1t}'s have been taken into account. This is equivalent with saying that any variables z_{2t} that *cause* z_{1t}, in Granger's sense, belong in z_t. It follows that any variables z_{2t} that Granger-cause z_{1t} and that appear in the agent's information set z_t will appear in the optimal decision function

$$u_t = h(z_t, x_t). \tag{3}$$

All of these remarks hold under Granger's general definition of causality, and also under the specialization of that definition to linear least-squares prediction theory that occupies most of his attention and all of Sims's. The specialization of Granger's general definition to the linear setup blends well with the applications in this volume which are mostly concerned with studying optimal linear decision rules. Granger causality as a construct influencing the modeler's choice of which variables belong in the agents' decision rules plays an important role in the papers of Sargent and Wallace (Chap. 22) and Sargent (Chaps. 23, 25), and is emphasized in the paper by Hansen and Sargent (Chap. 7) in Section 1. Econometric procedures similar to those described by Granger and Sims can be used to help determine the appropriate choice of z_t, or at least to check the appropriateness of given choices about z_t.

A second reason that the concept of Granger causality naturally interests students of rational expectations models is its link to the theory of martingales. There is a variety of examples of statistical models arrived at by writing down arbitrage conditions or Euler equations, models often motivated by appeals to "efficient markets." One example is the martingale model for the log of stock prices. This statistical model has the implication that *no* variables Granger-cause the first difference of the log of a stock price, an implication which can be tested using procedures described by Granger and Sims. In this volume, the paper by Hall (Chap. 26) uses such a procedure to test a statistical model derived from the Euler equations for a household's intertemporal maximization problem.

In Chapter 22, Sargent and Wallace reexamine some of the hyperinflations studied by Cagan (1956) to determine the directions of Granger causality between inflation and money creation. They find stronger evidence of Granger causality extending from inflation to money creation than in the reverse direction, a finding that at first glance would surprise someone committed to a monetary explanation of the hyperinflations. Sargent and Wallace go on to try to construct an explanation for this pattern of Granger causality by constructing a stochastic model of money creation and inflation in which Cagan's adaptive expectations model turns out to be consistent with rational expectations. The relationship of this research strategy to that used by Muth (Chap. 2) is evident. The paper by Sargent further pursues this strategy and discusses identification and estimation of the demand for money function in the context of that bivariate model of money creation and inflation that implies that Cagan's adaptive expectations model is rational.[3]

The Sargent paper on hyperinflation (Chap. 23) illustrates in a very simple context how estimation might proceed under the cross-equation restrictions on systems of stochastic difference equations that are imposed by rational expectations. The Sargent papers on the term structure of interest rates (Chap. 24) and on the demand for labor (25) are attempts to estimate models where the cross-equation restrictions are substantially

---

[3]In further work, Salemi and Sargent (1980) have studied models that relax the assumption that Cagan's adaptive expectation formulation is rational. Also for the German hyperinflation Salemi (1976) has studied the block Granger-causality structure among sets of variables including money creation, inflation, spot foreign exchange rates, and forward exchange rates, and has obtained interesting results that are usefully compared to those obtained by Frenkel (1977).

more complicated. All of these papers illustrate again how a characterizing feature of rational expectations models is their restrictions across lag distributions in different equations, that is, across the functions h and f.

Of all the applied papers in this volume, the one by Sargent on the demand for labor (Chap. 25) is the only one with a structure that fully matches the decision theory sketched above. That is, Sargent explicitly sets out particular versions of the functions f, Φ, V, and g, and then computes h as the solution of the agent's optimal control problem. The econometric model is specified and estimated in terms of the parameters of the functions f, V, and g; the parameters of h are not free.

Each of the remaining papers falls short of specifying parameters at the level of the functions f, V, and g. The papers (Chapters) of Sargent and Wallace (22), Sargent (23 and 24), and Hall (26) each specify their statistical model at the level of what might be interpreted as "Euler equations" or h's.[4] There is at present little cause to criticize these analyses for not specifying statistical models at the "deeper" level recommended above, since theoretical and econometric methods for doing this are still in the stage of early development. However, as comparison of Hansen and Sargent (Chaps. 7, 8) with the paper of Sargent (25) indicates, these developments are proceeding rapidly, so that more and more sophisticated and faithful applications of the decision theory above can soon be expected.

Among students of the business cycle, private agents' errors in forming forecasts about the future have long been suspected of playing an important role in business cycles. The papers in Section 5 are concerned with interpreting time-series data with models that assert that private agents' mistakes in forming expectations are the *sole* mechanism through which variations in aggregate demand provide impulses for the business cycle. These models assert that movements in aggregate demand that have been anticipated influence only prices, and do not contribute to business cycle fluctuations. Only unexpected movements in aggregate demand are posited to set off movements in real economic activity. In order to give empirical content to this view, it is necessary to posit both some restrictions on expectations formation and a model for aggregate demand. Barro (Chaps. 29, 30) and Sargent (Chap. 27) both impose rational expectations, while they use somewhat different statistical models of aggregate demand.

The papers of Barro and Sargent are attempts to represent particular versions of textbook classical macroeconomic models in a way suitable for confronting aggregate economic time series. The version of classical theory they sought to implement econometrically is represented at a variety of levels of rigor in Friedman (1968), Bailey (1962), and Lucas (1972), and is characterized by "neutrality" of output and employment with respect to

---

[4]Compare Cagan's demand schedule for money with the marginal condition for the consumer in Lucas (1972).

some movements in aggregate demand. Of course, we know from the work of Metzler (1951), that theoretical models that impose cleared markets and optimizing agents do not uniformly imply that expected movements in aggregate demand or money are neutral with respect to employment or output. The work of Barro and Sargent was motivated by the hunch that such deviations from neutrality are phenomena of secondary importance, and that the time-series data could be well accounted for by models in which expected movements in aggregate demand are neutral.

The papers in this section reveal that considerable subtlety is involved in distinguishing the view that expected aggregate demand changes are neutral from the view that they are not, at least on the basis of time-series observations drawn from an economy operating under a single regime. The paper by Sargent (Chap. 28) is devoted to discussing this problem, though a careful reading of the papers (Chapters) by Barro (29 and 30) and Sargent (27 and 9) also reveals that the authors are concerned with aspects of this "identification" or "interpretation" problem. Partly because of this problem, Sargent and Sims (1977) have been exploring other ways of statistically representing and testing the hypothesis of neutrality.

The matter of whether unexpected movements in aggregate demand have been the dominant demand impulse behind the business cycle is important from the viewpoint of whether systematic countercyclical policy *can* be effective, which is one message of the papers of Section 2 of this volume. This issue is not yet fully resolved. Resolving it will require some additional careful empirical studies to determine whether, in fact, unexpected movements in "aggregate demand" or "money" have been the prime impetus for business cycles.

Up to now, we have said nothing about the methods available for solving the control problem of maximizing (4) with respect to (1) and (2) over the class of control laws (3). At this point it is useful to make a few observations about the usual method of studying and solving such problems. We do so in the context of a version of the problem (1)–(4) that has been generalized to permit dependence on time of the functions $V, f, g,$ and h and the sets $S_1, S_2,$ and U. We consider the $(T + 1)$ period problem to maximize

$$E_0 \left\{ \sum_{t=0}^{T} \beta^t V_t(z_t, x_t, u_t) \right\} \tag{10}$$

subject to (z_0, x_0) given and

$$z_{t+1} = f_t(z_t, \epsilon_t), \qquad t = 0, \dots, T \tag{11}$$

$$x_{t+1} = g_t(z_t, x_t, u_t), \qquad t = 0, \dots, T. \tag{12}$$

Here $f_t : S_{1t} \times \mathcal{E} \to S_{1t+1}$; $g_t : S_{1t} \times S_{2t} \times U_t \to S_{2t+1}$; and $V_t : S_{1t} \times S_{2t} \times U_t \to R$. The sets S_{1t}, S_{2t}, and U_t are permitted to depend on time, as are the functions f_t, g_t, and V_t. At time t, the agent is assumed to observe (z_t, x_t), which completely describes the state of the system at that time. The maximization of (10) subject to (11) and (12) is over decision rules or policy functions of the form

$$u_t = h_t^T(z_t, x_t) \tag{13}$$

where $h_t^T : S_{1t} \times S_{2t} \to U_t$. The T superscript on h_t^T emphasizes that the optimal choice of policy function at time t in general depends on the horizon T. We continue to assume that ϵ_t is independently and identically distributed with cumulative distribution function Φ.[5]

This maximization problem has two distinctive features. First, the criterion function (10) is of a particular form, being additively separable in the triples (z_t, x_t, u_t). Second, decisions u_t at time t only influence the returns dated t and later, $V_s(z_s, x_s, u_s)$, $s \geq t$. This influence occurs directly on $V_t(z_t, x_t, u_t)$ and indirectly on $V_s(z_s, x_s, u_s)$, $s > t$, through the law of motion (12). Taken together, these features of the problem impart to it a sequential character which permits it to be solved via a recursive procedure.

To indicate the recursive solution procedure, we write the problem as being, subject to (11) and (12) and (z_0, x_0) given, to[6]

$$\underset{h_0^T, h_1^T, \ldots, h_T^T}{\text{maximize}} \quad E_0\{V_0[z_0, x_0, h_0^T(z_0, x_0)] + \beta V_1[z_1, x_1, h_1^T(z_1, x_1)]$$
$$+ \cdots + \beta^T V_T[z_T, x_T, h_T^T(z_T, x_T)]\}. \tag{14}$$

By the law of iterated mathematical expectations, we have that for any random variable y, $E_0 y = E_0(E_1 y) = \ldots = E_0[E_1(\ldots E_T y \ldots)]$.[7] Using this law, the above line can be written,

$$\underset{h_0^T, h_1^T, \ldots, h_T^T}{\max} E_0\{V_0[z_0, x_0, h_0^T(z_0, x_0)] + \beta E_1\{V_1[Z_1, x_1, h_1^T(z_1, x_1)]$$
$$+ \beta E_2\{V_2[z_2, x_2, h_2^T(z_2, x_2)] + \cdots \tag{15}$$
$$+ \beta E_T\{V_T[z_T, x_T, h_T^T(z_T, x_T)]\} \cdots \}\}\},$$

where the maximization is again subject to (11) and (12), with (z_t, x_t) known at time t. We now make use of the second property mentioned above, namely that the choice of $u_t = h_t^T(z_t, x_t)$ influences returns dated t and later, but has no influence on returns dated earlier than t. This fact, together with the additively separable nature of the criterion function (15)

---

[5]Control problems of this type are described in Bertsekas (1976).

[6]Where y is any random variable, we define $E_t(y) = Ey|(z_t, x_t)$. Thus, $E_t(E_{t+1} y) = E[Ey|(z_{t+1}, x_{t+1})|z_t, x_t]$.

[7]This law is also termed the "smoothing property" of conditional mathematical expectations.

permits repeatedly moving the maximization operation inside the brackets, so that (15) is equivalent with the problem,

$$\max_{h_0^T} E_0\{V_0[z_0, x_0, h_0^T(z_0, x_0)] + \beta \max_{h_1^T} E_1\{V_1[z_1, x_1, h_1^T(z_1, x_1)]$$

$$+ \beta \max_{h_2^T} E_2\{V_2[z_2, x_2, h_2^T(z_2, x_2)] + \cdots \quad (16)$$

$$+ \beta \max_{h_T^T} E_T\{V_T[z_T, x_T, h_T^T(z_T, x_T)]\} \cdots \}\}\}.$$

The maximization over h_t^T is subject to (z_t, x_t) being known and to the laws of motion (11) and (12) for x and z. The cascading of brackets indicates that the maximization over h_t^T takes account of the influence of h_t^T on returns dated t and later. In distributing the maximization operations above, we are exploiting the property that returns dated earlier than t are independent of the decision function $h_t^T(z_t, x_t)$ chosen at time t.

The equality of (14) and (16) implies that the original problem (14) can be solved recursively by "working backwards"; that is, by first solving the problem in the innermost bracket in (16) to determine h_T^T, then proceeding to solve the problems in the outer brackets in order. Thus, define the optimum value functions:

$$J_T^T(z_T, x_T) = \max_{h_T^T} E_T V_T[z_T, x_T, h_T^T(z_T, x_T)]$$

$$J_{T-1}^T(z_{T-1}, x_{T-1}) = \max_{h_{T-1}^T} E_{T-1}\{V_{T-1}[z_{T-1}, x_{T-1}, h_{T-1}^T(z_{T-1}, x_{T-1})]$$

$$+ \beta J_T^T(z_T, x_T)\} \quad (17)$$

$$\vdots$$

$$J_t^T(z_t, x_t) = \max_{h_t^T} E_t\{V_t[z_t, x_t, h_t^T(z_t, x_t)]$$

$$+ \beta J_{t+1}^T(z_{t+1}, x_{t+1})\}, \quad 0 \le t \le T-1.$$

The maximizations in (17) are assumed to take place recursively subject to the known laws of motion (11) and (12). By virtue of the equality of (14) with (16), it is optimal to choose h_T^T according to the first line of (17), h_{T-1}^T according to the second line, and so on. In effect, it is optimal first to solve for all (z_T, x_T) the one-period problem that will be faced at time T. Then for all (z_{T-1}, x_{T-1}) the two-period problem starting at time $T-1$ from state (z_{T-1}, x_{T-1}) is solved with period T states being valued according to $J_T^T(z_T, x_T)$, and so on. This recursive solution strategy takes into account the influence of h_t^T on returns dated t and later but exploits the fact that returns dated earlier than t are independent of h_t^T.

As this recursive solution procedure suggests, the optimal policy functions h_t^T are functions of $V_s, f_s,$ and g_s dated t and later. We can represent this formally by a mapping

$$h_t^T = T_t^T(V_s, f_s, g_s; s \ge t). \quad (18)$$

This mapping from (V_s, f_s, g_s) to earlier h_t^T's is produced through the process of "working backwards" in solving the problem via the recursions (17).

The preceding argument shows that if a sequence of policy functions $\{\tilde{h}_t^T : t = 0, 1, \ldots, T\}$ is optimal for the original problem (14), then the tail end of the plan $\{\tilde{h}_v^T : v = s, \ldots, T\}$ is optimal for the remainder of the problem at $s > 0$, to maximize

$$E_s \sum_{v=s}^{T} \beta^v V_v [z_v, x_v, h_v^T(z_v, x_v)]$$

subject to the laws of motion (11) and (12), starting from (z_s, x_s). This property is known as Bellman's "principle of optimality." Satisfaction of this principle means that the "agent" subsequently has an incentive to stick with the original plan $\{\tilde{h}_t^T : t = 0, \ldots, T\}$ which was found to be optimal at time 0. In addition, where it is applicable, the principle offers considerable computational gains, since it is not necessary to choose the $(T + 1)$ functions $\{h_t^T : t = 0, \ldots, T\}$ simultaneously. Instead, they can be computed recursively. In effect, one large optimization problem in $(T + 1)$ unknown functions can be broken down into $(T + 1)$ smaller problems in one unknown function each.

As indicated above, the principle of optimality is a consequence of the two special features of our problem, the additively separable nature of the criterion function, and the sequential nature of the problem. Below, we shall encounter an important instance in which the second feature fails to obtain, rendering the principle of optimality inapplicable.

In contrast to our earlier setup of (1)–(4), the optimum policy functions h_t^T emerging from (10)–(13) depend on time t. Two features of the setup (10)–(13) make it necessary for the optimal policy functions h_t^T to vary with t. First, there is the fact that the functions V_t, g_t, and f_t have been permitted to vary through time. Second, even if V_t, g_t, and f_t were time invariant, the finite horizon T would in general make it optimal for the policy functions h_t^T to vary with t. For econometric applications of the kind described in this book, it is especially convenient if the optimal policy functions and the preference and constraint functions V_t, f_t, and g_t are time invariant. In the interests of this convenience, V_t, f_t, and g_t, S_{1t}, S_{2t}, and U_t are commonly specified to be independent of time, as in (1)–(4). Further, it is common to take the limit of problem (10) as $T \to \infty$. Under suitable regularity conditions (see Blackwell 1965; Lucas and Prescott, Chap. 6; or Bertsekas 1976) with V_t, g_t, f_t, S_{1t}, S_{2t}, and U_t all independent of time, it follows that for fixed j,

$$\lim_{T \to \infty} h_j^T = h_j$$

and that for all i and j

$$\lim_{T \to \infty} h_i^T = \lim_{T \to \infty} h_j^T = h,$$

so that it is optimal to employ a time-invariant optimal policy function. For econometric applications, setups satisfying the regularity conditions needed for time invariance are highly convenient and probably the only tractable ones given current computer technology.

It is worth noting that restricting oneself to time-invariant return, constraint, and optimal policy functions $V, f, g,$ and h is not necessarily as confining as it may seem at first. For example, in some problems an element of nonstationarity may seem to be introduced by the assumption that the agent is learning about some parameters or variables as time passes. However, by defining the state of the system (z_t, x_t) to include variables that are sufficient statistics for the agent's beliefs, the time-invariant version of the model may still apply. The sufficient statistics for the distribution of the agent's beliefs in some applications themselves obey time invariant laws of motion. Jovanovic (1979), Prescott and Townsend (1980), and Bertsekas (1976) all exploit this idea. Econometric applications of this idea have not yet been made, but they seem feasible.

Applications of optimal control to macroeconomic policy problems, for example, by Poole (1970), Chow (1975), and Kareken, Muench, and Wallace (1973), have used precisely the control problem above, except with a different interpretation. Recall that the problem is

$$\max_{\{u_t\}} E_0 \left\{ \sum_{t=0}^{\infty} \beta^t V(z_t, x_t, u_t) \right\} \qquad (4)$$

subject to

$$z_{t+1} = f(z_t, \epsilon_t) \qquad \text{Prob } \{\epsilon_t \leq \epsilon\} = \Phi(\epsilon) \qquad (1)$$

$$x_{t+1} = g(z_t, x_t, u_t), \qquad (2)$$

where the optimization is over control laws of the form

$$u_t = h(z_t, x_t). \qquad (3)$$

In applications of this setup to determining optimal macroeconomic policy rules, u_t has been interpreted as a vector of policy instruments such as tax rates, government purchases, high-powered money, and so on; x_t is a set of endogenous variables determined by the model, including for example inflation rates, GNP, and unemployment; z_t is a vector of exogenous variables and random shocks appearing in the structural equations of the model; g is an econometric model of the economy; f and Φ describe the probability structure of the exogenous variables and random terms; V is an instantaneous return function expressing the policy authorities' preferences over states of the economy; and h is an optimal control law for the macroeconomic policy variables. The idea was to implement this setup in the context of particular concrete econometric models g to make careful quantitative statements about optimal monetary and fiscal policy rules h. This approach has contributed significantly to clarifying long-standing issues in the macroeconomic policy area. Examples are the studies by Poole and by Kareken, Muench, and Wallace of the desirability of the monetary authority's controlling interest rates or monetary aggregates.

These applications of the control model view the policymaking problem as a "game against nature." That is, the problem assumes that the functions f and g are both fixed, and independent of the policy authorities' choice of h. But recall that $x_{t+1} = g(z_t, x_t, u_t)$ and $z_{t+1} = f(z_t, \epsilon_t)$ constitute an econometric model of private agents' behavior. Included in the policymaker's g are the decision functions of private agents, many of whom are themselves supposed to face dynamic optimization problems. For example, the policymaker's g typically includes investment, consumption, and portfolio balance schedules, each of which is supposedly the outcome of a dynamic optimum problem of private agents. The assumption that g is independent of the government's choice of its h is in general inconsistent with the notion that private agents are solving *their* optimum problems properly. To see this, recall how above we imagined (1)–(4) to describe the choice problem facing private agents. In such problems, typically some elements of the z_t appearing in the private agents' return function will be relative prices or tax rates whose random behavior is partly or entirely determined by the government's choice of its feedback rule h. Thus the government's choice of its h influence the g and f functions that appear in private agents' decision problems. Similarly, private agents choose their h's which are elements of the government's constraint set, that is, its "econometric model" g.

These observations suggest that the single-agent decision theory outlined above is inadequate for fully analyzing the mutual interaction of the government's and private agents' decisions. We can analyze these interactions by replacing the setup described by (1)–(4) by a setting defining a differential game. We now distinguish between two representative agents, agent 1 and agent 2. We shall think of agent 1 as being "the government" and agent 2 as being "the public" or "the private agent."[8] The technology is now defined as

$$x_{t+1} = \bar{g}_t(z_t, x_t, u_{1t}, u_{2t}) \tag{19}$$

[8]In many applied problems, we would like a single government, agent 1, to face a large collection of private agents who act approximately competitively. For this purpose, we would use an N-agent game in which agent 1 is the government, and agents $2, \ldots, N$ are the private agents. Equation (19) would be replaced by $x_{t+1} = \tilde{g}_t(z_t, x_t, u_{1t}, u_{2t}, \ldots, u_{Nt})$, and (21) and (22) would be modified accordingly. For the N-agent setup, most of the remarks we make about the two-agent game apply. The advantage of the large N-agent game over the two-agent game is that it permits individual private agents to ignore the influences that economywide versions of the state variables which they are choosing exert on government policy variables through the government's policy rules. Lucas and Prescott (Chap. 6) distinguish between economywide state variables and the state variables of the representative private agent in order to build in competitive behavior of private agents with respect to the government. Using an N-agent game, and driving N toward infinity in the correct way accomplishes the same purpose.

where the function $\bar{g}_t$ maps $S_{1t} \times S_{2t} \times U_{1t} \times U_{2t} \rightarrow S_{2t+1}$ where $u_{1t} \in U_{1t}$ and $u_{2t} \in U_{2t}$, and where U_{1t} and U_{2t} are spaces in which the controls u_{1t} and u_{2t} lie. The variable u_{it} is the vector of control variables that is set by agent i. Here the state variables x_t and z_t and the spaces S_{1t} and S_{2t} are as defined above. We once again assume that

$$z_{t+1} = f_t(z_t, \epsilon_t) \tag{20}$$

where the ϵ_t are independent drawings from a cumulative distribution function Φ.

Agent 1 is supposed to maximize

$$E_0 \sum_{t=0}^{T} \beta_1^t V_{1t}(z_t, x_t, u_{1t}, u_{2t}), \qquad 0 < \beta_1 < 1, \tag{21}$$

given z_0, x_0, while agent 2 maximizes

$$E_0 \sum_{t=0}^{T} \beta_2^t V_{2t}(z_t, x_t, u_{1t}, u_{2t}), \qquad 0 < \beta_2 < 1, \tag{22}$$

given z_0, x_0, where V_{1t} and V_{2t} are the given instantaneous return functions of agents 1 and 2. We assume that at time t, each agent observes (z_t, x_t). The maximization of (21) is over sequences of policy functions of the form[9]

$$u_{1t} = \bar{h}_{1t}(z_t, x_t), \qquad t = 0, 1, \ldots, T, \tag{23}$$

where $\bar{h}_{1t} : S_{1t} \times S_{2t} \rightarrow U_{1t}$, while the maximization of (22) is over policy functions of the form

$$u_{2t} = \bar{h}_{2t}(z_t, x_t), \qquad t = 0, 1, \ldots, T, \tag{24}$$

where $\bar{h}_{2t} : S_{1t} \times S_{2t} \rightarrow U_{2t}$.

As described so far, the problems of maximizing (21) and (22), respectively, are not fully posed. We must describe completely the views that agent i has of agent j's decision rules $\bar{h}_{jt}$, so that the return functions and the constraints subject to which maximization occurs are fully specified. For example, agent 1's problem is to maximize (21) over policies $\bar{h}_{1t}$ subject to (19) and (20). Neither the return functions V_{1t} nor the constraints (19) are fully specified until one attributes to agent 1 a view about the functions $\bar{h}_{2t}(z_t, x_t)$ according to which u_{2t} is to be set.

One can imagine a variety of ways of specifying these views or, equivalently, a variety of ways of modeling the differential game being played by the agents. The papers in Section 6 of the book in effect utilize one or the other of two different ways of specifying these views and of defining an

[9]The optimal policy functions $\bar{h}_{1t}$ and $\bar{h}_{2t}$ depend on the horizon of the problem T. We omit a T superscript on $\bar{h}_{1t}$ and $\bar{h}_{2t}$ to get a less cumbersome notation, but its presence should be understood.

equilibrium of the game. These are the Nash equilibrium and the Stackelberg or dominant-player equilibrium.[10]

In the Nash equilibrium, agent i is supposed to maximize his criterion function (21) or (22) subject to (19), (20), *and* knowledge of the sequence of the policy functions $\bar{h}_{jt}$, $t = 0, \ldots, T$, of the other agent. The maximization is carried out taking as *given* the $\bar{h}_{jt}$ of the other agent, so that agent i assumes that his choice of the sequence of functions $\bar{h}_{it}$ has no effect on the policy functions $\bar{h}_{jt}$, $t = 0, \ldots, T$, being used by agent j. A Nash equilibrium is then a pair of sequences of functions $\bar{h}_{1t}$, $\bar{h}_{2t}$, $t = 0, \ldots, T$, such that $\bar{h}_{1t}$ maximizes

$$E_0 \sum_{t=0}^{T} \beta_1^t V_{1t} [z_t, x_t, u_{1t}, \bar{h}_{2t}(z_t, x_t)] \tag{25}$$

subject to

$$x_{t+1} = \bar{g}_t [z_t, x_t, u_{1t}, \bar{h}_{2t}(x_t, z_t)], \, u_{1t} = \bar{h}_{1t}(z_t, x_t)$$
$$z_{t+1} = g_t(z_t, \epsilon_t), \text{ given } z_0, x_0;$$

while $\bar{h}_{2t}$ maximizes

$$E_0 \sum_{t=0}^{T} \beta_2^t V_{2t} [z_t, x_t, \bar{h}_{1t}(z_t, x_t), u_{2t}] \tag{26}$$

subject to

$$x_{t+1} = \bar{g}_t [z_t, x_t, \bar{h}_{1t}(x_t, z_t), u_{2t}], \, u_{2t} = \bar{h}_{2t}(z_t, x_t)$$
$$z_{t+1} = f_t(z_t, \epsilon_t), \text{ given } z_0, x_0.$$

The Nash equilibrium of this differential game is known to have the property that the principle of optimality applies to the maximization problem of each player. This can be proved by noting that problem (25) or (26) is a version of the single-agent optimization problem (10)–(13) which we studied earlier. In particular, for problem (25) or (26), the assumptions needed to pass from expression (14) to expression (16) are met. That the principle of optimality is satisfied for each agent's problem means that recursive methods can in principle be used to calculate the Nash equilibrium policy functions $\{\bar{h}_{1t}, \bar{h}_{2t}; t = 0, \ldots, T\}$.[11]

The fact that in a Nash equilibrium each agent's problem satisfies the principle of optimality means that each agent has an incentive to adhere to the sequence of policy functions that he initially chooses. This is true so

[10]Cruz (1975) and the references he gives discuss alternative equilibrium concepts for differential games. A variety of information structures for the game could also be imagined, only some of which are mentioned by Cruz (1975).

[11]Nash equilibria of linear quadratic differential games are computed recursively using the matrix Riccati equations for each agent. See Cruz (1975) and the references given there.

long as the assumptions about each agent's perception of the independence of the other agent's policy from his own policy functions remain valid.

Via the same argument that led to (18) in the single-agent problem, it can be noted that the solution of agent i's problem can be described by a set of nontrivial mappings T_t^i such that

$$\bar{h}_{it} = T_t^i(V_{is}, f_s, \bar{g}_s, \bar{h}_{js}; s \geq t) \qquad \begin{array}{l} i = 1, 2 \\ j \neq i \\ t = 0, 1, \ldots, T \end{array} \qquad (27)$$

so that T_t^i maps the sequences of functions $\{V_{is}, f_s, \bar{g}_s, \bar{h}_{js}; s \geq t\}$ into the policy functions $\bar{h}_{it}$. The arguments of T_t^i are all the functions that influence present or future returns or constraints of agent i at time t. In the Nash equilibrium, each agent i is assumed to ignore the fact that his choice of the sequence $\{\bar{h}_{it}; t = 0, \ldots, T\}$ influences h_{jt} in a nontrivial way through the mappings T_t^j.

A second concept of equilibrium is the Stackelberg or dominant-player equilibrium. In the dominant-player equilibrium, one player j called the dominant player is assumed to take into account the mappings T_t^i of the other player. We will assume that the dominant player is the government, agent 1. Then it is assumed that agent 1 maximizes over $\{\bar{h}_{1t}, t = 0, \ldots, T\}$ the criterion

$$E_0 \sum_{t=0}^{T} \beta_1^t V_{1t}[z_t, x_t, \bar{h}_{1t}(z_t, x_t), T_t^2(V_{2s}, f_s, \bar{g}_s, \bar{h}_{1s}; s \geq t)(z_t, x_t)] \quad (28)$$

subject to

$$\begin{array}{l} x_{t+1} = \bar{g}_t[z_t, x_t, \bar{h}_{1t}(z_t, x_t), T_t^2(V_{2s}, f_s, \bar{g}_s, \bar{h}_{1s}; s \geq t)(z_t, x_t)] \\ z_{t+1} = f_t(z_t, x_t), \text{ given } (z_0, x_0). \end{array} \quad (29)$$

Since they are derived by substituting from (27) for $u_{2t} = \bar{h}_{2t}(z_t, x_t) = T_t^2(V_{2s}, f_s, \bar{g}_s, \bar{h}_{1s}; s \geq t)(z_t, x_t)$ into the functions $\bar{g}_t$ and V_{1t}, (28) and (29) express the notion that agent 1 is choosing the sequence of functions $\{\bar{h}_{1t}, t = 0, \ldots, T\}$, taking into account the effect of this choice on agent 2's sequence of policies $\bar{h}_{2t}, t = 0, \ldots, T$. The second agent, called the follower, is assumed to behave in the same fashion as is described for the Nash equilibrium. Thus, agent 2 solves his maximization problem taking the sequence of functions $\bar{h}_{1t}$ as given. The follower, agent 2, ignores the existence of the influence of his choice of $\bar{h}_{2t}, t = 0, \ldots, T$, on $\bar{h}_{1t}, t = 0, \ldots, T$, though the mappings (27) $\bar{h}_{1t} = T_t^1(V_{1s}, f_s, \bar{g}_s, \bar{h}_{2s}; s \geq t)$.

A dominant-player equilibrium is a pair of sequences $\{\bar{h}_{1t}; t = 0, \ldots, T\}$ and $\{\bar{h}_{2t}; t = 0, \ldots, T\}$ such that $\{\bar{h}_{2t}; t = 0, \ldots, T\}$ maximizes the follower's criterion function (26) given the sequence of functions $\{\overline{h}_{1t}, t = 0, \ldots, T\}$; and such that $\{\overline{h}_{1t}; t = 0, \ldots, T\}$ maximizes the leader's criterion (28) subject to (29) and given the mappings $\overline{h}_{2t} = T_t^2(V_{2s}, f_s, \overline{g}_s, \overline{h}_{1s}; s \geq t)$. As we shall remark further below, computing a dominant-player equilibrium is generally a more difficult task than is computing a Nash equilibrium.

Kydland and Prescott (Chap. 31) and Calvo (Chap. 32) both model the differential game played by the government and the public as a dominant-player game. This amounts to having the representative private agent choose its decision functions $\overline{h}_{2t}$ taking as given the government's policy functions for such control variables as government expenditures, tax rates, the "money supply," and so on.[12] On the other hand, the government is assumed to choose its policy functions $\overline{h}_{1t}$ taking into account the effect of this choice on private agents' rules $\overline{h}_{2t}$. One of the ultimate goals of much of the econometric work described in this volume is to develop a set of statistical tools that is in principle capable of giving the government the ability to estimate the parameters that are needed for it to be able to estimate the mapping $T_t^2(V_{2s}, f_s, \overline{g}_s, \overline{h}_{1s}, s \geq t)$. The government can accomplish this if it knows the functions V_{2t}, f_t, and $\overline{g}_t$. These are the objects that econometric procedures ought to be directed at estimating.

In the dominant-player equilibrium, the problem of the follower is readily shown to satisfy the principle of optimality. This follows because once again the follower's problem can be verified to be a version of problem (10)–(13). However, the optimum problem of the leader does *not* satisfy the principle of optimality. The reason is that, via the mappings T_t^2, the functions $\overline{h}_{1t}$ influence the returns of agent 1 for dates earlier than t. This fact means that the problem ceases to be a sequential one to which the principle of optimality applies. Thus, consider the leader's problem (28), and attempt to mimic the argument showing the equivalence of (14) and (16) for our earlier single agent problem (10)–(13). Criterion (28) can be written

$$\underset{\overline{h}_{10}, \overline{h}_{11}, \ldots, \overline{h}_{1T}}{\text{maximize}} E_0\{V_{10}[z_0, x_0, h_{10}(z_0, x_0), T_0^2(V_{2s}, f_s, \overline{g}_s, \overline{h}_{1s}; s \geq 0)(z_0, x_0)]$$

$$+ \beta_1 E_1\{V_{11}[z_1, x_1, \overline{h}_{11}(z_1, x_1)], T_1^2(V_{2s}, f_s, \overline{g}_s, \overline{h}_{1s}; s \geq 1)(z_1, x_1) \quad (30)$$

$$+ \cdots + \beta_1 E_T\{V_{1T}[z_T, x_T, h_{1T}(z_T, x_T), T_T^2(V_{2s}, f_s, \overline{g}_s, \overline{h}_{1s};$$

$$s = T)(z_T, x_T)]\} \cdots\}\}.$$

---

[12] At this point, a two-agent setting is excessively confining for analyzing the situation we have in mind, in which the government sets its policy variables as functions of economywide (or marketwide) aggregates over which individual agents imagine that they have no control. For example, if the government sets some tax rate as a function of economywide employment, we still want a model in which individual employers act as competitors (price takers) with respect to that tax rate. The two-agent model in the text or in Chow (Chap. 34) does not accommodate such competitive behavior. To analyze this kind of behavior, it is necessary to resort to one of the devices mentioned in note 8 above. While such devices lead to additional computational and econometric considerations, the analytics of the time-inconsistency issue are essentially the same as conveyed by the discussion of the two-agent setup in the text.

Expression (30) indicates that all $\{\bar{h}_{1s}; s = 0, \ldots, T\}$ appear in the return function V_{10} at time 0. More generally, $\{\bar{h}_{1s}; s = t, \ldots, T\}$ appear in the return function V_{1t} at time t. Furthermore, future values of h_{1s} also appear in the law of motion $x_{t+1} = g_t[z_t, x_t, \bar{h}_{1t}, T_t^2(V_{2s}, f_s, \bar{g}_s, \bar{h}_{1s}; s \geq t)(z_t, x_t)]$. These facts prevent the distribution of the maximization operation that occurred between (15) and (16), and that underlies the principle of optimality. The upshot is that the functions $\{h_{1s}, s = 0, \ldots, T\}$ cannot be calculated recursively. Furthermore, suppose that the particular sequence of functions $\{\bar{h}_{1t}^\circ, t = 0, \ldots, T\}$ is optimal for the original problem (28) or (30). It is *not* in general true for $s = 1, \ldots, T$ that the tail of the plan $\{h_{1v}^\circ; v = s, \ldots, T\}$ is optimal for the remainder of the problem, to maximize

$$E_s \sum_{v=s}^{T} \beta_1^v V_{1v}[z_v, x_v, \bar{h}_{1v}(z_v, x_v), T_v^2(V_{2k}, f_k, \bar{g}_k, \bar{h}_{1k}; k \geq v)(z_v, x_v)]$$

subject to the laws of motion (29) and starting from (z_s, x_s). This means that in general, at future points in time, the leader has an incentive to depart from a previously planned sequence of policy functions $\{h_{1t}; t = 0, \ldots, T\}$.

The reason that the principle of optimality fails to hold for the leader's problem is the appearance of future values of his own policy functions $\bar{h}_{1s}$ in the current return functions V_{1t} in (30). Future $\bar{h}_{1s}$'s occur in V_{1t} in (30) through the mappings $T_t^2(V_{2s}, f_s, \bar{g}_s, \bar{h}_{1s}; s \geq t) = \bar{h}_{2t}$ which summarize the influence of the leader's current and future policy functions $\bar{h}_{1s}$ on the follower's current policy function. In essence, the principle of optimality fails to hold for the leader's problem because he is taking account of the fact that he is playing a dynamic game against an intelligent agent who is reacting in systematic ways to his own choices of $\bar{h}_{1s}$. In particular, in choosing the policy function $\bar{h}_{1s}$, the leader, agent 1, takes into account the influence of his choice on the follower, agent 2's, choices in earlier periods.

Kydland and Prescott (Chap. 31) and Calvo (Chap. 32) use the term "time inconsistency of optimal plans" to refer to the fact that the principle of optimality does not characterize the leader's problem. At future points in time, the leader has an incentive to depart from a previously planned optimal strategy $\bar{h}_{1t}$ and to employ some different sequence of policy functions for the "tail" of the problem. However, if the leader actually gives in to the temptation to abandon the initially optimal rules $\bar{h}_{1t}$ in favor of new rules, this invalidates the assumptions used by the follower, agent 2, in solving his optimum problem. Once the follower catches on to this fact, the follower has an incentive not to behave as originally predicted, leading to a breakdown in an ability either to predict the behavior of the follower or to make an analytic statement about optimal government policy.

Kydland and Prescott (Chap. 31) and Calvo (Chap. 32) describe a variety of examples in which, in a dominant-player game with the public, the government has an incentive to depart from a contingency plan that was optimal at an earlier point in time. Calvo's example illustrates that this "time inconsistency" problem can emerge even in a setup in which the government shares the same objective as the representative private agent, namely, the maximization of the expected utility of the representative agent.

Kydland and Prescott (Chap. 31) introduce the concept of "time-consistent" government plans which do satisfy the principle of optimality. To obtain time-consistent plans, Kydland and Prescott in effect compute a Nash equilibrium of a differential game. While such an equilibrium obeys the principle of optimality, it leaves unexploited expected gains for the government since it ignores the influence that the government's choice of the policies $\bar{h}_{1t}$ has on $\bar{h}_{2t}$. Kydland and Prescott computed several numerical examples showing that various arbitrary time-invariant functions $\bar{h}_{1t} = \bar{h}_1$, to which the government commits itself forever, would dominate the time-consistent rules in terms of the expected value of the government's criterion function.

Kydland and Prescott interpret their work as supporting the case for using fixed rules for setting government policy variables. This amounts to restricting the policy functions $\bar{h}_{1t}$ to be time invariant, meaning $\bar{h}_{1t} = \bar{h}_1$ for all t. Such a restriction on the domain of the government's choice in general causes the resulting government rule to be suboptimal relative to the time-varying rules described above. Hence, a preference for time-invariant rules is not based on the formal results referred to above, but stems from the following considerations. Remember that the cornerstone of the material in this volume is the assumption that private agents are optimizing their criterion functions, subject to knowledge of the current and future laws of motion of the variables that influence their constraints and opportunities, among which are the laws of motion $\bar{h}_{1t}$ for the variables chosen by the government. How is the public presumed to figure out the laws of motion $\bar{h}_{1t}$? If the system is operating for a long time under a single time-invariant rule $\bar{h}_{1t} = \bar{h}_1$, there is some presumption that private agents will eventually catch on to the $\bar{h}_1$ rule under which the government is operating.[13] However, if the private agents are confronted with a planned sequence $\{\bar{h}_{1t}\}$ of time-varying government rules, it is harder to imagine that agents can successfully figure out the constraints that they face. Certainly, private agents' inference problem in this setup is much more complicated than it is under a constant $\{\bar{h}_1\}$ sequence. Our view is that the assumption of rational expectations is more plausible when agents are assumed to face a time-invariant $\{\bar{h}_{1t}\}$ sequence, and that more reliable predictions about the consequences of alternative regimes can be made under this assumption.

---

[13]This presumption can be formalized using Bayes's law in some setups.

John Taylor's paper (Chap. 33) provides a simple example of a model in which the government's optimal control problem in the dominant-player game can be solved computationally, when the government adopts a time-invariant feedback rule. Taylor estimates a macroeconomic model subject to the restrictions implied by rational expectations. He estimates parameters describing private sector behavior, parameters that his theory predicts are invariant with respect to interventions in the form of changes in the government's policy rule. This gives him the ability to predict private behavior under alternative government policy rules. Taylor goes on to compute the optimal policy rule for the government, where "optimal" is interpreted to mean minimizing the stationary variance of real output subject to a constraint on the variance of the inflation rate.

The paper by Gregory Chow (Chap. 34) describes computational methods for estimating parameters and solving optimal control problems in two-person, linear quadratic differential games. These methods can also be generalized to handle N-person games, and also by taking the limit as $N \to \infty$ in the correct way, the competitive game employed by Lucas and Prescott (Chap. 6) and Lucas (Chap. 5). Chow describes how the optimal rule for the "leader" can be solved in the dominant-player game, under the restriction that the leader binds itself to a time-invariant rule, $\bar{h}_{1t} = \bar{h}_1$ in our notation, for the duration of the game. Chow describes how various hill-climbing algorithms can be used to compute the optimal $\bar{h}_1$ function. To perform this calculation, notice how Chow needs estimates of the parameters of private agents' objective function and their constraints and opportunities, and that knowledge of private agents' past behavior as reflected in historical estimates of $\bar{h}_2$ will not suffice. Finally notice that even though the econometric model is linear in the variables, the dominant player's optimization problem is a nonlinear one due to the presence of the complicated nonlinear restrictions across the private agents' optimal rule $\bar{h}_2$ and their environment, which includes $\bar{h}_1$. The formulas developed by Hansen and Sargent (Chaps. 7, 8) express these cross-equation restrictions in a different way than does Chow (Chap. 34). It would be interesting to study control problems such as Chow's using these formulas, and to explore whether the numerical computations could be reduced.

III

Before concluding, we should add a few words concerning the principles which guided the selection of papers in this volume. First, with the exception of Muth's (Chap. 1), which could hardly have been left out, we have excluded papers which are reprinted elsewhere in book form. This rule also excluded several of Lucas's papers which will be published as a collection separately.

Second, as emphasized by the title of this collection, we have focused mainly on papers which offer something to the economist who wishes to apply the idea of rational expectations to problems of estimation, testing, policy evaluation, or control. Naturally, the economists who have contributed most along this line tend to be those who find the hypothesis promising and attractive. This imparts a certain "bias" to the collection, which we might have tried to "correct" by including some of the many critical papers which have also been published. We chose not to do this: the book is, frankly, a bandwagon, more appealing to some than to others.

Our emphasis on econometric applicability led us to exclude the many papers applying rational expectations in more abstract theoretical contexts, though there have been many fruitful connections made between this literature and that sampled here, and will be many more in the future. We need a different principle to rationalize the exclusion of the vast literature, stemming from Fama's work, applying similar ideas under the name "efficient markets." This work has a coherence of its own, but as noted elsewhere in this introduction, the reader of this volume will have no difficulty recognizing precursors of many of its ideas in this earlier empirical work on securities prices.

Finally, though we claim no priority for the general ideas used in this introduction to try to tie the various papers together, neither do we wish to implicate any of the papers' authors. These papers are individual products, each with its own motivation and point of view. Our reasons for recommending them to readers need bear no particular relationship to their authors' reasons for writing them.

Robert E. Lucas, Jr.
and
Thomas J. Sargent
April 1980

References

Bailey, Martin J. *National Income and the Price Level*. 1st ed. New York: McGraw Hill, 1962.

Bertsekas, Dimitri P. *Dynamic Programming and Stochastic Control*. New York: Academic Press, 1976.

Black, Stanley. "The Use of Rational Expectations in Models of Speculation." *Rev. Econ. and Statis.* 54, no. 2 (May 1972): 161–65.

Blackwell, David. "Discounted Dynamic Programming." *Ann. Math. Statis.* 36 (1965): 226–35.

Cagan, Phillip. "The Monetary Dynamics of Hyperinflation." In *Studies in the Quantity Theory of Money*, edited by M. Friedman. Chicago: Univ. Chicago Press, 1956.

Chow, Gregory C. *Analysis and Control of Dynamic Economic Systems*. New York: Wiley, 1975.

Cruz, José, Jr. "Survey of Nash and Stackelberg Equilibrium Strategies in Dynamic Games." *Ann. Econ. and Soc. Measurement* 4, no. 2 (Spring 1975): 339–44.

Frenkel, Jacob. "The Forward Exchange Rate, Expectations and the Demand for Money: The German Hyperinflation." *A.E.R.* 67, no. 4 (September 1977): 653–70.

Friedman, Milton. *A Theory of the Consumption Function.* Princeton, N.J. Princeton Univ. Press, 1956.

————. "The Role of Monetary Policy." *A.E.R.* 58, no. 1 (March 1968): 1–17.

Jovanovic, Boyan. "Job Matching and the Theory of Turnover." *J.P.E.* 87, no. 5, pt. 1 (October 1979): 972–90.

Kareken, J. A.; Muench, T.; and Wallace, N. "Optimal Open Market Strategy: The Use of Information Variables." *A.E.R.* 63, no. 1 (1973): 156–72.

Lucas, Robert E., Jr. "Expectations and the Neutrality of Money." *J. Econ. Theory,* 4, no. 2 (April 1972): 102–24.

Metzler, Lloyd. "Wealth, Savings, and the Rate of Interest." *J.P.E.* 59, no. 2 (1951): 93–116.

Phillips, P. C. B. "The Problem of Identification in Finite Parameter Continuous Time Models." *J. Econometrics* 1 (1973): 351–62.

Poole, William. "Optimal Choice of Monetary Policy Instruments in a Simple Stochastic Macro Model." *Q.J.E.* 84 (May 1970): 199–216.

Prescott, Edward C., and Townsend, Robert M. "Equilibrium under Uncertainty: Multi-Agent Statistical Decision Theory." In *Bayesian Analysis in Econometrics and Statistics.* Edited by Arnold Zellner. Amsterdam: North-Holland, 1980.

Salemi, Michael. "Hyperinflation, Exchange Depreciation, and the Demand for Money in Post World War I Germany." Ph.D. dissertation, Univ. Minnesota, 1976.

Salemi, Michael, and Sargent, T. J. "Estimation of Demand Functions for Money during Hyperinflations under Rational Expectations." *Internat. Econ. Rev.* 20, no. 3 (1979): 741–58.

Sargent, Thomas J. *Macroeconomic Theory.* New York: Academic Press, 1979.

Sargent, Thomas J., and Sims, Christopher A. "Business Cycle Modeling without Pretending to Have Too Much *A Priori* Economic Theory." In C. A. Sims, ed., *New Methods in Business Cycle Research: Proceedings from a Conference.* Edited by C. A. Sims. Minneapolis: Federal Reserve Bank of Minneapolis, 1977.

Simon, Herbert A. "Dynamic Programming under Uncertainty with a Quadratic Objective Function." *Econometrica* 24, no. 1 (January 1956): 74–81.

Sims, Christopher A. "Discrete Approximations to Continuous Time Lag Distributions in Econometrics." *Econometrica* 39, no. 3 (June 1971): 545–64.

Theil, Henri. *Optimal Decision Rules for Government and Industry.* Amsterdam: North-Holland, 1964.

PART 1 Implications of Rational Expectations and Econometric Practice

1

Rational Expectations and the Theory of Price Movements

John F. Muth

In order to explain fairly simply how expectations are formed, we advance the hypothesis that they are essentially the same as the predictions of the relevant economic theory. In particular, the hypothesis asserts that the economy generally does not waste information, and that expectations depend specifically on the structure of the entire system. Methods of analysis, which are appropriate under special conditions, are described in the context of an isolated market with a fixed production lag. The interpretative value of the hypothesis is illustrated by introducing commodity speculation into the system.

That expectations of economic variables may be subject to error has, for some time, been recognized as an important part of most explanations of changes in the level of business activity. The "ex ante" analysis of the Stockholm School—although it has created its fair share of confusion—is a highly suggestive approach to short-run problems. It has undoubtedly been a major motivation for studies of business expectations and intentions data.

As a systematic theory of fluctuations in markets or in the economy, the approach is limited, however, because it does not include an explanation

Research undertaken for the project, *Planning and Control of Industrial Operations,* under contract with the Office of Naval Research, contract N-onr-760-(01), project NR 047011. Reproduction of this paper in whole or in part is permitted for any purpose of the United States Government. An earlier version of this paper was presented at the Winter Meeting of the Econometric Society, Washington, D.C., December 30, 1959. I am indebted to Z. Griliches, A. G. Hart, M. H. Miller, F. Modigliani, M. Nerlove, and H. White for their comments. Author's note, 1981: Reference should be made to the implicit expectations of E. S. Mills ("The Theory of Inventory Decisions," *Econometrica* 25 [1957]: 222–38), which differs from rational expectations in its stochastic properties. The normality assumption in note 3 below is not required, and the reference to the work of Bossons and Modigliani is not correct. On this latter point, see J. Bossons and F. Modigliani, "Statistical vs. Structural Explanations of Understatement and Regressivity in 'Rational' Expectations," *Econometrica* 34 (1966): 347–53. Other references have not been updated.

[*Econometrica,* 1961, vol. 29, no. 6]

of the way expectations are formed. To make dynamic economic models complete, various expectations formulas have been used. There is, however, little evidence to suggest that the presumed relations bear a resemblance to the way the economy works.[1]

What kind of information is used and how it is put together to frame an estimate of future conditions is important to understand because the character of dynamic processes is typically very sensitive to the way expectations are influenced by the actual course of events. Furthermore, it is often necessary to make sensible predictions about the way expectations would change when either the amount of available information or the structure of the system is changed. (This point is similar to the reason we are curious about demand functions, consumption functions, and the like, instead of only the reduced form "predictors" in a simultaneous equation system.) The area is important from a statistical standpoint as well, because parameter estimates are likely to be seriously biased toward zero if the wrong variable is used as the expectation.

The objective of this paper is to outline a theory of expectations and to show that the implications are—as a first approximation—consistent with the relevant data.

1. The "Rational Expectations" Hypothesis

Two major conclusions from studies of expectations data are the following:

1. Averages of expectations in an industry are more accurate than naive models and as accurate as elaborate equation systems, although there are considerable cross-sectional differences of opinion.

2. Reported expectations generally underestimate the extent of changes that actually take place.

In order to explain these phenomena, I should like to suggest that expectations, since they are informed predictions of future events, are essentially the same as the predictions of the relevant economic theory.[2] At the risk of confusing this purely descriptive hypothesis with a pronouncement as to what firms ought to do, we call such expectations "rational." It is sometimes argued that the assumption of rationality in economics leads to theories inconsistent with, or inadequate to explain, observed phenomena, especially changes over time (e.g., Simon 1959). Our hypothesis is based on exactly the opposite point of view: that dynamic economic models do not assume enough rationality.

The hypothesis can be rephrased a little more precisely as follows: that expectations of firms (or, more generally, the subjective probability distribution of outcomes) tend to be distributed, for the same information set,

---

[1]This comment also applies to dynamic theories in which expectations do not explicitly appear. See, e.g., Arrow and Hurwicz (1958) and Arrow, Block, and Hurwicz (1959).

[2]We show in Section 4 that the hypothesis is consistent with these two phenomena.

about the prediction of the theory (or the "objective" probability distributions of outcomes).

The hypothesis asserts three things: (1) Information is scarce, and the economic system generally does not waste it. (2) The way expectations are formed depends specifically on the structure of the relevant system describing the economy. (3) A "public prediction," in the sense of Grunberg and Modigliani (1954), will have no substantial effect on the operation of the economic system (unless it is based on inside information). This is not quite the same thing as stating that the marginal revenue product of economics is zero, because expectations of a single firm may still be subject to greater error than the theory.

It *does not* assert that the scratch work of entrepreneurs resembles the system of equations in any way; nor does it state that predictions of entrepreneurs are perfect or that their expectations are all the same.

For purposes of analysis, we shall use a specialized form of the hypothesis. In particular, we assume: (1) The random disturbances are normally distributed. (2) Certainty equivalents exist for the variables to be predicted. (3) The equations of the system, including the expectations formulas, are linear. These assumptions are not quite so strong as may appear at first because any one of them virtually implies the other two.[3]

2. Price Fluctuations in an Isolated Market

We can best explain what the hypothesis is all about by starting the analysis in a rather simple setting: short-period price variations in an isolated market with a fixed production lag of a commodity which cannot be stored.[4] The market equations take the form

$$C_t = -\beta p_t \qquad \text{(demand)},$$
$$P_t = \gamma p_t^e + u_t \qquad \text{(supply)}, \quad (1)$$
$$P_t = C_t \qquad \text{(market equilibrium)},$$

where: P_t represents the number of units produced in a period lasting as long as the production lag, C_t is the amount consumed, p_t is the market price in the tth period, p_t^e is the market price expected to prevail during the tth period on the basis of information available through the $(t-1)$st

---

[3] As long as the variates have a finite variance, a linear regression function exists if and only if the variates are normally distributed (see Allen 1938 and Ferguson 1955). The certainty-equivalence property follows from the linearity of the derivative of the appropriate quadratic profit or utility function (see Simon 1956 and Theil 1957).

[4] It is possible to allow both short- and long-run supply relations on the basis of dynamic costs (see Holt *et al.* 1960, esp. chaps. 2–4, 19). More difficult are the supply effects of changes in the number of firms. The relevance of the cost effects has been emphasized by Buchanan (1939) and Akerman (1957). To include them at this point would, however, take us away from the main objective of the paper.

period, and u_t is an error term—representing, say, variations in yields due to weather. *All the variables used are deviations from equilibrium values.*

The quantity variables may be eliminated from (1) to give

$$p_t = -\frac{\gamma}{\beta}p_t^e - \frac{1}{\beta}u_t. \tag{2}$$

The error term is unknown at the time the production decisions are made, but it is known—and relevant—at the time the commodity is purchased in the market.

The prediction of the model is found by replacing the error term by its expected value, conditional on past events. If the errors have no serial correlation and $Eu_t = 0$, we obtain

$$Ep_t = -\frac{\gamma}{\beta}p_t^e. \tag{3}$$

If the prediction of the theory were substantially better than the expectations of the firms, then there would be opportunities for the "insider" to profit from the knowledge—by inventory speculation if possible, by operating a firm, or by selling a price forecasting service to the firms. The profit opportunities would no longer exist if the aggregate expectation of the firms is the same as the prediction of the theory:

$$Ep_t = p_t^e. \tag{4}$$

Referring to (3) we see that if $\gamma/\beta \neq -1$ the rationality assumption (4) implies that $p_t^e = 0$, or that the expected price equals the equilibrium price. As long as the disturbances occur only in the supply function, price and quantity movements from one period to the next would be entirely along the demand curve.

The problem we have been discussing so far is of little empirical interest, because the shocks were assumed to be completely unpredictable. For most markets it is desirable to allow for income effects in demand and alternative costs in supply, with the assumption that part of the shock variable may be predicted on the basis of prior information. By retracing our steps from (2), we see that the expected price would be

$$p_t^e = -\frac{1}{\beta + \gamma}Eu_t. \tag{5}$$

If the shock is observable, then the conditional expected value or its regression estimate may be found directly. If the shock is not observable, it must be estimated from the past history of variables that can be measured.

Expectations with Serially Correlated Disturbances
We shall write the u's as a linear combination of the past history of normally and independently distributed random variables ε_t with zero mean

and variance σ^2:

$$u_t = \sum_{i=0}^{\infty} w_i \varepsilon_{t-i}, \qquad E\varepsilon_j = 0, \qquad E\varepsilon_i \varepsilon_j = \begin{cases} \sigma^2 & \text{if } i = j, \\ 0 & \text{if } i \neq j. \end{cases} \qquad (6)$$

Any desired correlogram in the u's may be obtained by an appropriate choice of the weights w_i.

The price will be a linear function of the same independent disturbances; thus

$$p_t = \sum_{i=0}^{\infty} W_i \varepsilon_{t-i}. \qquad (7)$$

The expected price given only information through the $(t - 1)$st period has the same form as that in (7), with the exception that ε_t is replaced by its expected value (which is zero). We therefore have

$$p_t^e = W_0 E\varepsilon_t + \sum_{i=1}^{\infty} W_i \varepsilon_{t-i} = \sum_{i=1}^{\infty} W_i \varepsilon_{t-i}. \qquad (8)$$

If, in general, we let $p_{t,L}$ be the price expected in period $t + L$ on the basis of information available through the tth period, the formula becomes

$$p_{t-L,L} = \sum_{i=L}^{\infty} W_i \varepsilon_{t-i}. \qquad (9)$$

Substituting for the price and the expected price into (1), which reflect the market equilibrium conditions, we obtain

$$W_0 \varepsilon_t + \left(1 + \frac{\gamma}{\beta}\right) \sum_{i=1}^{\infty} W_i \varepsilon_{t-i} = -\frac{1}{\beta} \sum_{i=0}^{\infty} w_i \varepsilon_{t-i}. \qquad (10)$$

Equation (10) is an identity in the ε's; that is, it must hold whatever values of ε_j happen to occur. Therefore, the coefficients of the corresponding ε_j in the equation must be equal.

The weights W_i are therefore the following:

$$W_0 = -\frac{1}{\beta} w_0, \qquad (11a)$$

$$W_i = -\frac{1}{\beta + \gamma} w_i \qquad (i = 1,2,3,\ldots). \qquad (11b)$$

Equations (11) give the parameters of the relation between prices and price expectations functions in terms of the past history of independent shocks. The problem remains of writing the results in terms of the history of observable variables. We wish to find a relation of the form

$$p_t^e = \sum_{j=1}^{\infty} V_j p_{t-j}. \qquad (12)$$

We solve for the weights V_j in terms of the weights W_j in the following manner. Substituting from (7) and (8), we obtain

$$\sum_{i=1}^{\infty} W_i \varepsilon_{t-i} = \sum_{j=1}^{\infty} V_j \sum_{i=0}^{\infty} W_i \varepsilon_{t-i-j} = \sum_{i=1}^{\infty} \left(\sum_{j=1}^{i} V_j W_{i-j} \right) \varepsilon_{t-i}. \qquad (13)$$

Since the equality must hold for all shocks, the coefficients must satisfy the equations

$$W_i = \sum_{j=1}^{i} V_j W_{i-j} \qquad (i = 1, 2, 3, \ldots). \qquad (14)$$

This is a system of equations with a triangular structure, so that it may be solved successively for the coefficients $V_1, V_2, V_3, \ldots$.

If the disturbances are independently distributed, as we assumed before, then $w_0 = -1/\beta$ and all the others are zero. Equations (14) therefore imply

$$p_t^e = 0, \qquad (15a)$$

$$p_t = p_t^e + W_0 \varepsilon_t = -\frac{1}{\beta} \varepsilon_t. \qquad (15b)$$

These are the results obtained before.

Suppose, at the other extreme, that an exogenous shock affects all future conditions of supply, instead of only the one period. This assumption would be appropriate if it represented how far technological change differed from its trend. Because u_t is the sum of all the past ε_j, $w_i = 1$ $(i = 0,1,2,\ldots)$. From (11),

$$W_0 = -1/\beta, \qquad (16a)$$
$$W_i = -1/(\beta + \gamma). \qquad (16b)$$

From (14) it can be seen that the expected price is a geometrically weighted moving average of past prices:

$$p_t^e = \frac{\beta}{\gamma} \sum_{j=1}^{\infty} \left(\frac{\gamma}{\beta + \gamma} \right)^j p_{t-j}. \qquad (17)$$

This prediction formula has been used by Nerlove (1958) to estimate the supply elasticity of certain agricultural commodities. The only difference is that our analysis states that the "coefficient of adjustment" in the expectations formula should depend on the demand and the supply coefficients. The geometrically weighted moving average forecast is, in fact, optimal under slightly more general conditions (when the disturbance is composed of both permanent and transitory components). In that case the coefficient will depend on the relative variances of the two components as well as the supply and demand coefficients (see Muth 1960).

Deviations from Rationality

Certain imperfections and biases in the expectations may also be analyzed with the methods of this paper. Allowing for cross-sectional differences in expectations is a simple matter, because their aggregate effect is negligible as long as the deviation from the rational forecast for an individual firm is not strongly correlated with those of the others. Modifications are necessary only if the correlation of the errors is large and depends systematically on other explanatory variables. We shall examine the effect of over-discounting current information and of differences in the information possessed by various firms in the industry. Whether such biases in expectations are empirically important remains to be seen. I wish only to emphasize that the methods are flexible enough to handle them.

Let us consider first what happens when expectations consistently over- or underdiscount the effect of current events. Equation (8), which gives the optimal price expectation, will then be replaced by

$$p_t^e = f_1 W_1 \varepsilon_{t-1} + \sum_{i=2}^{\infty} W_i \varepsilon_{t-i}. \tag{18}$$

In other words the weight attached to the most recent exogenous disturbance is multiplied by the factor f_1, which would be greater than unity if current information is overdiscounted and less than unity if it is underdiscounted.

If we use (18) for the expected price instead of (8) to explain market price movements, then (11) is replaced by

$$W_0 = -\frac{1}{\beta} w_0, \tag{19a}$$

$$W_1 = -\frac{1}{\beta + f_1 \gamma} w_1, \tag{19b}$$

$$W_i = -\frac{1}{\beta + \gamma} w_i \qquad (i = 2,3,4,\ldots). \tag{19c}$$

The effect of the biased expectations on price movements depends on the statistical properties of the exogenous disturbances.

If the disturbances are independent (that is, $w_0 = 1$ and $w_i = 0$ for

$i \geqslant 1$), the biased expectations have no effect. The reason is that successive observations provide no information about future fluctuations.

On the other hand, if all the disturbances are of a permanent type (that is, $w_0 = w_1 = \cdots = 1$), the properties of the expectations function are significantly affected. To illustrate the magnitude of the differences, the parameters of the function

$$p_t^e = \sum_{j=1}^{\infty} V_j p_{t-j}$$

are compared in figure 1 for $\beta = 2\gamma$ and various values of f_1. If current information is underdiscounted ($f_1 = 1/2$), the weight V_1 attached to the latest observed price is very high. With overdiscounting ($f_1 = 2$), the weight for the first period is relatively low.

The model above can be interpreted in another way. Suppose that some of the firms have access to later information than the others. That is, there is a lag of one period for some firms, which therefore form price expectations according to (8). The others, with a lag of two periods, can only use the following:

$$p_t^{e'} = \sum_{i=2}^{\infty} W_i \varepsilon_{t-i}. \qquad (20)$$

Then the aggregate price expectations relation is the same as (18), if f_1 represents the fraction of the firms having a lag of only one period in obtaining market information (that is, the fraction of "insiders").

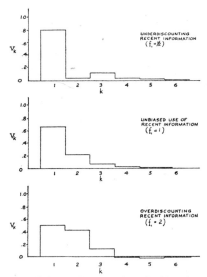

FIG. 1.—Autoregression coefficients of expectations for biased use of recent information ($w_0 = w_1 = \cdots = 1$).

3. Effects of Inventory Speculation

Some of the most interesting questions involve the economic effects of inventory storage and speculation. We can examine the effect by adjoining to (1) an inventory demand equation depending on the difference between the expected future price and the current price. As we shall show, the price expectation with independent disturbances in the supply function then turns out to have the form

$$p_t^e = \lambda p_{t-1}, \tag{21}$$

where the parameter λ would be between zero and one, its value depending on the demand, supply, and inventory demand parameters.

Speculation with moderately well-informed price expectations reduces the variance of prices by spreading the effect of a market disturbance over several time periods, thereby allowing shocks partially to cancel one another out. Speculation is profitable, although no speculative opportunities remain. These propositions might appear obvious. Nevertheless, contrary views have been expressed in the literature.[5]

Before introducing inventories into the market conditions, we shall briefly examine the nature of speculative demand for a commodity.

Optimal Speculation
We shall assume for the time being that storage, interest, and transactions costs are negligible. An individual has an opportunity to purchase at a known price in the tth period for sale in the succeeding period. The future price is, however, unknown. If we let I_t represent the speculative inventory at the end of the tth period,[6] then the profit to be realized is

$$\pi_t = I_t(p_{t+1} - p_t). \tag{22}$$

Of course, the profit is unknown at the time the commitment is to be made. There is, however, the expectation of gain.

The individual demand for speculative inventories would presumably be based on reasoning of the following sort. The size of the commitment depends on the expectation of the utility of the profit. For a sufficiently small range of variation in profits, we can approximate the utility function by the first few terms of its Taylor's series expansion about the origin:

$$u_t = \phi(\pi_t) = \phi(0) + \phi'(0)\pi_t + \frac{1}{2}\phi''(0)\pi_t^2 + \cdots \tag{23}$$

The expected utility depends on the moments of the probability distribution of π:

$$Eu_t = \phi(0) + \phi'(0)E\pi_t + \frac{1}{2}\phi''(0)E\pi_t^2 + \cdots \tag{24}$$

[5] See Baumol (1957). His conclusions depend on a nonspeculative demand such that prices would be a pure sine function, which may always be forecast perfectly.
[6] Speculative inventories may be either positive or negative.

From (22) the first two moments may be found to be

$$E\pi_t = I_t(p_{t+1}^e - p_t),\tag{25a}$$
$$E\pi_t^2 = I_t^2[\sigma_{t,1}^2 + (p_{t+1}^e - p_t)^2],\tag{25b}$$

where p_{t+1}^e is the conditional mean of the price in period $t + 1$ (given all information through period t) and $\sigma_{t,1}^2$ is the conditional variance. The expected utility may therefore be written in terms of the inventory position as follows:

$$Eu_t = \phi(0) + \phi'(0)I_t(p_{t+1}^e - p_t) + \frac{1}{2}\phi''(0)I_t^2[\sigma_{t,1}^2$$
$$+ (p_{t+1}^e - p_t)^2] + \cdots.\tag{26}$$

The inventory therefore satisfies the condition

$$\frac{dEu_t}{dI_t} = \phi'(0)(p_{t+1}^e - p_t) + \phi''(0)I_t[\sigma_{t,1}^2 + (p_{t+1}^e - p_t)^2] + \cdots = 0.\tag{27}$$

The inventory position would, to a first approximation, be given by

$$I_t = -\frac{\phi'(0)(p_{t+1}^e - p_t)}{\phi''(0)[\sigma_{t,1}^2 + (p_{t+1}^e - p_t)^2]}.\tag{28}$$

If $\phi'(0) > 0$ and $\phi''(0) < 0$, the above expression is an increasing function of the expected change in prices (as long as it is moderate).

At this point we make two additional assumptions: (1) the conditional variance, $\sigma_{t,1}^2$, is independent of p_t^e, which is true if prices are normally distributed, and (2) the square of the expected price change is small relative to the variance. The latter assumption is reasonable because the original expansion of the utility function is valid only for small changes. Equation (28) may then be simplified to[7]

$$I_t = \alpha(p_{t+1}^e - p_t),\tag{29}$$

where $\alpha = -\phi'(0)/\phi''(0)\sigma_{t,1}^2$.

Note that the coefficient α depends on the commodity in only one way: the variance of price forecasts. The aggregate demand would, in addition, depend on who holds the stocks as well as the size of the market. For some commodities, inventories are most easily held by the firms.[8] If an organized futures exchange exists for the commodity, a different population would be involved. In a few instances (in particular, durable goods), inventory accumulation on the part of households may be important.

The original assumptions may be relaxed, without affecting the results significantly, by introducing storage or interest costs. Margin requirements

---

[7]This form of the demand for speculative inventories resembles that of Telser (1959) and Kaldor (1939–40).

[8]Meat, e.g., is stored in the live animals or in any curing or ageing process.

may, as well, limit the long or short position of an individual. Although such requirements may primarily limit cross-sectional differences in positions, they may also constrain the aggregate inventory. In this case, we might reasonably expect the aggregate demand function to be nonlinear with an upper "saturation" level for inventories. (A lower level would appear for aggregate inventories approaching zero.)

Because of its simplicity, however, we shall use (29) to represent inventory demand.

Market Adjustments

We are now in a position to modify the model of Section 2 to take account of inventory variations. The ingredients are the supply and demand equations used earlier, together with the inventory equation. We repeat the equations below (P_t represents production and C_t consumption during the tth period):

$$C_t = -\beta p_t \qquad \text{(demand)}, \qquad (30a)$$

$$P_t = \gamma p_t^e + u_t \qquad \text{(supply)}, \qquad (30b)$$

$$I_t = \alpha(p_{t+1}^e - p_t) \quad \text{(inventory speculation)}. \qquad (30c)$$

The market equilibrium conditions are

$$C_t + I_t = P_t + I_{t-1}. \qquad (31)$$

Substituting (30) into (31), the equilibrium can be expressed in terms of prices, price expectations, and the disturbance, thus

$$-(\alpha + \beta)p_t + \alpha p_{t+1}^e = (\alpha + \gamma)p_t^e - \alpha p_{t-1} + u_t. \qquad (32)$$

The conditions above may be used to find the weights of the regression functions for prices and price expectations in the same way as before. Substituting from (6), (7), and (8) into (32), we obtain

$$-(\alpha + \beta) \sum_{i=0}^{\infty} W_i \varepsilon_{t-i} + \alpha \sum_{i=1}^{\infty} W_i \varepsilon_{t+1-i}$$

$$= (\alpha + \gamma) \sum_{i=1}^{\infty} W_i \varepsilon_{t-i} - \alpha \sum_{i=0}^{\infty} W_i \varepsilon_{t-1-i} + \sum_{i=0}^{\infty} w_i \varepsilon_{t-i}. \qquad (33)$$

In order that the above equation hold for all possible ε's, the corresponding coefficients must, as before, be equal. Therefore, the following system of equations must be satisfied:[9]

$$-(\alpha + \beta)W_0 + \alpha W_1 = w_0, \qquad (34a)$$

$$\alpha W_{i-1} - (2\alpha + \beta + \gamma)W_i + \alpha W_{i+1} = w_i \qquad (i = 1,2,3,\ldots). \qquad (34b)$$

[9]The same system appears in various contexts with embarrassing frequency (see Holt et al. 1960, and Muth 1960).

Provided it exists, the solution of the homogeneous system would be of the form

$$W_k = c\lambda_1^k, \qquad (35)$$

where λ_1 is the smaller root of the characteristic equation

$$\alpha - (2\alpha + \beta + \gamma)\lambda + \alpha\lambda^2 = \alpha(1 - \lambda)^2 - (\beta + \gamma)\lambda = 0. \qquad (36)$$

λ_1 is plotted against positive values of $\alpha/(\beta + \gamma)$ in figure 2.

A unique, real, and bounded solution to (34) will exist if the roots of the characteristic equation are real. The roots occur in reciprocal pairs, so that if they are real and distinct exactly one will have an absolute value less than unity. For a bounded solution the coefficient of the larger root vanishes; the initial condition is then fitted to the coefficient of the smaller root.

The response of the price and quantity variables will be dynamically stable, therefore, if the roots of the characteristic equation are real. It is easy to see that they will be real if the following inequalities are satisfied:

$$\alpha > 0, \qquad (37a)$$

$$\beta + \gamma > 0. \qquad (37b)$$

The first condition requires that speculators act in the expectation of gain (rather than loss). The second is the condition for Walrasian stability. Hence an assumption about dynamic stability implies rather little about the demand and supply coefficients. It should be observed that (37) are not necessary conditions for stability. The system will also be stable if both inequalities in (37) are reversed (!) or if $0 > \alpha/(\beta + \gamma) > -1/4$. If $\alpha = 0$, there is no "linkage" from one period of time to another, so the system is dynamically stable for all values of $\beta + \gamma$.

Suppose, partly by way of illustration, that the exogenous disturbances affecting the market are independently distributed. Then we can let $w_0 = 1$ and $w_i = 0$ $(i \geqslant 1)$. The complementary function will therefore be the complete solution to the resulting difference equation. By substituting

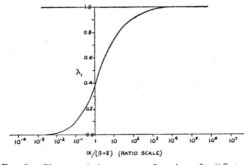

Fig. 2.—Characteristic root as a function of $\alpha/(\beta + \gamma)$

(35) into (34a), we evaluate the constant and find

$$W_k = -\frac{1}{(\alpha + \beta) - \alpha\lambda_1}\lambda_1^k. \tag{38}$$

The weights V_k may be found either from (14) or by noting that the resulting stochastic process is Markovian. At any rate, the weights are

$$V_k = \begin{cases} \lambda_1, & k = 1, \\ 0, & k > 1. \end{cases} \tag{39}$$

The expected price is therefore correlated with the previous price, and the rest of the price history conveys no extra information, i.e.,

$$p_t^e = \lambda_1 p_{t-1}, \tag{40}$$

where the parameter depends on the coefficients of demand, supply, and inventory speculation according to (36) and is between 0 and 1. If inventories are an important factor in short-run price determination, λ_1 will be very nearly unity so that the time series of prices has a high positive serial correlation.[10] If inventories are a negligible factor, λ_1 is close to zero and leads to the results of Section 2.

Effects of Inventory Speculation
Substituting the expected price, from (40) into (30), we obtain the following system to describe the operation of the market:

$$C_t = -\beta p_t, \tag{41a}$$

$$P_t = \gamma\lambda_1 p_{t-1} + \varepsilon_t, \tag{41b}$$

$$I_t = -\alpha(1 - \lambda_1)p_t. \tag{41c}$$

The market conditions can be expressed in terms of supply and demand by including the inventory carryover with production and inventory carry-foward with consumption; thus,

$$\begin{aligned} Q_t &= C_t + I_t & \text{(demand)}, \\ Q_t &= P_t + I_{t-1} & \text{(supply)}. \end{aligned} \tag{42}$$

Substituting from (41) we obtain the system:

$$Q_t = -[\beta + \alpha(1 - \lambda_1)]p_t \qquad \text{(demand)}, \tag{43a}$$

$$Q_t = [\gamma\lambda_1 - \alpha(1 - \lambda_1)]p_{t-1} + \varepsilon_t \qquad \text{(supply)}. \tag{43b}$$

The coefficient in the supply equation is reduced while that of the demand equation is increased. The conclusions are not essentially different from

---

[10]If the production and consumption flows are negligible compared with the speculative inventory level, the process approaches a random walk. This would apply to daily or weekly price movements of a commodity whose production lag is a year (see Kendall 1953).

TABLE 1

EFFECTS OF INVENTORY SPECULATION

Description	Symbol	General Formula	Approximation for Small α
1. Characteristic root	λ_1	[eq. (36)]	$\alpha/(\beta + \gamma)$
2. Standard deviation of prices	σ_p	$\lvert W_0 \rvert (1 - \lambda_1^2)^{-1/2}\sigma$	$\dfrac{1}{\beta}\left(1 - \dfrac{\alpha}{\beta}\right)\sigma$
3. Standard deviation of expected price	σ_p^e	$\lambda_1\sigma_p$	$\dfrac{\alpha}{\beta(\beta + \gamma)}\sigma$
4. Standard deviation of output	σ_P	$(\sigma^2 + \gamma^2\lambda_1^2\sigma_p^2)^{1/2}$	$\left[1 + \dfrac{\alpha\gamma}{2\beta(\beta + \gamma)}\right]\sigma$
5. Mean producers' revenue	$EP_t p_t$	$\gamma\lambda_1^2\sigma_p^2 + W_0\sigma^2$	$-\dfrac{1}{\beta}\left(1 - \dfrac{\alpha}{\beta}\right)\sigma^2$
6. Mean speculators' revenue	$EI_t(p_{t+1} - p_t)$	$\alpha(1 - \lambda_1)^2\sigma_p^2$	$\alpha\sigma^2$
7. Mean consumers' expenditure	$EC_t p_t$	$-\beta\sigma_p^2$	$-\dfrac{1}{\beta}\left(1 - \dfrac{2\alpha}{\beta}\right)\sigma^2$

NOTES.—(1) σ is the standard deviation of the disturbance in the supply function (30b) with $w_0 = 1$ and $w_1 = w_2 = \cdots = 0$. (2) $W_0 = -1/[\beta + \alpha(1 - \lambda_1)]$.

those of Hooton (1950). The change is always enough to make the dynamic response stable.

If price expectations are in fact rational, we can make some statements about the economic effects of commodity speculation. (The relevant formulas are summarized in table 1.) Speculation reduces the variance of prices by spreading the effect of a disturbance over several time periods. From figure 3, however, we see that the effect is negligible if α is much less than the sum of β and γ. The standard deviation of expected prices first increases with α because speculation makes the time series more predictable and then decreases because of the small variability of actual prices. The variability of factor inputs and production follows roughly the same pattern (cf. Kaldor 1939–40).

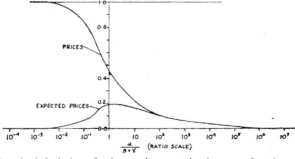

FIG. 3.—Standard deviation of prices and expected prices as a function of $\alpha/(\beta + \gamma)$ for $\beta = \gamma$.

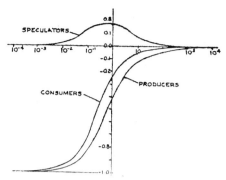

FIG. 4.—Mean income of producers and speculators, and mean expenditures of consumers as a function of $\alpha/(\beta + \gamma)$ for $\beta = \gamma$.

In figure 4 we see that mean income to speculators is always positive and has a maximum value slightly to the left of that for expected prices. Producers' revenue and consumers' expenditures both increase with α. Consumers' expenditures increase at first a little faster than the revenue of the producers. The effect of speculation on welfare is therefore not obvious.

The variability of prices for various values of γ/β is plotted as a function of α/β in figure 5. The general shape of the curve is not affected by values of γ/β differing by as much as a factor of 100. The larger the supply coefficient, however, the sharper is the cut-off in price variability.

4. Rationality and Cobweb Theorems

It is rather surprising that expectations have not previously been regarded as rational dynamic models, since rationality is assumed in all other aspects of entrepreneurial behavior. From a purely theoretical standpoint, there are good reasons for assuming rationality. First, it is a principle applicable to all dynamic problems (if true). Expectations in different markets and systems would not have to be treated in completely different

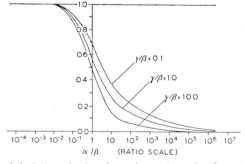

FIG. 5.—Standard deviation of prices for various values of γ/β as a function of α/β

ways. Second, if expectations were not moderately rational there would be opportunities for economists to make profits in commodity speculation, running a firm, or selling the information to present owners. Third, rationality is an assumption that can be modified. Systematic biases, incomplete or incorrect information, poor memory, etc., can be examined with analytical methods based on rationality.

The only real test, however, is whether theories involving rationality explain observed phenomena any better than alternative theories. In this section we shall therefore compare some of the empirical implications of the rational expectations hypothesis with those of the cobweb "theorem." The effects of rational expectations are particularly important because the cobweb theorem has often been regarded as one of the most successful attempts at dynamic economic theories (e.g., Goodwin 1947). Few students of agricultural problems or business cycles seem to take the cobweb theorem very seriously, however, but its implications do occasionally appear. For example, a major cause of price fluctuations in cattle and hog markets is sometimes believed to be the expectations of farmers themselves (Jesness 1958). Dean and Heady (1958) have also suggested more extensive governmental forecasting and outlook services in order to offset an increasing tendency toward instability of hog prices due to a secular decrease in the elasticity of demand.

Implications of Cobweb Theorems

If the market equilibrium conditions of (1) are subjected to independent shocks in the supply function, the prediction of the theory would be

$$E(p_t \mid p_{t-1}, p_{t-2}, \ldots) = -\frac{\gamma}{\beta} p_t^e. \tag{44}$$

As a result, the prediction of the cobweb theory would ordinarily have the sign opposite to that of the firms. This, of course, has been known for a long time. Schultz noted that the hypothesis implies farmers do not learn from experience, but added: "Such a behavior is not to be ruled out as extremely improbable" (1958, p. 78).

The various theories differ primarily in what is assumed about price expectations. The early contributors (through Ezekiel 1938) have assumed that the expected price is equal to the latest known price. That is,

$$p_t^e = p_{t-1}. \tag{45}$$

Goodwin (1947) proposed the extrapolation formula,

$$p_t^e = p_{t-1} - \rho(p_{t-1} - p_{t-2}). \tag{46}$$

That is, a certain fraction of the latest change is added on to the latest observed price. Depending on the sign of ρ, which should be between -1 and $+1$, we can get a greater variety of behavior. It is still the case, however, that farmers' expectations and the prediction of the model have the opposite sign.

A third expectations formula is much more recent. The adaptive expectations model, used by Nerlove (1958), satisfies the following equation:

$$p_t^e = p_{t-1}^e + \eta(p_{t-1} - p_{t-1}^e). \tag{47}$$

The forecast is changed by an amount proportional to the most recently observed forecast error. The solution of the difference equation gives the price expectation as a geometrically weighted moving average:

$$p_t^e = \eta \sum_{j=0}^{\infty} (1 - \eta)^j p_{t-j}. \tag{48}$$

Certain properties of the cobweb models are compared with the rational model in table 2 for shocks having no serial correlation. Such comparisons are a little treacherous because most real markets have significant income effects in demand, alternative costs in supply, and errors in both behavioral equations. To the extent that these effects introduce positive serial correlation in the residuals, the difference between the cobweb and rational models would be diminished. Subject to these qualifications, we shall compare the two kinds of models according to the properties of firms' expectations and the cyclical characteristics of commodity prices and output.

TABLE 2

PROPERTIES OF COBWEB MODELS

	Expectation p_t^e	Prediction $E(p_t\|p_{t-1,\dots})$	Stability Conditions
(A) Classical (Schultz-Tinbergen-Ricci)	p_{t-1}	$-\dfrac{\gamma}{\beta}p_t^e$	$\gamma < \beta$
(B) Extrapolative (Goodwin)	$(1 - \rho)p_{t-1} + \rho p_{t-2}$ $(-1 < \rho < 1)$	$-\dfrac{\gamma}{\beta}p_t^e$	$\dfrac{\gamma}{\beta} < \begin{cases} \dfrac{1}{1-2\rho}, & \rho \leqslant \dfrac{1}{3} \\ \dfrac{1}{\rho}, & \rho \geqslant \dfrac{1}{3} \end{cases}$
(C) Adaptive (Nerlove)	$\eta \sum_{j=1}^{\infty} (1 - \eta)^{j-1} p_{t-j}$ $(0 < \eta < 1)$	$-\dfrac{\gamma}{\beta}p_t^e$	$\dfrac{\gamma}{\beta} < \dfrac{2}{\eta} - 1$
(D) Rational	0	0	$\beta + \gamma \neq 0$
(E) Rational (with speculation)	$\lambda_1 p_{t-1}$ $(0 < \lambda_1 < 1)$	$\lambda_1 p_{t-1}$	$\alpha > 0$ $\beta + \gamma > 0$

NOTE.—The disturbances are normally and independently distributed with a constant variance.

Expectations of Firms
There is some direct evidence concerning the quality of expectations of
firms. Heady and Kaldor (1954) have shown that for the period studied,
average expectations were considerably more accurate than simple extrapolation, although there were substantial cross-sectional differences in expectations. Similar conclusions concerning the accuracy have been reached,
for quite different expectational data, by Modigliani and Weingartner
(1958).

It often appears that reported expectations underestimate the extent of
changes that actually take place. Several studies have tried to relate the
two according to the equation:

$$p_t^e = b p_t + v_t', \tag{49}$$

where v_t' is a random disturbance. Estimated values of b are positive, but
less than unity (see, e.g., Theil 1953). Such findings are clearly inconsistent
with the cobweb theory, which ordinarily requires a negative coefficient.
We shall show below that they are generally consistent with the rational
expectations hypothesis.

Bossons and Modigliani (N.D.) have pointed out that the size of the
estimated coefficient, $\hat{b}$, may be explained by a regression effect. Its relevance may be seen quite clearly as follows. The rational expectations hypothesis states that, in the aggregate, the expected price is an unbiased
predictor of the actual price. That is,

$$p_t = p_t^e + v_t, \qquad E p_t^e v_t = 0, \qquad E v_t = 0. \tag{50}$$

The probability limit of the least squares estimate of b in (49) would then
be given by

$$\text{Plim } \hat{b} = (\text{Var } p^e)/(\text{Var } p) < 1. \tag{51}$$

Cycles
The evidence for the cobweb model lies in the quasi-periodic fluctuations
in prices of a number of commodities. The hog cycle is perhaps the best
known, but cattle and potatoes have sometimes been cited as others which
obey the "theorem." The phase plot of quantity with current and lagged
price also has the appearance which gives the cobweb cycle its name.

A dynamic system forced by random shocks typically responds, however, with cycles having a fairly stable period. This is true whether or not
any characteristic roots are of the oscillatory type. Slutzky (1937) and Yule
(1927) first showed that moving-average processes can lead to very regular
cycles. A comparison of empirical cycle periods with the properties of the
solution of a system of differential or difference equations can therefore be
misleading whenever random shocks are present (Haavelmo 1940).

The length of the cycle under various hypotheses depends on how we
measure the empirical cycle period. Two possibilities are: the interval between successive "upcrosses" of the time series (i.e., crossing the trend line

TABLE 3

CYCLICAL PROPERTIES OF COBWEB MODELS

	Serial Correlation Of Prices, r_1	Mean Interval between Successive Upcrosses, L	Mean Interval between Successive Peaks or Troughs, L'
(A) Classical	$r_1 = -\dfrac{\gamma}{\beta} < 0$		
(B) Extrapolative	$r_1 = \dfrac{-\gamma(1 - \rho)}{\beta + \gamma\rho} < 0$	$2 \leqslant L \leqslant 4$	$2 \leqslant L' \leqslant 3$
(C) Adaptive	$-\dfrac{\eta\gamma}{\beta} \leqslant r_1 \leqslant 0$		
(D Rational	$r_1 = 0$	$L = 4$	$L' = 3$
(E) Rational— with storage	$r_1 = \lambda_1 > 0$	$L > 4$	$3 \leqslant L' \leqslant 4$

NOTE.—The disturbances are assumed to be normally and independently distributed with a constant variance. β and γ are both assumed to be positive.

from below), and the average interval between successive peaks or troughs. Both are given in table 3, which summarizes the serial correlation of prices and mean cycle lengths for the various hypotheses.[11]

That the observed hog cycles were too long for the cobweb theorem was first observed in 1935 by Coase and Fowler (1935, 1937). The graph of cattle prices given by Ezekiel (1938) as evidence for the cobweb theorem implies an extraordinarily long period of production (5–7 years). The interval between successive peaks for other commodities tends to be longer than three production periods. Comparisons of the cycle lengths should be interpreted cautiously because they do not allow for positive serial correlation of the exogenous disturbances. Nevertheless, they should not be construed as supporting the cobweb theorem.

References

Akerman, G. "The Cobweb Theorem: A Reconsideration." Q.J.E. 71 (February 1957): 151–60.

Allen, H. V. "A Theorem Concerning the Linearity of Regression." Statis. Res. Memoirs 2 (1938): 60–68.

Arrow, K. J., and Hurwicz, L. "On the Stability of Competitive Equilibrium, I." Econometrica 26 (October 1958): 522–52.

Arrow, K. J.; Block, H. D.; and Hurwicz, L. "On the Stability of Competitive Equilibrium, II." Econometrica 27 (January 1959): 82–109.

Baumol, W. J. "Speculation, Profitability, and Stability." Rev. Econ. and Statis. 39 (August 1957): 263–71.

Bossons, J. D., and Modigliani, F. "The Regressiveness of Short Run Business Expectations as Reported to Surveys: An Explanation and Its Implications." Manuscript, n.d.

Buchanan, N. S. "A Reconsideration of the Cobweb Theorem." J.P.E. 47 (February 1939): 67–81.

[11] See Kendall (1951, chaps. 29 and 30, esp. pp. 381 ff.) for the relevant formulas.

Coase, R. H. and Fowler, R. F. "Bacon Production and the Pig-Cycle in Great Britain." *Economica* 2 N.S. (1935): 143–67. Also "Reply" by R. Cohen and J. D. Barker, pp. 408–22, and "Rejoinder" by Coase and Fowler, pp. 423–28.

———. "The Pig-Cycle in Great Britain: An Explanation." *Economica* 4 N.S. (1937): 55–82.

Dean, G. W., and Heady, E. O. "Changes in Supply Response and Elasticity for Hogs." *J. Farm Econ.* 40 (November 1958): 845–60.

Ezekiel, M. "The Cobweb Theorem." *Q.J.E.* 52 (February 1938): 255–80. Reprinted in *Readings in Business Cycle Theory.*

Ferguson, T. "On the Existence of Linear Regression in Linear Structural Relations." *Univ. California Publications in Statis.* 2, no. 7 (1955): 143–66.

Goodwin, R. M. "Dynamical Coupling with Especial Reference to Markets Having Production Lags." *Econometrica* 15 (1947): 181–204.

Grunberg, E., and Modigliani, F. "The Predictability of Social Events." *J.P.E.* 62 (December 1954): 465–78.

Haavelmo, T. "The Inadequacy of Testing Dynamic Theory by Comparing Theoretical Solutions and Observed Cycles." *Econometrica* 8 (1940): 312–21.

Heady, E. O., and Kaldor, D. R. "Expectations and Errors in Forecasting Agricultural Prices." *J.P.E.* 62 (February 1954): 34–47.

Holt, C. C.; Modigliani, F.; Muth, J. F.; and Simon, H. A. *Planning Production, Inventories, and Work Force.* Englewood Cliffs, N.J.: Prentice-Hall, 1960.

Hooton, F. G. "Risk and the Cobweb Theorem." *Econ. J.* 60 (1950): 69–80.

Jesness, O. B. "Changes in the Agricultural Adjustment Program in the Past Twenty-five Years." *J. Farm Econ.* 40 (May 1958): 255–64.

Kaldor, N. "Speculation and Economic Stability." *Rev. Econ. Studies* 7 (1939–40): 1–27.

Kendall, M. G. *The Advanced Theory of Statistics.* Vol. 2. New York: Hafner, 1951.

———. "The Analysis of Economic Time Series—Part I: Prices." *J. Royal Statis. Soc.* 116 A (1953): 11–34.

Modigliani, F., and Weingartner, H. M. "Forecasting Uses of Anticipatory Data on Investment and Sales." *Q.J.E.* 72 (February 1958): 23–54.

Muth, J. F. "Optimal Properties of Exponentially Weighted Forecasts." *J. Amer. Statis. Assoc.* 55 (June 1960): 299–306.

Nerlove, M. "Adaptive Expectations and Cobweb Phenomena." *Q.J.E.* 73 (May 1958): 227–40.

———. *The Dynamics of Supply: Estimation of Farmers' Response to Price.* Baltimore: Johns Hopkins Press, 1958.

Schultz, H. *The Theory and Measurement of Demand.* Chicago: Univ. Chicago Press, 1958.

Simon, H. A. "Dynamic Programming under Uncertainty with a Quadratic Criterion Function." *Econometrica* 24 (1956): 74–81.

———. "Theories of Decision-Making in Economics." *A.E.R.* 49 (June 1959): 253–83.

Slutzky, E. "The Summation of Random Causes as the Source of Cyclic Processes." *Econometrica* 5 (April 1937): 105–46.

Telser, L. G. "A Theory of Speculation Relating Profitability and Stability." *Rev. Econ. and Statis.* 61 (August 1959): 295–301.

Theil, H. "A Note on Certainty Equivalence in Dynamic Planning." *Econometrica* 25 (April 1957): 346–49.

———. *Economic Forecasts and Policy.* Amsterdam: North-Holland, 1958.

Yule, G. U. "On a Method of Investigating Periodicity in Disturbed Series." *Trans. Royal Soc., London* A 226 (1927): 267–98.

2

Optimal Properties of Exponentially Weighted Forecasts

John F. Muth

The exponentially weighted average can be interpreted as the expected value of a time series made up of two kinds of random components: one lasting a single time period (transitory) and the other lasting through all subsequent periods (permanent). Such a time series may, therefore, be regarded as a random walk with "noise" superimposed. It is also shown that, for this series, the best forecast for the time period immediately ahead is the best forecast for *any* future time period, because both give estimates of the permanent component. The estimate of the permanent component is imperfect, and so the estimate of a regression coefficient is inconsistent in a relation involving the permanent component (e.g., consumption as a function of permanent income). Its bias is small, however.

Forecasts derived by weighting past observations exponentially (i.e., geometrically) have been used with some success in operations research and economics. Magee (1958), Winters (in press),[1] and Brown (1959) have used this approach in short-term forecasting of sales, primarily in inventory control. Distributed lags, while not always arising from explicit forecasts, have appeared in studies of capacity adjustment by Koyck (1954), demand for cash balances during hyperinflations by Cagan (1956), the consumption function by Friedman (1957), and agricultural supply functions by Nerlove (1958). Its main a priori justification as a forecasting relation has been that it leads to correction of persistent errors, without responding very much to random disturbances.

Because exponentially weighted forecasts have been successful in a variety of applications, it is worthwhile finding the statistical properties of time series for which the forecasting method would work well. The answer would allow the range of applicability of the forecasting method to be

This paper was written as part of the project, "The Planning and Control of Industrial Operation," under grant from the Office of Naval Research.

[1]See also Holt et al. (in press, chap. 14).

[*Journal of the American Statistical Association*, 1960, vol. 55, no. 290]

judged better and would ultimately lead to modifications when the conditions on the time series are not met. The methods we will use are related to those which have been moderately successful in control engineering.[2]

We shall consider only one estimation problem—the possible inconsistency in the regression coefficient of the forecasts because errors of measurement may be present. The reader is referred to Klein (1958) and Koyck (1954) for a discussion of other estimation problems.

1. "Adaptive Expectations" and Optimal Prediction

The exponentially weighted moving average forecast arises from the following model of expectations adapting to changing conditions. Let y_t represent that part of a time-series which cannot be explained by trend, seasonal, or any other systematic factors; and let y_t^e represent the forecast, or expectation, of y_t on the basis of information available through the $(t - 1)$st period. It is assumed that the forecast is changed from one period to the next by an amount proportional to the latest observed error. That is:

$$y_t^e = y_{t-1}^e + \beta(y_{t-1} - y_{t-1}^e), \qquad 0 \le \beta \le 1. \qquad (1)$$

The solution of the above difference equation gives the formula for the exponentially weighted forecast:

$$y_t^e = \beta \sum_{i=1}^{\infty} (1 - \beta)^{i-1} y_{t-i}. \qquad (2)$$

Since the weights attached to prior values of y_t add up to unity, the forecasting scheme does not in this respect introduce any systematic bias.

Now, suppose that the realizations of the random process can be written as some linear function of independent random shocks:

$$y_t = \varepsilon_t + \sum_{i=1}^{\infty} w_i \varepsilon_{t-i}, \qquad (3)$$

the shocks being independently distributed with mean zero and variance σ^2.

As long as the parameters w_i, which characterize the random process, are known, it is a relatively simple matter to find the expected value of y_t for any time period on the basis of previous outcomes. Suppose we wish to find the expectation of y_t given $\varepsilon_{t-1}, \varepsilon_{t-2}, \varepsilon_{t-3}, \cdots$ (i.e., the only information lacking to give the value of y_t exactly is the latest "shock," ε_t). Then

---

[2]Statistical problems in engineering control are ably discussed in Laning and Battin (1956).

we simply replace ε_t by its expected value, which is zero. Therefore we have:

$$y_t^e = E(y_t \,|\, \varepsilon_{t-1}, \varepsilon_{t-2}, \varepsilon_{t-3}, \cdots)$$

$$= \sum_{i=1}^{\infty} w_i \varepsilon_{t-i}.$$

(4)

In order to relate the regression functions above to the expression for the exponentially weighted forecast, we need to be able to write (4) in terms of the observed variables $y_{t-1}, y_{t-2}, \cdots$. That is, we need to find the coefficients of the following function:

$$y_t^e = \sum_{j=1}^{\infty} v_j y_{t-j}.$$

(5)

Substituting from (3), and rearranging terms, we obtain:

$$y_t^e = \sum_{j=1}^{\infty} v_j \left(\varepsilon_{t-j} + \sum_{i=1}^{\infty} w_i \varepsilon_{t-i-j} \right)$$

$$= v_1 \varepsilon_{t-1} + \sum_{i=2}^{\infty} \left(v_i + \sum_{j=1}^{i-1} v_j w_{i-j} \right) \varepsilon_{t-i}.$$

(6)

By comparing coefficients of equations (4) and (6), we have the necessary relation between the parameters, w_i, associated with the latent shocks and those, v_j, associated with the observable past history of the process:

$$w_1 = v_1$$

$$w_i = v_i + \sum_{j=1}^{i-1} v_j w_{i-j}, \qquad i = 2, 3, 4, \cdots.$$

(7)

In order to characterize the time series for which the exponentially weighted forecast is optimal, we substitute the weights

$$v_j = \beta(1 - \beta)^{j-1}, \qquad j = 1, 2, 3, \cdots$$

(8)

from equation (2) into equations (7). The result of the substitutions is the system:

$$w_1 = \beta$$

$$w_i = \beta(1 - \beta)^{i-1} + \beta \sum_{j=1}^{i-1} (1 - \beta)^{j-1} w_{i-j}, \qquad i = 2, 3, 4, \cdots.$$

(9)

It follows that

$$w_i = \beta \qquad \text{for all } i \geq 1.$$

(10)

Writing y_t in terms of the independent shocks, as in equation (3), we obtain:

$$y_t = \varepsilon_t + \beta \sum_{i=1}^{\infty} \varepsilon_{t-i}. \tag{11}$$

The shock associated with each time period has a weight of unity; its weight in successive time periods, however, is constant and somewhere between zero and one. Part of the shock in any period, therefore, has a permanent effect, while the rest affects the system only in the current period.[3]

We have assumed that the forecasts given by equation (2) were for the period immediately ahead. The best forecasts for all future periods, however, are the same. In order to prove this assertion, it is necessary to generalize the previous results. Let $y_{t,T}$ represent the value of y_{t+T}, forecasted on the basis of information available through period t (T is called the "forecast span"). By an argument similar to that leading to equation (4), we have the relation:

$$y_{t,T} = E(y_{t+T} | \varepsilon_t, \varepsilon_{t-1}, \varepsilon_{t-2}, \cdots)$$
$$= \sum_{i=0}^{\infty} w_{i+T} \varepsilon_{t-i}. \tag{12}$$

However, we wish to express the forecast in terms of the observables y_t, y_{t-1}, y_{t-2}, $\cdots$, rather than the latent variables ε_t, ε_{t-1}, ε_{t-2}, $\cdots$. The desired equation has the form:

$$y_{t,T} = \sum_{j=0}^{\infty} v_{T,j} y_{t-j}. \tag{13}$$

From a knowledge of the weights w, we need to find the coefficients v.

The appropriate relations, which are found in the same way as equations (7), are the following:

$$w_{i+T} = v_{T,i} + \sum_{j=0}^{i-1} v_{T,j} w_{i-j}, \qquad \begin{array}{l} i = 0, 1, 2, \cdots \\ T = 1, 2, 3, \cdots. \end{array} \tag{14}$$

To find the coefficients of equations (13), substitute from (10) into (14) to obtain the following system:

$$\beta = v_{T,i} + \beta \sum_{j=0}^{i-1} v_{T,j}, \qquad i = 0, 1, 2, 3 \cdots. \tag{15}$$

---

[3] Some ways in which the economic system might generate time series of this form is examined in Muth (in press).

Subtracting the conditions for $i = k - 1$ from those for $i = k$ ($k = 1, 2, 3, \cdots$), we obtain the difference equation:

$$v_{T,k} = (1 - \beta)v_{T,k-1}, \qquad k = 1, 2, 3, \cdots. \tag{16}$$

Since, from equation (15), $v_{T,0} = \beta$, we obtain the unique solution:

$$v_{T,k} = \beta(1 - \beta)^k, \qquad k = 0, 1, 2, \cdots. \tag{17}$$

The forecast weights are therefore independent of T, and the assertion is proved. This result is due to the fact that all prior shocks have the same weight, and that the forecasts only give an estimate of the permanent component of the shocks.

2. Expectations with Independent Components

The same type of forecasting rule is appropriate if the permanent and transitory components in each period are statistically independent rather than perfectly correlated as in the preceding case. Let $\bar{y}_t$ represent the permanent component of y_t and η_t the transitory component, so that:

$$y_t = \bar{y}_t + \eta_t. \tag{18}$$

The transitory components are assumed to be independently distributed with mean zero and variance σ_η^2. The permanent components are defined by the relationships:

$$\bar{y}_t = \bar{y}_{t-1} + \varepsilon_t = \sum_{i=1}^{t} \varepsilon_i, \tag{19}$$

where the ε's are serially independent with mean zero and variance σ_ε^2. The η's and ε's are also assumed to be independent (this assumption is not, however, an essential one).

The forecasting problem, then, is to find the coefficients $v_1, v_2, \cdots$ in the equation:

$$y_t^e = \sum_{j=1}^{\infty} v_j y_{t-j} \tag{20}$$

which minimize the error variance,

$$V = E(y_t - y_t^e)^2. \tag{21}$$

The methods used in Section 1 are not appropriate for the independent components because it is impossible to measure both the ε_t and the η_t from the one set of observed variables. We can, however, proceed as follows.

Substitute from equations (18)–(20) and write the forecast error in terms of the weights attached to past observations:

$$V = \sigma_\varepsilon^2 + \sigma_\eta^2 + \sigma_\varepsilon^2 \sum_{j=1}^{\infty} \left(1 - \sum_{i=1}^{j} v_i\right)^2 + \sigma_\eta^2 \sum_{j=1}^{\infty} v_j^2. \tag{22}$$

Setting the derivatives of V with respect to v_k equal to zero, we have the following conditions on the optimal weights:

$$\frac{\partial V}{\partial v_k} = -2\sigma_\varepsilon^2 \sum_{j=k}^{\infty} \left(1 - \sum_{i=1}^{j} v_i\right) + 2\sigma_\eta^2 v_k = 0, \qquad k = 1, 2, \cdots. \tag{23}$$

Taking second differences of the conditions above to eliminate the long summations, the optimal weights are the solution of the following difference equations:

$$\left(1 + \frac{\sigma_\varepsilon^2}{\sigma_\eta^2}\right) v_1 - v_2 = \frac{\sigma_\varepsilon^2}{\sigma_\eta^2} \tag{24a}$$

$$-v_{k-1} + \left(2 + \frac{\sigma_\varepsilon^2}{\sigma_\eta^2}\right) v_k - v_{k+1} = 0, \qquad k = 2, 3, \cdots. \tag{24b}$$

The characteristic equation of the system above is

$$-\frac{(1 - \lambda)^2}{\lambda} + \frac{\sigma_\varepsilon^2}{\sigma_\eta^2} = 0. \tag{25}$$

Because of the symmetry of equation (24b), the characteristic roots occur in a reciprocal pair. Only the root less than unity, say λ_1, is relevant, because the infinite sums in equations (22) and (23) would otherwise diverge. The relevant root may be written explicitly in terms of the variance ratio as follows:

$$\lambda_1 = 1 + \frac{1}{2}\frac{\sigma_\varepsilon^2}{\sigma_\eta^2} - \frac{\sigma_\varepsilon}{\sigma_\eta}\sqrt{1 + \frac{1}{4}\frac{\sigma_\varepsilon^2}{\sigma_\eta^2}}. \tag{26}$$

The solution will then be of the form: $v_k = c\lambda_1^k$, where λ_1 is the relevant characteristic root and c is a constant to be determined from equation (24a). Substituting from equation (25) into (24b), we find that $c = (1 - \lambda_1)/\lambda_1$. The weights appearing in the forecasting formula would therefore be the following:

$$v_k = (1 - \lambda_1)\lambda_1^{k-1}, \qquad k = 1, 2, 3, \cdots. \tag{27}$$

Note that the weights have the same form as those in equation (2) if $\beta = 1 - \lambda_1$. The forecast for the next period is the forecast for all future periods as well because it is an estimate of the permanent component, $\bar{y}_t$.

If the changes in the permanent component are small relative to the "noise," then λ_1 will be very nearly unity. The forecast then gives nearly equal weights to all past observations in order that the transitory components tend to cancel each other out. The forecasts then do not depend very much on recent information because it says very little about the future. On the other hand, if changes in the permanent component are large relative to the noise, λ_1 would be small so as to weight the recent information heavily.

It is, incidentally, not necessary to assume that ε_t and η_t are uncorrelated. If $E\varepsilon_t\eta_t = \sigma_{\varepsilon\eta}$ and $E\varepsilon_t\eta_s = 0$ $(t \neq s)$, it is only necessary to replace the ratio $\sigma_\varepsilon^2/\sigma_\eta^2$ in equations (24)–(26) by $\sigma_\varepsilon^2/(\sigma_\eta^2 + \sigma_{\varepsilon\eta})$.

3. Permanent and Transitory Components of Income

In the preceding sections we have characterized the time series for which the exponentially weighted moving average equals the conditional expected value. The important feature is that the time series consists of two random parts: one lasting a single time period, and the other lasting through all subsequent periods. The structure therefore resembles the hypothesis concerning permanent and transistory components of income, advanced by Friedman in his study of the consumption function (1957). The structure is not exactly the same, however, because Friedman intentionally left the definitions of "permanent" and "transitory" somewhat vague. We have had to be more specific in the definitions, according to equations (18) and (19), although nothing in the analysis states how long a "period" must be. Nevertheless, it appears that the exponentially weighted moving average is an appropriate measure of permanent income if Friedman's other hypotheses are true.

A problem which may be raised at this point concerns errors of estimating the marginal propensity to consume because of inaccurate measurements of the permanent component. Suppose that consumption depends on the true value of the permanent component of income, on the assumption that households can identify the two sources much better than is possible from aggregate time series. The propensity to consume estimated from the exponentially weighted moving average of income would then be biased downward because of the errors of measurement. We will show, however, that the bias should be small. The consumption model is:

$$c_t = \alpha\bar{y}_t + \delta_t, \tag{28}$$

where c_t is the consumption in the tth period, α the propensity to consume, and δ_t the error term of the equation assumed to be independent of the permanent component and its estimate.

The least-squares estimate of α (denoted by $\hat{\alpha}$) which results from using the value of the moving average, y^e_{t+1}, instead of the true permanent component, $\bar{y}_t$, is

$$\hat{\alpha} = \left(\sum c_t y^e_{t+1}\right)\bigg/\left(\sum y^e_{t+1}{}^2\right). \tag{29}$$

Its probability limit is

$$P \lim \hat{\alpha} = \alpha \, \mathrm{Cov}(\bar{y}_t, y^e_{t+1})/\mathrm{Var}\, y^e_{t+1}, \tag{30}$$

as long as δ_t is not correlated with y^e_t.

Assume that the process applies to the income of each household, with t denoting the age of the head of the household starting from the beginning of his working life.[4]

$$y_t = \eta_t + \sum_{i=1}^{t} \varepsilon_i. \tag{31}$$

From equations (20) and (27), y^e_{t+1} may similarly be expressed in terms of the independently distributed shocks:

$$y^e_{t+1} = (1 - \lambda_1) \sum_{k=1}^{t} \lambda_1^{k-1} y_{t+1-k}$$

$$= \sum_{k=1}^{t} [(1 - \lambda_1)\lambda_1^{k-1}\eta_{t+1-k} + (1 - \lambda_1^k)\varepsilon_{t+1-k}]. \tag{32}$$

The variance of y^e_{t+1} is therefore:

$$\mathrm{Var}\, y^e_{t+1} = (1 - \lambda_1)^2 \frac{1 - \lambda_1^{2t}}{1 - \lambda_1^2}\sigma_\eta^2 + \left(t - 2\lambda_1 \frac{1 - \lambda_1^t}{1 - \lambda_1} + \lambda_1^2 \frac{1 - \lambda_1^{2t}}{1 - \lambda_1^2}\right)\sigma_\varepsilon^2$$

$$= \left[t - \frac{\lambda_1}{1 - \lambda_1}(1 - \lambda_1^t)^2\right]\sigma_\varepsilon^2, \tag{33}$$

the latter equation arising from the dependence of λ_1 on the ratio $\sigma_\varepsilon^2/\sigma_\eta^2$ according to (25). The covariance between $\bar{y}_t$ and y^e_{t+1} may be similarly expressed as:

$$\mathrm{Cov}(\bar{y}_t, y^e_{t+1}) = \left[t - \frac{\lambda_1}{1 - \lambda_1}(1 - \lambda_1^t)\right]\sigma_\varepsilon^2. \tag{34}$$

The asymptotic bias, according to equations (30), is determined by the ratio of (34) to (33). Since this ratio is very nearly unity for moderately large values of t, it appears that this kind of measurement error of the permanent component would introduce very little asymptotic bias in the estimate of the propensity to consume.

---

[4]This uses one of the ideas of Modigliani and Brumberg (1954) in their approach to the theory of the consumption function.

References

Brown, R. G. *Statistical Forecasting for Inventory Control.* New York: McGraw-Hill, 1959.

Cagan, P. "The Monetary Dynamics of Hyper-Inflation." In *Studies in the Quantity Theory of Money,* edited by M. Friedman. Chicago: Univ. Chicago Press, 1956.

Friedman, M. *A Theory of the Consumption Function.* Princeton: Princeton Univ. Press, 1957.

Holt, C. C.; Modigliani, F.; Muth, J. F.; and Simon, H. A. *Planning Production, Inventories, and Work Force.* Englewood Cliffs, N.J.: Prentice Hall, in press.

Klein, L. R. "The Estimation of Distributed Lags." *Econometrica* 26 (1958): 553–61.

Koyck, L. M. *Distributed Lags and Investment Analysis.* Amsterdam: North-Holland, 1954.

Laning, J. H., Jr., and Battin, R. H. *Random Processes in Automatic Control.* New York: McGraw-Hill, 1956.

Magee, J. F. *Production Planning and Inventory Control.* New York: McGraw-Hill, 1958.

Modigliani, F., and Brumberg, R. "Utility Analysis and the Consumption Function: An Interpretation of Cross-Section Data." In *Post-Keynesian Economics.* New Brunswick, N.J.: Rutgers Univ. Press, 1954.

Muth, J. F. "Rational Expectations and the Theory of Price Movements." Forthcoming.

Nerlove, M. *The Dynamics of Supply: Estimation of Farmers' Response to Price.* Baltimore: Johns Hopkins Press, 1958.

Winters, P. R. "Forecasting Sales by Exponentially Weighted Moving Averages." *Management Sci.,* in press.

3

A Note on the "Accelerationist" Controversy

Thomas J. Sargent

Recent empirical tests of the Phelps-Friedman "accelerationist" view of the Phillips curve are marred by the fact that their validity is predicated on the adequacy of a very suspect maintained hypothesis.[1] Those tests all involve obtaining estimates of the notorious parameter "α" in the following equation designed to explain the movement of wages over time:

$$\frac{\Delta w_t}{w_{t-1}} = \alpha \pi_t + f(U_t, \cdots) + \varepsilon_t. \tag{1}$$

Here π_t is the public's anticipated rate of commodity price inflation, w_t is the wage rate at time t, U_t is the unemployment rate, and $f(U_t, \cdots)$ is the short-run Phillips curve with $\partial f/\partial U < 0$ and with the sequence of dots representing a list of other variables; ε_t is an unobservable random variable. In order to implement (1) empirically, an observable proxy for π_t must be obtained. Almost always this requirement is filled by using the Fisher-Cagan[2] equation

$$\pi_t = \sum_{i=0}^{m} v_i \frac{\Delta P_{t-i}}{P_{t-i-1}}, \qquad v_i \geq 0 \tag{2}$$

where P_t is the commodity price level at time t, and the v_i's are parameters. Substituting (2) into (1) yields the equation that has typically been estimated:

$$\frac{\Delta w_t}{w_{t-1}} = \alpha \sum_{i=0}^{m} v_i \frac{\Delta P_{t-i}}{P_{t-i-1}} + f(U_t, \cdots) + \varepsilon_t. \tag{3}$$

An estimated α of unity (or close to unity) is taken to confirm the Phelps-Friedman "accelerationist" position, while an α markedly lower than unity is taken to imply that there is a meaningful long-run trade-off be-

[1] Examples of recent empirical work on the matter are papers by Gordon (1970), Cagan (1968), Solow (1968), and Tobin (1968).

[2] See Fisher (1961) and Cagan (1956).

[*Journal of Money, Credit, and Banking*, 1971, vol. 8]

tween wage inflation and the unemployment rate.[3] Empirical investigations of the accelerationist hypothesis have focused on estimating α in (3).

Notice, however, that fitting a regression like (3) only permits estimating
$(m + 1)$ of the $(m + 2)$ parameters $\alpha, v_0, v_1, \cdots, v_m$. That is because the
weighted sum of current and past rates of inflation contains only $(m + 1)$
terms. Thus, in order to identify α, or any other of these $m + 2$ parameters,
some extraneous information must be imposed on those parameters. Almost always, the constraint that has been imposed is that the distributed
lag weights in (2) sum to unity:

$$\sum_{i=0}^{m} v_i = 1. \tag{4}$$

The quality of the estimates of α obtained is obviously predicated on the
adequacy of this restriction. Apparently, the restriction has been justified
by the following type of argument. Suppose that the rate of inflation
increases from zero, which has been its value for a long time (more than
$m + 1$ periods), to one percent per annum, staying there indefinitely. Then
it is reasonable to expect that eventually people will catch on and expect
inflation to continue at one percent per annum. This is taken to imply that
the weights in (2) sum to unity.

It is certainly reasonable to expect that a sustained, constant inflation
sooner or later would be fully anticipated. But this consideration is of very
little use in producing a reasonable restriction to impose on the v_i's of (3)
for the purposes of empirical estimation; for during the periods used in
estimation, inflation was never as sustained as is imagined in the mental
experiment described above. That experiment leads us to deduce a restriction on the weights in (3) by assuming a time path for the inflation rate
that bears little resemblance to the path that inflation has actually followed in the past. This is an important shortcoming because what form of
expectations generator is reasonable depends on the actual behavior of the
variable about which expectations are being formed.[4] When searching for
an identifying restriction on the sum of the weights in (3) to be used in
empirical work, it therefore seems most appropriate to ask what sort of

---

[3]This interpretation of α flows from the following argument. Suppose that commodity
price inflation is generated via the "mark-up" equation (a) $\Delta p_t/p_{t-1} = \Delta w_t/w_{t-1} + g(\cdots)$
where $g(\cdots)$ represents some unspecified influences on the inflation rate. In the long run, any
sustained rate of inflation will be fully anticipated, so that $\pi = \Delta p/p_{-1} = \Delta w/w_{-1} + g(\cdots)$.
Substituting the above expression for π into equation (3) yields the long-run Phillips curve
$\Delta w/w_{-1} = \alpha(\Delta w/w_{-1}) + \alpha g(\cdots) + f(U, \cdots)$ or $\Delta w/w_{-1} = 1/(1 - \alpha)f(U, \cdots) + \alpha/$
$(1 - \alpha) \cdot g(\cdots)$. The slope of the long-run Phillips curve, which indicates the extent to which
there exists a persistent trade-off between wage inflation and unemployment, equals
$1/(1 - \alpha)(\partial f/\partial U)$. The slope of the long-run Phillips curve approaches negative infinity as α
approaches unity from below.
[4]This point has been emphasized by Nerlove (1967).

expectations-generating scheme would be reasonable in light of the actual behavior of the inflation rate during the period being studied. In doing this, it seems natural to adopt assumptions about the evolution of the rate of inflation that are compatible with equation (2) being a "rational" (more precisely a minimum-mean-squared-error) generator of expectations. As is well known, one-period-forward expectations formed via (2) will be minimum-mean-squared-error forecasts if the actual rate of inflation evolves according to the $(m + 1)$th order autoregressive process

$$\frac{\Delta P_{t+1}}{P_t} = \sum_{i=0}^{m} v_i \frac{\Delta P_{t-1}}{P_{t-i-1}} + u_{t+1}, \tag{5}$$

where u_t is an independently, identically distributed random variable with

$$E(u_{t+1}) = 0,$$

$$E(u_t u_s) = \begin{cases} \sigma_u^2 & t = s \\ 0 & t \neq s. \end{cases}$$

Now the configuration of distributed lag weights in estimates of equation (3) will be plausible, or "rational" in the sense of Muth (1961), if they are consistent with the actual process generating inflation, which we approximate by equation (5). Hence the most reasonable restriction to impose on the sum of the weights is not that it necessarily equals unity, but that it be compatible with the observed evolution of the rate of inflation.

It is apparent that as long as the inflation rate can be approximated as a covariance-stationary stochastic process and the v_i's are nonnegative, the v_i's in (5) must sum to less than unity.[5] Were the weights in (5) to sum to

[5]Consider the $(m + 1)$th order autoregressive process

$$y_{t+1} = v_0 y_t + v_1 y_{t-1} + \cdots + v_m y_{t-m} + u_{t+1} \tag{6}$$

where u_{t+1} is an independently, identically distributed random variable with mean zero and finite variance, and $v_i > 0$, $i = 0, \cdots, m$. We transform (6) into a first-order system by defining the $(m + 1) \times 1$ vector x

$$x_i = \begin{bmatrix} x_{1t} \\ x_{2t} \\ \vdots \\ x_{m+1,t} \end{bmatrix} = \begin{bmatrix} y_{t-m} \\ y_{t-m+1} \\ \vdots \\ y_t \end{bmatrix},$$

the $(m + 1) \times (m + 1)$ matrix A,

$$A = \begin{bmatrix} 0 & 1 & 0 & \cdots & 0 \\ 0 & 0 & 1 & \cdots & 0 \\ \vdots & & & & \\ v_m & v_{m-1} & & \cdots & v_0 \end{bmatrix}$$

unity (or close to unity) the inflation rate would display extremely strong serial correlation or "drift." By this we mean that the spectral density of the inflation rate would display Granger's "typical spectral shape" (1966), having infinite (or very great) power at zero frequency. On the other hand, a relatively drift-free inflation rate would require that the weights in (5) sum to considerably less than unity.

Now even the most casual glance at the price history of the United States makes it clear that the inflation rate has not been a strongly drifting variable. The spectral density of the inflation rate for most U.S. data does not possess Granger's typical spectral shape, instead being quite flat or "white." Thus, the inflation rate has ordinarily displayed relatively little serial correlation, and would certainly be very poorly modeled by a Markov process with the lag weights summing to unity. This means that imposing restriction (4) amounts to supposing that the public's method of forming expectations of inflation was very irrational in the sense of being widely inconsistent with the actual inflation process.[6]

We conclude that imposing (4) on U.S. data is likely to lead to serious overestimation of the individual distributed lag weights, the v_i's, and to serious *under*estimation of α. It is not surprising, therefore, that most empir-

---

and the $(m + 1) \times 1$ vector B,

$$B = \begin{bmatrix} 0 \\ 0 \\ \vdots \\ 0 \\ 1 \end{bmatrix}.$$

Then (6) can be written as the equivalent first-order system

$$x_{t+1} = Ax_t + Bu_{t+1}. \tag{7}$$

Equation (7) describes a stationary system if and only if the maximum eigenvalue of A is less than unity in absolute value. Now since A is an indecomposable, nonnegative matrix, its maximum eigenvalue, say λ^*, satisfies the inequalities:

$$\min_i \sum_j A_{ij} < \lambda^* < \max_i \sum_j A_{ij}, \quad \text{unless} \quad \min_i \sum_j A_{ij} = \max_i \sum_j A_{ij},$$

in which case

$$\lambda^* = \min_i \sum_j A_{ij} = \max_i \sum_j A_{ij}.$$

(See, e.g., Lancaster 1968, p. 310.) It follows that (7) will be stationary only if $\sum_{i=0}^{m} v_i$ is less than unity.

[6]A somewhat deeper point can be made by extending the argument advanced in the text. Notice that equation (3) and equation (a) in note 3 form a system that has been assumed to govern the evolution of $\Delta w_t/w_{t-1}$ and $\Delta P_t/P_{t-1}$ over time. But the model has been constructed in such a way that the expectations of the public have been assumed *not* to be identical with the model's predictions of subsequent rates of inflation. The model is "irrational" in the sense of Muth (1961).

ical studies have estimated α to be markedly less than unity. Unfortunately, as usually interpreted, those estimates tell us virtually nothing about the validity of the accelerationist thesis.[7]

References

Cagan, Philip. "The Monetary Dynamics of Hyperinflation." In *Studies in the Quantity Theory of Money,* ed. by M. Friedman. Chicago: Univ. Chicago Press, 1956.

———. "Theories of Mild, Continuing Inflation: A Critique and Extension." In *Proceedings of a Symposium on Inflation: Its Causes, Consequences, and Control,* ed. by Stephen W. Rousseau. New York: New York Univ., 1968.

Fisher, Irving. *The Theory of Interest.* New York: Kelley, 1961.

Gordon, Robert J. "The Recent Acceleration of Inflation and Its Lessons for the Future." *Brookings Papers on Economic Activity* 1 (1970):8–41.

Granger, C. W. J. "The Typical Spectral Shape of an Economic Variable." *Econometrica* 34 (January 1966):150–61.

Lancaster, Kelvin. *Mathematical Economics.* New York: Macmillan, 1968.

[7]The discussion in the text, which proceeds in terms of one-period-forward forecasts, actually acquires more significance when it is extended to cover multiple-period horizons. Thus, let x_t be the actual rate of inflation. Then (5) can be written

$$x_{t+1} = \sum_{i=0}^{m} v_i x_{t-i} + u_{t+1}.$$

At time t, the least-squares forecast of x at time $t + 1$ is

$$\hat{x}_{t+1} = E(x_{t+1}|x_t, x_{t-1}, \cdots) = \sum_{i=0}^{m} v_i x_{t-i}.$$

At time t, the least-squares forecast of x at time $t + 2$ is

$$\hat{x}_{t+2} = E(x_{t+2}|x_t, x_{t-1}, \cdots) = v_0 \hat{x}_{t+1} + \sum_{i=0}^{m-1} v_{i+1} x_{t-i}$$

$$= \sum_{i=0}^{m-1} (v_0 v_i + v_{i+1}) x_{t-i} + v_0 v_m x_{t-m} = \sum_{i=0}^{m} w_i x_{t-i}$$

where $w_i = v_0 v_i + v_{i+1}, i = 0, \cdots, m - 1; w_m = v_0 v_m$. (See Nerlove [1967] and Sargent and Wallace [in press] for treatments of multiple-period forecasts.) On the assumptions in the text, it is easy to show that as long as $\Sigma_i v_i < 1$, then $\Sigma_i w_i < \Sigma_i v_i$. More generally, as long as Σv_i is less than unity, the sum of weights in the expectations generator

$$\hat{x}_{t+j} = \sum_{i=0}^{m} w_{ij} x_{t-i}$$

decreases as j increases. The relevance of this point can be seen when it is noted that in order to rationalize the presence of anticipated inflation in the wage equation, the standard practice is to cite the need to forecast as arising from the transactions costs that make it advisable to negotiate labor contracts of some minimal length. This rationalization suggests that, with quarterly data, the pertinent horizon over which anticipations are cast is probably between four and eight quarters. The above argument suggests that for multiple-period horizons, the appropriate sum of the weights is even smaller than the argument in the text implies.

Muth, John F. "Rational Expectations and the Theory of Price Movements." *Econometrica* 29 (July 1961): 315–35.

Nerlove, Marc. "Distributed Lags and Unobserved Components in Economic Time Series." In *Ten Economic Studies in the Tradition of Irving Fisher*, ed. by William Fellner et al. New York: Wiley, 1967.

Sargent, T., and Wallace, N. "Market Transaction Costs, Asset Demand Functions, and the Relative Potency of Monetary and Fiscal Policy." *J. Money, Credit, and Banking* (in press).

Solow, R. M. "Recent Controversy on the Theory of Inflation: An Eclectic View." In *Proceedings of a Symposium on Inflation: Its Causes, Consequences, and Control*, ed. by Stephen W. Rousseau. New York: New York Univ., 1968.

Tobin, James. "Discussion." In *Proceedings of a Symposium on Inflation: Its Causes, Consequences, and Control*, ed. by Stephen W. Rousseau. New York: New York Univ., 1968.

4

Distributed Lags and Optimal Investment Policy

Robert E. Lucas, Jr.

The literature on optimal investment policy for a single firm has grown rapidly in recent years.[1] It is now widely agreed that a satisfactory microeconomic theory of capital should account not only for the determination of the firm's "desired" capital stock, but also for the adjustment process by which this stock is attained (or approached). There are a number of plausible reasons why one might expect a present value maximizing firm to stagger its adjustment to a new equilibrium level of capital stock (assuming an equilibrium level exists) among which should be listed costs of accumulation which vary with its rapidity, gestation lags between initiation and completion of investment projects, lags between installation of capital equipment and its "decay," and uncertainty as to future demand and cost shifts. There is as yet no "general" theory of investment which analyzes simultaneously all of these factors: research to date has consisted of the singling out of one or another of these effects and the analysis of the structure of the optimal investment plan which results. The present paper is another step in this series of "partial analyses" of the investment decision. In particular, it is an attempt to determine the firm's optimal investment plan in the presence of gestation lags and under a wide variety of assumptions on depreciation patterns. The analysis is conducted under the assumptions of certainty and perfect markets used in Eisner and Strotz (1963) and Lucas (in press). In order to maintain contact with empirical investment studies, the discussion of each model concludes with the difference equation in gross or net investment which provides the natural discrete time approximation to the continuous optimal plan. It is found that with appropriate assumptions on lags and adjustment costs, any distributed lag investment function currently in use in empirical work can be given as sound an optimizing basis as that now enjoyed by the first-order "flexible accelerator."

I wish to thank Michael Lovell, John Muth, and Richard Schramm for their helpful criticism. [This paper was written in 1965. No attempt has been made to update the list of references to include the many more recent papers which bear on the subject of this paper.]

[1] E.g., see Arrow, Beckmann, and Karlin (1958); Eisner and Strotz (1963); Lucas (in press).

1. Statement of the Problem

Sections 2, 3, and 4 of this paper will be concerned with detailed examinations of the optimal investment policy for a single firm under several alternative sets of assumptions about production possibilities, depreciation, and gestation lags. In order to clarify the relationships among these various models, it will be helpful first to formulate a problem general enough to include those treated below as special cases.

Consider a firm whose receipts at time t depend on its capital stock $x(t)$, its gross rate of investment (purchases of capital goods) $y(t)$, its net rate of investment $\dot{x}(t)$, and the rate at which it is initiating new projects $z(t)$. The presence of $x(t)$ and $y(t)$ in a "receipts function" is, of course, standard, since the former provides productive services and the latter requires direct outlays. Insofar as production is disrupted by the installation of new capital goods, either $\dot{x}(t)$ or $y(t)$ or both may influence current receipts by inducing variation in output from a given $x(t)$ input, or, in other words, there may well be a cost in terms of output foregone of a rapid expansion of capital stock. Finally, if initiating investment projects involves research and planning in the search for and choice between proposed projects, an increased initiation rate will entail a diversion of resources from current production and a fall in output per unit of capital input. These considerations suggest a receipts function $R[x(t), \dot{x}(t), y(t), z(t)]$ with a positive marginal productivity of capital, negative marginal productivity of gross investment, and negative or zero marginal productivities for $\dot{x}(t)$ and $z(t)$. Throughout this paper we shall deal with a receipts function with these properties.

To complete the characterization of production possibilities, we relate initiated projects to gross investment, and investment to capital stock, as follows:

$$x(t) = \int_{-T}^{t} f(t - s) y(s) \, ds, \tag{1}$$

$$y(t) = \int_{-T}^{t} g(t - s) z(s) \, ds, \tag{2}$$

Assume that $f(u)$ is a piecewise continuous, nonincreasing function, with $f(0) = 1$ and $f(\infty) = 0$, and that g is piecewise continuous with

$$\int_{0}^{\infty} g(u) \, du = 1.$$

Note that any stronger restriction on f rules out such a popular depreciation hypothesis as $f(u) = 1$ for $0 < u \leq \tau$ and $f(u) = 0$ for $u > \tau$. Similarly, a stronger restriction on g would rule out the most commonly treated case of zero gestation time: $g(0) = 1, g(u) = 0$ for $u > 0$. Finally, note that

$x(t)$ can be related directly to initiations by:

$$x(t) = \int_{-T}^{t} w(t-s)z(s)\, ds, \tag{3}$$

where

$$w(u) = \int_{0}^{u} f(v)g(u-v)\, dv$$

is the convolution of f and g.

Given (1) and (2) [or (2) and (3)] together with an "endowment" $z(s)$, $-T < s < t$, of initiated projects it is evident that $x(s)$, $x(s)$, $y(s)$ and hence $R(s)$, $s > t$, are determined by the firm's choice of $z(s)$, $s > t$. We shall further restrict the function R by assuming that if $z^i(s)$, $i = 1, 2, s \geq t$, are two investment plans, with associated receipts streams $R^i(s)$, then for $0 < \theta < 1$,

$$R[\theta z^1(s) + (1-\theta)z^2(s)] > \theta R^1(s) + (1-\theta)R^2(s)$$

for any $z(s)$, $s \geq t$.

Next suppose that the firm obtains funds on a perfect capital market at a constant rate r, and that the receipts function R does not shift with time.[2] We shall then regard the firm's problem as that of initiating projects $z(t)$, $t \geq 0$, so as to maximize its present value, given by:

$$V(0) = \int_{0}^{\infty} e^{-rt}R(x, \dot{x}, y, z)\, dt,$$

subject to (1) and (2) and given an initial backlog of initiated projects $z(t)$, $-T \leq t < 0$. We assume that R is so restricted that a maximum for $V(0)$ exists for any initial backlog, so that there will be at least one optimal choice for $z(t)$, $t \geq 0$. In this event, there will be a *unique* optimal $z(t)$ path, in view of the concavity of R as specified in the previous paragraph.

The difficulty with this formulation is that, in the absence of additional restrictions on R, f, and g, it does not permit a very useful characterization of the optimal investment path. A direct variational approach (i.e., a comparison of a proposed optimal path $z^0[t]$ with $z^0[t] + \varepsilon v[t]$, ε "small") leads to an integral equation, or marginal equality involving discounted costs and returns, which sheds little light on the character of the optimal plan. For this reason, the remainder of this paper will treat the problem under alternative sets of simplifying restrictions. The restrictions we shall employ fall into two quite different categories. In Section 2 it is assumed that output depends only on $x(t)$ and $\dot{x}(t)$, so that $R(t)$ becomes $R(t) = pF(x, \dot{x}) - qy$, where p and q are the (constant) prices of output and

---

[2]The reader should be aware that the restriction that R does not shift over time is a strong one. For example, if prices enter into the function, this restriction requires that the firm treat the current ($t = 0$) price as permanent, and that future changes be wholly unanticipated.

capital goods, respectively. In this case, the linearity of $V(0)$ in $y(t)$, together with the linearity of (2) and (3) in $z(t)$ permits the conversion of the problem into a unconstrained maximum problem in which the integrand depends only on $x(t)$, $\dot{x}(t)$, and t. This conversion can be carried out with no further restrictions on f and g.

If R is not linear in $y(t)$ and $z(t)$, it will not be possible to convert the maximization of $V(0)$ into a problem involving $x(t)$ alone. Hence, to solve the problem for more general R functions, one must restrict f and g. This is done in Section 3, where these functions are assumed to possess *rational* LaPlace transforms. With this restriction, it is shown that the integral constraints (1) and (2) can be expressed as equivalent systems of differential constraints, and that with the constraints in this form the calculus of variations may be employed to characterize the optimal paths.

2. Solution When Receipts Are Linear in Gross Investment

In this section, we treat the problem stated in Section 1 with a receipts function of the form $R(t) = pF[x(t), \dot{x}(t)] - qy(t)$ where the prices p and q do not vary with time. The firm's present value is then:

$$V(0) = \int_0^\infty e^{-rt} R(t) \, dt = \int_0^\infty e^{-rt} [pF(x, \dot{x}) - qy] \, dt.$$

Note that $V(0)$ is the weighted sum of the LaPlace transforms of F and y. We shall use the constraints (2) and (3) to obtain an expression for the transform of $y(t)$ which involves only $x(t)$.

The right side of (3) can be written as the sum:

$$x(t) = \int_0^t w(t-s)z(s) \, ds + \int_{-T}^0 w(t-s)z(s) \, ds, \tag{4}$$

where the first term is the convolution of w and z and the second is a function of time, $m(t)$ say, which cannot be affected by decisions made subsequent to time 0. Applying the convolution theorem of LaPlace transforms to (4) gives:

$$\int_0^\infty e^{-rt} x(t) \, dt = L_r(x) = L_r(w)L_r(z) + L_r(m)$$
$$= L_r(f)L_r(g)L_r(z) + L_r(m). \tag{5}$$

Operating similarly on equation (2) gives:

$$L_r(y) = L_r(g)L_r(z) + L_r(n), \tag{6}$$

where

$$n(t) = \int_{-T}^0 g(t-s)z(s) \, ds.$$

Eliminating $L_r(z)$ between (5) and (6) gives:

$$L_r(y) = \frac{1}{L_r(f)} L_r(x) + \frac{L_r(n)L_r(f) - L_r(m)}{L_r(f)}. \tag{7}$$

Since only the first term on the right of (7) varies with the firm's choice of $z(t)$, $t \geq 0$, the $z(t)$ path which yields a maximum to $V(0)$ will be the same as that which maximizes

$$W(0) = \int_0^\infty e^{-rt}\left[pF(x, \dot{x}) - \frac{q}{L_r(f)} x\, dt \right].$$

Thus, under certain conditions, the original problem with integral constraints is easily converted to a classical problem in the calculus of variations. It should be noted, however, that this conversion will be useful only if the choice of $\dot{x}(t)$ is unrestricted, which requires that the choice of $z(t)$ be unrestricted *and* that $g(0) > 0$ (i.e., that an initiated project has some of its effect immediately). If these conditions do not hold, $\dot{x}(t)$ will be constrained and, further, the constraint at t will depend in a complicated fashion on decisions made prior to t.

In the event that $\dot{x}(t)$ *is* unrestricted, the problem of maximizing $W(0)$ is essentially identical to the problem analyzed in Eisner and Strotz (1963) and Lucas (in press) and requires no detailed discussion here. It can be shown that the optimal investment plan can be approximated by the stable, first-order flexible accelerator, with the stationary or desired capital stock given implicitly by

$$pF_x(x^0, 0) = \frac{q}{L_r(f)} - rpF_{\dot{x}}(x^0, 0). \tag{8}$$

The left side of (8) is the stationary marginal value product of capital. The second term on the right of (8) is the marginal cost, in terms of value of output foregone, of increasing the net accumulation rate from 0 to 1 unit. The first term on the right is an expression for the user cost or rental price of capital. With declining balance depreciation at a constant rate d, it reduces to $q(r + d)$; with "one hoss shay" depreciation with lifetime S, we have $q/L_r(f) = qr(1 - e^{-rS})^{-1}$. User costs for other depreciation schemes can easily be generated from a table of transforms.

Another feature of the converted problem which is worth noting is the absence in the integrand of $W(0)$ of the gestation lag function g. In other words, the nature of the gestation lag will have no effect on the optimal investment plan (although it will affect the value of the firm, given adoption of the optimal plan). This implausible result can be traced to the absence, in the formulation of the problem, of any penalties to the firm for initiating "too many" investment projects. An increase in product price, for example, will induce the firm to initiate a sufficient number of projects to put net investment *immediately* onto the optimal flexible accelerator path. As these projects "come due," it may be necessary to initiate a large volume of negative investment to remain on the optimal path, but however wild the fluctuation in initiations may be, it will have no effect on the firm's present value. To summarize, gestation lags, in the absence of appropriately specified initiation costs, will not affect the investment expenditures of an optimizing firm.

3. Solution When Lag Functions Have Rational Transforms

In the preceding section, the investment problem was examined under very general assumptions about the nature of the lag functions f and g, but under rather severe restrictions on the way in which initiated and completed investment projects affect the receipts of the firm. In this section, we require that f and g have rational LaPlace transforms, which will permit the conversion of the integral constraints (1) and (2) into a finite number of differential constraints. Once this conversion is accomplished, a much richer variety of problems can be handled by well-known variational techniques.

In order to permit the argument to proceed in the simplest way possible, we shall treat in detail a highly simplified problem in which gestation lags are excluded (so that $y[t] = z[t] = $ gross investment) and the receipts function takes the form $R(t) = rF[x(t)] - C[y(t)]$, where F and C are quadratic production and investment cost functions, respectively, and $F' > 0$, $F'' \leq 0$, $C' > 0$, $C'' > 0$. In fact, as will be noted at various points below, the methods used can be applied as well to the general problem posed in Section 1, provided only that f and g have rational transforms.

Assume, then, that the transform of the depreciation function f takes the form:

$$L_s(f) = \int_0^\infty e^{-st} f(t)\, dt = \frac{P(s)}{Q(s)},$$

where s is any complex number with nonnegative real part, and where:

$$P(s) = p_0 + p_1 s + \cdots + p_{n-1} s^{n-1}$$
$$Q(s) = q_0 + q_1 s + \cdots + q_{n-1} s^{n-1} + s^n.$$

Without loss of generality, it is also required that P and Q have no common roots. Functions f which satisfy this restriction can be written as a sum of terms like $A(t)e^{-\alpha t}$, where $A(t)$ is a polynomial in t. In this application, f is bounded, so that the real part of the parameter α must be positive. This restriction is considerably more stringent than the "smoothness" assumptions typically used in economic theory, but for the purposes of applied economics, it is essentially vacuous. While it rules out such familiar hypothesis as straight-line or "one hoss shay" depreciation (which were, of course, themselves introduced as approximations) it is compatible with any observed value-decline or survival curve.

The utility of the restriction for our purposes lies in the fact that it permits us to regard the constraint (1) as the solution for $x_1(t)$ of a system of n linear differential equations in $x_1(t), \ldots, x_n(t)$.[3] More precisely: *there is exactly one differential equation system of the form:*

$$\dot{x}_i = x_{i+1} + b_i y, \; i = 1, \ldots, n - 1,$$

$$\dot{x}_n = \sum_{j=1}^{n} a_{j-1} x_j + b_n y \tag{9}$$

$$x_i(-T) = 0, \; i = 1, \ldots, n$$

which yields as the solution for $x_1(t)$:

$$x_1(t) = \int_{-T}^{t} f(t - s) y(s) \, ds. \tag{10}$$

For the proof of this statement, and for subsequent arguments, it will be useful to develop some additional notation. Denote the $n \times n$ (companion) matrix of coefficients of the x_i in (9) by $A_0(0)$, and the matrix $[A_0(0) - \lambda I]$ by $A_0(\lambda)$. Denote by $A_j(\lambda), j = 1, \ldots, n - 1$, the submatrix of $A_0(\lambda)$ obtained by deleting the first j rows and columns. Then for $j = 0, 1, \ldots, n - 1$ the characteristic polynomial of $A_j(0)$ is

$$\det A_j(\lambda) = (-1)^{n-j}[a_j + a_{j+1}\lambda + \cdots + a_{n-1}\lambda^{n-j-1} + \lambda^{n-j}]$$
$$= (-1)^{n-j} g_j(\lambda),$$

where the second equality defines $g_0(\lambda), \ldots, g_{n-1}(\lambda)$. It is convenient to define $g_n(\lambda) = 1$.

With this notation established, we may proceed with the proof. Without loss of generality, assume that $T = 0$ (since the system can always be put in this form by a change in the time variable). Let $L_s(x_i)$ be the transform of $x_i(t)$ and $L_s(y)$ the transform of $y(t)$. In matrix form, the transformed system (9) is $A_0(s)L_s(x) = -bL_s(y)$, where $L_s(x) = \text{col}[L_s(x_i)]$ and $bL_s(y) = \text{col}[b_i L_s(y)]$. The first row of the inverse of $A_0(s)$ is the row vector whose jth element is $-g_j(s)/g_0(s)$. Hence the transform of the solution for $x_1(t)$ is:

$$L_s(x_1) = L_s(y) \sum_{i=1}^{n} b_i \frac{g_i(s)}{g_0(s)}.$$

---

[3] The notion of using the rational transform assumption to permit the conversion of an integral characterization of a distributed lag into a differential description has been exploited, in the discrete analogue, by Jorgenson (in press). The proof, which is given below, that this conversion is legitimate is essentially an adaptation of arguments associated with standard treatments of linear differential equations using LaPlace transforms. See, e.g., Widder (1961, chap. 14).

The solution for $x_1(t)$ is therefore:

$$x_1(t) = \int_0^t f^*(t - s)y(s)\,dz,$$

where $L_s(f^*) = \sum_{i=1}^n b_i[g_i(s)/g_0(s)]$. It remains only to show that there is a one-to-one correspondence between the coefficients p_i, q_i of $L_s(f)$ and the coefficients a_i, b_i of $L_s(f^*)$ such that $L_s(f) = L_s(f^*)$. This correspondence is given by $a_i = q_i$ for $i = 0, 1, \ldots, n - 1$; $b_1 = p_{n-1}$, $b_1a_{n-1} + b_2 = p_{n-2}$, $\ldots$, $b_1a_1 + \cdots + b_{n-1}a_{n-1} + r_n = p_0$.

The problem of the firm, stated at the beginning of this section, may now be restated in what we have shown to be the equivalent form:

$$\max_{\substack{y(t) \\ t \geq 0}} V(0) = \int_0^\infty e^{-rt}\{pF[x_1(t)] - C[y(t)]\}\,dt,$$

subject to

$$\dot{x}(t) = A_0(0)x(t) + by(t) \tag{11}$$

(where [11] is [9] in matrix form) and given $x_1(0), \ldots, x_n(0)$.[4] Of the n "state variables" $x_1(t), \ldots, x_n(t)$, only the first has a natural economic interpretation as the level of capital services at time t. The remaining $n - 1$ stocks are other weighted integrals of the initial endowment $y(s)$, $-T \leq s < 0$, of capital goods, and may be regarded as "auxiliary capital measures." It has long been recognized, of course, that it is not in general possible to summarize all the relevant information about the endowment $y(s)$ in a single capital measure, so that the novelty of this approach lies not in the use of more than one capital measure but rather in the effort to define these measures exactly.

To develop the necessary conditions for a maximum of $V(0)$, form the Lagrangean expression

$$H(x_1, \ldots, x_n, \lambda_1, \ldots, \lambda_n, y, t) = e^{-rt}[F(x_1) - C(y)$$

$$+ \sum_{i=1}^n \lambda_i(\dot{x}_i - \sum_{j=1}^n a_{ij}x_j - b_i\,y)],$$

where $(a_{ij}) = A_0(0)$. Any optimal path must satisfy the Euler-Lagrange conditions, given, after some simplification, by (11) and

$$0 = C'(y) + \sum_{i=1}^n \lambda_i b_i \tag{12}$$

$$0 = F'(x_1) + a_0\lambda_n + r\lambda_1 - \dot{\lambda}_1 \tag{13}$$

$$0 = -\lambda_{k-1} + a_{k-1}\lambda_n + r\lambda_k - \lambda_k - \dot{\lambda}_k, \quad k = 2, 3, \ldots, n, \tag{14}$$

[4]The values of $x_1(0) \ldots, x_n(0)$ are determined by (9), given $x_1(-T), \ldots, x_n(-T)$ and $y(s)$, $-T < s < 0$.

together with the endpoint conditions:

$$\lim_{t \to \infty} e^{-rt} \lambda_i(t) = 0, \; i = 1, \ldots, n. \tag{15}$$

To derive the implications of equations (11)–(15), we proceed in three steps. First, a stationary solution is found, and the effect of changes in the interest rate on the stationary levels of capital services and gross investment is determined. Secondly, this stationary solution is shown to be stable, and the unique optimal investment plan is determined explicitly. Finally, the distributed lag gross investment function which approximates the continuous solution is determined.

Denote by (11^0)–(14^0) the system of equations obtained from (11)–(14) by setting all time derivatives equal to zero. We seek a solution x^0, λ^0, y^0 to this system of $2n + 1$ linear equations. From (14^0) λ_j, $j = 1, \ldots, n - 1$ is obtained as a function of λ_n:

$$\lambda_j = \lambda_n g_j(r).$$

From (13^0):

$$\begin{aligned} F'(x_1) &= -a_0 \lambda_n - r \lambda_1 \\ &= -a_0 \lambda_n - r \lambda_n g_1(r) \\ &= -\lambda_n g_0(r). \end{aligned}$$

From (12^0):

$$\begin{aligned} C'(y) &= -\lambda_n \sum_{i=1}^{n} b_i g_i(r) \\ &= F'(x_1) \sum_{i=1}^{n} b_i \frac{g_i(r)}{g_0(r)} \end{aligned}$$

or:

$$F'(x_1) = \frac{C'(y)}{L_r(f)}. \tag{16}$$

A second relation between the stationary values of y and x_1 is obtained from (11^0):

$$x_1 = L_0(f) y = y \int_0^\infty f(u) \, du. \tag{17}$$

It is easily seen that if x_1^0 and y^0 are the unique solutions to (16) and (17), $dx_1^0/dr < 0$ and $dy^0/dr < 0$.

To obtain the general solution to (11)–(14), we first use (12) to eliminate $y(t)$ from the system, replacing $y(t)$ in (11) with:

$$y(t) = y^0 - \frac{1}{C''} \sum_{i=1}^{n} b_i [\lambda_i(t) - \lambda_i^0].$$

Then (11), (12), and (14) constitute a homogeneous system of $2n$ linear equations in the variables $x_i - x_i^0$ and $\lambda_i - \lambda_i^0$:

$$\begin{bmatrix} \dot{x} \\ \dot{\lambda} \end{bmatrix} = A \begin{bmatrix} x - x^0 \\ \lambda - \lambda^0 \end{bmatrix} = \begin{bmatrix} A_0(0) & B \\ C & -A_0'(r) \end{bmatrix} \begin{bmatrix} x - x^0 \\ \lambda - \lambda^0 \end{bmatrix}, \qquad (18)$$

where B is the $n \times n$ matrix whose i,j-th element is $(b_i b_j)/C''$ and C is the $n \times n$ matrix with F'' in the upper left corner and zeros elsewhere. We wish to find the $2n$ roots of the characteristic polynomial $P(q) = \det(A - qI)$ associated with this system.

Expanding $\det(A - qI)$ by the cofactors of the first column, we find that $P(q) = P_1(q) + P_2(q)$, where

$$P_1(q) = \det A_0(q) \cdot \det A_0(r - q) \cdot (-1)^n$$
$$= (-1)^n g_0(q) g_0(r - q),$$

and $P_2(q)$ is F'' times its cofactor. Expanding the cofactor of F'' by the cofactors of its first row one finds, after lengthy calculation, that

$$P_2(q) = (-1)^n \frac{F''}{C''} \left[\sum_{i=1}^{n} b_i g_i(q) \right] \left[\sum_{i=1}^{n} b_i g_i(r - q) \right].$$

Hence the roots of $P(q)$ occur in n pairs: if q is a root, so is $r - q$. We now wish to show that no root of $P(q)$ has a real part lying in the closed interval $[0, r]$. To do so, we proceed by contradiction.

The integral $L_s(f)$ converges for all complex s with nonnegative real parts, which implies that the roots of $g_0(q)$ all have strictly negative real parts.[5] Hence if q^0 (and thus also $r - q^0$) is a root of $P(q)$ with real part in $[0, r]$, we have $g_0(q^0) g_0(r - q^0) \neq 0$, and

$$0 = P(q^0) = g_0(q^0) g_0(r - q^0)(-1)^n \left[1 - \frac{F''}{C''} L_{q^0}(f) L_{r-q^0}(f) \right]. \qquad (19)$$

Since $F'' < 0$ and $C'' > 0$, (19) requires that the product $L_{q^0}(f) L_{r-q^0}(f)$ be real and negative. For complex $q^0 = q_1 + i q_2$, q_1 and q_2 real, we have

$$L_{q^0}(f) = \int_0^\infty e^{-q_1 t} \cos(q_2 t) f(t)\, dt + i \int_0^\infty e^{-q_1 t} \sin(q_2 t) f(t)\, dt,$$

and similarly for $L_{r-q^0}(f)$. Multiplying the two transforms expressed in this form, an expression for the real part of the product is obtained which may be regarded as a function of q_2 for fixed q_1. Examination of this function shows that it takes the positive value $L_{q_1}(f) L_{r-q_1}(f)$ when $q_2 = 0$, and further that its derivative with respect to q_2 is zero everywhere. Hence q^0 cannot satisfy (19) and is not, therefore, a root of $P(q)$. We conclude that *the matrix A of the system (18) has n roots with negative real parts and n roots with real parts exceeding* r.

----

[5] Recall that $L_s(f) = \sum_{i=1}^{n} b_i [g_i(s)]/[g_0(s)]$.

To write out the general solution to (18), let

$$T = \begin{bmatrix} T_{11} & T_{22} \\ T_{21} & T_{22} \end{bmatrix},$$

where T_{ij} are $n \times n$ blocks, be the nonsingular matrix such that:

$$T^{-1}AT = \begin{bmatrix} J_1 & 0 \\ 0 & J_2 \end{bmatrix}$$

where J_1 is the $n \times n$ Jordan matrix whose diagonal elements are those roots of A with negative real parts and J_2 is the Jordon matrix corresponding to the roots with positive real parts. The general solution to (18) is then:

$$\begin{bmatrix} x(t) - x^0 \\ \lambda(t) - \lambda^0 \end{bmatrix} = T \begin{bmatrix} e^{tJ_1} & 0 \\ 0 & e^{tJ_2} \end{bmatrix} T^{-1} \begin{bmatrix} x(0) - x^0 \\ \lambda(0) - \lambda^0 \end{bmatrix}.$$

The initial values $x_i(0)$ are determined by gross investment prior to time 0; $\lambda(0)$ is yet to be determined. Letting T^{ij}, $i, j = 1, 2$, be the blocks of T^{-1}, the solution for $\lambda(t)$ is

$$\begin{aligned} \lambda(t) = \lambda^0 &+ T_{21}e^{tJ_1}\{T^{11}[x(0) - x^0] + T^{12}[\lambda(0) - \lambda^0]\} \\ &+ T_{22}e^{tJ_2}\{T^{21}[x(0) - x^0] + T^{22}[\lambda(0) - \lambda^0]\}. \end{aligned} \tag{20}$$

If the necessary conditions (15) are to be satisfied, it is evident that the second term on the right of (20) must be zero, since any nonzero components will move away from zero at exponential rates exceeding r. This requires that

$$\lambda(0) - \lambda^0 = -(T^{22})^{-1}T^{21}[x(0) - x^0].$$

Hence, observing that $[T^{11} - T^{12}(T^{22})T^{21}] = T_{11}^{-1}$, the unique optimal paths for $\lambda(t)$ and $x(t)$ are:[6]

$$\lambda(t) = \lambda^0 + T_{21}e^{tJ_1}T_{11}^{-1}[x(0) - x^0], \tag{21}$$

$$x(t) = x^0 + T_{11}e^{tJ_1}T_{11}^{-1}[x(0) - x^0]. \tag{22}$$

To develop the implications for observed investment behavior of the solutions (21) and (22), three further steps are needed. First, (21) and (22) must be replaced by discrete time analogues or approximations. Second, provision must be made for changes over time in the determinants of x^0

---

[6]Equations (21) and (22) are asymptotically valid approximations to the optimal path even if F and C are not quadratic. In the nonquadratic case, (18) is regarded as a linear approximation to the true, nonlinear system obtained from the necessary conditions. Equation (20) *cannot*, however, be treated as an approximation to the general solution of this nonlinear system, since the matrix A has n positive roots. Hence, in the nonquadratic case, the conditions (15) cannot be used as above to rule out nonoptimal paths which satisfy (11)–(14). Nevertheless, (21) and (22) *are* valid approximations since they approximate *a* path satisfying (15) and the uniqueness of the optimal path assures that there is only one such path. For a fuller treatment along these lines, see Lucas (in press).

and λ^0 (in this case, the rate of interest). Third, the solution must be expressed in terms of gross investment only, since, in the absence of prior information on the depreciation function, no other variable involved in the problem can be observed.

In order to analyze the effects of interest rate changes, we adopt the convention that such changes occur at discrete points in time, one unit apart, that these changes are unanticipated, and that after a change the firm behaves as though it knows that the new rate will be maintained forever. We shall "measure" capital stocks at the beginning of a period and all other variables at the end of a period, so that x_t^0 and λ_t^0 will be functions of the rate r_t which has prevailed over the preceding one period. Note also that in considering the discrete case we take into account the effect of interest rate changes on x^0 and λ^0 while ignoring the effect of these changes on adjustment speeds. With these conventions established, define $R = T_{11}e^{J_1}T_{11}^{-1}$ and $S = T_{21}e^{J_1}T_{11}^{-1}$, and replace (21) and (22) with:

$$x_{t+1} = Rx_t + [I - R]x^0(r_t), \tag{23}$$
$$\lambda_t = \lambda^0(r_t) + S[x_t - x^0(r_t)]. \tag{24}$$

An equivalent form for the difference equations (23) is:

$$\begin{aligned} \rho_n x_{t+n} + \rho_{n-1}x_{t+n-1} + \cdots + \rho_1 x_{t+1} + \rho_0 x_t \\ = U_{n-1}x_{t+n-1}^0 + \cdots + U_1 x_{t+1}^0 + U_0 x_t^0, \end{aligned} \tag{25}$$

where $(-1)^n \Sigma_{i=0}^n \rho_i q^i (\rho_n = 1)$ is the characteristic polynomial of R, and

$$U_j = (\rho_{j+1}I + \rho_{j+2}R + \cdots + \rho_{n-1}R^{n-j-2} + R^{n-j-1})(I - R)$$

for $j = 0, 1, \ldots, n - 1$. Note that if $q_1, \ldots, q_n$ are the negative roots of A, then $e^{q_1}, \ldots, e^{q_n}$ are the roots of R, so that the difference equation (25) (or [23]) is stable. Further, we have

$$\sum_{j=0}^{n-1} U_j = I \sum_{i=0}^{n} \rho_i. \tag{26}$$

From the discrete version of (12) and from (24):

$$y_t - y_t^0 = -\frac{1}{C''}\sum_{i=1}^{n} b_i(\lambda_{it} - \lambda_{it}^0) = c'(x_t - x_t^0), \tag{27}$$

where $c' = -1/C''(b_1, \ldots, b_n)S$ is a $1 \times n$ vector of constants. Then from (25) and (27):

$$\sum_{i=0}^{n} \rho_i y_{t+i} = \sum_{i=1}^{n} \rho_i y_{t+i}^0 - \rho_n c' x_{t+n}^0 + c'\left[\sum_{i=0}^{n-1}(U_i - \rho_i I)x_{t+i}^0\right]. \tag{28}$$

From (11^0), each x_{it}^0 can be obtained as a constant times y_t^0, say $x_t^0 = ky_t^0$, $k = \text{col}(k_i)$. Then combining terms on the right of (28), the coefficient of $y_{t+i}^0, i = 0, 1, \ldots, n - 1$, is $\rho_i + c'(U_i - \rho_i I)k$ and the coefficient of y_{t+n}^0 is $\rho_n - \rho_n c'k$. Using (26), one finds that these $n + 1$ coefficients sum to $\Sigma_{i=0}^n \rho_i$. Finally, since y_t^0 is a linear function of r_t, we obtain the gross investment function:

$$y_{t+n} = \alpha_0 + \sum_{i=0}^n \beta_i r_{t+1} - \sum_{i=0}^{n-1} \rho_i y_{t+1}. \qquad (29)$$

The ratio $(\Sigma_{i=1}^n \beta_i)/(1 + \Sigma_{i=0}^{n-1} \rho_i)$ is equal to the "long-run" derivative of gross investment with respect to the interest rate. The theory predicts that this derivative will be negative, and in addition, that the difference equation (29) will be stable. Finally, from a given hypothetical depreciation function one could in principle deduce additional implications on $\beta_0, \ldots, \beta_n$ and $\rho_0, \ldots, \rho_{n-1}$. Reviewing the derivation of (29), however, one sees that there is little hope of obtaining a simple, general formula for obtaining these implications.

Before concluding the analysis of this problem, it is of some interest to note the simplification which results if we assume constant returns to scale, or more precisely, that $F''(x) = 0$. Returning to equation (18), $F''(x) = 0$ is seen to imply that the block C of the matrix A is the zero matrix, so that A is block-diagonal, with characteristic polynomial $P_1(q)$. The n negative roots of $P_1(q)$ are the roots of $A_0(0)$ (the poles of the transform $L_s[f]$). The solutions (21) and (22) become

$$x(t) = x^0 + e^{A_0(0)t}[x(0) - x^0],$$
$$\lambda(t) = \lambda^0$$

and the gross investment function is simply

$$y_t = \alpha + \beta r_t. \qquad (30)$$

Thus under constant returns, gross investment attains its stationary level instantaneously. The capital stock will either grow or decline until it reaches the level at which y^0 is just sufficient to maintain it.

This completes the analysis of the problem stated at the beginning of this section, in which there are no gestation lags separating the initiation and completion of an investment project and where the depreciation function is assumed to possess a rational LaPlace transform. To summarize the argument, it was shown that the integral constraint relating past gross investment to current capital services can be converted in a unique way to a system of differential constraints. This conversion requires the introduction into the analysis of a finite number of "auxiliary capital measures." With the problem in this more tractable form, the calculus of variations is used to obtain a differential equation system together with boundary conditions whose unique solution gives the optimal investment plan for the firm. When translated into discrete terms, this optimal plan yields a stable distributed lag investment function of the "general Pascal" form proposed by Jorgenson (in press).

It is evident that the methods used to attack this simple problem are easily extended to other cases. In particular, we are interested in the investment function which results when gestation lags are reintroduced into the problem, and the firm's problem is the maximization of:

$$V(0) = \int_0^\infty e^{-rt}[F(x) - C(z) - qy] \, dt,$$

subject to (1) and (2) and given the backlog of initiations $z(t)$, $-T < t < 0$. Let the functions f, F, and C be restricted as in the beginning of this section, and let the gestation function g have a rational transform, convergent for all s with nonnegative real parts. To solve this problem, (2) and (3) are converted to first-order systems separately, and the argument proceeds exactly as in the simpler case. If $L_s(g)$ has n_g poles and $L_s(w) = L_s(f)L_s(g)$ has n_w poles, then letting $n = n_g + n_w$, equation (29) gives the gross investment function for this case as well. Under constant returns to scale, (29) still holds, with $n = n_g$. For each of these cases, the "long-run" interest rate coefficient is predicted to be negative, and in each case the difference equation is stable. It should be noted, however, that the three theories which may underly (29) are *not* in principle indistinguishable from each other. In deriving (29) and the two stated implications, the only information on the lag functions which has been used is the assumption that their transforms converge on the right half of the complex plane. Depending on the additional restrictions one may wish to place on f or g or both, there will be additional implications on the coefficients of (29).

4. Discussion

This paper has been concerned with the examination of the optimizing basis underlying distributed lag investment demand functions for a single firm. Confining the argument to conditions of certainty and perfect capital markets, we have treated the firm's problem as one of present value maximization so that stationary or desired capital stocks and the optimal path of approach to these levels can be derived in a single operation. Within this framework, the implications of a variety of assumptions on the production function, the depreciation pattern of capital equipment, and the lag between the initiation and completion of an investment project, have been obtained. This analysis has suggested several observations on investment theory and econometric work which may be stated briefly before concluding.

First, and most important, the effect on investment behavior of lags of *any* sort depends critically on the way in which movements from one stock level to another affect the firm's costs and/or output. Thus in Section 2 it was found that the introduction of gestation lags has *no* effect on either desired stock or on the optimal approach to this stock as long as the initiation of projects is assumed to be costless. In view of this fact, it is not surprising that when the problem is formulated so that depreciation and gestation assumptions *do* affect the investment behavior of an optimizing firm, the relation between the assumed form of these lags and the form of the distributed lag investment function which results is far from simple. Only under constant returns to scale can the form of the lag structure of investment demand be inferred from knowledge of the functions f and g.

Second, it is evident from the analysis in Section 3 that the lag between initiation and completion of an investment project and the lag between installation and replacement of a piece of equipment can be treated in essentially identical fashion. For empirical study of investment demand, it is no more *necessary* that we know in advance the depreciation function f than it is necessary to know the form of the gestation lag g (although, of course, genuine a priori information on either is useful). Similarly, we are in as good a position to assert that initiated projects are a constant fraction of completed projects as we are to assert that depreciation is a constant fraction of completions (or of capital stock): both assertions are true for stationary or exponentially growing capital stocks; neither is true for irregularly moving "desired" or actual stocks such as are typically observed (unless, of course, the true f or g is exponential).

Finally, the analysis above may serve to underscore Griliches's (1963) insistence on the futility of a search for a single, "all purpose" measure of capital. What is, in fact, given to a firm is a backlog of initiated, partially or fully completed, investment projects. If by a capital measure is meant a weighted integral, or sum, of this backlog, the capital measurement problem may be rephrased as the question: what is the minimum number of such weighted integrals necessary to determine (a) the firm's optimal investment policy, and (b) the firm's present value under this policy? With exponential depreciation and no gestation lag, this minimum number is one: initial capital services contain all the necessary information. Under the assumptions of Section 2, one measure (initial capital services) suffices to answer (a), while a second $[V(0) - W(0)]$ must be added to answer (b). When these assumptions are relaxed, as is done in Section 3, one must require the lag functions to possess rational LaPlace transforms in order to define a finite number of "capital measures" needed to determine the optimal policy. In the absence of this or other restrictions on the lag functions, one cannot in general summarize a $y(t)$, $t < 0$, endowment in any finite number of capital measures.

References

Arrow, K. J.; Beckmann, M.; and Karlin S. "Optimal Expansion of the Capacity of the Firm." In *Studies in the Mathematical Theory of Inventory and Production,* ed. by K. J. Arrow, S. Karlin, and H. Scarf. Stanford: Stanford Univ. Press, 1958.

Eisner, R., and Strotz, R. H. "The Determinants of Business Investment." In Commission on Money and Credit, *Impacts of Monetary Policy.* Englewood Cliffs: Prentice-Hall, 1963.

Griliches, Z. "Capital Stock in Investment Functions: Some Problems of Concept and Measurement." In *Measurement in Economics: Studies in Mathematical Economics and Econometrics in Memory of Yehunda Grunfeld.* Stanford: Stanford Univ. Press, 1963.

Jorgenson, D. W. "Rational Distributed Lag Functions." *Econometrica* (in press).

Lucas, R. "Optimal Investment Policy and the Flexible Accelerator." *Internat. Econ. Rev.* (in press).

Widder, D. V. *Advanced Calculus.* Englewood Cliffs: Prentice-Hall, 1961.

5

Optimal Investment with Rational Expectations

Robert E. Lucas, Jr.

Most recent work in investment theory has been concerned with the present value maximization problem of an individual firm. That is, it is directed at the question: how should a firm with given production possibilities and initial assets respond to an anticipated pattern of future prices and interest rates? In many applications, it is of at least equal interest to restate the question at the *industry* level: how will a competitive industry, composed of optimizing firms, respond to shifts in its demand and factor supply functions? In particular, the latter statement of the problem is more relevant to econometric investment studies, most of which have utilized data at the industry or even sectoral level.

In a recent paper (Lucas 1967) I have analyzed the dynamic behavior of a competitive industry composed of firms which optimize over time. This model is restated in Section I below. The argument of this section proceeds in what would seem to be a natural "two-step" fashion: first, the supply response of an individual firm to changing current and expected prices is obtained; secondly, these supply functions are aggregated over firms and combined with a demand function to determine price and industry output. To conduct an analysis of this sort, it is necessary to make some assumption about the way in which firms form price expectations. For simplicity, I have assumed that firms' expectations are *static* in the sense that current price is believed to be permanent.

In Section II, an industry with the characteristics postulated in Section I is analyzed again, this time under the assumption that firms' expectations are *rational* (i.e., correct). In this context, the optimal supply response of firms and the industry as a whole must be determined simultaneously rather than sequentially as in Section I. The conclusion of this section is that, in the price-quantity plane, the behavior of the industry under the two expectations hypotheses is qualitatively identical. Under rational expectations, however, it turns out that the "equations of motion" of the industry may be interpreted as necessary conditions for the industry-wide maximization of a "discounted consumer surplus" integral.

This paper was written in 1966. No attempt has been made to update the list of references to include the many more recent papers which bear on the subject of this paper.

In Section III, the analysis of Section II is reinterpreted to provide a growth theory for a pure monopolist. Section IV discusses possible generalizations of the relationship between the maximization of consumer surplus and the equations governing industry behavior to models with different production possibilities.

I. A Model of a Competitive Industry

Consider an industry consisting of many small firms, each producing a single output $Q(t)$ by means of a single capital input $K(t)$. Capital in use at time t is determined by an initial stock $K(0)$ and a real, gross investment rate $I(t)$, according to

$$\dot{K}(t) = I(t) - \delta K(t), \tag{1}$$

where δ is constant. Output is determined by a "production function" which incorporates internal "costs of adjustment" arising from variations in the investment rate:

$$Q(t) = K(t)f[I(t)/K(t)] = K(t)f[u(t)], \tag{2}$$

where $u(t) = I(t)/K(t)$. The function f is defined for $u \geq 0$, has a continuous second derivative, and satisfies

$$f(0) > 0, f'(u) < 0, f''(u) < 0, \text{ and } f'(r + \delta - \alpha) = -\infty, \tag{3}$$

where r is the firms' cost of capital and α is some arbitrarily small, positive number.

With prices p and q in the output and capital goods markets, each firm's receipts are

$$R(t) = K(t)\{pf[u(t)] - qu(t)\},$$

and present value is

$$V(0) = \int_0^\infty e^{-rt}R(t)\, dt.$$

Our hypotheses both about the state of these markets (and about the capital funds market in which r is determined) and about the way in which firms form price expectations will be summarized in the assumption that each firm treats p, q, and r as constant at current levels.

Given these production possibilities and market opportunities, it is assumed that each firm selects a continuous investment plan $I(t)$ (or $u[t]$) for $t \geq 0$, satisfying $I(t) \geq 0$ for all t, so as to maximize $V(0)$, given $K(0)$ and subject to (1). It is also assumed that such a plan exists for all $K(0) \geq 0$. It can then be shown that the optimal investment plan is unique.

To determine the optimal plan, form the Hamiltonian expression:

$$H(u, K, \lambda, t) = e^{-rt}K(t)[pf(u) - qu + \lambda(u - \delta)].$$

Then if $[u(t), K(t)]$ is the optimal plan, there must exist a continuous function $\lambda(t)$ such that

$$\dot{\lambda} = (r + \delta - u)\lambda - pf(u) + qu, \tag{4}$$

and

$$\lim_{t \to \infty} e^{-rt}\lambda(t) = 0. \tag{5}$$

Further, $u(t)$ maximizes $H(u, K, \lambda, t)$ for all $t \geq 0$, and the constraint (1) is satisfied. From (3), H is maximized at a unique value of u for all K, λ, and t. At this value

$$pf'(u) - q + \lambda \leq 0, \tag{6}$$

where equality holds if the maximizing value of u is positive. Since (4) and (6) do not depend on $K(t)$, the determination of the optimal investment plan is reduced to that of finding a solution $[u(t), \lambda(t)]$ of (4) and (6) which satisfies (5). If such a solution is found, the optimal $K(t)$ is given by (1) and $K(0)$.

We next show that for all positive p, q, r, and δ, (4) and (6) have a stationary solution. Setting $\dot{\lambda} = 0$ and using (4) to eliminate λ, equation (6) becomes

$$p[f(u) + (r + \delta - u)f'(u)] \leq q(r + \delta), \tag{7}$$

with equality for $u > 0$. The determination of u by (7) is indicated diagrammatically in figure 1. From (3), the left side of (7) is defined at $u = 0$,

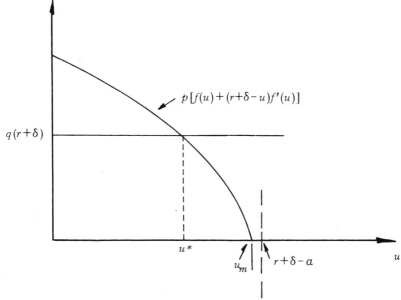

FIG. 1

is declining for $0 \leq u < r + \delta - \alpha$, and becomes an arbitrarily large (in absolute value) negative number as u approaches the right endpoint of this interval. Thus, if $p[f(0) + (r + \delta - u)f'(0)] \geq q(r + \delta)$, (7) is satisfied with equality for a unique $u = u^*$. If this inequality at $u = 0$ does not hold, $u = 0$ satisfies (7) with a strict inequality. The constant solution u^* (and the corresponding constant λ^*) so determined thus satisfy (4), (5), and (6). Since the optimal investment plan is unique, this stationary plan is the optimal one.

By rewriting (7), one obtains a marginal condition with a familiar interpretation:

$$p[f(u) - uf'(u)] \leq [q - pf'(u)][r + \delta], \tag{8}$$

with equality for $u > 0$. Since $f - uf'$ is the marginal physical product of capital, the left side of (8) is the marginal value product of capital. The term $q - pf'$ on the right of (8) is the marginal cost of accumulating capital, consisting of payments to suppliers (q) and the value of output foregone by increasing investment by one unit ($-pf'$). The term $r + \delta$ converts the right side of (8) to the units of a rental price or user cost of capital.

Equation (8) (or [7]) may be solved for u as a function of r and q/p. It is easily found that, for $u > 0$, $\partial u / \partial r < 0$ and $\partial u / \partial (q/p) < 0$. The function $u = D(r, q/p)$ with these properties is the firm's investment demand function. It is clear that if u satisfies (7), $f(u) > 0$; hence, output will always be positive. The function

$$Q(t) = K(t)f[D(r, q/p)] \tag{9}$$

is the firm's short-run supply function. Its derivatives are determined from those of f and D. Finally, the firm's planned capital stock and output growth are given by

$$\frac{\dot{K}(t)}{K(t)} = \frac{\dot{Q}(t)}{Q(t)} = D[r, q/p] - \delta. \tag{10}$$

In the remainder of this section we shall be concerned with an industry of firms behaving as the firm just described would. In this discussion, product price will vary through time, so that it will be useful first to consider the response of investment to price changes in somewhat more detail. Looking again at figure 1, it is seen that for fixed q and r, changes in p will induce proportional shifts in the ordinate of curve $p[f + (r + \delta - u)f']$ at each value of u. Thus there will always be some critical price $p_c > 0$ such that $u = 0$ for $p \leq p_c$. For $p \geq p_c$, investment is a rising function of price, or $D'(p) > 0$. At some $u = u_m < r + \delta - \alpha$ (where u_m does not depend on p) the curve $p[f + (r + \delta - u)f']$ will cross the u-axis. Also:

$$\lim_{p->\infty} D(p) = u_m.$$

The curve $u = D(p)$ must then have the form indicated in figure 2.

Turning next to the industry, note first that if all firms face the same prices and have the same production possibilities the individual investment demand, output supply, and growth functions (eqq. [10]) all aggregate perfectly to the industry level. We shall let $Q(t)$, $K(t)$, and $I(t)$ refer to industry aggregates without change in notation. It remains only to postulate a demand function for the industry. Let this function be

$$p(t) = g[z(t)], \tag{11}$$

where $z(t)$ is the ratio of output $Q(t)$ to a "shift variable" $S(t)$, with

$$S(t) = S(0)e^{\beta t}, \ \beta < r, \tag{12}$$

and where g has a continuous second derivative and satisfies

$$g'(z) < 0, \ g(0) = \infty, \ g(\infty) = 0. \tag{13}$$

From (10), (12), and the definition of $z(t)$, the long-run supply function of the industry is:

$$\frac{\dot{z}(t)}{z(t)} = D[p(t)] - \delta - \beta. \tag{14}$$

Combining (11) and (15) yields a first-order equation in $z(t)$ which, with $z(0)$, determines the movement over time of industry output and, via (11),

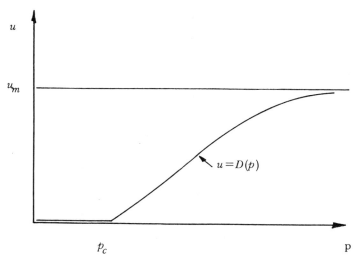

FIG. 2

of price. Initial output $Q(0)$ is determined by the intersection of the demand curve (11) and the short-run supply curve (9).[1]

The behavior over time of industry output and price for the case in which $D(p) = \beta + \delta$ has a solution p^* (i.e., for the case $u_m > \beta + \delta \geq 0$) is shown in figure 3. In this case, $z^* = g^{-1}(p^*)$ is a position of stable equilibrium for the industry: for any $z(0)$, $z(t)$ converges monotonically to z^*. Price $p(t)$ is determined by (11); $u(t)$, $K(t)$, and $Q(t)$ are determined in the manner indicated in the discussion of individual firm behavior.

In the event that either $u_m \leq \beta + \delta$ or $\beta + \delta < 0$, there is no price satisfying $D(p) = \beta + \delta$ and hence no equilibrium position for the industry. In the first case, in which demand is expanding "too rapidly," $\dot{z}/z < 0$ for all t, so that $z(t)$ will fall toward zero and price will rise without limit. In the second case, where demand is declining even more rapidly than capital is depreciating, $z(t)$ grows and price tends to zero.

One interesting feature of the industry just described is the fact that the firms which comprise it will grow at a rate independent of initial size (as measured by assets or output). Further, unit costs (however measured) will not vary across firms of different sizes, and estimation of a conventional cross-section production function will yield $Q = aK$ which is homogeneous of degree one. Finally, the present value of an optimally managed firm will

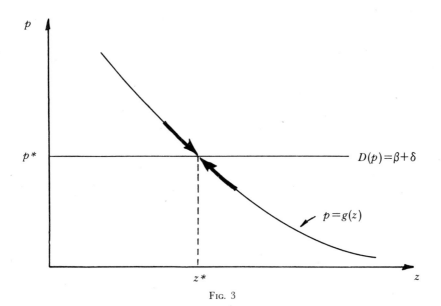

FIG. 3

---

[1]From what has been assumed so far, it follows that (9) and (11) are satisfied for at *least* one value of p, but it does *not* follow that the short-run market clearing price is unique. This possible lack of uniqueness has no effect on the stability argument.

be proportional to its asset holdings, so that there are no "scale incentives" for firms to merge or dissolve. In short, this model is consistent with the evidence generally cited in support of the static constant returns to scale hypothesis. Unlike the latter theory, however, the theory developed here *does* distinguish between short- and long-run behavior, and the optimal policy for each firm is determinate.

II. The Competitive Model under Rational Expectations

In the preceding section, firms were assumed to regard the current price at each moment of time as a "permanent" price, yet this expectation proved valid at one price only: the industry's long-run equilibrium price. In this section, it is assumed that the output price expectations of each firm are *rational*, or that the entire future price pattern, $p(t)$, $t \geq 0$, is correctly anticipated.[2] All other assumptions made in Section I will be maintained, including the assumption that expectations on prices other than $p(t)(q$ and $r)$ are static.

Letting price vary with time has no effect either on the statement of the firm's maximum problem or on the necessary conditions. Hence conditions (1) and (4)–(6) are valid under *any* price expectations hypothesis. Under rational expectations, the investment plans satisfying these conditions, aggregated to the industry level, must be consistent with the industry demand function (11). For convenience, we restate these five conditions, this time in terms of a new state variable: $x(t) = K(t)/S(t)$. These conditions are valid for firm variables and for industry aggregates.

$$0 \geq p(t)f'[u(t)] - q + \lambda(t) \tag{15}$$

with equality whenever $u(t) > 0$;

$$\dot{\lambda}(t) = [r + \delta - u(t)]\lambda(t) - p(t)f[u(t)] + qu(t), \tag{16}$$

$$\dot{x}(t) = x(t)[u(t) - \delta - \beta], \tag{17}$$

$$p(t) = g\{x(t)f[u(t)]\}, \tag{18}$$

$$0 = \lim_{t \to \infty} e^{-rt}\lambda(t). \tag{19}$$

Equations (15)–(19) have not been derived from a single maximum problem. Nevertheless, as one might expect from static theory, they can be given an interpretation as necessary conditions for a "consumer surplus"

---

[2]Muth (1961) defines a rational expectation as one with the same mean value as the true, future price, where both the expected and actual prices are random variables. With certainty, this definition reduces to that used here.

maximization problem. To define this problem, let $z(t) = x(t)f[u(t)]$, as in Section I, and for some fixed positive value z_0, let

$$\int g(z)\,dz = \begin{cases} \int_{z_0}^{z} g(y)\,dy & \text{for } z > z_0 \\[2ex] -\int_{z}^{z_0} g(y)\,dy & \text{for } z < z_0 \end{cases}$$

Clearly $\int g(z)\,dz$ is defined for $x > 0$. The functional

$$W = \int_{0}^{\infty} e^{-(r-\beta)t}[\int g(z)\,dz - qux]\,dt \tag{20}$$

may then be regarded as a dollar measure of discounted consumer surplus, in exact analogy to the area between the demand and supply curves in static analysis. It is easily verified that (15)–(19) are necessary conditions for the maximization of W, subject to (17) and given $x(0)$.

We next prove the strict concavity of W, regarded as a functional of $u(t)x(t)$, which will imply that, for given $x(0)$, (i) there is at most one solution of (15)–(18) which satisfies (19), and (ii) this solution, if it exists, maximizes W.

Let u_0x_0 and u_1x_1 be two distinct (for some t and hence, by continuity, for some interval of time) investment plans, yielding values W_0 and W_1 to W. For $0 < \lambda < 1$, let $u_\lambda x_\lambda = \lambda u_0 x_0 + (1 - \lambda)u_1 x_1$, and let W_λ be the value of W at $u_\lambda x_\lambda$. Let x_i and z_i $(i = 0, 1, \lambda)$ be the associated capital and output paths. From (17), $x_\lambda = \lambda z_0 + (1 - \lambda)z_1 = z_2$ (say). Then:

$$W_\lambda - \lambda W_0 - (1 - \lambda)W_1 = \int_{0}^{\infty} e^{-rt}[\int g(z_\lambda)\,dz_\lambda$$

$$- \lambda \int g(z_0)\,dz_0 - (1 - \lambda)\int g(z_1)\,dz_1]\,dt$$

$$= \int_{0}^{\infty} e^{-rt}[\int g(z_2)\,dz_2 - \lambda \int g(z_0)\,dz_0 - (1 - \lambda)\int g(z_1)\,dz_1]\,dt$$

$$+ \int_{0}^{\infty} e^{-rt}[\int g(z_\lambda)\,dz_\lambda - \int g(z_2)\,dz_2]\,dt.$$

The first term on the last line is strictly positive, since $\int g(z)\,dz$ is a strictly concave function of z (from [13]). The second term is nonnegative, since $g(z) > 0$ for all z and $z_\lambda \geq z_2$. Thus $W_\lambda - \lambda W_0 - (1 - \lambda)W_1 > 0$ as was to be shown.

It remains only to exhibit a solution to (15)–(18) which satisfies (19): if such a solution can be found, it is the only growth pattern for the industry consistent with both optimizing behavior and rational expectations.

The behavior of solutions to (15)–(18) will depend on whether or not (15) holds with equality. We begin, then, by dividing the positive quadrant of the (x, λ) plane into a region over which $u = 0$ and a region over which $u > 0$. The $u = 0$ region consists of those pairs (x, λ) satisfying:

$$\lambda \leq q - g[xf(0)]f'(0), \tag{21}$$

and the boundary of this region is the curve on which (21) holds with equality. This curve is downward sloping for all x; as $x \to \infty$, $\lambda \to q$; and as $x \to 0$, $\lambda \to \infty$. The $u = 0$ region is thus as indicated in figure 4.

The curve on which $\dot{x} = 0$ is, from (17), the curve on which $u = \beta + \delta$. Along this curve, (15) must hold with equality, or

$$\lambda = q - g[xf(\beta + \delta)]f'(\beta + \delta). \tag{22}$$

The $u = \beta + \delta$ curve thus has the same features as the $u = 0$ curve, with the former lying everywhere above the latter as indicated in figure 4. Above this curve, x is rising; below it, x is falling.

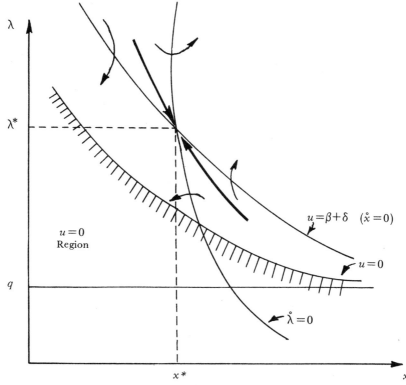

Fig. 4

Within the $u = 0$ region, the curve on which $\dot{\lambda} = 0$ is given by

$$\lambda = \frac{f(0)}{r + \delta} g[xf(0)]. \tag{23}$$

This curve intersects the boundary of the $u = 0$ region at the point $x = g^{-1}(p_c)/f(0)$, where p_c is as defined in Section I. As x increases from this value, λ falls, with $\lambda \to 0$ as $x \to \infty$. This portion of the $\lambda = 0$ curve is thus as indicated in figure 4.

In the $u > 0$ region, the curve relating λ and x for $\dot{\lambda} = 0$ (as well as the curve relating u and λ) is obtained by solving the two equations (16) (with $\dot{\lambda} = 0$) and (15) (with equality) for x and u as functions of λ. Since the relevant Jacobian is never zero, this may always be done. The slope of the function $x(\lambda)$ so obtained is, however, indeterminate (except near the boundary of the $u = 0$ region, where it is negative).

The stationary solutions of the system (15)–(18) must also be stationary solutions of the system with static expectations treated in Section I, and conversely. The system under rational expectations thus also has either one stationary solution or none. Referring to figure 4, the $\dot{\lambda} = 0$ curve either intersects the $\dot{x} = 0$ curve once (as drawn) or remains below the $\dot{x} = 0$ curve for all λ.

If the system does have a stationary solution, its stability may be determined by examining the linear system which is approximately valid near the stationary solution. The characteristic equation associated with this linear system is

$$0 = P(y) = y^2 - (r - \beta)y - xg'f[xg'(f')^2 + gf']^{-1}[f + (r - \beta)f'],$$

where the coefficients of $P(y)$ are evaluated at the stationary values of the variables. Since $xg'(f')^2 + gf'' < 0$ and $f + (r - \beta)f' > 0$, the constant term of $P(y)$ is negative. $P(y)$ then has two real roots, one negative and one exceeding $r - \beta$. This proves that the stationary solution is a saddle point, which implies that for any $x(0)$ there is exactly one solution to (15)–(18) which converges to the stationary point. Since this solution satisfies (19), it is the unique optimal one. This solution, as well as those which do not converge to the stationary point, is indicated by arrows in figure 4.

A comparison of industry behavior under the two alternative expectations hypotheses may also be made from figure 4. Under static expectations, condition (7) holds at each point in time, which implies that the industry remains continuously on the $\dot{\lambda} = 0$ curve of this diagram. Under rational expectations, the industry will move on a path to the left of this curve for $x(t)$ less than its equilibrium value, x^*, and on a path to the right of this curve for $x > x^*$. In other words, for any x, λ will be closer to its equilibrium value under rational than under static expectations. From (15), this implies that the industry will approach equilibrium *less* rapidly if expectations are rational. This result corresponds well to one's intuition: a once-and-for-all shift to the right in the demand curve (for example) induces a rise in current output price; firms with static expectations interpret this increase as permanent, and expand accordingly; when this expansion brings price down, they find their anticipations have been incorrect, and that they have "overreacted" to the initial price change.

The two expectations hypotheses may also be compared via the "consumer surplus" measure (20). For any $x(0)$ not equal to the equilibrium capital stock, any incorrect expectations will give this integral a smaller value than it will have under rational expectations. The difference is a measure of the "social cost" of errors in anticipations.

III. A Monopoly Model

With a slight reinterpretation of the function $g(z)$, figure 4 and the adjoining text describe the behavior through time of a pure monopolist. Consider an industry identical to the one just analyzed, but in which all assets are owned by a single monopolist. The total revenue of the monopolist is $pQ = g(z)zS$ and marginal revenue is $g(z) + zg'(z) = m(z)$ (say). Let the function m satisfy

$$m(z) > 0, \; m'(z) < 0, \; m(0) = \infty, \; m(\infty) = 0 \qquad (24)$$

for all $z > 0$. The monopolist's present value is then proportional to

$$V(0) = \int_0^\infty e^{-(r-\beta)t} [pxf(u) - qux] \, dt$$

$$= \int_0^\infty e^{-(r-\beta)t} \left[\int m(z) \, dz - qux \right] dt + K.$$

Comparing the last term on the right to the right side of (20), one sees that the monopolist's problem is identical in form (if [24] holds) to the problem analyzed in Section II.

IV. Generalizations of the Rational Expectations Model

In Section III it was shown that the equations governing the behavior through time of firms in a competitive industry with rational expectations could be regarded as necessary conditions for the maximization of "discounted consumer surplus." This conclusion was obtained under the assumption of production possibilities which appear to be the natural generalization of the static constant returns to scale hypothesis, namely, that output is homogeneous of degree one in fixed capital inputs *and* gross investment. The question arises as to whether the equations of motion for a competitive industry with rational expectations can *always* (i.e., for *any* production function) be derived from a consumer surplus maximization problem.

To deal with this question, consider an industry of n firms, each producing an output Q_i according to $Q_i = F(K_i, I_i)$. Let the industry demand curve be given by $p = g(Q, t)$ where $Q = \Sigma_i Q_i$. Then analogously with (20), discounted consumer surplus W is given by

$$W = \int_0^\infty e^{-rt} \left[g(Q, t)\, dQ - q \sum_i I_i \right] dt.$$

To complete the formulation of the problem, one must now decide whether capital is "fixed to the firm" or "fixed to the industry" or, in other words, whether there are adjustment costs associated with interfirm transfers of assets. If capital is fixed to each firm, then W is maximized subject to n separate constraints: $K_i = I_i - \delta K_i$, $i = 1, \dots, n$. It is easily verified that in this event, the necessary conditions for maximizing W are equivalent to the necessary conditions for present value maximization by each firm (under rational expectations).

If one regards a firm as composed of a number of distinct production units, or plants, the ownership of which may be transferred costlessly from firm to firm (or to newly organized firms), the assumption of n distinct net investment constraints is not appropriate. In this case, W is maximized subject to

$$\frac{d}{dt} \left\{ \sum_i K_i \right\} = \sum_i I_i - \delta \sum_i K_i.$$

Further, the number of firms n must also be regarded as a "choice variable." Maximization of W under these conditions requires that capital and gross investment at each point in time must be distributed across firms so as to maximize output. With identical production possibilities this requires, with $K = \Sigma_i K_i$ and $I = \Sigma_i I_i$, that $K_i = K/n$ and $I_i = I/n$. It also requires that n be chosen to maximize:

$$Q = nF\left(\frac{K}{n}, \frac{I}{n}\right)$$

for given K and I. Thus if, for example, F is strictly concave, W has no maximum, since Q is always rising with n (i.e., since the optimal firm size is zero). To summarize, if assets are freely transferable from firm to firm, consumer surplus maximization yields the equations of motion for the industry *only* if the industry is assumed to be optimally organized, in the above sense, at each moment of time.

References

Lucas, Robert E., Jr. "Adjustment Costs and the Theory of Supply." *J.P.E.* 75, no. 4, pt. 1 (1967): 321–34.
Muth, John F. "Rational Expectations and the Theory of Price Movements." *Econometrica* 29(1961): 315–35.

6

Investment under Uncertainty

Robert E. Lucas, Jr.,
Edward C. Prescott

This paper determines the time series behavior of investment, output, and prices in a competitive industry with a stochastic demand. It is shown, first, that the equilibrium development for the industry solves a particular dynamic programming problem (maximization of "consumer surplus"). This problem is then studied to determine the characteristics of the equilibrium paths.

Explanatory variables in empirical studies of the demand for investment goods fall into three broad classes: variables measuring anticipated, future demand—sales, profits, stock price indexes; variables measuring past decisions, the effects of which persist into the present—lagged capital stock and investment rates; and variables measuring current market opportunities—interest rates, factor prices, and, again, profits.[1] Existing investment theory has concerned itself largely with the latter two classes of variables, first by rationalizing the role of prices in determining a long-run "desired" capital stock using a static, profit maximizing hypothesis, later by discovering the optimizing basis for a staggered approach to the desired stock in "costs of adjustment" which penalize rapid change.[2] In the present paper, an uncertain future is introduced into an adjustment-cost type model of the firm, and the optimal response to this uncertainty is studied in an attempt to integrate variables of the first category into the existing theory.[3]

Briefly, we shall be concerned with a competitive industry in which product demand shifts randomly each period, and where factor costs remain stable. In this context, we attempt to determine the competitive

---

[1] For reviews of the empirical investment literature, see Eisner and Strotz (1963), or, more recently, Schramm (1966).

[2] We refer to the body of theory that stems from the work of Haavelmo (1960), Eisner and Strotz (1963), and Jorgenson (1963). More recent contributions are by Gould (1968), Lucas (1967a, 1967b), and Treadway (1967).

[3] A recent paper by Pashigian (1968) discusses one-period equilibrium in a competitive industry under supply and demand uncertainty, a problem closely related to that studied here.

[Econometrica, 1971, vol. 39, no. 5]

equilibrium time paths of capital stock, investment rates, output, and output price for the industry as a whole and for the component firms. From the viewpoint of firms in this industry, forecasting future demand means simply forecasting future output prices. The usual way to formulate this problem is to postulate some forecasting rule for firms, which in turn generates some pattern of investment behavior, which in turn, in conjunction with industry demand, generates an actual price series.

Typically the forecasting rule postulated takes the form of anticipated prices being a fixed function of past prices—"adaptive expectations." But it is clear that if the underlying disturbance (in our case, the demand shift) has a regular stochastic character (such as a Markov process), forecasting in this manner is adaptive only in a restrictive and not very interesting sense. Except for an unlikely coincidence, price forecasts and actual prices will have different probability distributions, and this difference will be persistent, costly to forecasters, and readily correctible.

To avoid this difficulty, we shall, in this paper, go to the opposite extreme, assuming that the actual and anticipated prices have the *same* probability distribution, or that price expectations are *rational*.[4] Thus we surrender, in advance, any hope of shedding light on the *process* by which firms translate current information into price forecasts. In return, we obtain an operational investment theory linking current investment to observable current and past explanatory variables, rather than to "expected" future variables which must, in practice, be replaced by various "proxy variables."

In the next section, our basic model of the industry is stated. In Section 2, we examine formally the investment decision from the viewpoint of the individual firm, clarifying the role of observable securities prices as evaluators of additions to capital stock. In Sections 3 and 4 competitive *industry* equilibrium is defined, and it is shown that equilibrium in this sense exists and is unique. In Sections 5 and 6, we investigate the long-run behavior of industry equilibrium under alternative assumptions on the nature of the demand shift process. Conclusions are summarized in Section 7.

1. Statement of the Model

Consider an industry consisting of many small firms, each producing a single output, q_t, by means of a single input, capital, k_t. We assume that production takes place under constant returns to scale so that with appropriate choice of units we may use k_t also to denote production at full

---

[4]This term is taken from Muth (1961), who applied it to the case where the expected and actual price (both random variables) have a common *mean value*. Since Muth's discussion of this concept applies equally well to our assumption of a common *distribution* for these random variables, it seems natural to adopt the term here.

capacity. Thus the production function is:

$$0 \leqslant q_t \leqslant k_t. \tag{1}$$

Denote gross investment by x_t. Investment and capacity are related in the nonlinear way:

$$k_{t+1} = k_t h(x_t/k_t), \tag{2}$$

where h is bounded, continuously differentiable, increasing, and strictly concave.[5] Assume that $\delta = h^{-1}(1)$ exists and satisfies $0 < \delta < 1$, so that $k_t \delta$ is the investment rate which will just maintain the stock k_t. Assume also that $h(0) > 0$, so that even with no investment in period t, some capital will remain in $t + 1$ if $k_t > 0$.

Given an initial stock k_0, (2) cannot be solved for k_t as a *linear* function of $k_0, x_0, \ldots, x_{t-1}$, as is possible with conventional depreciation hypotheses, so (2) requires some explanation. One entirely plausible possibility is that the true relationship between physical investment and plant capacity is, in fact, nonlinear, so that a given quantity of, say, machines, makes a better plant (yields more productive services) the longer the period over which they are assembled. Alternatively, one may assume that the relation between capacity and physical investment *is* linear, and regard x_t as the dollar value of investment. Then if investment costs per unit of capacity are a strictly convex function of physical investment per unit of capacity, (2) is implied.[6]

Denote the product price by p_t. Then ex post, the present value of the firm, using the discount factor $\beta = 1/(1 + r)$, where $r > 0$ is the cost of capital, is

$$V = \sum_{t=0}^{\infty} \beta^t [p_t q_t - x_t]. \tag{3}$$

It is evident that the allocation across firms of a given industry stock of capital is immaterial, so that in the following the notation k_t, x_t, and q_t will

[5]These assumptions on h imply that $kh(x/k)$, regarded as a function of the two variables x and k, is increasing in both arguments and concave. To see the latter property, let (k^θ, x^θ) be a convex combination of (k^0, x^0) and (k^1, x^1) and let $\phi = \theta k^0/k^\theta$, $0 \leqslant \phi \leqslant 1$. Then $x^\theta/k^\theta = \phi(x^0/k^0) + (1 - \phi)(x^1/k^1)$ and using the concavity of h,

$$k^\theta h(x^\theta/k^\theta) \geqslant \phi k^\theta h(x^0/k^0) + (1 - \phi)k^\theta h(x^1/k^1)$$
$$= \theta k^0 h(x^0/k^0) + (1 - \theta)k^1 h(x^1/k^1).$$

[6]The strict concavity of the function h gives rise to the "adjustment costs" referred to in the introduction. The main function of introducing such costs, to anticipate the development somewhat, is to assure that the model reflects observed, gradual changes in capital stocks, as opposed to immediate passage to a long-run equilibrium level. This feature is shared by the adjustment costs imposed in Eisner and Strotz (1963), Gould (1968), Lucas (1967a, 1967b), and Treadway (1967), although there are differences in form among all of these treatments and the present one. These differences will not be critical to any of the arguments which follow.

be used interchangeably for industry and firm variables. (Alternatively, think of a competitive industry with one firm.)

To complete the formulation of the problem of the individual firm, one must assume a particular stochastic structure for the price sequence $\{p_t\}$ and postulate an objective function for the firm. This will be done in Section 3, in the course of defining industry equilibrium. At this point, however, we already have enough information for a suggestive, if formal, examination of the decision problem faced by the individual firm. This is undertaken in the following section.

2. The Investment Decision of an Individual Firm

In this section, we suppose that the objective of the firm is the maximization of the mean value of the present value expression given in (3), with the stochastic behavior of prices somehow specified. Since we have omitted variable factors of production in our formulation, the firm's supply decision is trivial: produce at full capacity. Hence the only current decision is the choice of an investment level, in which the known (unit) cost of a unit of investment goods is compared to an expected, marginal return. To compute the latter, one must solve the present value maximization problem, but it will turn out (predictably) that "solving" this problem amounts to finding an appropriate "shadow price" to use in evaluating an addition to capital stock. From our (economists') point of view, this difficult task cannot be avoided, and we undertake it in the following sections, but from a firm's point of view it can be, and indeed is, avoided.

From the entrepreneur's viewpoint, the objective is to maximize the value of all *claims* to the income stream (3), and this value is the quantity of capital held times the value per unit of capital as *observed* on securities markets. Similarly, the appropriate valuation to place on an addition to next period's capital stock (current investment) is the price per unit, reflected in securities prices, expected to prevail next period. That is, the burden of evaluating the income stream produced by the firm is borne not by firms but by traders in the firms' securities.

This fact considerably simplifies the firm's decision problem (correspondingly complicating household's). In our formulation, additional simplification arises from the evident fact that the value placed on the claim to a unit of capital will not depend on the distribution of capital across firms. It is thus treated by each firm as a parametric market price. Denote by w_t the current value of a unit of capital, and by w_t^* the (undiscounted) value per unit expected to prevail next period. For a firm beginning period t with capital stock k_t, an investment x will lead to a next period value of $\beta k_t h(x/k_t) w_t^*$ (from [2]). The cost of this investment is $-x$. Hence the firm must solve:

$$\max_{x \geq 0} \left[-x + \beta k_t h(x/k_t) w_t^* \right].$$

The current value of the firm is, of course,

$$w_t k_t = p_t k_t - x + \beta k_t h(x/k_t) w_t^*. \tag{4}$$

If the maximum problem is correctly solved, and if there is agreement on w_t^*, we have a second condition:

$$0 \geqslant -1 + \beta h'(x/k_t) w_t^*, \qquad \text{with equality if } x > 0. \tag{5}$$

Solving (5) for x as a function of k_t, β, and w_t^* gives the investment demand function as seen by the firm. From the point of view of an outside observer (ourselves), however, (4) and (5) are solved *jointly* for x and w_t^* as functions of k_t, p_t, and w_t. This yields the observed investment function:

$$x_t = k_t g(w_t - p_t), \qquad g'(\cdot) > 0. \tag{6}$$

We remark at this point that (6) is essentially the function used by Grunfeld in his empirical study of the investment behavior of several United States corporations (1960). Grunfeld's justification for using w_t as an "explanatory" variable was that it served as a proxy for the firm's own estimation of future income streams. Our argument goes somewhat further, to assert that the firm need not even form its own estimation of the future, beyond forecasting the value placed on assets in its industry *next* period. (Of course, entrepreneurs, in common with other agents in securities markets, form judgments on the income streams of their own and other firms. The point is that these judgments are apart from, and irrelevant to, the investment goods demand decision.)

By aggregating (6) across firms (which leads to an equation of exactly the same form) one obtains an industry demand function for investment goods, given the value per unit, w_t. But this aggregate function tells us *nothing* about the development through time of capital stock, output, and prices, since the time path of w_t is, as yet, unknown. Equation (6) is a consistency requirement which must hold at each point in time, but it is not a theory of capital accumulation in the industry. To obtain such a theory, we must determine how investment and the price w_t are *jointly* determined on the basis of available information on current and future industry demand. This problem is studied in the following sections.

3. Industry Equilibrium: Definition

To answer the questions raised in the preceding section—that is, to obtain a theory of the development of the industry through time—we begin with a mathematical formulation of the stochastically shifting industry demand. Given this formulation, we propose a definition of industry equilibrium involving in addition to a market clearing requirement, a precise specification of firms' objective functions. In the next section, we show that there is a unique equilibrium development for the industry. Characterization of this development is then resumed in Sections 5 and 6.

The industry demand function is assumed to have the usual properties *and* is assumed to be subject to random shifts. Specifically,

$$p_t = D(q_t, u_t), \tag{7}$$

where $\{u_t\}$ is a Markov process taking values on the real line E, with a transition function $p(\cdot, \cdot)$ defined on $E^2 = E \times E$. For fixed u, $p(\cdot, u)$ is a probability distribution function on E; and $p(u, \cdot)$ is a Baire function on E.[7] Thus if A is a Borel subset of E, the probability that $u_{t+1} \in A$ conditional on $u_t = u$ is given by

$$\int_A p(dz, u),$$

where the notation indicates that the integration is with respect to the distribution $p(\cdot, u)$, u fixed. For given u_t, D is a continuous, strictly decreasing function of q_t, taking on the finite value $\bar{p}(u_t) \leqslant \bar{\bar{p}} < \infty$ at $q_t = 0$, and with $\int_0^q D(z, u_t)\, dz$ bounded uniformly in u_t and q. Assume that D is continuous and increasing in u_t, so that an increase in u_t means a shift to the right of the demand curve.[8]

To complete the formulation of the problem, we must specify the price-forecasting policies of firms, define what is meant by an investment-output policy, and postulate an objective function for firms. If the industry were in short-run (one period) equilibrium at each point in time, price and output would be determined for that period as functions of the shift variable u_t. From the vantage point of time 0, the price at time t will then depend on the initial state of the industry, (k_0, u_0), and on the realization $u_1, \ldots, u_t$ of the $\{u_t\}$ process between 0 and t. Hence it is natural to define an anticipated price process, for given (k_0, u_0), as a sequence $\{p_t\}$ of *functions* of $(u_1, \ldots, u_t)$, or functions with domain E^t. Similarly, one may think of an investment-output plan as a sequence $\{q_t, x_t\}$ of functions on E^t, or as a contingency plan indicating in advance how the firm will react to any possible realization of the $\{u_t\}$ process. Specifically, let L be the set of all sequences $x = \{x_t\}$, $t = 0, 1, \ldots$, where x_0 is a number and, for $t \geqslant 1$, x_t is a bounded Baire function on E^t, bounded in the sense that for all $x \in L$,

$$\|x\| = \sup_t \sup_{(u_1, \ldots, u_t) \in E^t} |x_t(u_1, \ldots, u_t)|$$

is finite. We restrict the sequences $\{p_t\}$, $\{q_t\}$, and $\{x_t\}$ to be elements of L^+: elements of L with non-negative terms for all $(t, u_1, \ldots, u_t)$. Then for any price-output-investment sequence, present value, V, is a well-defined random variable with a finite mean. We shall take as the objective of the firm

---

[7] Baire functions are all members of the class of functions consisting of all continuous functions, pointwise limits of sequences of continuous functions, pointwise limits of sequences of this larger class, and so on. Alternatively Baire functions are measurable with respect to the Borel sets.

[8] Further restrictions will be imposed, as needed, on $p(\cdot, \cdot)$ in Sections 5 and 6.

the maximization of the mean value of V with respect to the investment-output policy, given an anticipated price sequence.

It remains for us to link the anticipated price sequence to the actual price sequence—also a sequence of functions on E^t. Typically, this is done by postulating the *process* by which firms actually develop forecasts from actual past values and other information. In this paper, we shall not take this route but rather postulate a property of the *outcome* of this (unspecified) process. Specifically, we assume that expectations of firms are rational, or that the anticipated price at time t is the same function of $(u_1, \ldots, u_t)$ as is the actual price. That is, we assume that firms know the true distribution of prices for all future periods.

These considerations lead to the following notion of competitive equilibrium for the industry under study.[9]

DEFINITION: An *industry equilibrium* (for fixed initial state $[k, u]$ is an element $\{q_t^0, x_t^0, p_t^0\}$ of $L^+ \times L^+ \times L^+$ such that (7) is satisfied for all $(t, u_1, \ldots, u_t)$ and such that

$$E\left\{\sum_{t=0}^{\infty} \beta^t [p_t^0 q_t^0 - x_t^0]\right\} \geqslant E\left\{\sum_{t=0}^{\infty} \beta^t [p_t^0 q_t - x_t]\right\} \tag{8}$$

for all $\{q_t, x_t\} \in L^+ \times L^+$ satisfying (1) and (2). (In [8], the expectation of the tth term in the series is taken with respect to the joint distribution of $[u_1, \ldots, u_t]$.)

In the next section, we show that the industry has a unique equilibrium in the sense of the above definition, and, further, that this equilibrium can be obtained by solving a particular dynamic programming problem. Subsequent sections are devoted to developing various properties of this equilibrium.

4. Existence and Uniqueness of Equilibrium

In this section, we show that the industry described above has exactly one competitive equilibrium development through time. The device employed

---

[9]At this point, we make two rather defensive observations on the scope of the definition we are using. First, we regard firms as mean value maximizers, with respect to the distribution of the demand shift variable, u_t. If this distribution is interpreted as reflecting relative frequencies of certain physical events (such as rainfall), then this assumption implies risk-neutral preferences on the part of shareholders. Alternatively, by imagining this industry as set in an economy characterized by a "state-preference" model (see Arrow 1964, Debreu 1959, and Hirschleifer 1965), one can reinterpret this distribution as giving the structure of market interest rates, and our "cost of capital" r as the certainty interest rate. In this case, (8), implies nothing about risk preferences.

Second, now that the precise content of the "rationality" of expectations is made clear (in the following definition), we add a final comment on its "reasonableness": we can think of no objection to this assumption which is not better phrased as an objection to our hypothesis that the stochastic component of demand has a regular, stationary structure. If the demand shift assumption *is* reasonable, then expectations rational in our sense are surely more plausible than any simple, adaptive scheme. If the demand assumption is *un*reasonable, then adopting an alternative expectations hypothesis will certainly not improve matters.

to do this involves first showing that a competitive equilibrium development will lead the industry to maximize a certain "consumer surplus"
expression, and then showing that the latter maximum problem can be
solved using the techniques of dynamic programming.

Define the function $s(q, u)$, $q \geqslant 0$, $u \in E$, by

$$s(q, u) = \int_0^q D(z, u)\, dz,$$

so that for fixed u, $s(q, u)$ is a continuously differentiable, increasing,
strictly concave, positive, and bounded function of q, and for fixed q, s is
increasing in u. Thus $s(q_t, u_t)$ is the area under the industry's demand curve
at an output of q_t and with the state of demand u_t. Then define the discounted "consumer surplus," S, for the industry by:

$$S = E\left\{\sum_{t=0}^{\infty} \beta^t [s(q_t, u_t) - x_t]\right\}.$$

The quantity S is used in applied cost-benefit work as a measure of the
dollar value to society of a policy $\{q_t, x_t\}$. For our purposes, however, the
welfare significance of S is not important. We are interested only in using
the connection between the maximization of S and competitive equilibrium in order to determine the properties of the latter.

Associated with the problem of maximizing the quantity S is the functional equation

$$v(k, u) = \sup_{x \geqslant 0} \left\{ s(k, u) - x + \beta \int v\left[kh\left(\frac{x}{k}\right), z\right] p(dz, u) \right\}. \tag{9}$$

The main result of this section, linking (9) to the determination of industry
equilibrium, is the following theorem.

THEOREM 1: The functional equation (9) has a unique, bounded solu-
tion v on $(0, \infty) \times E$, and for all (k, u), the right side of (9) is attained by a
unique $x(k, u)$. In terms of this function, the unique industry equilibrium,
given k_0 and u_0, is given by:

$$x_t = x(k_t, u_t), \tag{10}$$

$$k_{t+1} = k_t h\left[\frac{x(k_t, u_t)}{k_t}\right], \tag{11}$$

$$q_t = k_t, \quad and \tag{12}$$

$$p_t = D(q_t, u_t), \tag{13}$$

for $t = 0, 1, 2, \ldots$, and all realizations of the $\{u_t\}$ process.

The remainder of this section is devoted to the proof of theorem 1, and
to obtaining some properties of the functions $v(k, u)$ and $x(k, u)$. The
reader interested primarily in the nature of the solutions to the difference
equations (10)–(13) (that is, in the characterization of the development of
the industry) should proceed directly to Section 5.

The proof of theorem 1 involves two distinct steps. First, one must connect the determination of industry equilibrium to the problem of maximizing consumer surplus. Second, the latter problem must be shown to lead to the functional equation (9). Both parts turn out to be complicated, although the outlines of each are familiar.

For the first part, we have the following lemma.

LEMMA 1: Suppose for given (k_0, u_0) the problem of maximizing S, subject to (1)–(2), over all $\{q_t, x_t\} \in L^+ \times L^+$ is solved by the sequence $\{q_t^0, x_t^0\}$. Then $\{q_t^0, x_t^0, p_t^0\}$, where p_t^0 is obtained from q_t^0 using (7), is an industry equilibrium. Conversely, suppose $\{q_t^0, x_t^0, p_t^0\}$ is an industry equilibrium. Then $\{q_t^0, x_t^0\}$ maximizes S, subject to (1)–(2), over $L^+ \times L^+$.

PROOF: The proof is an application of theorems 1 and 2 of Debreu (1954) and of Prescott and Lucas (in press). The basic space used in Debreu (1954) corresponds to our $L \times L$. The economy in our application consists of a single consumer whose preferences, given by S, are defined on $L^+ \times L^+$ (X in Debreu [1954]), and a single firm, whose production possibility set $Y \subset L^+ \times L^+$ consists of all elements satisfying (1) and (2). Pareto optimality in this economy is then equivalent to maximizing S over Y.

Assumptions I–V of Debreu (1954) (the convexity of X, the concavity of S, the continuity of S, the convexity of Y, and the existence of an interior point of Y) are readily verified. If $k_0 > 0$, the hypotheses of the Remark (Debreu 1954, p. 591) are valid. If $k_0 = 0$, the unique industry equilibrium occurs when output and investment are zero for all t; in the following, we assume $k_0 > 0$.

To prove the second part of the lemma, one applies theorem 1 of Debreu (1954).

To prove the first part of the lemma, we use theorem 2 of Debreu (1954), plus the Remark, which states that if $\{q_t^0, x_t^0\}$ maximizes S over Y, there exists a continuous linear form α on $L \times L$ such that $\{q_t^0, x_t^0\}$ maximizes $\alpha\{q_t, x_t\}$ over Y, and such that $\{q_t^0, x_t^0\}$ maximizes S over all elements of X which satisfy

$$\alpha(\{q_t, x_t\}) \leqslant \alpha(\{q_t^0, x_t^0\}).$$

It then follows from theorems 1 and 2 of Prescott and Lucas (in press) that there exist elements $\{\alpha_t\}$, $\{\gamma_t\}$ of L^+ such that $\{q_t^0, x_t^0\}$ maximizes

$$E\left\{\sum_{t=0}^{\infty} \beta^t [\alpha_t q_t - \gamma_t x_t]\right\} \tag{14}$$

over Y, and such that $\{q_t^0, x_t^0\}$ maximizes S over all elements of X which satisfy

$$E\left\{\sum_{t=0}^{\infty} \beta^t [\alpha_t q_t - \gamma_t x_t]\right\} \leqslant E\left\{\sum_{t=0}^{\infty} \beta^t [\alpha_t q_t^0 - \gamma_t x_t^0]\right\} \tag{15}$$

where the expectations in (14) and (15) are with respect to the distributions P_t of $(u_1, \ldots, u_t)$, $t = 1, 2, \ldots$.

We next show that for some constant $\lambda > 0$

$$\gamma_t \leqslant \lambda \tag{16}$$

almost everywhere, with equality a.e. on any Borel set A such that $E\{\gamma_t I_A x_t^0\} > 0$. ($I_A$ is the function taking the value 1 on $A \subset E^t$ and 0 elsewhere.) To verify (16), consider first the case $E\{\gamma_t I_A x_t^0\} = 0$ for all t, A. If (16) is false in this case, then for all $\lambda > 0$ one can find t, A such that $E\{\gamma_t I_A\} > \lambda E\{I_A\}$. Then S can always be improved, subject to (15), by increasing q_s^0 over some $B \subset E^s$ with $E\{I_B\} > 0$ and increasing x_t^0 over $A \subset E^t$ with $E\{\gamma_t I_A\}/E\{I_A\}$ sufficiently large, which is a contradiction.

For the case where $E\{\gamma_t I_A x_t^0\} > 0$ for some t, A, define λ by $E\{\gamma_t I_A\} = \lambda E\{I_A\}$. Now if s, B satisfy $E\{\gamma_s I_B\} > \lambda E\{I_B\}$, S can be increased, subject to (15), by increasing x_s^0 on B and decreasing x_t^0 on A. Similarly if $E\{\gamma_s I_B\} < \lambda E\{I_B\}$, S can be improved, subject to (15), by decreasing x_s^0 on B and increasing x_t^0 on A, unless $x_s^0 = 0$ almost everywhere on B. In the latter case, however, $E\{\gamma_s I_B x_s^0\} = 0$. Hence (16) is proved.

In view of (16) and the fact that $\{q_t^0, x_t^0\}$ maximizes the expression (14) over Y, we have

$$\sum_{t=0}^{\infty} \beta^t E\{\alpha_t q_t^0 - \gamma_t x_t^0\} \geqslant \sum_{t=0}^{\infty} \beta^t E\{\alpha_t q_t - \gamma_t x_t\} \geqslant \sum_{t=0}^{\infty} \beta^t E\{\alpha_t q_t - \lambda x_t\}$$

for all $\{q_t, x_t\} \in Y$, with equality if $\{q_t, x_t\} = \{q_t^0, x_t^0\}$. Then letting $p_t^0 = \lambda^{-1}\alpha_t$, we have shown that $\{q_t^0, x_t^0\}$ maximizes

$$\sum_{t=0}^{\infty} \beta^t E\{p_t^0 q_t - x_t\}$$

over Y, or that condition (8) of the definition of industry equilibrium is satisfied.

To show that (7) is satisfied (almost everywhere) by $\{q_t^0, x_t^0, p_t^0\}$, observe that if $\{q_t^0, x_t^0\}$ maximizes S over all elements of X satisfying (15), it also maximizes S over the subset of X on which $x_t = 0$ whenever $x_t^0 = 0$. Over this set, (16) (and the fact that x_t^0 is clearly 0 whenever $\gamma_t = 0$) implies that the constraint (15) is equivalent to

$$\sum_{t=0}^{\infty} \beta^t E\{p_t^0 q_t - x_t\} \leqslant \sum_{t=0}^{\infty} \beta^t E\{p_t^0 q_t^0 - x_t^0\}.$$

Since s is strictly increasing in q, this constraint will be binding, so that $\{q_t^0\}$ maximizes

$$\sum_{t=0}^{\infty} \beta^t E\{s(q_t, u_t) - p_t^0 q_t\}.$$

Then since $q_t^0 > 0$, we have

$$p_t^0 = s_1(q_t^0, u_t) = D(q_t^0, u_t),$$

which proves that (7) is satisfied (almost everywhere) and completes the proof of lemma 1.

We now turn to the study of the problem of maximizing S subject to (1) and (2), the solution to which will be, by the lemma just proved, the unique industry equilibrium. This will be done by studying the functional equation (9), which is related to the problem of maximizing S by the principle of optimality, a version of which is utilized in lemma 4, below.

To show the existence and uniqueness of a solution to (9) and to obtain some of its properties, we utilize the method of successive approximation as applied in Bellman (1957). As a convenient device in this argument, we employ the operator T, taking bounded Baire functions on $(0, \infty) \times E$ into the same set of functions, defined by

$$Tf(k, u) = \sup_{x \geqslant 0} \left\{ s(k, u) - x + \beta \int f\left[kh\left(\frac{x}{k}\right), z\right] p(dz, u) \right\}. \quad (17)$$

Then, clearly, solutions to (9) are coincident with solutions to $Tf = f$. The relevant properties of T are given by the next lemma.

LEMMA 2: (i) If f is nondecreasing in k, so is Tf; (ii) if f is concave in k, so is Tf; (iii) $Tf = f$ has a unique solution, f^*; and (iv) for any g, $\lim_{n \to \infty} T^n g = f^*$.

PROOF: To prove (i), observe that if f is nondecreasing, $s(k, u)$ and $\int f[kh(x/k), z] p(dz, u)$ are nondecreasing functions of k for all fixed x.

To prove (ii), note first that the concavity of f in k implies that f is continuous in k on $(0, \infty)$, so that the expression in brackets on the right of (7) is continuous in k. Further, this expression is finite at $x = 0$ and tends to $-\infty$ as x becomes large (since f is bounded). Hence, for any $k > 0$, $Tf(k, u)$ is attained by some $x \geqslant 0$. Let k^0 and k^1 be on $(0, \infty)$, let k^θ be a convex combination, and let x^0 and x^1 attain $Tf(k^0, u)$ and $Tf(k^1, u)$, respectively. Then:

$$Tf(k^\theta, u) = s(k^\theta, u) + \sup_{x \geqslant 0} \left\{ -x + \beta \int f[k^\theta h(x/k^\theta), z] p(dz, u) \right\}$$

$$\geqslant \theta s(k^0, u) - \theta x^0 + \theta \beta \int f[k^0 h(x^0/k^0), z] p(dz, u)$$

$$+ (1 - \theta) s(k^1, u) - (1 - \theta) x^1$$

$$+ (1 - \theta) \beta \int f[k^1 h(x^1/k^1), z] p(dz, u)$$

$$= \theta Tf(k^0, u) + (1 - \theta) Tf(k^1, u).$$

To prove (iii) and (iv), observe that T is monotone ($f \geqslant g$ for all (k, u) implies $Tf \geqslant Tg$) and if a is any constant, $T(f + a) = Tf + a\beta$. By theorem 5 of Blackwell (1965), these two facts imply (iii) and (iv).

Lemma 2 leads directly to a third lemma.

LEMMA 3: The functional equation (9) is satisfied by a unique bounded Baire function $v(k, u)$ on $(0, \infty) \times E$. The function $v(k, u)$ is continuous, nondecreasing, and concave in k for any fixed u. For any (k, u), $v(k, u)$ is attained by a unique investment rate $x(k, u)$ and $x(k, u)$ is a Baire function, continuous in k.

PROOF: Let $g(k, u) = s(k, u)$. Then by lemma 2, $\lim_{n \to \infty} T^n g = f^*$, where f^* is the unique bounded solution to (9). Let $v(k, u) = f^*$. Since $s(k, u)$ is increasing in both arguments and strictly concave in k, the limit function v is nondecreasing and concave in k. Since v is concave in k for fixed u, it is continuous in k on $(0, \infty)$.

It follows from these facts that the expression in brackets on the right side of (9) is a continuous, strictly concave function of x, positive at $x = 0$ and negative for x sufficiently large, so that it attains its supremum on $(0, \infty)$ at a unique x, depending on k and u. This defines the policy function $x(k, u)$.

To show that $x(k, u)$ is a Baire function, we must show that for all x^0,

$$S(x^0) = \{(k, u) \in (0, \infty) \times E: x(k, u) \leqslant x^0\}$$

is a Borel set. For $x^0 < 0$, this is trivial. Now denote the expression in brackets on the right of (9) by $H(x, k, u)$, and for $x^0 \geqslant 0$ and $\varepsilon > 0$, define

$$S(x^0, \varepsilon) = \{(k, u) \in (0, \infty) \times E: H(x^0, k, u) \geqslant H(x^0 + \varepsilon, k, u)\}.$$

Since H is a Baire function, $-H(x^0, k, u) + H(x^0 + \varepsilon, k, u)$ is a Baire function on $(0, \infty) \times E$, for each $\varepsilon > 0$. Hence $S(x^0, \varepsilon)$ is a Borel set. Let $\{\varepsilon_n\}$ be a decreasing sequence tending to 0 as n tends to infinity. Then

$$\bigcap_{n=1}^{\infty} S(x^0, \varepsilon_n)$$

is a Borel set, and since this set equals (using the concavity of H in x) the set $S(x^0)$, $x(k, u)$ is a Baire function. Since the expression in brackets varies continuously with k, $x(k, u)$ is continuous in k.[10]

The function $x(k, u)$ defines, for given (k_0, u_0), a sequence of Baire functions $\{k_t, x_t\}$ as given by (10) and (11). The next lemma shows that this sequence is the (essentially) unique optimal policy.

LEMMA 4: For any fixed $(k_0, u_0) \in (0, \infty) \times E$, the sequence $\{k_t^0, x_t^0\}$ defined by (10) and (11) is an element of Y, and this policy maximizes S over Y. Further, it is the unique optimal policy in the sense that any other element of Y yielding the same value of S differs from $\{k_t^0, x_t^0\}$ at most over sets of P_t measure zero.

---

[10] A theorem in Debreu (1959, p. 19), suitably specialized to this application, states that if $f(x, y)$ is continuous, the function $g(y) = \max_{x \in S} f(x, y)$, where S is compact, is continuous. Further, if $g(y)$ is attained at a unique $x(y)$ for each y, $x(y)$ is also continuous. This fact will be used at various points below, without reference.

Proof: From lemma 3 and the continuity of h, the terms of the sequence $\{k_t^0, x_t^0\}$ are Baire functions, and they clearly satisfy (1) and (2). To show that $\{k_t^0, x_t^0\} \in Y$, then, we need only show that k_t^0 and x_t^0 are bounded, uniformly in $(u_1, \ldots, u_t, t)$. Since the policy $x_t = 0$ for all t is always feasible, we have $v(k, u) > 0$ for all $k > 0$. Then from (9),

$$-x(k, u) + \beta \int v\left[kh\left(\frac{x(k, u)}{k}\right), z\right] p(dz, u) \geqslant \beta \int v[kh(0), z] p(dz, u) > 0$$

for all (k, u), $k > 0$. Let B be a bound for v so that the term on the left, above, is less than

$$-x(k, u) + \beta B.$$

Hence $x(k, u)$ is bounded from above by βB. Then if $k_t > (\beta B / \delta)$, $k_{t+1} < k_t$, so that $\max [(\beta B / \delta), k_0]$ is an upper bound for k_t.

To show that $\{k_t^0, x_t^0\}$ is optimal, it is sufficient to show that it yields the return $v(k_0, u_0)$ (Blackwell 1965, theorem 6, part f). Define the operator F_x, taking bounded Baire functions on $(0, \infty) \times E$ into the same set of functions, by

$$F_X f(k, u) = s(k, u) - x(k, u) + \beta \int f\left[kh\left(\frac{x(k, u)}{k}\right), z\right] p(dz, u).$$

The functional equation $F_X f = f$ has a unique solution, f^* (Blackwell 1965, theorem 5), and this solution, evaluated at (k_0, u_0), gives the value of S under the policy $\{k_t^0, x_t^0\}$. Since $F_X v = v$, $v = f^*$, which proves that $\{k_t^1, x_t^0\}$ is optimal.

To prove uniqueness, let $\{k_t^1, x_t^1\}$ yield the same value to S as $\{k_t^0, x_t^0\}$, and let A_t be the Borel subset of E^t on which x_t^1 and x_t^0 differ. Let t' be the first period in which the probability of A_t is nonzero. Then the returns from the policies differ by

$$\beta^{t'} E\left\{-x_{t'}^0 + v\left[k_{t'}^0 h\left(\frac{x_{t'}^0}{k_{t'}^0}\right), u_{t'+1}\right] + x_{t'}^1 - v\left[k_{t'}^0 h\left(\frac{x_{t'}^1}{k_{t'}^0}\right), u_{t'+1}\right]\right\} > 0,$$

where the expectation is taken with respect to P_{t+1}. This contradicts the assumed optimality of $\{k_t^1, x_t^1\}$, and completes the proof of the lemma.

The proof of theorem 1 now follows directly from lemmas 1, 3, and 4. In the next two sections, we pursue the study of the unique industry equilibrium as given by (10)–(13).

5. Long-Run Equilibrium with Independent Errors

Equations (10) and (11) and $p(\cdot, \cdot)$ determine a Markov process $\{k_t, u_t\}$ taking values on $(0, \infty) \times E$ which governs the development of k_t, x_t, and u_t through time, starting from a given (k_0, u_0). To determine the long-run characteristics of this process, it will be necessary to restrict the $\{u_t\}$ process further. In the present section, we treat the special but interesting case where u_t and u_s are independent for $s \neq t$, or where the transition function $p(z, u)$ does not depend on u.

In this case, the functional equation (9) becomes

$$v(k, u) = \max_{x \geq 0} \left\{ s(k, u) - x + \beta \int v\left[kh\left(\frac{x}{k}\right), z \right] p(dz) \right\}, \qquad (18)$$

from which it is clear that the optimal investment rate, $x(k, u)$, will not depend on u. It follows from (10) and (11) that the time path of capital stock will be deterministic, following the difference equation

$$k_{t+1} = k_t h\left[\frac{x(k_t)}{k_t} \right], \qquad (19)$$

where $x(k_t)$ is the unique investment rate attaining $v(k_t, u)$. Hence we turn our attention to the existence, uniqueness, and stability of stationary solutions to (19), with results summarized in theorem 2, below.

A capital stock $k^c > 0$ will be a stationary solution to (19) if and only if it is a solution to

$$x(k) = \delta k, \qquad (20)$$

since $h(\delta) = 1$. The solutions to (20) are described in the next lemma.

LEMMA 5: Equation (20) has a solution $k^c > 0$ if and only if

$$\int D(0, u) p(du) > \delta + \frac{r}{h'(\delta)}. \qquad (21)$$

A positive stationary solution, if it exists, must satisfy

$$\int D(k, u) p(du) = \delta + \frac{r}{h'(\delta)}, \qquad (22)$$

so there is at most one positive solution to (20).

PROOF: We first show that any solution to (20) satisfies (22). From (18),

$$v(k, u) \geq s(k, u) - \delta k + \beta \int v(k, z) p(dz)$$

(since $x = \delta k$ is always feasible) for all (k, u) with equality if and only if k satisfies (20). Then taking the mean of both sides with respect to $p(u)$ and collecting terms:

$$E\{v(k, u)\} \geq \frac{1}{1 - \beta} [E\{s(k, u)\} - \delta k] \qquad (23)$$

with equality if and only if k satisfies (20). If k^c satisfies (20), (18) implies

$$-\delta k^c + \beta E\{v(k^c, u)\} \geq -x + \beta E\{v(k^c h(x/k^c))\}$$

for all $x \geqslant 0$. Now applying (23), which holds with equality at k^c,

$$-\delta k^c + \frac{\beta}{1 - \beta}[E\{s(k^c, u)\} - \delta k^c]$$

$$\geqslant -x + \frac{\beta}{1 - \beta}[E\{s(k^c h(x/k^c))\} - \delta k^c h(x/k^c)],$$

for $x \geqslant 0$. At $x = \delta k^c$, this inequality holds with equality. At any other value of x, the right side takes on a smaller value, which is to say that δk^c maximizes the expression on the right. Then the first-order condition

$$E\{s_1(k^c, u)\} = E\{D(k^c, u)\} = \delta + \frac{r}{h'(\delta)}$$

is satisfied. If (21) does not hold, no $k^c > 0$ satisfies this condition, so the necessity of (21) is proved. Further, we have proved that positive stationary solutions satisfy (22) and, since D is strictly decreasing in k, that there is at most one such solution.

To show that (21) is sufficient for the existence of a positive solution to (20), we must rule out the possibilities that $x(k) > \delta k$ or $x(k) < \delta k$ for all $k > 0$. To rule out the former possibility, recall from lemma 4 that $x(k)$ is bounded, so that for k sufficiently large, $x(k) < \delta k$. Suppose, contrary to the lemma, that (22) has a positive solution k^c and that $x(k) < \delta k$ for all $k > 0$. Define the function $z(k)$ by

$$z(k) = \max\left\{\frac{E\{s(k, u)\} - \delta k}{1 - \beta}, 0\right\}$$

so that from (23), $z(k) < E\{v(k, u)\}$ for all $k > 0$. Now, define the operator F_X on bounded continuous functions on $(0, \infty)$ by

$$F_X y(k) = E\{s(k, u)\} - x(k) + \beta y\left[kh\left(\frac{x(k)}{k}\right)\right].$$

It is readily verified that for any y, z in the domain of F_X, $\|F_X y - F_X z\| \leqslant \beta \|y - z\|$. Also, $F_X E\{v(k, u)\} = E\{v(k, u)\}$ where v is the solution to (9), and for any y,

$$\lim_{n \to \infty} F_X^n y = E\{v(k, u)\}. \tag{24}$$

We next show that for $z(k)$ as defined above, $F_X z(k) < z(k)$ for all $k \leqslant k^c$. We have, directly from the definitions of z and F_X,

$$F_X z - z = \frac{\beta}{1 - \beta}\left[E\left\{s\left[kh\left(\frac{x(k)}{k}\right), u\right]\right\} - E\{s(k, u)\}\right]$$

$$- \frac{\beta}{1 - \beta}\delta k\left[h\left(\frac{x(k)}{k}\right) - 1\right] + \delta k - x(k). \tag{25}$$

The strict concavity of s and h implies

$$s\left[kh\left(\frac{x(k)}{k}\right), u\right] - x(k, u) \leqslant D(k, u)k\left[h\left(\frac{x(k)}{k}\right) - 1\right] \qquad (26)$$

and

$$h\left(\frac{x(k)}{k}\right) - 1 < h'(\delta)\left[\frac{x(k)}{k} - \delta\right]. \qquad (27)$$

Combining (25), (26), (27), and (22) then gives, for $k \leqslant k^c$,

$$F_\chi z < z. \qquad (28)$$

One may also verify that $y(k) < z(k)$ over the interval $(0, k^c)$ implies $F_\chi y(k) < F_\chi z(k)$ on this interval. Thus (24) and (28) together imply

$$E\{v(k, u)\} = \lim_{n \to \infty} F_\chi^n z(k) < z(k), \qquad k \in (0, k^c],$$

which contradicts (23). This completes the proof of lemma 5.

It can be shown that $v(k) = E\{v(k, u)\}$ is differentiable for $k > 0$.[11] Then from (18), $x(k)$ must satisfy

$$-1 + \beta v'\left[kh\left(\frac{x(k)}{k}\right)\right]h'\left[\frac{x(k)}{k}\right] \leqslant 0 \qquad (29)$$

with equality if $x(k) > 0$. Inspection of (29) reveals that $x(k)/k$ is a strictly decreasing function of k where $x(k) > 0$, and that $kh(x(k)/k)$ is a strictly increasing function of k. Hence if (20) has a solution, $k^c > 0$. Then the results of this section may be summarized in this theorem.

THEOREM 2: Under the hypothesis of independence of the $\{u_t\}$ process, there are two possibilities for the behavior of the optimal capital stock, k_t. If (21) holds, and if $k_0 > 0$, k_t will converge monotonically to the stationary value k^c, given implicitly by (22). If (21) fails to hold, or if $k_0 = 0$, capital will converge monotonically to zero.

The marginal condition (22), which is satisfied by the long-run capital stock, has a familiar interpretation. The left side of (22) is the expected marginal value product of capital. Since in our model the marginal physical product is unity, this becomes simply expected output price. The right side of (22) is a rental price or user cost of capital, equal to the sum of a depreciation cost term, δ, and a capital or interest cost term, $(r/h'(\delta))$.

While capital and investment are varying deterministically as described in theorem 2, output each period is supplied to the market inelas-

---

[11] If we let $g_n(k) = E\{T^n s(k, u)\}$ and $a_n(k) = g_n(k) - g_{n-1}(k)$, it can be shown that (i) $a_n(k) \leqslant \beta n B_1$, (ii) $a_n(0) = 0$, (iii) $a_n'(k) > 0$, and (iv) $|a_n''(k)| \leqslant B_2$ provided $h''(k)$ is bounded, for $k \geqslant k^* > 0$. Given these conditions, it follows $a_n'(k) \leqslant (\beta^{n/2}/2)B_1^{1/2}B_2$ proving $g_n'(k)$ converges uniformly for $k \geqslant k^*$. Since $g_n(k)$ converges to $v(k) = Ev(k, u)$, $v(k)$ is differentiable for all $k \geqslant k^*$. Since this result holds for all $k^* > 0$, $v'(k)$ exists for all $k > 0$.

tically, in a quantity given by the historically determined capacity of the industry. Fluctuations in demand then affect price only, in a manner which can be computed from the demand function (7). (It may be noted that if variable inputs were introduced, the short-run supply would be upward sloping but not vertical, so that *both* price and output would vary with demand shifts. Nevertheless, in this case as well the capital-invest- ment path will be deterministic.)

While the case of independent errors discussed in this section may ap- pear to be an unlikely specialization of our general model, it is interesting to note that it corresponds perhaps more closely than any other analytical model of the industry to the familiar geometrical dichotomy between short-run and long-run supply. In the short-run case, capacity is fixed and price and output are determined entirely by the *current* demand function and the short-run supply function. In determining the long-run equilib- rium, on the other hand, demand fluctuations play *no* role, with equilib- rium capacity determined entirely by average, or normal, demand.

6. Long-Run Equilibrium with Serially Dependent Errors

In the case of a serially independent $\{u_t\}$ process, as studied in the preced- ing section, a demand shift in period t results in a windfall gain (or loss) for firms in that period, but yields *no* information about what the state of demand in future periods is likely to be. As a result, the current state of demand has no effect on investment policy, and the capital stock of the industry follows a deterministic difference equation. In this section, we shall drop the assumption of independent demand shifts, replacing it with an assumption that these shifts are positively correlated in a particular way, so that, for example, an upward shift in demand not only increases price and profit *this* period but increases the probability that price will continue to be higher than average over the near future.

To study the case of dependent errors, it will be necessary to impose some additional restrictions on the $\{u_t\}$ process, with the general aim of assuring that the distribution of (k_t, u_t) will converge to a stationary distri- bution which is independent of the initial state of the industry, (k_0, u_0). First, we require, for all $v \in E$ and all nondegenerate intervals $A \subset E$,

$$\int_A p(du, v) > 0, \tag{30}$$

so that for any u_t and any nondegenerate subinterval of E, u_{t+1} will fall in that subinterval with positive probability. Similarly, it assures that u_{t+s} will fall in that subinterval with positive probability, or that

$$\mathrm{pr}\,[u_{t+s} \in A \,|\, u_t = u_0] > 0 \tag{31}$$

for all $u_0 \in E$ and all nondegenerate subintervals A of E. Assumption (30) does not preclude the possibility that the left side of (31) may approach 0 as s approaches infinity. We shall rule out this possibility explicitly by adding

$$\lim_{s \to \infty} \text{pr} \, [u_{t+s} \in A \, | \, u_t = u_0] > 0 \tag{32}$$

for all u_0, A as above, where the limiting value does not depend on the value of u_0. That is, u_t has a limiting distribution which does not depend on the initial value u_0 and which assigns positive probability to all non-degenerate intervals of E. It follows from (31) and (32) that for any fixed A the terms of the sequence (31), $s = 1, 2, \ldots$, are uniformly bounded away from zero.

We also wish to insure that the relation between current and future demands is always positive (so that a high demand this period *always* signals high demand for the future) by requiring that

$$\text{pr} \, \{u_{t+1} \geqslant x \, | \, u_t\} \tag{33}$$

be a strictly increasing function of u_t for all $x \in E$ and that

$$\begin{cases} \lim_{u_t \to \infty} \text{pr} \, \{u_{t+1} \geqslant x \, | \, u_t\} = 1, \\ \lim_{u_t \to -\infty} \text{pr} \, \{u_{t+1} \geqslant x \, | \, u_t\} = 0, \end{cases} \tag{34}$$

for all $x \in E$. An example of a process satisfying the restrictions (30), (32), (33), and (34) is:

$$u_{t+1} = \rho u_t + \varepsilon_t,$$

where $0 < \rho < 1$, and where $\{\varepsilon_t\}$ is a sequence of independent, identically distributed normal random variables. Finally, in addition to the assumption (Sec. 1) that $D(k, u)$ (and hence $s[k, u]$ also) is an increasing function of u, we add the restrictions that the limits

$$\overline{s}(k) = \lim_{u \to \infty} s(k, u), \tag{35}$$

$$\underline{s}(k) = \lim_{u \to \infty} s(k, u), \tag{36}$$

exist, and convergence is uniform in k.

Our first task, given these restrictions, is to decompose the set of possible states of the (k_t, u_t) process, the set $(0, \infty) \times E$, into transient sets (sets which cannot be entered, and which will be departed with probability ultimately approaching 1) and ergodic sets (sets which once entered cannot be departed, and which contain no transient subsets). To do this, we develop some additional notation and prove some preliminary lemmas.

Since $\int v(k, z) p(dz, u)$ is a bounded, increasing (by [33]) function of u, the limits

$$\bar{v}(k) = \lim_{u \to \infty} \int v(k, z) p(dx, u), \tag{37}$$

$$\underline{v}(k) = \lim_{u \to -\infty} \int v(k, z) p(dz, u), \tag{38}$$

exist for all fixed k. We wish to show that convergence is uniform in k and to exhibit functional equations solved by $\bar{v}(k)$ and $\underline{v}(k)$. To this end, we first introduce another lemma.

LEMMA 6: Let $f(k, u)$ be a bounded Baire function on $(0, \infty) \times E$, such that

$$\lim_{u \to \infty} f(k, u) = \bar{f}(k) \quad \text{and} \quad \lim_{u \to -\infty} f(k, u) = \underline{f}(k)$$

exist, and convergence is uniform. Then

$$\lim_{u \to \infty} \int f(k, z) p(dx, u) = \bar{f}(k) \quad \text{and} \quad \lim_{u \to -\infty} \int f(k, z) p(dx, u) = \underline{f}(k),$$

and convergence is uniform.

PROOF: Let B be a bound for f. Then for $x \in E$,

$$\left| \bar{f}(k) - \int f(k, z) p(dz, u) \right|$$

$$= \left| \int_{-\infty}^{x} [\bar{f}(k) - f(k, z)] p(dz, u) + \int_{x}^{\infty} [\bar{f}(k) - f(k, z)] p(dz, u) \right|$$

$$\leqslant 2B \int_{-\infty}^{x} p(dz, u) + \sup_{z \in [x, \infty)} |\bar{f}(k) - f(k, z)| \int_{x}^{\infty} p(dz, u).$$

For x sufficiently large, $|\bar{f}(k) - f(k, z)|$ is arbitrarily small, uniformly in k, while $\int_{x}^{\infty} p(dz, u)$ is bounded by 1. For any fixed x, however large, the first term on the right is made arbitrarily small by choosing u sufficiently large, applying (34). The proof for $\underline{f}(k)$ is similar.

As an application of lemma 6, we have the next lemma.

LEMMA 7: The function $\bar{v}(k)$, defined in (37), satisfies the functional equation

$$\bar{v}(k) = \sup_{x \geqslant 0} \left\{ \bar{s}(k) - x + \beta \bar{v} \left[kh \left(\frac{x}{k} \right) \right] \right\} \tag{39}$$

and an analogous functional equation is satisfied by $\underline{v}(k)$.

PROOF: We first show that

$$\lim_{u \to \infty} v(k, u) = \bar{v}(k) \tag{40}$$

uniformly in k. Define the operator T as in Section 2, and let $0(k, u) = 0$ on $(0, \infty) \times E$. Let $0_n(k, u) = T^n 0(k, u)$. Then, by lemma 3, $\lim_{n \to \infty} T^n 0 = v(k, u)$, uniformly in k and u. It will then be sufficient to show that $0_n(k, u)$ converges uniformly to the limit $\overline{0}_n(k)$ as $u \to \infty$, for all n. For $n = 1$, the proposition is true, since $0_1(k, u) = s(k, u)$, and $s(k, u)$ converges uniformly to $\overline{s}(k)$ by (35). Suppose $0_n(k, u)$ converges uniformly to $\overline{0}_n(k)$. By the definition of the operator T,

$$0_{n+1}(k, u) = \sup_{x \geqslant 0} \left\{ s(k, u) - x + \beta \int 0_n \left[kh\left(\frac{x}{k}\right), z \right] p(dz, u) \right\}.$$

Let

$$\overline{0}_{n+1}(k) = \overline{s}(k) + \sup_{x \geqslant 0} \left\{ -x + \beta \overline{0}_n \left[kh\left(\frac{x}{k}\right) \right] \right\}.$$

Since $\overline{0}_n(k) \geqslant 0_n(k, u)$,

$$0 \leqslant \overline{0}_{n+1}(k) - 0_{n+1}(k, u)$$

$$= \sup_{x \geqslant 0} \left\{ -x + \beta \overline{0}_n \left[kh\left(\frac{x}{k}\right) \right] \right\}$$

$$- \sup_{x \geqslant 0} \left\{ -x + \beta \int 0_n \left[kh\left(\frac{x}{k}\right), z \right] p(dz, u) \right\} + \overline{s}(k) - s(k, u)$$

$$\leqslant \beta \sup_{x \geqslant 0} \left| \overline{0}_n \left[kh\left(\frac{x}{k}\right) \right] - \int 0_n \left[kh\left(\frac{x}{k}\right), z \right] p(dz, u) \right|$$

$$+ \overline{s}(k) - s(k, u).$$

By lemma 6, the induction hypothesis, and (35), the term on the right is arbitrarily small, uniformly in $kh(x/k)$, for u sufficiently large. Thus $0_{n+1}(k, u)$ converges uniformly to $\overline{0}_{n+1}(k)$ and $\lim_{n \to \infty} \overline{0}_n(k)$. This completes the proof that the convergence in (40) is uniform.

Now

$$\overline{v}(k) = \lim_{u \to \infty} \sup_{x \geqslant 0} \left\{ s(k, u) - x + \beta \int v[kh(x/k)] p(dz, u) \right\}.$$

By (35), (40), and lemma 6, the expression in braces converges uniformly in k; thus, the supremum and limit operation can be interchanged to obtain (39). The proof for $\underline{v}(k)$ is similar.

The limit functions $\overline{v}(k)$ and $\underline{v}(k)$ share the properties of continuity, monotonicity, and concavity with $\int v(k, z) p(dz, u)$ regarded as a function of k for fixed u. Then, as in Section 3, $\overline{v}(k)$ and $\underline{v}(k)$ are attained at unique values $\overline{x}(k)$ and $\underline{x}(k)$, respectively, and these functions are continuous. Also as in Section 3, the functions $(1/k)\overline{x}(k)$ and $(1/k)\underline{x}(k)$ are decreasing and the functions $kh[(1/k)\overline{x}(k)]$ and $kh[(1/k)\underline{x}(k)]$ are increasing. Finally,

$$\overline{x}(k) = \lim_{u \to \infty} x(k, u)$$

and

$$\underline{x}(k) = \lim_{u \to -\infty} x(k, u)$$

for all k.

From (33), $x(k, u)$ is an increasing function of u, so that $\overline{x}(k) > \underline{x}(k)$ for all k such that $\overline{x}(k) > 0$. By an argument used to prove lemma 4, $\overline{x}(k) < \delta k$ for k sufficiently large. Let $\overline{k}$ be the least positive solution to $\overline{x}(k) = \delta k$ (or 0 if there is no positive solution) and let $\underline{k}$ be the greatest positive solution to $\underline{x}(k) = k$ (or 0 if there is no solution). Then since $\underline{x}(k) < \overline{x}(k)$ if $\overline{x}(k) > 0$, either $\underline{k} = \overline{k} = 0$, or $0 \leqslant \underline{k} < \overline{k} < \infty$.

We now prove another lemma.

LEMMA 8: (i) For all $k \geqslant \overline{k}$, there exists $h_0 < 1$ (not dependent on k) such that the event $h[(x(k, u)/k)] \leqslant h_0$ has positive probability, for all t and all u_0; (ii) for all $0 < k \leqslant \underline{k}$ there exists $h_1 > 1$ (not dependent on k) such that the event $h[(x(k, u/k)] \geqslant h_1$ has positive probability, for all t and all u_0.

PROOF: We prove (i) only, since the proofs of the two parts are essentially the same. For any k, the event $(1/k)\underline{x}(k) \leqslant (1/k)x(k, u) \leqslant (1/2k)[\overline{x}(k) + \underline{x}(k)]$ has positive probability, by (31) and the definitions of $\overline{x}(k)$ and $\underline{x}(k)$. For $k \geqslant \overline{k}$, $(1/k)\overline{x}(k) \leqslant (1/k)\overline{x}(\overline{k}) = \delta$, so that the occurrence of this event implies

$$\frac{1}{k}x(k, u) \leqslant \frac{\delta}{2} + \frac{1}{2k}\underline{x}(\underline{k}) < \delta.$$

Letting $h_0 = h[(\delta/2) + (1/2k)\underline{x}(k)] < 1$, (i) is proved.

Using lemma 8, we can prove the next lemma.

LEMMA 9: The sets $T_1 = (0, k) \times E$ and $T_2 = (\overline{k}, \infty) \times E$ are transient, and the set $B = (\underline{k}, \overline{k}) \times E$ contains all ergodic sets.

PROOF: Since $\{k_t, u_t\}$ takes values in $T_1 \cup B \cup T_2$ (for $k_0 > 0$), it is sufficient to show that (i) if $(k_0, u_0) \notin T_i (i = 1, 2)$, $(k_t, u_t) \notin T_i$ with probability 1 for all $t = 1, 2 \ldots$; and (ii) for all $(k_0, u_0) \in T_1 \cup T_2$,

$$\lim_{t \to \infty} \text{pr}\,[(k_t, u_t) \in B] = 1.$$

To prove (i), we show that $\text{pr}\,[k_{t+1} \geqslant \overline{k}\,|\,(k_t, u_t)] = 0$ for $(k_t, u_t) \in T_1 \cup B$. For $k_t < \overline{k}$, we have

$$k_{t+1} \leqslant k_t h\left(\frac{1}{k_t}\underline{x}(k_t)\right) < \overline{k}h\left(\frac{1}{k}\overline{x}(\overline{k})\right) = \overline{k},$$

since $kh((1/k)\overline{x}(k))$ is an increasing function of k. A similar argument rules out passage into T_1 from $B \cup T_2$.

To prove (ii), let $(k_0, u_1) \in T_2$. Since $x(k_0, u) \leqslant \delta k_0$ for all u, we have $k_t \leqslant k_0$ for all t. Let $h_0 \leqslant 1$ be the number whose existence was established in lemma 8. For some t^*, $k_0 h_0^{t^*} < \overline{k}$. Hence if the event $h[(x(k, u)/k)] \leqslant h_0$

occurs t^* times in t periods, $k_t < \bar{k}$. Since the probability that this event occurs is bounded away from zero, the probability that it will not occur t^* times in t periods goes to zero as t becomes large. A similar argument applies if $(k_0, u_0) \in T_1$.

Next, we have the final lemma.

LEMMA 10: The set $B = (\underline{k}, \bar{k}) \times E$ constitutes the single ergodic set.

PROOF: It has been shown (lemma 9) that all ergodic sets are contained in B. To show that B is a single ergodic set, it is sufficient to show that for some $t \geqslant 1$, all $(k_0, u_0) \in B$, and all nondegenerate rectangular subsets A of B, that

$$\text{pr}\left[(k_t, u_t) \in A \,|\, (k_0, u_0)\right] > 0.$$

Let $A = \{(k, u) \in B: k_a \leqslant k \leqslant k_b, u_a \leqslant u \leqslant u_b\}$, where $\underline{k} \leqslant k_a < k_b \leqslant \bar{k}$ and $u_a < u_b$, $u_a, u_b \in E$. Suppose, to be specific, that $k_0 < k_a$. Then for any finite t one can choose $\theta_2 > \theta_1 > 1$ such that $k_0 \theta_1^t = k_a$ and $k_0 \theta_2^t = k_b$, and $\lim_{t \to \infty} \theta_1 = 1$. By choosing t large enough, the event $h[x(k, u)/k] \geqslant \theta_1$ has positive probability for all $k \leqslant k_a$, so that the event

$$\theta_1 \leqslant h[x(k, u)/k] \leqslant \theta_2$$

has positive probability. Hence the probability that this event will occur t consecutive times is positive, as is the probability that $u_a \leqslant u_t \leqslant u_b$, for any u_{t-1}. Hence the lemma is proved.

Lemmas 9 and 10 accomplish the division of the set $(0, \infty) \times E$ of possible states of the $\{k_t, u_t\}$ process into two transient sets and a single ergodic set. In doing this, nothing has been assumed to assure that the ergodic set B is non-empty, or equivalently, that $\bar{x}(k) = \delta k$ has a positive solution $\bar{k}$. The following theorems characterize the long-run behavior of the system under the hypothesis that B is non-empty. We return to the questions of verifying this hypothesis, and of characterizing the system when it is false, below.

THEOREM 3: If B is not empty, for all (k, u) and all (k_0, u_0), the limit

$$\lim_{t \to \infty} \text{pr}\,\{k_t \leqslant k, u_t \leqslant u \,|\, (k_0, u_0)\} = P(k, u)$$

exists, and does not depend on (k_0, u_0). The function $P(k, u)$ is a probability distribution on $(0, \infty) \times E$, assigning probability zero to all subsets of $T_1 \cup T_2$ and positive probability to all Borel subsets of B with positive area.

PROOF: See Doob (1953, theorem 5.7, p. 214, and surrounding text).

Since under the limiting distribution, k_t lies on a bounded interval with probability 1, the mean of k, k^*, say, exists and is positive. Then we have the following "stability" theorem.

THEOREM 4: *If B is not empty, then for any initial state (k_0, u_0),*

$$\lim_{T \to \infty} \frac{1}{T} \sum_{t=0}^{T} k_t = k^*$$

with probability 1.

PROOF: The result follows from Doob (1953, theorem 6.2, p. 220).

To verify the hypotheses of theorems 3 and 4, we wish to determine when the equation $\bar{x}(k) = \delta k$ has a positive solution. This question is analogous to the question of the existence of a positive solution to $x(k) = \delta(k)$ studied (and solved) in the preceding section. We have the following theorem.

THEOREM 5: *The ergodic set E is non-empty ($\bar{x}[k] = \delta k$ has a positive solution) if and only if*

$$\lim_{u \to \infty} D(0, u) > \delta + \frac{r}{h'(\delta)}. \tag{41}$$

PROOF: The proof follows that of lemma 5, with the operator $\int f(u)p(du)$ on functions f replaced by $\lim_{u \to b} f(u)$. This replacement is justified by lemma 7.

If (41) fails to hold, capital stock in the industry will go to zero with probability one, since $x(k_t, u_t) < \delta k_t$ for all (k_t, u_t). Thus theorems 3, 4, and 5 provide a complete description of the long-run behavior of the industry under the assumptions of this section.

7. Conclusions

The object of this paper has been the extension of "cost-of-adjustment" type investment theory to situations involving demand uncertainty. In doing so, we have tried to go beyond formulations of the "price expectations affect supply, which in turn affects actual price" variety, to consider the *simultaneous* determination of anticipated and actual prices. This involves studying the determination of industry equilibrium, in addition to the individual firm's optimizing behavior, a step which radically alters the nature of the problem.

Generally, the equilibrium behavior of capital stock, output, and price through time is similar to the certainty case studied in Lucas (1967a): the interplay of shifting demand and the costs of varying capacity leads to a difference equation in capital stock. The stationary character of the demand shifts leads capital stock to settle down, either with certainty or "on average," to a long-run equilibrium level, determined by interest rates, adjustment costs, and average demand levels.

An interesting feature of our theory is the role played by securities prices in informing firms of the *market* (not "shadow") price placed on additions to capital stock. We have found (Sec. 2) that securities prices as a variable in a firm level investment function have a much stronger justification than simply as a "proxy" variable for future demand.

References

Arrow, K. J. "The Role of Securities in the Optimal Allocation of Risk Bearing." *Rev. Econ. Studies* 31 (1964): 91–96.

Bellman, Richard. *Dynamic Programming.* Princeton, N.J.: Princeton University Press, 1957.

Blackwell, David. "Discounted Dynamic Programming." *Ann. Math. Statis.* 36 (1965): 226–35.

Debreu, Gerard. *Theory of Value.* New York: Wiley, 1959.

———. "Valuation Equilibrium and Pareto Optimum." *Proc. Nat. Acad. Sci.* 40 (1954): 588–92.

Doob, J. L. *Stochastic Processes.* New York: Wiley, 1953.

Eisner, Robert, and Strotz, Robert. "Determinants of Business Investment" (with bibliography by G. R. Post). In *Impacts of Monetary Policy* by the Commission on Money and Credit. Englewood Cliffs, N.J.: Prentice-Hall, 1963.

Gould, J. P. "Adjustment Costs in the Theory of Investment of the Firm." *Rev. Econ. Studies* 35 (1968): 47–55.

Grunfeld, Yehuda. "The Determinants of Corporate Investment." In A. C. Harberger (Editor), *The Demand for Durable Goods,* edited by A. C. Harberger. Chicago: Univ. Chicago Press, 1960.

Haavelmo, Trygve. *A Study of the Theory of Investment.* Chicago: Univ. Chicago Press, 1960.

Hirshleifer, J. "Investment Decision under Uncertainty: Choice Theoretic Approaches." *Q.J.E.*, vol. 79 (1965).

Jorgenson, Dale W. "Capital Theory and Investment Behavior." *A.E.R.* 53 (1963): 247–59.

Lucas, Robert E., Jr. "Adjustment Costs and the Theory of Supply." *J.P.E.* 75 (1967): 321–34.

———. "Optimal Investment Policy and the Flexible Accelerator." *Internat. Econ. Rev.* 8 (1967): 78–85.

Muth, John F. "Rational Expectations and the Theory of Price Movements." *Econometrica* 29 (1961): 315–35.

Pashigian, B. Peter. "Supply Uncertainty and the Theory of a Competitive Industry." Univ. Chicago working paper, 1968.

Prescott, Edward C., and Lucas, Robert E., Jr. "A Note on Price Systems in Infinite Dimensional Spaces." *Internat. Econ. Rev.*, in press.

Schramm, Richard. "Optimal Adjustment of Factors of Production and the Study of Investment Behavior." Ph.D. dissertation, Carnegie Inst. Tech., 1966.

Treadway, Arthur. "Rational Entrepreneurial Behavior and the Dynamics of Investment." Ph.D. dissertation, Univ. Chicago, 1967.

7

Formulating and Estimating Dynamic Linear Rational Expectations Models

Lars Peter Hansen
Thomas J. Sargent

This paper describes methods for conveniently formulating and estimating dynamic linear econometric models under the hypothesis of rational expectations. An econometrically convenient formula for the cross-equation rational expectations restrictions is derived. Models of error terms and the role of the concept of Granger causality in formulating rational expectations models are both discussed. Tests of the hypothesis of strict econometric exogeneity along the lines of Sims's are compared with a test that is related to Wu's.

This paper describes research which aims to provide tractable procedures for combining econometric methods with dynamic economic theory for the purpose of modeling and interpreting economic time series. That we are short of such methods was a message of Lucas's (1976) criticism of procedures for econometric policy evaluation. Lucas pointed out that agents' decision rules, e.g., dynamic demand and supply schedules, are predicted by economic theory to vary systematically with changes in the stochastic processes facing agents. This is true according to virtually any dynamic theory that attributes some degree of rationality to economic agents, e.g., various versions of "rational expectations" and "Bayesian learning" hypotheses. The implication of Lucas's observation is that instead of estimating the parameters of decision rules, what should be estimated are the parameters of agents' objective functions and of the random processes that they faced historically. Disentangling the parameters governing the stochastic processes that agents face from the parameters of their objective functions would enable the econometrician to predict how

This research was supported by the Federal Reserve Bank of Minneapolis. The views expressed herein are solely those of the authors and do not necessarily represent the views of the Federal Reserve Bank of Minneapolis or the Federal Reserve System. Helpful comments on an earlier draft were made by John Taylor.

[*Journal of Economic Dynamics and Control*, 1980, vol. 2]

agents' decision rules would change across alterations in their stochastic environment. Accomplishing this task is an absolute prerequisite of reliable econometric policy evaluation. The execution of this strategy involves estimating agents' decision rules jointly with models for the stochastic processes they face, subject to the cross-equation restrictions implied by the hypothesis of rational expectations.[1] However, even for very simple models, these cross-equation restrictions are of a complicated form, so that in applications substantial technical problems exist even about the best way of expressing these restrictions mathematically. This paper aims to extend what is known about conveniently characterizing these restrictions and estimating models subject to them.

Our work here involves a setup in which the environment and agents' decision rules can be modeled as time invariant linear stochastic difference equations. Such setups are attractive because they are ones for which the dynamic stochastic optimization theory is tractable analytically, and because it is convenient for econometric reasons to remain within the well-developed domain of time invariant linear stochastic difference equations. In this paper, we adopt the device of carrying out the entire discussion in terms of a simple example, that of a firm devising a contingency plan for the employment of a single factor of production subject to quadratic costs of adjustment and uncertain technology and factor rental processes. This has the advantage of keeping the discussion simple and concrete, while setting aside several technical complications that arise in more general settings, e.g., models with multiple factors. Virtually every issue we deal with here appears in the more complicated setups. Included among the topics treated in this paper are the following:

1. *Derivation of a convenient expression for the decision rule.* Having tractable expressions for the restrictions across the parameters of stochastic processes that agents face and their decision rules is necessary in order to make rational expectations modeling applicable to problems of even moderate dimension. Success in this part of our work will in effect extend the size of rational expectations systems that are manageable.

2. *Delineation of the natural role played by "Granger causality" in these models.* Formulating and estimating models of this type naturally requires use of the concept of Granger causality (1969). In dynamic problems, agents' decision rules typically involve predictions of future values of the stochastic processes, say w_t, that they care about but can't control, e.g., in competitive models output prices and/or input prices. Theory asserts that current and past values of any stochastic processes that help predict w_t belong in the decision rules. This is equivalent with saying that all processes agents see and that Granger cause w_t belong in agents' decision rules. Further, given the appropriate conditioning set or universe with respect to which

---

[1]Examples of such cross-equation restrictions in simple setups are in Lucas (1972), Sargent (1978a, 1978b), and Taylor (1978, 1979).

Granger causality is defined, it is usually correct to assume that the decision variable of a competitive firm fails to Granger cause w_t. It is for these reasons that analysis of such models naturally leads to heavy utilization of the concept of Granger causality. However, it should be recognized that in some settings w_t fails to be Granger caused by the firm's decision variable only when the firm's information set used to forecast w_t includes marketwide totals of the firm's decision variable. This occurs, for example, when marketwide employment contributes to the determination of the factor wage w_t.

3. *Delineation of the relationship between Granger causality and econometric exogeneity.* Sims (1972) has shown that if x_t is to be strictly exogenous in a behavioral relationship expressing n_t as a one-sided distributed lag of x_t, then n_t must fail to Granger cause x_t. So failure of n_t to Granger cause x_t is a necessary condition for x_t to be strictly exogenous. It is not a sufficient condition, however, which will be evident in the context of this paper. Below we develop a statistical test of a stronger sufficient condition which is applicable to situations in which the economic behavioral relationship in question is a decision rule expressing n_t as a one-sided distributed lag of x_t. The restrictions that the assumption of rational expectations imposes across the decision rule and the stochastic process for x_t are essential in making the test feasible. This test is related to Wu's (1973) test for exogeneity so that a useful by-product of this paper is to clarify the relationship between Wu's test for exogeneity and Sims's test.

4. *Development of models of the error terms in estimated decision rules.* This paper develops two different models of the error terms in behavioral equations. Both models use versions of the assumption that private agents observe and respond to more data than the econometrician possesses. Each model imposes substantial structure on the error term and limits the freedom of the econometrician in certain respects to be described. Together with variants of "errors in variables" models, these models are about the only plausible models of the error processes that we can imagine. The rational expectations or equilibrium modelling strategy virtually forces the econometrician to interpret the error terms in behavioral equations in one of these ways. The reason is that the dynamic economic theory implies that agents' decision rules are *exact* (nonstochastic) functions of the information they possess about the relevant state variables governing the dynamic process they wish to control. The econometrician must resort to *some* device to convert the exact equations delivered by economic theory into inexact (stochastic) equations susceptible to econometric analysis.

5. *Development of estimation strategies for rational expectations models.* The discussion of this topic will draw heavily on each of the preceding four topics as we discuss methods for the tractable, consistent, and asymptotically efficient estimation of rational expectations models.

It should be emphasized that the techniques we describe are applicable to an entire class of problems of which our factor demand example is only one member. Other setups that involve identical conceptual and estimation problems include linear–quadratic versions of Lucas and Prescott's (1971) model of investment under uncertainty (e.g., Blanco 1978 or Sargent 1979), versions of Cagan's model of portfolio balance during hyperinflations (e.g., Salemi and Sargent 1980, and Sargent 1977), and rational expectations versions of Friedman's permanent income theory of consumption (e.g., Hall 1978 or Sargent 1978a). The essential characteristic of these examples is that each can be reduced to a problem in which an agent is choosing a linear dynamic contingency plan for a single variable. Extensions to multivariable dynamic choice problems are deferred to a sequel to this paper.[2]

1. Formulas for Decision Rules

A firm employing a single factor of production chooses a contingency plan for that factor n_t to maximize its expected present value

$$
\lim_{N \to \infty} E_t \sum_{j=0}^{N} \beta^j [(\gamma_0 + a_{t+j} - w_{t+j})n_{t+j} - (\gamma_1/2)n_{t+j}^2 \\
- (\delta/2)(n_{t+j} - n_{t+j-1})^2], \tag{1}
$$

subject to n_{t-1} given, where n_t is employment of the factor at time t, w_t is the real factor rental, and a_t is a random shock to technology which is seen by the firm but unobserved by the econometrician.[3] We shall think of n_t as being employment of the single factor labor and w_t as the real wage, but it would be equally appropriate to regard n_t as the stock of capital and w_t as the real rental on capital.[4] In (1) γ_0, γ_1, and δ are each positive constants, while the constant discount factor β satisfies $0 < \beta < 1$. The notation $E_t(y)$ denotes the mathematical expectation of the random variable y, conditioned on information available at time t, an information set to be

---

[2]Aspects of estimating models under rational expectations are discussed by McCallum (1976), Shiller (1972), Wallis (1980), Taylor (1978, 1979), and Revankar (1980). While our estimation problems share many common features with the ones treated in these papers, our setup tends to impose more structure on the estimation problem because the process that we estimate is in effect a "closed-loop-system" resulting from the solution of an optimum problem by a private agent or by a fictitious planner. The paper by Kennan (1979) estimates parameters of a model similar to ours by estimating the stochastic Euler equation.

[3]The price of the output good has not been included in our formulation. One can view this as a world in which there is only one consumption good. Alternatively, we could formally introduce the output price into the analysis. However γ_1 would have to be set to zero so that no third-order terms enter into the objective function.

[4]In particular, we could assume that the firm chooses capital k_t to maximize

$$
V_t = E_t \sum_{j=0}^{\infty} \beta^j [(\gamma_0 + a_{t+j})k_{t+j} - (\gamma_1/2)k_{t+j}^2 \\
- J_{t+j}(k_{t+j} - k_{t+j-1}) - (\delta/2)(k_{t+j} - k_{t+j-1})^2],
$$

specified shortly. The firm faces a stochastic process for a_t of the form

$$a_t = \alpha_1 a_{t-1} + \cdots + \alpha_q a_{t-q} + v_t^a,$$

or

$$\alpha(L)a_t = v_t^a,$$

where L is the lag operator and where $\alpha(L) = 1 - \alpha_1 L - \cdots - \alpha_q L^q$, α_j being a scalar for all j. We assume that w_t is the first element of a vector autoregressive process x_t that satisfies

$$\zeta(L)x_t = v_t^x,$$

where x_t and v_t^x are each ($p \times 1$), and where

$$\zeta(L) = I - \zeta_1 L - \cdots - \zeta_r L^r.$$

The matrix ζ_j is $p \times p$ and so is conformable in dimension with the vector x_t for $j = 1, \ldots, r$. Here (v_t^a, v_t^x) are the innovations for the joint (a_t, x_t) process. More particularly, we assume

$$v_t^a = a_t - E[a_t | a_{t-1}, a_{t-2}, \ldots, x_{t-1}, x_{t-2}, \ldots],$$
$$v_t^x = x_t - E[x_t | x_{t-1}, x_{t-2}, \ldots, a_{t-1}, a_{t-2}, \ldots].$$

It follows that $Ev_t^a | \Omega_{t-1} = 0$ and $Ev_t^x | \Omega_{t-1} = 0$, where $\Omega_{t-1} = \{a_{t-1}, a_{t-2}, \ldots, x_{t-1}, x_{t-2}, \ldots\}$. At time t, the firm is assumed to know $\Omega_t \cup \{n_{t-1}, n_{t-2}, \ldots\}$. We further assume that a_t and x_t are jointly covariance stationary stochastic processes. Sufficient conditions for this are that the roots of $\alpha(z) = 0$ and det $\zeta(z) = 0$ lie outside the unit circle. Actually, for much of our work, the assumption of covariance stationarity can be relaxed somewhat and be replaced by the assumption that a_t and x_t are of mean exponential order less than $1/\sqrt{\beta}$.[5]

We solve the firm's problem by using the discrete time calculus of variations.[6] Differentiating the objective function (1) with respect to n_{t+j},

---

subject to k_{t-1} given. Here J_t is the relative price of capital at time t, relative to the firm's output. Using "summation by parts" it is easy to verify that the above expression is equivalent with

$$V_t = E_t J_t k_{t-1} + E_t \sum_{j=0}^{\infty} \beta^j [(\gamma_0 + a_{t+j})k_{t+j} - (\gamma_1/2)k_{t+j}^2$$
$$- (J_{t+j} - \beta E_{t+j} J_{t+j+1})k_{t+j} - (\delta/2)(k_{t+j} - k_{t+j-1})^2].$$

Since k_{t-1} is given, the same decision rule for k_t will be found by maximizing (1) in the text with $k_t = n_t$ and $J_t - \beta E_t J_{t+1} = w_t$. Here $J_t - \beta E_t J_{t+1}$ can be interpreted as the rental rate on capital.

[5]Sufficient conditions for this requirement of mean exponential order less than $1/\sqrt{\beta}$ are that the zeroes of $\alpha(z)$ and det $\zeta(z)$ be greater than $\sqrt{\beta}$ in absolute value. This is the general condition on uncontrolled random processes required for the class of problems we are studying.

[6]See Sargent (1979) for an exposition of this technique and application to some simple models.

$j = 0, \ldots, N - 1$, and setting each derivative equal to zero gives the system of stochastic Euler equations

$$\beta E_{t+j} n_{t+j+1} + \phi n_{t+j} + n_{t+j-1} = (1/\delta)(w_{t+j} - a_{t+j} - \gamma_0),$$

$$j = 0, \ldots, N - 1, \tag{2}$$

where $\phi = -[(\gamma_1/\delta) + 1 + \beta]$. Differentiating with respect to the last term n_{t+N} gives the terminal or transversality condition

$$\lim_{N \to \infty} E_t \beta^N [\gamma_0 + a_{t+N} - w_{t+N} - \gamma_1 n_{t+N} - \delta(n_{t+N} - n_{t+N-1})] = 0. \tag{3}$$

To solve the Euler equations for $j = 0, \ldots, \infty$, subject to the terminal condition (3) and the given initial employment n_{t-1}, first obtain the factorization of the characteristic polynomial of (2),

$$[1 + (\phi/\beta)z + (1/\beta)z^2] = (1 - \rho_1 z)(1 - \rho_2 z).$$

Given our assumptions about the signs and magnitudes of β, γ_1, and δ, it can readily be shown that $0 < \rho_1 < 1$ and that $\rho_2 = 1/\beta\rho_1$.[7] It follows that the unique solution of the Euler equations that satisfies the transversality condition is

$$n_t = \rho_1 n_{t-1} - (\rho_1/\delta) \sum_{j=0}^{\infty} \lambda^j E_t [w_{t+j} - a_{t+j} - \gamma_0], \tag{4}$$

where $\lambda \equiv \rho_2^{-1} = \beta\rho_1$. Equation (4) is derived from the Euler equation (2) by solving the stable root backwards, and the unstable root forwards in order to satisfy the transversality condition. See Sargent (1979) for more details. Equation (4) exhibits the certainty equivalence or separation property. That is, the same solution for n_t would emerge if we had maximized the criterion formed by replacing (a_{t+j}, w_{t+j}) by $(E_t a_{t+j}, E_t w_{t+j})$ and dropping the operator E_t from outside the sum in the objective function (1).

Equation (4) is not yet a decision rule, for the terms $E_t w_{t+j}$ and $E_t a_{t+j}$ must be eliminated by expressing them as functions of variables known by agents at time t. We shall use the classic Wiener–Kolmogorov formulas to derive a closed form for the decision rule.[8] To derive the decision rule we shall tentatively restrict our specification of the stochastic processes for w_t and a_t to require that the roots of det $\zeta(z) = 0$ and of $\alpha(z) = 0$ be outside the unit circle. These conditions on roots guarantee that a_t and w_t are covariance stationary, thereby justifying the use of the Wiener–Kolmogorov prediction formulas. It will turn out, however, that while our

[7] See Sargent (1979).
[8] These formulas are derived by Whittle (1963).

formulas were initially derived on the assumption that these roots are outside the unit circle, the formulas remain valid under wider conditions, in fact under the conditions on the exponential orders of w_t and a_t indicated in footnote 5.

In Appendix A we shall derive expressions for the terms on the right-hand side of (4) using complex analysis. That derivation seems worthwhile to us in its own right, since it illustrates a method useful in other contexts and also carries insights into the nature of the "annihilation operator" used in solving linear least-squares prediction problems. Here we shall derive the formula in a technically less demanding way using tools more familiar to economists. We desire formulas for the terms

$$U \sum_{j=0}^{\infty} \lambda^j E_t x_{t+j} = \sum_{j=0}^{\infty} \lambda^j E_t w_{t+j} \quad \text{and} \quad \sum_{j=0}^{\infty} \lambda^j E_t a_{t+j},$$

where U is the $(1 \times p)$ unit row vector with 1 in the first place and zeroes elsewhere. The moving average representations for a_t and x_t, which exist by the assumptions on the zeroes of $\alpha(z)$ and det $\zeta(z)$, are

$$a_t = \alpha(L)^{-1} v_t^a = \chi(L) v_t^a = \left[\sum_{j=0}^{\infty} \chi_j L^j \right] v_t^a,$$

and

$$x_t = \zeta(L)^{-1} v_t^x = \xi(L) v_t^x = \left[\sum_{j=0}^{\infty} \xi_j L^j \right] v_t^x.$$

The Wiener–Kolmogorov prediction formula is

$$E_t x_{t+k} = [\xi(L)/L^k]_+ v_t^x,$$

where $[\ \ ]_+$ is the annihilation operator that instructs us to ignore negative powers of L. In other words,

$$E_t x_{t+k} = \left[\sum_{j=k}^{\infty} \xi_j L^{j-k} \right] v_t^x.$$

Then we have

$$\sum_{k=0}^{\infty} \lambda^k E_t x_{t+k} = \left[\sum_{k=0}^{\infty} \lambda^k \sum_{j=k}^{\infty} \xi_j L^{j-k} \right] v_t^x = \psi(L) v_t^x,$$

where

$$\psi(L) = \sum_{k=0}^{\infty} \sum_{j=k}^{\infty} \lambda^k \xi_j L^j L^{-k}.$$

Interchanging orders of summation gives

$$\psi(L) = \sum_{j=0}^{\infty} \sum_{k=0}^{j} \lambda^k \xi_j L^j L^{-k}$$

$$= \sum_{j=0}^{\infty} \xi_j L^j \sum_{k=0}^{j} \lambda^k L^{-k}$$

$$= \sum_{j=0}^{\infty} \xi_j L^j [(1 - \lambda^{j+1} L^{-j-1})/(1 - \lambda L^{-1})]$$

$$= \left(\sum_{j=0}^{\infty} \xi_j L^j - \lambda L^{-1} \sum_{j=0}^{\infty} \xi_j \lambda^j \right) \Big/ (1 - \lambda L^{-1})$$

$$= [\xi(L) - \lambda L^{-1} \xi(\lambda)]/(1 - \lambda L^{-1}).$$

Even though the above expression for $\psi(L)$ contains both positive and negative powers of L, by construction the polynomial in the lag operator $\psi(L)$ contains only nonnegative powers of L. In summary it has been shown that

$$\sum_{k=0}^{\infty} \lambda^k E_t x_{t+k} = \{[\xi(L) - L^{-1} \lambda \xi(\lambda)]/(1 - \lambda L^{-1})\} v_t^x. \tag{5}$$

Equation (5) is a closed form that is especially useful for estimation in the frequency domain. The corresponding formula for a_t is

$$\sum_{k=0}^{\infty} \lambda^k E_t a_{t+k} = \{[\chi(L) - L^{-1} \lambda \chi(\lambda)]/(1 - \lambda L^{-1})\} v_t^a. \tag{6}$$

For time domain estimation, it is desirable to replace the right-hand sides of equations (5) and (6) with equivalent expressions in terms of current and past values of x_t and a_t, respectively. Using

$$v_t^x = \zeta(L) x_t = \xi(L)^{-1} x_t,$$

we can substitute into equation (5) to obtain

$$\sum_{k=0}^{\infty} \lambda^k E_t x_{t+k} = \{[\xi(L) - L^{-1} \lambda \xi(\lambda)]/(1 - \lambda L^{-1})\} \xi^{-1}(L) x_t$$

$$= \{[I - L^{-1} \lambda \xi(\lambda) \xi^{-1}(L)]/(1 - \lambda L^{-1})\} x_t$$

$$= \{[I - L^{-1} \lambda \zeta(\lambda)^{-1} \zeta(L)]/(1 - \lambda L^{-1})\} x_t,$$

Now calculate $\zeta(L)/(1 - \lambda L^{-1})$ by using polynomial long division on $(-L^r \zeta_r - L^{r-1} \zeta_{r-1} - \cdots - L\zeta + I)/(1 - \lambda L^{-1})$ to obtain

$$\zeta(L)/(1 - \lambda L^{-1})$$
$$= -\zeta_r L^r - (\zeta_{r-1} + \lambda \zeta_r) L^{r-1} - \cdots - (\zeta_1 + \lambda \zeta_2 + \cdots + \lambda^{r-1} \zeta_r) L$$
$$+ (I - \lambda \zeta_1 - \cdots - \lambda^r \zeta_r)/(1 - \lambda L^{-1}).$$

It follows that

$$L^{-1}\lambda\zeta(\lambda)^{-1}\zeta(L)/(1-\lambda L^{-1})$$
$$= L^{-1}\lambda\zeta(\lambda)^{-1}[-\zeta_r L^r - (\zeta_{r-1} + \lambda\zeta_r)L^{r-1}$$
$$- \cdots - (\zeta_1 + \lambda\zeta_2 + \cdots + \lambda^{r-1}\zeta_r)L] + L^{-1}\lambda I/(1-\lambda L^{-1}).$$

Therefore

$$[I - L^{-1}\lambda\zeta(\lambda)^{-1}\zeta(L)]/(1-\lambda L^{-1})$$
$$= L^{-1}\lambda\zeta(\lambda)^{-1}[\zeta_r L^r + (\zeta_{r-1} + \lambda\zeta_r)L^{r-1}$$
$$+ \cdots + (\zeta_1 + \lambda\zeta_2 + \cdots + \lambda^{r-1}\zeta_r)L]$$
$$+ I/(1-\lambda L^{-1}) - L^{-1}\lambda I/(1-\lambda L^{-1})$$
$$= I + \zeta(\lambda)^{-1}[\lambda\zeta_r L^{r-1} + (\lambda\zeta_{r-1} + \lambda^2\zeta_r)L^{r-2}$$
$$+ \cdots + (\lambda\zeta_1 + \lambda^2\zeta_2 + \cdots + \lambda^r\zeta_r)].$$

Thus we have

$$[I - L^{-1}\lambda\zeta(\lambda)^{-1}\zeta(L)]/(1-\lambda L^{-1})$$
$$= \zeta(\lambda)^{-1}[\zeta(\lambda) + (\lambda\zeta_1 + \lambda^2\zeta_2 + \cdots + \lambda^r\zeta_r)$$
$$+ \lambda\zeta_r L^{r-1} + (\lambda\zeta_{r-1} + \lambda^2\zeta_r)L^{r-2}$$
$$+ \cdots + (\lambda\zeta_2 + \lambda^2\zeta_3 + \cdots + \lambda^{r-1}\zeta_r)L].$$

Recalling that $\zeta(\lambda) = I - \zeta_1\lambda - \zeta_2\lambda^2 - \cdots - \zeta_r\lambda^r$, we have

$$[I - L^{-1}\lambda\zeta(\lambda)^{-1}\zeta(L)]/(1-\lambda L^{-1})$$
$$= \zeta(\lambda)^{-1}[I + (\lambda\zeta_2 + \lambda^2\zeta_3 + \cdots + \lambda^{r-1}\zeta_r)L$$
$$+ \cdots + (\lambda\zeta_{r-1} + \lambda^2\zeta_r)L^{r-2} + \lambda\zeta_r L^{r-1}],$$

or

$$[I - L^{-1}\lambda\zeta(\lambda)^{-1}\zeta(L)]/(1-\lambda L^{-1})$$
$$= \zeta(\lambda)^{-1}\left[I + \sum_{j=1}^{r-1}\left(\sum_{k=j+1}^{r}\lambda^{k-j}\zeta_k\right)L^j\right]. \tag{7}$$

Using an analogous argument we have

$$[1 - L^{-1}\lambda\alpha(\lambda)^{-1}\alpha(L)]/(1-\lambda L^{-1})$$
$$= \alpha(\lambda)^{-1}\left[1 + \sum_{j=1}^{q-1}\left(\sum_{k=j+1}^{q}\lambda^{k-j}\alpha_k\right)L^j\right]. \tag{8}$$

Substituting from (5), (6), (7), and (8) into (4) gives a closed form expression for the decision rule for n_t.

$$n_t = \rho_1 n_{t-1} - \frac{\rho_1}{\delta}U\zeta(\lambda)^{-1}\left[I + \sum_{j=1}^{r-1}\left(\sum_{k=j+1}^{r}\lambda^{k-j}\zeta_k\right)L^j\right]x_t$$
$$+ \frac{\rho_1}{\delta}\alpha(\lambda)^{-1}\left[1 + \sum_{j=1}^{q-1}\left(\sum_{k=j+1}^{q}\lambda^{k-j}\alpha_k\right)L^j\right]a_t + \frac{\rho_1\gamma_0}{\delta}\left(\frac{1}{1-\lambda}\right), \tag{9}$$

where $\alpha(L)a_t = v_t^a$, and $\zeta(L)x_t = v_t^x$. Equation (9) is a convenient closed
form that expresses the restrictions imposed across the decision rule and
the parameters of the stochastic processes for x_t and a_t. Notice that current
and $(r - 1)$ lagged values of x_t are in the decision rule, while current and
$(q - 1)$ lagged values of a_t appear. So the numbers of lagged x's and a's in
the decision rule are one less than the orders of the autoregressive processes
for x_t and a_t respectively. Further, notice that current and lagged x's appear in the decision rule because they help predict future values of the
wage. Thus, any stochastic processes that both Granger cause the wage
and that are included in the firm's information set appear in the decision
rule for n_t. The above derivation took place under the assumptions that x_t
had an rth order vector autoregressive representation and a_t a qth order
univariate autoregressive representation. Analogous formulas have been
obtained when x_t and a_t are permitted to be mixed autoregressive moving
average processes and when other variables observed by the firm are useful
in forecasting future values of a_t (see Hansen and Sargent 1979).

   The solution method leading to (9) is usefully compared with the standard dynamic programming algorithm for computing the optimal decision
rule (e.g., Bertsekas 1976 or Kwakernaak and Sivan 1972). It is straightforward to show that our problem is a linear optimal regulator problem with
a system representation that is detectable and stabilizable.[9] The optimal
value function of the problem can be determined by solving the matrix
"algebraic Riccati" equation, from which the optimum decision rule is
directly calculable. The algebraic Riccati equation is solved either by
iterating on the Riccati matrix difference equation until convergence is
obtained, or else by Vaughan's (1970) procedure of calculating the eigenvalues and eigenvectors of the state–costate transition matrix. Such procedures do not lead to closed forms but require the use of iterative procedures either to solve for the stationary solution of a matrix difference
equation or else to calculate eigenvalues of the state–costate transition
matrix. Evidently, the solution method leading to (9) dominates these
dynamic programming procedures both in terms of speedier computation,
and in terms of delivering expressions for the decision rules which can
conveniently be differentiated with respect to the free parameters. Each of
these features is of substantial practical importance since the decision rule
and its derivatives with respect to the free parameters $\{\gamma_0, \gamma_1, \delta, \alpha(L),$
$\zeta(L)\}$ will have to be evaluated repeatedly in the course of nonlinear
maximum likelihood estimation.

   It should be mentioned that we are able to obtain a closed form solution
in (9) because the costs of adjustment have a simple first-order form,
permitting us analytically to factor the characteristic polynomial
$[1 + (\phi/\beta)z + (1/\beta)z^2]$. In models with higher-order characteristic polynomials, which result either when there are higher-order adjustment costs

---

[9]But not controllable (see Kwakernaak and Sivan 1972).

or when there are interrelated costs of factor adjustment, the characteristic polynomial cannot be factored analytically. In such models, one cannot obtain a completely closed form expression for the decision rule. Still, the method leading to equation (9) remains useful in such models, and enables one to get "as close as possible" to a closed form solution. The application of our method of solution to models with higher-order dynamics will be described in a sequel to this paper.

2. Restrictions on the Error Process

In this section we illustrate how our methods can be used to provide guidance for interpreting the disturbance or error term in a regression equation. We shall take the view that a_t is a random process that is observed by private agents but is not observed by the econometrician. This indeed is a well-known way for justifying the presence of a disturbance term. Under this interpretation, equation (9) imposes substantial structure on the error process in the equation to be fit by the econometrician. Recalling that $a_t = \alpha(L)^{-1}v_t^a$, the disturbance in equation (9) is given by

$$e_t = \frac{\rho_1}{\delta}\alpha(\lambda)^{-1}\left[1 + \sum_{j=1}^{q-1}\left(\sum_{k=j+1}^{q}\lambda^{k-j}\alpha_k\right)L^j\right]\alpha(L)^{-1}v_t^a.$$

We can rewrite this equation as

$$\alpha(L)e_t = \pi(L)v_t^a, \tag{10}$$

where

$$\pi(L) = \frac{\rho_1}{\delta}\alpha(\lambda)^{-1}\left[1 + \sum_{j=1}^{q-1}\left(\sum_{k=j+1}^{q}\lambda^{k-j}\alpha_k\right)L^j\right].$$

Here v_t^a is the serially uncorrelated random process of innovations in a_t, i.e., v_t^a is "fundamental" for a_t.[10]

Equation (10) shows that the error term in the decision rule (9) is a mixed moving average, autoregressive process with autoregressive order q and moving average order $q - 1$. The parameters of the autoregressive component $\alpha(L)$ are inherited from the qth order Markov specification for the technology shock a_t. The moving average part $\pi(L)$ is entirely determined by the parameters of $\alpha(L)$ and the parameters of the objective function (1). Furthermore the roots of $\pi(z)$ can in general be on either side of the unit circle.[11] This means that the moving average polynomial $\pi(L)$ may not have a stable inverse in nonnegative powers of L. Consequently, even though v_t^a is fundamental for a_t, it is not necessarily fundamental for

---

[10]Some authors impose the additional requirement that the contemporaneous covariance matrix of the serially uncorrelated process be the identity matrix as one of the conditions for being "fundamental." In our exposition we do not impose this additional requirement.

[11]Throughout this paper we will continually make substitutions of z for L and vice versa. It should be remembered that $\pi(L)$ is an operator defined on the space of stochastic processes while $\pi(z)$ is an analytic function.

e_t. That is, v_t^a need not lie in the space spanned by square-summable linear combinations of current and lagged e's.[12]

It is of interest to contrast our specification for e_t with other time series specification strategies. Unrestricted moving average components of a mixed autoregressive moving average process have multiple representations in the sense that different moving average specifications imply the same covariance structure of the process. A common strategy in this situation is to achieve identification by focusing on the moving average specification that is invertible, i.e., the specification for which the zeroes of the moving average polynomial do not lie inside the circle. In our setup we have restrictions across the autoregressive and moving average parameters. In particular, we are not free to assume that the zeroes of $\pi(z)$ lie outside the circle because the parameters of $\pi(L)$ are completely determined by the other parameters of our model. This has important implications which will be discussed below. Before proceeding to the discussion of these implications, we should emphasize that the restrictions which we have derived on the disturbance term depend critically on the assumption that agents use current and past observations of only the technology shock to forecast future values of the technology shock, i.e., no other processes observable to agents Granger cause a_t. As noted previously, it is possible to relax this assumption and instead operate under the notion that the firm observes a vector b_t whose first element is a_t and whose other elements are useful in forecasting future values of a_t. Unfortunately, the parameters governing the b_t process will not necessarily be identifiable. This can create problems in identifying the criterion function parameters of the firm's optimization problem except when the b_t process is orthogonal to the x_t process.

Some widely used estimation procedures for models with mixed moving average, autoregressive errors, such as those of Box and Jenkins (1970), require that the error term be written in a form for which the moving average component is invertible. If such an estimation strategy is to be used, then it is required to rewrite e_t in terms of a new process v_t^e such that $\alpha(L)e_t = \theta(L)v_t^e$, where v_t^e is fundamental for e_t. The condition that v_t^e be fundamental for e_t amounts to choosing $\theta(L)$ so that $\pi(z)\pi(z^{-1}) = \theta(z)\theta(z^{-1})$ for $|z| = 1$, where $\theta(z)$ has no zeroes inside the unit circle. To be more specific, if $z_1, \ldots, z_j$ are the zeroes of $\pi(z)$ that are inside the unit circle, then by multiplying $\pi(z)$ by Blaschke factors, we obtain[13]

$$\theta(z) = \pi(z)[(1 - z_1 z)/(z - z_1)] \ldots [(1 - z_j z)/(z - z_j)],$$

[12]We have produced examples in which some of the roots of $\pi(z)$ are inside the unit circle. This happens only if $q \geq 3$. For $q = 2$, $\pi(L)$ turns out to be $(1 - \hat{\alpha}_1 \hat{\alpha}_2 \lambda L)$, where $(1 - \alpha_1 L - \alpha_2 L^2) = (1 - \hat{\alpha}_1 L)(1 - \hat{\alpha}_2 L)$. Since $|\hat{\alpha}_1| < 1$, $|\hat{\alpha}_2| < 1$, it follows that the zero of $(1 - \hat{\alpha}_1 \hat{\alpha}_2 \lambda z)$ is outside the unit circle.

[13]The factor multiplying $\pi(z)$ is an example of the "Blaschke factors" described, e.g., by Saks and Zygmund (1971, p. 221). The Blaschke factors that we employ differ from the standard form by a constant and a conjugation. We have left out the constant because it has modulus equal to one, and we have left out the conjugation since the complex zeroes of $\pi(z)$ come in conjugate pairs.

which satisfies the above requirements. Other estimation procedures are available that do not require that the moving average polynomial for the error process e_t in (10) be invertible. Such procedures are directly applicable without need to replace $\pi(L)v_t^a$ by $\theta(L)v_t^e$. We shall describe these procedures in Section 4.

An alternative to the model of the error term described above can be derived by simply positing that the error term e_t in the decision rule (9) is an mth order autoregressive process, and then to work backwards and determine what assumptions are implied about the a_t process in the objective function. In particular, suppose that

$$e_t = \varepsilon_1 e_{t-1} + \cdots + \varepsilon_m e_{t-m} + v_t^e,$$

or

$$\varepsilon(L)e_t = v_t^e, \qquad (11)$$

where $\varepsilon(L) = 1 - \varepsilon_1 L - \cdots - \varepsilon_m L^m$, e_t is covariance stationary and v_t^e is the innovation in the e_t process. We then can invert (11), to get

$$e_t = \varepsilon(L)^{-1}v_t^e,$$

since $\varepsilon(z)$ has its zeroes outside the unit circle by the assumption of covariance stationarity.

Let

$$\Delta(L) = [\varepsilon(L)^{-1}(L - \lambda) + \lambda\varepsilon(0)^{-1}]/L.$$

It is easily verified that $\Delta(L)$ is one-sided, i.e., that the expansion for $\Delta(z)$ about zero contains only nonnegative powers of L. Define $a_t = \Delta(L)v_t^e$, and assume that v_t^e is contained in agents' information set at time t. We know that the technology shock a_t must be related to the disturbance e_t in the decision rule by

$$e_t = \frac{\rho_1}{\delta} \sum_{j=0}^{\infty} \lambda^j E_t a_{t+j} = [L\Delta(L)/(L - \lambda)]_+ v_t^e. \qquad (12)$$

Using the formula (A3) in Appendix A we have that

$$\begin{aligned}
[L\Delta(L)/(L - \lambda)]_+ &= [L\Delta(L) - \lambda\Delta(\lambda)]/(L - \lambda) \\
&= [\varepsilon(L)^{-1}(L - \lambda) + \lambda\varepsilon(0)^{-1} - \lambda\varepsilon(0)^{-1}]/(L - \lambda) \\
&= \varepsilon(L)^{-1}.
\end{aligned}$$

Substituting into (12) we have that $e_t = \varepsilon(L)^{-1}v_t^e$, and therefore equation (11) has been verified. We should note that $\Delta(z)$ is not necessarily invertible. Consequently, v_t^e might not be recoverable from current and past observations on a_t, so that for this model of the error term it must be assumed that agents observe the v_t^e process itself and not just the a_t process.

A disadvantage of this model for e_t as a purely autoregressive process is that it requires that the covariance structure of the technology shock a_t be linked in a particular way to parameters in the firm's criterion function. In our view, this is not plausible; thus we prefer the model (10) for e_t.

3. Granger Causality and Econometric Exogeneity

Let us write the dynamic demand schedule for labor, i.e., the firm's decision rule for n_t, as

$$n_t = \rho_1 n_{t-1} + \mu(L)x_t + \pi(L)a_t,$$

where

$$\mu(L) = -\frac{\rho_1}{\delta}U\zeta(\lambda)^{-1}\left[I + \sum_{j=1}^{r-1}\left(\sum_{k=j+1}^{r}\lambda^{k-j}\zeta_k\right)L^j\right],$$

$$\pi(L) = \frac{\rho_1}{\delta}\alpha(\lambda)^{-1}\left[1 + \sum_{j=1}^{q-1}\left(\sum_{k=j+1}^{q}\lambda^{k-j}\alpha_k\right)L^j\right].$$

For the sake of simplicity, the constant term has been omitted. Solving for n_t as a function of current and past x's and a's we have that

$$n_t = (1 - \rho_1 L)^{-1}\mu(L)x_t + (1 - \rho_1 L)^{-1}\pi(L)a_t. \tag{13}$$

This provides us with an expression for the firm's demand schedule for n_t as a sum of distributed lags of current and past x's and current and past a's. Recalling that $x_t = \zeta(L)^{-1}v_t^x$ and $a_t = \alpha(L)^{-1}v_t^a$, we can substitute into equation (13) to obtain

$$n_t = (1 - \rho_1 L)^{-1}\mu(L)\zeta(L)^{-1}v_t^x + (1 - \rho_1 L)^{-1}\pi(L)\alpha(L)^{-1}v_t^a. \tag{14}$$

Since (v_t^a, v_t^x) are the innovations in the joint (a_t, x_t) process, it follows that v_t^a and v_t^x are serially uncorrelated and that $Ev_t^a v_{t-j}^x = 0$ for $j \neq 0$. Contemporaneous correlation between v_t^a and v_t^x cannot in general be ruled out.

Let us introduce a new process c_t such that $c_t = v_t^a - \nu v_t^x$, where $Ec_t v_t^x = 0$ and ν is a $(1 \times p)$ row vector. This defines νv_t^x as the linear least-squares predictor of v_t^a given v_t^x. In the case in which v_t^a and v_t^x are uncorrelated, ν is equal to zero and $c_t = v_t^a$. Substituting into equation (14) we have

$$n_t = (1 - \rho_1 L)^{-1}[\mu(L)\zeta(L)^{-1} + \pi(L)\alpha(L)^{-1}\nu]v_t^x \\ + (1 - \rho_1 L)^{-1}\pi(L)\alpha(L)^{-1}c_t. \tag{15}$$

As argued in the previous section, $\pi(z)$ may not be invertible. Thus if we define a disturbance term

$$d_t = (1 - \rho_1 L)^{-1}\pi(L)\alpha(L)^{-1}c_t, \tag{16}$$

c_t may not be fundamental for d_t. Using the transformation with Blaschke factors described in Section 2, there exists a $\theta(L)$ such that $\pi(z)\pi(z^{-1}) =$

$\theta(z)\theta(z^{-1})$ for $|z| = 1$, where $\theta(z)$ does not have any zeroes inside the unit circle. This allows us to define a new serially uncorrelated process v_t^d that is fundamental for d_t such that

$$d_t = (1 - \rho_1 L)^{-1}\theta(L)\alpha(L)^{-1}v_t^d. \tag{17}$$

Since $Ec_t v_{t-j}^x = 0$ for all j it follows that $Ed_t v_{t-j}^x = 0$ and consequently $Ev_t^d v_{t-j}^x = 0$ for all j. We can substitute equations (17) and (16) into (15) and determine that

$$
\begin{aligned}
n_t = {} & (1 - \rho_1 L)^{-1}[\mu(L)\zeta(L)^{-1} + \pi(L)\alpha(L)^{-1}\nu]v_t^x \\
& + (1 - \rho_1 L)^{-1}\theta(L)\alpha(L)^{-1}v_t^d.
\end{aligned} \tag{18}
$$

Equation (18) together with the fact that $x_t = \zeta(L)^{-1}v_t^x$ provides us with the representation of the joint (n_t, x_t) process given below

$$
\begin{bmatrix} n_t \\ x_t \end{bmatrix} =
$$

$$
\begin{bmatrix} (1 - \rho_1 L)^{-1}\theta(L)\alpha(L)^{-1} & (1 - \rho_1 L)^{-1}\{\mu(L)\zeta(L)^{-1} + \pi(L)\alpha(L)^{-1}\nu\} \\ 0 & \zeta(L)^{-1} \end{bmatrix}
$$

$$
\times \begin{bmatrix} v_t^d \\ v_t^x \end{bmatrix}. \tag{19}
$$

This system expresses (n_t, x_t) as one-sided square-summable moving averages of the serially uncorrelated processes v_t^d and v_t^x which satisfy $Ev_t^x v_{t-j}^d = 0$ for all j. The joint (v_t^d, v_t^x) process is fundamental for the joint (n_t, x_t) process. Thus (19) provides us with a Wold moving average representation of the joint (n_t, x_t) process. Note that we have a zero restriction in this representation in that x_t is not dependent upon v_t^d. The triangular character of this moving average representation together with Sims's theorem 1 (1972) imply that n_t fails to Granger cause x_t.[14]

Sims's theorem 2 informs us that if n_t fails to Granger cause x_t then there exists a representation of the form

$$n_t = \eta(L)x_t + u_t, \tag{20}$$

where

$$\eta(L) = \sum_{j=0}^{\infty} \eta_j L^j.$$

The coefficients of $\eta(L)$, i.e., the η_j's, are square-summable matrices and u_t is a covariance stationary stochastic process obeying the orthogonality conditions $Ex_t u_{t-j} = 0$ for all j. These orthogonality conditions say that x_t is strictly exogenous in (20) and that the projection of n_t onto the entire x_t

[14]Formally Sims's theorems are for a bivariate process; however, they readily generalize to a partitioned vector process.

process is one-sided on present and past x's. So Sims's theorem 2 informs us that if n_t fails to Granger cause x_t then there exists a regression of n_t on a one-sided distributed lag of x_t in which x_t is strictly exogenous. A candidate for the representation guaranteed by Sims's theorem is the dynamic labor demand schedule (13).[15] Our purpose here is to indicate that this schedule need not be the representation in which x_t is strictly exogenous. The upshot is that econometric exogeneity of x_t in the firm's decision rule for n_t is a stricter condition than the Granger noncausality of x_t by n_t. As we have seen, this latter condition is an implication of the assumptions we have used in our model derivation.

It is useful to substitute $v_t^x = \zeta(L)x_t$ and equation (17) into equation (18) yielding

$$n_t = (1 - \rho_1 L)^{-1}[\mu(L) + \pi(L)\alpha(L)^{-1}\nu\zeta(L)]x_t + d_t. \qquad (21)$$

Since $Ed_t v_{t-j}^x = 0$ for all j, it follows that $Ed_t x_{t-j} = 0$ for all j. Letting $u_t = d_t$, and

$$\eta(L) = (1 - \rho_1 L)^{-1}[\mu(L) + \pi(L)\alpha(L)^{-1}\nu\zeta(L)],$$

we see that equation (21) is the representation insured by Sims's theorem. In other words, x_t is strictly exogenous in equation (21). Comparing equations (13) and (21) it is immediately apparent that equation (21) is the labor demand schedule if and only if $\nu = 0$. The condition $\nu = 0$ is equivalent to the requirement that $Ev_t^x v_t^a = 0$.

Summarizing our argument, Sims's theorem 1 indicates that the failure of n_t to Granger cause x_t is manifest in the existence of a triangular moving average representation for the joint (n_t, x_t) process. Equation system (19) displays such a representation for our model. The existence of this triangular moving average representation is a necessary condition for x_t to be strictly exogenous in the firm's demand schedule for labor as Sims's theorems 1 and 2 show, but it is not a sufficient condition. Sufficient conditions are both that (a) there exists a triangular moving average representation, i.e., n_t does not Granger cause x_t, and (b) the vector of regression parameters $\nu = 0$, i.e., $Ev_t^x v_t^a = 0$. Thus the conditions under which x_t is exogenous in the labor demand schedule are more stringent than the conditions under which n_t fails to Granger cause x_t.

The hypothesis that n_t fails to Granger cause x_t is a key one in formulating the model. Further, any variable that Granger causes the real wage w_t ought to be included in the vector x_t, at least if there is a presumption that that variable was observable by the firm. Using the standard tests of Granger and Sims, these specifications can be subjected to empirical checks, before proceeding with estimation of the model. Now it happens that the parameters of the model, i.e., the parameters of the firm's objec-

---

[15]We are identifying the labor demand schedule as the representation of n_t in terms of current and past x's and a's.

tive function and the Markov processes governing x_t and a_t, are all identifiable without imposing the exogeneity assumption that $\nu = 0$. Consistent estimators of these parameters can be constructed imposing only the Granger noncausality of x_t by n_t, but leaving ν unrestricted in (21). Then, under the maintained hypotheses that n_t does not Granger cause x_t and that the other specifications of the model are correct, the null hypothesis that $\nu = 0$ can be tested.

This latter test is similar in spirit to the test for exogeneity proposed by Wu (1973) in a classical simultaneous equations setting. The idea of Wu's test for exogeneity was to examine the covariance between the disturbance of the reduced form equation for a stochastic regressor appearing in a particular structural equation and the disturbance term in that same structural equation. In the context of our model, this is analogous to testing whether $Ev_t^x v_t^a = 0$, which is equivalent to $\nu = 0$. It should be pointed out, however, that the estimation environment which we are considering differs somewhat from the one which Wu considered, in that we are allowing for serial correlation in disturbance terms and that we achieve parameter identification via nonlinear cross-equation restrictions implied by the hypothesis of rational expectations.

The preceding amounts to a description of the representation theory underlying our proposed test for strict exogeneity under the maintained hypothesis of the model. That is, we have shown that the hypothesis of strict econometric exogeneity in the labor demand schedule in terms of current and past n's and a's translates into the hypothesis that $\nu = 0$ in the population Wold representation (19). We now briefly describe two statistical procedures for testing the null hypothesis $\nu = 0$, each of which has a justification in terms of asymptotic distribution theory. The first procedure involves first estimating all of the free parameters of (19) by a quasi-maximum likelihood procedure,[16] including ν among the free parameters. Then the model (19) is reestimated imposing the strict exogeneity assumption $\nu = 0$. On the null hypothesis that $\nu = 0$, the likelihood ratio statistic is asymptotically distributed as chi-square with p degrees of freedom, where ν is a $(p \times 1)$ vector.

A second testing procedure is closely related. It involves estimating (19) with ν a free parameter by a quasi-maximum likelihood procedure, and then using the asymptotic covariance matrix of the estimated ν to test the null hypothesis that $\nu = 0$.

The preceding representation of the hypothesis of strict exogeneity maintains the hypothesis that the specification of the model is correct. As it happens, the model often imposes overidentifying restrictions on the lag distribution of x_t on the right-hand side of (21). This means that (21) is a regression equation (i.e., $Ed_t x_{t-j} = 0$ for $j \geqq 0$) only if the overidentifying

---

[16]For a precise definition of the term "quasi-maximum likelihood procedure," see Section 4.

restrictions are true. One can compute various specification tests for the model, which are closely related to exogeneity tests, and are based on estimates of the sample moments corresponding to $Ed_t x_{t-j}$ for $j \geq 0$. Rejection of the hypothesis that these moments are zero can be viewed as evidence against the specification of the model. Failing such a test would leave open whether the specification is faulty because of an incorrect criterion function being attributed to the maximizing agent, or because of a failure of x_t to be Granger noncaused by n_t, as the model assumes. Presumably, careful application of Granger causality tests in the "model-free" setting of Granger and Sims could be used to help isolate the source of failure.

4. Estimation of the Model Parameters

The system that we want to estimate is

$$n_t = (1 - \rho_1 L)^{-1}[\mu(L) + \pi(L)\alpha(L)^{-1}\nu\zeta(L)]x_t$$
$$+ (1 - \rho_1 L)^{-1}\pi(L)\alpha(L)^{-1}c_t \qquad (22)$$
$$\zeta(L)x_t = v_t^x,$$

where

$$\pi(L) = \frac{\rho_1}{\delta}\alpha(\lambda)^{-1}\left[1 + \sum_{j=1}^{q-1}\left(\sum_{k=j+1}^{q}\lambda^{k-j}\alpha_k\right)L^j\right],$$

$$\mu(L) = \frac{\rho_1}{\delta}\zeta(\lambda)^{-1}\left[I + \sum_{j=1}^{r-1}\left(\sum_{k=j+1}^{r}\lambda^{k-j}\zeta_k\right)L^j\right],$$

$$Ec_t c_{t-j} = 0, \qquad Ev_t^x v_{t-j}^{x'} = 0 \qquad \text{for} \quad j \neq 0,$$
$$Ec_t v_{t-j}^x = 0 \qquad \text{for all } j.$$

Equation system (22) can be estimated by using the method of quasision equations which emerge from our model. The underlying parameters which are to be estimated are ν, ρ_1, δ, λ, and the parameters of $\alpha(L)$ and $\zeta(L)$.[17] As was noted in Section 3, x_t is strictly exogenous in the first equation of this system.

Equation system (22) can be estimated by using the method of quasi-maximum likelihood with a normal density function. The word "quasi" is included because it is not necessary to assume that the stochastic processes are Gaussian in order to obtain the desired asymptotic properties of the maximum likelihood estimates, e.g., consistency and asymptotic efficiency.

---

[17]In actuality, one may be interested in knowing β and γ_1, since β, γ_1 and δ are the parameters of agents' objective functions. The parameters β and γ_1 can easily be recovered from the other parameters being estimated.

Suppose that we have a sample on (n_t, x_t) for $t = 1, \ldots, T$. Let us stack the observations into vectors $(\bar{n}_T, \bar{x}_T)$, where

$$\bar{n}_T = \begin{bmatrix} n_1 \\ n_2 \\ \vdots \\ n_T \end{bmatrix}, \quad \bar{x}_T = \begin{bmatrix} x_1 \\ x_2 \\ \vdots \\ x_T \end{bmatrix}.$$

Now write the Wold moving average representation (19) in the form

$$\begin{pmatrix} n_t \\ x_t \end{pmatrix} = \Phi(L) \begin{pmatrix} v_t^d \\ v_t^x \end{pmatrix}, \tag{23}$$

where $\Phi(L)$ is the matrix of polynomials in L on the right-hand side of (19), and where

$$E \begin{pmatrix} v_t^d \\ v_t^x \end{pmatrix} (v_t^d v_t^{x'}) = V = \begin{pmatrix} V_{11} & 0 \\ 0 & V_{22} \end{pmatrix}.$$

(Recall that by construction $Ev_t^d v_t^x = 0$.) Then the covariance generating function for the joint (n_t, x_t) process is $\Phi(z)V\Phi(z^{-1})'$. We can use the covariance generating function for the (n_t, x_t) process to generate the population elements of the covariance matrix of the stacked random vector $(\bar{n}_T', \bar{x}_T')$ in terms of the underlying parameters of the model. Let the covariance matrix of $(\bar{n}_T', \bar{x}_T')$ be

$$\Gamma_T = E \begin{pmatrix} \bar{n}_T \\ \bar{x}_T \end{pmatrix} \begin{pmatrix} \bar{n}_T \\ \bar{x}_T \end{pmatrix}'.$$

(Recall that the mean of $[\bar{n}_T', \bar{x}_T']$ is zero by virtue of the means having been subtracted off.)

The normal log likelihood function for $(\bar{n}_T, \bar{x}_T)$ is given by

$$\mathcal{L}_T = -\tfrac{1}{2}(T + Tp) \log 2\pi - \tfrac{1}{2} \log \det \Gamma_T - \tfrac{1}{2} [\bar{n}_T' \bar{x}_T'] \Gamma_T^{-1} \begin{bmatrix} \bar{n}_T \\ \bar{x}_T \end{bmatrix}. \tag{24}$$

Directly maximizing the log likelihood function is difficult computationally, since Γ_T is a complicated function of the underlying parameters of the model, and since inversion of the large $(T + Tp) \times (T + Tp)$ matrix Γ_T is required for each evaluation of the likelihood function.[18] An alternative strategy is to express the normal likelihood function as a product of conditional likelihood functions and to employ recursive prediction algorithms to evaluate the conditional means and variances (see Rissanen and Caines 1979). This relinquishes the burden of inverting the Γ_T matrix but requires

---

[18]This is a well-known problem in models with moving average errors (see Anderson 1975, chap. 5; or Hannan 1970, chap. 6).

the use of recursive formulas in order to evaluate the likelihood function. By virtue of the highly nonlinear nature of the cross-equation rational expectations restrictions, the likelihood function will have to be maximized via some numerical method which requires repeated evaluation of the likelihood. For this reason, we mention a pair of strategies for simplifying the calculations by approximating the likelihood function.

Likelihood Conditional on Some Initial Observations

It is convenient to rewrite system (19) or (22) in the regression equation form

$$\alpha(L)(1 - \rho_1 L)n_t = [\alpha(L)\mu(L) + \pi(L)\nu\zeta(L)]x_t + \theta(L)v_t^d,$$
$$\zeta(L)x_t = v_t^x. \tag{25}$$

The equations express n_t as a mixed moving average autoregressive process with an exogenous driving process x_t. In the first equation of (25), there are $(q + 1)$ lagged n's, $(q + r - 1)$ lagged x's, and $(q - 1)$ lagged v_t^d's.

Now represent the joint density f_J of $(\bar{n}_T', \bar{x}_T')$ by

$$F_J(\bar{n}_T, \bar{x}_T) = f_c(\bar{n}_T \mid \bar{x}_T) \cdot f_m(\bar{x}_T), \tag{26}$$

where f_c is the density function for $\bar{n}_T$ conditioned on $\bar{x}_T$ and f_m is the marginal density of $\bar{x}_T$. It is convenient to approximate each density on the right-hand side of (26) with a density conditioned on some initial observations. First, approximate $f_m(\bar{x}_T)$ by

$$
\begin{aligned}
&f_m(x_T, x_{T-1}, \ldots, x_1) \\
&\approx g_m(x_T, x_{T-1}, \ldots, x_{r+1} \mid x_r, x_{r-1}, \ldots, x_1) \\
&= g_c(x_T \mid x_{T-1}, \ldots, x_{T-r}) g_c(x_{T-1} \mid x_{T-2}, \ldots, x_{T-r-1}) \\
&\quad \cdots g_c(x_{r+1} \mid x_r, x_{r-1}, \ldots, x_1),
\end{aligned} \tag{27}
$$

where g_m and g_c are the appropriate marginal and conditional density functions. Taking logarithms on both sides of (27) we obtain

$$
\begin{aligned}
&\log g_m(x_T, x_{T-1}, \ldots, x_{r+1} \mid x_r, x_{r-1}, \ldots, x_1) \\
&= \sum_{t=r+1}^{T} \log g_c(x_t \mid x_{t-1}, \ldots, x_{t-r}).
\end{aligned} \tag{28}
$$

Using the normal density and equation (25) we have

$$
\begin{aligned}
&\log g_c(x_t \mid x_{t-1}, \ldots, x_{t-r}) \\
&= -\frac{p}{2} \log 2\pi - \frac{1}{2} \log \det V_{22} \\
&\quad -\frac{1}{2}\left(x_t - \sum_{j=1}^{r} \zeta_j x_{t-j}\right)' V_{22}^{-1}\left(x_t - \sum_{j=1}^{r} \zeta_j x_{t-j}\right).
\end{aligned}
$$

Using this expression for $\log g_c$ in (27) gives

$$\log g_m(x_T, x_{T-1}, \ldots, x_{r+1} \mid x_r, x_{r-1}, \ldots, x_1)$$

$$= -\frac{p(T-r)}{2} \log 2\pi - \left(\frac{T-r}{2}\right) \log \det V_{22} \qquad (29)$$

$$-\tfrac{1}{2} \sum_{t=r+1}^{T} \left(x_t - \sum_{j=1}^{r} \zeta_j x_{t-j}\right)' V_{22}^{-1} \left(x_t - \sum_{j=1}^{r} \zeta_j x_{t-j}\right).$$

Next approximate the term $f_c(\bar{n}_T \mid \bar{x}_T)$ in (26) with

$$f_c(n_T, n_{T-1}, \ldots, n_1 \mid x_T, x_{T-1}, \ldots, x_1)$$

$$\approx h_m(n_T, n_{T-1}, \ldots, n_{q+r} \mid n_{q+r-1}, \ldots, n_1, x_T, x_{T-1}, \ldots, x_1, v_{q+r-1}^d, \ldots, v_1^d)$$

$$= h_c(n_T \mid n_{T-1}, \ldots, n_{T-(q+1)}, x_T, \ldots, x_{T-(q+r-1)}, v_{T-1}^d, \ldots, v_{T-(q-1)}^d)$$

$$\cdot h_c(n_{T-1} \mid n_{T-2}, \ldots, n_{T-(q+2)}, x_{T-1}, \ldots, x_{T-(q+r-2)}, v_{T-2}^d, \ldots, v_{T-q}^d)$$

$$\cdot \ldots \cdot h_c(n_{q+r} \mid n_{q+r-1}, \ldots, n_{r-1}, x_{q+r}, \ldots, x_1, v_{q+r-1}^d, \ldots, v_{r+1}^d), \qquad (30)$$

where h_m and h_c are the appropriate marginal and conditional densities.[19]
The normal density with (25) leads to

$$h_c(n_t \mid n_{t-1}, \ldots, n_{t-(q+1)}, x_t, \ldots, x_{t-(q+r-1)}, v_{t-1}^d, \ldots, v_{t-(q-1)}^d)$$

$$\sim \mathfrak{N}\Big(\{[-\alpha(L)(1-\rho_1 L)]/L\}_+ n_{t-1} + [\alpha(L)\mu(L) + \pi(L)\nu\zeta(L)]x_t$$

$$+ [\theta(L)/L]_+ v_{t-1}^d, \theta_0^2 V_{11}\Big).$$

Substituting the normal density into (30) and taking logs leads to

$$\log h_m(n_T, n_{T-1}, \ldots, n_{q+r} \mid n_{q+r-1}, \ldots, n_1, x_T, \ldots, x_1, v_{q+r-1}^d, \ldots, v_1^d)$$

$$= -\{[T+1-(q+r)]/2\} \log 2\pi - \{[T+1-(q+r)]/2\} \log \theta_0^2 V_{11}$$

$$-\tfrac{1}{2}(1/\theta_0^2 V_{11}) \sum_{t=q+r}^{T} \{\alpha(L)(1-\rho_1 L)n_t - [\alpha(L)\mu(L)$$

$$+ \pi(L)\nu\zeta(L)]x_t - [\theta(L)/L]_+ v_{t-1}^d\}^2. \qquad (31)$$

Adding (29) and (31) and viewing the result as an approximation to the log of (26) leads to the approximate log likelihood function

$$\mathscr{L}_T^* = \{-[p(T-r)/2] \log 2\pi - [(T-r)/2] \log \det V_{22}$$

$$-\tfrac{1}{2} \sum_{t=r+1}^{T} [\zeta(L)x_t]' V_{22}^{-1} (\zeta(L)x_t]\}$$

---

[19] Recall that by virtue of the invertibility built into representation (19) or (23), v_t^d is in the space spanned by current and lagged n's and x's. In effect, lagged v^d's are conditioned on in (30) as proxies for the more extensive set of lagged n's and x's whose information they fully summarize.

$$+ \Big(-\{[T + 1 - (q + r)]/2\} \log 2\pi$$

$$-\{[T + 1 - (q + r)]/2\} \log \theta_0^2 V_{11} \tag{32}$$

$$-\tfrac{1}{2}(1/\theta_0^2 V_{11}) \sum_{t=q+r}^{T} \{\alpha(L)(1 - \rho_1 L)n_t$$

$$-[\alpha(L)\mu(L) + \pi(L)\nu\zeta(L)]x_t$$

$$-[\theta(L)/L]_+ v_{t-1}^d\}^2 \Big).$$

This approximation to the log likelihood is to be maximized over the free parameters ν, ρ_1, δ, λ, $\alpha(L)$, $\zeta(L)$, and V subject to the cross-equation restrictions exhibited in (22). The expression (32) for the approximate log likelihood indicates that it is desirable to estimate all of the equations of (22) jointly, even though x_t is strictly exogenous in the first equation of (22). The reason for joint estimation is that the parameters of $\zeta(L)$ appear in the first equation of (22) via the assumption of rational expectations. Evidently, estimating $\zeta(L)$ by maximizing the term in braces in (32) and then maximizing the second term in large parentheses,[20] taking $\zeta(L)$ as given, leads to a lower value of the approximate likelihood.

Since the initial values $v_{q+r-1}^d, \ldots, v_{r+1}^d$ are unobservable, implementing the approximation (32) requires one additional approximation be used to generate estimates of these initial values of v^d. Box and Jenkins (1970) describe several ways to select the initial v_t^d's. One permissible procedure would be to set the initial values of the v_t^d's at their unconditional means of zero. The invertibility built into the Wold representation (19) guarantees that the impact of these initial v's becomes negligible as $T \to \infty$.

Spectral Approximations

Hannan (1970) has suggested an alternative approximation to the log likelihood function $\mathfrak{L}_T$ in (24).[21] Using the compact representation (23), we know that the theoretical spectral density matrix of the (n_t, x_t) process is given by $S(\omega) = \Phi(e^{-i\omega})V\Phi(e^{i\omega})'$. Let $I(\omega_j)$ be the periodogram for the (n_t, x_t) process at frequency $\omega_j = 2\pi j/T$. Now make the following approximations:

$$[\bar{n}_T' \bar{x}_T'] \Gamma_T^{-1} \begin{bmatrix} \bar{n}_T \\ \bar{x}_T \end{bmatrix} \approx \sum_{j=1}^{T} \text{tr}\, [S(\omega_j)^{-1} I(\omega_j)],$$

[20]This amounts to estimating the second equation of (22) for the exogenous process x_t first, and then estimating the first equation of (22) taking the estimate of $\zeta(L)$ as given.
[21]See Hannan 1970, chap. 6, secs. 4 and 5.

and   (33)

$$\log\,(\det\,\Gamma_T) \approx \sum_{j=1}^{T} \log\,\{\det\,[S(\omega_j)]\}.$$

Substituting into (24), the corresponding approximate log likelihood function is

$$\mathcal{L}_T^{**} = -\tfrac{1}{2}(T + Tp)\log 2\pi - \tfrac{1}{2}\sum_{j=1}^{T} \log\,\{\det\,[S(\omega_j)]\}$$

$$-\tfrac{1}{2}\sum_{j=1}^{T} \text{tr}\,[S(\omega_j)^{-1}I(\omega_j)].$$

(34)

The computational gain in employing $\mathcal{L}_T^{**}$ instead of $\mathcal{L}_T$ is evident by the fact that evaluation of $\mathcal{L}_T$ requires inversion of the $(T + Tp) \times (T + Tp)$ matrix Γ_T whereas evaluation of $\mathcal{L}_T^{**}$ requires the inversion of the much smaller $(p + 1) \times (p + 1)$ matrices $S(\omega_j)$ for $j = 1, 2, \ldots, T$. The justification for approximating $\mathcal{L}_T$ by $\mathcal{L}_T^{**}$ relies on the sample size T being large. In contrast to $\mathcal{L}_T^{*}$ defined in expression (32), computation of $\mathcal{L}_T^{**}$ does not compel one to shift to the invertible representation for (n_t, x_t).

A note of caution about these approximate likelihood functions is pertinent. In a somewhat different context, Phadke and Kedem (1978) show that when a zero of the moving average polynomial is close to unity in modulus, maximization of approximate likelihood functions analogous to $\mathcal{L}_T^{*}$ and $\mathcal{L}_T^{**}$ can give rise to parameter estimates that are substantially inferior to the ones obtained by maximizing the actual likelihood function. They found this especially to be true for the frequency domain approximization.[22]

In situations in which the parameter vector v is specified to be zero, an alternative estimation procedure is available. The linear least-squares projection of n_t on current and past x's is not dependent on the parameters of the generating equation of the a_t process. This can be witnessed by examining equation (21). The serial correlation properties of the disturbance term of this projection can be consistently estimated by employing the residuals obtained from least-squares estimation of the projection. Using a variant of generalized least squares, the projection and the autoregression for x_t can then be estimated jointly subject to the cross-equation restrictions implied by the model, thus delivering estimates of the criterion function parameters of the firm's dynamic optimization problem.

In practice, the selected approximation to the likelihood function would

---

[22]Phadke and Kedem (1978) ran Monte Carlo simulations on estimators obtained from maximizing the approximate likelihood functions and the exact likelihood function for finite order vector moving average processes.

be maximized by using an "acceptable gradient method." Let Ψ_∞ be the free parameters of the model and let Ψ_0 be an initial estimate. (Where the model is overidentified, i.e., if p and r are large enough, there is a variety of ways to get an initial consistent estimate.) Then the approximate likelihood function is maximizing by iterating on

$$\Psi_{i+1} = \Psi_i - \Lambda_i Q_i G_i, \tag{35}$$

where Λ_i is a scalar step size, Q_i a positive definite matrix, and G_i the gradient of the approximate log likelihood function. The reader is referred to Bard (1974) for a detailed description of alternative procedures for choosing Λ_i and Q_i and for calculating the gradient G_i. For present purposes it suffices to point out that the explicit closed form solution (22) exhibiting the cross-equation restrictions makes it possible to calculate the gradient G_i analytically fairly directly. Similarly, for methods in which Q_i is set equal to H_i^{-1} where H_i is the second derivative matrix of the approximate likelihood, the formulas in (22) make analytical calculation of the Hessian feasible. The explicit formulas (22) are thus of potential advantage both in facilitating rapid and accurate computation of estimates, and in facilitating computation of the asymptotic covariance matrix of the estimates.

Next, we note that where $Q_i = H_i^{-1}$, asymptotically efficient estimates can be obtained by taking one-step with (35) starting from an initial consistent estimate Ψ_0. A variety of such two step estimators that exploit the locally quadratic character of the normal log likelihood function have been proposed in contexts somewhat similar to the present one.

Finally, hypotheses can be tested either using the estimated asymptotic covariance matrix of the coefficients or likelihood ratio tests. For example, where the model is overidentified, the model can be tested by nesting it within a more loosely specified model, say one that does not impose the cross-equation rational expectations restrictions, and then computing a likelihood ratio statistic. Examples of this specification test strategy are given by Sargent (1977, 1978b).

5. An Omitted Information Variables Model for the Error Term

In this section, we describe an alternative model of the error term which is related to a model of the error proposed by Shiller (1972) in another context. This model of the disturbance term permits estimation of the parameters of the firm's objective function under conditions which are more stringent in some respects but less stringent in other respects than are required for the model of the error term used in the preceding parts of this paper.

Let us write the demand schedule for employment as

$$n_t = \rho_1 n_{t-1} - (\rho_1/\delta) \sum_{j=0}^{\infty} \lambda^j E w_{t+j} \mid X_t + \pi(L) a_t, \qquad (36)$$

where $X_t = \{x_t, x_{t-1}, \ldots\}$. Let us partition x_t as $x_t' = (x_{1t}', x_{2t}')$. Hence x_t is a $(p \times 1)$ vector and x_{1t} a $(p_1 \times 1)$ vector. We assume that x_{1t} includes at least w_t. Let $X_{1t} = \{x_{1t}, x_{1t-1}, \ldots\}$. We make the following assumptions: (i) The firm uses the entire information set X_t to form its expectations of future w's, so that (13) or (36) is the appropriate demand schedule for employment. (ii) The econometrician has access only to a subset of the information $X_{1t} \subseteq X_t$ which private agents use. (iii) The random shock a_t obeys the extensive orthogonality conditions $E a_t x_{1t-j} = 0$ for all j. Notice that the model (36) can be rewritten as

$$n_t = \rho_1 n_{t-1} - (\rho_1/\delta) \sum_{j=0}^{\infty} \lambda^j E w_{t+j} \mid X_{1t}$$

$$+ \pi(L) a_t + (\rho_1/\delta) \sum_{j=0}^{\infty} \lambda^j (E w_{t+j} \mid X_{1t} - E w_{t+j} \mid X_t),$$

or

$$n_t = \rho_1 n_{t-1} - (\rho_1/\delta) \sum_{j=0}^{\infty} \lambda^j E w_{t+j} \mid X_{1t} + \pi(L) a_t + s_t,$$

where

$$s_t = (\rho_1/\delta) \sum_{j=0}^{\infty} \lambda^j (E w_{t+j} \mid X_{1t} - E w_{t+j} \mid X_t).$$

Let x_{1t} have the vector autoregressive representation $\zeta^1(L) x_{1t} = v_t^1$, where

$$v_t^1 = x_{1t} - E(x_{1t} \mid x_{1t-1}, x_{1t-2}, \ldots),$$

and

$$\zeta^1(L) = I - \zeta_1^1 L - \ldots \zeta_{r_1}^1 L^{r_1},$$

and assume that the roots of $\det \zeta^1(z) = 0$ are outside the unit circle. Then equation (22) can be written as

$$n_t = \rho_1 n_{t-1} + \mu^1(L) x_{1t} + \pi(L) a_t + s_t, \qquad (37)$$

where

$$\mu^1(L) = (-\rho_1/\delta) U_1 \zeta^1(\lambda)^{-1} \left[I + \sum_{j=1}^{r_1-1} \left(\sum_{k=j+1}^{r_1} \lambda^{k-j} \zeta_k^1 \right) L^j \right], \qquad (38)$$

and U_1 is the unit vector conformable to x_{1t} with 1 in the (first) place corresponding to w_t and zeroes elsewhere.

Now the random term a_t has been assumed orthogonal to x_{1t-j} for all integer j. Therefore $\pi(L)a_t$ is orthogonal to x_{1t-j} for all integer j. Further, by the law of iterated projections, we have for all $j \geq 0$,

$$E[(Ew_{t+j}|X_{1t} - Ew_{t+j}|X_t)|X_{1t}] = Ew_{t+j}|X_{1t} - Ew_{t+j}|X_{1t} = 0.$$

It follows that $Es_t | X_{1t} = 0$. Therefore, we have that $Es_t x_{1t-j} = 0$ for $j \geq 0$ so that the random variable s_t is orthogonal to x_{1t-j} for $j \geq 0$. We have therefore established that the composite error term $\pi(L)a_t + s_t$ is orthogonal to x_{1t-j} for $j \geq 0$, i.e.,

$$E\{[\pi(L)a_t + s_t]x'_{1t-j}\} = 0 \quad \text{for} \quad j \geq 0. \tag{39}$$

However, $\pi(L)a_t + s_t$ is not in general orthogonal to n_{t-1}, since lagged values of both $\pi(L)a_t$ and s_t influence n_{t-1}, and since both $\pi(L)a_t$ and s_t may be serially correlated.

Under our current model assumptions we cannot rule out the possibility that for the joint (n_t, x_{1t}) process, n_t Granger causes x_{1t}. Even though n_t fails to Granger cause the complete block x_t, relative to the information set $\{n_t, x_{1t}\}$, n_t may Granger cause x_{1t}, for "omitted variable" reasons (see Granger 1969). Thus no claim can be made that x_{1t} is exogenous in equation (27). As noted above, the composite error term in equation (37) may be serially correlated. Without specifically modeling the joint covariance properties of the variables unobservable to the econometrician, fully efficient parameter estimation procedures such as quasi-maximum likelihood are not feasible. Indeed, a more richly specified model is needed in order even to write down the joint likelihood function for (n_t, x_{1t}). One possible strategy is to trace through the restrictions that our model places on the moving average representation for the joint (n_t, x_{1t}) process. Although conceptually this is a feasible approach, the restrictions are cumbersome and estimation of the moving average representation subject to these restrictions appears to be computationally impractical. Rather than pursue this line further, we consider an alternative, computationally simpler strategy. This procedure can be viewed as a generalization of the method of moments, and it exploits the orthogonality conditions implied by our model. We now examine these orthogonality conditions in more detail.

Solving equation (37) for $\pi(L)a_t + s_t$ and writing out the orthogonality conditions (39) for $j = 0, 1, \ldots, r_1 - 1$ gives

$$E\left[n_t - \rho_1 n_{t-1} - \sum_{k=0}^{r_1-1} \mu_k^1 x_{1t-k}\right] x'_{1t-j} = 0,$$

or

$$En_t x'_{1t-j} - \rho_1 En_{t-1} x'_{1t-j} - \sum_{k=0}^{r_1-1} \mu_k^1 Ex_{1t-k} x'_{1t-j} = 0,$$

or

$$C_{nx}(j) - \rho_1 C_{nx}(j-1) - \sum_{k=0}^{r_1-1} \mu_k^1 C_{xx}(j-k) = 0, \quad j = 0, \ldots, r_1 - 1, \quad (40)$$

where[23] $C_{nx}(j) = En_t x'_{1t-j}$ and $C_{xx}(j) = Ex_{1t} x'_{1t-j}$. Each μ_k^1 is a $(1 \times p_1)$ row vector while each x_{1t-j} is a $(p_1 \times 1)$ column vector. So (39) is a system of $p_1 \cdot r_1$ equations in the $(p_1 \cdot r_1 + 1)$ parameters $(\mu_0^1, \mu_1^1, \ldots, \mu_{r_1-1}^1, \rho_1)$. Therefore, the normal equations (39) by themselves are incapable of identifying this list of parameters. But recall that not all of the parameters in this list are free. For the model imposes the extensive set of restrictions across the μ^1's and the parameters of $\zeta^1(L)$ which are summarized in formula (38). The parameters of $\zeta^1(L)$ are identified from the vector autoregression $\zeta^1(L)x_{1t} = v_t^1$ and its normal equations

$$C_{xx}(j) - \sum_{k=1}^{r_1} \zeta_k^1 C_{xx}(j-k) = 0. \quad (41)$$

Given that $\zeta^1(L)$ is sufficiently rich (i.e., p_1 and r_1 are large enough—and for the current problem each can be quite small, namely, one) the free parameters of $\mu^1(L)$ in (37) and ρ_1 are identified or overidentified by the population orthogonality conditions (40) and (41). It is clearly the presence of the cross-equation restrictions summarized in (38) that allows the orthogonality conditions (40) and (41) to identify the free structural parameters despite the fact that we are one orthogonality condition short in (40). Thus, (36) fails to be a regression equation, yet consistent estimation of the free parameters is still possible because of the presence of the cross-equation restrictions delivered by rational expectations.

A generalized method of moments estimator of the model parameters can be obtained by replacing the population moments in the orthogonality conditions (40) and (41) with the corresponding sample moments. When the model parameters are overidentified there are more orthogonality conditions than there are parameters to be estimated. Consequently, it is not in general possible to select parameter estimates that allow all of the sample orthogonality conditions to equal zero. This necessitates an alternative strategy for obtaining parameter estimates that allows linear combinations of the sample orthogonality conditions to be as close to zero as possible. The number of linear combinations is dictated by the number of underly-

---

[23]Additional orthogonality conditions can be obtained by allowing j to exceed $r_1 - 1$. In particular, it may be desirable to exploit as many orthogonality conditions as there are sample moments that can be computed. The determination of the appropriate number of these orthogonality conditions is dependent on the serial correlation properties of the composite residual. We intentionally choose not formally to specify these residual properties and instead to focus on a fixed number of orthogonality conditions, i.e., the number of orthogonality conditions we use is not dependent on sample size.

ing parameters to be estimated. Discussions of consistency for generalized method of moments estimators of this form when the underlying stochastic processes are stationary and ergodic are provided in Hansen (1979).[24]

Given that there is latitude as to the choice of which linear combinations of the sample orthogonality conditions to employ, a question remains as to what is the "best" choice. In this context we mean best in sense of delivering the smallest asymptotic covariance matrix among the class of estimators under consideration. In other words, all other estimators in this class have an asymptotic covariance matrix that exceeds the "best" estimator by a positive definite matrix. It turns out that the "best" choice is dependent upon the serial correlation properties of the composite residual term. Consistent estimators of the residual covariances can be obtained from some first step consistent parameter estimates. In Appendix B we show how to determine the optimal or best weighting scheme for the sample orthogonality conditions as well as how to compute the asymptotic covariance matrix for the parameter estimates. These results are developed in much more detail in Hansen (1979).

6. Conclusions

A hallmark of rational expectations models is that they typically impose restrictions across parameters in agents' decision rules and the parameters of equations that describe the uncontrollable random processes that agents face passively. These cross-equation restrictions are an important source of identification in rational expectations models, a source that helps to fill the vacuum created by the fact that in these models there are often too few exclusion restrictions of the classic Cowles commission variety to achieve identification.[25] The cross-equation restrictions play a critical role in the statistical models and tests proposed in this paper. For example, it is the presence of overidentifying cross-equation restrictions on the labor demand schedule that makes it feasible to test both the necessary and sufficient conditions that assure that x_t is strictly exogenous in the labor demand schedule. Again, the feasibility of consistent estimation with the "omitted information variable" model of the error term rests on the presence of cross-equation restrictions which compensate for what would be a short-fall of orthogonality conditions in their absence. Again, the presence of restrictions across the parameters of the processes generating the exogenous and endogenous variables is the reason that joint estimation of the

---

[24]Sims has illustrated that a wide class of econometric estimators is encompassed in the generalized method of moments framework. He has demonstrated this in his graduate econometrics course at the University of Minnesota.

[25]The implications of rational expectations models for achieving identification with exclusion restrictions are discussed by Sims (1980), Lucas and Sargent (1978), and Sargent and Sims (1977).

parameters of the exogenous and endogenous processes is required for statistical efficiency, in contrast to the more familiar case in which the parameters of the strictly exogenous processes can be efficiently estimated by themselves.

The methods that we have described in this paper are fairly directly applicable to a host of problems that can be reduced to that of an agent choosing a linear dynamic contingency plan for a single variable.[26] It is desirable and nontrivial to extend our methods to the case where the agent is choosing linear contingency plans for a vector of interrelated variables. An interrelated dynamic factor demand model would be a good example. This generalization will be described in a sequel to this paper (see Hansen and Sargent 1981).

Appendix A

This appendix contains a derivation of formulas (5) and (6) of the text obtained by using some analytic function theory. We use results from elementary complex analysis that can be found in many good books on the subject, e.g., Churchill (1960) and Saks and Zygmund (1971). The technique delivers a fast way of evaluating the annihilation operator $[\Psi(z)]_+$ by employing a partial-fractions-like decomposition of $\Psi(z)$. This method turns out to be useful in solving a variety of classical signal extraction problems in addition to our present application.

Let us begin with a two-sided lag operator $\Psi(L)$ where

$$\Psi(L) = \sum_{j=-\infty}^{+\infty} \Psi_j L^j \quad \text{and} \quad \sum_{j=-\infty}^{+\infty} \Psi_j^2 < +\infty.$$

The "z transform" of this operator is given by

$$\Psi(z) = \sum_{j=-\infty}^{+\infty} \Psi_j z^j = \Psi^+(z) + \Psi^-(z),$$

where

$$\Psi^+(z) = \sum_{j=0}^{+\infty} \Psi_j z^j \quad \text{and} \quad \Psi^-(z) = \sum_{j=1}^{+\infty} \Psi_{-j} z^{-j}.$$

$\Psi^+(z)$ defines an analytic function for $|z| < 1$ and $\Psi^-(z)$ defines an analytic function for $|z| > 1$. Furthermore

$$\lim_{z \to \infty} \Psi^-(z) = 0.$$

Using a result from Zygmund (1959), it follows that

$$\lim_{R \uparrow 1} \Psi^+(Re^{i\omega}) = \Psi^+(e^{i\omega}), \qquad \lim_{R \downarrow 1} \Psi^-(Re^{i\omega}) = \Psi^-(e^{i\omega})$$

exist for almost all $\omega \in [0, 2\pi]$.[27] Thus $\Psi(z)$ is at least well defined almost everywhere for $|z| = 1$, and in particular

$$h(\omega) = \Psi(e^{i\omega}) = \Psi^+(e^{i\omega}) + \Psi^-(e^{i\omega})$$

---

[26] A linear version of the Lucas–Prescott (1971) model of investment under uncertainty fits in since their fictitious "planner" faces a problem of this form.

[27] See Zygmund 1959, p. 276.

is the transfer function for the linear filter $\Psi(L)$. The annihilation operator $[\ \ ]_+$ applied to z transforms is defined by $[\Psi(z)]_+ = \Psi^+(z)$. In other words the annihilation operator instructs us to ignore negative powers of z. We now restrict ourselves to cases in which $\Psi^-(z)$ defines an analytic function for $|z| > R$ for some $R < 1$. By this we simply mean that the power series

$$\sum_{j=1}^{\infty} \Psi_{-j} z^{-j}$$

is convergent for $|z| > R$. Under this additional assumption, $\Psi(z)$ defines an analytic function in the annular region $R < |z| < 1$. This prepares us for consideration of the following lemma:

LEMMA. Suppose $A(z)$ is a regular function in $|z| < 1$ such that (i) $A(z) = \Psi(z)$ for $R < |z| < 1$, (ii) $A(z)$ has at most a finite number of singularities $z_1, z_2, \ldots, z_k$ in $|z| < 1$, with $P_1(z), P_2(z), \ldots, P_k(z)$ denoting the corresponding principal parts of the Laurent series expansion of $A(z)$ at these points.[28] Then

$$[\Psi(z)]_+ = A(z) - \sum_{j=1}^{k} P_j(z).$$

PROOF. Let $B(z) \equiv A(z) - \sum_{j=1}^{k} P_j(z)$. A standard result from analytic function theory assures us that $B(z)$ is analytic in $|z| < 1$.[29] Since (i) is true, $R > \max\{|z_1|, |z_2|, \ldots, |z_k|\}$. $P_j(z)$ is analytic for $|z| \neq z_j$ and

$$\lim_{z \to \infty} P_j(z) = 0.$$

Hence $D(z) \equiv \sum_{j=1}^{k} P_j(z)$ is analytic for $|z| > R$ and

$$\lim_{z \to \infty} D(z) = 0.$$

Using these results we have that

$$B(z) = \sum_{j=0}^{\infty} B_j z^j \quad \text{for} \quad |z| < 1,$$

and

$$D(z) = \sum_{j=1}^{\infty} D_j z^{-j} \quad \text{for} \quad |z| > R.$$

Since $A(z) = B(z) + D(z)$, it follows that

$$\sum_{j=0}^{\infty} B_j z^j + \sum_{j=1}^{\infty} D_j z^{-j}$$

[28]Let the Laurent series expansion of $A(z)$ about z_j be given by

$$A(z) = \sum_{m=-\infty}^{\infty} A_m (z - z_j)^m.$$

The principal part is given by $\sum_{m=-\infty}^{-1} A_m (z - z_j)^m$. The function $A(z)$ is said to be regular in the region $|z| < 1$ if it is analytic in that region except at isolated singularities.

[29]See Saks and Zygmund 1971, p. 146.

is the Laurent series expansion for $A(z) = \Psi(z)$ in the region $R < |z| < 1$. Since this expansion is unique,

$$\Psi^+(z) = \sum_{j=0}^{\infty} B_j z^j = B(z).$$

This lemma provides a simple and computationally convenient formula for computing $[\Psi(z)]_+$. In order to see the value of this computational technique, let us reconsider the prediction problem examined in the text. We are interested in determining the linear least-squares predictor of

$$y_t = \sum_{k=0}^{\infty} \lambda^k x_{t+k}, \tag{A1}$$

given information available up until time t. We assume that the only information useful for predicting y_t is current and past observations of x_t. We also assume that x_t is a linearly indeterministic, covariance stationary process. Wold's theorem

$$x_t = \sum_{j=0}^{\infty} \xi_j v_{t-j}^x, \tag{A2}$$

where v_t^x is the linear least-squares one-step-ahead prediction error and $E v_t^x v_{t-j}^{x'} = 0$ for $j \neq 0$. Current and past v^x's encompass the same information set as current and past x's. Wold's theorem also assures us that the elements of $\{\xi_j\}$ are square summable. The z transform of $\sum_{k=0}^{+\infty} \lambda^k L^{-k}$ is

$$\sum_{k=0}^{+\infty} \lambda^k z^{-k} = 1/(1 - \lambda z^{-1}) = z/(z - \lambda) \quad \text{for} \quad |z| > \lambda.$$

The z transform corresponding to the Wold representation is

$$\xi(z) = \sum_{j=0}^{+\infty} \xi_j z^j \quad \text{for} \quad |z| < 1.$$

Combining (A1) and (A2) we can represent

$$y_t = \sum_{j=-\infty}^{+\infty} \Psi_j v_{t-j}^x,$$

where

$$\Psi(z) = \sum_{j=-\infty}^{+\infty} \Psi_j z^j = z\xi(z)/(z - \lambda) \quad \text{for} \quad \lambda < |z| < 1.$$

The linear least-squares predictor of y_t is $E_t y_t = [\Psi(L)]_+ v_t^x$. Thus we need to compute $[\Psi(z)]_+$.

Now $A(z) \equiv z\xi(z)/(z - \lambda)$ is regular in $|z| < 1$ and has a simple pole at λ $A(z) = \Psi(z)$ for $\lambda < |z| < 1$. In the Laurent series expansion of $A(z)$ around λ, the residue of $A(z)$ is given by

$$\lim_{z \to \lambda} (z - \lambda)A(z) = \lambda\xi(\lambda).$$

This informs us that the principal part of the expansion of $A(z)$ at λ is $\lambda\xi(\lambda)/(z - \lambda)$. Using the lemma we have that

$$[\Psi(z)]_+ = z\xi(z)/(z - \lambda) - \lambda\xi(\lambda)/(z - \lambda)$$
$$= [\xi(z) - \lambda z^{-1}\xi(\lambda)]/(1 - \lambda z^{-1}).$$

This agrees with equation (5) in the text.

In the text it is claimed that the covariance stationarity assumption for a_t and x_t can be relaxed. We shall examine this claim for x_t and assert that the logic for a_t is completely analogous. We make an rth order vector Markov specification $\zeta(L)x_t = v_t^x$ for $t \geqq 0$, where $\zeta(L) = I - \zeta_1 L - \ldots - \zeta_r L^r$, where $x_{-1}, \ldots, x_{-r}$ are given initial values, and where v_t^x is a contemporaneously uncorrelated vector white noise. We assume that the roots of $\det \zeta(z) = 0$ lie outside the region $|z| < \sqrt{\beta}$.

Define $x_t = 0$ for $t < -r$, and let $v_t^x = \zeta(L)x_t$ for $t < 0$.

Using the assumption on the roots of $\det \zeta(z)$, we know that $\zeta(z)$ has an inverse with elements analytic for $|z| < \sqrt{\beta}$. Taking the Taylor series expansion about zero we have

$$\zeta(z)^{-1} = \xi(z) = \sum_{j=0}^{\infty} \xi_j z^j.$$

Since $v_t^x = 0$ for $t < -r$, $\zeta(L)v_t^x$ is a well-defined stochastic process and

$$x_t = \xi(L)v_t^x. \qquad (A3)$$

Even though the coefficients ξ_j may not be bounded, equation (A3) provides a valid representation of the x_t process to which the Wiener-Kolmogorov prediction formulas can be applied.

As was argued in the text $\lambda < \sqrt{\beta}$. Therefore $\Psi(z) = z\xi(z)/(z - \lambda)$ is analytic for $\lambda < |z| < \sqrt{\beta}$. Its Laurent series expansion, given by

$$\Psi(z) = \sum_{j=-\infty}^{+\infty} \Psi_j z^j,$$

provides a representation for y_t of the form

$$y_t = \sum_{j=-\infty}^{+\infty} \Psi_j v_{t-j}^x.$$

Using the Wiener-Kolmogorov solution to the prediction problem we know that

$$E[y_t \mid x_t, x_{t-1}, \ldots, x_{-r}] = [\Psi(L)]_+ v_{t-j}^x.$$

If we modify the domain specified in the lemma to be $|z| < \sqrt{\beta}$, we conclude that

$$[\Psi(z)]_+ = [z\xi(z) - \lambda\xi(\lambda)]/(z - \lambda).$$

This extends our prediction formula to nonstationary finite order Markov processes.

The lemma turns out to be handy in solving classical signal extraction problems of the kind discussed by Whittle (1963, p. 66). For example, let a signal y_t be governed by an rth order Markov process

$$(1 - \rho_1 L)(1 - \rho_2 L) \ldots (1 - \rho_r L)y_t = e_t, \qquad |\rho_j| < 1,$$

while $x_t = y_t + u_t$. Here $Eu_t e_{t-j} = 0 = Eu_t = Ee_t$ for all t and j, where u_t and e_t are serially uncorrelated white noises. The problem is to form the linear least-squares projection $[y_t \,|\, x_t, x_{t-1}, \ldots]$. This can be solved using formula (3) of Whittle (1963, p. 66). The lemma is useful in solving this problem since it makes application of the annihilation operator $[\quad]_+$ fairly routine.

Appendix B

In this appendix we discuss the asymptotic distribution of the family of generalized method of moments estimators proposed in Section 5. We abstain from a detailed presentation and refer the interested reader to Hansen (1979). Both Hansen's discussion and the present discussion exploit a framework developed by Sims in lectures to his graduate econometrics class at the University of Minnesota.

In this appendix we adopt different notation than is used in the text. We do this in order to facilitate the presentation. We let x_t denote the underlying observable vector process including both endogenous and exogenous variables and all relevant lags of these variables. We assume that this process is stationary and ergodic. β_∞ denotes the vector of parameters to be estimated and is of dimension k. The sample orthogonality conditions discussed in Section 5 are compactly written

$$O_T(\beta) = (1/T) \sum_{t=1}^{T} f(x_t, \beta).$$

The dimensionality of O_T is assumed to be $p \geq k$. Our model assumptions imply that $Ef(x_t, \beta_\infty) = 0$ for all t, and therefore $EO_T(\beta_\infty) = 0$.

Let us introduce a matrix A that is $q \times p$, where $k \leq q \leq p$ and define β_T to be that value of β such that $|AO_T(\beta_T)|$ is as small as possible. We assume that β_T converges in probability to β_∞. Let

$$B = E[\partial f(x_t, \beta_\infty)/\partial \beta],$$

and let

$$R_j = E[f(x_t, \beta_\infty) f(x_{t-j}, \beta_\infty)'].$$

The infinite sum

$$S = \sum_{j=-\infty}^{+\infty} R_j$$

is assumed to converge absolutely. Employing some mild side conditions Hansen obtains the result that $\sqrt{T}(\beta_T - \beta_\infty)$ converges in distribution to a normally distributed random variable with zero mean and covariance matrix

$$(B'A'AB)^{-1}B'A'ASA'AB(B'A'AB)^{-1}.$$

In order for this covariance matrix to be as small as possible, it is desirable to select A so that $A'A = S^{-1}$, and the resulting covariance matrix is $(B'S^{-1}B)^{-1}$. The "best" choice of A is dependent on S, which is not known a priori and must therefore be estimated. Consistent estimators of S can be obtained from a first step estimator of β_∞ employing a not necessarily "optimal" choice of A. This allows us to obtain a sequence $A_T'A_T = S_T^{-1}$, that converges in probability to S^{-1}. If we substitute A_T for A in our definition of β_T we still obtain the same asymptotic distribution for $\sqrt{T}(\beta_T - \beta_\infty)$. This provides the "optimal" estimator alluded to in Section 5.

References

Anderson, T. W. *The Statistical Analysis of Time Series*. New York: Wiley, 1975.

Bard, Yonathan. *Nonlinear Parameter Estimation*. New York: Academic Press, 1974.

Barro, Robert J. "Unanticipated Money Growth and Unemployment in the United States." *A.E.R.* 67 (1977): 101–15.

———. "Unanticipated Money, Output, and the Price Level in the United States." *J.P.E.* 86 (1978): 549–80.

Bertsekas, Dimitri P. *Dynamic Programming and Stochastic Control.* New York: Academic Press, 1976.

Blanco, Herminio. "Investment under Uncertainty: An Empirical Analysis." Ph.D. dissertation, Univ. Chicago, 1978.

Box, C. E. P., and Jenkins, G. M. *Time Series Analysis, Forecasting and Control.* San Francisco: Holden-Day, 1970.

Churchill, R. V. *Complex Variables and Applications.* New York: McGraw-Hill, 1960.

Granger, C. W. J. "Investigating Causal Relations by Econometric Models and Cross-Spectral Methods." *Econometrica* 37 (1969): 424–38.

Graves, R., and Telser, L. *Functional Analysis in Mathematical Economics.* Chicago: Univ. Chicago Press, 1971.

Hall, Robert E. "Stochastic Implications of the Life Cycle–Permanent Income Hypothesis: Theory and Evidence." *J.P.E.* 86 (1978): 971–87.

Hannan, E. J. *Multiple Time Series.* New York: Wiley, 1970.

Hansen, L. P. "Large Sample Properties of Generalized Method of Moments Estimators." Manuscript, 1979.

Hansen, L. P., and Sargent, T. J. "A Note on Wiener-Kolmogorov Prediction Formulas for Rational Expectations Models." Manuscript, 1979.

———. "Linear Rational Expectations Models for Dynamically Interrelated Variables." In *Rational Expectations and Econometric Practice,* ed. by R. E. Lucas, Jr., and T. J. Sargent. Minneapolis: Univ. Minnesota Press, 1981.

Holt, C.; Modigliani, F.; Muth, J. F.; and Simon, H. A. *Planning Production, Inventories, and Work Force.* Englewood Cliffs, N.J.: Prentice-Hall, 1960.

Kennan, John. "The Estimation of Partial Adjustment Models with Rational Expectations." *Econometrica* 47 (1979): 1441–56.

Kushner, Harold. *Introduction to Stochastic Control.* New York: Holt, Rinehart, and Winston, 1971.

Kwakernaak, H., and Sivan, R. *Linear Optimal Control Systems.* New York: Wiley, 1972.

Lucas, R. E., Jr. "Econometric Testing of the Natural Rate Hypothesis." In *The Econometrics of Price Determination Conference,* ed. by Otto Eckstein. Washington: Board of Governors of the Federal Reserve System, 1972.

———. "Econometric Policy Evaluation: A Critique." In *The Phillips Curve and Labor Markets,* ed. by K. Brunner and A. H. Meltzer. Carnegie-Rochester Conferences on Public Policy 1. Amsterdam: North-Holland, 1976.

Lucas, R. E., Jr., and Prescott, E. "Investment under Uncertainty." *Econometrica* 39 (1971): 659–81.

Lucas, R. E., Jr., and Sargent, T. J. "After Keynesian Macroeconomics." In *After the Phillips Curve: Persistence of High Inflation and High Unemployment.* Boston: Federal Reserve Bank of Boston, 1978.

McCallum, B. T. "Rational Expectations and the Natural Rate Hypothesis: Some Consistent Estimates." *Econometrica* 44 (1976): 43–52.

Phadke, M. S., and Kedem, G. "Computation of the Exact Likelihood Function of Multivariate Moving Average Models." *Biometrika* 65 (1978): 511–19.

Revankar, N. S. "Asymptotic Relative Efficiency Analysis of Certain Tests of Independence in Structural Systems." *Internat. Econ. Rev.* 19 (1978): 165–80.

———. "Testing of the Rational Expectations Hypothesis." *Econometrica* (1980), in press.

Rissanen, J., and Caines, P. E. "The Strong Consistency of Maximum Likelihood Estimators for ARMA Processes." *Ann. Statis.* 7 (1979): 297–315.

Saks, S., and Zygmund, A. *Analytic Functions.* New York: Elsevier, 1971.

Salemi, M., and Sargent, T. J. "The Demand for Money during Hyperinflations under Rational Expectations, II." *Internat. Econ. Rev.* 1980, in press.

Sargent, T. J. "The Demand for Money during Hyperinflations under Rational Expectations, I." *Internat. Econ. Rev.* 18 (1977): 59–82.

———. "Rational Expectations, Econometric Exogeneity, and Consumption." *J.P.E.* 86 (1978): 673–700.

———. "Estimation of Dynamic Labor Demand Schedules under Rational Expectations." *J.P.E.* 86 (1978): 1009–1044.

———. *Macroeconomic Theory.* New York: Academic Press, 1979.

Sargent, T. J., and Sims, C. A. "Business Cycle Modeling without Pretending to Have Too Much a Priori Economic Theory." In *New Methods in Business Cycle Research,* ed. by C. A. Sims. Minneapolis: Federal Reserve Bank of Minneapolis, 1977.

Shiller, R. "Rational Expectations and the Structure of Interest Rates." Ph.D. dissertation, Massachusetts Inst. Tech., 1972.

Sims, C. A. "Money, Income, and Causality." *A.E.R.* 62 (1972): 540–52.

———. "Macroeconomics and Reality." *Econometrica* (1980), in press.

Taylor, John B. "Output and Price Stability: An International Comparison." Manuscript, 1978.

———. "Estimation and Control of a Macroeconomic Model with Rational Expectations." *Econometrica* (1980), in press.

Tunnicliffe Wilson, G. "The Estimation of Parameters in Multivariate Time Series Models. *J. Royal Statis. Soc.* Series B 35 (1973): 76–85.

Vaughan, D. R. "A Nonrecursive Algebraic Solution for the Discrete Riccati Equation. *IEEE Transactions on Automatic Control* 15 (1970): 597–99.

Wallis, Kenneth F. "Econometric Implications of the Rational Expectations Hypothesis." *Econometrica* 48, no. 1 (1980): 49–72.

Whittle, P. *Regulation and Prediction by Linear Least-Square Methods.* Princeton: Van Nostrand, 1963.

Wu, De-Min. "Alternative Tests of Independence between Stochastic Regressors and Disturbances." *Econometrica* 41 (1973): 733–50.

Zygmund, A. *Trigonometric Series.* Vol. I. Cambridge: University Press, 1959.

8

Linear Rational Expectations Models for Dynamically Interrelated Variables

Lars Peter Hansen
Thomas J. Sargent

This paper aims to develop procedures for the rapid numerical computation and convenient mathematical representation of a class of multiple variable, linear stochastic rational expectations models. A variety of examples from this class of models can be imagined. These include versions of interrelated factor demand models like Mortensen's (1973) formed by blending the model of Nadiri and Rosen (1973) with the adjustment cost models of Lucas (1967a, b), Gould (1968), and Treadway (1969, 1971); models of exhaustible resource extraction along the lines of Epple and Hansen (1979); and dynamic linear models of interrelated industries, such as the corn and hog industries. Our desires for rapid computation and convenient representation are motivated by practical considerations, since our ultimate goal is to devise methods for estimating multiple variable, rational expectations models of time series by versions of the method of maximum likelihood. Rapid computation of equilibria for different points in the parameter space is required for inexpensive maximization of the likelihood function. Convenient mathematical representation is valuable for a closely related reason, since it is desirable to be able to differentiate the likelihood function analytically in as many directions as possible. For this reason, a goal of the paper is to get "as close as possible" to a closed form summarizing the (highly nonlinear) cross-equation restrictions that are the hallmark of rational expectations models. It will become clear later what we mean by the phrase "as close as possible," since we shall indicate why a closed form analytic expression for the equilibrium cannot, in general, be calculated for the multiple endogenous variable models of the class that we consider.

The views expressed herein are solely those of the authors and do not necessarily represent the views of the Federal Reserve Bank of Minneapolis or the Federal Reserve System. The research described in this paper was supported by the Federal Reserve Bank of Minneapolis. The computer programming was performed by Ian Bain, Thomas Doan, and Paul O'Brien. Ian Bain made extensive and very helpful comments on an earlier draft.

This paper is a sequel to our earlier paper, Hansen and Sargent (1980). We extend the methods of estimating and formulating models that we have described in the single endogenous variable case to the case of several interrelated endogenous variables. We exploit several results obtained in the previous paper. Other important precursors to the work we do here include the work of Nadiri and Rosen (1973), the paper by Lucas and Prescott (1971) on investment, and the books of Holt et al. (1960) and Graves and Telser (1971). Graves and Telser consider a certainty version of a problem close to our "standard problem." Our paper proposes a simple method for factoring the spectral-density-like matrix encountered in Graves and Telser's problem, and extends the computation of equilibria to the stochastic case by using a formula developed by Hansen and Sargent (1980).

This paper is devoted solely to issues of model formulation. We have avoided issues of econometric estimation, including models or interpretations of "error terms," since these issues are extensively discussed in our earlier paper (1980). The estimation procedures and models of error terms described in that paper extend rather directly to the present class of setups. On the other hand, moving from a single endogenous variable to multiple variables does involve some nontrivial technical complications. It is these that we concentrate on in this paper.

The paper is organized as follows. Section I gives three examples of models that fall within the general class of models we study. The distinguishing characteristic of these models is that all are the solutions of quadratic dynamic optimum problems subject to linear constraints, and that to solve each one a spectral-density-like matrix must be factored. Section II describes the standard dynamic programming algorithm for solving our general problem, while sections III and IV describe algorithms that are "faster" and "more revealing." Section V gives an example designed to illustrate the relative computation costs associated with the different algorithms. Section VI then mentions a certain kind of "identification" or interpretation problem that can characterize some models of this class.

I. Three Examples

This section contains three examples of models that are included in the class of models analyzed in subsequent sections. The first two examples are related and are versions of interrelated factor demand models. We begin with the simpler of these models first; which is a model at the firm level and takes as given the factor price random processes and the output price random process. The second model then takes into account that, in the aggregate, firms' decisions influence output price. A third example indicates how the state and decision variables can be defined to model decisions about depletion of exhaustible resources.

Example (i): A Firm's Interrelated Demand for Factors

Letting E_0 be the mathematical expectation operator conditioned on information known at time 0, a firm is supposed to maximize

$$E_0 \sum_{t=0}^{\infty} \beta^t \left\{ P_t y_t - W_t n_t - J_t(k_t - k_{t-1}) - \begin{bmatrix} \Delta k_t \\ \Delta n_t \end{bmatrix}' D \begin{bmatrix} \Delta k_t \\ \Delta n_t \end{bmatrix} \right\} \qquad (1)$$

subject to (k_{-1}, n_{-1}) given, and the linear production function

$$y_t = d' \begin{bmatrix} k_t \\ n_t \end{bmatrix} \qquad (2)$$

where d is a 2 $\times$ 1 vector of positive constants. Here β is a discount factor with $0 < \beta < 1$, P_t is product price, k_t is the stock of capital, n_t the stock of employment of labor, W_t the wage rate of labor, J_t the price of capital goods, and D a positive definite matrix reflecting costs of adjusting factors of production. The model is a linear decision rule, quadratic objective function, multiple factor version of the costly adjustment models of Lucas (1967a, b), Treadway (1969, 1971), Gould (1968), and Mortensen (1973). The positive definite quadratic form in D represents interrelated costs of adjustment.

The firm maximizes (1) by choosing a contingency plan for setting

$$\begin{bmatrix} k_t \\ n_t \end{bmatrix}, \ t \geq 0,$$

as a function of information known to become available when period t rolls around. At time t, the firm is supposed to have an information set $\Omega_t = \{X_t, X_{t-1}, \ldots\}$, where X_t is a $p \times 1$ vector ($p \geq 3$), whose first three elements are P_t, J_t, and W_t. The vector X_t also contains any other variables that the firm finds useful to forecast the process (P, J, W). Of course, at time t, the firm also knows the lagged values k_{t-1} and n_{t-1}. We assume that the vector process X follows the rth-order vector autoregressive scheme

$$\delta(L)X_t = V_t^x \qquad (3)$$

where $\delta(L) = I - \delta_1 L - \ldots - \delta_r L^r$, where $EV_t^x | \Omega_{t-1} = 0$, and where the roots of det $\delta(z) = 0$ are in modulus all greater than $\sqrt{\beta}$. The process for X is assumed to be taken as given by the firm and to be uninfluenced by the firm's decision process.

Substituting the production function (2) into the objective (1), and using summation by parts and the law of iterated projections to rearrange the expressions in $J_t(k_t - k_{t-1})$ in terms of $(J_t - \beta E_t J_{t+1})k_t$, the objective function can be rewritten

$$E_0 \sum_{t=0}^{\infty} \beta^t \left\{ P_t d' \begin{bmatrix} k_t \\ n_t \end{bmatrix} - W_t n_t - R_t k_t - \begin{bmatrix} \Delta k_t \\ \Delta n_t \end{bmatrix}' D \begin{bmatrix} \Delta k_t \\ \Delta n_t \end{bmatrix} \right\} + J_{-1} k_{-1}$$

where $R_t = J_t - \beta E_t J_{t+1}$. The variable R_t has an interpretation as the rental rate on capital at time t.

The solution of this problem is a linear decision rule of the form

$$\begin{bmatrix} k_t \\ n_t \end{bmatrix} = g_0 + g_1 \begin{bmatrix} k_{t-1} \\ n_{t-1} \end{bmatrix} + h_0 X_t + h_1 X_{t-1} + \cdots h_{r-1} X_{t-r+1}$$

where the g_j's and h_j's are matrices of constants which are complicated functions of the parameters of d, D, and $\delta(L)$. In subsequent sections, we describe quick ways of computing the g_j's and h_j's, and of characterizing their properties.

Example (ii): Market Equilibrium with
Interrelated Demand for Factors

This is a linear, multiple factor version of the model proposed by Lucas and Prescott (1971). We retain the objective function (1), but change the assumption about how the firm forms expectations about the product market price P. In particular, we now take account of the fact that the product price P follows a law of motion that is influenced by the capital accumulation decisions of the aggregate of firms in the industry. First, we assume that R_t and W_t are the first two elements of a $(p \times 1)$ vector Z_t $(p \geq 2)$ which is governed by the rth-order autoregressive process

$$\theta(L)Z_t = V_t^z \tag{4}$$

where $\theta(L) = I - \theta_1 L - \cdots - \theta_r L^r$, where $EV_t^z = E[V_t^z \mid Z_{t-1}, Z_{t-2}, \ldots, U_{t-1}, U_{t-2}, \ldots] = 0$, where U is a demand shock to be described below, and where the roots of det $\theta(z) = 0$ are all greater than $\sqrt{\beta}$ in modulus. Note that P_t is excluded from Z_t. The firm, which is now one of m identical firms, takes the process (4) governing Z as given.

The industry demand curve is

$$P_t = A_0 - A_1 Y_t + U_t; \; A_0, A_1 > 0 \tag{5}$$

where U_t is a random process with mean zero and Y_t is market output. There are m identical firms, so we have

$$Y_t = m y_t = m d' \begin{bmatrix} k_t \\ n_t \end{bmatrix} = d' \begin{bmatrix} K_t \\ N_t \end{bmatrix} \tag{6}$$

where $K_t = m k_t$ and $N_t = m n_t$. Here K_t and N_t are marketwide stocks of capital and employment, respectively.

We assume that the demand shock U follows the qth-order autoregressive specification

$$\xi(L)U_t = V_t^u \tag{7}$$

where $\xi(L) = 1 - \xi_1 L - \cdots - \xi_q L^q$, and where $EV_t^u = E[V_t^u | Z_{t-1}, Z_{t-2}, \ldots, U_{t-1}, U_{t-2}, \ldots] = 0$. We also assume that the zeroes of det $\xi(z)$ exceed $\sqrt{\beta}$ in modulus. To complete the model we must specify the firm's beliefs about the motion of K and N, which influence the evolution of the market price P and which the firm has an incentive to forecast. We assume that the representative firm believes that marketwide capital and labor obey the law of motion.

$$
\begin{bmatrix} K_t \\ N_t \end{bmatrix} = B_0 + B_1 \begin{bmatrix} K_{t-1} \\ N_{t-1} \end{bmatrix} + G_0 Z_t + \cdots + G_{r-1} Z_{t-r+1} \\
+ F_0 U_t + \cdots + F_{q-1} U_{t-q+1}. \tag{8}
$$

Further, the representative firm is assumed to know K_{t-1} and N_{t-1} at t.

Now substituting the demand schedule (5) and production function (6) into the objective function, the individual firm's problem is to maximize

$$
E_0 \sum_{t=0}^{\infty} \beta^t \left\{ \left(A_0 - A_1 d' \begin{bmatrix} K_t \\ N_t \end{bmatrix} + U_t \right) d' \begin{bmatrix} k_t \\ n_t \end{bmatrix} - W_t n_t \right.
$$
$$
\left. - R_t k_t - \begin{bmatrix} \Delta k_t \\ \Delta n_t \end{bmatrix}' D \begin{bmatrix} \Delta k_t \\ \Delta n_t \end{bmatrix} \right\} + J_{-1} k_{-1} \tag{9}
$$

subject to k_{-1}, n_{-1}, K_{-1}, N_{-1} given and known, and the given laws of motion as in (8), (4), and (7). At time t, the firm's known state variables consist of k_{t-1}, n_{t-1}, K_{t-1}, N_{t-1}, and the information variables $\{Z_t, Z_{t-1}, \ldots, U_t, U_{t-1}, \ldots\}$. A solution to this problem is a contingency plan for setting $[k_t, n_t]$ of the linear form

$$
\begin{bmatrix} k_t \\ n_t \end{bmatrix} = b_0 + b_1 \begin{bmatrix} k_{t-1} \\ n_{t-1} \end{bmatrix} + b_2 \begin{bmatrix} K_{t-1} \\ N_{t-1} \end{bmatrix} + g_0 Z_t + \cdots + g_{r-1} Z_{t-r+1} \\
+ f_0 U_t + \cdots + f_{q-1} U_{t-q+1}. \tag{10}
$$

A rational expectations equilibrium is a pair of functions (8) and (10) such that

$$
\begin{bmatrix} K_t \\ N_t \end{bmatrix} = m \begin{bmatrix} k_t \\ n_t \end{bmatrix}
$$

identically. This equality between the perceived law of motion for (K, N) and the actual law is readily shown to hold if

$$
B_0 = m b_0, \; B_1 = (b_1 + m b_2), \; G_j = m g_j, \; F_j = m f_j. \tag{11}
$$

The restrictions (11) guarantee that the individual firm's perception of the law of motion of (K, N) turns out to be accurate, that is, is implied by optimizing behavior of the individual firms composing the industry. It is to be emphasized that the individual firms are assumed to behave competitively with respect to the market price, and to take as given the process governing the evolution of the marketwide stocks of factors, which influence the evolution of the market price.

Notice how the definition of the rational expectations equilibrium builds in: (*a*) accurate perceptions on the part of firms of the laws of motion for the state processes (K, N, Z, and U) that are beyond their control, (*b*) optimizing behavior of firms, and (*c*) market clearing in the output market. However, notice that the model does not analyze "the other side" of the market for inputs, but simply takes the stochastic process Z as given.[1]

The methods that we describe can readily be used to compute the equilibrium of the model, that is, the parameters $\{B_0, B_1, G_0, \ldots, G_{r-1}, F_0, \ldots, F_{q-1}\}$ as functions of the underlying parameters d, D, A_0, A_1, $\theta(L)$, and $\delta(L)$. We give an example of such calculations in Section *V*.

Example (*iii*): *Exhaustible Resource Depletion*

Epple and Hansen (1979) have formulated a model for the purpose of studying the extraction of exhaustible resources. Their model fits a slightly modified version of the "general problem" that we analyze in Sections II and III.

Epple and Hansen study a situation in which a vector of resources is being extracted from a single reservoir or mine. They model the exhaustible nature of these resources by positing that marginal exploitation costs increase as a function of the cumulated amount of the resource vector that has been extracted. Resource extraction cost at time t is assumed to be given by $\Delta y_t' d + \Delta y_t' S_t + \Delta y_t' D_1 \Delta y_t + \Delta y_t' D_2(1/2\,\Delta y_t + y_{t-1})$ where y_t denotes the cumulated amount of the resource extracted as of time t, D_1 and D_2 are positive definite symmetric matrices, d is a column vector, and S is a vector random process representing shocks to the extraction process. The exhaustible nature of the resource is represented by the presence of the quadratic term $\Delta y_t' D_2(1/2\,\Delta y_t + y_{t-1})$.

Let P_t be the price vector at time t for the resources. The owner of the resource is assumed to maximize

$$E_0 \sum_{t=0}^{\infty} \beta^t \{ P_t' \Delta y_t - \Delta y_t' d - \Delta y_t' S_t$$

$$- \Delta y_t D_1 \Delta y_t - \Delta y_t' D_2 \left(\frac{1}{2} \Delta y_t + y_{t-1} \right) \} \tag{12}$$

---

[1] The model could be extended in various ways to model the determination of J_t and W_t in terms of the demands for factors generated here interacting with supply curves for these factors.

subject to y_{-1} given and subject to the random processes $\delta(L)X_t = V_t^x$ and $\alpha(L)S_t = V_t^s$ where P_t is the first component of the $(p \times 1)$ vector X_t, $EV_t^x | \Omega_{t-1} = 0$, $EV_t^s | \Omega_{t-1} = 0$, and $\Omega_{t-1} = \{X_{t-1}, X_{t-2}, \ldots, S_{t-1}, S_{t-2}, \ldots\}$. The polynomials in the lag operator $\delta(L)$ and $\alpha(L)$ satisfy properties analogous to those specified in example (i). The solution of the owner's maximum problem is a linear contingency plan for setting y_t as a function of $\{y_{t-1}, X_t, X_{t-1}, \ldots, S_t, S_{t-1}, \ldots\}$. In this example, the supplier faces the random process X as a price taker.

The example could be altered to handle the case where the supplier is a monopolist facing a flow demand curve of the linear form

$$P_t = A_0 - A_1 \Delta y_t + U_t, \quad A_0, A_1 > 0 \tag{13}$$

where U_t is a random shock to demand. Alternatively, the example could be modified along the lines of example (ii) to be a model of a competitive industry with a large number of price taking firms with a market flow demand curve such as (13).

II. The General Problem

We consider the following setup. Let

y_t be an $n \times 1$ vector of variables, typically stocks of things that enter an agent's objective function

h be an $n \times 1$ vector of constants

β be a discount factor, with $0 < \beta < 1$

S_{1t} be an $n \times 1$ vector of stochastic processes of mean exponential order less than $1/\sqrt{\beta}$.

$S_t = \begin{bmatrix} S_{1t} \\ S_{2t} \end{bmatrix}$ be a $(p \times 1)$ vector of stochastic processes of mean exponential order less than $1/\sqrt{\beta}$. Here $p \geq n$, and S_{1t} is the first n rows of S_t.

H be an $n \times n$ positive definite symmetric matrix

$D(L) = D_0 + D_1 L + \cdots + D_m L^m$, D_j an $n \times n$ matrix, where D_0 is of full rank, $j = 0, \ldots, m$.

We assume that the $p \times 1$ vector stochastic process S obeys the rth-order autoregression $S_t = \delta_1 S_{t-1} + \cdots + \delta_r S_{t-r} + V_t^s$ or $\delta(L)S_t = V_t^s$ where $\delta(L) = I - \delta_1 L - \cdots - \delta_r L^r$, where δ_j is $p \times p$, and where the zeroes of $det\ \delta(z)$ are assumed to be greater than $\sqrt{\beta}$ in modulus. This condition on the zeroes of $det\ \delta(z)$ is equivalent with the condition that S be of mean expotential order less than $(\sqrt{\beta})^{-1}$.

Let E be the mathematical expectations operator. We assume that $E[V_t^s | S_{t-1}, S_{t-2}, \ldots, y_{t-1}, y_{t-2}, \ldots] = 0$ for all t, and $EV_t^s V_t^{s\prime} = \Sigma_t$ where

Σ_t is a positive semidefinite matrix for all $t.$[2] At time t, the agent is assumed to have an information set Ω_t including at least $y_{t-1}, \ldots, y_{t-m}$ and S_t, $S_{t-1}, \ldots, S_{t-r+1}$.

The problem is then to choose a linear decision rule or contingency plan for setting y_t as a function of elements in Ω_t, in order to maximize the objective function

$$\lim_{N \to \infty} E_0 \sum_{t=0}^{N} \beta^t \{(h + S_{1t})'y_t - y_t'Hy_t - [D(L)y_t]'[D(L)y_t]\} \quad (14)$$

where $E_t(x) = Ex|\Omega_t$. The maximization is subject to $y_{-1}, \ldots, y_{-m}$ given and the given law of motion for S_{1t}

$$\delta(L)\begin{bmatrix} S_{1t} \\ S_{2t} \end{bmatrix} = V_t^s. \quad (15)$$

This problem can be solved as follows by using standard dynamic programming methods for problems with quadratic objectives and linear constraints (e.g., see Bertsekas 1976, Kushner 1971, or Kwakernaak and Sivan 1972). Define the *state* vector $X_t' = [y_{t-1}', y_{t-2}', \ldots, y_{t-m}', 1, S_t', S_{t-1}', \ldots, S_{t-r+1}']$. Define the *control* vector $v_t = D_0 y_t + D_1 y_{t-1} + \cdots + D_m y_{t-m}$. The *transition equation* for the system is then

$$\begin{bmatrix} y_t \\ y_{t-1} \\ \vdots \\ y_{t-m+2} \\ y_{t-m+1} \\ 1 \\ S_{t+1} \\ S_t \\ \vdots \\ S_{t-r+3} \\ S_{t-r+2} \end{bmatrix} = \begin{bmatrix} -D_0^{-1}D_1 & -D_0^{-1}D_2 & \cdots & -D_0^{-1}D_{m-1} & -D_0^{-1}D_m & 0 & 0 \\ I_n & 0 & & 0 & 0 & 0 & 0 \\ \vdots & & & & & & \\ 0 & 0 & & 0 & 0 & 0 & 0 \\ 0 & 0 & & I_n & 0 & 0 & 0 \\ 0 & 0 & & 0 & 0 & 1 & 0 \\ 0 & 0 & & 0 & 0 & 0 & \delta_1 \\ 0 & 0 & & 0 & 0 & 0 & I_p \\ \vdots & & & & & & \\ 0 & 0 & & 0 & 0 & 0 & 0 \\ 0 & 0 & \cdots & 0 & 0 & 0 & 0 \end{bmatrix}$$

$$
\begin{bmatrix}
0 & \cdots & 0 & 0 \\
0 & & 0 & 0 \\
& & & \vdots \\
0 & & 0 & 0 \\
0 & & 0 & 0 \\
0 & & 0 & 0 \\
\delta_2 & & \delta_{r-1} & \delta_r \\
0 & & 0 & 0 \\
& & & \vdots \\
0 & & 0 & 0 \\
0 & \cdots & I_p & 0
\end{bmatrix}
\begin{bmatrix}
y_{t-1} \\
y_{t-2} \\
\vdots \\
y_{t-m+1} \\
y_{t-m} \\
1 \\
S_t \\
S_{t-1} \\
\vdots \\
S_{t-r+2} \\
S_{t-r+1}
\end{bmatrix}
+
\begin{bmatrix}
D_0^{-1} \\
0 \\
\vdots \\
0 \\
0 \\
0 \\
0 \\
0 \\
\vdots \\
0 \\
0
\end{bmatrix}
v_t
+
\begin{bmatrix}
0 \\
0 \\
\vdots \\
0 \\
0 \\
0 \\
V_{t+1}^s \\
0 \\
\vdots \\
0 \\
0
\end{bmatrix}
$$

or $X_{t+1} = AX_t + Bv_t + U_{t+1}$, where A, B, and U_{t+1} correspond to the matrices in the line above.

Let $\beta X_t' R X_t$ and $v_t' Q v_t$ be the quadratic forms

$$
\begin{bmatrix}
y_{t-1} \\
y_{t-2} \\
\downarrow \\
y_{t-m} \\
1 \\
S_t \\
S_{t-1} \\
\downarrow \\
S_{t-r+1}
\end{bmatrix}
\begin{bmatrix}
-H & 0 & \cdots & \frac{1}{2}h & 0 & \frac{1}{2}\phi & \cdots & 0 \\
0 & 0 & & 0 & 0 & 0 & & 0 \\
& \vdots & & & & & & \vdots \\
0 & 0 & & 0 & 0 & 0 & & 0 \\
\frac{1}{2}h' & 0 & & 0 & 0 & 0 & & 0 \\
0 & 0 & & 0 & 0 & 0 & & 0 \\
\frac{1}{2}\phi' & 0 & & 0 & 0 & 0 & & 0 \\
& \vdots & & & & & & \vdots \\
0 & 0 & \cdots & 0 & 0 & 0 & \cdots & 0
\end{bmatrix}
\begin{bmatrix}
y_{t-1} \\
y_{t-2} \\
\downarrow \\
y_{t-m} \\
1 \\
s_t \\
s_{t-1} \\
\downarrow \\
S_{t-r+1}
\end{bmatrix}
$$

and $v_t' Q v_t = -v_t' I v_t$ where $\phi = [I\ 0]$ and is dimensional $n \times p$. Notice that the $(mn) \times (mn)$ submatrix in the upper-left-hand corner of R is negative semidefinite by virtue of the assumption that H is positive definite.

With these definitions of X_t, U_t, v_t, A, B, Q, and R, the problem (14) becomes to maximize

$$
\lim_{N \to \infty} E_0 \sum_{t=0}^{N} \beta^t \{ X_t' R X_t + v_t' Q v_t \} \tag{16}
$$

subject to X_0 given and

$$
X_{t+1} = AX_t + Bv_t + U_{t+1}. \tag{17}
$$

The solution of this control problem is a feedback rule of the linear form

$$
v_t = -F X_t \tag{18}
$$

where

$$F = \beta(Q + \beta B'PB)^{-1}B'PA \qquad (19)$$

and where P is the "appropriate" solution[3] of the algebraic matrix Riccati equation

$$P = \beta A'PA + R - \beta^2 A'PB(Q + \beta B'PA)^{-1}B'PA. \qquad (20)$$

The desired solution of equation (20) is obtained by iterations on the matrix Riccati difference equation

$$P_{k+1} = \beta A'P_kA + R - \beta^2 A'P_kB(Q + \beta B'P_kB)^{-1}B'P_kA \qquad (21)$$

starting from $P_0 = 0$. For our problem, conditions are satisfied that are sufficient to guarantee that iterations on (21) converge to the appropriate solution of the algebraic Riccati equation (20).[4] The conditions on our problem that are sufficient to guarantee this convergence are (i) that the matrix H is positive definite, and (ii) that the zeroes of $det\ \delta(z)$ all exceed $\sqrt{\beta}$ in modulus. Furthermore, the conditions on our problem guarantee that the asymptotic closed loop system matrix $(A - BF)$ has all of its eigenvalues less than $1/\sqrt{\beta}$ in modulus.[5]

Problems like ours have special features—namely, the presence of a distinctive pattern of zeroes in A and B in (17)—that permit a quicker method of solving problem (16). Let us partition the state X_t as $X_t' = [X_{1t}', X_{2t}']$ where $X_{1t}' = [y_{t-1}', \ldots, y_{t-m}'], X_{2t}' = [1, S_t', \ldots, S_{t-r+1}']$. For applications of the problems that we will study, the dimension of X_1 will generally be much smaller than the dimension of X_2. That is, both the

---

[3] For problems with negative semidefinite matrices R, the "appropriate" solution of (18) is the unique negative definite solution P. For our problem, R fails to be negative semidefinite, and so does the appropriate solution of (18). However, the submatrix R_{11} defined below is negative semidefinite, and so is the associated P_{11}. This is enough to make our problem well posed, and to support the claims about appropriate solutions that are made in the text. These claims are proved in Sargent (1980).

[4] For details, see Sargent (1980).

[5] This can be established as follows. In (16) define the transformed variables $\tilde{X}_t = \beta^{t/2}X_t$, and $\tilde{v}_t = \beta^{t/2}v_t$. Problem (16) is equivalent to the undiscounted linear regulator problem, to maximize

$$\lim_{N \to \infty} E_0 \sum_{t=0}^{N} \{\tilde{X}_t'R\tilde{X}_t + \tilde{v}_t'Q\tilde{v}_t\}$$

subject to $\tilde{X}_{t+1} = \beta^{1/2}A\tilde{X}_t + \beta^{1/2}B\tilde{v}_t + \beta^{(t+1)/2}\xi_{t+1}$. The optimizer is a control law $\tilde{v}_t = \tilde{F}\tilde{X}_t$, from which the optimizer of the original problem $v_t = \tilde{F}X_t$ can be calculated. For A, B, R, and Q defined as in the text, it can be verified that the pair $(\beta^{1/2}A, \beta^{1/2}B)$ is stabilizable. Further, letting the rank of R be r, choose a matrix G with r rows such that $G'G = R$. Then for our problem, it can be verified that the pair $(\beta^{1/2}A, G)$ is detectable. The stabilizability of $(\beta^{1/2}A, \beta^{1/2}B)$ and the detectability of $(\beta^{1/2}A, G)$ imply that the closed loop system matrix $(\beta^{1/2}A - \beta^{1/2}B\tilde{F})$ has all of its eigenvalues less than unity in modulus. From this and the observation that $\tilde{F} = F$, it follows that the eigenvalues of $(A - BF)$ are bounded by $\beta^{-1/2}$ in modulus. For a more detailed treatment, see Sargent (1980). Kwakernaak and Sivan (1972) and Kailath (1979) are good references on the results from linear optimal control theory we are appealing to.

number of variables n being chosen by the "agent" and the number of lags m inherited from the criterion function will be small relative to the number of variables p in S and the order r of the autoregression for S. Partitioning the rest of the transition equation conformably with $[X'_{1t}, X'_{2t}]$, we have

$$\begin{bmatrix} X_{1t+1} \\ X_{2t+1} \end{bmatrix} = \begin{bmatrix} A_{11} & 0 \\ 0 & A_{22} \end{bmatrix} \begin{bmatrix} X_{1t} \\ X_{2t} \end{bmatrix} + \begin{bmatrix} B_1 \\ 0 \end{bmatrix} v_t + U_{t+1}. \tag{22}$$

This system is in "controllability canonical form," under the assumption that the D_0 is of full rank. This follows from the fact that the pair (A_{11}, B_1) is controllable.[6] Further, the eigenvalues of A_{22} are all less than $1/\sqrt{\beta}$ by virtue of the assumption that the zeroes of $\det \delta(z)$ all exceed $\sqrt{\beta}$ in modulus. Now let us partition P and R conformably with the partition (X'_{1t}, X'_{2t}) so that

$$P = \begin{bmatrix} P_{11} & P_{12} \\ P'_{12} & P_{22} \end{bmatrix} \qquad R = \begin{bmatrix} R_{11} & R_{12} \\ R'_{12} & R_{22} \end{bmatrix},$$

where for our problem $R_{22} = 0$. Note again that R_{11} is negative semi-definite by virtue of the assumption that H is positive definite.

By partitioning the algebraic matrix Riccati equation (20), it is possible to show that P_{11} is the unique negative definite solution of

$$\begin{aligned} P_{11} = \beta A'_{11} P_{11} A_{11} + R_{11} \\ - \beta^2 A'_{11} P_{11} B_1 (Q + \beta B'_1 P_{11} B'_1)^{-1} B'_1 P_{11} A_{11} \end{aligned} \tag{23}$$

and that P_{11} is the limit as $k \to \infty$ of

$$\begin{aligned} P_{11,k+1} = \beta A'_{11} P_{11,k} A_{11} + R_{11} \\ - \beta^2 A'_{11} P_{11,k} B_1 (Q + \beta B'_1 P_{11,k} B_1)^{-1} B'_1 P_{11,k} A_{11} \end{aligned} \tag{24}$$

starting from $P_{11,0} = 0$. Also, P_{12} is the stationary point of the difference equation

$$\begin{aligned} P_{12,k+1} = \beta A'_{11} P_{12,k} A_{22} + R_{12} \\ - \beta^2 A'_{11} P_{11,k} B_1 (Q + \beta B'_1 P_{11,k} B_1)^{-1} B'_1 P_{12,k} A_{22} \end{aligned} \tag{25}$$

starting from $P_{12,0} = 0$, where the "forcing function" $\{P_{11,k}\}_{k=0}^{\infty}$ is the solution of (24) starting from $P_{11,0} = 0$.[7]

---

[6]Necessary and sufficient conditions for iterations on (19) to converge are readily stated in terms of the controllability canonical form (22). The necessary and sufficient conditions are (a), that the pair (A_{11}, B_1) be controllable, and (b) that the eigenvalues of the matrix A_{22} have moduli all less than $1/\sqrt{\beta}$. The necessary and sufficient condition for controllability is that the matrix $[B_1, A_{11}B_1, \ldots, A_{11}^{mn-1}B_1]$ have rank mn, where m is the number of lags in $D(L)$ and n is the dimension of y_t. Condition (b) on the eigenvalues of A_{22} is guaranteed by our assumption that the roots of $\det \delta(z) = 0$ are all greater than $\sqrt{\beta}$ in modulus. These conditions are derived mainly by adapting results summarized by Kwakernaak and Sivan (1972) for the undiscounted case to the discounted case. See Sargent (1980) for details.

[7]Again, for details see Sargent (1980).

Now partition the control law F in (18) conformably with $[X'_{1t}, X'_{2t}]$, so that

$$v_t = -[F_1 F_2]\begin{bmatrix} X_{1t} \\ X_{2t} \end{bmatrix}.$$

Then it follows from partitioning (19) that

$$F_1 = \beta(Q + \beta B'_1 P_{11} B_1)^{-1} B'_1 P_{11} A_{11} \tag{26}$$

$$F_2 = \beta(Q + \beta B'_1 P_{11} B_1)^{-1} B'_1 P_{12} A_{22}. \tag{27}$$

The piece $F_1 X_{1t}$ of the control law is sometimes called the "feedback" part of the control law, while $F_2 X_{2t}$ is called the "feedforward" part.

From the matrix Riccati equation (23) for P_{11} and from the formula (26) for F_1, it follows that the feedback matrix F_1 depends only on the matrices A_{11}, B_1, and R_{11}, and is independent of the parameters characterizing the random process S. Recall that the feedback matrix F_1 gives the dependence of the control law for v_t on the initial state variables $X'_{1t} = [y'_{t-1}, y'_{t-2}, \ldots, y'_{t-m}]$. From inspection of the Riccati equation (23) for P_{11} and the formula (26) for F_1, it follows that the parameters of F_1 are exactly those that come from solving the following smaller-dimensional, non-stochastic optimization problem: maximize

$$\sum_{t=0}^{\infty} \beta^t(X'_{1t} R_{11} X_{1t} + v'_t Q v_t)$$

subject to $X_{1t+1} = A_{11} X_{1t} + B_1 v_t$, with X_{10} given. The solution of this problem is the feedback law $v_t = -F_1 X_{1t}$ where F_1 is given by equation (26). Further, notice that $(A_{11} - B_1 F_1)$ is just the upper left square of $(A - BF)$, which has the block triangular form

$$\begin{bmatrix} A_{11} - B_1 F_1 & A_{12} - B_1 F_2 \\ 0 & A_{22} \end{bmatrix}$$

It follows from the earlier result that the eigenvalues of $(A - BF)$ are bounded in modulus by $\beta^{-1/2}$ that the eigenvalues of $(A_{11} - B_1 F_1)$ are bounded in modulus by $\beta^{-1/2}$. This bound on the modulus of the eigenvalues of $(A_{11} - B_1 F_1)$ is an important feature of our problem, which we propose to exploit in devising an alternative solution procedure in the following section of this paper. In particular, it is this feature of our problem that verifies that the particular solution that we choose to the Euler equations described in the following section is the optimizing choice.[8]

Now it happens that, given F_1, the parameters of F_2 can be found directly without the need to use (27) and without the need to iterate on (25).

---

[8] The assumption that H is positive definite, and not only semidefinite, plays a role in delivering the bound of $\beta^{-1/2}$ on the modulus of the eigenvalues of $A_{11} - B_1 F_1$. If H were only assumed to be positive semidefinite, more restrictions than have been imposed above on $D(L)$ would be required to assure that the eigenvalues of $(A_{11} - B_1 F_1)$ are bounded in modulus by $\beta^{-1/2}$. In particular, sufficient conditions would have to be imposed to satisfy the detectability condition described in note 5.

This is true because of a certain kind of symmetry between the feedback and feedforward parts of the optimal control law. Below, we note this symmetry for our problem and show how it can be combined with the Wiener-Kolmogorov theory of linear least-squares prediction to compute F_2 directly from knowledge of F_1 and $\delta(L)$. There will be computational and other advantages from pursuing this strategy.

III. Solutions Using Wiener-Kolmogorov Formulas

We return to our problem (14). We propose to solve the problem by using the certainty equivalence principle. That is, we shall first solve a version of the problem assuming that $\{S_{1t}\}$ is a known sequence, rather than a stochastic process. We derive an expression for the decision rule in which y_t depends linearly on lagged y's and actual future $S_{1t+j}, j \geq 0$. By the certainty equivalence principle, the correct rule under uncertainty can be derived from this rule by replacing S_{1t+j} for $j \geq 1$ with $E_t S_{1t+j}$, the linear least-squares forecast of S_{1t+j} based on information available at time t. We use earlier results of Hansen and Sargent (1980), which are based on the classic Wiener-Kolmogorov prediction theory, to derive a convenient operational expression for the part of the decision rule that implicitly reflects the $E_t S_{1t+j}$'s. This procedure leads to the optimal linear decision rule.

We first solve the certainty version of our problem: maximize

$$J = \lim_{N \to \infty} \sum_{t=0}^{N} \beta^t \{(h + S_{1t})' y_t - y_t' H y_t - [D(L)y_t]'[D(L)y_t]\} \quad (28)$$

where $\{S_{1t}\}_{t=0}^{\infty}$ is regarded as a known sequence, and where the maximization is over sequences $\{y_t\}_{t=0}^{\infty}$. The initial conditions $y_{-1}, \ldots, y_{-m}$ are all given. To solve the problem, we fix $N \gg m$, and consider first the N-period problem (28) with N fixed. We shall obtain a set of first-order necessary conditions for a maximum of (28) with N fixed.

Consider first the term

$$I = \sum_{t=0}^{N} \beta^t [D(L)y_t]'[D(L)y_t]$$

$$= \sum_{t=0}^{N} \beta^t (y_t' D_0' + y_{t-1}' D_1' + \cdots + y_{t-m}' D_m')(D_0 y_t + \cdots + D_m y_{t-m}).$$

Differentiating I with respect to y_t for $t = 0, \ldots, N - m$ gives

$$\begin{aligned}
(\partial I)/(\partial y_t) &= \beta^t D_0' D(L)y_t + \beta^{t+1} D_1' D(L)y_{t+1} + \cdots + \beta^{t+m} D_m' D(L)y_{t+m} \\
&\quad + \beta^t \{[D(L)y_t]' D_0\}' + \beta^{t+1}\{[D(L)y_{t+1}]' D_1\}' \\
&\quad + \cdots + \beta^{t+m}\{[D(L)y_{t+m}]' D_m\}' \quad (29) \\
&= 2\beta^t [D_0' D(L) + \beta L^{-1} D_1' D(L) + \cdots + \beta^m L^{-m} D_m' D(L)]y_t \\
&= 2\beta^t D(\beta L^{-1})' D(L)y_t.
\end{aligned}$$

Therefore, to maximize (28) with N taken fixed, we have the Euler equations

$$(\partial J)/(\partial y_t) = \beta^t[(h + S_{1t}) - 2Hy_t - 2D(\beta L^{-1})'D(L)y_t] = 0$$
$$t = 0, 1, \ldots, N - m. \tag{30}$$

For the infinite time problem obtained by driving N to infinity, the Euler equations (30) are also first-order necessary conditions. However, as there exists more than one solution of the Euler equations (30) that satisfies the $m \times n$ initial conditions $y_{-1}, \ldots, y_{-m}$, we need additional conditions to pick out the unique optimum path of y_t. For the certainty version of our problem, it can be proved that, as $N \to \infty$, the optimum of criterion function (28) is bounded below.[9] This means that the optimum path for y_t satisfies

$$\sum_{t=0}^{\infty} \beta^t y_t' H y_t < +\infty. \tag{31}$$

This condition is shown in Appendix A uniquely to determine the solution of the Euler equations that our procedure selects. Equivalently, our procedure is known to be correct because it selects the unique solution of the Euler equations that gives rise to a closed loop system with zeroes of its characteristic polynomial that are bounded in modulus by $\beta^{-1/2}$. As indicated in Section II, this is known to be a property of the optimal closed loop system.

Write the Euler equation as

$$[H + D(\beta L^{-1})'D(L)]y_t = \frac{1}{2}(h + S_{1t}). \tag{32}$$

The Euler equations (32) can be solved subject to (31) and $n \cdot m$ initial conditions, $y_{-1}, \ldots, y_{-m}$, by the following procedure. First, we note that the roots of $det\,[H + D(\beta z^{-1})'D(z)] = 0$ come in pairs: if z_0 is a root, so is βz_0^{-1}. It is, in general, possible to factor the matrix polynomial $H + D(\beta z^{-1})'D(z)$ so that

$$H + D(\beta z^{-1})'D(z) = C(\beta z^{-1})'C(z) \tag{33}$$

where $C(z)$ is an mth-order, $n \times n$ matrix polynomial in nonnegative powers of z, $C(z) = C_0 + C_1 z + \cdots + C_m z^m$, and where all of the roots of $det\,C(z) = 0$ in modulus are greater than $\sqrt{\beta}$. For each root z_0 of $det\,C(z) = 0$, there is a root βz_0^{-1} of $det\,C(\beta z^{-1}) = 0$. The roots of $det\,C(\beta z^{-1}) = 0$ in modulus are all less than $\sqrt{\beta}$. The factorization (33) is

---

[9]This follows from the stabilizability and detectability of the transformed system (see n. 5) and from results in linear optimal control theory (see Kwakernaak and Sivan 1972, and Sargent 1980).

unique up to premultiplication of $C(L)$ by an orthogonal matrix. These assertions about (33) are proved in Appendix B.

Using the factorization (33), we can write the Euler equations (32) as $C(\beta L^{-1})'C(L)y_t = 1/2(h + S_{1t})$. The solution of this equation that satisfies condition (31) is then

$$C(L)y_t = \frac{1}{2}[C(\beta L^{-1})']^{-1}(h + S_{1t}) \tag{34}$$

or

$$C_0 y_t + C_1 y_{t-1} + \cdots + C_m y_{t-m} = \tag{35}$$

$$\frac{1}{2}(C_0' + C_1'\beta L^{-1} + \cdots + C_m'\beta^m L^{-m})^{-1}(h + S_{1t}).$$

As shown in Appendix A, condition (31) and the initial conditions impel us to solve the "stable roots backwards and the unstable roots forwards." Now premultiplying both sides of (35) by C_0^{-1} gives

$$y_t + C_0^{-1}C_1 y_{t-1} + \cdots + C_0^{-1}C_m y_{t-m} = \tag{36}$$

$$\frac{1}{2}(C_0'C_0 + C_1'C_0\beta L^{-1} + \cdots + C_m'C_0\beta^m L^{-m})^{-1}(h + S_{1t}).$$

From Section II we have a quick and feasible method of obtaining F_1', which together with $D(L)$ directly gives the "feedback" polynomial in (36)—namely, $(I + C_0^{-1}C_1 L + C_0^{-1}C_2 L^2 + \cdots + C_0^{-1}C_m L^m)$. Given this polynomial, we shall now describe a method for obtaining a tractable expression for the "feedforward" part of the solution in (36)—namely, $1/2(C_0'C_0 + C_1'C_0\beta L^{-1} + \cdots + C_m'C_0\beta^m L^{-m})^{-1}(h + S_{1t})$.

First, by multiplying the polynomials in L, it is established that

$$C(\beta L^{-1})'C(L) = \sum_{j=-m}^{m} \tilde{C}_j L^j$$

where

$$\tilde{C}_0 = C_0'C_0 + \beta C_1'C_1 + \cdots + \beta^m C_m'C_m$$
$$\tilde{C}_1 = C_0'C_1 + \beta C_1'C_2 + \cdots + \beta^{m-1}C_{m-1}'C_m$$
$$\tilde{C}_2 = C_0'C_2 + \beta C_1'C_3 + \cdots + \beta^{m-2}C_{m-2}'C_m \tag{37}$$
$$\vdots$$
$$\tilde{C}_m = C_0'C_m$$
$$\tilde{C}_{-j} = \beta^j \tilde{C}_j' \text{ for } j = 1, \ldots, m.$$

Similarly, where $D(\beta L^{-1})'D(L) = \Sigma_{j=m}^{m} \tilde{D}_j L^j$, it is established that

$$\tilde{D}_0 = D_0'D_0 + \beta D_1'D_1 + \cdots + \beta^m D_m'D_m$$
$$\vdots$$
$$\tilde{D}_m = D_0'D_m \tag{38}$$
$$\tilde{D}_{-j} = \beta^j \tilde{D}_j', j = 1, \ldots, m.$$

Therefore, given $D(L)$, it is evident from (37), (38), and (33) that

$$C_0'C_m = D_0'D_m. \tag{39}$$

Next, since $C_0^{-1}C_1, \ldots, C_0^{-1}C_m$ are all known from the feedback polynomial in (36), we can calculate $C_0'C_0$ using (33) from $C_0'C_0 = C_0'C_m(C_0^{-1}C_m)^{-1}$ or

$$C_0'C_0 = (D_0'D_m)(C_0^{-1}C_m)^{-1}. \tag{40}$$

Equation (40) expresses $C_0'C_0$ in terms of known parameters. Given $C_0'C_0$, we can obtain $C_j'C_0$ from

$$C_j'C_0 = (C_0^{-1}C_j)'C_0'C_0, \; j = 1, \ldots, m. \tag{41}$$

So equations (40) and (41) together with the known values of $D_0'D_m$ and $C_0^{-1}C_j$ determine all the matrices that appear on the right side of (36): $M(\beta z^{-1}) = C_0'C_0 + C_1'C_0\beta z^{-1} + \cdots + C_m'C_0\beta^m z^{-m}$.

In order to compute the equilibrium decision rule (36), we shall need a convenient algorithm for computing the inverse of $M(z)$, since the inverse of $M(\beta L^{-1})$ appears on the right side of (36). We now describe convenient formulas for computing $M(z)^{-1}$ via the identity $M(z)^{-1} = adj\, M(z)/det\, M(z)$. We proceed by describing algorithms for computing both $adj\, M(z)$ and $det\, M(z)$. These calculations ultimately lead to equation (45) below. The intervening calculations are useful technical details which can be skipped on first reading.

Our procedure is an adaptation of one proposed by Emre and Hüseyin (1975). We begin by evaluating $det\, M(z)$. To accomplish this task we note that

$$\begin{aligned}
\frac{\partial\, det\, M(z)}{\partial z} &= trace\left[\frac{\partial\, det\, M(z)}{\partial M(z)}\frac{\partial M(z)'}{\partial z}\right] \\
&= det\, M(z)\, trace\left[\frac{\partial M(z)}{\partial z}M(z)^{-1}\right]
\end{aligned} \tag{42}$$

Let $\tilde{M}(z) = [\partial M(z)/\partial z]M(z)^{-1}$ and write its Taylor series expansion about zero as $\tilde{M}(z) = \tilde{M}_0 + \tilde{M}_1 z + \tilde{M}_2 z^2 + \cdots$. Now

$$\begin{aligned}
\tilde{M}(z)M(z) &= \frac{\partial M(z)}{\partial z} \\
&= C_1'C_0 + 2C_2'C_0 z + \cdots + mC_m'C_0 z^{m-1}.
\end{aligned}$$

Equating coefficients in the Taylor series we know that

$$\tilde{M}_0 C_0'C_0 = C_1'C_0 \quad \text{or} \quad \tilde{M}_0 = C_1'C_0'^{-1}$$

$$\tilde{M}_1 C_0'C_0 + \tilde{M}_0 C_1'C_0 = 2C_2'C_0 \quad \text{or} \quad \tilde{M}_1 = 2C_2'C_0'^{-1} - \tilde{M}_0 C_1'C_0'^{-1}$$

$$\vdots$$

$$\tilde{M}_j C_0'C_0 + \cdots + \tilde{M}_0 C_j'C_0 = (j+1)C_{j+1}'C_0 \quad \text{or}$$

$$\tilde{M}_j = (j+1)C_{j+1}'C_0'^{-1} - \tilde{M}_{j-1}C_1'C_0'^{-1} - \cdots - \tilde{M}_0 C_j'C_0'^{-1}$$

where $C_j = 0$ for $j > m$. This provides us with recursive formulas for the $\tilde{M}_j$'s. Let $k = m \cdot n$ and write

$$det\, M(z) = d_0 + d_1 z + \cdots + d_k z^k.$$

Differentiating with respect to z we obtain

$$\frac{\partial\, det\, M(z)}{\partial z} = d_1 + 2d_2 z + \cdots + kd_k z^{k-1}.$$

We can rewrite equation (42) as

$$\frac{\partial\, det\, M(z)}{\partial z} = det\, M(z)(trace\, \tilde{M}_0 + trace\, \tilde{M}_1 z + trace\, \tilde{M}_2 z^2 + \cdots).$$

Again we equate coefficients to obtain

$$d_1 = d_0\, trace\, \tilde{M}_0$$

$$2d_2 = d_0\, trace\, \tilde{M}_1 + d_1\, trace\, \tilde{M}_0 \quad \text{or} \quad d_2 = \frac{1}{2}(d_0\, trace\, \tilde{M}_1 + d_1\, trace\, \tilde{M}_0)$$

$$\vdots$$

$$kd_k = d_0\, trace\, \tilde{M}_{k-1} + \cdots + d_{k-1}\, trace\, \tilde{M}_0 \quad \text{or}$$

$$d_k = \frac{1}{k}(d_0\, trace\, \tilde{M}_{k-1} + \cdots + d_{k-1}\, trace\, \tilde{M}_0)$$

Noting that $d_0 = det\,(C_0'C_0)$ we have now derived recursive formulas for the d_j's and thus the polynomial coefficients for $det\, M(z)$. Using these coefficients and a numerical factorization algorithm we can express $det\, M(z) = d_k(z - z_1)(z - z_2) \ldots (z - z_k)$, where $z_1, \ldots, z_k$ are the roots of $det\, M(z)$. These roots are greater than $\sqrt{\beta}$ in magnitude.

In order to proceed to the second step of the inversion of $M(z)$, we shall write

$$M(z)^{-1} = \frac{adj\, M(z)}{d_k(z - z_1)(z - z_2) \ldots (z - z_k)} \tag{43}$$

where $adj\, M(z)$ is the adjoint of $M(z)$. Thus our second step involves deriving a formula for $adj\, M(z)$. The Taylor series expansion about zero for $adj\, M(z)$ can be written $adj\, M(z) = M_0^* + M_1^* z + \cdots + M_{k-m}^* z^{k-m}$. Notice that $[adj\, M(z)]M(z) = [det\, M(z)]I$; equating coefficients of the Taylor series expansion of both sides of this equation gives

$$M_0^* C_0' C_0 = d_0 I \quad \text{or} \quad M_0^* = d_0(C_0'C_0)^{-1}$$

$$M_0^* C_1' C_0 + M_1^* C_0' C_0 = d_1 I \quad \text{or} \quad M_1^* = d_1(C_0'C_0)^{-1} - M_0^* C_1' C_0'^{-1}$$

$$\vdots$$

$$M_0^* C_{k-m}' C_0 + \cdots + M_{k-m}^* C_0' C_0 = d_{k-m} I \quad \text{or}$$

$$M_{k-m}^* = d_{k-m}(C_0'C_0)^{-1} - M_0^* C'_{k-m} C_0'^{-1} \cdots - M_{k-m-1}^* C_1' C_0'^{-1}.$$

This provides us with recursive formulas for the M_j^*'s.

The third step in our inversion formula for $M(z)$ amounts to expanding (43) by matrix partial fractions to obtain

$$M(z)^{-1} = \frac{N_1}{(z - z_1)} + \cdots + \frac{N_k}{(z - z_k)} \tag{44}$$

where

$$N_j = \frac{1}{d_k \prod_{\substack{i \neq j \\ 1 \leq i \leq k}} (z_j - z_i)} [M_0^* + M_1^* z_j + \cdots + M_{k-m}^* (z_j)^{k-m}].$$

Equation (44) can be rewritten

$$M(z)^{-1} = \frac{-\frac{1}{z_1} N_1}{\left(1 - \frac{1}{z_1} z\right)} + \cdots + \frac{-\frac{1}{z_k} N_k}{\left(1 - \frac{1}{z_k} z\right)} \tag{45}$$

Finally, substituting βz^{-1} for z gives

$$M(\beta z^{-1})^{-1} = (C_0' C_0 + C_1' C_0 \beta z^{-1} + \cdots + C_m' C_0 \beta^m z^{-m})^{-1}$$

$$= \frac{-\frac{1}{z_1} N_1}{1 - \frac{1}{z_1} \beta z^{-1}} + \cdots + \frac{-\frac{1}{z_k} N_k}{1 - \frac{1}{z_k} \beta z^{-1}} \tag{46}$$

Applying equation (46) to the right side of (36) gives the decision rule for y_t:

$$y_t + C_0^{-1} C_1 y_{t-1} + \cdots + C_0^{-1} C_m y_{t-m}$$

$$= \frac{1}{2} \sum_{j=1}^{k} \left(\frac{-\lambda_j N_j}{1 - \lambda_j \beta L^{-1}} \right) (h + S_{1t}) \tag{47}$$

where $\lambda_j = 1/z_j$. Using the expansion $[1 - (\lambda_j)\beta L^{-1}]^{-1} = \Sigma_{i=0}^{\infty} (\lambda_j \beta)^i L^{-i}$, (47) can be written

$$y_t = -(C_0^{-1} C_1 y_{t-1} + \cdots + C_0^{-1} C_m y_{t-m})$$

$$- \frac{1}{2} \sum_{j=1}^{k} \lambda_j N_j \left[\sum_{i=0}^{\infty} (\lambda_j \beta)^i (S_{1t+i} + h) \right] \tag{48}$$

Equation (47) or (48) expresses the optimal choice of y_t as a function of m lagged y's and the sum of k geometric sums of all future values of the vector sequence S_1.

It is now a simple step to add uncertainty. Where S is a random process obeying the assumptions we have imposed above, the optimal rule is obtained by replacing S_{1t+i} with $E_t S_{1t+i}$ in (48):

$$y_t = -(C_0^{-1}C_1 y_{t-1} + \cdots + C_0^{-1}C_m y_{t-m})$$
$$-\frac{1}{2}\sum_{j=1}^{k}\lambda_j N_j\left[\sum_{i=0}^{\infty}(\lambda_j\beta)^i(E_t S_{1t+i} + h)\right]. \quad (49)$$

By using a formula of Hansen and Sargent (1980), the geometric sum in expected S_{1t+i}'s can be written

$$\sum_{i=0}^{\infty}(\lambda_j\beta)^i E_t S_{1t+i} = \phi\delta(\lambda_j\beta)^{-1}\left\{I + \sum_{s=1}^{r-1}\left[\sum_{i=s+1}^{r}(\lambda_j\beta)^{i-s}\delta_i\right]L^s\right\}S_t, \quad (50)$$

where ϕ is an $n \times p$ matrix of the form $[I\ 0]$. The classic Wiener-Kolmogorov prediction formulas are embedded in (50), as described by Hansen and Sargent (1980). Substituting (50) into (49), we obtain the decision rule

$$y_t = -(C_0^{-1}C_1 y_{t-1} + \cdots + C_0^{-1}C_m y_{t-m})$$
$$-\frac{1}{2}\sum_{j=1}^{k}\lambda_j N_j\phi\,\delta(\lambda_j\beta)^{-1}\left\{I + \sum_{s=1}^{r-1}\left[\sum_{i=s+1}^{r}(\lambda_j\beta)^{i-s}\delta_i\right]L^s\right\}S_t \quad (51)$$
$$-\frac{1}{2}\sum_{j=1}^{k}\lambda_j N_j\left(\frac{1}{1-\lambda_j\beta}\right)h.$$

Equation (51) expresses the optimal choice of y_t as a function of m lagged y's and current and $(r - 1)$ lagged values of S. The "state" variables thus match up with the setup of Section II.

In Section V, we shall exhibit speeds of calculating a particular numerical example of a Lucas-Prescott equilibrium of investment uncertainty, using both the method of Section II and the method leading up to (51). This will give the reader some sense of how much quicker the method of this section can be than the earlier one. Before proceeding to this example, in the next section we describe a modification of the present procedure which differs in that it factors the matrix $H + D(\beta L^{-1})'D(L)$ by a different method.

IV. Another Solution Procedure

The previous two sections have indicated two different but related methods for solving our general problem. The first method involved casting the problem in the form of a "stochastic linear optimal regulator" problem, and solving it by iterating on the matrix Riccati difference equation. This approach in effect solved the "optimization" and "prediction" pieces of the problem jointly. The second method explicitly separated the optimization and the prediction problems, used the recursive method to factor the spectral density-like matrix $[H + D(\beta L^{-1})D(L)]$ involved in the "optimization" piece of the problem, but used analytic, nonrecursive formulas to solve the "prediction" aspects of the problem.

A third procedure is also available in principle, and it is practical in sufficiently small systems (n and m should be small). The method involves using the procedure described by Rozanov (1967) to factor $[H + D(\beta L^{-1})'D(L)]$.[10] By using this procedure, the requirement for nonanalytic procedures (i.e., numerical or recursive procedures) can be reduced to the minimum extent possible, namely, to the need to find the roots of several univariate polynomials. In general, the procedure can be described as follows. The matrix characteristic polynomial for the Euler equations can be represented, as in Appendix B, as

$$H + D(\beta L^{-1})'D(L) = H + \bar{D}(\sqrt{\beta}L^{-1})'\bar{D}\left(\frac{1}{\sqrt{\beta}}L\right) \tag{52}$$

where $\bar{D}_j = D_j(\sqrt{\beta})^j$. We use Rozanov's procedure to factor the "spectral density" matrix

$$H + \bar{D}(z^{-1})'\bar{D}(z) = G(z^{-1})'G(z) \tag{53}$$

where $G_j = \Sigma_{j=0}^m G_j z^j$, and the roots of $det\ G(z) = 0$ are all outside the unit circle. As in Appendix B, the Euler equations for the certainty version of our problem can be written as

$$G(\sqrt{\beta}L^{-1})'G\left(\frac{1}{\sqrt{\beta}}L\right)y_t = \frac{1}{2}(h + S_{1t}) \tag{54}$$

or

$$C(\beta L^{-1})'C(L)y_t = \frac{1}{2}(h + S_{1t}) \tag{55}$$

where $C_j = (1/\sqrt{\beta})^j G_j$. Once $C(L)$ has been obtained, the solution for the feedback rule can be obtained exactly as described in Section III.

The advantage of using the method described by Rozanov over the methods of Sections II and III is that Rozanov's delivers closed form expressions (or "nearly" closed form expressions, depending on the size of m and n). The disadvantage of Rozanov's method vis-à-vis using the recursive method of Section III is that the algebraic calculations required for Rozanov's method are tedious.

[10]The procedure suggested by Rozanov (1967) involves obtaining an initial noninvertible triangular factorization and then multiplying by appropriate Blaschke factor matrices in order to shift roots from inside the unit circle to outside the unit circle. An alternative procedure for factoring a vector moving average, discrete time spectral density matrix, has been offered by Whittle (1963) and more recently by Murthy (1973). It amounts to inverting the spectral density, thus converting a vector moving average problem into a vector autoregressive problem. The orthogonality conditions associated with the vector autoregression are then used to determine the invertible factorization. From the standpoint of this paper, we are concerned only with the factorization of spectral densities of vector moving average processes. However, the procedures discussed by Rozanov, Whittle, and Murthy are appropriate for arbitrary rational spectral densities.

In Appendix C, we report explicit closed form formulas for factoring $H + \bar{D}(z)'\bar{D}(z)$ for the case in which $n = 2, m = 1$. These formulas were derived by following the instructions provided by Rozanov (1967). When combined with formulas (42)–(51), the formulas in Appendix C give a completely closed form expression for the decision rule in the $n = 2, m = 1$ case.

V. An Illustration

We illustrate these computational methods by computing the equilibrium of a multiple factor version of the Lucas-Prescott model, which was the second example in Section I. Recall that the firm is assumed to maximize

$$E_0 \sum_{t=0}^{\infty} \beta^t \left[P_t d' \binom{k_t}{n_t} - W_t n_t - R_t k_t - \binom{\Delta k_t}{\Delta n_t}' D \binom{\Delta k_t}{\Delta n_t} \right] \tag{56}$$

subject to

$$P_t = A_0 - A_1 Y_t + U_t \tag{57}$$

$$\binom{K}{N}_t = B_0 + B_1 \binom{K_{t-1}}{N_{t-1}} + G_0 Z_t + \cdots + G_{r-1} Z_{t-r+1}$$
$$+ F_0 U_t + \cdots + F_{q-1} U_{t-q+1} \tag{58}$$

$$\theta(L) Z_t = V_t^z \tag{59}$$

$$\xi(L) U_t = V_t^u \tag{60}$$

where the rentals R_t and W_t are the first two elements of the $(p \times 1)$ vector process Z_t. At time t, the firm is assumed to know the state variables $\{k_{t-1}, n_{t-1}, K_{t-1}, N_{t-1}\}$ and the information variables $\{Z_t, Z_{t-1}, \ldots, U_t, U_{t-1}, \ldots\}$. The firm knows the parameters of the laws of motion for $(K, N)'$, Z, and U, and also the parameters of the demand schedule.

To compute the equilibrium law of motion for $(K_t, N_t) \equiv (mk_t, mn_t)$, we follow Lucas and Prescott (1971) or Sargent (1979) and solve the following social planning problem: to maximize[11]

$$E_0 \sum_{t=0}^{\infty} \beta^t \left[A_0 md' \binom{k_t}{n_t} - \frac{1}{2} A_1 m^2 \binom{k_t}{n_t}' dd' \binom{k_t}{n_t} \right.$$
$$+ md' \binom{k_t}{n_t} U_t - m \binom{R_t}{W_t}' \binom{k_t}{n_t}$$
$$\left. - m \binom{k_t - k_{t-1}}{n_t - n_{t-1}}' D \binom{k_t - k_{t-1}}{n_t - n_{t-1}} \right]. \tag{61}$$

[11]Note that in this example the matrix $H = A_1 m^2 dd'$, and so is positive semidefinite but not positive definite. However, it can be verified that the problem does satisfy sufficient conditions for the closed loop system matrix $(A_{11} - B_1 F_1)$ to have eigenvalues bounded in modulus by $\beta^{-1/2}$. In particular, the zeroes of what corresponds to the matrix polynomial $det\ D(z)$ of Section III are less than $\beta^{-1/2}$ in modulus, which delivers the required detectability condition (see n. 5).

In (61), the maximization is over contingency plans for (k_t, n_t) given the laws of motion (59) and (60), and given $(k_{t-1}, n_{t-1}, Z_t, Z_{t-1}, \ldots, U_t, U_{t-1}, \ldots)$. Once the contingency plan for the representative firm's stocks (k_t, n_t) that maximizes (61) has been obtained, the competitive equilibrium for (K_t, N_t) can be obtained by multiplying by m, that is, by using $(K_t, N_t) = (mk_t, mn_t)$. It should be noted that the contingency plan for (k_t, n_t) that maximizes the social planning criterion (61) is not the optimum contingency plan (10) of the representative firm of Section I, but is simply m^{-1} times the equilibrium law of motion (8) for (K, N). That the competitive equilibrium described in Section I implicitly maximizes (61) can be verified directly by using an argument analogous to that of Sargent (1980).

Using each of our three methods, we have calculated a rational expectations equilibrium by maximizing (61). For the Z process (59) we assumed

$$\begin{pmatrix} R_t \\ W_t \end{pmatrix} = \begin{pmatrix} .6 & .2 \\ .7 & -.1 \end{pmatrix}\begin{pmatrix} R_{t-1} \\ W_{t-1} \end{pmatrix} + \begin{pmatrix} -.2 & .3 \\ .1 & -.1 \end{pmatrix}\begin{pmatrix} R_{t-2} \\ W_{t-2} \end{pmatrix}$$

$$+ \begin{pmatrix} -.1 & -.4 \\ .3 & .2 \end{pmatrix}\begin{pmatrix} R_{t-3} \\ W_{t-3} \end{pmatrix} + \begin{pmatrix} .1 & .0 \\ -.1 & .2 \end{pmatrix}\begin{pmatrix} R_{t-4} \\ W_{t-4} \end{pmatrix} + V_t^z.$$

For (60), we assumed for simplicity that $U_t \equiv 0$, so that demand shocks are suppressed. (It would be very cheap to include demand shocks with our second and third computational methods, somewhat more expensive with the first method.) We assumed that $A_1 = .00005$, $m = 1000$, $\beta = .9$, and $d' = (.25, .75)$. We chose D to obey

$$mD = \begin{pmatrix} 2 & 1 \\ 1 & 1.5 \end{pmatrix}.$$

To match the objective function (61) of the social planning problem with the objective function (14) of the general optimization problem described in Section II above, we set $H = (1/2)A_1 m^2 dd'$, $h = A_0 md$,

$$[D(L)y_t]'[D(L)y_t] = \begin{pmatrix} k_t - k_{t-1} \\ n_t - n_{t-1} \end{pmatrix}' (mD) \begin{pmatrix} k_t - k_{t-1} \\ n_t - n_{t-1} \end{pmatrix},$$

and

$$S_t \equiv S_{1t} = -m\begin{pmatrix} R_t \\ W_t \end{pmatrix}.$$

Also, we set $A_0 = 0$, which amounts to setting constant terms in the equilibrium (K, N) process to zero. The resulting equilibrium should then be thought of as describing variables measured in deviations from their means.[12]

[12]We did not carry along the constant terms in the demand function or compute them for the equilibrium. The latter constants would be easy to compute given the former.

We calculated the equilibrium three ways: with the method of Section II which involves iterating on the full matrix Riccati difference equation (21), with the "short" method of Section III, and with the "shorter" method of Section IV. The equilibrium can be written as

$$\begin{pmatrix} k_t \\ n_t \end{pmatrix} = \begin{pmatrix} 1.1021 & .3064 \\ -.3404 & -.0213 \end{pmatrix} \begin{pmatrix} k_{t-1} \\ n_{t-1} \end{pmatrix}$$
$$+ \begin{pmatrix} -.4977 & .0627 \\ .1747 & -.0542 \end{pmatrix} \begin{pmatrix} mR_t \\ mW_t \end{pmatrix} + \begin{pmatrix} .0815 & .0378 \\ -.0275 & -.0122 \end{pmatrix} \begin{pmatrix} mR_{t-1} \\ mW_{t-1} \end{pmatrix} \quad (62)$$
$$+ \begin{pmatrix} -.0139 & .1960 \\ .0053 & -.0661 \end{pmatrix} \begin{pmatrix} mR_{t-2} \\ mW_{t-2} \end{pmatrix} + \begin{pmatrix} -.0493 & .0094 \\ .0167 & -.0036 \end{pmatrix} \begin{pmatrix} mR_{t-3} \\ mW_{t-3} \end{pmatrix}.$$

To express the equilibrium in terms of (K_t, N_t), simply multiply both sides of (62) by $m = 1000$.

To implement the first two computational methods, which are iterative, a convergence criterion had to be adopted. We used the following convergence criterion. We calculated successive iterates on the feedback law, namely, $F_k = \beta(Q + \beta B'P_k B)^{-1}B'P_k A$, where iterations on the matrix Riccati difference equation (20) were started from $P_0 = 0$. Then we computed the norm defined as the maximum absolute value over elements of $(F_{k+1} - F_k)$. For convergence, we insisted that this norm had to be less than 10^{-5}. For the (k_t, n_t) law that maximized (61), all three methods gave identical answers to at least five digits, as expected. (The results for the third method involve no iteration and are exact.)

Table 1 gives the time taken for each method in central processor time on the Cyber 172 at the University of Minnesota. Generally, we would expect the relative speed advantage of the shorter methods in calculating the equilibrium to increase the closer is β to unity and the larger is the dimensionality of the S process both in terms of the number of lags in its autoregression, and the number of variables in S. For our example, since central processor time costs about 8 cents per second, one evaluation of the equilibrium costs about half a penny by the short methods, about 25 cents by the full Riccati method. The relative costliness of these computational procedures clearly will vary from problem to problem.

TABLE 1

CENTRAL PROCESSOR TIME TO CALCULATE RATIONAL EXPECTATIONS
EQUILIBRIUM (IN SECONDS)

Method	Time
Full Riccati (Sec. II)	3.247
Short Riccati (Sec. III)	0.075
Spectral Factorization (Sec. IV)	0.052

NOTE.—Computed on Cyber 172 Computer, University of Minnesota.

VI. A Possible Identification Problem

Let us represent the decision rule (51), using (35) in the compact form

$$C(L)y_t = E_t \left\{ \frac{1}{2} [C(\beta L^{-1})']^{-1}(h + S_{1t}) \right\} \tag{63}$$

where $\delta(L)S_t = v_t^s$. Here it is understood that E_t stands for the expectation or linear projection conditioned on $\{S_t, S_{t-1}, \ldots\}$.

Suppose the econometrician sees enough of the (y, S) process to permit him to estimate the parameters of $C(L)$ and h. Let us pose the following question. Is it possible to work backwards to obtain a unique H and $D(L)$ such that $H + D(\beta L^{-1})'D(L) = C(\beta L^{-1})'C(L)$? In other words, can we identify the criterion function parameters H and $D(L)$ from the decision rule parameters $C(L)$? First of all, there is a relatively trivial sense in which the answer to this question is no. Both $C(L)$ and $D(L)$ are identified only up to a premultiplication by an orthogonal matrix. From the standpoint of criterion function identification, this problem is not particularly interesting because premultiplication of $D(L)$ by an orthogonal matrix does not effect the term $[D(L)y_t]'[D(L)y_t]$ that enters into the criterion function. In other words if Λ is an orthogonal matrix conformable with $D(L)$, then $[\Lambda D(L)y_t]'[\Lambda D(L)y_t] = [D(L)y_t]\Lambda'\Lambda[D(L)y_t] = [D(L)y_t]' [D(L)y_t]$. This suggests that all we should really care about is identification of $D(L)$ up to a premultiplication by an orthogonal matrix since elements in this class of $D(L)$'s all give rise to the same criterion function.

It turns out that there is another sense in which the criterion function parameters cannot be identified from the decision rule parameters. Using the procedure suggested in Section IV and Appendix C, we see the link between factoring a spectral density function and solving for $C(L)$ from $D(L)$ and H. Appealing to linear prediction theory and using the development provided in Appendix B it is possible to show that a whole family of H's and $D(L)$'s lead to the same decision rule. This turns out to be a simple corollary to the result that a covariance stationary stochastic process has multiple moving average representations.[13] Thus, without further restrictions there is a whole family of objective functions that are consistent with decision rule (63). In absence of additional restrictions we cannot hope completely to identify the objective function parameters.

Fortunately, for many purposes, the fact that only a class of objective functions can be identified is of no practical concern. The reason is that all objective functions that imply the same decision rule give rise to exactly the same predictions about the response of economic agents to interventions in the form of changes in $\delta(L)$. For econometric policy evaluation,

---

[13]Multiple moving average representations can be obtained both by "flipping" roots inside and outside the unit circle via multiplication by Blaschke factors and by altering the number of underlying orthogonal white noise processes employed in the representation. See Rozanov (1967) for details.

then, it is enough to identify the decision rule without having completely to identify the objective function.

In circumstances in which either more data are available or in which a priori restrictions are imposed on $D(L)$ it is often possible substantially to reduce the family of objective functions consistent with $C(L)$. For example, the econometrician may have observations on "output" q_t which obeys

$$q_t = (h + S_{1t})'y_t - y_t'Hy_t \tag{64}$$

where S_1 is not observed by the econometrician. The idea here is that observations on q permit estimation of H via (64). In addition it is supposed that the cost term $[D(L)y_t]'[D(L)y_t]$ in (14) represents costs that are "internal" to the firm or the unit whose decisions are being modeled, so that $D(L)$ cannot be estimated from direct observations on inputs and outputs. In this example, H is uniquely identified; however, $D(L)$ cannot necessarily be completely pinned down from estimates of $C(L)$. A different example is where the form of $D(L)$ is restricted so that $(y_t - y_{t-1})'\bar{H}(y_t - y_{t-1}) = [D(L)y_t]'[D(L)y_t]$. Even without observations on q_t, it is possible to recover both $\bar{H}$ and H from $C(L)$ and hence the objective function parameters are all identified.

VII. Conclusions

This paper has been devoted to describing quick and revealing ways of calculating optimal decision rules or dynamic equilibria for linear stochastic rational expectations models. The full value of such methods becomes evident only when we recall that our purpose is ultimately to estimate models of this class by using interpretations of the errors and estimators along the lines described in our earlier paper (Hansen and Sargent 1980). For example, there we describe maximum likelihood procedures for the estimation of single-endogenous variable, dynamic models of the class considered here. For the purposes of implementing maximum likelihood methods, it is a substantial advantage to have quick algorithms for evaluating the likelihood function, which requires evaluating the optimal decision rule or equilibrium stochastic process. It is also an advantage to have formulas as close to being in closed form as possible, since this facilitates computing analytic derivatives of the likelihood function. The general principles of estimation and interpretation of error terms described in our earlier paper extend in a fairly straightforward way to the present context.

Appendix A

In this appendix we examine the solutions to discrete time Euler equations for the infinite time problem. We take the following steps in order to characterize these solutions. First, write the Euler equations

$$[H + D(\beta L^{-1})'D(L)]y_t = S_t^* \text{ for } t = 0, 1, \ldots. \tag{A1}$$

Second, obtain a partial fractions decomposition of $[H + D(\beta z^{-1})'D(z)]^{-1}$ of the form

$$[H + D(\beta z^{-1})'D(z)]^{-1} = \frac{G_1^*}{z - z_1} + \cdots + \frac{G_k^*}{z - z_k} +$$
$$\frac{H_1^*}{z - \beta z_1^{-1}} + \cdots + \frac{H_k^*}{z - \beta z_k^{-1}}$$

where $z_1, \ldots, z_k$ are assumed to be distinct and are greater than $\sqrt{\beta}$ in modulus. We assume that $(1/\sqrt{\beta})^t S_t^* \to 0$ as $t \to \infty$. Third, we obtain a particular solution to (A1) of the form

$$y_t^p = \frac{-G_1^*}{z_1} \sum_{j=0}^{\infty} (z_1)^{-j} S_{t-j}^* - \cdots - \frac{-G_k^*}{z_k} \sum_{j=0}^{\infty} (z_k)^{-j} S_{t-j}^* +$$
$$H_1^* \sum_{j=0}^{\infty} (\beta z_1^{-1})^j S_{t+j+1}^* + \cdots + H_k^* \sum_{j=0}^{\infty} (\beta z_k^{-1})^j S_{t+j+1}^*$$

for $t = -m, -m + 1, \ldots$ where $S_j^* = 0$ for $j < 0$. Let $A_1^*, \ldots, A_k^*, B_1^*, \ldots, B_k^*$ be n dimensional nonzero vectors such that $[H + D(\beta z_j^{-1})'D(z_j)]A_j^* = 0$ and $[H + D(z_j)'D(\beta z_j^{-1})]B_j^* = 0$. The general solution to the homogenous equation is

$$y_t^h = c_1 A_1^* z_1^{-t} + \cdots + c_k A_k^* z_k^{-t} +$$
$$f_1 B_1^* (\beta z_1^{-1})^{-t} + \cdots + f_k B_k^* (\beta z_k^{-1})^{-t}$$

where $c_1, \ldots, c_k, f_1, \ldots, f_k$ are arbitrary scalar constants. Fifth, obtain a general representation of the solutions to (A1) by adding y_t^p and y_t^h.

We have $m \times n = k$ initial conditions $y_{-1}, y_{-2}, \ldots, y_{-m}$. We also have the requirement that

$$\sum_{t=0}^{\infty} \beta^t y_t' H y_t < \infty \tag{A2}$$

where H is positive definite. Note that for nonzero f_j

$$\sum_{t=0}^{\infty} \beta^t f_j^2 (\beta z_1^{-1})^{-2t} B_j^{*'} H B_j^*$$

is not finite. Thus, (A2) is satisfied only if $f_j = 0$ for $j = 1, \ldots, k$. The initial condition vectors $y_{-1}, \ldots, y_{-m}$ uniquely determine $c_1, \ldots, c_k$. The solution provided in the text corresponds to the solution for y_t described above.

Appendix B

This appendix proves the assertions in the text about the factorization of the characteristic polynomial associated with the system of Euler equations. We state the assertions in the form of the following

LEMMA: The matrix polynomial in z, $[H + D(\beta z^{-1})'D(z)]$, has a representation

$$H + D(\beta z^{-1})'D(z) = C(\beta z^{-1})'C(z) \tag{B1}$$

where

$$C(z) = \sum_{j=0}^{m} C_j z^j,$$

each C_j is an $(n \times n)$ matrix, and all the roots of $det\ C(z) = 0$ in modulus are not less than $\sqrt{\beta}$. The factorization (B1) is unique up to premultiplication of $C(z)$ by an orthogonal matrix.

PROOF: Define the polynomial in z

$$J(z) = H + D(\beta z^{-1})'D(z)$$
$$\equiv H + \bar{D}(\sqrt{\beta}z^{-1})'\bar{D}\left(\frac{1}{\sqrt{\beta}}z\right)$$

(B2)

where

$$D(z) = \sum_{j=0}^{m} D_j z^j = \sum_{j=0}^{m} D_j(\sqrt{\beta})^j\left(\frac{1}{\sqrt{\beta}}z\right)^j.$$

So we have defined

$$\bar{D}(z) = \sum_{j=0}^{m} \bar{D}_j z^j$$

where $\bar{D}_j \equiv D_j(\sqrt{\beta})^j$. Notice that

$$D(\beta z^{-1})' = \sum_{j=0}^{m} D_j'(\sqrt{\beta})^j(\sqrt{\beta}z)^{-j}$$
$$= \bar{D}(\sqrt{\beta}z^{-1})'.$$

Also $D(z) = \bar{D}[(1/\sqrt{\beta})z]$. Now consider the function $F(z)$ defined as $F(z) = H + \bar{D}(z^{-1})'\bar{D}(z)$. The function $F(z)$ is the matrix cross covariance generating function of the n-dimensional covariance stationary stochastic process W defined by $W_t = Y_t + X_t$ where

$$EY_t Y_{t-s}' = \begin{cases} H & s = 0 \\ 0 & s \neq 0 \end{cases}$$

and $EY_t = 0$, $X_t = \bar{D}(L)'U_t$, $EU_t = 0$, $EU_t U_t' = I$, and $EY_t U_{t-s} = 0$ for all s. It follows from the factorization theorem for spectral density matrices (see Rozanov 1967) that we have the factorization of $F(z)$,

$$H + \bar{D}(z^{-1})'\bar{D}(z) = G(z^{-1})'G(z)$$

(B3)

where the roots of $G(z)$ do not lie inside the unit circle. The factorization is unique up to premultiplication of $G(z)$ by an orthogonal matrix. It immediately follows from (B2) that

$$H + D(\beta z^{-1})'D(z) = G(\sqrt{\beta}z^{-1})'G[(1/\sqrt{\beta})z]$$
$$\equiv C(\beta z^{-1})'C(z)$$

(B4)

where

$$C(z) = \sum_{j=0}^{m} C_j z^j$$

and $C_j = (1/\sqrt{\beta})^j G_j$. From the spectral factorization theorem we know that $det\ G(z) = \mu_0(1 - \mu_1 z)\ldots(1 - \mu_s z)$ where $s = nm$, and where $|\mu_j| \leq 1$. Thus,

$$det\ C(z) = det\ G\left(\frac{1}{\sqrt{\beta}}z\right) = \mu_0\left(1 - \mu_1\frac{1}{\sqrt{\beta}}z\right)\ldots\left(1 - \mu_s\frac{1}{\sqrt{\beta}}z\right).$$

(B5)

From (B5) we know that the roots of $det\ C(z)$ are not less than $\sqrt{\beta}$ in modulus. It also follows that the roots of $det\ C(\beta z^{-1})$ do not exceed $\sqrt{\beta}$ in modulus. This concludes the proof of the lemma.

Appendix C

This appendix provides explicit formulas for factoring $H + \bar{D}(z^{-1})'\bar{D}(z)$ where $n = 2$ and $m = 1$. Let $H + \bar{D}(z^{-1})'\bar{D}(z) = F(z)$, where we write

$$F(z) = \begin{bmatrix} f_{11}(z) & f_{12}(z) \\ f_{21}(z) & f_{22}(z) \end{bmatrix}$$

where we let

$$f_{11}(z) = \alpha_1 z^{-1} + \alpha_0 + \alpha_1 z$$
$$f_{22}(z) = \beta_1 z^{-1} + \beta_0 + \beta_1 z$$
$$f_{12}(z) = \gamma_{-1} z^{-1} + \gamma_0 + \gamma_1 z$$
$$f_{21}(z) = \gamma_1 z^{-1} + \gamma_0 + \gamma_{-1} z.$$

The factorization procedure involves the following three steps:

Step 1: Set $f_{11}(z) = \rho_0(1 - \rho_1 z)(1 - \rho_1 z^{-1})$, $|\rho_1| < 1$, $\rho_0 > 0$. This is accomplished by setting

$$\rho_1 = \frac{-\alpha_0 \pm \sqrt{\alpha_0^2 - 4\alpha_1^2}}{2\alpha_1} \qquad \text{subject to } |\rho_1| < 1$$

$$\rho_0 = -\frac{\alpha_1}{\rho_1}.$$

Step 2: Form $det\, F(z)$ and find the factorization $det\, F(z) = \kappa_0(1 - \kappa_1 z)(1 - \kappa_2 z)(1 - \kappa_1 z^{-1})(1 - \kappa_2 z^{-1})$, where $\kappa_0 > 0$, $|\kappa_1| < 1$, $|\kappa_2| < 1$. This is accomplished as follows. Let

$$a_2 = \alpha_1 \beta_1 - \gamma_{-1} \gamma_1$$
$$a_1 = \alpha_0 \beta_1 + \alpha_1 \beta_0 - \gamma_0(\gamma_1 + \gamma_{-1})$$
$$a_0 = \alpha_0 \beta_0 + 2\alpha_1 \beta_1 - \gamma_{-1}^2 - \gamma_1^2 - \gamma_0^2.$$

If $a_2 \neq 0$, set

$$\hat{\kappa}_1 = \frac{\dfrac{-a_1}{a_2} + \sqrt{\dfrac{a_1^2}{a_2^2} - 4\left(\dfrac{a_0}{a_2} - 2\right)}}{2}$$

$$\hat{\kappa}_2 = \frac{\dfrac{-a_1}{a_2} - \sqrt{\dfrac{a_1^2}{a_2^2} - 4\left(\dfrac{a_0}{a_2} - 2\right)}}{2}$$

$$\kappa_1 = \frac{\hat{\kappa}_1 \pm \sqrt{\hat{\kappa}_1^2 - 4}}{2} \qquad \text{subject to } |\kappa_1| < 1$$

$$\kappa_2 = \frac{\hat{\kappa}_2 \pm \sqrt{\hat{\kappa}_2^2 - 4}}{2} \qquad \text{subject to } |\kappa_2| < 1$$

$$\kappa_0 = \frac{a_2}{\kappa_1 \kappa_2}.$$

If $a_2 = 0$, set

$$\kappa_1 = 0$$

$$\kappa_2 = \frac{-a_0 \pm \sqrt{a_0^2 - 4a_1^2}}{2a_1} \qquad \text{subject to } |\kappa_2| < 1$$

$$\kappa_0 = -\frac{a_1}{\kappa_2}.$$

Step 3: Compute $G(z)$ where $G(z^{-1})'G(z) = F(z)$, where

$$G(z) = \begin{bmatrix} g_{11}(z) & g_{12}(z) \\ g_{21}(z) & g_{22}(z) \end{bmatrix}.$$

We compute $G(z)$ as follows. Define

$$\xi_0 = \gamma_{-1} + \gamma_0\rho_1 + \gamma_1\rho_1^2,$$
$$\xi_1 = \sqrt{\kappa_0}(1 - \kappa_1\rho_1)(1 - \kappa_2\rho_1)$$
$$\xi_2 = \sqrt{\xi_0^2 + \xi_1^2}$$
$$\psi_0 = \xi_0/\xi_2$$
$$\psi_1 = \xi_1/\xi_2$$
$$\kappa_3 = -(\kappa_1 + \kappa_2)$$

Then

$$g_{11}(z) = \psi_0\sqrt{\rho_0}(z - \rho_1)$$
$$g_{21}(z) = -\psi_1\sqrt{\rho_0}(1 - \rho_1 z)$$
$$g_{12}(z) = \frac{\psi_0\gamma_{-1} + \psi_1\sqrt{\kappa_0} + (\psi_0\gamma_0 + \rho_1\psi_0\gamma_{-1} + \rho_1\psi_1\sqrt{\kappa_0} + \psi_1\sqrt{\kappa_0}\kappa_3)z}{\sqrt{\rho_0}}$$
$$g_{22}(z) = \frac{\psi_1\gamma_{-1} - \psi_0\sqrt{\kappa_0} + (\psi_1\gamma_0 + \psi_1\gamma_{-1}\rho_1^{-1} - \psi_0\sqrt{\kappa_0}\kappa_3 - \psi_0\sqrt{\kappa_0}\rho_1^{-1})z}{\sqrt{\rho_0\rho_1}}.$$

References

Bertsekas, Dimitri P. *Dynamic Programming and Stochastic Control.* New York: Academic Press, 1976.

Emre, Erol, and Hüseyin, Özay. "Generalization of Leverrier's Algorithm to Polynomial Matrices of Arbitrary Degree." *IEEE Transactions on Automatic Control* (February 1975), p. 136.

Epple, D., and Hansen, L. "An Econometric Model of U.S. Petroleum Supply with Optimal Endogenous Depletion." Manuscript, April 1979.

Gould, J. P. "Adjustment Costs in the Theory of Investment of the Firm." *Rev. Econ. Studies* 35(1), no. 101 (1968): 47–56.

Granger, C. W. J. "Investigating Causal Relations by Econometric Models and Cross-Spectral Methods." *Econometrica* 37 (July 1969): 424–38.

Graves, R., and Telser, L. *Functional Analysis in Mathematical Economics.* Chicago: Univ. Chicago Press, 1971.

Hansen, Lars P., and Sargent, Thomas. "Formulating and Estimating Dynamic Linear Rational Expectations Models," *J. Econ. Dynamics and Control* 2 (February 1980): 7–46 [also chap. 7 in this vol.].

Holt, C.; Modigliani, F.; Muth, T. F.; and Simon, H. A. *Planning Production, Inventories and Work Force,* Englewood Cliffs, N.J.: Prentice Hall, 1960.

Kailath, Thomas. *Linear Systems.* Englewood Cliffs, N.J.: Prentice Hall, 1979.

Kennan, John. "The Estimation of Partial Adjustment Models with Rational Expectations." *Econometrica* (1980), in press.

Kushner, Harold. *Introduction to Stochastic Control.* New York: Holt, Rinehart & Winston, 1971.

Kwakernaak, H., and Sivan, R. *Linear Optimal Control Systems.* New York: Wiley, 1972.

Lucas, R. E., Jr. "Optimal Investment Policy and the Flexible Accelerator." *Internat. Econ. Rev.* 8, no. 1 (February 1967): 78–85. (*a*)

———. "Adjustment Costs and the Theory of Supply." *J.P.E.* 75, no. 4, pt. 1 (1967): 321–34. (*b*)

————. "Econometric Testing of the Natural Rate Hypothesis." In *The Econometrics of Price Determination Conference*, edited by Otto Eckstein. Washington: Board of Governors, Federal Reserve System, 1972.

————. "Econometric Policy Evaluation: A Critique." In *The Phillips Curve and Labor Markets*, edited by K. Brunner and A. H. Meltzer. Carnegie-Rochester Conference Series on Public Policy, vol. 1. Amsterdam: North-Holland, 1976.

Lucas, R. E., Jr., and Prescott, E. "Investment under Uncertainty." *Econometrica* 39 (September 1971): 659–81.

Mortensen, Dale. "Generalized Costs of Adjustment and Dynamic Factor Demand Theory." *Econometrica* 41 (1973): 657–65.

Murthy, D. N. P. "Factorization of Discrete-Process Spectral Matrices." *IEEE Transactions on Information Theory* (September 1973), pp. 693–96.

Nadiri, M., and Rosen, S. *A Disequilibrium Model of Demand for Factors of Production*. New York: Columbia Univ. Press, 1973.

Rozanov, Yu. A. *Stationary Random Processes*. San Francisco: Holden-Day, 1967.

Sargent, Thomas J. *Macroeconomic Theory*. New York: Academic Press, 1979.

————. "Lecture Notes on Linear Prediction and Control." Manuscript, Winter 1980.

Taylor, John B. "Output and Price Stability: An International Comparison." Manuscript, June 1978.

————. "Estimation and Control of a Macroeconomic Model with Rational Expectations." *Econometrica* (in press).

Treadway, Arthur B. "On Rational Entrepreneurial Behavior and the Demand for Investment." *Rev. Econ. Studies* 36(2), no. 106 (1969): 227–40.

————. "The Rational Multivariate Flexible Accelerator." *Econometrica* 39, no. 5 (September 1971): 845–55.

Whittle, P. *Regulation and Prediction by Linear Least Squares Methods*, Princeton, N.J.: Van Nostrand, 1963.

PART 2 Macroeconomic Policy

9

Rational Expectations, the Real Rate of Interest, and the Natural Rate of Unemployment

Thomas J. Sargent

The interaction of expected inflation and nominal rates of interest is a topic that has received its share of attention since Milton Friedman gave Irving Fisher's theory a prominent role in his presidential address to the American Economic Association in 1967.[1] The relationship between interest and expected inflation depends intricately on the interactions of the real and financial sectors of the economy, so that the subject of this paper lies in the domain of macroeconomic analysis. Partial equilibrium analysis won't do. Therefore, even though my main subject is the relationship between interest rates and expected inflation, there is no way to avoid such matters as the nature of the Phillips curve, the way expectations are formed, and, in some formulations, the sizes of various interest elasticities: those of the demand and supply for money and those of aggregate demand and its components.

Thus, consider Irving Fisher's theory. In one interpretation, it asserts that an exogenous increase in the rate of inflation expected to persist over a given horizon will produce an equivalent jump in the nominal yield on bonds of the corresponding maturity. That assertion concerns the way the whole economy is put together; in particular, it is about the reduced form equations for nominal rates of interest. If it is to hold, various restrictions must be imposed on the parameters of the structural equations of a macroeconomic model, which in turn imply important restrictions on the reduced form equations for endogenous variables besides the interest rate—for example, aggregate income and prices, variables that properly concern

The research underlying this paper was financed by the Federal Reserve Bank of Minneapolis, and earlier research that was an indirect input was supported by the National Bureau of Economic Research. Neither institution is responsible for the paper's conclusions. I benefited from discussions with Neil Wallace, Arthur Rolnick, Christopher A. Sims, and members of the Brookings panel, none of whom, however, can be held responsible for any errors. Thomas Turner provided valuable help with the calculations.

[1] Friedman (1968). One statement of Fisher's theory can be found in Fisher (1930).

[Brookings Papers on Economic Activity, 1973, vol. 2, ed. by Arthur M. Okun and George L. Perry]

policymakers more than do nominal interest rates. For example, in standard IS-LM-Phillips curve models,[2] the response of the interest rate to an
exogenous shock in expected inflation, like the response to any other shock
that affects aggregate demand, is distributed over time.[3] A once-and-for-
all jump in expected inflation eventually leaves the real rate of interest
unaltered, but in the short run drives it down and output up.[4] Only in the
special case in which the LM curve is vertical, the IS curve is horizontal, or
the short-run Phillips curve is vertical (price adjustments being instantaneous whenever employment threatens to deviate from full employment)
does an increase in expected inflation produce an immediate, equivalent
jump in the nominal interest rate.[5] These special sets of parameter values
obviously impart a very monetarist or classical sort of behavior to the
model.

On this interpretation of Fisher's theory, all of the parameters influencing the slopes of the IS, LM, and Phillips curves are pertinent in evaluating its adequacy. Conversely, evidence that the theory seems adequate
contains indirect implications about the parameters of the macroeconomic
structure, and therefore might have some clues relevant for evaluating the
relative efficacy of monetary and fiscal policies.

While the preceding statement of Fisher's theory may be of interest in
highlighting its macroeconomic content, the theory can be stated in an
alternative and less confining form, which probably comes closer to what
modern adherents to Fisher's doctrine have in mind. This statement is less
confining because its truth does not require any restrictions on the magnitudes of the slopes of the IS, LM, and short-run Phillips curves. Furthermore, it does not involve pursuing the implications of an exogenous jump
in expected inflation. Instead, expectations of inflation are assumed to be
endogenous to the system in a very particular way: they are assumed to be
"rational" in Muth's sense[6]—which is to say that the public's expectations
are not systematically worse than the predictions of economic models. This
amounts to supposing that the public's expectations depend, in the proper
way, on the things that economic theory says they ought to. Beyond this,
the alternative statement of Fisher's theory assumes that the Phelps-Friedman hypothesis of a natural rate of unemployment is true, and thus that
no (systematic) monetary or fiscal policies can produce a permanent effect
on the unemployment rate.[7] Given these two hypotheses (which are re-

---

[2] See, e.g., Bailey (1962, esp. pp. 49–54), which contains a good exposition of Fisher's theory
from the standpoint of the standard macroeconomic model.

[3] This point has been made by Kane (1973), among others.

[4] Some of Keynes' views about the effect of an increase in expected inflation on interest and
employment are contained in Keynes (1936, pp. 141–43).

[5] E.g., see Sargent (1972).

[6] Some very important implications of assuming rationality in Muth's (1961) sense in
certain kinds of models of forward markets were pointed out by Samuelson (1965).

[7] See Phelps 1972.

lated to one another, since it seems impossible to give the natural rate hypothesis a proper formal statement without invoking the hypothesis of rationality), it follows that the real rate of interest is independent of the systematic, or foreseen, part of the money supply, which therefore can influence the nominal rate only through effects on expected inflation.

The notion that the real rate of interest is independent of the systematic part of the money supply embodies the key aspect of Fisher's theory appealed to by Friedman in his presidential address. To obtain this property for the real rate requires no assumptions about the slopes of the IS, LM, and short-run Phillips curves, for rationality and the natural unemployment rate hypothesis are sufficient to support it. From this point of view, then, the important thing is not the response of the system to an exogenous shift in expected inflation.

It is important to determine the relationship that the standard way of empirically implementing Fisher's theory bears to the preceding statement of the theory. Irving Fisher and most of his followers[8] have implemented the theory by estimating a model of the form

$$r_t = \rho + \pi_t + u_t$$

$$\pi_t = \sum_{i=0}^{n} w_i(p_{t-i} - p_{t-i-1}),$$

where r_t is the nominal rate of interest, ρ is a constant, π_t is the unobservable expected rate of inflation, p_t is the logarithm of the price level, w_i and n are parameters, and u_t is a random error assumed to be distributed independently of past, present, and future values of p. These two equations have typically been combined to yield the equation

$$r_t = \sum_{i=0}^{n} w_i(p_{t-i} - p_{t-i-1}) + u_t + \rho,$$

which has been estimated by a variant of the method of least squares. The w_i's have been interpreted as estimates of the distributed lags by which the public forms its expectations of inflation. (Some of Fisher's followers have added some regressors in an effort to improve his equation.)[9]

Generally speaking, the results of estimating this equation have reflected poorly on the model. For data extending over very long periods of time, estimates of the w_i's depict extraordinarily long distributed lags, much too long to be useful in forming predictions of inflation. Consequently, the estimated w_i's do not seem to provide a plausible description of the way

---

[8] E.g., see Gibson 1970, and Yohe and Karnosky 1969.
[9] E.g., see Feldstein and Eckstein 1970.

people form expectations of inflation—at least if they do so in an informed way.[10] For this reason, Fisher's empirical results have often been viewed with suspicion.[11]

As it turns out, such negative empirical results carry no implications about the validity of the version of Fisher's theory considered here. Even if the theory is correct, there is in general no reason to expect that regressions of nominal interest rates on current and lagged rates of inflation should give distributed lag functions that could reasonably be used to form expectations of inflation. The theory cannot be tested by running regressions like Fisher's.

This paper is organized as follows. The first section describes a very simple and fairly standard macroeconomic model within which to analyze the relationship between interest and inflation. The second section takes a short detour from the main theme of the paper to analyze the interest-inflation relationship that obtains when expectations of inflation are generated by the standard "adaptive" mechanism, the usual assumption in empirical work. Here I briefly outline the restrictions on the macroeconomic structure necessary to rationalize the kind of procedure used by Fisher in his empirical work. Next comes a description of the behavior of the model embodying "rational" expectations; I show that under this assumption, the natural unemployment rate hypothesis and a version of Fisher's theory about the interest rate and expected inflation form a package. Proper empirical tests of the model are also discussed, and two of them are implemented. As it turns out, the most straightforward way to test the model is to test the natural unemployment rate hypothesis.

The argument in this paper is heavily dependent on the analysis of the natural rate hypothesis carried out by Lucas in a series of papers.[12] The proposition that the real interest rate is independent of the systematic part of the money supply, given both rationality and the natural rate hypothesis, follows quite directly from Lucas's work. In important ways, the structure of the argument in this paper resembles that of Friedman's presidential address, in which the close connection between the hypothesis of a natural rate of unemployment and Fisher's theory of the real rate of interest was brought out.

---

[10]This point has been made by Cagan (1965).

[11]Nerlove has proposed comparing regressions of dependent variables (like r_t) on current and lagged proxies for psychological expectations (like $p_t, p_{t-1}, \ldots$) with the distributed lags associated with the optimal forecast of the variables about which expectations are being formed (in this case inflation) on the basis of the regressors. See Nerlove (1967). An application of such a comparison to Fisher's equation, with the results confirming Cagan's doubts about the plausibility of long lags, is contained in Sargent (1973).

[12]Lucas and Rapping 1969; Lucas 1972, 1973a, 1973b, in press.

A Simple Macroeconomic Model

I assume a macroeconomic structure that can be described by the following equations:

Aggregate supply schedule: (1)

$$y_t = k_t + \gamma(p_t - {}_tp^*_{t-1}) + U_t, \qquad \gamma > 0;$$

Aggregate demand schedule, or IS curve: (2)

$$y_t = k_t + c[r_t - ({}_{t+1}p^*_t - p_t)] + dZ_t + \varepsilon_t, \qquad c < 0;$$

Portfolio balance schedule: (3)

$$m_t = p_t + y_t + br_t + \eta_t, \qquad b \leq 0.$$

Here y_t, p_t, and m_t are the natural logarithms of real national income, the price level, and the exogenous money supply, respectively; r_t is the nominal rate of interest itself (not its logarithm), while Z_t is a vector of exogenous variables. The parameters c, γ, and b are assumed to be scalars, while d is a vector conformable to Z_t.[13] The variables U_t, ε_t, and η_t are mutually uncorrelated, normally distributed random variables. They may be serially correlated. The variable ${}_{t+1}p^*_t$ is the public's psychological expectation as of time t of the logarithm of the price level expected to prevail at time $t + 1$. The variable k_t is a measure of "normal" productive capacity, such as the logarithm of the stock of labor or of capital or some linear combination of the two; it is assumed to be exogenous.

Equation (1) is an aggregate supply schedule relating the deviation of output from normal productive capacity directly to the gap between the current price level and the public's prior expectation of it. Unexpected rises in the price level thus boost aggregate supply, because suppliers mistakenly interpret surprise increases in the aggregate price level as increases in the relative prices of the labor or goods they are supplying. This mistake occurs because suppliers receive information about the prices of their own goods faster than they receive information about the aggregate price level. This is the kind of aggregate supply schedule that Lucas and Rapping (1969) have used to explain the inverse correlation between observed inflation and unemployment depicted by the Phillips curve.

Equation (2) is an aggregate demand or IS schedule showing that the deviation of aggregate demand from capacity is inversely related to the real rate of interest, which, in turn, equals the nominal rate r_t minus the

---

[13] All of the results carry through if c and b are assumed to be polynomials in the lag operator, so that the equations in which they appear involve distributed lags. Also, almost all of them carry through if the random terms are permitted to be correlated across equations. The only exceptions occur where the assumption that they are uncorrelated is used to rationalize a version of Fisher's equation under "adaptive" expectations.

rate of inflation expected by the public, $_{t+1}p_t^* - p_t$. The rate r_t is assumed to be the yield to maturity on a one-period bond. Aggregate demand also depends on a vector of exogenous variables, Z_t, which includes government expenditures and tax rates.[14]

Equation (3) summarizes the condition for portfolio balance. Owners of bonds and equities (which are assumed to be viewed as perfect substitutes for one another) are satisfied with the division of their portfolios between money, on the one hand, and bonds and equities, on the other, when equation (3) is satisfied. Equation (3) posits that the demand for real balances depends directly on real income and inversely on the nominal rate of interest.

To complete the model requires an hypothesis explaining the formation of the public's expectations of the price level. Here the behavior of the model will be analyzed under two such hypotheses: first, with one particular kind of ad hoc, extrapolative expectations, consistent with the formulation adopted in almost all empirical work on the Fisher relationship; and subsequently with the assumption that the public's expectations are "rational."

The Interest-Inflation Relationship under "Adaptive" Expectations

To equations (1), (2), and (3) I temporarily add the hypothesis

$$_{t+1}p_t^* = \sum_{i=0}^{\infty} v_i p_{t-i} \equiv v^* p_t, \tag{4}$$

where the v's are a set of parameters. Equation (4) is an example of the so-called adaptive expectations hypothesis proposed by Cagan (1956) and Friedman (1957). Given the exogenous variables m_t, k_t, and Z_t and the random terms U_t, ε_t, and η_t, equations (1)–(4) form a system that is capable of determining y_t, p_t, r_t, and $_{t+1}p_t^*$.

To obtain a version of the equation estimated by Fisher, substitute the expectation hypothesis (4) into the aggregate demand schedule (2), and solve for the nominal rate of interest:

$$r_t = v^* p_t - p_t + c^{-1}(y_t - k_t) - c^{-1}dZ_t - c^{-1}\varepsilon_t. \tag{5}$$

---

[14]The results would apply if c and d were polynomials in the lag operator; choosing those polynomials appropriately would be equivalent to putting lagged y's and k's in the aggregate demand schedule. For these results, an important thing about equation (2) is that it excludes as arguments both the money supply and the price level, apart from the latter's appearance as part of the real rate of interest. This amounts to ruling out direct real balance effects on aggregate demand. It also amounts to ignoring the expected rate of real capital gains on cash holdings as a component of the disposable income terms that belong in the expenditures schedules that underlie equation (2). Ignoring these things is usual in macroeconometric work.

This equation has a disturbance term, $-c^{-1}\varepsilon_t$, which is simply a linear function of the disturbance in the aggregate demand schedule, and so is in general correlated both with p and with $y - k$. Because of this correlation, single-equation methods like least squares ought not to be expected to provide reliable estimates of the parameters of (5). In general, random shocks to aggregate demand affect r, p, and $y - k$, contributing to the existence of a relationship between r and p quite apart from any effects of expected inflation on the interest rate. This influence poisons the data from the point of view of extracting estimates of the parameters of (5) by single-equation methods.

However, some restrictions can be placed on the parameters of the model so as to make p and $y - k$ independent of current and lagged ε's, thus rationalizing the statistical procedures used by Fisher and his followers. In particular, suppose that in the portfolio balance schedule, $b = 0$, so that the demand for money is independent of the nominal rate of interest. It is also essential that k_t, the measure of productive capacity, be exogenous and not dependent on current or past values of either the nominal or the real rate of interest. This requirement amounts to ruling out effects of the real rate of interest on the rate of formation of productive capacity. Given that $b = 0$, nominal aggregate output is determined by the portfolio balance schedule (3), which can be arranged to read

$$p_t + y_t = m_t - \eta_t. \tag{6}$$

The division of nominal output between real output and the price level is then determined by the aggregate supply schedule (1) and the expectations generator (4):

$$y_t - k_t = \gamma p_t - \gamma v^* p_{t-1} + U_t. \tag{7}$$

Equations (6) and (7) jointly determine p and y, so that aggregate demand plays no role in affecting either p or $y - k$; that is, the LM curve is vertical, so that shifts in the IS curve have no effects on output. The interest rate bears the full burden of equilibrating the system when shocks to aggregate demand occur. In such a system, ε is uncorrelated with both p and $y - k$, so that application of least squares to (5) can be expected to produce statistically consistent estimates. Note that if k depends on lagged values of the real rate of interest, it also depends on lagged values of ε. But then serial correlation of the ε's implies that least-squares estimates of (5) are not consistent, even if $b = 0$. Hence, k_t must be assumed independent of lagged real rates of interest in order to rationalize least-squares estimation of equation (5).

But the problem is more than a simple matter of statistical technique. Unless $b = 0$, a jump in expected inflation is not fully reflected immediately in the nominal rate of interest. To see this, let $(_{t+1}p_t^* - p_t)$ in equation (2) and $_t p_{t-1}^*$ in equation (1) both be exogenous, thus abandoning (4).

Then an exogenous jump in $(_{t+1}p_t^* - p_t)$ has the readily apparent effect of shifting the IS curve upward in the r, $(y - k)$ plane by exactly the amount of the shift. Unless $b = 0$, making the LM curve vertical, the upward shift in the IS curve increases r, but by less than the increase in $(_{t+1}p_t^* - p_t)$; $y - k$ also increases. How much of the adjustment to a jump in expected inflation is borne by the nominal interest rate and how much by real output depends on the slopes of the IS curve, the LM curve, and the short-run Phillips curve. The nominal interest rate bears more of the burden of adjustment the steeper is the LM curve, the flatter is the IS curve, and the more responsive are prices to output in the short-run Phillips curve—that is, the steeper is the short-run Phillips curve.[15]

In summary, useful estimates of the parameters of Fisher's equation (5) can be expected only where both $b = 0$ and k_t is independent of current and past real rates of interest. The first restriction is extremely "monetarist" in character, implying a "quantity theory" world. Many economists would have little faith in the correctness of these restrictions, making estimation of (5) an endeavor of questionable value from their point of view. But at least there exists a set of restrictions on the economic structure that makes (5) a sensible equation to estimate. As far as I can determine, no set of restrictions on the parameters of a standard Keynesian model, like the one formed by equations (1)-(4), can be used to rationalize some of the equations fitted in the literature on price expectations and the interest rate.[16]

Behavior of the Model under Rational Expectations

The implementation of Fisher's theory described in the preceding section is subject to two severe limitations. First, its appropriateness depends on the adequacy of some very tight restrictions on the slopes of the LM curve, the IS curve, and the short-run Phillips curve. Second, equation (4) has often been criticized as an excessively naive theory of expectations, since it fails to incorporate the possibility that people form expectations about the price level by using information other than current and lagged prices. One tractable way of meeting this second criticism is to hypothesize that the

---

[15]On this, see Bailey (1962), and Sargent (1972).

[16]E.g., Robert J. Gordon has regressed a nominal interest rate on current and past inflation and current and past velocity (i.e., the nominal income-money ratio), interpreting the coefficients on current and lagged inflation as estimates of the weights that people use in forming price expectations. I know of no way of interpreting such an equation either as a structural equation or as a reduced form equation, at least within the class of Keynesian macroeconomic models of which the simple model here is a member. See Gordon (1970, pp. 8-47). Also see Gordon's "Discussion" in *Econometrics of Price Determination*. The point being made here is developed in greater detail in Sargent (1973). It should be noted that Gordon (1971) has estimated a much improved equation. That equation can be regarded as the reduced form for the interest rate, on the assumption that prices are exogenous.

expectations of the public are rational in the sense of Muth (1961) and
Samuelson (1965), and are thus equivalent with the optimal predictions of
economic and statistical theory. For purposes of the analysis here, this
hypothesis would involve assuming that the public (a) knows the true
reduced form for the price level, (b) knows the probability distributions or
rules governing the evolution of the exogenous variables, and (c) combines
this information to form optimal (least-squares) forecasts of the price level.
Two reasons might be given for entertaining the hypothesis that expectations are rational. First, it makes concrete and operational the appealing
notion that people use information besides past prices in forming their
forecasts of the price level. Second, in certain instances it has been possible
to test the hypothesis empirically by using the test proposed by Samuelson,
and the hypothesis has fared pretty well when tested on data on stock
prices, commodities prices, and interest rates (Samuelson 1965).[17]

When (4) is replaced with the assumption that expectations are rational,
the system formed by equations (1), (2), and (3) implies a version of Fisher's theory in which the real rate of interest is statistically independent of
the systematic part of the money supply, so that foreseen changes in the
money supply affect the nominal rate of interest only to the extent that
they alter the expected rate of inflation. This result holds regardless of the
magnitudes of the slopes of the IS, LM, and short-run Phillips curves. (In
fact, for the model to possess an equilibrium, b must be strictly less than
zero.) In this section, I propose to show that the invariance of the real rate
of interest with respect to the systematic part of the money supply requires
only (a) the assumption of an aggregate supply schedule like (1), and (b)
the assumption that expectations are rational.

To close the model formed by equations (1), (2), and (3), I now posit
that expectations about the logarithm of the price level are rational. This
amounts to requiring that

$$_{t+1}p_t^* = \underset{t}{E}\, p_{t+1},\tag{8}$$

where $\underset{t}{E}\, p_{t+1}$ is the conditional mathematical expectation of p_{t+1} formed
using the model and information about the exogenous and endogenous
variables available as of time t. Equation (8) asserts equality between the
psychological expectation $_{t+1}p_t^*$ and the objective conditional expectation
$\underset{t}{E}\, p_{t+1}$.

To complete the model under (8), I must specify the behavior of the
exogenous variables and random terms that condition the expectation in

[17]The evidence is reviewed by Fama (1970). Evidence that the hypothesis of rational
expectations can be combined with the expectations theory of the term structure to produce a
workable explanation of the term structure is presented in Shiller (1972). Also see Modigliani
and Shiller (1973).

(8). I assume that the money supply is governed by the linear feedback rule

$$
\begin{aligned}
m_{t+1} = &\sum_{i=0}^{\infty} w_i m_{t-i} + \sum_{i=0}^{\infty} v_i^1 \varepsilon_{t-i} + \sum_{i=0}^{\infty} v_i^2 U_{t-i} \\
&+ \sum_{i=0}^{\infty} v_i^3 \eta_{t-i} + \sum_{i=0}^{\infty} v_i^4 k_{t-i} + \sum_{i=0}^{\infty} v_i^5 Z_{t-i} + \xi_{mt+1},
\end{aligned}
\tag{9}
$$

where the w_i's and v_i^j's are parameters and ξ_{mt} is a normally distributed, serially uncorrelated random variable with mean zero; ξ_{mt+1} satisfies $E(\xi_{mt+1}|m_t, m_{t-1}, \ldots, \varepsilon_t, \varepsilon_{t-1}, \ldots, Z_t, \ldots) = 0$ and represents the random part of the money supply that cannot be predicted on the basis of past variables. This part might well result from deliberate policymaking decisions, but simply cannot be predicted on the basis of information about the state of the economy. The remaining, systematic, part of the money supply, which in (9) is represented by distributed lags in all of the disturbances and exogenous variables appearing in the model, can be predicted perfectly, given the values of all current and lagged exogenous variables and disturbances. Since each endogenous variable is a linear combination of the exogenous variables and the disturbances, any sort of linear feedback from the exogenous and endogenous variables to the money supply can be represented by (9). Thus, one justification for assuming (9) is that it is a very general rule capable of encompassing feedback from, for example, prices, output, and the interest rate to the money supply. Furthermore, for a linear model with known coefficients and a quadratic loss function, feedback rules of the form (9) with $\xi_{mt+1} = 0$ are known to be optimal.[18]

The random terms ε_t, U_t, and η_t, and the exogenous variables Z_t and k_t are each governed by an autoregressive process

$$
\begin{aligned}
\varepsilon_{t+1} &= \rho_\varepsilon^* \varepsilon_t + \xi_{\varepsilon t+1} \\
U_{t+1} &= \rho_U^* U_t + \xi_{U t+1} \\
\eta_{t+1} &= \rho_\eta^* \eta_t + \xi_{\eta t+1} \\
k_{t+1} &= \rho_k^* k_t + \xi_{k t+1} \\
Z_{t+1} &= \rho_Z^* Z_t + \xi_{Z t+1},
\end{aligned}
\tag{10}
$$

where $\rho_\varepsilon^* \varepsilon_t \equiv \Sigma_{i=0}^{\infty} \rho_{\varepsilon_i} \varepsilon_{t-i}$, and so on. Here the ξ's are mutually uncorrelated, serially uncorrelated, normally distributed random variables with means zero.

The public is assumed to know, or at least to have estimated, the parameters of (9) and (10). Where required, it uses this knowledge to calculate the pertinent expectations or least-squares forecasts. Then, given the sys-

---

[18]Except for the fact that I have added the stochastic term ξ_{mt}, this is an example of the kind of linear feedback rule studied by Chow (1970).

tem formed by equations (1), (2), (3), (8), (9), and (10), the equilibrium price level can be written as a function of current and past m, k, Z, ε, η, and U:

$$p_t = R(m_t, m_{t-1}, \ldots, k_t, k_{t-1}, \ldots, Z_t, Z_{t-1}, \ldots,$$
$$\varepsilon_t, \varepsilon_{t-1}, \ldots, \eta_t, \eta_{t-1}, \ldots, U_t, U_{t-1}, \ldots),$$
$$(11)$$

which is the reduced form for the price level. This reduced form equation builds in the fact that p_t is influenced by $\underset{t}{E} p_{t+1}$. But p_{t+1} will be influenced by $\underset{t+1}{E} p_{t+2}$, so that $\underset{t}{E} p_{t+1}$ will depend on $\underset{t}{E} p_{t+2}$, and so on, and this must be taken into account under rationality. Appendix A, where R is calculated explicitly, shows how forecasts of next period's price are forced, through this dependence, to take into account forecasts of the values of the exogenous variables influencing the price level in all subsequent periods.[19] In forming these expectations, individuals consider the money supply rule (9) and the autoregressions for the disturbances and exogenous variables (10). The parameters of equations (9) and (10) are thereby built into the reduced form R of (11).Consequently, the parameters of the reduced form R depend on *both* the structural parameters of the model and the parameters of the monetary rule (9) and the autoregressions (10). The parameters of (11) will thus not be invariant with respect to systematic changes in the money supply rule that have either been publicly announced or in effect long enough for the public to detect them.[20]

The reduced form equation (11) can be combined with the money supply rule (9) and the laws governing the random terms and exogenous variables (10) to yield the probability distribution of p_{t+1}, conditional on data observed up through time t:

$$Prob(p_{t+1} < F \mid m_t = m_0, m_{t-1} = m_1, \ldots, k_t = k_0, k_{t-1} = k_1, \ldots,$$
$$Z_t = Z_0, Z_{t-1} = Z_1, \ldots, \varepsilon_t = \varepsilon_0, \varepsilon_{t-1} = \varepsilon_1, \ldots,$$
$$U_t = U_0, U_{t-1} = U_1, \ldots, \eta_t = \eta_0, \eta_{t-1} = \eta_1, \ldots) \quad (12)$$
$$= H(F, m_0, m_1, \ldots, k_0, k_1, \ldots, Z_0, Z_1, \ldots,$$
$$\varepsilon_0, \varepsilon_1, \ldots, U_0, U_1, \ldots, \eta_0, \eta_1, \ldots).$$

The conditional expectation in (8) is evaluated with respect to (12):

$$\underset{t+1}{p_t^*}$$
$$= E(p_{t+1} \mid m_t, m_{t-1}, \ldots, k_t, k_{t-1}, \ldots, Z_t, Z_{t-1}, \ldots, \varepsilon_t, \ldots, U_t, \ldots, \eta_t) \quad (13)$$
$$= \int_{-\infty}^{\infty} F \, dH(F \mid m_t, m_{t-1}, \ldots, k_t, k_{t-1}, \ldots, Z_t, Z_{t-1}, \ldots, \varepsilon_t, \ldots, U_t, \ldots, \eta_t).$$

[19] Such an equilibrium is calculated for a nonstochastic model by Hall (1971). For a linear, stochastic model, an example of such an equilibrium is calculated by Sargent and Wallace (1973). Also see Lucas (1972).

[20] The implications for the theory of economic policy of this characteristic of models with rational expectations are carefully drawn out by Lucas (in press).

For convenience, let θ_t denote the set of variables upon which the expectation (13) is conditioned, so that

$$_{t+1}p_t^* = E(p_{t+1}|\theta_t), \tag{13'}$$

where θ_t includes all observations on m, k, Z, ε, U, and η dated t and earlier.

It is now easy to show that the system is described by two intimately related propositions that reflect central aspects of the monetarist point of view. First, a natural rate of output exists in the sense that the deviation of output from its normal level is statistically independent of the systematic parts of monetary and fiscal policies; that is, widely known changes in the w's and v's of equation (9) and in the ρz's of equation (10) have no effects on the expected value of ($y - k$). Second, the real rate of interest is independent of the systematic part of the money supply; that is, alterations in the w's and v's of the feedback rule (9) have no effects on the expected value of the real rate. (Random movements in the money supply, represented by ξ_{mt}, do have effects on both aggregate supply and the real rate of interest.)

The first of these propositions, which is due to Lucas (1972, 1973a, in press), follows from a simple and well-known property that, under rationality, characterizes the prediction error that appears in the aggregate supply schedule (1). Using (13'), the prediction error is

$$p_t - E(p_t|\theta_{t-1}).$$

The regression of the prediction error on θ_{t-1} is

$$E\{[p_t - E(p_t|\theta_{t-1})]|\theta_{t-1}\} = E(p_t|\theta_{t-1}) - E(p_t|\theta_{t-1}) = 0,$$

which shows that the prediction error is independent of all elements of θ_{t-1}. Substituting this result into the conditional expectation of equation (1) gives

$$E[(y_t - k_t)|\theta_{t-1}] = E(U_t|\theta_{t-1}) = E(U_t|U_{t-1}, U_{t-2}, \ldots). \tag{14}$$

Since U_t depends only on lagged U's, equation (14) shows that $y - k$ is independent of all components of θ_{t-1} except lagged values of U. That part of the current money supply (or the fiscal policy variables in Z_t) that can be expressed as a linear combination of the elements of θ_{t-1} (that is, the "systematic" part of policy) therefore has no effect on the expected value of $y_t - k_t$, regardless of the parameters of that linear combination.

The second proposition—that the real rate of interest is independent of the systematic part of the money supply rule—stands and falls with Lucas's natural rate proposition.[21] Solving equation (2) for the nominal

[21] The result requires that both m and p be excluded from the aggregate demand schedule, except for the latter's appearance as part of the term $E_t p_{t+1} - p_t$. As mentioned in note 14, this seems to be a standard specification in macroeconometric models. It is, however, well known that including a real balance effect in the aggregate demand schedule modifies Fisher's theory in a static, full employment context. See Mundell (1963). The expected rate of inflation can be viewed as the rate of tax on real balances. Where $m_t - p_t$ appears in the

rate of interest gives

$$r_t = c^{-1}(y_t - k_t) - \frac{d}{c}Z_t + E(p_{t+1}|\theta_t) - p_t - c^{-1}\varepsilon_t. \tag{15}$$

Taking expectations in (15) conditional on θ_{t-1} and substituting from (14) gives

$$E\{[r_t - E(p_{t+1}|\theta_t) + p_t]|\theta_{t-1}\}$$
$$= -\frac{d}{c}E(Z_t|\theta_{t-1}) + c^{-1}E(U_t|\theta_{t-1}) - c^{-1}E(\varepsilon_t|\theta_{t-1}). \tag{16}$$

Equation (16) states that the real rate of interest is correlated with elements of θ_{t-1} only to the extent that they help predict subsequent values of the random variables U_t and ε_t and subsequent fiscal policy—that is, the variables in Z_t. Of course, U_t depends only on lagged U's, while ε_t depends only on lagged ε's. The real rate of interest is therefore a function of the systematic parts of fiscal policy, but is independent of the parameters that determine the systematic part of the money supply. In this system changes in the money supply at t that can be foreseen as of time $t-1$ leave the real interest rate at t unchanged. It follows that the systematic part of the money supply affects the nominal rate of interest only to the extent that it influences the expected rate of inflation. The only part of the money supply at t that affects the real rate at t is the random component ξ_{mt}.

Results of Changing Aspects of the Model

These two propositions will characterize models much more complicated than the one used here so long as expectations are assumed to be rational and aggregate supply is governed by an equation like (1).[22] For example,

---

aggregate demand schedule—either alone, as in the real balance effect, or multiplied by minus the expected rate of inflation, as implied by some definitions of disposable income— changes in the expected rate of inflation bring about changes in the real rate of interest, just as do changes in the other tax rates included in Z_t.

[22] The behavior of the model under rational expectations would not be sustantially altered if the aggregate supply hypothesis were expanded to be

$$y_t - k_t = \gamma\left[p_t - \underset{t-1}{E}\,p_t - \left(\frac{1}{n}\sum_{j=1}^{n_1}\underset{t}{E}\,p_{t+j} - \frac{1}{n}\sum_{j=1}^{n}\underset{t-1}{E}\,p_{t+j}\right)\right] + U_t,$$

which states that aggregate supply responds to the "surprise" component of this period's price level minus the amount by which an average of expectations of prices in n future periods is revised as a result of new information received this period. The above equation embodies the notion that aggregate supply responds to the part of the prediction error $p_t - \underset{t-1}{E}\,p_t$ that is viewed as transitory. The argument in the above equation still possesses all of the properties of prediction errors that are used in the text to show the behavior of the model under rationality.

By invoking the expectations theory of the term structure of interest rates, yields on bonds with maturities greater than one period could be included in the model. It would be straightforward, for example, to enter an n-period rate in the aggregate demand schedule, modifying the price expectation term accordingly, while keeping a one-period rate in the portfolio balance curve.

the two propositions would continue to hold if the assumption of exogenous productive capacity k_t is abandoned and instead k_t is assumed to depend on past values of output and the real rate of interest. This specification would permit growth in capacity to be influenced by capital accumulation, which in turn could be governed by a version of the distributed lag accelerator.

For another modification that would leave the two propositions intact, (1) might be replaced with the alternative aggregate supply schedule

$$y_t - k_t = \gamma(p_t - Ep_t | \theta_{t-1}) + \sum_{i=1}^{q} \lambda_i (y_{t-i} - k_{t-i}) + U_t, \qquad (1')$$

which application of the Koyck-Jorgenson transformation shows to be equivalent to

$$y_t - k_t = \gamma \sum_{i=0}^{\infty} \phi_i [p_{t-i} - E(p_{t-i} | \theta_{t-i-1})] + \sum_{i=0}^{\infty} \phi_i U_{t-1}, \qquad (1'')$$

where the ϕ_i's are functions of the λ_i's. According to $(1')$, deviations of aggregate supply from normal capacity output display some persistence, so that $y_t - k_t$ depends partly on a distributed lag of prediction errors, as equation $(1'')$ shows. If $(1'')$ replaces (1) in the version of the model with rational expectations, both $y_t - k_t$ and the real rate of interest remain independent of the systematic part of the money supply. To see this, one has only to note that the systematic parts of current and lagged values of the money supply contribute nothing to the prediction errors that appear in $(1'')$, nor do they influence the U's. Of course, the random parts of the money supply, ξ_m, will still influence $y - k$. Under $(1'')$, the effects of ξ_m on $y - k$ will be distributed over time, but the two propositions about the systematic parts of policy variables remain unaltered.

In essence, two features of the model must hold to validate these propositions. First, expectations must be rational. Second, the model must possess "super-neutrality," by which I mean that proportionate changes in either the levels or the rates of change of all endogenous and exogenous variables denominated in dollars (prices, wages, and stocks of paper assets of fixed dollar value such as money and bonds) do not disturb an initial equilibrium. It should be noted that current and expected values of endogenous and exogenous nominal variables are among those changed proportionately in the experiment defining super-neutrality.

Appendix B demonstrates that key features of the results remain intact even when individuals have much less information and wisdom than I have imputed to them so far, so long as they have access to information at least about lagged prices and use it rationally in forecasting the price level. Appendix B also shows that dropping the assumption that bonds and equities are perfect substitutes does not change the essential character of the model.

Testing the Model

A "Wrong" Test

The usual way of implementing Fisher's theory about interest and expected inflation has been to regress nominal interest rates on current and lagged values of the logarithm of the price level, interpreting the coefficients as estimates of the distributed lag by which the public seems to form its expectations about inflation. The implausibility of those distributed lags as devices for forming predictions of inflation has weakened the appeal of Fisher's doctrine. However, according to the version of the model with rational expectations described here, these regressions are not a valid test. In particular, there is no reason to expect that the distributed lags estimated in such regressions provide the basis for plausible, or in some sense optimal, forecasts of inflation. This is so even though the model predicts that the real rate of interest is independent of the money supply rule, a proposition that can be taken as capturing the essence of Fisher's theory.

To establish the inappropriate nature of the standard regressions, I use equation (15) to calculate the regression of the nominal interest rate on current and lagged prices:

$$E(r_t \mid p_t, p_{t-1}, \ldots) = E[(p_{t+1} - p_t) \mid p_t, p_{t-1}, p_{t-2}, \ldots]$$
$$+ c^{-1}E(U_t \mid p_t, p_{t-1}, \ldots) - \frac{d}{c}E(Z_t \mid p_t, p_{t-1}, \ldots) \tag{17}$$
$$+ c^{-1}\gamma E\{[p_t - E(p_t \mid \theta_{t-1})] \mid p_t, p_{t-1}, \ldots\}$$
$$- c^{-1}E(\varepsilon_t \mid p_t, p_{t-1}, \ldots).$$

Regressions of interest on current and lagged prices have been interpreted as yielding estimates of the regression $E[(p_{t+1} - p_t) \mid p_t, p_{t-1}, \ldots]$. In the model here, however, that interpretation is erroneous because of the presence of the second, third, fourth, and fifth terms in (17). The model predicts that the exogenous variables Z_t will be correlated with current and perhaps past values of the price level. The model also predicts that ε_t and U_t will be correlated with the current price level: a positive "pip" in ε_t increases both r_t and p_t, an effect that has nothing to do with the formation of expectations of inflation.[23] The presence of this effect pollutes the relationship between r and p from the point of view of extracting an estimate of $E[(p_{t+1} - p_t) \mid p_t, p_{t-1}, \ldots]$. The presence of the third and fourth terms similarly biases the regression of r on current and past p's taken as a device for recovering forecasts of inflation.

The biases pinpointed by equation (17) could easily be spectacularly large and could in principle give rise to the presence of a Gibson paradox in data generated by the model. Very long and implausible distributed

---

[23]This is presumably the kind of effect that Tobin (1968) had in mind when he questioned Irving Fisher's explanation of the Gibson paradox.

lags of interest on inflation could be generated, since the model embodies sources of dependence between the interest rate and price *level* that are not accounted for by the presence of expected inflation. This fact implies that demonstrations of the "implausibility" of regressions of interest on inflation cannot refute the version of Fisher's theory embodied in the model.

A "Proper" Test

The straightforward approach to testing the model would be to subject the theory's centerpiece, the natural rate hypothesis, to an empirical test. However, as Lucas (1972) has forcefully pointed out, almost all such work has been wholly inadequate. Basically, these improper tests[24] have all involved fitting a structure that can be rearranged to yield an expression for unemployment of the following form:

$$Un_t = \widehat{\beta}(p_t - \sum_{i=1}^{n} \widehat{v}_i p_{t-i}) + \text{residual}_t, \qquad (18)$$

where the unemployment rate Un_t can be regarded as an inverse index of $y_t - k_t$. In every case, $\widehat{\beta}$ has been less than 0, indicating a short-run trade-off between inflation and employment. The standard test of the natural rate hypothesis has been to determine whether, according to the estimates of equation (18), a once-and-for-all increase in the rate of inflation implies a permanent change in the unemployment rate.[25] But even if it doesn't, a once-and-for-all jump in some higher-order difference in the (log of the) price level will always imply a permanent change in the unemployment rate in the context of equation (18) with any fixed set of $\widehat{v}_i$'s. Thus, if the authorities can make the price level follow a path

$$p_t = \sum_{i=1}^{n} \widehat{v}_i p_{t-i} + \phi,$$

they can, by increasing ϕ by $d\phi$, have a permanent, predictable effect on unemployment of $\widehat{\beta}d\phi$. This conclusion, however, is incompatible with the natural rate hypothesis, which requires that certain, foreseen, once-and-

---

[24] The test was described by both Robert Solow and James Tobin in their contributions to the *Proceedings of a Symposium on Inflation.* One of the best-known applications of the test is Gordon (1970).

[25] Usually, the weights are constrained to satisfy $\sum_{i=1}^{\infty} \widehat{v}_i = 1$, so that a once-and-for-all jump in the log of the price level is *not* permitted to imply a permanent change in the unemployment rate.

for-all jumps in *any* order difference of the price level have no permanent effect on the unemployment rate. Put another way, the natural rate hypothesis requires that changing from one deterministic (and hence perfectly predictable) process for the price level to another will leave the unemployment rate unaltered. *No* values of the $\hat{v}_i$'s of equation (18) are capable of representing that hypothesis, given the way the estimated $\hat{v}_i$'s are manipulated in the test. The test, therefore, cannot possibly be fair (again, see Lucas 1972).

Lucas (1973*b*) has described and implemented two proper tests of the rational expectations version of the natural rate hypothesis. One involves testing a set of cross-equation restrictions implied by the hypothesis, the other, testing across countries for a relationship between the slope of a country's short-run inflation-unemployment tradeoff and the variance of its nominal aggregate demand implied by the hypothesis. Lucas is unable to reject the natural rate hypothesis on the basis of either of these tests.

Although, to my knowledge, Lucas's are the only proper tests of the natural rate hypothesis implemented to date, there are other tests of the natural rate hypothesis. One exploits the implications under rationality of the hypothesis that aggregate supply is a function of the error in predicting the current price level on the basis of data available at some previous moment. Using the unemployment rate Un_t as an inverse index of $y_t - k_t$, the aggregate supply schedule (1′) can be written

$$ Un_t = \beta(p_t - Ep_t \,|\, \theta_{t-1}) + \sum_{i=1}^{q} \lambda_i Un_{t-i} + u_t, \qquad \beta < 0. \qquad (19) $$

Here u_t is a random disturbance assumed to be normally distributed and to obey $E(u_t \,|\, \theta_{t-1}, u_{t-1}, u_{t-2}, \ldots) = E(u_t \,|\, u_{t-1}, u_{t-2}, \ldots)$. To take a special example that will illustrate the idea behind the test, suppose that u_t is not serially correlated and that all of the λ_i's equal zero. Taking expectations in (19) conditional on any subset θ_{lt-1} of θ_{t-1} gives $E(Un_t \,|\, \theta_{lt-1}) = 0$, an implication that could be tested empirically by regressing Un_t on components of θ_{lt-1}. However, the presence of nonzero λ_i's or serial correlation in u_t would destroy this implication, since then

$$ E(Un_t \,|\, \theta_{lt-1}, Un_{t-1}, \ldots, Un_{t-q}) = \sum_{i=1}^{q} \lambda_i Un_{t-i} + E(u_t \,|\, \theta_{lt-1}) \neq 0. $$

The term $\sum_{i=1}^{q} \lambda_i Un_{t-i}$ obviously would not be zero; if u_t is serially correlated, then $E(u_t \,|\, \theta_{lt-1})$ also departs from zero to the extent that components of θ_{lt-1} proxy for lagged u's.

To illustrate how a feasible test could be carried out under these circumstances, suppose that u_t follows the first-order Markov process

$u_t = \rho u_{t-1} + \xi_{ut}$, with $|\rho| < 1$, where ξ_{ut} is a normally distributed, serially uncorrelated random variable. Then notice that (19) can be written as

$$Un_t = (\lambda_1 + \rho)Un_{t-1} + \sum_{i=2}^{q} (\lambda_i - \rho\lambda_{i-1})Un_{t-i} - \rho\lambda_q Un_{t-q-1} \qquad (20)$$

$$+ \beta(p_t - Ep_t|\theta_{t-1}) - \beta\rho(p_{t-1} - Ep_{t-1}|\theta_{t-2}) + \xi_{ut}.$$

Taking expectations in (20) conditional on $Un_{t-1}, \ldots, Un_{t-q-1}$ and any subset θ_{lt-2} of θ_{t-2} yields

$$E(Un_t \mid Un_{t-1}, \ldots, Un_{t-q-1}, \theta_{lt-2}) = (\lambda_1 + \rho)Un_{t-1}$$

$$+ \sum_{i=2}^{q} (\lambda_i - \rho\lambda_{i-1})Un_{t-i} - \rho\lambda_q Un_{t-q-1} \qquad (21)$$

$$- \rho\beta E[(p_{t-1} - Ep_{t-1}|\theta_{t-2})| Un_{t-1}].$$

Equation (21) holds because the prediction error $p_t - Ep_t|\theta_{t-1}$ is independent of all components of θ_{t-1}, which include the regressors in (21), while the lagged prediction error is independent of $Un_{t-2}, \ldots, Un_{t-q-1}$ and θ_{lt-2}, but not of Un_{t-1}. According to (21), the regression of the unemployment rate against $Un_{t-1}, \ldots, Un_{t-q-1}$, and some components of θ_{t-2} ought, on the natural rate hypothesis, to have zero coefficients on components of θ_{t-2}. This implication can be tested empirically by calculating the regression indicated in (21). If $\rho = 0$, then (20) implies that

$$E(Un_t \mid Un_{t-1}, \ldots, Un_{t-q-1}, \theta_{t-1}) = E(Un_t \mid Un_{t-1}, \ldots, Un_{t-q-1}),$$

so that if the u's in (19) are serially uncorrelated, components of θ_{t-1} ought not to obtain coefficients significantly different from zero when they are added to a regression of Un_t on enough lagged values of itself. On the other hand, if u_t is governed by an nth order autoregressive process

$$u_t = \sum_{i=1}^{n} \rho_i u_{t-i} + \xi_{ut},$$

where ξ_{ut} has the same properties imputed to it above, then it is readily shown that the natural rate hypothesis implies only that

$$E(Un_t \mid Un_{t-1}, Un_{t-2}, \ldots, Un_{t-n-q}, \theta_{lt-n-1})$$
$$= E(Un_t \mid Un_{t-1}, Un_{t-2}, \ldots, Un_{t-n-q}).$$

The higher the order of serial correlation in the u's, the more periods components of θ_t must be lagged to warrant the implication that their coefficients are zero.

    One can view the test from a slightly different perspective by considering the following very general mixed autoregressive, moving-average representation of the unemployment rate,

$$Un_t = \sum_{i=1}^{q} \lambda_i Un_{t-i} + \sum_{i=0}^{f} \alpha_i \xi_{ut-i}, \tag{22}$$

where the λ_i's and α_i's are parameters and where ξ_{ut} is again a serially uncorrelated, normally distributed random variable. The natural rate hypothesis can be viewed as permitting ξ_{ut} to be correlated with values of endogenous variables dated t and later, but as requiring ξ_{ut} to be uncorrelated with past endogenous and exogenous variables, so that $E(\xi_{ut} \mid \theta_{t-1}) = 0$. This means that the "innovation," or new random part of the unemployment rate, cannot be predicted from past values of any variables, and that it cannot be affected by movements in past values of government policy variables. This specification captures the heart of the natural unemployment rate hypothesis, and implies that there is no better way to predict subsequent rates of unemployment than fitting and extrapolating a mixed autoregressive, moving-average process in the unemployment rate itself. This suggests that the natural unemployment rate hypothesis can be tested against specific competing hypotheses by setting up statistical prediction "horse races." My proposed regression test is an alternative test, and exploits the notion that, if $E(\xi_{ut} \mid \theta_{t-1}) = 0$, then (22) implies that

$$E(Un_t \mid Un_{t-1}, \ldots, Un_{t-q}, \theta_{t-f-1}) = \sum_{i=1}^{q} \lambda_i Un_{t-i}.$$

To provide material for the test, regressions (1), shown below, are autogressions for the unemployment rate.

$$Un_t = 0.418 + 1.715 \, Un_{t-1} - 1.046 \, Un_{t-2} + 0.245 \, Un_{t-3} \tag{1}$$
$$(0.164) \quad (0.116) \qquad (0.199) \qquad \quad (0.115)$$

$\bar{R}^2 = 0.9245$, standard error of estimate $= 0.318$, Durbin-Watson statistic $= 1.984$.
Period of fit: 1952:1–1970:4.

$$Un_t = 0.538 + 1.553 \, Un_{t-1} - 0.665 \, Un_{t-2},$$
$$(0.158) \quad (0.089) \qquad (0.089)$$

$\bar{R}^2 = 0.9208$, standard error of estimate $= 0.325$, Durbin-Watson statistic $= 1.616$.
Period of fit: 1952: 1–1970:4.

where Un is the unemployment rate for all civilian workers, seasonally adjusted, and t indicates time (data for regressions [1], and for regressions [2] and [3] below, unless stated otherwise, were obtained from the data bank for the Wharton Econometric Model). The numbers in parentheses here and in the following regressions are standard errors.

Regressions (2) and (3) include various components of θ_{t-1}, as well as lagged values of the unemployment rate. In regression (2), these components are the logarithm of the GNP deflator (p), seasonally adjusted, lagged one through four quarters, and the log of average hourly earnings in manufacturing corrected for overtime payments, not seasonally adjusted (w), lagged one through four quarters (from various issues of *Employment and Earnings*).

$$Un_t = -0.723 + 1.600\, Un_{t-1} - 0.722\, Un_{t-2}$$
$$\quad\;\; (1.806) \quad (0.097) \qquad\quad (0.101)$$
$$- 20.982 p_{t-1} + 15.805 p_{t-2} + 0.153 p_{t-3} + 2.574 p_{t-4}$$
$$\;\;(13.607) \qquad (20.223) \qquad (20.087) \qquad (14.002)$$
$$+ 5.509 w_{t-1} + 3.152 w_{t-2} - 3.807 w_{t-3} - 3.080 w_{t-4}.$$
$$\quad (8.960) \qquad\;\; (10.125) \qquad (10.014) \qquad (8.327)$$

$$(2)$$

$\bar{R}^2 = 0.917$, standard error of estimate $= 0.333$, Durbin-Watson statistic $= 1.684$.
$$F(8,65) = 0.594.$$

The F-statistic pertinent for testing the null hypothesis that the coefficients on lagged p and lagged w are zero is 0.594, which implies that the null hypothesis cannot be rejected at the 95 percent confidence level. Accordingly, the natural unemployment rate hypothesis cannot be rejected on the basis of this regression. The adjusted standard error of the residuals in regression (2) (0.333) is actually larger than that obtained by excluding the p's and w's (0.325), reported in regressions (1).

Regression (3) implements the test by employing a much larger set of elements of θ_{t-1}. In addition to three lagged values of the unemployment rate, the regression includes values of the logarithm of the money supply (currency plus demand deposits), seasonally adjusted (m), the federal and state and local government deficit on the national income accounts basis (Def); and the logs of the GNP deflator, seasonally adjusted (p), of the implicit deflator for personal consumption expenditures (pc), of the average hourly wage rate in manufacturing, seasonally adjusted (wr), of government purchases of goods and services (g), of total federal and state and local government employment, seasonally adjusted (ng), and of GNP (y). Each of these arguments is included lagged one, two, and three periods.

$$Un_t = 39.622 + 1.223\, Un_{t-1} - 0.546\, Un_{t-2} - 0.129\, Un_{t-3}$$
$$\quad\;\; (12.427) \quad (0.136) \qquad\;\; (0.211) \qquad\quad (0.169)$$
$$- 3.852 m_{t-1} - 11.835 m_{t-2} + 16.801 m_{t-3} + 0.023\, Def_{t-1}$$
$$\;\; (9.839) \qquad (15.926) \qquad (9.620) \qquad (0.016)$$
$$- 0.006\, Def_{t-2} + 0.020\, Def_{t-3} + 26.268 p_{t-1} - 25.552 p_{t-2}$$
$$\;\; (0.020) \qquad\quad (0.018) \qquad\quad (21.702) \qquad (24.210)$$
$$+ 27.416 p_{t-3} - 7.807\, pc_{t-1} + 28.701\, pc_{t-2} - 57.719\, pc_{t-3}$$
$$\;\; (19.511) \qquad (20.868) \qquad (24.375) \qquad (20.328)$$

$$(3)$$

$$- 1.631 wr_{t-1} + 1.461 wr_{t-2} + 8.567 wr_{t-3} + 3.448 g_{t-1}$$
$$(8.068) \qquad (10.286) \qquad (7.623) \qquad (2.917)$$
$$- 1.508 g_{t-2} + 3.812 g_{t-3} + 4.909 ng_{t-1} - 13.424 ng_{t-2}$$
$$(3.723) \qquad (2.662) \qquad (10.333) \qquad (14.168)$$
$$+ 4.725 ng_{t-3} + 1.151 y_{t-1} - 8.560 y_{t-2} - 3.824 y_{t-3}.$$
$$(10.053) \qquad (6.228) \qquad (7.913) \qquad (6.879)$$

$\bar{R}^2 = 0.9497$, standard error of estimate $= 0.259$, Durbin-Watson statistic $= 2.161$. $F(24,48) = 2.503$.

For regression (3) the pertinent F-statistic for testing the null hypothesis that elements of θ_{t-1} (other than lagged rates of unemployment) have zero coefficients is 2.503. This statistic is distributed with 24,48 degrees of freedom and so is significant at the 99 percent confidence level. As a result, the null hypothesis must be rejected. The adjusted standard error of estimate falls from the 0.318 reported in (1) to 0.259 when the components of θ_{t-1} are added to the regression, indicating a modest but statistically significant gain in explanatory power. Consequently, this application of the test requires rejection of the version of the natural rate hypothesis that assumes rational expectations formed on the basis of at least the information contained in the particular set θ_{lt-1} used in the regression under discussion.

Several reasons suggest caution in interpreting the verdict of this test. First, as shown above, the test assumes that the u's in equation (19) are not serially correlated. If, in fact, they are, the test becomes biased in favor of rejecting the natural rate hypothesis. Second, the essence of the natural rate hypothesis could stand unrefuted even though tests using large subsets θ_{lt-1} find systematic effects of θ_{lt-1} on Un_t. This can occur if individuals form their expectations rationally on less information than is represented by θ_{lt-1}. In this regard, it is noteworthy that the natural rate hypothesis cannot be rejected on the basis of regression (2), which includes only lagged w's and p's as components of θ_{lt-1}. Third, the test could lead to rejection of the natural rate hypothesis if the u's are correlated with components of θ_{lt-1}. This might occur, because, for example, current and lagged θ's have a direct effect on unemployment that requires no movement in the price level, contrary to the hypothesis in (19). In this event, systematic changes in the price level could still leave the unemployment rate unaffected, so that policymakers confront no "cruel choice" between the average rate of inflation and the average unemployment rate.

Finally, it should be noted that the results of the test reported in (3) have not been shown to be of comfort to advocates of any particular alternatives to the natural rate hypothesis. That is, it has not been shown that an autoregression for unemployment yields ex ante predictions of unemployment inferior to those of a particular structural macroeconometric model that embodies a particular aggregate supply theory other than the natural rate hypothesis. A particular alternative aggregate supply hypothesis might well be able to predict unemployment better than an autoregressive moving-average process, but there is no way of knowing for sure until a horse race is held.[26]

Another Test

An alternative test of the natural unemployment rate hypothesis can be carried out by directly estimating the parameters of a version of equation (19), where u_t is now assumed to be a serially uncorrelated random term satisfying $E(u_t | \theta_{t-1}) = 0$. Equation (19) embodies the null hypothesis to be tested, the natural unemployment rate hypothesis.[27] I propose to test it against the following alternative hypothesis:

$$Un_t = \sum_{i=1}^{q} \lambda_i Un_{t-i} + \beta(p_t - Ep_t | \theta_{t-1})$$

$$+ \beta(1 - \alpha)(Ep_t | \theta_{t-1} - p_{t-1}) + u_t. \quad (23)$$

Equation (23) states that if $\alpha < 1(\alpha > 1)$, then increases in the systematic part of the rate of inflation decrease (increase) the unemployment rate, contrary to the natural rate hypothesis. On the natural rate hypothesis, $\alpha = 1$, which makes (23) equivalent to equation (19). My strategy is to estimate (23) and to test the null hypothesis, $\alpha = 1$, against the alternative hypothesis, $\alpha \neq 1$.[28]

In conducting this test, two econometric problems must be overcome. First, macroeconomic theory implies that Un_t (or equivalently $y_t - k_t$) and

---

[26]Charles Nelson found that the predictions of the unemployment rate from a version of the Fed-M.I.T. model were inferior to the predictions from an autoregression. This was so, even though for my purposes Nelson's procedure is biased in favor of the Fed-M.I.T. model because he permits it to use the actual values of the exogenous variables at the same date for which unemployment is being forecast (see Nelson 1972).

[27]It is common to write the natural rate hypothesis in a way that, under rational expectations, would take the form

$$Un_t = \sum_{i=1}^{q} \lambda_i Un_{t-1} + \beta[(p_t - p_{t-1}) - E(p_t - p_{t-1}) | \theta_{t-1}] + u_t, \quad (a)$$

so that the surprise increase in the rate of inflation is what boosts aggregate supply. But so long as p_{t-1} is one of the variables in θ_{t-1}, it is straightforward to show that

$$(p_t - p_{t-1}) - E[(p_t - p_{t-1}) | \theta_{t-1}] = p_t - Ep_t | \theta_{t-1}.$$

It follows, then, that (a) is equivalent with (19) in the text.

[28]The test here is related to Lucas's (1972), which tests the restrictions across the reduced forms for the price level and for output that are implied by rational expectations in conjunction with an aggregate supply schedule like (1). For the test used here it is necessary neither to specify nor to estimate the full reduced forms for aggregate supply and the price level. The test requires that a list of some predetermined variables influencing the price level be available; but there is no necessity to have a complete list of the predetermined variables appearing in the reduced form for the price level.

p_t are simultaneously determined, implying that u_t and p_t may be correlated. For example, take a standard macroeconomic model in which aggregate demand, $(y - k)_d$, depends inversely on the current price level, while aggregate supply, $(y - k)_s$, responds directly to the current price level. With predetermined expectations, equation (1) or (19) is an example of such an aggregate supply schedule, while an aggregate demand schedule in the $p, y - k$ plane is derived by using the portfolio balance schedule (3) to eliminate the nominal interest rate from the IS curve (2). It is evident that an increase in u_t causes the aggregate supply schedule to shift upward in the $p, y - k$ plane, causing the price level to rise, $y - k$ to fall, and unemployment to rise. This leads to a positive correlation between u_t and p_t, provided, for example, that u is uncorrelated with the disturbances in the aggregate demand schedule in the $p, y - k$ plane. The correlation between u and p makes least-squares estimation of (19) or (23) inappropriate. This problem can be overcome in the standard way, by using the technique of instrumental variables: replacing p_t in (23) by $\hat{p}_t$, the predicted value of p_t from a first-stage regression including a constant, Un_{t-1} through Un_{t-q}, and predetermined variables including lagged prices, lagged values of other variables thought to be endogenous to the system, and current and lagged values of exogenous variables.

The second econometric challenge is to produce an appropriate proxy for $Ep_t \mid \theta_{t-1}$. Here I am assuming that the regression $Ep_t \mid \theta_{t-1}$ is linear in θ_{t-1}, so that $Ep_t \mid \theta_{t-1}$ is in effect formed as if it were the prediction from a least-squares regression of p_t on θ_{t-1}, and therefore

$$Ep_t \mid \theta_{t-1} = \delta\theta_{t-1}$$
$$p_t = \delta\theta_{t-1} + e_t \equiv \tilde{p}_t + e_t,$$

where $\widehat{\delta}$ is a vector of least-squares parameter estimates conformable to θ_{t-1}, while e_t is a least-squares residual vector that is orthogonal to θ_{t-1} by construction. I propose to use $\tilde{p}_t$ in place of $Ep_t \mid \theta_{t-1}$ in equation (23).[29]

---

[29] Suppose that instead of using θ_{t-1} to obtain $\tilde{p}_t$, $\tilde{p}_t^0$ is obtained from a regression of p_t on some subset θ_{lt-1} of θ_{t-1}, so that

$$p_t = \delta_0\theta_{lt-1} + e_{0t} = \tilde{p}_t^0 + e_{0t},$$

where $\widehat{\delta}_0$ is a vector of least-squares coefficients conformable to θ_{lt-1} and e_{0t} is a least-squares residual. But individuals' expectations really equal the $\tilde{p}_t$ of the text. Then

$$\tilde{p}_t = \tilde{p}_t^0 + e_{0t} - e_t,$$

so that (24) can be written

$$Un_t = \sum_{i=1}^{q} \lambda_i Un_{t-1} + \beta(p_t - \tilde{p}_t^0) + (1 - \alpha)\beta(\tilde{p}_t^0 - p_{t-1}) + u_t - \alpha\beta(e_{0t} - e_t). \quad \text{(b)}$$

So long as θ_{lt-1} includes the constant, Un_{t-1} through Un_{t-q}, and p_{t-1}, $e_{0t} - e_t$ is orthogonal to all arguments of (b) except $p_t - \tilde{p}_t^0$. It can readily be shown that using $\tilde{p}_t^0$ rather than $\tilde{p}_t$ leads to statistical inconsistency only in the estimate of β, and in particular that its use does not produce an inconsistent estimate of $(1 - \alpha)\beta$, the parameter that must be estimated to test the natural rate hypothesis.

I then substitute $\tilde{p}_t$ for $Ep_t \mid \theta_{t-1}$ in (23) to obtain

$$Un_t = \sum_{i=1}^{q} \lambda_i Un_{t-i} + \beta(p_t - \tilde{p}_t) + (1 - \alpha)\beta(\tilde{p}_t - p_{t-1}) + u_t. \quad (24)$$

Since it is assumed that $E(u_t \mid \theta_{t-1}) = 0$, it follows that u_t is uncorrelated with $\tilde{p}_t$. Furthermore, by construction $(p_t - \tilde{p}_t)$ is orthogonal both to Un_{t-1} through Un_{t-q}, to p_{t-1}, and to $\tilde{p}_t$, by the orthogonality of least-squares residuals to regressors. However, as I have argued above, simultaneity leads to a prediction that u_t and p_t, and hence u_t and $p_t - \tilde{p}_t$, are positively correlated. Under these circumstances, in which $p_t - \tilde{p}_t$ is correlated with the disturbance while the remaining regressors are orthogonal both to the disturbance and to $p_t - \tilde{p}_t$, it follows that least squares yields consistent estimates of the coefficients on all regressors except $p_t - \tilde{p}_t$.[30] Consequently, in (24), application of least squares yields consistent estimates of $(1 - \alpha)\beta$ and the λ_i's, but inconsistent estimates of β. On the hypothesis that $\beta \neq 0$, a consistent estimate of $(1 - \alpha)\beta$ is really all that is required to test the natural rate hypothesis, $\alpha = 1$.

As mentioned above, the inconsistency in the estimates of β can be eliminated by replacing p_t by $\widehat{p}_t$ in (24) to obtain

$$Un_t = \sum_{i=1}^{q} \lambda_i Un_{t-i} + \beta(\widehat{p}_t - \tilde{p}_t)$$
$$+ (1 - \alpha)\beta(\tilde{p}_t - p_{t-1}) + u_t + \beta f_t, \quad (24')$$

where f_t is a least-squares residual in the first-stage regression used to form $\widehat{p}_t$; f_t is orthogonal to $\widehat{p}_t$, $\tilde{p}_t$, p_{t-1}, and the lagged Un's, so long as p_{t-1}, the lagged Un's, and all the "first-stage" variables used to obtain $\tilde{p}_t$ are used in the first stage to obtain $\widehat{p}_t$. Since u_t and p_t are expected to be positively correlated, and since the u's, the f's, and $(p - \tilde{p})$s are orthogonal to the other regressors in (24'), estimating (24) rather than (24') should produce an estimate of β that is biased upward in large samples.

In summary, my strategy is to decompose the rate of inflation into two parts: a systematic part that is predictable from variables known in the past, and a random part that cannot be predicted from past data. The natural unemployment rate hypothesis permits the random part of the log of the price level (which equals the random part of the rate of inflation) to have an effect on the unemployment rate, but denies that the systematic part of the rate of inflation can affect unemployment. That hypothesis can be tested by regressing the unemployment rate against lagged values of itself and the random and systematic parts of the rate of inflation.

Table 1 reports the results of applying the test to quarterly data for the United States over the period 1952:1–1970:4. Two measures of the price

---

[30]Theil's (1971) specification theorem is being invoked here.

TABLE 1
REGRESSION RESULTS FOR ALTERNATIVE TESTS OF THE NATURAL
UNEMPLOYMENT RATE HYPOTHESIS

Variable and Regression Statistic	Regression			
	4.1	4.2	5.1	5.2
Variable:				
Constant	0.2380 (2.172)	0.2380	0.694 (0.216)	0.694
Unemployment rate lagged 1 quarter, Un_{-1}	1.717 (0.116)	1.717	1.667 (0.116)	1.667
Unemployment rate lagged 2 quarters, Un_{-2}	−1.029 (0.199)	−1.029	−0.999 (0.196)	−0.999
Unemployment rate lagged 3 quarters, Un_{-3}	0.246 (0.115)	0.246	0.216 (0.114)	0.216
Random (unexpected) part of inflation, based on the GNP deflator, p, or the wage index, w:				
$p - \bar{p}$	−8.694 (19.656)	...	...	...
$\hat{p} - \bar{p}$	...	−75.156 (68.672)	...	...
$w - \bar{w}$	...	...	−11.884 (10.053)	...
$\hat{w} - \bar{w}$	...	...	...	−50.500 (52.109)
Systematic (expected) part of inflation:				
$\bar{p} - p_{-1}$	14.085 (11.130)	14.085 (11.903)	...	...
$\bar{w} - w_{-1}$	...	...	−13.215 (6.925)	−13.215 (7.634)
Regression statistic:				
$\bar{R}^2$	0.924	...	0.928	...
Durbin-Watson statistic	1.980	...	1.952	...
$\hat{\alpha}$	2.62	1.19	0.11	0.74
t-statistic	1.27	1.19	−1.91	−1.73

SOURCE.—Derived from equations (24) and (24′), using relevant official U.S. series from the data bank of the Wharton Econometric Model.

NOTE.—The period of fit is 1952:1–1970:4. The dependent variable is the unemployment rate. Standard errors are in parentheses. The standard errors of coefficients for regressions (4.2) and (5.2) are asymptotic. For detailed definitions of symbols see discussion in text.

level were used: the logarithm of the GNP deflator (p), and the log of a straight-time wage index in manufacturing (w).[31] Regressions (4.1) and (4.2) are estimates of equations (24) and (24′) for p, while regressions (5.1) and (5.2) are estimates of the same two equations using w as the index of the price level.

The data that form the raw material for these regressions are plotted in figures 1 and 2. In each figure, panel (a) depicts the estimated innovation

[31]To form $\bar{p}$ or $\bar{w}$, p or w was regressed against a constant, time, and three lagged values each of p and w, as well as three lagged values each of pc, g, Def, m, y, ng, Un, and wr, where each of these variables is defined as in regression (3). To obtain $\hat{p}$ or $\hat{w}$, p or w was regressed against all of the variables just listed and also the current values of g, ng, m, and Def.

THOMAS J. SARGENT

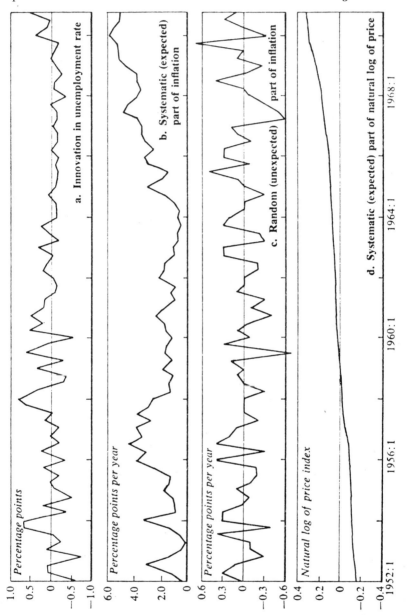

FIG. 1.—Innovation in the unemployment rate, and decomposition of inflation into systematic and random parts, using the GNP deflator to measure inflation. Derived from the relevant official U.S. series from the data bank for the Wharton Econometric Model. Here and in fig. 2, equal vertical distances on various panels do not necessarily signify equal changes. Innovation in the unemployment rate is the residual in a regression of the unemployment rate against a constant and three lagged values of itself.

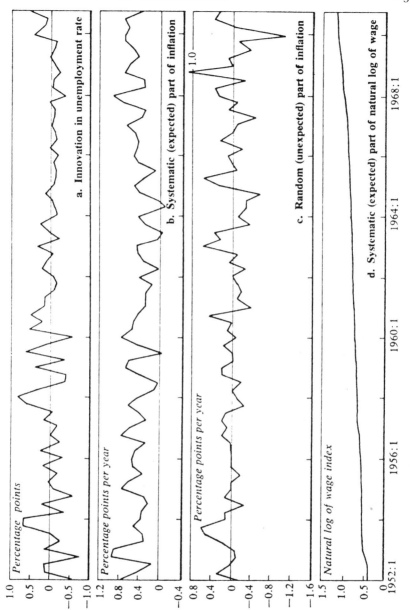

FIG. 2.—Innovation in the unemployment rate, and decomposition of inflation into systematic and random parts, using the manufacturing wage index to measure inflation (for source and explanation, see fig. 1.).

in the unemployment rate—that is, the residual in a regression of the unemployment rate against a constant and three lagged values of itself. The natural unemployment rate hypothesis permits this innovation to be inversely related to the random or unexpected part of the current price level, but denies that it is related to the systematic or expected part of the price level or rate of inflation. Panels (b) depict $\tilde{p} - p_{-1}$ and $\tilde{w} - w_{-1}$, respectively, and panels (c) report the unexpected parts, $\hat{p} - \tilde{p}$ and $\widehat{w} - \tilde{w}$. Panels (d) report the paths of $\tilde{p}$ and $\tilde{w}$. What is claimed for these numbers is that, on my assumptions, they represent appropriate decompositions of $\tilde{w}, \hat{p}, \widehat{w} - w_{-1}$, and $\hat{p} - p_{-1}$ for the purpose of estimating equation (24').

Regressions (4.1), (4.2), (5.1), and (5.2) test the natural rate hypothesis against the alternative hypothesis that the systematic part of the rate of inflation affects the unemployment rate. The coefficient on $\tilde{p}_t - p_{t-1}$ or $\tilde{w}_t - w_{t-1}$ estimates $\beta(1 - \alpha)$ and should equal zero on the natural rate hypothesis. The t-statistic reports the ratio of the coefficient on $\tilde{p}_t - p_{t-1}$ ($\tilde{w}_t - w_{t-1}$) to its standard error, and provides the basis for a statistical test of the null hypothesis. Regressions (5.1) and (5.2) come closest to supporting a rejection of the natural rate hypothesis. The t-statistic for regression (5.1) is -1.91 and is distributed according to the t-distribution with 70 degrees of freedom; its absolute value is thus slightly below the critical value of 1.99 for a two-tailed test at the 95 percent confidence level. However, for a one-tailed test, which is pertinent for testing the hypothesis $\alpha = 1$ against the alternative $\alpha < 1$, the critical value of the t-statistic is 1.66 at the 95 percent confidence level, so that the natural rate hypothesis can be rejected at that confidence level on a one-tailed test. The t-statistic for regression (5.2), being based on instrumental variable estimates, has only an asymptotic justification. Its absolute value is below the critical level for a normal variate of 1.96 for a two-tailed test at the 95 percent confidence level, but exceeds the critical value of 1.65 for a one-tailed test at this level. The regressions using w thus provide some evidence for rejecting the natural rate hypothesis, although not at an unusually high confidence level. On the other hand, the t-statistics for regressions (4.1) and (4.2) fail to support rejection of the hypothesis. The point estimates in regressions (5.1) and (5.2) indicate an inverse tradeoff ($\alpha < 1$) between unemployment and the expected change in w, a tradeoff consistent with a negatively sloped long-run Phillips curve. But the point estimates in regressions (4.1) and (4.2) indicate a direct tradeoff ($\alpha > 1$) between unemployment and the systematic part of inflation in the GNP deflator, and are thus not compatible with a negatively sloped long-run Phillips curve. Yet the short-run Phillips curve in regression (4.2) has the usual slope.

The coefficients on $\hat{p} - \tilde{p}$ and $\widehat{w} - \tilde{w}$ in regressions (4.2) and (5.2) exceed in absolute value the coefficients on $p - \tilde{p}$ and $w - \tilde{w}$ in regressions (4.1) and (5.1), respectively. This is consistent with the argument that in large samples the least-squares estimate of the coefficient on $p - \bar{p}$ is biased upward due to simultaneous-equations bias.

The coefficients on all regressors except $p - \bar{p}$ or $\hat{p} - \bar{p}(w - \bar{w}$ or $\hat{w} - \bar{w})$ are identical in the pairs of regressions (4.1) and (4.2) and (5.1) and (5.2). This is no accident but stems from the fact that, by construction, $p - \bar{p}$ and $\hat{p} - \bar{p}(w - \bar{w}$ and $\hat{w} - \bar{w})$ are each orthogonal to the remaining regressors, which are the same in these pairs of regressions. Consequently, the coefficients on those remaining regressors are the same whichever of these two "random" terms is included in the regression.

The magnitudes of the coefficients in regressions (4.2) and (5.2) support Lucas's notion that the surprise, or random, part of the rate of inflation has a much larger effect on the unemployment rate than does the systematic part. However, in each regression, the t-statistic for the coefficient on the surprise part of inflation indicates statistical insignificance. If anything, there seems to be less evidence for a stable relationship between unemployment and the surprise in inflation than between unemployment and expected inflation. The results suggest that it is difficult to isolate even a stable short-run tradeoff between inflation and unemployment in these data. Some evidence remains for an inverse tradeoff between the unemployment rate and the systematic part of the rate of inflation in the straight-time wage index, w, but it is not strong enough to reject the natural rate hypothesis at a very high confidence level. I imagine that that evidence would not be sufficiently compelling to persuade someone to abandon a strongly held prior belief in the natural rate hypothesis.

Conclusion

This paper has set out a macroeconomic model for which a version of Irving Fisher's theory about the relationship between interest rates and expected inflation is correct. The model turns out to be characterized by a number of properties that monetarists have attributed to the economy. Its structural equations themselves do not differ from those of the standard IS-LM-Phillips curve models used to rationalize Keynesian prescriptions for activist, countercyclical monetary and fiscal policies. In fact, the statics of the model with fixed or exogenous expectations about the price level are of the usual Keynesian variety.[32] Where the model does differ from standard implementations of the IS-LM-Phillips curve model is in the replacement of the usual assumption of fixed-weight, extrapolative or "adaptive" expectations by the assumption that expectations about future prices are rational and do not differ systematically from the predictions of the model.

[32]There are models that, with exogenous expectations, display static properties that are very much more "monetarist" than those possessed by the model in this paper. An example is Tobin (1955).

The result of this change in assumptions is to produce a model with the following implications:

1. The rate of output is independent of the systematic parts of both the money supply and fiscal policy variables.

2. The real rate of interest is independent of the systematic part of the money supply.

3. The monetary authority should not adopt a systematic policy of pegging the nominal interest rate at some fixed level over many periods. Such a policy would be very inflationary or deflationary, since strictly speaking, no equilibrium price level exists under it.

4. The distributed lag coefficients of money income behind money are variables, being dependent on, among other things, the money supply rule. Changes in the rule have the effect of altering the lag of money income behind money. More generally, the distributed lags in all of the reduced form equations change with changes in the rule governing any policy variable.

These four implications of the model are among the most prominent doctrines associated with the Chicago school. Furthermore, the model's assumption that expectations are rational and its stress on the distinction between the effects of random and systematic movements in the price level have long been important elements of macroeconomics at Chicago. For example, Milton Friedman (1969) has written:

> . . . it is argued that once it becomes widely recognized that prices are rising, the advantages [in terms of higher real output] . . . will disappear: escalator clauses or their economic equivalent will eliminate the stickiness of prices and wages and the greater stickiness of wages than of prices; strong unions will increase still further their wage demands to allow for price increases; and interest rates will rise to allow for the price rise. If the advantages are to be obtained, the rate of price rise will have to be accelerated and there is no stopping place short of runaway inflation. From this point of view, there may clearly be a major difference between the effects of a superficially similar price rise, according as it is an undesigned and largely unforeseen effect of such impersonal events as the discovery of gold, or a designed result of deliberative policy action by a public body.

While the model described in this paper is consistent with a number of policy prescriptions associated with monetarism, or the Chicago school, it does not embody the naive monetarism of textbooks, which requires either a vertical LM curve or a horizontal IS curve or a vertical short-run Phillips curve. On the contrary, the model requires only weak "sign" restrictions on the parameters of those three curves.

Given the empirical evidence of which I am aware, there is room for disagreement about the usefulness of the kind of model described in this paper. On the one hand, one test of the natural unemployment rate hypothesis above—which is the model's centerpiece—points to rejection of that hypothesis and seems to imply some scope for policymakers to influence the mean of the unemployment rate via a suitable policy rule. On the other hand, I am aware of no evidence that shows that any particular existing structural model embodying a specific alternative to the natural rate hypothesis can outperform it in predicting the course of the unemployment rate. Such evidence ought to be in hand before it is reasonable to believe that economists know enough to design policies that can affect the expected value of the unemployment rate.

Appendix A: Equilibrium of the Model with Rational Expectations

To determine the equilibrium of the system formed by equations (1), (2), (3), and (8), I first solve (3) for r_t:

$$r_t = b^{-1}m_t - b^{-1}p_t - b^{-1}y_t - b^{-1}\eta_t.$$

Substituting the above equation and (8) into (2) yields

$$y_t = k_t + cb^{-1}m_t - cb^{-1}p_t - cb^{-1}y_t - cb^{-1}\eta_t - c\,E_t\,p_{t+1} + cp_t + \varepsilon_t + dZ_t.$$

Solving this equation for $y_t - k_t$, and equating the result to the expression for $y_t - k_t$ derived by substituting (8) into (1), gives

$$\gamma p_t - \gamma\,\underset{t-1}{E}\,p_t + U_t = \frac{cb^{-1}}{1 + cb^{-1}}m_t + \frac{c(1 - b^{-1})}{(1 + cb^{-1})}p_t - \left(\frac{c}{1 + cb^{-1}}\right)\underset{t}{E}\,p_{t+1}$$
$$- \frac{cb^{-1}}{1 + cb^{-1}}\eta_t + \left(\frac{1}{1 + cb^{-1}}\right)\varepsilon_t - \left(\frac{cb^{-1}}{1 + cb^{-1}}\right)k_t + \frac{d}{1 + cb^{-1}}Z_t.$$

Solving this equation for p_t gives

$$p_t = B_0\,\underset{t-1}{E}\,p_t + B_1 m_t + B_2\,\underset{t}{E}\,p_{t+1} + B_3 \eta_t + B_4 \varepsilon_t + B_5 U_t + B_6 k_t + B_7 Z_t, \quad \text{(A1)}$$

where

$$B_0 = \left(\frac{\gamma}{\phi}\right)$$

$$B_1 = \frac{cb^{-1}}{1 + cb^{-1}}/\phi > 0$$

$$B_2 = -\frac{c}{1 + cb^{-1}}/\phi > 0$$

$$B_3 = -B_1 < 0$$

$$B_4 = \frac{1}{1 + cb^{-1}}/\phi > 0$$

$$B_5 = -\frac{1}{\phi} < 0$$

$$B_6 = B_3 < 0$$

$$B_7 = dB_4$$

$$\phi = \gamma - \frac{c(1 - b^{-1})}{1 + cb^{-1}} > 0.$$

To simplify the notation, I define the (5×1) vector

$$\mu_t = [B_3\eta_t, B_4\varepsilon_t, B_5U_t, B_6k_t, B_7Z_t]'.$$

Defining I as the 1×5 vector $[1, 1, 1, 1, 1]$, (A1) can be written as

$$p_t = B_0 \underset{t-1}{E} p_t + B_1 m_t + B_2 \underset{t}{E} p_{t+1} + I\mu_t. \tag{A2}$$

To derive an expression for $\underset{t}{E} p_{t+1}$, shift equation (A2) forward one period and take expectations conditional on information available at time t:

$$\underset{t}{E} p_{t+1} = \frac{B_1}{1 - B_0} \underset{t}{E} m_{t+1} + \frac{B_2}{1 - B_0} \underset{t}{E} p_{t+2} + \frac{1}{1 - B_0} I \underset{t}{E} \mu_{t+1}. \tag{A3}$$

More generally, for any $j \geq 1$,

$$\underset{t}{E} p_{t+j} = \frac{B_1}{1 - B_0} \underset{t}{E} m_{t+j} + \frac{B_2}{1 - B_0} \underset{t}{E} p_{t+j+1} + \frac{1}{1 - B_0} I \underset{t}{E} \mu_{t+j}. \tag{A4}$$

Repeatedly substituting (A4) into (A3) yields the following expression for $\underset{t}{E} p_{t+1}$:

$$\underset{t}{E} p_{t+1} = \frac{B_1}{1 - B_0} \sum_{j=1}^{\infty} \delta^{j-1} \underset{t}{E} m_{t+j} + \frac{1}{1 - B_0} \sum_{j=1}^{\infty} \delta^{j-1} I \underset{t}{E} \mu_{t+j}, \tag{A5}$$

where

$$\delta = \frac{B_2}{1 - B_0} = \frac{\dfrac{-c}{1 + cb^{-1}}/\phi}{1 - \dfrac{\gamma}{\phi}}$$

or

$$0 < \delta = \frac{1}{1 - b^{-1}} < 1.$$

Here I am imposing the terminal condition

$$\lim_{j \to \infty} \delta^{j-1} \underset{t}{E} p_{t+j} = 0,$$

which rules out speculative bubbles. Equation (A5) states that under rationality, the currently held expectation of the price level for next period depends on current expectations about the whole future course of the money supply, as well as that of the vector μ, which includes as components U, ε, η, k, and Z. Notice that as long as $b < 0$, the parameter δ is between zero and unity, which permits the infinite sums in (12) to converge.

To make (A5) operational, I must specify how the expectations of future m and μ are formed. I do this by positing that m and μ are governed by autoregressive processes known to the public, and that the public properly takes into account the nature of those processes in forecasting the variables. For example, the money supply is assumed to be governed by the known feedback rule

$$m_{t+1} = \sum_{i=0}^{\infty} w_i m_{t-i} + \sum_{i=0}^{\infty} v_i \mu_{t-i} + \xi_{mt+1}, \tag{A6}$$

where ξ_{mt} is a serially uncorrelated random term that is normally distributed with mean zero, while the w_i's are fixed parameters and each v_i is a 1×5 vector of parameters, $i = 0, \ldots, \infty$. The random variable ξ_m denotes the component of the money supply that cannot be predicted on the basis of past m's or μ's (the part perhaps attributable to discretion). The (5×1) vector μ is assumed to be governed by the autoregressive process

$$\mu_{t+1} = \sum_{t=0}^{\infty} X_i \mu_{t-i} + \psi_{t+1}, \tag{A7}$$

where each X_i is a diagonal (5×5) matrix of parameters and ψ_{t+1} is a (5×1) vector of mutually uncorrelated, serially uncorrelated, normally distributed random variables with means zero.

Given (A6) and (A7), Wold's "chain rule of forecasting" (see Wold 1964) can be used to give the expected value of m_{t+j} for any j, conditional on information available at t. These forecasts have the form

$$\underset{t}{E} m_{t+j} = \sum_{i=0}^{\infty} w_{ji} m_{t-i} + \sum_{i=0}^{\infty} X_{ji} \mu_{t-i}, \tag{A8}$$

where the w_{ji}'s are known functions of the w_i's of (A6), and the (1×5) X_{ji}'s are known functions of the v_i's of (A6) and the X_i's of (A7).

Using (A8), the first term on the right side of equation (A5) becomes

$$\frac{B_1}{1 - B_0} \sum_{j=1}^{\infty} \delta^{j-1} \left(\sum_{i=0}^{\infty} w_{ji} m_{t-i} + \sum_{i=0}^{\infty} X_{ji} \mu_{t-i} \right) = \sum_{i=0}^{\infty} W_i m_{t-i} + \sum_{i=0}^{\infty} V_i \mu_{t-i},$$

where

$$W_i = \frac{B_1}{1 - B_0} \sum_{j=1}^{\infty} \delta^{j-1} w_{ji},$$

$$V_i = \frac{B_1}{1 - B_0} \sum_{j=1}^{\infty} \delta^{j-1} X_{ji},$$

a (1×5) matrix. Using this procedure, equation (A5) can be rewritten to express $\underset{t}{E} p_{t+1}$ in terms of current and past values of m_t and μ_t:

$$\underset{t}{E} p_{t+1} = \sum_{i=0}^{\infty} W_i m_{t-i} + \sum_{i=0}^{\infty} \tilde{V}_i \mu_{t-i} = W * m_t + \tilde{V} * \mu_t, \tag{A9}$$

where

$$W * m_t \equiv \sum_{i=0}^{\infty} W_i m_{t-i},$$

and so on, and where each $\tilde{V}_i$ is a (1×5) matrix. Here the $\tilde{V}_i$'s depend on the parameters of the monetary "rule" (A6), the parameters of autoregressive processes that underlie (A7), and the parameters of the economic structure, equations (1), (2), and (3). The W_i's depend both on the model's structural parameters and on the parameters w_i of the monetary rule.

The expression for $\underset{t}{E} p_{t+1}$ can now be substituted into equation (A2) to get the reduced form for the price level:

$$p_t = B_0 W * m_{t-1} + B_0 \tilde{V} * \mu_{t-1} + B_1 m_t + I \mu_t$$
$$+ B_2 W * m_t + B_2 \tilde{V} * \mu_t. \tag{A10}$$

Equation (A10) is the reduced form equation that appears as equation (11) in the text, while equation (A9) corresponds to the conditional expectation (13) in the text.

Appendix B: Modifications to the Model

A More Realistic Portfolio Sector

Building in a more realistic portfolio sector forces a modification of the proposition that the real rate of interest is independent of the systematic part of the money supply. Suppose the assumption that bonds and equities are viewed as perfect substitutes by owners of wealth were abandoned and replaced by separate demand schedules for equities and bonds of various maturities, perhaps assuming that the assets are gross substitutes (see Tobin 1969). It would then be standard to assume that the pertinent interest rate to enter in the aggregate demand schedule is the yield on equities (see Tobin 1969; Modigliani and Miller 1958). The real yields on all of the paper assets would appear in each member of the set of equations describing the conditions for portfolio balance—that is, equations expressing equality of the stock demand for each paper asset with the quantity of each in existence. In such a system, it remains true that the real yield on equities that appears in the aggregate demand schedule is independent of the systematic part of the money supply. Systematic, predictable movements in the money supply are thus not able to influence the equity yield, which can be characterized as the "critical" yield from the point of view of affecting aggregate demand (see Tobin 1969). However, by conducting debt management or open market operations, the monetary authority can systematically influence both the relationships borne by the yields on other paper assets to the equity yield and the relationships among those other yields. In this way, debt management can have systematic effects on the yields of certain assets, whose strength depends on the extent to which wealth owners regard alternative paper assets as good substitutes for one another. In such a system, debt management operations might well permit the monetary authority to peg the nominal rate on, say, 3-month Treasury bills. But that pegging would have no persistent effect on the critical yield on equities that governs aggregate demand.[33]

It might be useful to consider an additional change in the system that would further modify the second proposition, without, I believe, touching any of the policy implications of the model. Assume again the existence of various paper assets that are imperfect substitutes for one another; but abandon the notion that the real rate of return on one single asset, such as the yield on a certain class of equities, is the one crucial yield that belongs in the aggregate demand schedule, and instead, assume that aggregate demand depends on the real rates of return on all n assets, so that, instead of text equation (2), the aggregate demand schedule becomes

$$y_t - k_t = \sum_{i=1}^{n} c_i r_{it} + dZ_t + \varepsilon_t, \qquad (2')$$

[33]The literature on the term structure of interest rates has in large part been devoted to attempting to detect evidence of imperfect substitutability among bonds of different maturities (e.g., see Modigliani and Sutch 1967; Meiselman 1962). Very little convincing evidence has been assembled that debt management has important effects on the yield curve.

where $c_i \leq 0$ for all i, and r_{it} is the *real* rate of return on the ith paper asset. Define an index $\bar{r}_t$ of real yields as

$$\bar{r}_t \equiv \sum_{i=1}^{n} \frac{c_i}{\sum\limits_{j=1}^{n} c_j} r_{it}.$$

Then notice that equation (2′) can be rewritten as

$$y_t - k_t = \left(\sum_{j=1}^{n} c_j\right) \bar{r}_t + dZ_t + \varepsilon_t. \tag{2''}$$

In the system that is formed by replacing (2) with (2′) and replacing (3) as before with a system of portfolio equilibrium conditions for a set of assets, it is easily shown that the real yield index $\bar{r}_t$ is independent of the systematic part of the money supply. Moreover, this yield index certainly qualifies as the "crucial" yield affecting aggregate demand, if anything does. In such a system, debt management policies are able systematically to affect the relationships among the real rates that are components of $\bar{r}_t$, but that is irrelevant from the point of view of affecting $\bar{r}_t$ and aggregate output.

The Model with "Partly Rational" Expectations

One criticism that has been made of the kind of model presented here is that it seems to require extraordinary amounts of wisdom and information on the part of those whose expectations are described by equation (13).[34] They are assumed to act as if they know the probability distribution (12) and then use it together with data on all of the conditioning variables to form their expectation about next period's price level. While assuming such a well-informed public may or may not strain credulity, the key aspects of the theory carry through even if the public is much less wise and knowledgeable.

First, the orthogonality of the public's prediction errors to the set of variables on which its expectations are based applies when the public gets its knowledge of the conditional expectation of p_{t+1} as if it were simply computing a linear least-squares regression of the price level on lagged values of the conditioning variables for the historical data available. The well-known properties of least-squares prediction errors—in particular, their orthogonality to the regressors in the sample period—will guarantee that the prediction error in the aggregate supply schedule is uncorrelated with past values of the conditioning variables. That in turn implies that $y - k$ will be independent of lagged values of those conditioning variables.

Now to indicate the minimal amount of information and wisdom that must be imputed to the public in order to preserve the key policy implications of the model, assume for the moment that in forming its forecast of the price level, the public has access to information only about lagged prices (and by implication lagged values of its own forecasts). The public again is assumed to put this information together in such a way as to extract the best (least-squares) forecast of p_t, so that

$$_t p_{t-1}^* = E(p_t \mid p_{t-1}, p_{t-2}, \ldots) \equiv E[p_t \mid \theta_{lt-1}],$$

[34] E.g., see Tobin's discussion of Lucas' paper in Tobin (1972).

where θ_{lt-1} includes only past values of p_t.[35] Taking note of the fact that the variables $p_{t-1} - {}_{t-1}p^*_{-t2}, p_{t-2} - {}_{t-2}p^*_{-3}, \ldots$ form a subset of the variables in θ_{lt-1} conditioning the above expectation, I calculate the regression of the current prediction error on past prediction errors,

$$E[(p_t - {}_tp^*_{t-1}) \,|\, p_{t-1} - {}_{t-1}p^*_{t-2}, p_{t-2} - {}_{t-2}p^*_{t-3}, \ldots] = 0,$$

which establishes that the prediction errors are serially uncorrelated.

Now combine the above hypothesis about expectations formation with the modified aggregate supply hypothesis (1'):

$$y_t - k_t = \gamma(p_t - Ep_t\,|\,\theta_{lt-1}) + \sum_{i=1}^{q} \lambda_i(y_{t-i} - k_{t-i}) + U_t.$$

Taking expectations conditional on θ_{t-1}, I obtain

$$E[(y_t - k_t)\,|\,\theta_{t-1}] = \gamma(Ep_t\,|\,\theta_{t-1} - Ep_t\,|\,\theta_{lt-1})$$

$$+ \sum_{i=1}^{q} \lambda_i(y_{t-i} - k_{t-i}) + E(U_t\,|\,U_{t-1}, U_{t-2}, \ldots).$$

In general, the term $Ep_t\,|\,\theta_{t-1} - Ep_t\,|\,\theta_{lt-1}$ will not be zero: one obtains a better prediction of p_t by taking into account the components of θ_{t-1} that are excluded from θ_{lt-1}. Consequently, on the hypothesis that the public's expectation is conditioned only on past prices, the forecast error $p_t - Ep_t\,|\,\theta_{lt-1}$ that appears in the aggregate supply schedule is not in general independent of the elements of θ_{t-1} that are excluded from θ_{lt-1}. In particular, the forecast error is generally correlated with past values of the money supply. This means that by choosing the money supply rule (9) appropriately, the monetary authority can systematically influence the forecast errors that appear in the aggregate supply schedule. The systematic part of the money supply then has effects on both the rate of output and the real rate of interest, so that neither of the two propositions about the neutrality of the systematic part of the money supply continues to hold.

But the potential accomplishments of stabilization policy are still severely circumscribed. While the monetary authority can have a systematic effect on the prediction errors in the aggregate supply schedule, there exists no feedback policy that is capable of inducing serial correlation in those forecast errors. So long as the forecasts are conditioned on at least lagged prices, the errors will be serially uncorrelated. The monetary authority's ability systematically to affect the public's forecast errors then comes down to an ability to affect the variance of those errors without being able to affect their mean or serial correlation properties. It follows that there are no feedback rules for the money supply and fiscal policy variables that can be expected to produce "runs" of forecast errors that will in themselves be a source of persistent movements in output. Under the assumptions here, then, the monetary and the fiscal authorities still face no "cruel choice" between the average rate of inflation they shoot for and the expected value of the unemployment rate. But there remains a nontrivial problem in choosing stabilization policies, for different deterministic feedback rules deliver different variances for the public's errors in forecasting the price level, and thereby are associated with different variances for the unemployment rate.

[35]Changing the assumption about ${}_{t+1}p^*_t$ in this way will itself change the form of the probability distribution (12) that governs p_{t+1}, as can be seen easily by pursuing the kind of calculations reported in Appendix A. The arguments of (12) would remain the same, however.

References

Bailey, Martin. *National Income and the Price Level: A Study in Macrotheory.* New York: McGraw-Hill, 1962.

Cagan, Phillip. "The Monetary Dynamics of Hyperinflation." In *Studies in the Quantity Theory of Money,* edited by Milton Friedman. Chicago: Univ. Chicago Press: 1956.

——. *Determinants and Effects of Changes in the Stock of Money, 1875–1960.* New York: Columbia Univ. Press for the Nat. Bur. Econ. Res., 1965.

Chow, Gregory C. "Optimal Stochastic Control of Linear Economic Systems." *J. Money, Credit, and Banking* 2(August 1970): 291–302.

Fama, Eugene F. "Efficient Capital Markets: A Review of Theory and Empirical Work." *J. Finance* 25, no. 2 (May 1970): 383–417.

Feldstein, Martin, and Eckstein, Otto. "The Fundamental Determinants of the Interest Rate." *Rev. Econ. and Statis.* 52 (November 1970): 363–75.

Fisher, Irving. *The Theory of Interest.* New York: Macmillan, 1930.

Friedman, Milton. *A Theory of the Consumption Function.* Princeton, N.J.: Princeton Univ. Press for the Nat. Bur. Econ. Res., 1957.

——. "The Role of Monetary Policy." *A.E.R.* 58 (March 1968): 1–17.

——. "The Supply of Money and Changes in Prices and Output." In *The Optimum Quantity of Money and Other Essays.* Chicago: Aldine, 1969. Orig. in *The Relationship of Prices to Economic Stability and Growth,* compendium of papers submitted by panelists appearing before the Joint Economic Committee, 85 Cong. 2 sess. (1958).

Gibson, William E. "Price-Expectations Effects on Interest Rates." *J. Finance* 25 (March 1970): 19–34.

Gordon, Robert J. "The Recent Acceleration of Inflation and Its Lessons for the Future." *Brookings Papers on Economic Activity,* no. 1 (1970), pp. 8–47.

——. "Inflation in Recession and Recovery." *Brookings Papers on Economic Activity,* no. 1 (1971), pp. 145–47.

Hall, R. E. "The Dynamic Effects of Fiscal Policy in an Economy with Foresight." *Rev. Econ. Studies* 38 (April 1971): 229–44.

Kane, Edward J. "The Rasche and Andersen Papers, A Comment by Edward J. Kane." *J. Money, Credit, and Banking* 5, pt. 1 (February 1973): 39–42.

Keynes, John Maynard. *The General Theory of Employment, Interest and Money.* New York: Harcourt, Brace, 1936.

Lucas, Robert E., Jr. "Econometric Testing of the Natural Rate Hypothesis." In *The Econometrics of Price Determination Conference,* edited by Otto Eckstein, sponsored by the Board of Governors of the Federal Reserve System and Social Science Research Council. Washington: Federal Reserve Bank, 1972.

——. "Expectations and the Neutrality of Money." *J. Econ. Theory* 4 (April 1973): 103–24. (*a*)

——. "Some International Evidence on Output-Inflation Tradeoffs." *A.E.R.* 63 (June 1973): 326–34. (*b*)

——. "Econometric Policy Evaluation: A Critique." *J. Money, Credit, and Banking* (in press).

Lucas, Robert E., Jr., and Rapping, Leonard A. "Real Wages, Employment, and Inflation." *J.P.E.* 77 (September/October 1969): 721–54.

Meiselman, David. *The Term Structure of Interest Rates.* Englewood Cliffs, N.J.: Prentice-Hall, 1962.

Modigliani, Franco, and Miller, Merton H. "The Cost of Capital, Corporation Finance and the Theory of Investment." *A.E.R.* 48 (June 1958): 261–97.

Modigliani, Franco, and Shiller, Robert J. "Inflation, Rational Expectations and the Term Structure of Interest Rates." *Economica* N.S. 40 (February 1973): 12–43.

Modigliani, Franco, and Sutch, Richard. "Debt Management and the Term Structure of Interest Rates: An Empirical Analysis of Recent Experience." *J.P.E.* 75, pt. 2 (August 1967): 569–89.

Mundell, Robert. "Inflation and Real Interest." *J.P.E.* 71 (June 1963): 280–83.

Muth, John F. "Rational Expectations and the Theory of Price Movements." *Econometrica* 29 (July 1961): 315–35.

Nelson, Charles R. "The Prediction Performance of the FRB-MIT-PENN Model of the U.S. Economy." *A.E.R.* 62 (December 1972): 902–17.

Nerlove, Marc. "Distributed Lags and Unobserved Components in Economic Time Series." In *Ten Economic Studies in the Tradition of Irving Fisher,* by William Fellner et al. New York: Wiley, 1967.

Phelps, Edmund S. *Inflation Policy and Unemployment Theory: The Cost-Benefit Approach to Monetary Planning.* New York: Norton, 1972.

Samuelson, Paul A. "Proof that Properly Anticipated Prices Fluctuate Randomly." *Indus. Management Rev.* 6 (Spring 1965): 41–49.

Sargent, Thomas J. "Anticipated Inflation and the Nominal Rate of Interest." *Q.J.E.* 86 (May 1972): 212–25.

———. "Interest Rates and Prices in the Long Run: A Study of the Gibson Paradox." *J. Money, Credit, and Banking* 5, pt. 2 (February 1973): 385–449.

———. The Fundamental Determinants of the Interest Rate: A Comment." *Rev. Econ. and Statis.* 55 (August 1973): 391–93.

Sargent, Thomas J., and Wallace, Neil. "Rational Expectations and the Dynamics of Hyperinflation." *Internat. Econ. Rev.* 14 (June 1973): 328–50.

Shiller, Robert J. "Rational Expectations and the Structure of Interest Rates." Ph.D. dissertation, Massachusetts Inst. Tech., 1972.

Theil, Henri. *Principles of Econometrics.* New York: Wiley, 1971.

Tobin, James. "A Dynamic Aggregative Model." *J.P.E.* 63 (February 1955): 103–15.

———. "Comment." In *Proceedings of a Symposium on Inflation: Its Causes, Consequences, and Control.* Wilton, Conn.: Kazanjian Econ. Found., 1968.

———. "A General Equilibrium Approach to Monetary Theory." *J. Money, Credit, and Banking* 1 (February 1969): 15–29.

———. "The Wage-Price Mechanism: Overview of the Conference." In *Econometrics of Price Determination Conference,* edited by Otto Eckstein. Washington: Federal Reserve Bank, 1972.

Wold, Herman O. A., ed. *Econometric Model Building: Essays on the Causal Chain Approach.* Amsterdam: North-Holland, 1964.

Yohe, William P., and Karnosky, Denis S. "Interest Rates and Price Level Changes, 1952–69." Federal Reserve Bank of St. Louis, *Review* 51 (December 1969): 18–38.

"Rational Expectations": A Correction

I have discovered an error in the computations of regression (3) and the regressions in table 1 in my paper, "Rational Expectations, the Real Rate of Interest, and the Natural Rate of Unemployment" (above). With the exception of the lagged unemployment rates in those regressions, the instrumental variables in θ_t were all inadvertently lagged four more quarters than is reported in the paper. For example, m_{t-1} in equation (3) is actually m_{t-5}. The correct calculations are reported here in regression (3) and table 1. [Note: I would like to thank Thomas Turner for performing the calculations.]

The F-statistic for regression (3) is now 4.5, which exceeds the value of 2.503 reported in my paper, and so is even more significant statistically. Thus, the test continues to point toward rejection of the natural rate hypothesis. The corrected results for table 1 now detect neither a short-run

TABLE 1

REGRESSION RESULTS FOR ALTERNATIVE TESTS OF THE NATURAL
UNEMPLOYMENT RATE HYPOTHESIS

Variable and Regression Statistic	Regression			
	4.1	4.2	5.1	5.2
Variable:				
Constant	0.420 (0.218)	0.420	0.696 (0.220)	0.696
Unemployment rate lagged 1 quarter, Un_{-1}	1.715 (0.115)	1.715	1.666 (0.116)	1.666
Unemployment rate lagged 2 quarters, Un_{-2}	-1.046 (0.198)	-1.046	-0.999 (0.196)	-0.999
Unemployment rate lagged 3 quarters, Un_{-3}	0.245 (0.115)	0.245	0.216 (0.114)	0.216
Random (unexpected) part of inflation, based on the GNP deflator, p, or the wage index, w:				
$p - \widetilde{p}$	30.322 (19.976)	. . .	. . .	. . .
$\widehat{p} - \widetilde{p}$	. . .	61.848 (37.420)	. . .	. . .
$w - \widetilde{w}$	. . .	. . .	-11.924 (9.447)	. . .
$\widehat{w} - \widetilde{w}$	. . .	. . .	. . .	-100.852 (56.064)
Systematic (expected) part of inflation:				
$\widetilde{p} - p_{-1}$	-0.170 (11.380)	-0.170 (11.627)	. . .	. . .
$\widetilde{w} - w_{-1}$	. . .	. . .	-13.282 (7.154)	-13.282 (10.361)
Regression Statistic:				
$\overline{R}^2$	0.925	. . .	0.928	. . .
Durbin-Watson statistic	1.935	. . .	1.958	. . .
$\widehat{\alpha}$	1.01	1.00	-0.11	0.87
t-statistic	-0.01	-0.01	-1.86	-1.28

SOURCE.—Derived from equations (24) and (24′) of original article, using relevant official U.S. series from the data bank of the Wharton Econometric Model.

NOTE.—The period of fit is 1952:1–1970:4. The dependent variable is the unemployment rate. Standard errors are in parentheses. The standard errors for coefficients for regression (4.2) and (5.2) are asymptotic. For detailed definitions of symbols, see text of original article.

nor a long-run Phillips curve using the log of the GNP deflator, p, the coefficient on the systematic part of Δp having t-statistics close to zero. The t-statistic on the systematic part of wage inflation in regression (5.2) is now -1.28, and fails to support rejection of the natural rate hypothesis. However, the coefficient on the "random" part of w in (5.2) is now larger than before both in absolute value and in statistical significance, so that the amended results for w are more favorable to the hypothesis of a tradeoff between unemployment and the surprise component of wage inflation.

$$
Un_t = 54.556 + 0.773\,Un_{t-1} - 0.357\,Un_{t-2} - 0.027\,Un_{t-3}
$$
$$
(15.819)\quad (0.175)\qquad\quad (0.212)\qquad\quad (0.136)
$$
$$
-\ 2.809\,m_{t-1} - 10.046\,m_{t-2} + 4.868\,m_{t-3} - 0.003\,Def_{t-1}
$$
$$
(7.109)\qquad\quad (12.522)\qquad (7.434)\qquad\quad (0.013)
$$
$$
-\ 0.240\,Def_{t-2} - 0.023\,Def_{t-3} - 17.151\,p_{t-1} - 7.967\,p_{t-2}
$$
$$
(0.018)\qquad\quad (0.016)\qquad\quad (17.468)\qquad (21.767)
$$
$$
-\ 14.502\,p_{t-3} + 28.156\,pc_{t-1} + 13.122\,pc_{t-2} + 10.917\,pc_{t-3}
$$
$$
(18.157)\qquad (20.014)\qquad\quad (22.101)\qquad\quad (19.059) \tag{3}
$$
$$
+\ 13.274\,wr_{t-1} - 11.730\,wr_{t-2} + 11.546\,wr_{t-3} + 2.536\,g_{t-1}
$$
$$
(6.969)\qquad\quad (9.164)\qquad\quad (7.079)\qquad\quad (2.620)
$$
$$
-\ 7.224\,g_{t-2} + 0.345\,g_{t-3} - 11.132\,ng_{t-1} + 2.311\,ng_{t-2}
$$
$$
(3.652)\qquad (2.745)\qquad\quad (7.237)\qquad\quad (11.061)
$$
$$
-\ 0.938\,ng_{t-3} - 16.814\,y_{t-1} + 15.477\,y_{t-2} + 3.840\,y_{t-3}
$$
$$
(8.519)\qquad\quad (5.240)\qquad\quad (6.562)\qquad\quad (5.544)
$$

$\bar{R}^2 = 0.9652$; standard error of estimate $= 0.216$; Durbin-Watson statistic $= 1.941$; $F(24,48) = 4.500$.

10

Rational Expectations and the Theory of Economic Policy

Thomas J. Sargent
Neil Wallace

There is no longer any serious debate about whether monetary policy should be conducted according to rules or discretion. Quite appropriately, it is widely agreed that monetary policy should obey a rule, that is, a schedule expressing the setting of the monetary authority's instrument (e.g., the money supply) as a function of all the information it has received up through the current moment. Such a rule has the happy characteristic that in any given set of circumstances, the optimal setting for policy is unique. If by remote chance, the same circumstances should prevail at two different dates, the appropriate settings for monetary policy would be identical.

The central practical issue separating monetarists from Keynesians is the appropriate form of the monetary policy rule. Milton Friedman has long advocated that the monetary authority adopt a simple rule having no feedback from current and past variables to the money supply. He recommends that the authority cause the money supply to grow at some rate of

This paper is intended as a popular summary of some recent work on rational expectations and macroeconomic policy and was originally prepared for a conference on that topic at the Federal Reserve Bank of Minneapolis in October 1974. The paper was previously published as paper 2 of the *Studies in Monetary Economics* series of the Federal Reserve Bank of Minneapolis. To make the main points simple, the paper illustrates things by using simple ad hoc, linear models. However, the ideas cannot really be captured fully within this restricted framework. The main ideas we are summarizing are due to Robert E. Lucas, Jr., and were advanced by him most elegantly in the context of a stochastic general equilibrium model (see Lucas 1972b). Lucas's paper analyzes policy questions in what we regard to be the proper way, namely, in the context of a consistent general equilibrium model. The present paper is a popularization that fails to indicate how Lucas's neutrality propositions are derived from a consistent general equilibrium model with optimizing agents. It is easy to overturn the "neutrality" results that we derive below from an ad hoc structure by making ad hoc changes in that structure. The advantage of Lucas's model is that ad hockeries are given much less of a role and, consequently, the neutrality proposition he obtains is seen to be a consequence of individual agents' optimizing behavior. In summary, this paper is not intended to be a substitute for reading the primary sources, mainly Lucas (1972a, 1972b, 1973, in press).

[*Journal of Monetary Economics,* 1976, vol. 2]

© 1976 by North-Holland Publishing Company

x percent per year without exception. In particular, the Fed ought not to try to "lean against the wind" in an effort to attenuate the business cycle.

Within the context of macroeconometric models as they are usually manipulated, Friedman's advocacy of a rule without feedback seems indefensible. For example, suppose that a variable y_t, which the authority is interested in controlling, is described by the stochastic difference equation,

$$y_t = \alpha + \lambda y_{t-1} + \beta m_t + u_t, \tag{1}$$

where u_t is a serially independent, identically distributed random variable with variance σ_u^2 and mean zero; m_t is the rate of growth of the money supply; and α, λ, and β are parameters. The variable y_t can be thought of as the unemployment rate or the deviation of real GNP from "potential" GNP. This equation should be thought of as the reduced form of a simple econometric model.

Suppose that the monetary authority desires to set m_t in order to minimize the variance over time of y_t around some desired level y^*. It accomplishes this by appropriately choosing the parameters g_0 and g_1 in the feedback rule,

$$m_t = g_0 + g_1 y_{t-1}. \tag{2}$$

Substituting for m_t from (2) into (1) gives

$$y_t = (\alpha + \beta g_0) + (\lambda + \beta g_1) y_{t-1} + u_t. \tag{3}$$

From this equation the steady-state mean of y is given by

$$E(y) = (\alpha + \beta g_0)/[1 - (\lambda + \beta g_1)], \tag{4}$$

which should be equated to y^* in order to minimize the variance of y around y^*. From (3) the steady-state variance of y around its mean (and hence around y^*) is given by

$$\operatorname{var} y = (\lambda + \beta g_1)^2 \operatorname{var} y + \sigma_u^2$$

or

$$\operatorname{var} y = \sigma_u^2/[1 - (\lambda + \beta g_1)^2]. \tag{5}$$

The monetary authority chooses g_1 to minimize the variance of y, then chooses g_0 from equation (4) to equate $E(y)$ to y^*. From equation (5), the variance of y is minimized by setting $\lambda + \beta g_1 = 0$, so that g_1 equals $-\lambda/\beta$. Then from equation (4) it follows that the optimal setting of g_0 is $g_0 = (y^* - \alpha)/\beta$. So the optimal feedback rule for m_t is

$$m_t = (y^* - \alpha)/\beta - (\lambda/\beta) y_{t-1}. \tag{6}$$

Substituting this control rule into (1) gives

$$y_t = y^* + u_t,$$

which shows that application of the rule sets y_t equal to y^* plus an irreducible noise. Notice that application of the rule eliminates all serial correlation in y, since this is the way to minimize the variance of y. Use of rule (6) means that the authority always expects to be on target, since its forecast of y_t at time $t-1$ is

$$\widehat{y}_t = \alpha + \lambda y_{t-1} + \beta m_t,$$

which under rule (6) equals y^*.

Friedman's x-percent growth rule in effect sets g_1 equal to zero. So long as λ is not zero, that rule is inferior to the feedback rule (6).

This example illustrates all of the elements of the usual proof that Friedman's simple x-percent growth rule is suboptimal. Its logic carries over to larger stochastic difference equation models, ones with many more equations and with many more lags. It also applies where criterion functions have more variables. The basic idea is that where the effects of shocks to a goal variable (like GNP) display a stable pattern of persistence (serial correlation), and hence are predictable, the authority can improve the behavior of the goal variable by inducing offsetting movements in its instruments.

The notion that the economy can be described by presumably a large system of stochastic difference equations with fixed parameters underlies the standard Keynesian objections to the monism of monetarists who argue that the monetary authority should ignore other variables such as interest rates and concentrate on keeping the money supply on a steady growth path. The view that, on the contrary, the monetary authority should "look at (and respond to) everything," including interest rates, rests on the following propositions:[1] (a) the economic structure is characterized by extensive simultaneity, so that shocks that impinge on one variable, e.g., an interest rate, impinge also on most others; (b) due to lags in the system, the effects of shocks on the endogenous variables are distributed over time, and so are serially correlated and therefore somewhat predictable; and (c) the "structure" of these lags is constant over time and does not depend on how the monetary authority is behaving. These propositions imply that variables that the authority observes very frequently, e.g., daily, such as interest rates, carry information useful for revising its forecasts of future value of variables that it can't observe as often, such as GNP and unemployment. This follows because the same shocks are affecting both the observed and the unobserved variables, and because those shocks have effects that persist. It follows then from (c) that the monetary authority should in general revise its planned setting for its policy instruments each time it receives some new and surprising reading on a variable that is

---

[1] See Kareken, Muench, and Wallace (1973) for a detailed presentation of this view.

determined simultaneously with a variable, like GNP or unemployment, that it is interested in controlling. Such an argument eschewing a simple x-percent growth rate rule in favor of "looking at everything" has been made by Samuelson (1970):

> . . . when I learned that I had been wrong in my beliefs about how fast M was growing from December, 1968 to April, 1969, this news was just one of twenty interesting items that had come to my knowledge that week. And it only slightly increased my forecast for the strength of aggregate demand at the present time. That was because my forecasts, so to speak, do not involve "action at a distance" but are loose Markov processes in which a broad vector of current variables specify the "phase space" out of which tomorrow's vector develops. (In short, I knowingly commit that most atrocious of sins in the penal code of the monetarists— I pay a great deal of attention to all dimensions of "credit conditions" rather than keeping my eye on the solely important variable $\dot{M}/M$.)
>
> . . . often, I believe, the prudent man or prudent committee can look ahead six months to a year and with some confidence predict that the economy will be in other than an average or "ergodic" state. Unless this assertion of mine can be demolished, the case for a fixed growth rate for M, or for confining M to narrow channels around such a rate, melts away.
>
> These general presumptions arise out of what we know about plausible models of economics and about the findings of historical experience.[2]

There can be little doubt about the inferiority of an x-percent growth rule for the money supply in a system satisfying propositions (a), (b), and (c) above. A reasonable disagreement with the "look at everything, respond to everything" view would seemingly have to stem from a disbelief of one of those three premises. In particular, proposition (c) asserting the invariance of lag structures with respect to changes in the way policy is conducted would probably not be believed by an advocate of a rule without feedback.

Thus, returning to our simple example, a critical aspect of the proof of the suboptimality of Friedman's rule is clearly the assumption that the

[2]Perhaps the "look at everything" view goes some way toward rationalizing the common view that policy ought not to be made by following a feedback rule derived from an explicit, empirically estimated macroeconometric model. It might be argued that the models that have been estimated omit some of the endogenous variables that carry information about the shocks impinging on the system as a whole. If the authority has in mind an a priori model that assigns those variables an important role, it is appropriate for it to alter its policy settings in response to new information about those variables. Perhaps this is what some people mean by "discretion," although we aren't sure.

parameters α, λ, and β of the reduced form (1) are independent of the settings for g_0 and g_1 in the feedback rule. Macroeconometric models are almost always manipulated under such an assumption. However, Lucas (in press) has forcefully argued that the assumption is inappropriate, and that the parameters of estimated reduced forms like (1) in part reflect the policy responses in operation during the periods over which they are estimated. This happens because in the reduced forms are embedded the responses of expectations to the way policy is formed. Changes in the way policy is made then ought not to leave the parameters of estimated reduced forms unchanged.

To illustrate this point while continuing with our example, suppose that our reduced form (1) has been estimated during some sample period and suppose that it comes from the "structure":

$$y_t = \xi_0 + \xi_1(m_t - E_{t-1}m_t) + \xi_2 y_{t-1} + u_t, \tag{7}$$

$$m_t = g_0 + g_1 y_{t-1} + \varepsilon_t, \tag{8}$$

$$E_{t-1}m_t = g_0 + g_1 y_{t-1}. \tag{9}$$

Here ξ_0, ξ_1, and ξ_2 are fixed parameters; ε_t is a serially independent random term with mean zero. We assume that it is statistically independent of u_t. Equation (8) governed the money supply during the estimation period. The variable $E_{t-1}m_t$ is the public's expectation of m_t as of time $t - 1$. According to (9), the public knows the monetary authority's feedback rule and takes this into account in forming its expectations. According to equation (7), unanticipated movements in the money supply cause movements in y, but anticipated movements do not. The above structure can be written in the reduced form

$$y_t = (\xi_0 - \xi_1 g_0) + (\xi_2 - \xi_1 g_1)y_{t-1} + \xi_1 m_t + u_t, \tag{10}$$

which is in the form of (1) with $\alpha = (\xi_0 - \xi_1 g_0)$, $\lambda = (\xi_2 - \xi_1 g_1)$ and $\beta = \xi_1$. While the form of (10) is identical with that of (1), the coefficients of (10) are clearly functions of the control parameters, the g's, that were in effect during the estimation period.

Suppose now that the monetary authority desires to design a feedback rule to minimize the variance of y around y^* under the assumption that the public will know the rule it is using and so use the currently prevailing g's in (8) in forming its expectations, rather than the old g's that held during the estimation period. The public would presumably know the g's if the monetary authority were to announce them. Failing that, the public might be able to infer the g's from the observed behavior of the money supply and other variables. In any case, on the assumption that the public knows what g's the authority is using, α and λ of equation (1) come to depend on the authority's choice of g's. This fundamentally alters the preceding analysis, as can be seen by substituting $g_0 + g_1 y_{t-1}$ for m_t in (10) to arrive at

$$y_t = (\xi_0 - \xi_1 g_0) + (\xi_2 - \xi_1 g_1)y_{t-1} + \xi_1(g_0 + g_1 y_{t-1} + \varepsilon_t) + u_t$$

or

$$y_t = \xi_0 + \xi_2 y_{t-1} + u_t + \xi_1 \varepsilon_t. \tag{11}$$

According to (11), the stochastic process for y_t does not even involve the parameters g_0 and g_1. Under different values of g_0 and g_1, the public's method of forming its expectations is also different, implying differences in the values of α and λ in (1) under different policy regimes. In our hypothetical model, the resulting differences in α and λ just offset the differences in g_0 and g_1, leaving the behavior of y identical as a result. Put somewhat differently, our old rule "set $g_1 = -\lambda/\beta$" can no longer be fulfilled. For on the assumption that the public uses the correct g's in forming its expectations, it implies

$$g_1 = -\lambda/\beta = (\xi_1 g_1 - \xi_2)/\xi_1 = g_1 - \xi_2/\xi_1$$

or

$$0 = -\xi_2/\xi_1,$$

which is an equality not involving the g's, and one that the monetary authority is powerless to achieve. The rule "$g_1 = -\lambda/\beta$" in no way restricts g_1.

The point is that estimated reduced forms like (1) or (10) often have parameters that depend partly on the way unobservable expectations of the public are correlated with the variables on the right side of the equation, which in turn depends on the public's perception of how policymakers are behaving. If the public's perceptions are accurate, then the way in which its expectations are formed will change whenever policy changes, which will lead to changes in the parameters α and λ of the reduced-form equation. It is consequently improper to manipulate that reduced form as if its parameters were invariant with respect to changes in g_0 and g_1. According to this argument, then, the above "proof" of the inferiority of a rule without feedback is fallacious. The argument for the "look at everything, respond to everything" view is correspondingly vitiated.

The simple model above is one in which there is no scope for the authority to conduct countercyclical policy by suitably choosing g_0 and g_1 so as to minimize the variance of y. Indeed, one choice of the g's is as good as another, so far as concerns the variance of y, so that the authority might as well set g_1 equal to zero, thereby following a rule without feedback. It seems, then, that our example contains the ingredients for constructing a more general defense of rules without feedback. These ingredients are two: first, the authority's instrument appears in the reduced form for the real variable y only as the discrepancy of the instrument's setting from the public's prior expectation of that setting; and second, the public's psychological expectation of the setting for the instrument equals the objective mathematical expectation conditioned on data available when the expectation was formed. The first property in part reflects a homogeneity of degree zero of supply with respect to prices and expected prices, the natural unemployment rate hypothesis. But it also derives partly from the second property, which is the specification that the public's expectations are "rational," that is, are formed using the appropriate data and objective probability distributions.

The natural rate hypothesis posits that fully anticipated increases in prices have no effects on the rate of real economic activity, as indexed for example by the unemployment rate. A Phillips curve that obeys the natural rate hypothesis can be written as

$$p_t - p_{t-1} = \phi_0 + \phi_1 U_t + {}_{t-1}p_t^* - p_{t-1} + \varepsilon_t, \qquad \phi_1 < 0, \qquad (12)$$

or

$$p_t - {}_{t-1}p_t^* = \phi_0 + \phi_1 U_t + \varepsilon_t, \qquad (13)$$

where U_t is the unemployment rate, p_t is the log of the price level, ${}_{t-1}p_t^*$ is the log of the price level that the public expects to prevail at time t as of time $t - 1$, and ε_t is a random term. According to (12), the Phillips curve shifts up by the full amount of any increase in expected inflation. That implies, as indicated by equation (13), that if inflation is fully anticipated, so that $p_t = {}_{t-1}p_t^*$, then the unemployment rate is unaffected by the rate of inflation, since (13) becomes one equation,

$$0 = \phi_0 + \phi_1 U_t + \varepsilon_t,$$

that is capable of determining the unemployment rate independently of the rate of inflation.

As Phelps (1972) and Hall (in press) have pointed out, in and of itself, the natural rate hypothesis does not weaken the logical foundations for "activist" Keynesian macroeconomic policy, i.e., rules with feedback. This fact has prompted some to view the natural rate hypothesis as an intellectual curiosity, having but remote policy implications.[3] To illustrate, we complete the model by adding to (13) a reduced form aggregate demand schedule and an hypothesis about the formation of expectations. We subsume "Okun's Law" in the former and assume it takes the form

$$p_t = am_t + bx_t + cU_t, \qquad c > 0, \qquad (14)$$

where m_t is the log of the money supply, the authority's instrument; and x_t is a vector of exogenous variables that follows the Markov scheme $x_t = \delta x_{t-1} + u_t$, u_t being a vector of random variables. For price expectations, we posit the ad hoc, in general "irrational" scheme,

$$_{t-1}p_t^* = \lambda p_{t-1}, \qquad (15)$$

[3]E.g., see the remarks attributed to Franco Modigliani in Sargent (1973), p. 480.

where λ is a parameter. Using (13)–(15), we can easily solve for unemployment as a function of m_t and x_t,

$$U_t = [\phi_0 - a(m_t - \lambda m_{t-1}) - b(x_t - \lambda x_{t-1}) + c\lambda U_{t-1} + \varepsilon_t]/(c - \phi_1). \tag{16}$$

It follows that the current setting for m_t affects both current and future values of unemployment and inflation. Given that the authority wishes to minimize a loss function that depends on current and future unemployment and perhaps inflation, the choice of m_t is a nontrivial dynamic optimization problem, the solution to which can often be characterized as a control rule with feedback. The optimal policy rule will depend on all of the parameters of the model and on the parameters of the authority's loss function. The policy problem in this context has been studied by Hall and Phelps. The authority can improve the characteristics of the fluctuations in unemployment and inflation by setting m so as to offset disturbances to the x's.

In this system, if the authority has a "humane" loss function that assigns regret to unemployment and that discounts the future somewhat, the authority should to some extent exploit the trade-off between inflation and unemployment implied by (14) and (16). As Hall (in press) has emphasized, the authority is able to do this by fooling people:

> the benefits of inflation derive from the use of expansionary policy to trick economic agents into behaving in socially preferable ways even though their behavior is not in their own interests. . . . The gap between actual and expected inflation measures the extent of the trickery. . . . The optimal policy is not nearly as expansionary when expectations adjust rapidly, and most of the effect of an inflationary policy is dissipated in costly anticipated inflation.

Hall has pinpointed the source of the authority's power to manipulate the economy. This can be seen by noting that removing the assumption that the authority can systematically trick the public eliminates the implication that there is an exploitable trade-off between inflation and unemployment in *any* sense pertinent for making policy. The assumption that the public's expectations are "rational" and so equal to objective mathematical expectations accomplishes precisely this. Imposing rationality amounts to discarding (15) and replacing it with

$$_{t-1}p_t^* = E_{t-1}p_t, \tag{17}$$

where E_{t-1} is the mathematical expectation operator conditional on information known at the end of period $t - 1$. If (17) is used in place of (15), equation (16) must be replaced with[4]

$$U_t = [a(m_t - E_{t-1}m_t) + b(x_t - E_{t-1}x_t) - \varepsilon_t]/(\phi_1 - c) - \phi_0/\phi_1. \qquad (18)$$

To solve the model for U_t, it is necessary to specify how the authority is behaving. Suppose we assume that the authority uses the feedback rule,

$$m_t = G\theta_{t-1} + \eta_t, \qquad (19)$$

where θ_{t-1} is a set of observations on variables dated $t - 1$ and earlier, and η_t is a serially uncorrelated error term obeying $E[\eta_t|\theta_{t-1}] = 0$; G is a vector conformable with θ_{t-1}.

If the rule is (19) and expectations about m are rational, then

$$E_{t-1}m_t \equiv Em_t|\theta_{t-1} = G\theta_{t-1}, \qquad (20)$$

since $E[\eta_t|\theta_{t-1}] = 0$. So we have

$$m_t - E_{t-1}m_t = \eta_t. \qquad (21)$$

Substituting from (21) into (18) we have

$$U_t = [a\eta_t + b(x_t - E_{t-1}x_t) - \varepsilon_t]/(\phi_1 - c) - \phi_0/\phi_1. \qquad (22)$$

Since the parameters G of the feedback rule don't appear in (22), we can conclude that the probability distribution of unemployment is independent of the values chosen for G. The distribution of the random, unpredictable component of m, which is η, influences the distribution of unemployment but there is no way in which this fact provides any logical basis for employing a rule with feedback. The η's have a place in (22) only because they are unpredictable noise. On the basis of the information in θ_{t-1}, there is no way that the η's can be predicted, either by the authority or the public.

In this system, there is no sense in which the authority has the option to conduct countercyclical policy. To exploit the Phillips curve, it must somehow trick the public. But by virtue of the assumption that expectations are rational, there is no feedback rule that the authority can employ and expect to be able systematically to fool the public. This means that the authority cannot expect to exploit the Phillips curve even for one period.

[4]Using (17), compute E_{t-1} of both sides of (13) and subtract the result from (13) to get

$$p_t - {}_{t-1}p_t^* = \phi_1(U_t - E_{t-1}U_t) + \varepsilon_t. \qquad (i)$$

Perform the same operation on (14) to get

$$p_t - {}_{t-1}p_t^* = a(m_t - E_{t-1}m_t) + b(x_t - E_{t-1}x_t) + c(U_t - E_{t-1}U_t). \qquad (ii)$$

Solve (i) for $(U_t - E_{t-1}U_t)$ and substitute the result into (ii) to get

$$(1 - c/\phi_1)(p_t - {}_{t-1}p_t^*) = a(m_t - E_{t-1}m_t) - (c/\phi_1)\varepsilon_t + b(x_t - E_{t-1}x_t). \qquad (iii)$$

Upon substituting the implied expression for $(p_t - {}_{t-1}p_t^*)$ into (13), we get (18).

Thus, combining the natural rate hypothesis with the assumption that expectations are rational transforms the former from a curiosity with perhaps remote policy implications into an hypothesis with immediate and drastic implications about the feasibility of pursuing countercyclical policy.[5]

As indicated above, by a countercyclical policy we mean a rule with feedback from current and past economic variables to the authority's instrument, as in a regime in which the authority "leans against the wind." While the present model suggests reasons for questioning even the possibility of a successful countercyclical policy aimed at improving the behavior of the unemployment rate or some closely related index of aggregate activity, the model is compatible with the view that there is an optimal rule for the monetary authority, albeit one that need incorporate no feedback. Such an optimal rule could be determined by an analysis that determines the optimal rate of expected inflation, along the lines of Bailey (1956) or Tobin (1968). If there is an optimal expected rate of inflation, it seems to imply restrictions on the constant and trend terms (and maybe the coefficients on some slowly moving exogenous variables like the labor force) of a rule for the money supply, but is not a cause for arguing for a feedback rule from endogenous variables to the money supply. The optimal rate of inflation, if there is one, thus has virtually no implications for the question of countercyclical policy. Furthermore, there is hardly any theoretical agreement about what the optimal rate of expected inflation is, so that it seems to be a weak reed for a control rule to lean on.

The simple models utilized above illustrate the implications of imposing the natural rate and rational expectations hypotheses in interpreting the statistical correlations summarized by the reduced forms of macroeconometric models, reduced forms that capture the correlations between monetary and fiscal variables on the one hand, and various real variables on the other hand. What is there to recommend these two hypotheses? Ordinarily, we impose two requirements on an economic model: first, that it be consistent with the theoretical core of economics-optimizing behavior within a coherent general equilibrium framework; and second, that it not be refuted by observations. Empirical studies have not turned up much evidence that would cause rejection at high confidence levels of models incorporating our two hypotheses.[6] Furthermore, models along these lines seem to be the only existing ones consistent with individuals' maximizing behavior that are capable of rationalizing certain important correlations,

[5]The original version of such a "neutrality" result is due to Lucas (1972b). His formulation is much deeper and more elegant than the one here, since his procedure is to start from individual agents' objectives and their information and then to investigate the characteristics of general equilibria. Less elegant formulations of neutrality results are in Sargent (1973) and Sargent and Wallace (1975).

[6]See Lucas (1973) and Sargent (in press) for empirical tests of the natural rate hypothesis.

such as the Phillips curve, that exist in the data and are summarized by the reduced forms of macroeconometric models. The key feature of models that imply our hypotheses has been described by Lucas (1973): "All formulations of the natural rate theory postulate rational agents, whose decisions depend on *relative* prices only, placed in an economic setting in which they cannot distinguish relative from general price movements." Their inability separately to identify relative and overall nominal price changes is what gives rise to reduced forms like (1). But their rationality implies that only the surprise components of the aggregate demand variables enter. And this has the far-reaching policy implications described above.

Several reasons can be given for using the hypotheses of rational expectations. An important one is that it is consistent with the findings that large parts of macroeconometric models typically fail tests for structural change (essentially versions of Chow tests).[7] As equation (10) illustrates, if expectations are rational and properly take into account the way policy instruments and other exogenous variables evolve, the coefficients in certain representations of the model (e.g., reduced forms) will change whenever the processes governing those policy instruments and exogenous variables change. A major impetus to work on rational expectations is thus that it offers one reason, but probably not the only reason, that macroeconometric models fail tests for structural change. Indeed, the hypothesis of rational expectations even offers some hope for explaining how certain representations of the model change out of the sample.

A second reason for employing the hypothesis of rational expectations is that in estimating econometric models it is a source of identifying restrictions. The usual method of modelling expectations in macroeconometric models—via a distributed lag on the own variable—leaves it impossible to sort out the scalar multiplying the public's expectations from the magnitude of the weights in the distributed lag on own lags by which expectations are assumed to be formed. Therefore, the coefficients on expectations are generally underidentified econometrically. The way out of this has usually been to impose a unit sum on the distributed lag whereby expectations are formed. The problem is that this is an ad hoc identifying restriction with no economic reason to recommend it. It is generally incompatible with the hypothesis of rational expectations, which can be used to supply an alternative identifying restriction.[8]

A third reason for using the rational expectations hypothesis is that it accords with the economist's usual practice of assuming that people behave in their own best interests. This is not to deny that some people are irrational and neurotic. But we have no reason to believe that those irrationalities cause *systematic and predictable* deviations from rational behavior

[7]E.g., see Muench et al. (1974).
[8]See Lucas (1972a, 1973) and Sargent (1971).

that a macroeconomist can model and tell the monetary authority how to compensate for. In this regard, it should be noted that the rational expectations hypothesis does not require that people's expectations equal conditional mathematical expectations, only that they equal conditional mathematical expectations plus what may be a very large random term (random with respect to the conditioning information). Thus we need only assume, for example, that

$$_{t-1}p_t^* = E_{t-1}p_t + \phi_t, \tag{18a}$$

where $E_{t-1}\phi_t = 0$, and ϕ_t is a random "mother-in-law" term allowing for what may be very large random deviations from rationality. It is easy to verify that all of our results about countercyclical policy go through when (18a) is assumed. Therefore, in the context of the natural rate hypothesis, random deviations from perfectly rational expectations buy the monetary authority no leverage in making countercyclical policy. To be able to conduct a countercyclical policy, there must be systematic deviations from rational expectations which the monetary authority somehow knows about and can predict.

A fourth reason for adopting the hypothesis of rational expectations is the value of the questions it forces us to face. We must specify exactly the horizon over which the expectations are cast and what variables people are assumed to see and when, things that most macroeconometric models are silent on. In doing policy analysis under rational expectations, we must specify whether a given movement in a policy variable was foreseen beforehand or unforeseen, an old and important distinction in economics, but one that makes no difference in the usual evaluations of policy made with macroeconometric models.

Although the imposition of the natural rate and rational expectations hypotheses on reduced-form equations like (1) has allowed us to state some important results, such reasoning is no substitute for analysis of the underlying microeconomic models. Manipulation of such reduced forms even under the interpretation given by equations (7)–(9), which imposes the natural rate and rational expectations hypotheses, can be misleading because it leaves implicit some of the dependencies between parameters and rules. (E.g., the "structure" consisting of [7]–[9] is itself a reduced form suggested by Lucas [1973], some of whose parameters depend on the variance of ε_t in [8].) Also, a welfare analysis using such a model can be misleading because it requires adoption of an ad hoc welfare criterion, like the "humane" loss function described above. In general, such a loss function is inconsistent with the usual welfare criterion employed in models with optimizing agents—Pareto optimality.

Finally, we want to take note of a very general implication of rationality that seems to present a dilemma. Dynamic models that invoke rational expectations can be solved only by attributing to the agents whose behavior is being described a way of forming views about the dynamic processes governing the policy variables. Might it not be reasonable at times to attribute to them a systematically incorrect view? Thus suppose an economy has been operating under one rule for a long time when secretly a new rule is adopted. It would seem that people would learn the new rule only gradually as they acquired data and that they would for some time make what from the viewpoint of the policymaker are forecastable prediction errors. During this time, a new rule could be affecting real variables.

A telling objection to this line of argument is that new rules are not adopted in a vacuum. Something would cause the change—a change in administrations, new appointments, and so on. Moreover, if rational agents live in a world in which rules can be and are changed, their behavior should take into account such possibilities and should depend on the process generating the rule changes. But invoking this kind of complete rationality seems to rule out normative economics completely by, in effect, ruling out freedom for the policymaker. For in a model with completely rational expectations, including a rich enough description of policy, it seems impossible to define a sense in which there is any scope for discussing the optimal design of policy rules. That is because the equilibrium values of the endogenous variables already reflect, in the proper way, the parameters describing the authorities' prospective subsequent behavior, including the probability that this or that proposal for reforming policy will be adopted.

Thus, suppose that a policy variable x_t is described by the objective probability distribution function,

$$\text{Prob}[x_{t+1} < F \mid Y_t, Z_t] = G[F, Y_t, Z_t; g_1, \ldots, g_p], \qquad (23)$$

where $Y_t = [y_t, y_{t-1}, \ldots]$ is a set of observations on current and past values of an endogenous variable, or vector of endogenous variables y; and where $Z_t = [z_t, z_{t-1}, \ldots]$ is a set of observations on current and past values of a list of n exogenous variables and disturbances z_t^i, $i = 1, \ldots, n$. The probability distribution has p parameters $g_1, \ldots, g_p$.

The probability distribution in (23) represents a very general description of the prospects about policy. It obviously can describe a situation in which policy is governed by a deterministic feedback rule, in which case the probability distribution collapses to a trivial one. The probability distribution in (23) can also model the case in which the monetary authority follows a feedback rule with random coefficients, coefficients that themselves obey some probability law. This situation is relevant where the monetary authority might consider changing the feedback rule from time to time for one reason or another. The probability distribution (23) can also model the case in which policy is in part simply random. The parameters

$[g_1, \ldots, g_p]$ determine the probability function (23) and summarize all of the factors making up the objective prospects for policy. Policy settings appear to be random drawings from the distribution given in (23).

Now consider a rational expectations, structural model for y_t leading to a reduced form,

$$y_t = h(x_t, x_{t-1}, \ldots, Z_t, E_t y_{t+1}), \qquad (24)$$

where $E_t y_{t+1}$ is the objective expectation of y_{t+1} conditioned on information observed up through time t. The Z_t's are assumed to obey some probability distribution functions,

$$\text{Prob}[z_{t+1}^1 < H^1, z_{t+1}^2 < H^2, \ldots, z_{t+1}^n < H^n \mid Z_t]$$
$$= F[H^1, H^2, \ldots, H^n, Z_t].$$

A final form solution for the model is represented by an equation of the form

$$y_t = \phi(x_t, x_{t-1}, \ldots, Z_t; \bar{g}), \qquad (25)$$

with the property that

$$E_t y_{t+1} = \int \int \phi(x_{t+1}, x_t, \ldots, Z_{t+1}; \bar{g}) \, dG \, dF,$$

so that the expectation of y_{t+1} equals the prediction from the final form. The parameters $\bar{g} = [g_1, \ldots, g_p]$ turn out to be parameters of the final form (25), which our notation is intended to emphasize. Those parameters make their appearance in (25) via the process of eliminating $E_t y_{t+1}$ from (24) by expressing it in terms of the x's and Z's. The parameters of F also are embedded in ϕ for the same reason. That is, the function ϕ must satisfy the equation

$$\phi(x_t, x_{t-1}, \ldots, Z_t; \bar{g})$$

$$= h[x_t, x_{t-1}, \ldots, Z_t, \int \int \phi(x_{t+1}, x_t, \ldots, Z_{t+1}; \bar{g}) \, dG \, dF],$$

in which the parameters of F and G make their appearance by virtue of the integration with respect to G and F.

The final form (25) formally resembles the final forms of the usual macroeconometric models without rational expectations. But there is a crucial difference, for in (25) there are no parameters that the authority is free to choose. The parameters in the vector $\bar{g}$ describe the objective characteristics of the policymaking process and cannot be changed. They capture all of the factors that determine the prospects for policy. The authority in effect makes a random drawing of x from the distribution described by (23). The persons on the committee and staffs that constitute the authority "matter" in the sense that they influence the prospects about policy and so are represented by elements of $\bar{g}$. But the authority has no freedom to influence the parameters of the final form (23), since the objective prospects that it will act wisely or foolishly are known to the public and are properly embedded in the final form (25).

The conundrum facing the economist can be put as follows. In order for a model to have normative implications, it must contain some parameters whose values can be chosen by the policymaker. But if these can be chosen, rational agents will not view them as fixed and will make use of schemes for predicting their values. If the economist models the economy taking these schemes into account, then those parameters become endogenous variables and no longer appear in the reduced-form equations for the other endogenous variables. If he models the economy without taking the schemes into account, he is not imposing rationality.

References

Bailey, M. "The Welfare Cost of Inflationary Finance." *J.P.E.* 64, no. 2 (April 1956): 93–110.

Hall, R. G. "The Phillips Curve and Macroeconomic Policy." In *The Phillips Curve and Labor Markets*, edited by K. Brunner. *J. Monetary Econ.*, suppl., in press.

Kareken, J. H.; Muench, T.; and Wallace, N. "Optimal Open Market Strategy: The Use of Information Variables." *A.E.R.* 63 (March 1973): 156–72.

Lucas, R. E., Jr. "Econometric Testing of the Natural Rate Hypothesis." In *The Econometrics of Price Determination Conference*, edited by O. Eckstein. Board of Governors of the Federal Reserve System and Social Science Research Council, 1972 (a)

———. "Expectations and the Neutrality of Money." *J. Econ. Theory* 4 (April 1972): 103–24. (b)

———. "Some International Evidence on Output–Inflation Tradeoffs." *A.E.R.* 63 (June 1973): 326–34.

———. "Econometric Policy Evaluation: A Critique." In *The Phillips Curve and Labor Markets*", ed. by K. Brunner and A. H. Meltzer. Carnegie-Rochester Conferences on Public Policy, 1. Amsterdam: North-Holland, 1976.

Muench, T.; Rolnick, A.; Wallace, N.; and Weiler, W. "Tests for Structural Change and Prediction Intervals for the Reduced Forms of Two Structural Models of the U.S.: The FRB-MIT and Michigan Quarterly Models." *Ann. Econ. and Soc. Measurement* 3, no. 3 (1974): 449–519.

Phelps, E. S. *Inflation Policy and Unemployment Theory.* New York: Norton, 1972.

Samuelson, P. A. "Reflections on Recent Federal Reserve Policy." *J. Money, Credit, and Banking* 2, no. 1 (February 1970): 33–44.

Sargent, T. J. "A Note on the Accelerationist Controversy," *J. Money, Credit, and Banking* 3, no. 3 (August 1971): 721–25.

———. "Rational Expectations, the Real Rate of Interest, and the Natural Rate of Unemployment." *Brookings Papers on Economic Activity*, no. 2 (1973): 429–80.

———. "A Classical Macroeconometric Model for the United States." *J.P.E.*, in press.

Sargent, T. J., and Wallace, N. "Rational Expectations, the Optimal Monetary Instrument, and the Optimal Money Supply Rule." *J.P.E.* 83, no. 2 (March–April 1975): 241–54.

Tobin, J. "Notes on Optimal Monetary Growth." *J.P.E.* 76, no. 4, pt. II (1968).

11

"Rational" Expectations, the Optimal Monetary Instrument, and the Optimal Money Supply Rule

Thomas J. Sargent and Neil Wallace

Alternative monetary policies are analyzed in an ad hoc macroeconomic model in which the public's expectations about prices are rational. The ad hoc model is one in which there is long-run neutrality, since it incorporates the aggregate supply schedule proposed by Lucas. Following Poole, the paper studies whether pegging the interest rate or pegging the money supply period by period minimizes an ad hoc quadratic loss function. It turns out that the probability distribution of output—dispersion as well as mean—is independent of the particular deterministic money supply rule in effect, and that under an interest rate rule the price level is indeterminate.

This paper analyzes the effects of alternative ways of conducting monetary policy within the confines of an ad hoc macroeconomic model. By ad hoc we mean that the model is not derived from a consistent set of assumptions about individuals' and firms' objective functions and the information available to them. Despite this deplorable feature of the model, it closely resembles the macroeconomic models currently in use, which is our excuse for studying it. Following Poole (1970), we compare two alternative strategies available to the monetary authority. One is to peg the interest rate period by period, letting the supply of money be whatever it must be to satisfy the demand for it. The other is to set the money supply period by period, accepting whatever interest rate equilibrates the system. We study the effects of such policies for two versions of the model: an autoregressive version in which the public's expectations are assumed formed via fixed autoregressive schemes on the variables being forecast, and a rational-expectations version in which the public's expectations are

Work on this paper was supported by the Federal Reserve Bank of Minneapolis, which does not necessarily endorse the conclusions. Robert Barro, Milton Friedman, John Kareken, and Robert E. Lucas made useful comments on an earlier version of the paper.

[*Journal of Political Economy*, 1975, vol. 83, no. 2]

assumed equal to objective (mathematical) expectations that depend on, among other things, what is known about the rules governing monetary and fiscal policy (see Muth 1961).

The two versions have radically different policy implications. In the rational-expectations version, (a) the probability distribution of output is independent of the deterministic money supply rule in effect, (b) if the loss function includes quadratic terms in the price level, then the optimal deterministic money supply rule is that which equates the expected value of next period's price level to the target value, and (c) a unique equilibrium price level does not exist if the monetary authority pegs the interest rate period by period, regardless of how its value varies from period to period. None of these results emerges from the autoregressive version. It, instead, exhibits all the usual exploitable tradeoffs between output and inflation, implies that minimization of the above loss function is a well-defined nontrivial dynamic problem giving rise to a unique optimal deterministic feedback rule either for the money supply or for the interest rate, and has a unique period-by-period equilibrium if the interest rate is pegged. Thus, in the autoregressive version of the model, which in principle is merely a variant of Poole's model, whether an interest rate feedback rule or a money supply feedback rule is superior depends, just as Poole asserted, on most of the parameters of the model including the covariance matrix of the disturbances.

In the rational-expectations version of the model, one deterministic money supply rule is as good as any other, insofar as concerns the probability distribution of real output. In this weak sense, an X percent growth rule for the money supply is optimal in this model, from the point of view of minimizing the variance of real output. Thus, switching from the assumption of autoregressive expectations to that of rational expectations has drastic policy implications. In particular, making that change transforms the model in which following Friedman's X percent growth rule would in general be foolish into one in which such a rule can be defended as being the best the authority can do.

1. The Ad Hoc Model

We assume a structure described by the following equations:[1]

aggregate supply schedule:

$$y_t = a_1 k_{t-1} + a_2(p_t - {}_t p_{t-1}^*) + u_{1t}, \qquad a_i > 0, i = 1, 2; \quad (1)$$

aggregate demand schedule or "IS" curve:

$$y_t = b_1 k_{t-1} + b_2[r_t - ({}_{t+1}p_{t-1}^* - {}_t p_{t-1}^*)] + b_3 Z_t + u_{2t}, \qquad b_1 > 0, b_2 < 0; \quad (2)$$

[1] The structure closely resembles the model used by Sargent (1973).

portfolio balance or "*LM*" schedule:

$$m_t = p_t + c_1 y_t + c_2 r_t + u_{3t}, \qquad c_1 > 0, c_2 < 0; \tag{3}$$

determination of productive capacity:

$$k_t = d_1 k_{t-1} + d_2[r_t - ({}_{t+1}p_{t-1}^* - {}_t p_{t-1}^*)] + d_3 Z_t + u_{4t}, \qquad d_2 < 0; \tag{4}$$

evolution of the exogenous variables:

$$Z_t = \sum_{j=1}^{q} \rho_j Z_{t-j} + \xi_t,$$

$$u_{it} = \sum_{j=1}^{q} \rho_{ij} u_{i,t-j} + \xi_{i,t}. \tag{5}$$

Here y_t, p_t, and m_t are the natural logarithms of output, the price level, and the money supply, respectively; r_t is the nominal rate of interest itself (not its logarithm); while Z_t is the vector of exogenous variables. The variable ${}_{t+i}p_{t-j}^*$ is the public's psychological expectation of the log of the price level to prevail at $t + i$, the expectation being held as of the end of period $t - j$. The variable k_{t-1} is a measure of productive capacity, such as the logarithm of the stock of capital or labor or some linear combination of the logarithms of those stocks at the end of period $t - 1$.

Equation (1) is an aggregate supply schedule relating output directly to productive capacity and the gap between the current price level and the public's prior expectation of the current price level. Unexpected increases in the price level thus boost aggregate supply, the reason being that suppliers of labor and goods mistakenly interpret surprise increases in the aggregate price level as increases in the relative prices of the labor and goods they are supplying. This happens because suppliers receive information about the prices of their own goods faster than they receive information about the aggregate price level. This is the kind of aggregate supply schedule that Lucas (1973) has used to explain the inverse correlation between observed inflation and unemployment depicted by the Phillips curve.

Equation (2) is an aggregate demand or "*IS*" schedule showing the dependence of aggregate demand on the real rate of interest and capacity, a measure of wealth. The real rate of interest equals the nominal rate r_t minus the rate of inflation between t and $t + 1$ expected by the public as of the end of period $t - 1$, namely, ${}_{t+1}p_{t-1}^* - {}_t p_{t-1}^*$. The rate r_t is assumed to be the yield to maturity on a one-period bond. Aggregate demand also depends on a vector of exogenous variables Z_t which includes government expenditures and tax rates.

Equation (3) summarizes the condition for portfolio balance. Owners of bonds and equities (assumed to be viewed as perfect substitutes for one another) are satisfied with the division of their portfolios between money, on the one hand, and bonds and equities, on the other hand, when equation (3) is satisfied. Equation (3) posits that the demand for real balances depends directly on real income and inversely on the nominal rate of interest.

Equation (4) determines productive capacity for the next period, while equation (5) describes autoregressive processes for the exogenous variables. The ζ's, which are sometimes called the "innovations" in the Z and u processes, are serially uncorrelated random variables.

To complete the model, we need equations describing $_{t+1}p^*_{t-1}$ and $_t p^*_{t-1}$. Adding those equations to (1)–(5) then results in a system capable of determining the evolution over time of y_t, p_t, r_t, $_{t+1}p^*_{t-1}$, and $_t p^*_{t-1}$ and k_t.

2. The Stabilization Problem

In order to discuss policy within the context of an ad hoc model, we must adopt an ad hoc loss function. The most familiar such function is the quadratic loss function

$$L = E_0 \sum_{t=1}^{\infty} \delta^{t-1}\left[(y_t, p_t)K(y_t, p_t)' + (y_t, p_y)(K_1, K_2)' + \frac{K_1^2}{4} + \frac{K_2^2}{4} \right],$$

where K is diagonal with elements $K_{ii} > 0$, $i = 1, 2$; K_1 and K_2 are parameters; and $0 < \delta < 1$. This function is separately quadratic in y and p and implies that $L = 0$, its lower bound, at particular constant values of y and p, the target values $-K_1/2K_{11}$ for y and $-K_2/2K_{22}$ for p. This function is easy to work with because it is quadratic, additive over time, and stationary in that the function of y and p whose expectation is to be minimized does not depend on t.

To minimize L, the monetary authority compares two strategies. The first is to peg r_t via a deterministic linear feedback rule

$$r_t = G\theta^*_{t-1}, \tag{6}$$

where θ^*_t represents the set of current and past values of all of the endogenous and exogenous variables in the system as of the end of period t, and G is a vector of parameters conformable to θ^*_{t-1}. The monetary authority chooses the parameters in G to minimize L. It must then compare the minimum loss associated with an interest rate rule having those G's with the loss associated with the best money supply feedback rule of the form

$$m_t = H\theta^*_{t-1}. \tag{7}$$

Whichever rule delivers the lower loss is the one that should be used.

3. The Autoregressive Expectations Version

Here we assume that the psychological expectations $_t p^*_{t-1}$ and $_{t+1} p^*_{t-1}$ are governed by the distributed-lag or "adaptive" schemes

$$_{t+1} p^*_t = \sum_{i=0}^{q} v_{1i} p_{t-i}, \tag{8}$$

$$_{t+2} p^*_t = \sum_{i=0}^{q} v_{2i} p_{t-i}, \tag{9}$$

where the v_{1i}'s and v_{2i}'s are fixed numbers. Given that the money supply is used as the monetary instrument, the system formed by equations (1)–(5), (8), and (9) can be reduced to a difference equation of the form

$$Y_{1t} = \sum_{i=1}^{q'} A_i Y_{1t-i} + \sum_{i=0}^{q'} B_i m_{t-i} + \phi_{1t}, \tag{10}$$

where $Y'_{1t} = (y_t, p_t, r_t, k_{t-1}, Z_t)$ and ϕ_{1t} is a vector of serially un-correlated random variables, the components of which are functions of the ξ_t's in equations (5). The A_i's are vectors conformable with Y_{1t} and the B_i's are scalars; both the A_i's and B_i's depend on the parameters of equations (1)–(5), (8), and (9). To find the best money-supply feedback rule, the monetary authority chooses the parameters H of the rule (7) to minimize the loss L subject to (10). Where loss is quadratic and the model is linear with known coefficients, rules of the linear form of (7) are known to be optimal.[2]

To find the optimal interest rate rule, the system formed by equations (1)–(5), (8), and (9) is written as

$$Y_{2t} = \sum_{i=1}^{q'} C_i Y_{2t-i} + \sum_{i=0}^{q'} D_i r_{t-i} + \phi_{2t}, \tag{11}$$

where $Y'_{2t} = (y_t, p_t, m_t, k_{t-1}, Z_t)$. The optimal interest rate rule is the one with the G's of (6) chosen so as to minimize loss L subject to (11).[3]

To show that (1)–(5), (8), and (9) yield versions of (10) and (11) that give rise to well-defined, nontrivial dynamic problems, it is enough to examine the one-period reduced forms for y_t and p_t.

With the money supply as the monetary instrument, we solve (1)–(3) for y, r, and p and get as a reduced form for p_t

$$p_t = J_0(_t p^*_{t-1}) + J_1(_{t+1} p^*_{t-1}) + J_2 m_t + X_t, \tag{12}$$

---

[2] See Chow (1970).

[3] Chow (1970) describes how optimal rules of the form (6) or (7) are found for a system like (10) or (11).

where X_t is a linear function (involving the parameters of [1]–[3]) of k_{t-1}, Z_t, and the u_{it}'s and where

$$J_0 = [a_2(1 + b_2c_2^{-1}) + b_2]/[a_2(1 + b_2c_2^{-1}) + b_2c_2^{-1}] < 1,$$

$$J_1 = (1 - J_0)/(1 - c_2^{-1}),$$

$$J_2 = -c_2^{-1}J_1.$$

Substitution of p_t from equation (12) into equation (1) gives the one-period reduced form for y_t. Taking E_{t-1} of p_t and y_t from these reduced forms and eliminating m_t gives the set of pairs $(E_{t-1}y_t, E_{t-1}p_t)$ attainable by choice of m_t. The set is a line whose slope is neither infinity nor zero. Its position, obviously, depends on lagged values of p, via the p^* variables, and on lagged values of other endogenous variables, the distributions of which depend on lagged values of m. In other words, the choice for the deterministic part of m_t has effects in future periods, which is what we mean when we say that (10) gives rise to a nontrivial dynamic problem.

With the interest rate as the monetary instrument, equation (2) is the one-period reduced form for y_t while that for p_t is obtained by substituting the solution for y_t into equation (1) and solving for p_t. The solution for p_t is

$$a_2p_t = (a_2 + b_2)_t p_{t-1}^* - b_2(_{t+1}p_{t-1}^*) + b_2r_t$$
$$+ (b_1 - a_1)k_{t-1} + b_3Z_t - u_{1t} + u_{2t}. \tag{13}$$

Again, if we take E_{t-1} of equation (2) and equation (13) and eliminate r_t, we find the set of pairs $(E_{t-1}y_t, E_{t-1}p_t)$ attainable by choice of r_t. That set again depends on lagged values of p, which shows that (11) also gives rise to a nontrivial dynamic problem.

The monetary authority is supposed to solve each of the two dynamic problems, minimizing loss first under an m rule and then under an r rule. Which policy is superior depends on which delivers the smaller loss, which in turn depends on all of the parameters of the model, including the covariance matrix of the disturbances. Which rule is superior is therefore an empirical matter, an outcome which is completely consistent with Poole's analysis.

4. The Rational-Expectations Version under a Money Supply Rule

Here we impose the requirement that the public's expectations be rational by requiring that

$$_{t+i}p_{t-j}^* = E_{t-j}p_{t+i}, \tag{14}$$

where $E_{t-j}p_{t+i}$ is the mathematical expectation of p_{t+i} calculated using the model (i.e., the probability distribution of p_{t+i}) and all information assumed to be available as of the end of period $t - j$. The available information is assumed to consist of data on current and past values of all endogenous and exogenous variables observed as of the end of period $t - j$, that is, θ^*_{t-j}.

To begin, we again solve the system (1)–(3) for y, r, and p given m. With expectations given by (14), what is now a pseudo-reduced-form equation for p is

$$p_t = J_0 E_{t-1} p_t + J_1 E_{t-1} p_{t+1} + J_2 m_t + X_t. \tag{15}$$

Computing $E_{t-1} p_t$ from (15) and subtracting the result from (15) we get

$$p_t - E_{t-1} p_t = J_2(m_t - E_{t-1} m_t) + X_t - E_{t-1} X_t$$
$$= X_t - E_{t-1} X_t, \tag{16}$$

where the last equality follows from the assumption that a deterministic rule of the form (7) is being followed. But since $X_t - E_{t-1} X_t$ is a linear combination of the innovations in the exogenous processes, it follows that $p_t - E_{t-1} p_t$ is an exogenous process, unaffected by the rule chosen for determining the money supply.

Using (14) and (16), we can write equation (1) as

$$y_t = a_1 k_{t-1} + a_2(X_t - E_{t-1} X_t) + u_{1t}. \tag{17}$$

If we substitute the right-hand side for y_t in equation (2), we can obtain the real interest rate as a function of k_{t-1} and exogenous processes. Substituting that function into equation (4), we get a difference equation in k driven by exogenous processes. This proves that k is an exogenous process, which by (17) implies that y is an exogenous process, that is, has a distribution independent of the deterministic rule for the money supply. So we have proved assertion (a) above: the distribution of output does not depend on the parameters of the feedback rule for the money supply.

To prove assertion (b), we write the tth term of the loss function L as

$$L_t = E_0[E_{t-1}(K_2 p_t + K_{22} p_t^2 + K_1 y_t + K_{11} y_t^2)],$$

where the insertion of E_{t-1} is valid for $t > 0$. Using $E(x^2) = E[(x - Ex)^2] + (Ex)^2$, we have

$$L_t = E_0[K_{0t} + K_2 E_{t-1} p_t + K_{22}(E_{t-1} p_t)^2],$$

where

$$K_{0t} = E_{t-1}[K_{22}(p_t - E_{t-1} p_t)^2 + K_1 y_t + K_{11} y_t^2]$$

and where, given the exogeneity of y_t and $p_t - E_{t-1} p_t$ proved above, K_0 is an exogenous process. Moreover, it is possible, as we shall show below, to find a rule for m that implies choosing $E_{t-1} p_t$ to minimize

$$K_{0t} + K_2 E_{t-1} p_t + K_{22}(E_{t-1} p_t)^2.$$

And, because K_{0t} is unaffected by settings for the money supply at any other time, a rule which minimizes L_t also minimizes L.

To show that there exists such a rule for m, we must solve the model. Again, we take $E_{t-1}p_t$ in (15) and write the result as

$$(1 - J_0)E_{t-1}p_t = J_1 E_{t-1}p_{t+1} + J_2 E_{t-1}m_t + E_{t-1}X_t. \qquad (18)$$

Since this holds for all t, it follows that

$$(1 - J_0)E_{t-1}p_{t+j} = J_1 E_{t-1}p_{t+j+1} + J_2 E_{t-1}m_{t+j} \\ + E_{t-1}X_{t+j}. \qquad (19)$$

By repeated substitution from (19) into (18), we obtain

$$(1 - J_0)E_{t-1}p_t = \sum_{j=0}^{n} [J_1/(1 - J_0)]^j (E_{t-1}X_{t+j} + J_2 E_{t-1}m_{t+j}) \\ + [J_1/(1 - J_0)]^{n+1} E_{t-1}p_{t+n+1}, \qquad (20)$$

where

$$0 < J_1/(1 - J_0) = 1/(1 - c_2^{-1}) < 1.$$

We assume that the limit as $n \to \infty$ of the second term on the right-hand side of (20) is zero, which is a terminal condition that has the effect of ruling out "speculative bubbles." Then, from (20),

$$(1 - J_0)E_{t-1}p_t = \sum_{j=0}^{\infty} [J_1/(1 - J_0)]^j E_{t-1}(X_{t+j} + J_2 m_{t+j}). \qquad (21)$$

Since this holds for all t, we may replace t by $t + 1$ and compute E_{t-1} of the result to get

$$(1 - J_0)E_{t-1}p_{t+1} = \sum_{j=0}^{\infty} [J_1/(1 - J_0)]^j \\ \times E_{t-1}(X_{t+j+1} + J_2 m_{t+j+1}). \qquad (22)$$

For an arbitrary money supply rule of the form (7), substituting (21) and (22) into (15) gives the solution for p_t; substituting (21) and (22) into (2) gives the solution for r_t. This assumes that the rule is not such as to imply too explosive a process for $X_{t+j} + J_2 m_{t+j}$.[4]

---

[4] A workable "reduced form" for p_t can be obtained by substituting (20) into (15) and then by using (5) and (7) to replace $E_{t-1}m_{t+j}$ and $E_{t-1}X_{t+j}$ with the linear functions of past variables that they equal. These linear functions are easily calculated from the feedback rule for m_t and the autoregressions governing components of X_t. While the resulting "reduced form" for p_t formally resembles the corresponding equation in the system with "adaptive" expectations, there is a crucial difference. Now changes in the parameters of the feedback rule for m_t produce changes in the parameters of the reduced form for p_t. This feature of the system is what renders Poole's results inapplicable. For an explicit illustration of the dependence of the reduced-form parameters on the form of the policy rule, see Sargent and Wallace (1973, pp. 332–33).

To find the optimal money supply rule, multiply (22) by $J_1/(1 - J_0)$ and subtract the result from (21) to get

$$(1 - J_0)E_{t-1}p_t - J_1 E_{t-1}p_{t+1} = E_{t-1}X_t + J_2 m_t. \tag{23}$$

The value of $E_{t-1}p_t$ that minimizes L_t for all t is

$$E_{t-1}p_t = -K_2/2K_{22}, \tag{24}$$

so that

$$E_{t-1}p_{t+1} = -K_2/2K_{22}. \tag{25}$$

The optimal rule for the money supply is obtained by substituting (24) and (25) into (23). The resulting expression for m_t is a feedback rule of the form (7).

Thus, in the rational-expectations version of our model, the choice among deterministic rules for the money supply is a trivial problem. One argument of the loss function, y, is unaffected by the rule, so the problem becomes the simplest kind of one target–one instrument problem. Moreover, a definite rule emerges only because we have assumed in specifying L that there is a target value for the price level. If, instead, loss were made dependent only on the variance of the price level, then one deterministic rule would be as good as any other.

The reason that the distribution of real output is independent of the systematic money supply rule can be summarized as follows. In order for the monetary authority to induce fluctuations in real output, it must induce unexpected movements in the price level by virtue of the aggregate supply curve (1). But by virtue of the assumption that expectations about the price level are rational, the unexpected part of price movements is independent of the systematic part of the money supply, as long as the authority and the public share the same information. There is no systematic rule that the authority can follow that permits it to affect the unexpected part of the price level. Of course, the authority could add an unpredictable random term to the systematic part of the money supply, so that (7) would be amended to become

$$m_t = H\theta^*_{t-1} + \psi_t, \tag{7'}$$

where ψ_t is a random variable obeying $E\psi_t \mid \theta^*_{t-1} = 0$. Then the distribution of unexpected price movements and of real output will depend on the distribution of ψ_t. But clearly, there is no way the authority can base a countercyclical policy on this particular nonneutrality, since there is no way the authority can regularly choose ψ_t in response to the state of economic affairs in order to offset other disturbances in the system.

This follows since ψ_t is that part of the money supply obeying $E\psi_t \mid \theta_{t-1}^* = 0$. Furthermore, in our model it is optimal to set $\psi_t = 0$ for all t.

5. The Rational-Expectations Version under an Interest Rate Rule

Above we showed that a certain terminal condition implied the existence of a unique equilibrium price level for the rational-expectations version under a money supply rule that is not too explosive. That analysis took as a starting point the difference equation (18). With the interest rate determined by the feedback rule (6), a seemingly analogous difference equation is obtained by imposing rationality, equation (14), in (13) and taking E_{t-1} of the result

$$
\begin{aligned}
0 = {} & b_2(E_{t-1}p_t - E_{t-1}p_{t+1}) + b_2 r_t + (b_1 - a_1)k_{t-1} \\
& + b_3 E_{t-1}(Z_t - u_{1t} + u_{2t}).
\end{aligned}
\tag{26}
$$

If we solve (26) by recursion, proceeding as we did in deriving (20) from (18), we find

$$
\begin{aligned}
E_{t-1}p_t = {} & -\sum_{j=0}^{n} E_{t-1}\{r_{t+j} + [(b_1 - a_1)/b_2]k_{t+j-1} + (b_3/b_2) \\
& \times (Z_{t+j} - u_{1t+j} + u_{2t+j})\} + E_{t-1}p_{t+n+1}.
\end{aligned}
\tag{27}
$$

To obtain a particular solution for $E_{t-1}p_t$ from (27) requires imposing a terminal condition in the form of taking as exogenous a value of $E_{t-1}p_{t+j}$ for some $j \geq 0$. This is obviously a very much stronger terminal condition than we had to impose on (20), a consequence of (26) being a non-convergent difference equation. Thus, when the interest rate is pegged, the model cannot determine a path of expected prices $E_{t-1}p_{t+j}$, $j = 0, 1, \ldots,$ and by implication cannot determine the price level p_t. Neither can it determine the money supply.

The economics behind the underdetermined expected price level is pretty obvious. Under the interest rate rule (6), the public correctly expects that the monetary authority will accommodate whatever quantity of money is demanded at the pegged interest rate. The public therefore expects that, *ceteris paribus*, any increase in p_t will be met by an equal increase in m_t. But that means that one $E_{t-1}p_t$ is as good as any other from the point of view of being rational. There is nothing to anchor the expected price level. And this is not simply a matter of choosing the "wrong" level or rule for the interest rate. There is no interest rate rule that is associated with a determinate price level.

At least since the time of Wicksell it has been known that, in the context of a static analysis of a full-employment model with wages and prices that are flexible instantaneously, it can happen that the price level is indeterminate if the monetary authority pegs the interest rate.[5] In such a static analysis, the indeterminacy of the price level depends critically on output and employment being exogenous with respect to shocks to aggregate demand or portfolio balance; that is, the Phillips curve must be vertical. In our model, however, the Phillips curve is not vertical, but Wicksell's indeterminacy still arises.

6. An Information Advantage for the Monetary Authority

Here we shall examine some consequences of the monetary authority having more information than the public. We shall first show that if the monetary authority follows the money supply rule that is optimal if there is no information discrepancy, then the loss attained is the same as attained when there is no information discrepancy. Then we consider whether that rule is optimal given an information discrepancy.

We shall write E_{t-1} for the expectation conditional on what the monetary authority knows at the end of period $t-1$ and $E_{\theta, t-1}$ for the expectation conditional on what the public knows at the end of period $t-1$, where θ is a subset of what the monetary authority knows. Then in place of (14) we impose

$$_{t+i}p_{t-j}^* = E_{\theta, t-j}p_{t+i},$$ (28)

so that in place of (15) we have

$$p_t = J_0 E_{\theta, t-1}p_t + J_1 E_{\theta, t-1}p_{t+1} + J_2 m_t + X_t.$$ (29)

Then, taking $E_{\theta, t-1}$ of p_t and subtracting from p_t, we have

$$p_t - E_{\theta, t-1}p_t = J_2(m_t - E_{\theta, t-1}m_t) + (X_t - E_{\theta, t-1}X_t).$$ (30)

The rule that we found to be optimal without an information discrepancy is

$$J_2 m_t = -(K_2/2K_{22})(1 - J_0 - J_1) - E_{t-1}X_t.$$ (31)

From this it follows that

$$J_2(m_t - E_{\theta, t-1}m_t) = -E_{t-1}X_t + E_{\theta, t-1}X_t.$$ (32)

Substituting into (30), we have

$$p_t - E_{\theta, t-1}p_t = X_t - E_{t-1}X_t.$$ (33)

[5] See Olivera (1970). In both our model and the standard static model, the aggregate demand schedule must exclude any components of real wealth that vary with the price level if Wicksell's indeterminacy is to arise. For example, if the anticipated rate of capital gains on real (outside) money balances is included in the aggregate demand schedule, the price level is determinate with a pegged interest rate. However, such a system has peculiar stability characteristics, since stability hinges on the sign of the expected rate of inflation.

Upon substituting from (33) into equation (1) of the structure, we get equation (17). And if we substitute for y_t in equation (2) the right-hand side of (17), we obtain $[r_t - E_{\theta, t-1}(p_{t+1} - p_t)]$ as a function of k_{t-1} and the exogenous processes, the same function that we previously found for $r_t - E_{t-1}(p_{t+1} - p_t)$. Then, substituting this function into equation (5) of the structure, we get the same first-order difference equation in k as we had without an information discrepancy. This proves that under the rule given by (31), the distribution of k does not depend on the information discrepancy. It follows then from equation (17) that the same is true for y.

To find the distribution of p_t, we proceed to solve the difference equation

$$(1 - J_0)E_{\theta, t-1}p_t = J_1 E_{\theta, t-1}p_{t+1} + J_2 E_{\theta, t-1}m_t + E_{\theta, t-1}X_t, \qquad (34)$$

which is obtained by taking $E_{\theta, t-1}$ of (29). Then, proceeding as we did for (18), we obtain expressions exactly like (21) and (22) except that in place of E_{t-1} on the left and right we have $E_{\theta, t-1}$.

But from (31)

$$X_{t+j} + J_2 m_{t+j} = -(K_2/2K_{22})(1 - J_0 - J_1) + X_{t+j} - E_{t-1}X_{t+j},$$

so for $j > 0$

$$E_{\theta, t-1}(X_{t+j} + J_2 m_{t+j}) = -(K_2/2K_{22})(1 - J_0 - J_1)$$

$$= E_{t-1}(X_{t+j} + J_2 m_{t+j}).$$

Thus, use of the rule given by (31) implies $E_{\theta, t-1}p_{t+j} = E_{t-1}p_{t+j}$, $j = 0, 1$, which by (29) implies that under the rule given by (31) the distribution of p does not depend on θ, that is, does not depend on the information discrepancy. It follows that the loss attained under the rule given by (31) does not depend on the information discrepancy.

This shows that the monetary authority can do as well given an information discrepancy as it can do if there is none. But can it do better? Can it, as it were, take advantage of the presence of an information discrepancy? We are not sure. But within our structure, the answer seems to be that it can take advantage of a discrepancy, although necessarily in a limited and rather subtle way.

To indicate why, let us focus first on how the distribution of y depends on the rule for m. Under present assumptions, equation (1) of the structure is

$$y_t = a_1 k_{1-t} + a_2(p_t - E_{\theta, t-1}p_t) + u_{1t}. \qquad (35)$$

It follows that as of the end of $t - 1$, $E_{\theta, t-1}y_t$ is unaffected by the choice of m_t, since

$$E_{\theta, t-1}y_t = a_1 E_{\theta, t-1}k_{t-1} + E_{\theta, t-1}u_{1t}. \qquad (36)$$

To find the variance of y_t, we subtract (36) from (35) and obtain $\tilde{y}_t = a_1 \tilde{k}_{t-1} + a_2 \tilde{p}_t + \tilde{u}_{1t}$, where $\tilde{x}_t \equiv x_t - E_{\theta, t-1}x_t$. The variance of

y_t around $E_{\theta,t-1} y_t$ is, therefore,

$$E_{\theta,t-1}(\tilde{y}_t^2) = E_{\theta,t-1}[(a_1 \hat{k}_{t-1} + \hat{u}_{1t})\hat{p}_t] + E_{\theta,t-1}(\hat{p}_t^2)$$
$$+ \text{ other terms,} \tag{37}$$

where $\hat{x}_t \equiv E_{t-1} x_t - E_{\theta,t-1} x_t$ and where the omitted terms are un-affected by the setting for the deterministic part of m_t. Thus, setting m_t according to (31) (i.e., setting $\hat{p}_t = 0$) minimizes $E_{\theta,t-1}(\tilde{y}_t^2)$ only if the first term on the right-hand side of (37) cannot be made negative. That term can be made negative by a rule different from (31) if $a_1 \hat{k}_{t-1} + \hat{u}_{1t} \neq 0$, that is, if the monetary authority knows more about either the k_{t-1} or the u_1 process than does the public. Of course, to take advantage of this information discrepancy, the monetary authority must know precisely how the public's information differs from its own.

Similar conclusions hold for the distribution of k_t. The expectation $E_{\theta,t-1} k_t$ is unaffected by the setting for m_t, but, in general, the variance $E_{\theta,t-1}(\tilde{k}_t^2)$ depends on it and is not minimized by use of the rule given by (31).[6] And since the setting for m_t affects the distribution of (y_{t+j}, p_{t+j}) for $j > 0$ by way of its effect on the distribution of k_t, this means that, given an information discrepancy, our structure gives rise to a non-trivial dynamic problem.

But this should not be taken to mean that we are back in the setting produced by the assumption that expectations are formed on the basis of fixed autoregressive schemes. The information discrepancy assumption does not produce any simple tradeoff between the means of output and the price level. The fact that $E_{\theta,t-1} y_t$ and $E_{\theta,t-1} k_t$ are unaffected by m_t is very limiting if θ contains, say, as little as $(1, p_{t-1}, y_{t-1})$. Second, to exploit the information discrepancy, the monetary authority must know what it is. To assume that it does seems farfetched. Indeed, we suspect that estimating the discrepancy is a very subtle and perhaps intractable econometric problem.

For these reasons, we think some comfort can be taken from the first result established in this section. Use of the rule given by (31) is optimal if the public is as well informed as the monetary authority. The loss attained under that rule does not depend on how well informed the public is, and implementation of the rule does not required knowledge of how well informed the public is.

This does not, of course, deny that there is a gain from learning more about the exogenous processes. Settings for the money supply under the rule given by (31) depend on what the monetary authority knows. Operating under that rule, loss is smaller the more the monetary authority knows about the exogenous processes.

---

[6] The reader may verify this by finding k_t as a function of k_{t-1} and $p_t - E_{\theta,t-1} p_t$ using (35) and equations (2) and (5) of the structure.

7. Concluding Remarks

Given that our conclusions are derived from an ad hoc model, should they be taken seriously? In one sense, they should not be. Because of their ad hoc nature, neither the structure set out in section 1 nor the loss function of section 2 should be accepted as providing a suitable context within which to study macroeconomic policy. Nevertheless, some aspects of our model cannot be dismissed so easily. First, the hypothesis that expectations are rational must be taken seriously, if only because its alternatives, for example, various fixed-weight autoregressive models, are subject to so many objections. Second, the aggregate supply hypothesis is one that has some microeconomic foundations,[7] and it has proved difficult to dispose of empirically.[8] It is precisely these two aspects of our model—rational expectations in conjunction with Lucas's aggregate supply hypothesis—that account for most of our results. We believe that the results concerning systematic countercyclical macroeconomic policy are fairly robust to alterations of other features of the model, such as the aggregate demand schedule and the portfolio balance condition. In particular, the dramatically different implications associated with assuming rational expectations, on the one hand, or fixed autoregressive expectations, on the other hand, will survive such alterations.

References

Chow, Gregory C. "Optimal Stochastic Control of Linear Economic Systems." *J. Money, Credit and Banking* 2 (August 1970): 291–302.

Lucas, Robert E., Jr. "Some International Evidence on Output-Inflation Tradeoffs." *A.E.R.* 63 (June 1973): 326–34.

Muth, John F. "Rational Expectations and the Theory of Price Movements." *Econometrica* 29 (July 1961): 315–35.

Olivera, Julio H. "On Passive Money." *J.P.E.* 78, no. 4, suppl. (July/August 1970): 805–14.

Poole, William. "Optimal Choice of Monetary Policy Instruments in a Simple Stochastic Macro Model." *Q.J.E.* 84 (May 1970): 197–216.

Sargent, Thomas. *"Rational" Expectations, the Real Rate of Interest, and the "Natural" Rate of Unemployment.* Brookings Papers on Economic Activity, no. 2. Washington: Brookings Inst., 1973.

Sargent, Thomas, and Wallace, Neil. "Rational Expectations and the Dynamics of Hyperinflation." *Internat. Econ. Rev.* 14 (June 1973): 328–50.

[7] For example, see Lucas (1973).

[8] Tests of the aggregate supply hypothesis are reported by Lucas (1973) and Sargent (1973).

12

Rational Expectations and the Role of Monetary Policy

Robert J. Barro

The purpose of this paper is to analyze the role of monetary policy in a model with three major characteristics: (1) prices and quantities are competitively determined by market-clearing relationships—that is, by the solution of a competitive equilibrium system; (2) information is imperfect; and (3) expectations of future variables are formed rationally, in the sense of being optimal predictions based on the available information. The focus of the analysis is on the effects of monetary expansion on prices and outputs.

Part 1 of the paper generates a Phillips-curve-type relation in a framework that builds on the work of Friedman (1968) and Lucas (1973). The source of the Phillips curve is a lack of full current information that prevents individuals from dichotomizing unanticipated price movements into relative and absolute components. Hence, although suppliers and demanders in any market form their expectations about future prices (in other markets) in a rational manner, the implied behavior of output in each market does not separate unanticipated supply and demand shifts into relative and aggregate parts. In this framework changes in money that are not fully perceived as nominal disturbances can lead to movements in output. It also follows here that an increase in the variance of the monetary growth rate (which is one component of the variance of aggregate excess demand) induces individuals to attribute a larger fraction of observed price movements to monetary forces, and thereby leads to a reduced responsiveness of output to a given monetary disturbance. Thus, as in Lucas's model, the magnitude of the Phillips curve slope is inversely related to the variance of the monetary growth rate.

Part 1 of the paper also discusses the determination of the variance of

This research was supported by a grant from the Liberty Fund. I have benefited from discussions of earlier versions of this paper at the Federal Reserve Bank of Minneapolis Seminar on Rational Expectations, and at seminars at Chicago, M.I.T., Rochester, and Pennsylvania. I am particularly grateful to Bob Lucas for a number of important suggestions.
[*Journal of Monetary Economics*, 1976, vol. 2]
© 1976 by North-Holland Publishing Company

relative prices and the variance of future prices about their currently predictable values. One interesting conclusion is that an increase in the variance of aggregate excess demand would lead to an increase in the variance of relative prices.

The second part of the paper follows Sargent and Wallace (1975) by inquiring into the role of monetary policy in this type of rational expectations model. Pure variance of money leads to an increase in the variance of output about its full current information position and to an increased variance of future prices about their currently predictable values. Essentially, an additional amount of monetary noise makes it more difficult for individuals to isolate real shifts, and therefore tends to move output away from full information output. Accordingly, to the extent that direct costs of controlling money are neglected, a zero variance of money would be optimal.

I then consider the implications of feedback effects from observed economic variables to money. When the monetary authority lacks superior information, it turns out that this sort of feedback is irrelevant to the determination of output. Essentially, when individuals know the form of the feedback rule and also perceive the variables to which money is reacting, this type of monetary behavior would be taken into account in the formation of expectations. When the monetary authority possesses superior information there is the potential for beneficial countercyclical policy. However, the provision of the superior information to the public has identical implications for output if the costs of providing this information are neglected.

Finally, I consider the case where the monetary authority has superior information about its own monetary rule. This situation might permit a form of systematic policy deception in the "short run," when the public does not appreciate the nature of the deception. However, in my model where the policy criterion concerns the gap between actual and full information output, this type of policy deception is not desirable.

1. A Rational Expectations Model with Imperfect Information

A. Setup of the Model

The model is an extension to the one developed by Lucas (1973). There is one type of nondurable commodity, denoted by y, that can be viewed as a personal service. With this view, the supply of the commodity corresponds to the supply of factor services, and the demand for the commodity corresponds to the demand for factor services. The commodity is transacted in various markets, indexed by $z = 1, \ldots, n$, that are at physically separated locations. The variety of locations for a single good is intended to serve as a proxy for markets in a variety of goods, since the multilocation context seems easier to formalize. There is assumed to be an instantaneous flow of information within any market, but a lag in the flow of information across markets. Hence, at a given point in time, there can be a different commodity price across markets, but only a single price within each market.

The model is constructed in a discrete time period framework, where the length of the period signifies the time delay with which information travels across markets. In the present setup market participants possess full information about the relevant economy-wide variables with a one-period lag. During a single period an individual can visit any of the n markets, but it is assumed to be impossible to visit more than one market during a period.[1] Further, it is supposed that there is sufficient information about last period's prices across markets so that current arbitrage insures that all markets offer the same ex ante distribution of price. In this respect the setup resembles the one used by Mortensen (in press).

Aside from lagged knowledge of aggregate variables, a participant in market z also possesses current information that is assumed to be limited to an observation of the current price in that market, $P_t(z)$. The crucial idea is that certain types of local information are received more rapidly than some aspects of global information—such as prices in other markets. It is this differential information structure that allows for a confusion between relative and absolute shifts, and thereby allows for temporary real effects of unpreceived money movements. Of course, the use of a fixed-length information lag and the distinction of only two types of information, local and global, are abstractions made solely for technical convenience.

Aside from the nondurable commodity, the only other good in the economy is fiat money, M.[2] Money is held by individuals because it is the only available store of value. New money enters the economy as transfer payments from the government. These transfers are received by individuals at the start of each period in an amount that is independent of each individual's money holding during the previous period. It is assumed, for simplicity, that the government does not participate directly in the commodity markets.

In order to keep the model analytically manageable, I have constructed the equations in log-linear form. All of the variables used below in these equations are to be interpreted in logarithmic terms.

[1] The present analysis does not deal with optimal search for information across markets. Further, the manner in which aggregate information is transmitted (with a one-period lag) is not explored. Extensions to incorporate optimal search could be very interesting.

[2] Sargent and Wallace (1975) have constructed a model that is similar in some respects, but which also includes a capital market. As Bob Lucas has pointed out to me, the existence of a single, economy-wide capital market implies that the observation of the price (rate of return) on this market conveys important aggregate information. This sort of current aggregate information is very different from the current local information that I assume is available in the present model. I plan to deal at a later time with the different type of information structure that is implied by the existence of an economy-wide capital market.

The supply of the commodity at date t in market z, denoted by $y_t^s(z)$, is assumed to depend on the following set of variables: (1) A systematic supply term, $k_t^s(z)$, that is intended to capture systematic changes in technology, population, etc. (2) A term that measures the current price of output in market z, $P_t(z)$, relative to the price that is expected to prevail next period.[3] Because all of next period's markets have the same ex ante distribution of price, it can be assumed that this expectation applies to P_{t+1}, the (geometric, unweighted) average of prices across the markets at date $t + 1$. If $I_t(z)$ denotes the information possessed at date t by participants in market z,[4] then $E P_{t+1} | I_t(z)$ is the relevant price expectation. A positive response of supply to the term $P_t(z) - E P_{t+1} | I_t(z)$ can be viewed as an effect of speculation over time associated with the intertemporal substitutability of leisure. This type of effect has been discussed in Lucas and Rapping (1969) and Lucas (1972). (3) A wealth variable, measured as $[M_t + E \Delta M_{t+1} | I_t(z) - E P_{t+1} | I_t(z)]$,[5] that is assumed to have a positive effect on desired leisure, and hence a negative effect on factor supply and a negative effect on $y_t^s(z)$. The inclusion of the (log of the) aggregate money stock, M_t, reflects a simplifying assumption that the total money possessed by participants in market z, $M_t(z)$, is always the same fraction of the aggregate money stock.[6] The term $E \Delta M_{t+1} | I_t(z)$, where $\Delta M_{t+1} \equiv M_{t+1} - M_t$, accounts for the expected governmental transfer at the start of the next period. (4) Random terms u_t^s and $\varepsilon_t^s(z)$, where u_t^s is a shift term on aggregate supply, and $\varepsilon_t^s(z)$ is a shift term on relative supply in market z. The sample mean of $\varepsilon_t^s(z)$ across the markets is zero by definition. Other properties of the distributions of these random variables will be discussed below, after the introduction of the demand side of the model.

The specific form of the supply function (in log-linear terms) is

$$
\begin{aligned}
y_t^s(z) = k_t^s(z) + \alpha_s[P_t(z) - E P_{t+1} | I_t(z)] \\
- \beta_s[M_t + E \Delta M_{t+1} | I_t(z) - E P_{t+1} | I_t(z)] + u_t^s + \varepsilon_t^s(z),
\end{aligned}
\tag{1}
$$

where α_s and β_s are, respectively, the (absolute values of the) relative price and wealth elasticities of current commodity supply. It should be noted that the wealth term in equation (1) does not hold constant the appropriate measure of wealth when $P_t(z)$ changes. The price deflator for the

---

[3] The inclusion of expected prices at dates further into the future does not seem to have any important effects in the present model.

[4] The present framework is sufficiently simple so that all participants in a single market at a given point in time have the same information set. In this respect, Lucas (1975) considers a more complicated setup.

[5] It would seem preferable to subtract off the expected desired real money holding at date $t + 1$. However, this change would complicate the exposition of the model without affecting the main results. See the discussion at the end of Appendix 2.

[6] Lucas (1972) develops a model in which this fraction is a random variable. In my model the random relative disturbance terms, discussed next, serve the same purpose.

wealth term should be a (weighted) price index that includes $P_t(z)$ as well as $E P_{t+1}$. The full effect of $P_t(z)$ on $y_t^s(z)$ includes a positive substitution effect plus a reinforcing effect that derives from the reduction in appropriately measured wealth. However, this wealth effect would be negligible if the weight of the current period, during which $P_t(z)$ applies, is small relative to the weight of the future period(s), during which $E P_{t+1}$ applies. Subsequently, the important issue concerns the net effect of $E P_{t+1}$ on $y_t^s(z)$, which depends from equation (1) on the sign of $\beta_s - \alpha_s$. If the current period is viewed as short relative to the length of the future, then the substitution effect, as measured by α_s, would tend to dominate over the wealth effect β_s. It is assumed below that the substitution effect is dominant, so that $\alpha_s > \beta_s$ and the net effect of $E P_{t+1}$ on $y_t^s(z)$ is negative.

The specification of the demand side of the model is parallel to that of the supply side,

$$
\begin{aligned}
y_t^d(z) = k_t^d(z) &- \alpha_d[P_t(z) - E P_{t+1} | I_t(z)] \\
&+ \beta_d[M_t + E \,\Delta M_{t+1} | I_t(z) - E P_{t+1} | I_t(z)] + u_t^d + \varepsilon_t^d(z).
\end{aligned} \tag{2}
$$

Price speculation by demanders implies a negative effect of $[P_t(z) - E P_{t+1} | I_t(z)]$ on $y_t^d(z)$, as measured by the elasticity $-\alpha_d$. Note that demanders in market z are assumed to possess the same information set, $I_t(z)$, as suppliers to this market.[7] The positive effect of wealth on commodity demand is measured by the elasticity β_d. As discussed in the case of supply, it is assumed that the substitution effect of $E P_{t+1}$ is dominant, so that $\alpha_d > \beta_d$ applies. Finally, u_t^d and $\varepsilon_t^d(z)$ are stochastic shift terms that are analogous to those introduced into the supply function.

B. Market-Clearing Determination of Prices and Outputs

Before deriving the market-clearing conditions, it is useful to define the excess demand variables,

$$
\begin{aligned}
k_t(z) &\equiv k_t^d(z) - k_t^s(z), \\
u_t &\equiv u_t^d - u_t^s, \\
\varepsilon_t(z) &\equiv \varepsilon_t^d(z) - \varepsilon_t^s(z).
\end{aligned}
$$

The determination of prices depends solely on excess demand measures, but the determination of output (below) requires also the specification of

---

[7]In the present setup an individual supplies and demands commodities simultaneously in the same market. It would be possible to allow each individual to visit two markets in each period, one for supply and one for demand, but the resulting complications in information sets are considerable. Separate concepts of supply and demand can be maintained here if one thinks of the commodity that an individual supplies as not being identical to those he demands (e.g., back-scratching services?).

separate supply and demand functions. I assume in the main text that u_t is generated by a random walk process,

$$u_t = u_{t-1} + v_t,$$
$$v_t \sim N(0, \sigma_v^2),$$

where N refers to the normal distribution. The random variable v_t is serially independent and represents the current period's "innovation" to real aggregate excess demand. Because u_t has a one-to-one effect on u_{t+1}, the v-innovations are "permanent" in the sense of determining the most likely position of all future values of u. I consider in Appendix 1 the implications of substituting a first-order Markov process, $u_t = \lambda u_{t-1} + v_t$, where $0 \leqq \lambda \leqq 1$. In this formulation, smaller values of λ signify that v_t has more of a transitory and less of a permanent effect on excess demand.

I assume that $\varepsilon_t(z)$ is serially independent and independent of u_t,[8] where $\varepsilon_t(z) \sim N(0, \sigma_\varepsilon^2)$. The ε-shifts are purely transitory, in the sense of lasting only one period. This assumption seems best viewed as reflecting substantial arbitrage possibilities across markets over one period of time, rather than implying that relative shifts in taste, technology, etc., are short-lived.

Finally, it is useful to define the (absolute value of the) price elasticity of excess demand, $\alpha \equiv \alpha_s + \alpha_d$, and the wealth elasticity, $\beta \equiv \beta_s + \beta_d$. The earlier assumptions on the dominance of substitution effects imply $\alpha > \beta$.

The price at date t in market z is determined to equate supply and demand in that market.[9] Equating the expressions in equations (1) and (2), and using the above definitions, leads to the market-clearing condition for market z,

$$\alpha P_t(z) = (\alpha - \beta)E P_{t+1} | I_t(z) + \beta[M_t + E \Delta M_{t+1} | I_t(z)] \\ + k_t(z) + u_t + \varepsilon_t(z). \tag{3}$$

It is apparent from the form of equation (3) and the assumed serial independence of $\varepsilon_t(z)$ that the distribution of $P_t(z)$ can be independent of the market index, z, only if $k_t(z)$ is constant across markets. That is, the arbitrage condition that ensures that all markets have the same ex ante distri-

---

[8]Since the sample mean of $\varepsilon_t(z)$ is zero by definition, the distribution of $\varepsilon_t(z)$ would actually depend on the number of markets. However, this consideration seems unimportant if the number of markets is large, as I am implicitly assuming. It is also possible that certain markets have positive or negative correlations of their relative excess demand shifts with the aggregate excess demand shifts (u_t or the monetary disturbance that is discussed below). In that case there would be different information about the aggregate picture in different markets. The analysis would then have to consider the implications of this differential information on the choice of which market to enter. I do not deal with these possibilities here.

[9]The model does not include any elements of adjustment costs for price changes that would inhibit price flexibility. In this respect see Barro (1972). In particular, there is no consideration of the role of long-term nominal contracting in the present analysis. The role of price stickiness in Keynesian models is discussed in detail in Barro and Grossman (1975, chap. 2). It would be of interest to incorporate price adjustment costs into a rational-expectations-type model.

bution of price is that the ratio of systematic demand to supply, $k_t(z) \equiv k_t^d(z) - k_t^s(z)$, be the same for all markets.[10] It is then permissible to drop the z subscript from the $k_t(z)$ term in equation (3).

Equation (3) indicates that $P_t(z)$ is determined by a set of "demand-pull" variables that include the money stock plus expected next period's transfer and the sum of systematic and random excess demand terms, $k_t + u_t + \varepsilon_t(z)$. There is also a "cost-push" term, $\mathrm{E}P_{t+1}|I_t(z)$,[11] that has an effect in the direction of the sign of $\alpha - \beta$. Under the assumption of a dominant substitution effect, the impact of $\mathrm{E}P_{t+1}$ on $P_t(z)$ is positive.

The key element of the rational expectations approach is that the $\mathrm{E}P_{t+1}$ term in equation (3) is not determined by an ad hoc expectations mechanism from outside of the model, but is instead based on the knowledge— implied by an assumed knowledge of the model—that prices are determined by market-clearing conditions of the form of equation (3). Hence, current market-clearing prices and (the set of) expectations about future prices are determined through a simultaneous process. In order to implement this approach, it is necessary to complete the specification of the model by describing the processes that generate M_t and k_t. I assume, provisionally, that changes in money are generated by a constant growth rate, g, plus a random term, denoted by m_t. That is,

$$M_t - M_{t-1} \equiv \Delta M_t = g + m_t,$$
$$m_t \sim N(0, \sigma_m^2), \tag{4}$$

where m_t is assumed to be serially independent, as well as uncorrelated with v_t and the array of $\varepsilon_t(z)$. I examine the implications of more complicated money supply processes in a later part of the paper. In order to focus on the short-run, cyclical effects of money, I also abstract in the main text from long-term monetary growth—that is, $g = 0$ is assumed. This abstraction amounts to neglecting the effects of systematic inflation. Appendix 2 deals with the case where $g \neq 0$. When $g = 0$, equation (4) implies that $E\,\Delta M_{t+1}|I_t(z) = 0$.

I assume that the k_t process takes the form,

$$k_t = k_0 - \beta\rho t, \tag{5}$$

where $k_0 = 0$ can be assumed subsequently through an appropriate normalization of output units. It turns out, as shown in Appendix 2, that the form for k_t in equation (5) amounts to assuming that the systematic growth rate of output is equal to ρ. Again, it is convenient to abstract in the main text from the effects of long-term growth so that $\rho = 0$ is as-

---

[10]Alternatively, if some serial dependence in $\varepsilon_t(z)$ had been introduced, then $k_t(z)$ could be such as to just offset the implications of this serial dependence for $P_t(z)$.

[11]The terms on the right side of equation (3) can be viewed equivalently as negative forces on the current excess demand for money.

sumed. Since $k_t = 0$ in this case, the systematic excess demand term no longer appears in the analysis. Appendix 2 deals with the case where $\rho \neq 0$.

The next step is to solve the model in the sense of determining prices and outputs as functions of exogenous variables. The simplest procedure for solving the model involves, first, writing out the (log-linear) form of the solution for $P_t(z)$ in terms of a vector of unknown coefficients on the set of relevant independent variables. Second, the market-clearing condition expressed in equation (3) is used to determine the values of the unknown coefficients. This solution method has been used before in a parallel context by Lucas (1972, 1973). The procedure is analogous to applying the method of undetermined coefficients to a trial solution in the case of differential or difference equations. In the present situation $P_t(z)$ depends on the following variables (in a log-linear form),[12]

$$P_t(z) = \Pi_1 M_{t-1} + \Pi_2 m_t + \Pi_3 v_t + \Pi_4 \varepsilon_t(z) + \Pi_5 u_{t-1}, \tag{6}$$

where the Π's are the unknown coefficients. Since M_{t-1} is included in current information sets, previous values of M do not appear in the price solution. Since m_t, v_t and $\varepsilon_t(z)$ are serially independent, past values of these variables do not appear.[13] Since, for a given value of v_t, u_t depends only on u_{t-1}, it follows that values of u prior to $t - 1$ do not appear.

If individuals know that prices in each period are determined by equation (6), then the expected price for next period must be

$$\begin{aligned}
EP_{t+1} \mid I_t(z) &= \Pi_1 EM_t \mid I_t(z) + \Pi_5 Eu_t \mid I_t(z) \\
&= \Pi_1 E(M_{t-1} + m_t) \mid I_t(z) + \Pi_5 E(u_{t-1} + v_t) \mid I_t(z),
\end{aligned}$$

since the expected values of m_{t+1}, v_{t+1} and $\varepsilon_{t+1}(z)$, conditioned on $I_t(z)$, are all zero. The information set, $I_t(z)$, is assumed to include observations (or sufficient data to infer the values) of M_{t-1} and u_{t-1}. The additional information contributed by an observation of $P_t(z)$[14] amounts, from equation (6), to an observation of the sum $\Pi_2 m_t + \Pi_3 v_t + \Pi_4 \varepsilon_t(z)$. The key to the formation of price expectations is then the calculation of the two expectations, Em_t and Ev_t, conditioned on the observation of $P_t(z)$. In effect, these

[12]In the case where g and ρ are nonzero, the solution includes the additional terms $\Pi_6 t + \Pi_7$—that is, a time trend and a constant term. See Appendix 2.

[13]If a variable such as v_{t-1} had been entered, it would eventually be determined that its associated Π-coefficient was zero.

[14]I have not included an individual's own value of ΔM_t, which arrives as a government transfer, as an additional element of $I_t(z)$. This exclusion is satisfactory if the relation between individual and aggregate transfers is sufficiently noisy so that the individual transfer provides a negligible increment of information over $P_t(z)$. This assumption need not be inconsistent with my earlier simplifying assumption that $M_t(z)$ was a constant fraction of M_t, since $M_t(z)$ refers to the total money contained in market z. If individual and aggregate M were always proportionately related, then M_t would, itself, become an element of $I_t(z)$, and the principal information gap in the model would disappear.

two conditional expectations are obtained by running regressions of m_t and v_t, respectively, on the observed sum $\Pi_2 m_t + \Pi_3 v_t + \Pi_4 \varepsilon_t(z)$. That is,

$$E m_t \mid I_t(z) = \frac{\theta_1}{\Pi_2} [\Pi_2 m_t + \Pi_3 v_t + \Pi_4 \varepsilon_t(z)],$$

where

$$\theta_1 = \frac{(\Pi_2)^2 \sigma_m^2}{(\Pi_2)^2 \sigma_m^2 + (\Pi_3)^2 \sigma_v^2 + (\Pi_4)^2 \sigma_\varepsilon^2},$$

and

$$E v_t \mid I_t(z) = \frac{\theta_2}{\Pi_3} [\Pi_2 m_t + \Pi_3 v_t + \Pi_4 \varepsilon_t(z)], \tag{7}$$

where

$$\theta_2 = \frac{(\Pi_3)^2 \sigma_v^2}{(\Pi_2)^2 \sigma_m^2 + (\Pi_3)^2 \sigma_v^2 + (\Pi_4)^2 \sigma_\varepsilon^2}.$$

The θ_1-coefficient measures the fraction of the total price variance (of $P_t[z]$ about its best estimate given I_{t-1}) that is produced by (aggregate) money variance m, and the θ_2 coefficient measures the fraction produced by aggregate real variance v. The remaining fraction of price variance, $1 - \theta_1 - \theta_2$, is attributable to relative real variance ε. The expected price at $t + 1$ can then be written as

$$E P_{t+1} \mid I_t(z) = \Pi_1 M_{t-1} + \left(\frac{\Pi_1 \theta_1}{\Pi_2} + \frac{\Pi_5 \theta_2}{\Pi_3} \right) [\Pi_2 m_t + \Pi_3 v_t + \Pi_4 \varepsilon_t(z)] + \Pi_5 u_{t-1}. \tag{8}$$

The Π-coefficients must be such that the market-clearing condition, equation (3), holds as an identity, given equations (6) and (8). This identity relation implies five (independent) conditions corresponding to term-by-term coefficient equalities for the variables that appear in equation (6). The algebra is straightforward and I will limit the discussion here to a presentation and interpretation of the results. The five Π-coefficients can be determined to be

$$\begin{aligned}
\Pi_1 &= 1, \\
\Pi_2 &= (\theta_1 + \theta_2) + (\beta/\alpha)(1 - \theta_1 - \theta_2), \\
\Pi_3 &= \Pi_2/\beta, \\
\Pi_4 &= \Pi_2/\beta, \\
\Pi_5 &= 1/\beta.
\end{aligned} \tag{9}$$

These coefficients imply the price solution

$$\begin{aligned}
P_t(z) = M_{t-1} &+ [\theta_1 + \theta_2 + (\beta/\alpha)(1 - \theta_1 - \theta_2)] \\
&\times \{m_t + (1/\beta)[v_t + \varepsilon_t(z)]\} + (1/\beta) u_{t-1}.
\end{aligned} \tag{10}$$

Before discussing this result, it is convenient to define the variance of the total aggregate disturbance, $\beta m_t + v_t$, as $\sigma_A^2 \equiv \beta^2 \sigma_m^2 + \sigma_v^2$. The θ-coefficients in equation (10) are then determined, using equations (7) and (9), as

$$\theta_1 + \theta_2 = \frac{\beta^2 \sigma_m^2 + \sigma_v^2}{\beta^2 \sigma_m^2 + \sigma_v^2 + \sigma_\varepsilon^2} = \frac{\sigma_A^2}{\sigma_A^2 + \sigma_\varepsilon^2}. \tag{11}$$

An aggregate "price index," P_t, can be calculated for future reference as a (geometric, unweighted) average of the prices determined in equation (10),

$$\begin{aligned} P_t = M_{t-1} &+ [\theta_1 + \theta_2 + (\beta/\alpha)(1 - \theta_1 - \theta_2)][m_t + (1/\beta)v_t] \\ &+ (1/\beta)u_{t-1}. \end{aligned} \tag{12}$$

The relative disturbances, $\varepsilon_t(z)$, are averaged out in determining P_t.

The main results for $P_t(z)$ in equation (10) can be interpreted as follows. First, M_{t-1}, which is contained in the information set $I_t(z)$, has a proportional effect on $P_t(z)$ ($\Pi_1 = 1$). On the other hand, m_t, the random part of M_t, is not a part of $I_t(z)$. Since market participants do not have separate observations of $P_t(z)$ and the aggregate price index, P_t, they cannot separate the impact of m_t from the impact of the other excess demand shifts, $v_t + \varepsilon_t(z)$. Hence, m_t and $(1/\beta)[v_t + \varepsilon_t(z)]$ enter with a common coefficient in equation (10). This coefficient is less than one as long as the substitution effect of a change in EP_{t+1} outweighs the income effect ($\alpha > \beta$). Because m_t has a coefficient that generally differs from one, it also turns out that this part of money can have a nonzero effect on output.

The expected future price level follows from equations (8) and (9) as

$$\begin{aligned} EP_{t+1}|I_t(z) = M_{t-1} &+ (\theta_1 + \theta_2)\{m_t + (1/\beta)[v_t + \varepsilon_t(z)]\} \\ &+ (1/\beta)u_{t-1}. \end{aligned} \tag{13}$$

Note that $\theta_1 + \theta_2$ is the fraction of total excess demand variance that is accounted for by aggregate shifts (m and v). Since M and u are generated by random walk processes, it follows that the m_t and v_t shifts persist into the next period and therefore continue to affect P_{t+1}. On the other hand, the $\varepsilon_t(z)$ shift is transitory and does not affect P_{t+1}. Accordingly, the current excess demand shift, $m_t + (1/\beta)[v_t + \varepsilon_t(z)]$, is weighted by $\theta_1 + \theta_2$ in forming EP_{t+1}. This weighting would change if the processes that generated M_t, u_t, and $\varepsilon_t(z)$ were altered. Appendix 2 deals with the case where u_t is no longer a random walk.

The difference between current observed price in market z and the expected future price (in any market) is determined from equations (10) and (13) as

$$P_t(z) - EP_{t+1}|I_t(z) = (\beta/\alpha)(1 - \theta_1 - \theta_2)\{m_t + (1/\beta)[v_t + \varepsilon_t(z)]\}. \tag{14}$$

The weighting term on the current demand shift depends on $1 - \theta_1 - \theta_2$, which measures the fraction of total excess demand variance that is attributable to relative (hence, in this model, transitory) shifts.

The price solutions from equations (13) and (14) can be substituted into either the supply or demand function for commodities (equations [1] or [2]) to obtain an expression for output. It is convenient to define here the parameter $H \equiv \alpha_s \beta_d - \alpha_d \beta_s$. Then, the result for output is[15]

$$
\begin{aligned}
y_t(z) = &(H/\alpha)(1 - \theta_1 - \theta_2)m_t + (1/\alpha)[\alpha_s - (H/\beta)(\theta_1 + \theta_2)][v_t^d + \varepsilon_t^d(z)] \\
&+ (1/\alpha)[\alpha_d + (H/\beta)(\theta_1 + \theta_2)][v_t^s + \varepsilon_t^s(z)] + (\beta_s/\beta)u_{t-1}^d \quad (15) \\
&+ (\beta_\alpha/\beta)u_{t-1}^s.
\end{aligned}
$$

There are a number of interesting aspects of the output expression. First, (only) the unperceived part of the current money stock, m_t, has an impact on output. The sign of the effect depends on the substitution and wealth elasticities of the commodity supply and demand functions, as measured by the combination $H \equiv \alpha_s \beta_d - \alpha_d \beta_s$. In Lucas's (1973) model, the substitution effect on demand, α_d, and the wealth effect on supply, β_s, were both assumed to be zero. In that case unperceived monetary expansion has, unambiguously, a positive effect on output. More generally, this result follows if the substitution effect on supply, α_s, and the wealth effect on demand, β_d, are the dominant influences.[16] I will treat the case where $H > 0$ as the normal one, although there is nothing in my particular model that suggests that this case would typically arise.[17]

Second, the magnitude of the effect of m_t on $y_t(z)$—which could be called a (reverse) Phillips curve slope—depends, through the $1 - \theta_1 - \theta_2$ term, on the relation between the variances of relative and aggregate disturbances. In particular,

$$
1 - \theta_1 - \theta_2 = \frac{\sigma_\varepsilon^2}{\sigma_A^2 + \sigma_\varepsilon^2} = \frac{\sigma_\varepsilon^2}{\beta^2 \sigma_m^2 + \sigma_v^2 + \sigma_\varepsilon^2}
$$

is the fraction of total excess demand variance that is attributable to relative disturbances. For given variances of the real disturbances, σ_ε^2 and σ_v^2, the magnitude of the Phillips-type response diminishes with the variance of the monetary growth rate, σ_m^2.[18] That is, when the monetary growth rate

---

[15]The output expression neglects any differences in the sizes of markets—that is, there are no remaining systematic effects on $y_t(z)$ that are associated with the z-index.

[16]Barro and Grossman (1975, chap. 7) contains a related discussion for a model that has separate labor and commodity markets, but which treats expectations in an ad hoc manner.

[17]In an overlapping-generations model with a retirement period, this case may be typical. In this sort of model working households would have a small fraction of total wealth, so that β_s would be small. Further, the retired households, with a relatively large fraction of total wealth, would have short time horizons, so that β_d would be large.

[18]If monetary disturbances had differential effects across markets—either systematic or random—one would anticipate a positive association between σ_m^2 and σ_ε^2. However, if the movement in σ_ε^2 is much less than one-to-one with σ_m^2, the qualitative conclusion about the Phillips curve slope would remain valid.

is less predictable, individuals are more inclined to associate observed price fluctuations in their markets with (aggregate) monetary movements. In that case, the reaction of output to a given monetary disturbance, m_t, would be correspondingly smaller. This type of effect has been discussed previously by Lucas (1973, p. 330), and it can be appropriately called the Lucas-hypothesis on the Phillips curve slope.[19] Given the negative effect of σ_m^2 on the Phillips slope, there is a sense in which more variable monetary growth has a "stabilizing" effect on output. However, since this process reflects a monetary clouding that lessens the extent to which observed prices are a signal about relative prices, it seems intuitive that this type of stabilization would not be desirable in a full sense. Section 2A of this paper confirms that intuition.

Third, this type of model does not yield real effects of monetary disturbances that persist beyond one period—that is, only the current value of m_t enters into equation (15). Some elements that could result in persistent effects are (1) the recognition that aggregate information is attained only gradually over time, rather than fully with a one-period lag; (2) elements of capital accumulation that would allow current changes in stocks to have a continued effect into subsequent periods; (3) adjustment costs in the supply and demand functions. Lucas's (1975) paper contains aspects of the first two of these elements. However, my analysis in the present paper does not incorporate any of these effects.

Fourth, the manner in which the current real shifts affect output brings out the key aspect of the information structure of the model—namely, each aggregate shift, v_t^d or v_t^s, has the same effect as the corresponding relative shift, $\varepsilon_t^d(z)$ or $\varepsilon_t^s(z)$. This behavior derives from the underlying assumption that participants in market z cannot tell what fraction of the observed movement in $P_t(z)$ reflects a relative price shift rather than an absolute shift. The precise way in which individuals would like to discriminate between these two types of shifts will be brought out below in Section 2A. It can also be noted here that the existence of an effect of unperceived monetary expansion on output, as discussed above, depends entirely on the inability of market participants to distinguish immediately between relative and absolute price shifts.

C. Price Distributions

Given the price solutions in equations (10) and (12), the model determines distributions of prices both across markets and over time. It is convenient to focus the discussion of these distributions on the problem of predicting

[19] I am currently attempting to test this hypothesis for the United States over the period 1890 to 1973. Lucas (1973) has performed some related tests for a cross-section of countries during the post-World War II period. Lucas's results support the hypothesis, but his main evidence seems to rest on two outlying Latin American cases.

the future price in a (randomly-selected) market z', based on information currently possessed by participants in market z. That is, I focus on the gap between $P_{t+1}(z')$ and $\mathrm{E}\,P_{t+1}\,|\,I_t(z)$.[20] This gap can be usefully broken down into three independent components,

$$
\begin{aligned}
P_{t+1}(z') - \mathrm{E}\,P_{t+1}\,|\,I_t(z) &\equiv [P_{t+1}(z') - P_{t+1}] + [P_{t+1} - \mathrm{E}\,P_{t+1}\,|\,I_t] \\
&+ [\mathrm{E}\,P_{t+1}\,|\,I_t - \mathrm{E}\,P_{t+1}\,|\,I_t(z)],
\end{aligned}
\tag{16}
$$

where I_t denotes full current information. The information set I_t includes separate observations of m_t and v_t, whereas $I_t(z)$ includes only the combination of m_t, v_t, and $\varepsilon_t(z)$ that is implicit in an observation of $P_t(z)$. It turns out that the three components in equation (16) are independently, normally distributed with zero mean, so that the variance of each component fully specifies its distribution. I will refer to these variances as τ_1^2, σ^2, and τ_2^2, respectively, and will use the symbol V to denote the sum of the three variances.

The first component corresponds to the distribution of relative prices at a point in time. Equations (10) and (12) (updated by one period) imply

$$
P_{t+1}(z') - P_{t+1} = (1/\beta)[\theta_1 + \theta_2 + (\beta/\alpha)(1 - \theta_1 - \theta_2)]\varepsilon_{t+1}(z'),
$$

which has zero mean (conditioned on $I_t[z]$). Using the expression for $\theta_1 + \theta_2$ in equation (11), the variance of relative prices can then be determined as

$$
\begin{aligned}
\tau_1^2 &\equiv \mathrm{E}[P_{t+1}(z') - P_{t+1}]^2\,|\,I_t(z) \\
&= \frac{\sigma_\varepsilon^2[\sigma_A^2 + (\beta/\alpha)\sigma_\varepsilon^2]^2}{\beta^2(\sigma_A^2 + \sigma_\varepsilon^2)^2}.
\end{aligned}
\tag{17}
$$

Not surprisingly, a key determinant of the relative price variance is σ_ε^2, the variance of relative excess demand.[21] More interestingly, there is also an effect of σ_A^2. This effect is positive as long as $\alpha > \beta$ holds, as I have been assuming. Therefore, an increase in the variance of aggregate excess demand leads to an increase in the variance of relative prices.[22] The reasoning for this effect is as follows. When σ_A^2 increases, the responsiveness of excess demand to locally observed prices diminishes, because individuals are less inclined to associate price movements with shifts in relative excess

---

[20] Recall that $\mathrm{E}\,P_{t+1}(z') = \mathrm{E}\,P_{t+1}$ for all z' in this model.

[21] However, the effect is not unambiguously positive. Two sufficient conditions for a positive effect are $\alpha < 3\beta$ or $\sigma_\varepsilon^2 < \sigma_A^2$.

[22] Vining (1974) has a preliminary, I believe inconclusive, discussion of some post-World War II United States evidence on this issue. Graham (1930, p. 175) discusses some observations from the German hyperinflation that appear to support this hypothesis. Cairnes (1873) discusses the general idea that changes in money (gold) would have short-run effects on the dispersion of relative prices. His emphasis is on the (nonproportional) manner in which new money enters different parts of the economy, and on differences in the responsiveness of supply and demand for various types of commodities. Mills (1927 pp. 252–69) calculates measures of price dispersion for the United States from 1891 to 1926.

demand. Accordingly, a given-size relative disturbance, $\varepsilon_t(z)$, requires a larger price movement in order to achieve clearing of the local market. This accentuated response of $P_t(z)$ to $\varepsilon_t(z)$ implies the increase in relative price variance, τ_1^2.

The second component of equation (16) is the future price net of the price that is predictable based on full current information, I_t. Equations (12) and (13) imply

$$P_{t+1} - E P_{t+1} | I_t = (1/\beta)[\theta_1 + \theta_2 + (\beta/\alpha)(1 - \theta_1 - \theta_2)](\beta m_{t+1} + v_{t+1}).$$

Note that this component has zero mean (conditioned on $I_t[z]$) and is independent of the first component. The variance of the future absolute price level can then be calculated as

$$\sigma^2 \equiv E[P_{t+1} - E P_{t+1} | I_t]^2 | I_t(z)$$

$$= \frac{\sigma_A^2 [\sigma_A^2 + (\beta/\alpha)\sigma_\varepsilon^2]^2}{\beta^2(\sigma_A^2 + \sigma_\varepsilon^2)^2}. \tag{18}$$

The effect of σ_A^2 on σ^2 is unambiguously positive if $\alpha > \beta$. The effect of σ_ε^2 is negative when $\alpha > \beta$ holds.

Finally, the third component in equation (16) involves the distribution of relative information in terms of its implications for $E P_{t+1}$. Equations (12) and (13) imply

$$E P_{t+1} | I_t - E P_{t+1} | I_t(z) = (1/\beta)[(1 - \theta_1 - \theta_2)(\beta m_t + v_t) - (\theta_1 + \theta_2)\varepsilon_t(z)].$$

It can be verified that this expression has zero mean conditioned on $I_t(z)$. This component is also independent of the first two components. The variance of relative information can then be calculated as

$$\tau_2^2 = E[E P_{t+1} | I_t - E P_{t+1} | I_t(z)]^2 | I_t(z)$$

$$= \frac{\sigma_A^2 \sigma_\varepsilon^2}{\beta^2(\sigma_A^2 + \sigma_\varepsilon^2)}. \tag{19}$$

This variance is increasing in both σ_A^2 and σ_ε^2.

The full variance of $P_{t+1}(z')$ about $E P_{t+1} | I_t(z)$ is the sum of the three component variances,

$$V \equiv E[P_{t+1}(z') - E P_{t+1} | I_t(z)]^2 | I_t(z)$$

$$= \tau_1^2 + \sigma^2 + \tau_2^2 \tag{20}$$

$$= \frac{1}{\beta^2(\sigma_A^2 + \sigma_\varepsilon^2)} \{[\sigma_A^2 + (\beta/\alpha)\sigma_\varepsilon^2]^2 + \sigma_A^2 \sigma_\varepsilon^2\}.$$

It can be shown by straightforward differentiation that V is unambiguously increasing in σ_ε^2,[23] and is unambiguously increasing in σ_A^2 as long as $\alpha > \beta$.

[23]That is, the positive effect on τ_2^2 in equation (19) and the ambiguous (though likely positive) effect on τ_1^2 in equation (17) dominate over the negative effect on σ^2 in equation (18).

One aspect of the next part of the paper is an analysis of the impact of monetary policy on the predictability of future prices, as measured inversely by V in equation (20). That analysis would be more meaningful if price predictability played some direct role in the commodity supply and demand functions—perhaps by affecting the costs of long-term nominal contracting. However, the present treatment does not incorporate this type of effect.

2. Monetary Policy

Following Sargent and Wallace (1975), I now consider the role of monetary policy in a rational expectations framework. Monetary policy is identified here with a stochastic control rule for determining the time path of the money stock. My procedure differs from that of Sargent and Wallace in two major respects: first, the criterion for evaluating policy is different; and second, my analysis incorporates the dependence of certain coefficients of the model—in particular, the Phillips curve slope—on the underlying distributions of the excess demand shifts. Sargent and Wallace (1975, p. 5) evaluate policy by using a loss function that gives credit to stabilizing a measure of aggregate output, where this output measure is an aggregate analogue to my equation (15). Their model corresponds in essential respects to dealing with the (geometric) average of the $y_t(z)$'s across the markets, where this averaging of equation (15) over the n markets leads to an aggregate output expression in which the relative excess demand shifts, $\varepsilon_t^s(z)$ and $\varepsilon_t^d(z)$, do not appear. Stabilizing this measure of aggregate output would amount to giving no credit to changes in the composition of output that were responses to changes in relative supply and demand—that is, to changes in the composition of tastes, technology, etc. It seems clear that a loss function based on this simple measure of aggregate output would not be appropriate.

My earlier discussion of the output expression in equation (15) stressed that the key aspect of the partial information structure of the model is the confusion between aggregate and relative shifts. It is possible to determine the output that would arise in each market if all participants were able to discriminate perfectly between these shifts—that is, under full current information where $I_t(z)$ includes observations on P_t and M_t. The output level under full current information (subsequently called full information output) can be compared with the output level determined in equation (15). My proposed criterion for monetary policy is to minimize the expected squared gap between actual and full information output in each market.[24]

[24]My basic idea for this measure is that it should serve as an approximation to the expected loss of consumer surplus. Ideally, the criterion would be based directly on the behavior of individual expected utilities. Unfortunately, the present model is not set up to proceed in that fashion.

A. Prices and Outputs under Full Current Information

This model coincides with the one developed in Part 1 except that P_t and M_t (and, hence, m_t, v_t and $\varepsilon_t[z]$) are now included in $I_t(z)$. The analysis proceeds as in Section 1B until the derivation of $EP_{t+1}|I_t(z)$. Given the new information assumption, equation (8) is now replaced by the simpler expression,

$$EP_{t+1}|I_t(z) = \Pi_1(M_{t-1} + m_t) + \Pi_5 u_t.$$

The remainder of the analysis follows the form of Section 1B. Using an asterisk to denote the full (current) information situation, the price level in market z turns out to be

$$P_t^*(z) = M_{t-1} + m_t + (1/\beta)(u_{t-1} + v_t) + (1/\alpha)\varepsilon_t(z). \tag{21}$$

It is convenient to rewrite here the price that arises under partial information, from equation (10),

$$P_t(z) = M_{t-1} + [\theta_1 + \theta_2 + (\beta/\alpha)(1 - \theta_1 - \theta_2)]\{m_t + (1/\beta)[v_t + \varepsilon_t(z)]\} + (1/\beta)u_{t-1}.$$

In contrast with its effect on $P_t(z)$, the unanticipated change in the money stock, m_t, has a one-to-one effect on $P_t^*(z)$. Further, the current real disturbances, v_t and $\varepsilon_t(z)$, have different effects on $P_t^*(z)$. In particular, if $\alpha > \beta$, the response of $P_t^*(z)$ to the aggregate disturbance, v_t, is larger than that to the relative disturbance, $\varepsilon_t(z)$.

The result for full information output is

$$y_t^*(z) = (1/\alpha)(\alpha_s - H/\beta)v_t^d + (1/\alpha)(\alpha_d + H/\beta)v_t^s + (\alpha_s/\alpha)\varepsilon_t^d(z) \\ + (\alpha_d/\alpha)\varepsilon_t^s(z) + (\beta_s/\beta)u_{t-1}^d + (\beta_d/\beta)u_{t-1}^s, \tag{22}$$

where $H \equiv \alpha_s\beta_d - \alpha_d\beta_s$. Again, it is convenient to rewrite the partial information result, this time from equation (15),

$$y_t(z) = (H/\alpha)(1 - \theta_1 - \theta_2)m_t + (1/\alpha)[\alpha_s - (H/\beta)(\theta_1 + \theta_2)] \\ \times [v_t^d + \varepsilon_t^d(z)] + (1/\alpha)[\alpha_d + (H/\beta)(\theta_1 + \theta_2)][v_t^s + \varepsilon_t^s(z)] \\ + (\beta_s/\beta)u_{t-1}^d + (\beta_d/\beta)u_{t-1}^s.$$

There are several interesting contrasts between the results for $y_t(z)$ and those for $y_t^*(z)$. First, m_t has no effect on $y_t^*(z)$, which corresponds to the one-to-one effect of m_t on $P_t^*(z)$. Second, each aggregate shift, v_t^d or v_t^s, has a different effect on $y_t^*(z)$ from the corresponding relative shift, $\varepsilon_t^d(z)$ or $\varepsilon_t^s(z)$. From inspection of the $y_t(z)$ and $y_t^*(z)$ expressions, it is clear that the two responses to the v_t's would coincide if $\theta_1 + \theta_2 = 1$. This result obtains because $\theta_1 + \theta_2 = 1$ signifies $\sigma_\varepsilon^2 = 0$, so that the aggregate–relative confusion cannot arise, and all aggregate shifts induce the appropriate output response. Note that the effect of m_t on $y_t(z)$ is zero in this case. It also follows that the response of $y_t(z)$ and $y_t^*(z)$ to the ε_t's would coincide if $\theta_1 + \theta_2 = 0$, since $\sigma_A^2 = 0$ in that case. When $\theta_1 + \theta_2$ is between zero and one, there will be divergences between the responses of $y_t(z)$ and $y_t^*(z)$ to m_t, v_t and $\varepsilon_t(z)$. This observation can be seen more easily by writing out an expression for the gap between actual and full information output,

$$y_t(z) - y_t^*(z) = (H/\alpha\beta)[(1 - \theta_1 - \theta_2)(\beta m_t + v_t) - (\theta_1 + \theta_2)\varepsilon_t(z)]. \quad (23)$$

If $H > 0$ and $0 < \theta_1 + \theta_2 < 1$, it is clear from equation (23) that (in relation to the full information situation) $y_t(z)$ reacts too much to the aggregate shifts, m_t and v_t, and not enough to the relative shifts, $\varepsilon_t(z)$. Equation (23) also indicates again that the important informational division is between aggregate shifts, $\beta m_t + v_t$, and relative shifts, $\varepsilon_t(z)$. In a more general model it would also become relevant to separate the βm_t part of the aggregate shifts from the v_t part—or, put another way, to separate the monetary shift, m_t, from the real shift, $v_t + \varepsilon_t(z)$. For example, this other type of informational division would arise if u_t were no longer generated by a random walk. Appendix 1 deals with this case and clarifies some aspects of the two types of information divisions: aggregate versus relative and monetary versus real.

The proposed criterion for monetary policy is to minimize the expected squared gap between $y_t(z)$ and $y_t^*(z)$, which is denoted by Ω. Substituting for $\theta_1 + \theta_2$ from equation (11) and using equation (23), the result is

$$\begin{aligned} \Omega &\equiv E[y_t(z) - y_t^*(z)]^2 \,|\, I_t(z) \\ &= \frac{H^2\sigma_A^2\sigma_\varepsilon^2}{(\alpha\beta)^2(\sigma_A^2 + \sigma_\varepsilon^2)}. \end{aligned} \quad (24)$$

This expression for the variance of output about its full information position will be used in the subsequent discussion of monetary policy.

B. The Optimal Money Variance

Before introducing the possibility of monetary policy through feedback control on observed values of prices, outputs, etc., I consider here the role played by pure variance of money—that is, by σ_m^2. First, it is clear from equation (23) that, if all the coefficients including $\theta_1 + \theta_2$ were fixed, then an increase in σ_m^2 would lead to an increased variance of $y_t(z)$ about $y_t^*(z)$. Accordingly, in the Sargent and Wallace model, where all coefficients are fixed, it is trivial that $\sigma_m^2 = 0$ would be optimal (and, hence, they do not discuss this issue). On the other hand, in my model an increase in σ_m^2 has effects that operate through the θ-coefficients. Specifically, the coefficient on the aggregate disturbance term in equation (23) is

$$1 - \theta_1 - \theta_2 = \frac{\sigma_\varepsilon^2}{\beta^2\sigma_m^2 + \sigma_v^2 + \sigma_\varepsilon^2},$$

and this coefficient declines with σ_m^2. As σ_m^2 increases, individuals attribute a larger fraction of observed price movements to aggregate shocks and are, therefore, fooled less—in terms of the departure of $y_t(z)$ from $y_t^*(z)$—for a given value of the aggregate shock, $\beta m_t + v_t$. In fact, as $\sigma_m^2 \to \infty$, the contribution of the aggregate disturbance term in equation (23) to the output variance Ω, as calculated in equation (24), approaches zero.[25] However, the contribution to Ω of the relative disturbance term in equation (23), $(\theta_1 + \theta_2)\varepsilon_t(z)$, is an increasing function of σ_m^2, so that the overall effect on Ω depends on two offsetting forces.

The nature of the net effect is apparent from equation (24). The form of this expression implies that Ω is an increasing function of both σ_A^2 (which equals $\beta^2\sigma_m^2 + \sigma_v^2$) and σ_ε^2. Hence, it is true in this model that the variance of output about its full information position is minimized by setting $\sigma_m^2 = 0$.[26] The reason for this result is that the policy criterion dictates getting output as close as possible to its full information position. An increase in any of the underlying variances, σ_m^2, σ_v^2, or σ_ε^2, clouds the picture, in the sense of making current price information a less accurate signal for market participants, and therefore makes it more difficult for individuals to get output close to full information output. To the extent that the variance of money, σ_m^2, can be controlled,[27] the smallest possible value would be optimal.[28]

The conclusion that $\sigma_m^2 = 0$ is optimal is basically in the spirit of the constant growth rate rule that has been advocated particularly by Friedman (e.g., Friedman 1960, chap. 4) and earlier by Simons (1948, pp. 181–83). The present result indicates that monetary policy is best when it is most predictable. In particular, an increase in money variance is nonneutral and leads to an increased variance of output about its full information position because money variance clouds the real picture and reduces the value of observed prices as allocative signals.

It is also useful to note here that the predictability of future prices is maximized by setting $\sigma_m^2 = 0$. That is, the variance V of $P_{t+1}(z')$ about

[25]Because $(1 - \theta_1 - \theta_2)^2$ approaches zero faster than σ_m^2 approaches infinity.

[26]In an earlier version of this paper I obtained the result that $\sigma_m^2 = 0$ would minimize Ω only under some configurations of the underlying parameters, and that $\sigma_m^2 = \infty$ was optimal in some other cases. Those conclusions depended on a misspecification in which EP_t, rather than EP_{t+1}, entered into the supply and demand functions. Another way to end up with $\sigma_m^2 = \infty$ as an answer is to change the objective function to the minimization of the variance of "aggregate" output y_t about $Ey_t \mid I_{t-1}$ (essentially the Sargent and Wallace criterion), where the aggregation eliminates the $\varepsilon_t(z)$ terms from the output expression of equation (15). This objective would definitely call for $\sigma_m^2 = \infty$ if aggregate real shifts were absent; that is, if $u_t^d \equiv u_t^s \equiv 0$. In the case where aggregate real shifts are present, the criterion would typically lead to a positive, but finite, value for σ_m^2.

[27]If there are significant money-control-type costs associated with reducing σ_m^2, then these costs would have to be weighed against the benefits from a lower variance. This sort of tradeoff would lead to the choice of a positive value for σ_m^2.

[28]This result remains valid when the u_t process is no longer a random walk. See Appendix 1.

$E P_{t+1} | I_t(z)$, which is indicated in equation (20), is an increasing function of σ_A^2 (and, hence, of σ_m^2) as long as $\alpha > \beta$ holds. Therefore, the introduction of a price variance criterion into the objective function would not alter the above result.

C. Monetary Policy as Feedback Control

I now consider the implications of complicating the money supply rule from the simple form of equation (4) to include feedback effects from observed economic variables. This extension would allow the monetary authority to perform the countercyclical function of increasing money more rapidly when output is relatively low or prices are relatively high, and expanding money less rapidly in the reverse situations. The implications of this sort of monetary behavior depend crucially on the information set that is available to the monetary authority. There are two cases that have sharply divergent implications. In the first case, the monetary authority does not have more information than any of the market participants. Formally, the authority's current information set is I_{t-1}, which includes all relevant information with a one-period lag, but does not include an observation on P_t.[29] In this situation monetary policy can react (say, countercyclically) only to economic variables that have already been perceived by market participants. In the second case, the monetary authority has superior information about (some) current economic variables. In an extreme case the authority's information set would be I_t, which includes an observation on P_t. In this case the authority's feedback rule for ΔM_t can include some economic variables, such as aggregate values of current prices and outputs, which are not yet fully perceived by market participants. Not surprisingly, it turns out that countercyclical policy can be more potent under the second case than under the first (and, further, that policy may have zero potency under the first case). Finally, I assume in both cases that the market participants and the monetary authority have the same information about the form of the monetary rule. That is, the form of the rule is, itself, assumed to be a part of the information set I_{t-1} (and, hence, of $I_t[z]$). I consider in a later section some implications of differential information about the form of the monetary rule.

The Monetary Authority Lacks Superior Information about the Economy

I consider first the situation where the monetary authority's information set is I_{t-1}. The feedback control problem can be illustrated in this case by prescribing a monetary rule of the form,

$$\Delta M_t = m_t - \gamma v_{t-1}, \tag{25}$$

[29]In this situation the monetary authority actually has less information than any of the market participants since each individual has a current price observation, $P_t(z)$, in his information set, $I_t(z)$.

where, as before, $m_t \sim N(0, \sigma_m^2)$. Since v_{t-1} is last period's real shift to aggregate excess demand, the rule described by equation (25) amounts to a countercyclical reaction to (one determinant of) last period's absolute price level if $\gamma > 0$. The form of the rule could be complicated to include a separate reaction to last period's "aggregate" output or money stock, which would amount to introducing m_{t-1} and separate terms for v_{t-1}^d and v_{t-1}^s into equation (25). The rule could also be extended to incorporate observations from period $t - 2$ or earlier periods. However, these complications to the form of equation (25) turn out to yield no additional insights, as should become clear from the subsequent discussion.[30]

When money is generated by the rule in equation (25), the model can be solved out for prices and outputs using the same type of procedure as in Section 1B.[31] Since the formal procedure involves no important new elements, I will confine attention here to a presentation and discussion of the results. The solutions for $P_t(z)$, $\mathrm{E}\,P_{t+1} \,|\, I_t(z)$, and $\mathrm{E}\,\Delta M_{t+1} \,|\, I_t(z)$ turn out to be

$$P_t(z) = M_{t-1} + [\theta_1 + \theta_2 + (\beta/\alpha)(1 - \theta_1 - \theta_2) - \gamma\beta\theta_2]$$
$$\times [m_t + \{1/\beta)[v_t + \varepsilon_t(z)]\} + (1/\beta)u_{t-1} - \gamma v_{t-1},$$
$$\mathrm{E}\,P_{t+1} \,|\, I_t(z) = M_{t-1} + (\theta_1 + \theta_2 - \gamma\beta\theta_2)\{m_t + (1/\beta)[v_t + \varepsilon_t(z)]\}$$
$$+ (1/\beta)u_{t-1} - \gamma v_{t-1},$$
$$\mathrm{E}\,\Delta M_{t+1} \,|\, I_t(z) = -\gamma\beta\theta_2\{m_t + (1/\beta)[v_t + \varepsilon_t(z)]\}.$$

In contrast to the earlier case in which there were no feedbacks to money (equations [4], [10], and [13], and $\mathrm{E}\,\Delta M_{t+1} \,|\, I_t[z] = 0$), the new elements concern the γ-terms. These terms are of two types: those pertaining to v_{t-1} and those associated with v_t. First, v_{t-1} is contained in the information set, $I_t(z)$. Hence, the negative effect of v_{t-1} on M_t, as implied by equation (25) if $\gamma > 0$, is fully perceived. As is generally the case for the perceived part of M_t, $P_t(z)$ moves in proportion to money—that is, the $-\gamma v_{t-1}$ term appears in the $P_t(z)$ expression. Since equation (25) implies that the effect of v_{t-1} on M_t would also carry over to M_{t+1}, it follows that $\mathrm{E}\,P_{t+1} \,|\, I_t(z)$ also moves in accordance with $-\gamma v_{t-1}$. Therefore, the negative reaction of ΔM_t to v_{t-1} does not produce any gaps either between $P_t(z)$ and $\mathrm{E}\,P_{t+1} \,|\, I_t(z)$ or between $M_t + \mathrm{E}\,\Delta M_{t+1} \,|\, I_t(z)$ and $\mathrm{E}\,P_{t+1} \,|\, I_t(z)$.

A second type of effect arises because the current excess demand shift, v_t, will have an effect next period on ΔM_{t+1}. Since v_t is not contained in $I_t(z)$,

---

[30]I have not discussed the possibility of monetary reaction to the array of $\varepsilon_{t-1}(z)$. Since the monetary authority is assumed to possess only the aggregate instrument, ΔM_t, one would not expect the pattern of relative excess demands to be an important input into policy decisions. In any event introducing the array of $\varepsilon_{t-1}(z)$ into equation (25) would not change the basic results.

[31]The form of the $P_t(z)$ solution in equation (6) would now include the addition term, $\Pi_6 v_{t-1}$.

market participants form an estimate of the feedback effect on next period's money based on the expectation $\gamma \mathrm{E} v_t | I_t(z) = \gamma \beta \theta_2 \{ m_t + (1/\beta)[v_t + \varepsilon_t(z)] \}$. This term appears in the above expressions for $\mathrm{E} \Delta M_{t+1} | I_t(z)$, $\mathrm{E} P_{t+1} | I_t(z)$, and $P_t(z)$. Again, the response of ΔM_{t+1} to v_t does not produce any gaps either between $P_t(z)$ and $\mathrm{E} P_{t+1} | I_t(z)$[32] or between $M_t + \mathrm{E} \Delta M_{t+1} | I_t(z)$ and $\mathrm{E} P_{t+1} | I_t(z)$.

The two feedback channels alter neither $P_t(z)$ relative to $\mathrm{E} P_{t+1}$ nor the wealth term, $M_t + \mathrm{E} \Delta M_{t+1} - \mathrm{E} P_{t+1}$. It follows that there will be no effect on commodity supply and demand, as given in equations (1) and (2), and therefore no effect on output, $y_t(z)$. Because the market participants know the form of the money rule, and take this behavior into account in forming expectations of future prices and monetary growth rates, the feedback from v_{t-1} to M_t has no effect on the entire distribution of output.[33] The level of output continues to be determined by equation (15). It follows trivially that the choice of the feedback parameter, γ, is irrelevant to the determination of the variance of output about its full information position, as determined in equation (24).[34]

The Monetary Authority Possesses Superior Information about the Economy

The conclusions on the output effect of feedback control are radically different when the monetary authority has superior information that can be included in the money rule. The situation can be illustrated in the case where the authority has the information set I_t, which includes an observation of v_t.[35] In this case a possible form of the monetary rule is

$$\Delta M_t = m_t - \delta v_t. \tag{26}$$

[32] Note that the supply and demand functions in equations (1) and (2) depend only on the expected real value of next period's money, $M_t + \mathrm{E} \Delta M_{t+1} - \mathrm{E} P_{t+1}$, which accords with the role of money as a store of value in this model. The current real money stock in market z, $M_t - P_t(z)$, might also enter these functions if the model incorporated the role of money as a mechanism for economizing on transaction costs (or if current real balances were simply included as a direct argument of individual utility functions). In that case $P_t(z)$ would not respond as much as $\mathrm{E} P_{t+1} | I_t(z)$ to the expected movement in ΔM_{t+1}. The implied gap between $P_t(z)$ and $\mathrm{E} P_{t+1}$ would then lead to effects on output, though the effects on actual and full information output would coincide. This sort of effect is analogous to the effect of systematic money growth on actual and full information output, as discussed in Appendix 2.

[33] This type of result was first presented by Sargent and Wallace (1975, sec. 4). Their assumptions about the monetary authority's information set are analogous to those that I make in this section.

[34] Generally, there will be a nonzero effect of changes in γ on the predictability of future prices. The main effect is the following. When γ is high, the effect of v_{t+1} on P_{t+1} is attenuated because of the offsetting feedback effect on ΔM_{t+2}. Hence (at least if γ is not too large) P_{t+1} can be made more predictable, based on $I_t(z)$, by setting a positive value of γ.

[35] I do not consider here the possibility of superior information about the configuration of the ε_t's. Since the policymaker is assumed to possess only the aggregate instrument, ΔM_t, this sort of information would, in any case, be of only second-order use. Further, it seems much less plausible that the policymaker would actually have superior information about the relative shifts.

Again, $\delta > 0$ describes a countercyclical monetary policy, but this time the response of ΔM_t is to v_t, which is not a part of the individual information sets, $I_t(z)$. Again, the solution for prices and outputs can be derived from a procedure of the type discussed in Section 1B. The price results are now[36]

$$P_t(z) = M_{t-1} + [\theta_1 + \theta_2 + (\beta/\alpha)(1 - \theta_1 - \theta_2)]$$
$$\times \{m_t + (1/\beta)[(1 - \beta\delta)v_t + \varepsilon_t(z)]\} + (1/\beta)u_{t-1},$$
$$\mathrm{E}\,P_{t+1} | I_t(z) = M_{t-1} + (\theta_1 + \theta_2)\{m_t + (1/\beta)[(1 - \beta\delta)v_t + \varepsilon_t(z)]\}$$
$$+ (1/\beta)u_{t-1}. \tag{27}$$

The feedback from v_t to ΔM_t implies that $\beta m_t + (1 - \beta\delta)v_t$ is now the aggregate excess demand shift that affects $P_t(z)$ and $\mathrm{E}\,P_{t+1} | I_t(z)$. Therefore, the variance of aggregate demand is now $\sigma_A^2 = \beta^2 \sigma_m^2 + (1 - \beta\delta)^2 \sigma_v^2$. It is apparent that raising the feedback parameter, δ, will reduce σ_A^2 as long as $\delta < 1/\beta$ applies. Further, setting $\delta = 1/\beta$ would minimize σ_A^2 for a given value of σ_m^2. (The combination of $\delta = 1/\beta$ and $\sigma_m^2 = 0$ would yield $\sigma_A^2 = 0$.)

The formula for Ω, the variance of output about its full information position,[37] is still that given in equation (24), and the formula for V, the variance of the absolute future price level, is still that given in equation (20). In particular, reductions in σ_A^2 unambiguously reduce Ω, and such reductions also unambiguously reduce V if $\alpha > \beta$ applies. It is then clear that $\delta = 1/\beta$ (along with $\sigma_m^2 = 0$) yields the optimal money rule of the form of equation (26). This parameter choice implies that the aggregate excess demand shift is $m_t + (1 - \beta\delta)v_t \equiv 0$. That is, there would be sufficient feedback from v_t to ΔM_t so that the direct effect of v_t on excess demand would be fully offset by an inverse movement of ΔM_t.[38]

Although the above form of stabilization policy seems obvious under the assumed superiority in the monetary authority's information set, the way that it works is somewhat subtle. In particular, the stabilization policy does not operate to eliminate any output effects of shifts in v_t^d or v_t^s, but, rather, it works by removing discrepancies between the movements of ac-

---

[36]Given equation (26), it follows that $\mathrm{E}\,\Delta M_{t+1} | I_t(z) = 0$.

[37]The formula for $y_t(z)$ from equation (15) is modified only in the coefficients of v_t^d and v_t^s. The new terms are

$$(1/\alpha)\{\alpha_s - (H/\beta)[(1 - \beta\delta)(\theta_1 + \theta_2) + \beta\delta]\}v_t^d,$$
$$(1/\alpha)\{\alpha_d + (H/\beta)[(1 - \beta\delta)(\theta_1 + \theta_2) + \beta\delta]\}v_t^s.$$

The formula for $y_t(z) - y_t^*(z)$ in equation (23) is modified only by replacing v_t with $(1 - \beta\delta)v_t$. However, the $\theta_1 + \theta_2$ coefficient that appears in this expression now involves $(1 - \beta\delta)^2\sigma_v^2$, rather than σ_v^2 (see equation (11)).

[38]This result can be generalized to a case where the policymaker has only partial information about current variables. As long as the monetary authority possesses some information that is not possessed by all market participants, there would be some potential role for countercyclical adjustments in money.

tual and full information output. Assume, for example, that there is no monetary feedback ($\delta = 0$), and that v_t^d is positive while v_t^s is zero. According to equation (27), this unanticipated aggregate demand shift would affect prices in all markets equiproportionately—that is, there would be a shift in the absolute price level, but no shift in relative prices. However, participants in market z would not be able fully to distinguish this shift from a relative price change, and, therefore, the movement in output would depart from the movement in full information output. In the case where $H > 0$, equation (23) indicates that actual output would increase too much in this situation. Suppose, now, that a stabilization policy is adopted that implies a negative response of ΔM_t to v_t so that the net disturbance, $(1 - \beta\delta)v_t$, is maintained at zero. Equation (27) indicates that neither relative nor absolute prices would then be affected by the positive value of v_t^d. In that case there is no possibility of a confusion between absolute and relative shifts, and the movement in v_t^d cannot lead to a departure of actual from full information output. Further, as is clear from equation (22), the movement in ΔM_t itself does not affect the response of full information output. Therefore, in this example, both actual and full information output would increase with the positive value of v_t^d in accordance with the coefficient shown in equation (22).

Since the stabilization policy works by preventing a confusion between absolute and relative price changes, it is also clear that an alternative to the active stabilization policy would be the provision of the information about current economic variables. If the monetary authority actually had more rapid observations of v_t, they could convey this information to the public. This information would then augment the information set, $I_t(z)$, that is used to form expectations about P_{t+1}. Once v_t is observable, it is clear that shifts in v_t can no longer lead to confusions between relative and absolute price changes. Hence, as in the case of the countercyclical monetary policy described above, movements in v_t would not produce discrepancies between actual and full information output. In other words, when the monetary authority has superior information about the economy, the provision of the information to the public is an alternative to an active stabilization policy. An argument for the superiority of stabilization policy would have to be based on the costs of transmitting and using the relevant information.[39] In particular, it could be argued that the existence of an active stabilization policy motivates individuals to reduce expenditures that are aimed at augmenting their information sets. If there are econo-

[39]The active stabilization policy and the information-provision policy do have different implications for the predictability of future prices. The information-provision policy ($\delta = 0$) in equation (26), but with v_t contained in $I_t(z)$, would involve a higher variance of future prices. Essentially, the movements in v_t and the associated movements in P_t would be perceived currently, but these movements would still not be predictable at date $t - 1$. On the other hand, the stabilization policy described above completely eliminates fluctuations in P_t associated with movements in v_t, and therefore makes P_t more predictable at date $t - 1$.

mies-of-scale in information production, there could be a net social gain along these lines.[40]

The Monetary Authority Has Superior Information about the Monetary Rule

Taylor (1975) has stressed the idea that individuals would not have perfect information about the form of the monetary rule. In this situation it is plausible that the monetary authority would have better information than the general public about its own future actions. In fact, this situation seems most plausible when the policymaker lacks a consistent objective function, such as the minimization of the variance of output about its full information position.[41] In any case, if the monetary authority has better information about its monetary rule, there is the possibility of controlling money so as to systematically fool the public. Taylor has pointed out that this sort of deception can be carried out during "transition" periods during which individuals are modifying their beliefs (along Bayesian adaptation lines) about the form of policy.[42] In Taylor's model there is also an optimal, nonzero amount of this deception. His model appears to support this type of action because the policymaker's objective function does not reflect individual preferences.[43] In my model, there appears to be no basis for policy deception as long as the policymaker's objective is based on minimizing the gap between actual and full information output.[44]

A simple form of policy deception arises when individuals believe that $\Delta M_t = m_t$, where $m_t \sim N(0, \sigma_m^2)$, but where the monetary authority knows (determines) that m_t is generated by a distribution other than $N(0, \sigma_m^2)$. Consider, for example, the case where m_t can be set by the monetary authority at any desired level, while, in the "short run," holding fixed people's belief that m_t has zero mean and variance σ_m^2.[45] In this case it is

---

[40]Of course, once this sort of information externality is introduced, it is also natural to consider the negative externalities associated with governmental incentive and control.

[41]An unpredictable objective function would be one possible rationale for the existence of m_t, the stochastic part of money.

[42]Sargent and Wallace (1974, p. 16) argue that there is no way for the monetary authority to systematically fool the public, even in the short run.

[43]His objective function gives positive credit to reducing unemployment throughout the relevant range. The analogy to my model would be to credit expansions of output even when it was already above its full information position.

[44]The normative case for policy deception could be based on external effects, such as income taxation, unemployment compensation, etc., that are not incorporated into my model. This idea is discussed by Phelps (1972) and also by Hall (1976), who argues: ". . . the benefits of inflation derive from the use of expansionary policy to trick economic agents into behaving in socially preferable ways even though their behavior is not in their own interest." Prescott (1975) downplays the importance of external effects in this context. In any case the possible external effects seem to have more pertinence for long-term allocative policies, such as the design of tax and welfare system, than for countercyclical monetary policy.

[45]The monetary authority might, instead, be reacting to v_{t-1} by a feedback rule of the form of equation (25), but individuals currently believe that $\gamma = 0$.

clear that the choice of m_t has a systematic effect on current output, as determined in equation (15). However, it is also clear from equation (23) that the expected squared gap between actual and full information output would be minimized by choosing $m_t = 0$.[46] Given the objective of minimizing gaps between actual and full information output, it is not surprising that optimal behavior rules out policy deception. In this sort of framework the best monetary policy is always the policy that is most predictable.[47] The obvious policy implication is for the monetary authority to make known in advance its intentions about money growth,[48] which is again the basic philosophy behind the constant growth rate rule.

3. Conclusions

I will conclude by highlighting some of the main results that deal with the effects of money variance and with the role of monetary policy. An increased variance of money makes it more difficult for individuals to react appropriately to the real shifts in the economy. There are two important types of responses to an increased money variance. First, since individuals react by attributing a larger fraction of observed price movements to monetary causes, there is a smaller effect of a given size monetary disturbance on output—that is, the magnitude of the Phillips curve slope is smaller. Second, the associated compounding of individual information problems leads both to a higher variance of output about its full (current) information position and to a reduced predictability of future prices. It also leads to an increase in the variance of relative prices across markets.

From the standpoint of monetary policy, it is clear that pure variance of money is harmful, essentially because it clouds the real picture for individuals. The analysis of monetary policy as feedback control is more complicated since the results hinge on the relative information positions of the monetary authority and the public. When the authority lacks superior information, the feedback to money must be based on economic variables that have already been perceived by the public. In this circumstance the choice of feedback control parameters has no implications for the entire distribution of output. On the other hand, if the monetary authority has superior information about the economy—which, for some reason, it does not provide to the public directly—then the appropriate feedback re-

---

[46]If the monetary authority sets $m_t = 0$ continually, this action would also lead people to believe (along Bayesian lines) that $\sigma_m^2 = 0$. I have not dealt explicitly with the effects of fooling people about the value of σ_m^2. Presumably, the variance of actual about full information output is minimized when perceptions about σ_m^2 are correct.

[47]There is a sense in which this conclusion is violated for the case where the monetary authority has superior information about the economy. In particular, the feedback rule from v_t to ΔM_t described by equation (26) would be ineffective if people fully perceived the countercyclical money response, $-\delta v_t$, while still remaining in the dark about v_t. On the other hand, it is desirable even in this case for people to know the form of the monetary rule.

[48]More specifically, the Federal Reserve should publicize, as rapidly as possible, the proceedings of its Open Market Committee.

sponse to the extra information can move output closer to its full information position.

Basically, the conclusions for monetary policy are in accord with the
philosophy behind Friedman's proposal for a constant growth rate rule. It
is only to the extent that the monetary authority has superior economic
information (as well as the appropriate objectives), and to the extent that
providing information to the public is costly, that there is a call for departures from the constant growth rate rule. Further, if the attempt to use
countercyclical policy to exploit the superior information results in a
higher variance of money, σ_m^2, there would be a tradeoff between the
beneficial effects from the countercyclical elements (the negative correlation between v_t and ΔM_t) and the adverse effects from pure monetary
variance.[49]

It may be useful to discuss the role of feedback control of money in the
case of a concrete example.[50] The United States economy in 1974 was
affected by two important real shocks: the oil cartel and the shortfall of
agricultural harvests. Although my model has been constructed to deal
with a closed economy, it seems that either of these shocks can be represented by a downward movement in aggregate real supply, v_t^s, and a lesser
downward movement in aggregate real demand, v_t^d. (I am abstracting here
from effects on relative supply and demand, which would be quantitatively important for these shocks, but which would not affect the essential
parts of my story.) It follows that output (in a "typical" market which
experiences zero relative shifts) would fall while prices would rise. What is
the role for monetary policy in this situation? The present analysis suggests
that there is a substantive role only to the extent that the monetary authority has better information than the public about the disturbances, or,
possibly, about their implications for the economy. Perhaps the most obvious observation about the oil and agricultural shocks is the extent to which
they are perceived. Hence, the approach in this paper argues that there is
no role for monetary policy in offsetting these real shifts.[51] Adverse shifts
like the oil and agricultural crises will reduce output and cause painful
relative adjustments no matter what the reaction of the monetary authority. Added monetary noise would only complicate and lengthen the process of adjustment.

[49]This type of tradeoff is discussed in Friedman (1953).

[50]Gordon (1975) discusses the same example. Perhaps not surprisingly, he reaches very
different conclusions.

[51]Further, to the extent that there is any role it would be a contraction of ΔM_t in response
to the positive value of $v_t \equiv v_t^d - v_t^s$. The present analysis implies that having the monetary
authority announce that there had been an oil or agricultural crisis (or, perhaps, telling
people that these crises meant lower output and higher prices) would be equivalent to the
appropriate active response of money. In this case it seems that both the announcement and
the active policy would have negligible effects. In fact, the announcement would be somewhat preferable since it would not involve the danger of introducing added variance into the
money supply.

Appendix 1: Results when u_t Is a First-Order Markov Process

I consider here the case where the real excess demand shift, u_t, is generated by a first-order Markov Process, $u_t = \lambda u_{t-1} + v_t$, where $0 \leqq \lambda \leqq 1$. Under this specification the magnitude of λ determines the extent to which the current shift, v_t, persists in its effect on u_{t+1}, and, hence, on P_{t+1}. The case treated in the main text corresponds to $\lambda = 1$—that is, to the situation where v_t affects u_{t+1} on a one-to-one basis.

The solution for prices and outputs can be derived in accordance with the general procedure developed in Section 1B of the text. Since no new elements are involved, I will simply indicate the results. It is convenient to define the parameter, $\widehat{\lambda} = \lambda/[\lambda + (\alpha/\beta)(1 - \lambda)]$. If $\alpha > \beta$ then the $\widehat{\lambda}$ parameter satisfies the conditions $0 \leqq \widehat{\lambda} \leqq \lambda \leqq 1$, $\widehat{\lambda} \to 0$ as $\lambda \to 0$, and $\widehat{\lambda} \to 1$ as $\lambda \to 1$. Recalling that $H \equiv \alpha_s \beta_d - \alpha_d \beta_s$, the results for prices and outputs are now

$$P_t(z) = M_{t-1} + [\theta_1 + \widehat{\lambda}\theta_2 + (\beta/\alpha)(1 - \theta_1 - \widehat{\lambda}\theta_2)]$$
$$\times \{m_t + (1/\beta)[v_t + \varepsilon_t(z)]\} + (\widehat{\lambda}/\beta)u_{t-1},$$

$$\mathrm{E}\,P_{t+1}|I_t(z) = M_{t-1} + (\theta_1 + \widehat{\lambda}\theta_2)\{m_t + (1/\beta)[v_t + \varepsilon_t(z)]\}$$
$$+ (\lambda\widehat{\lambda}/\beta)u_{t-1},$$

$$y_t(z) = (H/\alpha)(1 - \theta_1 - \widehat{\lambda}\theta_2)m_t + (1/\alpha)[\alpha_s - (H/\beta)(\theta_1 + \widehat{\lambda}\theta_2)]$$
$$\times [v_t^d + \varepsilon_t^d(z)] + (1/\alpha)[\alpha_d + (H/\beta)(\theta_1 + \widehat{\lambda}\theta_2)][v_t^s + \varepsilon_t^s(z)]$$
$$+ \lambda\left[\frac{\alpha_s(1 - \lambda) + \beta_s\lambda}{\alpha(1 - \lambda) + \beta\lambda}\right]u_{t-1}^d + \lambda\left[\frac{\alpha_d(1 - \lambda) + \beta_d\lambda}{\alpha(1 - \lambda) + \beta\lambda}\right]u_{t-1}^s,$$

$$y_t^*(z) = (1/\alpha)[\alpha_s - (H/\beta)\widehat{\lambda}]v_t^d + (1/\alpha)[\alpha_d + (H/\beta)\widehat{\lambda}]v_t^s + (\alpha_s/\alpha)\varepsilon_t^d(z)$$
$$+ (\alpha_d/\alpha)\varepsilon_t^s(z) + \lambda\left[\frac{\alpha_s(1 - \lambda) + \beta_s\lambda}{\alpha(1 - \lambda) + \beta\lambda}\right]u_{t-1}^d$$
$$+ \lambda\left[\frac{\alpha_d(1 - \lambda) + \beta_d\lambda}{\alpha(1 - \lambda) + \beta\lambda}\right]u_{t-1}^s,$$

$$y_t(z) - y_t^*(z) = (H/\alpha\beta)\{\beta m_t + \widehat{\lambda}v_t - (\theta_1 + \widehat{\lambda}\theta_2)[\beta m_t + v_t + \varepsilon_t(z)]\},$$
$$\Omega \equiv \mathrm{E}[y_t(z) - y_t^*(z)]^2|I_t(z)$$
$$= \frac{H^2}{(\alpha\beta)^2(\sigma_A^2 + \sigma_\varepsilon^2)}[(1 - \widehat{\lambda})^2\beta^2\sigma_m^2\sigma_v^2 + \beta^2\sigma_m^2\sigma_\varepsilon^2 + (\widehat{\lambda})^2\sigma_v^2\sigma_\varepsilon^2],$$

where $\sigma_A^2 \equiv \beta^2\sigma_m^2 + \sigma_v^2$ in the last expression. The original results in Section 1B of the text correspond, in each case, to $\lambda = \widehat{\lambda} = 1$.

The principal new results from allowing $\widehat{\lambda} \neq 1$ are brought out in the above expression for Ω. When $\widehat{\lambda} = 1$, the aggregate real shift, v_t, is permanent, in the sense of affecting u_{t+1} on a one-to-one basis. More importantly, the monetary variable, M_t, and the aggregate real shift, u_t, are in this case generated by processes of the same form—that is, by random walks. In this situation the current disturbance associated with money, βm_t, and the current movement in the aggregate real disturbance, v_t, have identical implications for the future price level, P_{t+1}. Therefore, when $\widehat{\lambda} = 1$, it is unnecessary for individuals who are interested in forecasting P_{t+1} to separate out the βm_t part of the current excess demand shift from the v_t part. The only concern is with separating the total aggregate shift, $\beta m_t + v_t$, from the relative shift, $\varepsilon_t(z)$ (since $\varepsilon_t[z]$ is purely transitory and has no impact on P_{t+1}). In the Ω-expression, $\widehat{\lambda} = 1$ implies that the $\sigma_m^2\sigma_v^2$ interaction term vanishes, and the remaining terms can be combined into an interaction term between σ_ε^2 and $\beta^2\sigma_m^2 + \sigma_v^2 \equiv \sigma_A^2$ (as in equation [24]). In this case the problem of separating permanent from transitory shifts in order to forecast P_{t+1} amounts to separating aggregate from relative shifts.

The other polar case is $\widehat{\lambda} = 0$, which corresponds to the v_t shifts being purely transitory. In that case v_t and $\varepsilon_t(z)$ are generated by processes of the same form and the $\sigma_v^2 \sigma_\varepsilon^2$ interaction term vanishes from the Ω-expression. The remaining terms can then be combined into an interaction term involving $\beta^2 \sigma_m^2$ and $\sigma_v^2 + \sigma_\varepsilon^2$. That is, the separation between permanent and transitory reduces in this case to a separation between monetary and real.

In the general case where $\widehat{\lambda}$ is in the interval between zero and one, all three interaction terms appear in the Ω-expression. Individuals would then be concerned with the full separation of the current excess demand shift, $\beta m_t + v_t + \varepsilon_t(z)$, into its three components. The separation between permanent and transitory would entail two types of divisions of current excess demand shifts: aggregate versus relative and monetary versus real.

From the standpoint of monetary policy, the important aspect of the extended model is that Ω is still a strictly increasing function of σ_m^2. (This property can be verified from straightforward differentiation of the Ω-expression.) Hence, the compounding of the information problem to include a separation of monetary versus real along with a separation of aggregate versus relative does not alter the conclusion that monetary noise makes the information problem more difficult.

Finally, it can be noted that the extension of the model to a first-order Markov process for u_t has been carried out within the framework where the monetary disturbance, m_t, and the relative shift, $\varepsilon_t(z)$, are purely white noise processes. It would be possible to introduce some serial dependence into these processes. However, it is already apparent from the above discussion of the u_t process that the crucial consideration is the relation between the processes that generate M_t, u_t and $\varepsilon_t(z)$. When these three processes assume different forms there will be an information problem associated with dividing currently observed excess demand shifts into its three components. The above case, in which the u_t-process is first-order Markov (with $\widehat{\lambda} \neq 0$ or 1) and m_t and $\varepsilon_t(z)$ are white noise, is one way in which the processes for M_t, u_t, and $\varepsilon_t(z)$ can take on different forms. Further alteration of the m_t or $\varepsilon_t(z)$ processes would not seem to change the basic picture, at least in terms of the implications for money variance, σ_m^2.

Appendix 2: Systematic Growth in Money and Output

This section extends the analysis of the text in two respects. First, the systematic growth rate of money, g in equation (4), is allowed to be nonzero. Second, the growth rate of k_t, the systematic part of excess demand which is defined as $-\beta\rho$ in equation (5), is allowed to be nonzero. It is clear that the introduction of these systematic growth elements (which are included in the information set, $I_t[z]$) would not affect the gap between actual and full information output. Therefore, the present discussion is limited to the effects of systematic growth on $P_t(z)$, $E P_{t+1} | I_t(z)$, and $y_t(z)$. The analysis here returns to the case where u_t is generated by a random walk ($\widehat{\lambda} = 1$, in the terminology of Appendix 1).

Formally, the extended model can be solved by the method of Section 1B of the text if the solution form for $P_t(z)$ in equation (6) is extended to include a time trend and a constant term—that is, $\Pi_6 t + \Pi_7$. Additional complications to the systematic parts of M_t and k_t—for example, to allow nonconstant growth rates—would be reflected as additional terms in the solution form for $P_t(z)$. Given the extended form of the solution, the procedure for solving the model is the same as that employed in Section 1B.

The solution for $P_t(z)$ coincides with equation (10) except for the inclusion of systematic effects associated with g and ρ. The extended result is

$$P_t(z) = M_{t-1} + g + [\theta_1 + \theta_2 + (\beta/\alpha)(1 - \theta_1 - \theta_2)]\{m_t + (1/\beta)[v_t + \varepsilon_t(z)]\}$$
$$+ (1/\beta)u_{t-1} - \rho t + (\alpha/\beta)(g - \rho) + \rho.$$

Since $M_{t-1} + g$ is now the fully perceived part of M_t, this term has a one-to-one effect on $P_t(z)$. The $-\rho t$ term indicates that the systematic growth of k_t at rate $-\beta\rho$ would generate a systematic growth in the price level at rate $-\rho$ if M were constant. With M growing steadily at rate g, the net systematic growth rate of the price level is $g - \rho$. This systematic rate of inflation appears additionally in the term $(\alpha/\beta)(g - \rho)$ as a positive effect on $P_t(z)$ for a given value of the nominal money stock. Equivalently, systematic inflation reduces the (expected) holding of real balances. I will discuss below the meaning of the final term, $+\rho$, in the $P_t(z)$ expression.

The expected price level for next period is now

$$\mathrm{E}\,P_{t+1}\mid I_t(z) = M_{t-1} + 2g + (\theta_1 + \theta_2)\{m_t + (1/\beta)[v_t + \varepsilon_t(z)]\}$$
$$+ (1/\beta)u_{t-1} - \rho(t + 1) + (\alpha/\beta)(g - \rho) + \rho.$$

In particular, the gap between $P_t(z)$ and $\mathrm{E}\,P_{t+1}\mid I_t(z)$ now includes the term $-(g - \rho)$, which is the negative of the systematic rate of inflation. In this model, where commodity supply and demand depend on $P_t(z) - \mathrm{E}\,P_{t+1}\mid I_t(z)$, it is this effect of systematic growth that leads to influences on output.

The solution for output is determined by substituting the price results into the commodity supply or demand function, as given in equations (1) and (2). The result for $y_t(z)$ coincides with equation (15) except for the new systematic effects,

$$y_t(z) = (\beta_s/\beta)k_t^d + (\beta_d/\beta)k_t^s - (H/\beta)(g - \rho) + \cdots,$$

where the terms that appear in equation (15) have been omitted. In determining output it is necessary to specify separately the systematic demand and supply, k_t^d and k_t^s, as well as the excess demand, k_t. I assume that individuals plan the systematic growth rate of real balances (real wealth) to equal the systematic growth rate of output. From the above expressions for $P_t(z)$ and $\mathrm{E}\,P_{t+1}\mid I_t(z)$, it is clear that the systematic growth rate of real balances is ρ. From the $y_t(z)$ expression it is clear that the systematic growth rate of output depends on the systematic growth rates of k_t^d and k_t^s. The condition that the systematic growth of real balances coincides with the systematic growth of output therefore implies a condition on the time paths of k_t^d and k_t^s. Using also the condition that $k_t = -\beta\rho t$, and setting $k_0^d = k_0^s = 0$ for convenience, it can be determined that

$$k_t^d = \rho(1 - \beta_s)t,$$
$$k_t^s = \rho(1 + \beta_d)t.$$

Substitution into the above expression for $y_t(z)$ yields

$$y_t(z) = \rho t - (H/\beta)(g - \rho) + \cdots.$$

That is, the systematic growth rate of output is, indeed, equal to ρ.

The other property of the output expression is that an increase in the systematic inflation rate, $g - \rho$, reduces output (both actual and full information) if $H > 0$. The mechanism is as follows. An increase in $g - \rho$ implies a lower real rate of return on money, which is the only store of value in the model. Accordingly, there is a substitution effect that reduces current labor supply and raises current consumption demand.[52] This shift raises output when $H > 0$. Of course, this sort of effect is operative here because money serves as the only store of value. Further, the present analysis does not deal with any benefits of holding money that are associated with transaction costs. For these reasons, it seems that the present model is probably more useful for an analysis of unperceived monetary change than for an analysis of systematic inflation.

Finally, I can now comment on the presence of the $+\rho$ terms in the above price expressions. In equations (1) and (2), excess commodity demand depends on expected next period's real balances, $M_t + \text{E}\,\Delta M_{t+1}\,|\,I_t(z) - \text{E}\,P_{t+1}\,|\,I_t(z)$. This formulation is reasonable as long as desired real balances are constant. More generally, it is a gap between expected and desired real balances that would produce an effect on excess commodity demand. It is now apparent that (desired) real balances grow at rate ρ in this model. If the effects of real balances on excess commodity demand are adjusted to take account of this systematic growth in desired real balances, the $+\rho$ terms would no longer appear in the above price expressions. The expression for $y_t(z)$ would be unaffected by this adjustment. Of course, no adjustment at all is required for the case in the text where $\rho = 0$ was assumed.

References

Barro, R. J. "A Theory of Monopolistic Price Adjustment." *Rev. Econ. Studies* 39 (January 1972): 17–26.

Barro, R. J., and Grossman, H. I. *Money, Employment, and Inflation.* Cambridge: Cambridge Univ. Press, 1975.

Cairnes, J. E. "The Course of Depreciation." In *Essays in Political Economy.* London: Kelley, 1873.

Friedman, M. "The Effects of a Full-Employment Policy on Economic Stability: A Formal Analysis." In *Essays in Positive Economics.* Chicago: Univ. Chicago Press, 1953.

———. *A Program for Monetary Stability.* New York: Fordham, 1960.

———. "The Role of Monetary Policy." *A.E.R.* 58 (March 1968): 1–17.

Gordon, R. J. "Alternative Responses of Policy to External Supply Shocks." *Brookings Papers on Economic Activity,* no. 1 (1975).

Graham, F. D. *Exchange, Prices and Production in Hyper-inflation: Germany, 1920–23* Princeton: Princeton Univ. Press, 1930.

Hall, R. E. "The Phillips Curve and Macroeconomic Policy." In *The Phillips Curve and Labor Markets,* edited by K. Brunner and A. Meltzer. Amsterdam: North-Holland, 1976.

Lucas, R. "Expectations and the Neutrality of Money." *J. Econ. Theory* 4 (April 1972): 103–24.

———. "Some International Evidence on Output-Inflation Tradeoffs." *A.E.R.* 63 (June 1973): 326–34.

———. "An Equilibrium Model of the Business Cycle." *J.P.E.* 83 (December 1975): 1113–44.

Lucas, R., and Rapping, L. "Real Wages, Employment, and Inflation." *J.P.E.* 77 (September/October 1969): 721–54.

Mills, F. C. *The Behavior of Prices.* New York: Nat. Bur. Econ. Res., 1927.

Mortensen, D. T. "Job Matching under Imperfect Information." In *Evaluating the Labor Market Effects of Social Programs,* edited by O. Ashenfelter (in press).

[52] In a life-cycle model these effects would also alter the distribution of wealth by age. I have not dealt with this type of distribution effect.

Phelps, E. S. *Inflation Policy and Unemployment Theory*. New York: Norton, 1972.

Prescott, E. C. "Efficiency of the Natural Rate." *J.P.E.* 83 (December 1975): 1229–36.

Sargent, T., and Wallace, N. "Rational Expectations and the Theory of Economic Policy." Presented at the Seminar on Rational Expectations at the Federal Reserve Bank of Minneapolis, October 1974.

————. "'Rational' Expectations, the Optimal Monetary Instrument, and the Optimal Money Supply Rule." *J.P.E.* 83 (April 1975): 241–54.

Simons, H. *Economic Policy for a Free Society*. Chicago: Univ. Chicago Press, 1948.

Taylor, J. "Monetary Policy during a Transition to Rational Expectations." *J.P.E.* 83 (October 1975): 1009–22.

Vining, D. "The Relationship between Relative and General Prices." Manuscript, 1974.

13

Long-Term Contracts, Rational Expectations, and the Optimal Money Supply Rule

Stanley Fischer

The paper is concerned with the role of monetary policy and argues that activist monetary policy can affect the behavior of real output, rational expectations notwithstanding. A rational expectations model with overlapping labor contracts is constructed, with each labor contract being made for two periods. These contracts inject an element of short-run wage stickiness into the model. Because the money stock is changed by the monetary authority more frequently than labor contracts are renegotiated, and, given the assumed form of the labor contracts, monetary policy has the ability to affect the short-run behavior of output, though it has no effects on long-run output behavior.

This paper is concerned with the role of monetary policy in affecting real output and argues that activist monetary policy can affect the short-run behavior of real output, rational expectations notwithstanding. Recent contributions[1] have suggested that the behavior of real output is invariant to the money supply rule chosen by the monetary authority if expectations are formed rationally. The argument to the contrary advanced below turns on the existence of long-term contracts in the economy and makes the empirically reasonable assumption that economic agents contract in nominal terms for periods longer than the time it takes the monetary authority to react to changing economic circumstances—in this paper the relevant contracts are labor contracts.

I am indebted to Rudiger Dornbusch for extensive discussions, to Edmund Phelps for a suggestive discussion some years ago and for his comments on the first draft of this paper, and to Robert Barro, Benjamin Friedman, and Thomas Sargent for comments. An argument similar to the thesis of this paper is contained in an independent paper by Phelps and Taylor (1977); the details are sufficiently different that the two papers should be regarded as complementary. Note 19 below discusses the relationship between the two papers. Research support from the National Science Foundation is gratefully acknowledged.

[1] Notably that of Sargent and Wallace (1975); this paper is henceforth referred to as SW.

[*Journal of Political Economy*, 1977, vol. 85, no. 1]

The literature on the policy implications of rational expectations is relatively technical. It is therefore worthwhile setting the issue in recent historical perspective. Since the discovery of the Phillips curve in 1958,[2] the logic of the evolution of professional views on the ability of monetary policy to affect real output has tended toward a position similar to the empirically based early postwar Keynesian view—that monetary policy can play no significant role in determining the behavior of output.

The Phillips curve was originally seen as a stable long-run relationship providing those combinations of unemployment and inflation rates among which policymakers could choose in accord with their preferences. The theoretical rationalization due to Lipsey (1960), based on the "law of supply and demand" in the labor market, did not affect that particular view of the curve.[3]

The famous "Phillips loops" around the long-run relationship, discussed in the original Phillips article, suggested that the short-run trade-off differed from the long-run relationship. The distinction between the short- and long-run trade-offs formed the basis for the originally startling natural rate hypothesis of Friedman (1968) and Phelps (1967) which argued that, while there was a short-run Phillips trade-off, there was in the long run a natural unemployment rate, independent of the steady state rate of inflation. More dramatically, the natural rate hypothesis implies that the long-run Phillips curve is vertical.

The arguments rested on the point that the short-run trade-off was the result of expectational errors by economic agents. In Friedman's version, suppliers of labor at the beginning of an inflationary period underestimate the price level that will prevail over the period of the work contract, accordingly overestimate the real wage, and offer a greater supply of labor at the prevailing nominal wage than they would if expectations were correct. The result is employment in excess of the equilibrium level and a trade-off between output and unanticipated inflation.[4] However, the expectational errors cannot persist so that employment returns to its equilibrium level—and unemployment returns to its natural rate—as expectations adjust to reality. Subsequent work by Phelps and others (1970) provided a better worked out theoretical foundation for the short-run trade-off.[5]

The dependence of the short-run trade-off on expectational errors did not by itself preclude any effects of monetary policy on output provided

[2] Despite Fisher's (1926) earlier discovery of the unemployment-inflation relationship, it was not until the publication of Phillips's 1958 article that the relationship began to play a central role in policy discussions.

[3] However, Harry Johnson (1969) in his inflation survey expressed doubts as to the ability of policymakers to exploit the Phillips tradeoff (see pp. 132–33).

[4] The level of employment and the rate of unemployment move inversely in Friedman's exposition.

[5] These developments are summarized by Gordon (1976).

the monetary authority could produce a rate of inflation that was not anticipated. Indeed the widespread use of adaptive expectations suggested that an ever-accelerating rate of inflation could maintain an unemployment rate below the natural rate—hence adherents of the natural rate hypothesis were for a time known as accelerationists. The accelerationist version of the natural rate hypothesis had two important consequences. First, by making the short-run trade-off depend on expectational errors it brought to the fore the question of the optimality of the natural rate.[6]

Second, the reliance of the accelerationist hypothesis on expectational errors made it possible that some expectations mechanism other than adaptive expectations would imply that there is no trade-off usable by policymakers. Rational expectations is that hypothesis.[7]

Briefly, rational expectations as applied in the context of economic models is the hypothesis that expectations are the predictions implied by the model itself, contingent on the information economic agents are assumed to have.[8] In particular, if economic agents are assumed to know the policy rule being followed by the monetary authority, that rule itself will affect expectations. For instance, consider the consequences for the expected price level of a current price level that is higher than had been expected. Adaptive expectations implies that the price level currently expected for next period will be higher than the price level that was expected last period to prevail in this period. Under rational expectations, the expected price level will change in a manner dependent on the money supply rule: if monetary policy accommodates inflationary shocks, the expected price level will rise; if monetary policy counteracts inflationary shocks, the expected price level may be lower than the level expected for this period.

Now consider the implications of the rational expectations hypothesis for the effects on output of alternative preannounced monetary rules in an economy that has an expectational Phillips curve of the Lucas form:[9]

$$Y_t = \alpha + \beta(P_t - {}_{t-1}P_t) + u_t, \qquad \beta > 0, \qquad (1)$$

where α and β are constant parameters, Y_t the level of output, P_t the logarithm of the price level, and ${}_{t-1}P_t$ the expectation taken at the end of period $(t - 1)$ of P_t, and u_t is a stochastic disturbance term.

The only way in which monetary policy can affect output, given (1), is by creating a difference between the actual price level and the expected price level. However, if the money supply rule is known to economic

---

[6] This issue, among others, was analyzed by Tobin (1972); it is taken up by Prescott (1975).

[7] The fundamental application of the rational expectations hypothesis in a Phillips curve context is by Lucas (1972); see also Lucas (1973) and SW.

[8] See Barro and Fischer (1976) for an extended discussion of rational expectations.

[9] This is similar to the aggregate supply function of SW and also Lucas (1973).

agents and is based on the same information as those agents have (for example, the money supply may be adjusted on the basis of lagged values of prices and output), then the predictable effects of the money supply on prices are embodied in $_{t-1}P_t$ and monetary policy can affect output only by doing the unexpected. Alternatively, if the monetary authority has superior information to private economic agents, say because it receives data more rapidly than they do, it can affect the behavior of output.[10] Superior information is, however, a weak reed on which to base the argument for the effectiveness of monetary policy because useful information has a habit of becoming available, perhaps through inference based on the actions of the monetary authority.

The argument made in this paper for the effectiveness of monetary policy depends instead on the existence of nominal long-term contracts in the economy. The aggregate supply equation (1) implies that the only expectation relevant to the behavior of output is the expectation formed one period earlier. The length of the period is not specified, but for the result to be interesting one supposes that it is a year or less. Since there are contracts that are made for more than a year, expectations of P_t made in periods earlier than $(t - 1)$ are likely to be relevant to the behavior of output.

In this paper I construct a model similar in spirit to the simple rational expectations models such as that of Sargent and Wallace (1975) (SW) and assume that expectations are formed rationally. If all contracts in the model economy are made for one period, the SW result on the irrelevance of the money supply rule for the behavior of output obtains; if there are some longer-term nominal contracts, then even fully anticipated monetary policy affects the behavior of output and there is room for a stabilizing monetary policy. The use of longer-term nominal contracts puts an element of stickiness into the nominal wage which is responsible for the effectiveness of monetary policy.

The paper does not provide a microeconomic basis for the existence of long-term nominal contracts, though the transaction costs of frequent price setting and wage negotiations must be part of the explanation. It will be seen below that the essential element needed for the effectiveness of monetary policy in this paper is that long-term contracts not be written in such a way as to duplicate the effects of a succession of single-period contracts, or the use of spot markets. It is reasonable to conjecture that the costs of wage setting lead to the use of long-term contracts and that the difficulties of contract writing prevent the emergence of contracts that are equivalent to the use of spot markets.

Section I introduces the model and demonstrates the fundamental rational expectations result on the irrelevance of monetary policy in a

---

[10] SW examine a case in which the monetary authority has superior information; see also Barro (1976).

world where all contracts are made for only one period. Section II presents a model with overlapping labor contracts in which all labor contracts are made for two periods and in which at any one time half the firms are operating in the first year of a 2-year contract and the other half in the second year of a contract. In this model monetary policy can affect the behavior of output. Section III considers various indexed labor contracts. Conclusions and further discussion are contained in Section IV.

I. The Model with One-Period Contracts

The model used to study monetary policy in this paper has three elements: wage setting behavior, an output supply equation, and an aggregate demand equation. The economy is stationary in that the analysis abstracts from growth in the capital stock and an increasing price level though the latter is readily included. A potential role for stabilization policy is created by the assumption that the economy is subjected to random disturbances—real supply disturbances and nominal demand disturbances —that affect output and the price level in each period. Depending on the details of wage setting, monetary policy may be able to offset some of the effects of these disturbances on real output.

First we consider wage setting behavior. The nominal wage is treated as predetermined throughout the paper in that it is known at the beginning of the period while output and the price level adjust during the period. The assumption that the wage is predetermined is based on the empirical observation that wages are usually set in advance of employment.

It is assumed that the nominal wage is set to try to maintain constancy of the real wage, which is equivalent in this model to maintaining constancy of employment and/or labor income; this assumption is based on recent work on the labor contract.[11] However, it should be emphasized that no substantive results of the paper would be affected if a nominal wage *schedule* (e.g., specifying overtime payments) were to be negotiated, rather than simply a nominal wage *rate*.[12]

If labor contracts are made every period, and assuming the goal of nominal wage setting is to maintain constancy of the real wage:

$$_{t-1}W_t = \gamma + {}_{t-1}P_t, \tag{2}$$

where $_{t-1}W_t$ is the logarithm of the wage set at the end of period $t - 1$ for period t; γ is a scale factor in the determination of the real wage and will be set at zero for convenience.

[11] See Azariadis (1975), Baily (1974), and Grossman (1975); Gordon (1976) discusses these contributions.

[12] The derivation of the aggregate supply function (4) below for the case of a nominal wage schedule is available from the author on request. The function has the same form as (4) but with different coefficients; no subsequent argument is affected by those differences.

Second, the supply of output is assumed to be a decreasing function of the real wage:

$$Y_t^s = \alpha + (P_t - W_t) + u_t, \tag{3}$$

where, again, the coefficient β of (1) has been set equal to unity for convenience, and where α will be taken to be zero; P_t is the logarithm of the price level and Y_t the level of output. It is assumed that firms operate on their demand curves for labor, that is, that the level of employment is determined by demand. Substituting from (2) into (3):[13]

$$Y_t^s = (P_t - {}_{t-1}P_t) + u_t. \tag{4}$$

This is similar to the standard rational expectations supply function (1). The form of the aggregate supply function is essentially unaffected if the firm faces a nominal wage schedule in which the wage rises as labor input is increased.[14] The term u_t is a stochastic "real" disturbance that impinges on production in each period; its properties will be specified below.

It remains now to close the model by taking demand considerations into account, and the simplest way of doing so is to specify a velocity equation

$$Y_t = M_t - P_t - v_t \tag{5}$$

where M_t is the logarithm of the money stock in period t and v_t is a disturbance term.[15]

Disturbances aside, this very simple macro model would be assumed in equilibrium to have the real wage set at its full employment level, would imply the neutrality of money, and would obviously have no role for monetary policy in affecting the level of output. Note again that (2) implies that all wages are set each period—there are only one-period labor contracts. A potential role for monetary policy is created by the presence of the disturbances u_t and v_t that are assumed to affect the level of output each period. Each of the disturbances is assumed to follow a first-order autoregressive scheme:

$$u_t = \rho_1 u_{t-1} + \varepsilon_t, \qquad |\rho_1| < 1, \tag{6}$$

$$v_t = \rho_2 v_{t-1} + \eta_t, \qquad |\rho_2| < 1, \tag{7}$$

where ε_t and η_t are mutually and serially uncorrelated stochastic terms with expectation zero and finite variances σ_ε^2 and σ_η^2, respectively.

[13] By setting α in (3) at zero, we appear to make negative levels of output possible. Any reader worried by that possibility should either set α to a positive value or else view (4) as a relationship that applies to deviations of output from a specified level. Note also that (3) can be viewed as a markup equation with the markup dependent on the level of output.

[14] See n. 12 above.

[15] SW are interested in the question of the optimal monetary instrument and thus specify two additional equations: an aggregate demand or IS equation, and a portfolio balance or LM equation. I use the single equation (5) to avoid unnecessary detail. A model with overlapping labor contracts and separate goods and money markets is presented in the appendix to Fischer (forthcoming).

We shall assume that expectations are formed rationally. Eliminating Y_t between (4) and (5)—which is equivalent to assuming the price level adjusts each period to equate aggregate supply and demand—we get:

$$2P_t = M_t + {}_{t-1}P_t - (u_t + v_t). \tag{8}$$

Now, taking expectations as of the end of $(t - 1)$ in (8), and noting that $E_{t-1}({}_{t-1}P_t) = {}_{t-1}P_t$:

$$ {}_{t-1}P_t = {}_{t-1}M_t - {}_{t-1}(u_t + v_t) \tag{9}$$

where ${}_{t-1}X_t$ is the expectation of X_t conditional on information available at the end of $(t - 1)$.

Assume the monetary rule is set on the basis of disturbances which have occurred up to and including period $(t - 1)$:

$$M_t = \sum_{i=1}^{\infty} a_i u_{t-i} + \sum_{i=1}^{\infty} b_i v_{t-i}. \tag{10}$$

The disturbances can be identified ex post so that there is no difficulty for the monetary authority in following a rule such as (10) or for the public in calculating the next period's money supply. From (10) it follows that

$$ {}_{t-1}M_t = M_t \tag{11}$$

and thus:

$$
\begin{aligned}
P_t - {}_{t-1}P_t &= \frac{M_t}{2} - \frac{{}_{t-1}P_t}{2} - \frac{u_t + v_t}{2} \\
&= \frac{{}_{t-1}(u_t + v_t)}{2} - \frac{u_t + v_t}{2} \\
&= \tfrac{1}{2}[\rho_1 u_{t-1} + \rho_2 v_{t-1} - (\rho_1 u_{t-1} + \varepsilon_t + \rho_2 v_{t-1} + \eta_t)] \\
&= -\tfrac{1}{2}(\varepsilon_t + \eta_t).
\end{aligned}
\tag{12}
$$

The disturbances in (12) are current shocks that can be predicted by neither the monetary authority nor the public and thus cannot be offset by monetary policy.

Substituting (12) into (4) it is clear that the parameters a_i and b_i of (10) have no effect on the behavior of output. Of course, as SW note, the monetary rule does affect the behavior of the price level, but since that is not at issue, there is no point in exploring the relationship further. The explanation for the irrelevance of the money supply rule for the behavior of output in this model is simple: money is neutral, and economic agents know each period what next period's money supply will be. In their wage setting they aim only to obtain a specified real wage and the nominal wage is accordingly adjusted to reflect the expected price level.

Thus, the model with only one-period contracts confirms the SW result of the irrelevance of the monetary rule for the behavior of output.

II. The Model with Two-Period Nonindexed Labor Contracts

We now proceed to inject an element of stickiness into the behavior of the nominal wage. Suppose that all labor contracts run for two periods and that the contract drawn up at the end of period t specifies nominal wages for periods $(t + 1)$ and $(t + 2)$.[16] Assuming again that contracts are drawn up to maintain constancy of the real wage, we specify:

$$_{t-i}W_t = {}_{t-i}P_t, \qquad i = 1, 2, \tag{13}$$

where $_{t-i}W_t$ is the wage to be paid in period t as specified in contracts drawn up at $(t - i)$, and $_{t-i}P_t$ is the expectation of P_t evaluated at the end of $(t - i)$. To prevent misunderstanding it should be noted that the use of a one-period, and not a two-period, labor contract is optimal from the viewpoint of minimizing the variance of the real wage; as discussed in the introduction, there must be reasons other than stability of the real wage, such as the costs of frequent contract negotiations and/or wage setting, for the existence of longer-term contracts.

In period t, half the firms are operating in the first year of a labor contract drawn up at the end of $(t - 1)$ and the other half in the second year of a contract drawn up at the end of $(t - 2)$. There is only a single price for output.[17] Given that the wage is predetermined for each firm, the aggregate supply of output is given by:

$$Y_t^s = \tfrac{1}{2} \sum_{i=1}^{2} (P_t - {}_{t-i}W_t) + u_t. \tag{14}$$

$$Y_t^s = \tfrac{1}{2} \sum_{i=1}^{2} (P_t - {}_{t-i}P_t) + u_t. \tag{14'}$$

Now, using rational expectations again, by combining (14') and (5), and noting that $E_{t-2}({}_{t-1}P_t) = {}_{t-2}P_t$:

$$_{t-2}P_t = {}_{t-2}M_t - {}_{t-2}(u_t + v_t) \tag{15}$$

$$_{t-1}P_t = \tfrac{2}{3}{}_{t-1}M_t + \tfrac{1}{3}{}_{t-2}M_t - \tfrac{1}{3}{}_{t-2}(u_t + v_t) - \tfrac{2}{3}{}_{t-1}(u_t + v_t). \tag{16}$$

[16] Akerlof (1969) uses a model with overlapping labor contracts, in which prices charged differ among firms.

[17] The extreme assumption is made here that labor is attached to a particular set of firms and that the state of excess supply or demand for labor in firms operating in mid-contract does not affect the starting wage in the new contracts of the remaining firms. Some labor mobility between firms could be incorporated in the analysis without affecting the results so long as mobility is not sufficiently great to eliminate all wage differentials between the two types of firms in a given period.

Note that since, by assumption, M_t is a function only of information available up to the end of period $(t - 1)$, $_{t-1}M_t = M_t$.

Accordingly,

$$2P_t = \tfrac{4}{3}M_t + \tfrac{2}{3}{}_{t-2}M_t - (u_t + v_t) - \tfrac{1}{3}{}_{t-1}(u_t + v_t) - \tfrac{2}{3}{}_{t-2}(u_t + v_t), \tag{17}$$

and

$$Y_t = \frac{M_t - {}_{t-2}M_t}{3} + \tfrac{1}{2}(u_t - v_t) + \tfrac{1}{6}{}_{t-1}(u_t + v_t) + \tfrac{1}{3}{}_{t-2}(u_t + v_t). \tag{18}$$

Let the money supply again be determined by the rule of equation (10) so that

$$_{t-2}M_t = a_1\rho_1 u_{t-2} + \sum_{i=2}^{\infty} a_i u_{t-1} + b_1\rho_2 v_{t-2} + \sum_{i=2}^{\infty} b_i v_{t-i} \tag{19}$$

and

$$M_t - {}_{t-2}M_t = a_1(u_{t-1} - \rho_1 u_{t-2}) + b_1(v_{t-1} - \rho_2 v_{t-2})$$
$$= a_1\varepsilon_{t-1} + b_1\eta_{t-1}. \tag{20}$$

The difference between the actual money stock in period t and that stock as predicted two periods earlier arises from the reactions of the monetary authority to the disturbances ε_{t-1} and η_{t-1} occurring in the interim. It is precisely these disturbances that cannot influence the nominal wage for the second period of wage contracts entered into at $(t - 2)$.

Substituting (20) and (10) into (18) it is clear that the parameters a_i and b_i of the money supply rule, for $i \geq 2$, have no effect on the behavior of output, and for purposes of this paper can be set at zero.[18] Thus:

$$Y_t = \tfrac{1}{3}[a_1(u_{t-1} - \rho_1 u_{t-2}) + b_1(v_{t-1} - \rho_2 v_{t-2})]$$
$$+ \tfrac{1}{2}(u_t - v_t) + \tfrac{1}{6}{}_{t-1}(u_t + v_t) + \tfrac{1}{3}{}_{t-2}(u_t + v_t) \tag{21}$$
$$= \tfrac{1}{2}(\varepsilon_t - \eta_t) + \tfrac{1}{3}[\varepsilon_{t-1}(a_1 + 2\rho_1) + \eta_{t-1}(b_1 - \rho_2)] + \rho_1^2 u_{t-2}.$$

Before we examine the variance of output as a function of the parameters a_1 and b_1, it is worth explaining why the values of those parameters affect the behavior of output, even when the parameters are fully known. The essential reason is that between the time the two-year contract is drawn up and the last year of operation of that contract, there is time for the monetary authority to react to new information about recent economic disturbances. Given the negotiated second-period nominal wage, the way the monetary authority reacts to disturbances will affect the real wage for the second period of the contract and thus output.

[18] From the viewpoint of the behavior of the price level it might be desirable to have nonzero values of those parameters, but we are focusing strictly on the behavior of output.

Calculating the asymptotic variance of Y from (21) we obtain:

$$\sigma_Y^2 = \sigma_\varepsilon^2 \left[\tfrac{1}{4} + \tfrac{4}{9}\rho_1^2 + \frac{\rho_1^4}{1 - \rho_1^2} + \frac{a_1(4\rho_1 + a_1)}{9} \right]$$
$$+ \sigma_\eta^2 \left[\tfrac{1}{4} + \tfrac{1}{9}\rho_2^2 - \frac{b_1}{9}(2\rho_2 - b_1) \right]. \tag{22}$$

The variance minimizing values of a_1 and b_1 are accordingly:

$$a_1 = -2\rho_1$$
$$b_1 = \rho_2 \tag{23}$$

which yield output variance of

$$\sigma_Y^2 = \sigma_\varepsilon^2 \left[\frac{1}{4} + \frac{\rho_1^4}{1 - \rho_1^2} \right] + \tfrac{1}{4}\sigma_\eta^2. \tag{24}$$

To interpret the monetary rule, examine the second equality in (21). It can be seen there that the level of output is affected by current disturbances $(\varepsilon_t - \eta_t)$ that cannot be offset by monetary policy, by disturbances $(\varepsilon_{t-1}$ and $\eta_{t-1})$ that have occurred since the signing of the older of the existing labor contracts, and by a lagged real disturbance (u_{t-2}). The disturbances ε_{t-1} and η_{t-1} can be wholly offset by monetary policy and that is precisely what (23) indicates. The u_{t-2} disturbance, on the other hand, was known when the older labor contract was drawn up and cannot be offset by monetary policy because it is taken into account in wage setting. Note, however, that the stabilization is achieved by affecting the real wage of those in the second year of labor contracts and thus should not be expected to be available to attain arbitrary levels of output—the use of too active a policy would lead to a change in the structure of contracts.

For a more general interpretation of the monetary rule, note from (17) that u—the real disturbance—and v—the nominal disturbance—both tend to reduce the price level. The rule accordingly is to accommodate real disturbances that tend to increase the price level and to counteract nominal disturbances which tend to increase the price level. Such an argument has been made by Gordon (1975).

The monetary rule can alternately be expressed in terms of observable variables as

$$M_t = \rho_2 M_{t-1} + (2\rho_1 - \rho_2)P_{t-1} - (2\rho_1 + \rho_2)Y_{t-1}$$
$$- \rho_1(_{t-2}W_{t-1} + _{t-3}W_{t-1}) \tag{25}$$

and it is also possible to substitute out for the wage rates in (25) to obtain a money supply rule solely in terms of lagged values of the money stock, prices, and income.

III. Indexed Contracts

The only way in which monetary policy can lose its effectiveness when there are long-term labor contracts is for the wage to be indexed in a way which duplicates the effects of one-period contracts. However, it will be seen (in [28] below) that such indexing is not of the type generally encountered. Other types of indexing do allow monetary policy that can affect output.

If the wage is set such that

$$_{t-i}W_t = {}_{t-1}P_t, \qquad i = 1, 2, \ldots \tag{26}$$

then the results of Section I above obtain, and, in particular, output is given by

$$Y_t = \tfrac{1}{2}(\varepsilon_t - \eta_t) + \rho_1 u_{t-1}. \tag{27}$$

However, the indexing formula implied by (26) is unlike anything seen in practice. It is:

$$W_t = -\rho_2 M + (\rho_1 + \rho_2)P_{t-1} + (\rho_2 - \rho_1)Y_{t-1} - \rho_1 W_{t-1} \tag{28}$$

where M_t is assumed constant at M since the monetary rule is of no consequence for the behavior of output. For $\rho_1 < 0$—negative serial correlation of real disturbances—and $\rho_1 + \rho_2 > 0$ the above formula could be similar to a wage contract which specifies both indexation to the price level and profit sharing, but it is certainly not in general the type of contract which is found. Probably the major reason such contracts are not seen in practice is that calculation of their terms would be difficult since industry and firm specific factors omitted from this simple model are relevant to contracts that duplicate the effects of a full set of spot markets.

The variance of output obtaining with the general indexing formula (28) for wage determination is

$$\sigma_Y^2 = \sigma_\varepsilon^2 \left(\frac{1}{4} + \frac{\rho_1^2}{1 - \rho_1^2}\right) + \tfrac{1}{4}\sigma_\eta^2. \tag{29}$$

This exceeds the variance of output with optimal monetary policy in the nonindexed economy with two-period contracts; this is because the criterion for wage setting, attempting to maintain constancy of the real wage, is not equivalent to the criterion of minimizing the variance of output. This result may be part of the explanation for the continued hostility of stabilization authorities to indexation.

If any indexation formula for wages other than (28) is used, and there are contracts which last more than one period, there is again room for stabilizing monetary policy. For instance, consider a wage indexed to the price level such that

$$_{t-i}W_t = {}_{t-i}W_{t-i+1} + P_{t-1} - P_{t-i} \tag{30}$$

in which the wage paid in period t on a contract made at the end of $(t - i)$ is the wage specified for the first year of the contract adjusted for inflation over the intervening period. We also specify that

$$_{t-i}W_{t-i+1} = {}_{t-i}P_{t-i+1}, \tag{31}$$

that is, that the wage for the first year of the contract minimizes the variance of the real wage in that period.

Assuming 2-year contracts, the supply equation (14), the velocity equation (5), and rational expectations in determining the expected price level in (31), one obtains, using the lag operator L:

$$Y_t(6 - 4L + 2L^2) = 2M_t(1 - L)^2 + u_t[3 - (1 - \rho_1)L + \rho_1 L^2]$$

$$- v_t[3 - (3 + \rho_2)L + (2 - \rho_2)L^2], \tag{32}$$

where use has been made of the fact that $M_t = {}_{t-1}M_t$.

Since M_t enters the output equation, it is clear that monetary policy does have an effect on the behavior of output. In this case it is actually possible for monetary policy to offset the effects of all lagged disturbances by using the rule

$$M_t = Lu_t[-(1 + 4\rho_1) + (1 + \rho_1)L - \rho_1 L^2][2(1 - L)^2]^{-1}$$

$$- Lv_t[(1 - 2\rho_2) + (-1 + 3\rho_2)L - \rho_2 L^2][2(1 - L)^2]^{-1} \tag{33}$$

which leaves

$$\sigma_y^2 = \frac{\sigma_\varepsilon^2}{4} + \frac{\sigma_\eta^2}{4}. \tag{34}$$

In the face of real disturbances, the monetary rule (33) destabilizes the real wage relative to its behavior under the optimal monetary policy in the nonindexed two-period contract model, and a fortiori relative to its behavior when there are single-period contracts. Given that the assumed aim of labor is to have stable real wages, an indexed contract like (30) would be less attractive to labor than the nonindexed contracts of Section II.

IV. Conclusions

The argument of this paper about active monetary policy turns on the revealed preference of economic agents for long-term contracts. The only long-term contracts discussed here are labor contracts, which generally provide a Keynesian-like element of temporary wage rigidity that provides a stabilizing role for monetary policy even when that policy is fully anticipated.[19] Monetary policy loses its effectiveness only if long-term contracts are indexed in an elaborate way that duplicates the effects of single-period contracts, as indicated at the beginning of Section III— and it should not be doubted that the labor contract of equation (28) is a very simplified version of the long-term contract that would in practice be needed to duplicate the effects of contracts negotiated each period.

The effectiveness of monetary policy does not require anyone to be fooled. In the model of Section II, with two-period contracts, monetary policy is fully anticipated but because it is based on information which becomes available after the labor contract is made, it can affect output. If the monetary authority wants to stabilize output, it can do so; in the model of Section II its optimal policy from the viewpoint of output stabilization is to accommodate real disturbances that tend to increase the price level and counteract nominal disturbances that tend to increase the price level. Stabilization of output in the face of real disturbances implies a less stable real wage than would obtain with one-period contracts while output stabilization in the face of nominal disturbances implies a real wage as stable as that obtained with one-period contracts.

Despite the different implications of this model from that of SW for the effectiveness of monetary policy in affecting output, the implied aggregate supply functions are only subtly different. An aggregate supply function such as that used by Lucas (1973) in which monetary policy cannot affect the behavior of output can be written

$$Y_t = \sum_{i=0}^{\infty} \gamma_i(P_{t-i} - {}_{t-i-1}P_{t-i}) + u_t. \tag{35}$$

That is, output is determined as a distributed lag on one-period forecast errors of the price level. A general aggregate supply function implying the potential effectiveness of monetary policy would be

$$Y_t = \sum_{i=0}^{\infty} \theta_i(P_t - {}_{t-i}P_t) + u_t. \tag{36}$$

In this case output is determined as a function of one and more period forecast errors of the price level.[20] The two formulations could be difficult to distinguish empirically.

[19] The major difference between this paper and that of Phelps and Taylor (1977) (PT) is that in most of PT it is price, rather than wage, rigidity that provides the element of nominal stickiness from which monetary policy derives its effectiveness. At the end of their paper, PT do present a model with (single-period) price and wage stickiness. Persistence effects in the present paper arise from the overlapping contracts and serial correlation of disturbances while in PT inventory accumulation produces persistence of past disturbances.

[20] Obviously, a more general form of (36) could involve terms like

$$\sum_{j=0}^{\infty} \phi_j \sum_{i=0}^{\infty} \theta_i(P_{t-j} - {}_{t-i-j}P_{t-j}).$$

Before concluding, we should note that there is no dispute that monetary policy can affect price level behavior. To the extent that price changes are costly, it would be desirable to maintain price stability. In the face of autocorrelated disturbances of the sort discussed in this paper, and even if all contracts are one period, an activist monetary policy would be needed to maintain stable prices. Thus an argument for the desirability of an activist monetary policy could be constructed even if there were no potential role for monetary policy in affecting output.

While the paper argues that an active monetary policy can affect the behavior of output if there are long-term contracts, and is desirable in order to foster long-term contracts, one of the important lessons of the rational expectations literature should not be overlooked:[21] the structure of the economy adjusts as policy changes. An attempt by the monetary authority to exploit the existing structure of contracts to produce behavior far different from that envisaged when contracts were signed would likely lead to the reopening of the contracts and, if the new behavior of the monetary authority were persisted in, a new structure of contracts. But given a structure of contracts, there is some room for maneuver by the monetary authorities—which is to say that their policies can, though will not necessarily, be stabilizing.

References

Akerlof, George A. "Relative Wages and the Rate of Inflation." *Q.J.E.* 83, no. 3 (August 1969): 353–74.
Azariadis, Costas. "Implicit Contracts and Underemployment Equilibria." *J.P.E.* 83, no. 6 (December 1975): 1183–202.
Baily, Martin N. "Wages and Employment under Uncertain Demand." *Rev. Econ. Studies* 41, no. 1 (January 1974): 37–50.
Barro, Robert J. "Rational Expectations and the Role of Monetary Policy." *J. Monetary Econ.*, vol. 2 (1976), in press.
Barro, Robert J., and Fischer, Stanley. "Recent Developments in Monetary Theory." *J. Monetary Econ.* 2, no. 2 (April 1976): 133–68.
Fischer, Stanley. "Wage Indexation and Macro-Economic Stability." Forthcoming in public policy suppl., *J. Monetary Econ.*
Fisher, Irving. "A Statistical Relation between Unemployment and Price Changes." *International Labor Review* (June 1926), reprinted in *J.P.E.* 81, no. 2 (March/April 1973): 496–502.
Friedman, Milton. "The Role of Monetary Policy." *A.E.R.* 58, no. 1 (March 1968): 1–17.
Gordon, Robert J. "Alternative Responses of Policy to External Supply Shocks." *Brookings Papers on Economic Activity*, no. 1 (1975), pp. 183–206.
———. "Recent Developments in the Theory of Inflation and Unemployment." *J. Monetary Econ.* 2, no. 2 (April 1976): 185–220.
Grossman, Herschel I. "The Nature of Optimal Labor Contracts: Towards a Theory of Wage and Employment Adjustment." Unpublished paper, Brown University, 1975.

[21] Lucas (1976).

Johnson, Harry G. "A Survey of Theories of Inflation." In *Essays in Monetary Economics*, by H. G. Johnson. 2d ed. Cambridge, Mass.: Harvard Univ. Press, 1969.

Lipsey, Richard G. "The Relation between Unemployment and the Rate of Money Wage Changes in the United Kingdom, 1862–1957: A Further Analysis." *Economica* 27, no. 105 (February 1960): 1–31.

Lucas, Robert E. "Expectations and the Neutrality of Money." *J. Econ. Theory* 4, no. 2 (April 1972): 103–24.

———. "Some International Evidence on Output-Inflation Trade-Offs." *A.E.R.* 63, no. 3 (June 1973): 326–34.

———. "Econometric Policy Evaluation: A Critique." In *The Phillips Curve and Labor Markets*, edited by Karl Brunner and Allan H. Meltzer. *J. Monetary Econ.*, suppl. (1976), pp. 19–46.

Phelps, Edmund S. "Phillips Curves, Expectations of Inflation, and Optimal Unemployment Over Time." *Economica* 34, no. 135 (August 1967): 254–81.

Phelps, Edmund S., and Taylor, John B. "Stabilizing Powers of Monetary Policy under Rational Expectations." *J.P.E.* 85, no. 1 (February 1977): 163–190.

Phelps, Edmund S., et al. *Microeconomic Foundations of Employment and Inflation Theory*. New York: Norton, 1970.

Phillips, A. W. "The Relation between Unemployment and the Rate of Change of Money Wage Rates in the United Kingdom, 1862–1957." *Economica* 25, no. 100 (November 1958): 283–99.

Prescott, Edward C. "Efficiency of the Natural Rate." *J.P.E.* 83, no. 6 (December 1975): 1229–36.

Sargent, Thomas J., and Wallace, Neil. " 'Rational' Expectations, the Optimal Monetary Instrument, and the Optimal Money Supply Rule." *J.P.E.* 83, no. 2 (April 1975): 241–54.

Tobin, James. "Inflation and Unemployment." *A.E.R.* 62, no. 1 (March 1972): 1–18.

14

Price-Level Stickiness and the Feasibility of Monetary Stabilization Policy with Rational Expectations

Bennett T. McCallum

This paper considers the validity of the Lucas-Sargent Proposition, which concerns the ineffectiveness of countercyclical monetary policy when expectations are rational, under the assumption that prices are "sticky." The model of Sargent and Wallace is modified so as to incorporate stickiness as follows: in each period the price adjusts to the market-clearing value only if the latter is far from the expected value (i.e., when the cost of maintaining an inappropriate price exceeds the lump-sum cost of a revision). Otherwise the price equals the value previously expected. Given this modification, the proposition remains valid.

Several recent papers have demonstrated a striking theoretical result concerning the feasibility of countercyclical monetary policy.[1] This result, which I shall refer to as the Lucas-Sargent Proposition, may be stated as follows: if aggregate-supply fluctuations are initiated by informational errors[2] and if economic agents' expectations are formed rationally, then countercyclical monetary policy will be entirely ineffective.[3] This proposition provides powerful intellectual support for Milton Friedman's proposal that monetary authorities abandon attempts to "lean against" prevailing cyclical tendencies, acting instead so as to

I am indebted to Robert Barro, Herschel Grossman, Robert Lucas, John Taylor, and John Whitaker for valuable comments on an earlier draft. Special thanks are due Thomas Sargent for suggesting an important modification.

[1] The result was first given a clear and explicit statement by Sargent (1973), who built upon the ideas of Lucas (1972, 1973, 1976). More recent developments are provided by Sargent and Wallace (1975, 1976) and Barro (1976), while an insightful but informal early discussion is presented by Gordon and Hynes (1970).

[2] Fluctuations *initiated* by expectational errors may persist: see Sargent (1973, p. 445).

[3] That is, the probability distribution of output will be independent of parameters describing the systematic portion of the authorities' responses to cyclical conditions.

[*Journal of Political Economy*, 1977, vol. 85, no. 3]

generate steady growth of the nominal money stock at some constant rate.[4]

In reaction, Edmund Phelps and John Taylor (1977) have developed a model, similar in some respects to the one used by Sargent and Wallace (1975), in which there is a role for activist monetary policy even though expectations are formed rationally. While there are several ways in which their model differs from that of Sargent and Wallace, the one stressed by Phelps and Taylor is the assumption that prices are "sticky"—that is, the aggregate price level does not adjust "flexibly" so as to equate aggregate supply and demand in each period. As it is widely agreed that prices are in fact sticky (in some sense), the Phelps-Taylor argument might appear to cast doubt on the relevance, for the design of monetary policy, of the Lucas-Sargent Proposition.[5]

Actually, however, it is not price stickiness per se that accounts for the Phelps-Taylor result. Instead, it is the combination of their particular (and extreme) method of incorporating stickiness *together with* a second change vis-à-vis Sargent and Wallace, namely, the replacement of the Lucas-type supply function with an "output determination equation" that relates departures from capacity output to differences between the expected "natural" and real rates of interest.[6] In fact, if one modifies the Sargent-Wallace model in a way that incorporates price stickiness of a less extreme degree but leaves intact its other features, the Lucas-Sargent Proposition will continue to hold. The purpose of the present note is to establish the validity of this assertion

I. The Model

Let us begin by writing the model of Sargent and Wallace in a manner that will prove to be convenient. For simplicity, we take (the log of) productive capacity, k_t, to be exogenously determined.[7] Excepting the money stock, which will be discussed below, the other exogenous variables are represented by the vector Z_t. The endogenous variables are y_t = log of aggregate output or supply; e_t = log of aggregate expenditure or demand; p_t = log of price level; and r_t = nominal interest rate. The structural equations of the model, which determine y_t, e_t, p_t, and r_t, are

---

[4] This point is stressed by Sargent and Wallace (1976).

[5] This has been suggested by Gordon (1976) and Nordhaus (1976).

[6] The rationale for this equation is not entirely clear, but the specific nature of the Phelps-Taylor stickiness assumption makes *some* replacement almost imperative. More discussion appears below, esp. in n. 8.

[7] As Phelps and Taylor take capacity to be constant, the question of its exogeneity (considered by Sargent and Wallace [1975]) is evidently not at issue.

as follows:

$$y_t = k_t + a_1(p_t - {}_{t-1}p_t^*) + u_{1t}, \tag{1}$$

$$e_t = b_1 k_t + b_2[r_t - ({}_{t-1}p_{t+1}^* - {}_{t-1}p_t^*)] + b_3 Z_t + u_{2t}, \tag{2}$$

$$m_t = p_t + c_1 e_t + c_2 r_t + u_{3t}, \tag{3}$$

and

$$y_t = e_t. \tag{4}$$

Here equation (1) is a Lucas-type aggregate-supply function (see Lucas 1973), in which ${}_{t-1}p_t^*$ represents the value of p_t expected by the public on the basis of information available at the end of period $t - 1$. Note that we have reversed the role of the p^* subscripts, in comparison with Sargent and Wallace (1975). Moreover, in what follows we shall delete the leading subscript whenever it equals $t - 1$, writing p_t^* instead of ${}_{t-1}p_t^*$. Equation (2) is an IS schedule relating demand for consumption and investment goods to an indicator of wealth (k_t) and the real rate of interest, while (3) is a conventional LM or portfolio-balance equation. The final relationship, (4), implies that the price level adjusts so as to equate aggregate supply and demand in each period. The model is completed by the specification of stochastic processes generating Z_t and u_{it} $(i = 1, 2, 3)$ plus the assumption that expectations are formed rationally. The zero-mean, constant-variance disturbances u_{it} may be autocorrelated but are generated by processes independent of those that yield Z_t.

The focus of attention in what follows is the feasibility of the monetary authority choosing a policy that will keep y_t closer to k_t, on average, than it would be in the absence of a stabilization policy. Again following Sargent and Wallace, let us presume that the authority's policy is describable as a deterministic feedback rule of the form

$$m_t = h_1 X_{t-1} + h_2 X_{t-2} + \cdots, \tag{5}$$

where X_t denotes the set of observations on all relevant variables as of period t, while each h_j is a vector of parameters conformable with X_{t-j}. Then the Lucas-Sargent Proposition is that the probability distribution of y_t in the foregoing model is not dependent upon the policy parameters. If the authorities alter the value of one or more elements of one or more of the h_j vectors, the distribution of y_t will be unaffected. This was proved by Sargent and Wallace (1975) and earlier, for a slightly different model, by Sargent (1973).

Our object now is to modify the foregoing model by replacing equation (4) with a relation that reflects price-level stickiness. At present there is no generally accepted way of representing this sort of phenomenon, except in analyses in which it is adequate simply to hold the relevant variable fixed at some constant value. The approach taken by Phelps and Taylor is to make each period's price *predetermined* and thus entirely unresponsive to current conditions. To be precise, Phelps and Taylor assume that each period's price is equal—apart from the effect of a purely random disturbance unrelated to any other aspect of the model—to the value that was expected one period earlier to be the market-clearing value.[8] The idea evidently is that last-minute price revisions are costly, that is, require the use of real resources.[9]

As the notion that price revisions are costly is quite appealing, it will be retained in our formulation. Our approach will also reflect, however, a second notion: that real (opportunity) costs are incurred whenever prices depart from market-clearing levels. Thus we presume that the cost of making a price change (which is taken to be of the lump-sum variety) must be balanced against the cost of maintaining an inappropriate price (which is taken to depend on the extent of the discrepancy). From the point of view implied by this pair of notions, the Phelps-Taylor analysis embodies an implicit assumption that the former cost is *always* greater than the latter, no matter how far current conditions depart from those expected one period earlier. Our presumption suggests that a more satisfactory method of representing price-level stickiness would be to specify the following: the price level in period t will equal the expected price p_t^* whenever the current market-clearing value is sufficiently close to p_t^*. Otherwise, when the market-clearing price is far from the expected value, the price will adjust to its market-clearing level. In the former case, y_t and e_t will be unequal. Thus we assume that additions (subtractions) to existing inventory stocks are made whenever output exceeds (falls short of) aggregate demand.

Formally, let us define the (log of the) market-clearing price as $p_t^\dagger$, the value that would equate aggregate supply and demand. Setting $e_t = y_t$ in equations (1)–(3) and solving, we obtain

$$p_t^\dagger = \pi_1 k_t + \pi_2 m_t + \pi_3 p_t^* + \pi_4 p_{t+1}^* + \pi_5 Z_t$$
$$+ \pi_6 u_{1t} + \pi_7 u_{2t} + \pi_8 u_{3t}, \qquad (6)$$

---

[8] This one change from the Sargent-Wallace model would not alone yield the Phelps-Taylor result: with rational expectations, the value of $p_t - p_t^*$ would be pure noise, so the supply function (1) would amount to $y_t = k_t + u_{1t} +$ noise. Accordingly, Phelps and Taylor drop (1), replacing it with an output equation that involves the value of p_{t+1} expected as of $t - 1$. It is the combination of this equation with the predetermined price level that provides their result: the money supply for t—which has an influence on p_{t+1}— is set *after* the price for t is fixed, hence with additional data available. Thus the effect is similar to supposing that there exists an informational advantage for the monetary authority (even though the private sector obtains information at the same time as the authority). There is, as a result, scope for useful countercyclical monetary policy: as shown by Sargent and Wallace (1975) and Barro (1976), an informational advantage will render monetary stabilization policy effective even in models with completely flexible, market-clearing prices.

[9] Phelps and Taylor explicitly mention but do not model the costs of making price changes.

where the coefficients $\pi_1 - \pi_8$ are definitionally related to the parameters of (1)–(3). Then taking δ_1 and δ_2 to be positive constants, we assume that p_t obeys the relationship

$$p_t = \begin{cases} p_t^* & \text{if } p_t^* - \delta_1 < p_t^\dagger < p_t^* + \delta_2, \\ p_t^\dagger & \text{otherwise.} \end{cases} \tag{7}$$

Clearly, this specification permits various degrees of stickiness, with relatively small values of δ_1 and δ_2 representing relatively flexible prices and vice versa.[10] Of course we have not given any full-blown justification for the specification, but the analysis of Barro (1972) provides some support.[11] In any event, relationship (7) certainly provides one way of modeling stickiness, appears no more ad hoc than other possibilities, and is less extreme than the Phelps-Taylor assumption.

II. Analysis

Our next task is to prove that the Lucas-Sargent Proposition holds in the model described by equations (1), (2), (3), (6), and (7). Let us begin by noting that this model incorporates the two features stressed by Sargent and Wallace (1975, p. 254),[12] namely, the Lucas-type output function and expectational rationality. Next, notice that the first of these features implies that the (unconditional) distribution of y_t can be affected by monetary policy only if that policy affects the distribution of the expectational error $p_t - p_t^*$. But the rationality assumption requires that p_t^* be formed in such a way that the expectational error will be unrelated to data available at $t - 1$. Thus $p_t - p_t^*$ will have a distribution that will depend in *no* way on available data, so there can be no policy feedback rule for m_t, based on such data, that will influence the distribution of y_t.

As there are some unorthodox aspects to the argument in the present context, some elaboration may be appropriate. For simplicity, let us delete the exogenous Z_t variables and assume that the u_{it} processes are serially independent.[13] Now the expectational error can be expressed as

$$p_t - p_t^* = \begin{cases} 0 & \text{if } -\delta_1 < p_t^\dagger - p_t^* < \delta_2, \\ p_t^\dagger - p_t^* & \text{otherwise.} \end{cases} \tag{8}$$

Furthermore, if we define

$$\xi_t \equiv \pi_6 u_{1t} + \pi_7 u_{2t} + \pi_8 u_{3t}, \tag{9}$$

---

[10] With $\delta_1 = \delta_2 = 0$, prices are entirely flexible.

[11] Barro shows that a rule like (7), but with p_{t-1} appearing in place of p_t^*, would be used by a profit-seeking monopolist with costs of the types described by our two "notions."

[12] And earlier by Sargent (1973, p. 444).

[13] If they were not, it would be possible to eliminate the u_{it} in favor of serially independent "innovations" and proceed as in the case considered.

we can write

$$p_t^\dagger - p_t^* = \pi_1 k_t + \pi_2 m_t + (\pi_3 - 1)p_t^* + \pi_4 p_{t+1}^* + \xi_t \qquad (10)$$

and observe that ξ_t is stochastically independent of the other variables on the right-hand side of (10), all of which are included in the set of available data[14] $\Phi_{t-1} \equiv \{X_{t-1}, X_{t-2}, \dots\}$. Thus the rationality assumption, which requires the error to depend in no way on any subset of Φ_{t-1}, may be imposed by means of the condition

$$\pi_1 k_t + \pi_2 m_t + (\pi_3 - 1)p_t^* + \pi_4 p_{t+1}^* \equiv 0. \qquad (11)$$

Accordingly, (8) reduces immediately to

$$p_t - p_t^* = \begin{cases} 0 & \text{if } -\delta_1 < \xi_t < \delta_2, \\ \xi_t & \text{otherwise,} \end{cases} \qquad (12)$$

from which it is clear, since ξ_t represents irreducible noise, that the choice among deterministic monetary feedback rules will have no effect on the distribution of $p_t - p_t^*$. Consequently, the choice will likewise have no effect on the distribution of y_t—which is the proposition asserted above.

It will be observed that our definition of rationality is not the one most frequently encountered, according to which p_t^* is taken to be the mathematical expectation, conditional on Φ_{t-1}, of p_t.[15] If there is no asymmetry in the model—that is, if $\delta_1 = \delta_2$ and the distribution of ξ_t is symmetric about its mean value of zero—then our definition will be fully consistent with the usual one, although slightly more stringent.[16] Moreover, the imposition of such symmetry requirements should not be deemed entirely unreasonable, as one such requirement is implicit in the usual notion that the conditional expectation is an "optimal" predictor of p_t.[17] It would be possible, therefore, to avoid any unusual implication of our definition by simply assuming that the symmetry conditions are satisfied.

I can see, however, no compelling theoretical reason for adding these requirements just to avoid the fact that our definition will, in the presence of asymmetries, make p_t^* unequal to $E(p_t \mid \Phi_{t-1})$. When an asymmetry does exist, it is surely "reasonable" that $p_t^* \neq E(p_t \mid \Phi_{t-1})$, for the effect in the model is to reduce the probability of the more costly type of

[14] Or, as in the case of m_t, are deterministically dependent upon variables in Φ_{t-1}.

[15] The Phelps-Taylor rationality condition is also somewhat unorthodox. Instead of setting p_t^* equal to $E(p_t \mid \Phi_{t-1})$, their procedure is to use the model to determine p_t^* and then generate p_t by adding a pure noise disturbance to the latter.

[16] That $E(p_t - p_t^* \mid \Phi_{t-1}) = 0$ in this case can be deduced from expression (12). If $F(\xi)$ is the distribution function for ξ_t, then the expectation equals $\int \xi dF(\xi)$ over the area outside $(-\delta_1, \delta_2)$, which will be zero.

[17] In particular, optimality is defined relative to a mean-squared-error criterion, which implies symmetry in the loss or cost structure.

discrepancy between p_t and $p_t^\dagger$, the market-clearing price. An example may be useful. Suppose that the distribution of ξ_t is symmetric but that any given absolute discrepancy between p_t and $p_t^\dagger$ is more costly for $p_t > p_t^\dagger$ than for $p_t < p_t^\dagger$. Then δ_1 will by design be smaller than δ_2, so that the more costly type of discrepancy will occur with lower probability. But this implies that the set of negative values of $p_t - p_t^*$ with nonzero probability of occurrence is larger than the corresponding set of positive values, so the mean value of the expectational error must be negative. This sort of example can, however, only serve to *illustrate* the fundamental justification for our definition of rationality, which is that *any* systematic relationship between expectational errors and available data would imply[18] the existence of unexploited profit opportunities.

III. Extension and Conclusion

Thus we have established our main point: recognition of price-level stickiness does not, in and of itself, negate the Lucas-Sargent Proposition. Furthermore, it appears that this conclusion could survive various changes in the specification of the foregoing model, provided that they do not alter equations (1) or (7). To provide some support for this conjecture, let us briefly sketch the analysis of one such change, which involves a slight extension of the model. Suppose that firms are more concerned with their inventory holdings than our previous discussion has implied and specifically assume that their desired end-of-period holdings are given by

$$i_t^d = d_1 k_t + d_2[r_t - (p_{t+1}^* - p_t^*)] + u_{4t}, \tag{13}$$

an inventory demand function of the "supply-of-storage" type. Given this modification, the market-clearing price $p_t^\dagger$ must now be defined not as the value that equates y_t and e_t but, rather, as the value that satisfies the condition[19]

$$y_t = e_t + i_t^d - i_{t-1}. \tag{14}$$

Consider then the extended model consisting of equations (1), (2), (3), (7), (13), and the counterpart of (6)—implied by (14)—which can be written as

$$p_t = \gamma_1 k_t + \gamma_2 m_t + \gamma_3 p_t^* + \gamma_4 p_{t+1}^* + \gamma_5 Z_t$$
$$+ \gamma_6 u_{1t} + \gamma_7 u_{2t} + \gamma_8 u_{3t} + \gamma_9 i_{t-1} + \gamma_{10} u_{4t}. \tag{6'}$$

Clearly the analysis of this model would proceed just as in Section II, with the only qualitative changes being the inclusion of an i_{t-1} term in the counterpart of condition (10) and a redefinition of ξ_t that incorporates

---

[18] In the absence of information collection and processing costs.
[19] When $p_t \neq p_t^\dagger$, actual inventory holdings will depart from the desired level.

the additional disturbance u_{4t}. Thus the Lucas-Sargent result would hold as before.

Finally, we might add that all of the foregoing discussion is applicable to the stabilization aspects of countercyclical fiscal policy as well as monetary policy. Thus in the model at hand there is no fiscal feedback rule, utilizing information available as of period $t - 1$, that can be used to control expectational errors or output.[20] Of course fiscal policy could be used to affect the real interest rate and thereby capacity output.[21] But activist *stabilization* policy, concerned with the distribution of $y_t - k_t$, will be ineffective unless it is based on more recent information than is available for private expectation formation. The combination of rational expectations and the supply function (1) negates output effects of counter-cyclical *demand* policy, not just monetary policy.

References

Barro, R. J. "A Theory of Monopolistic Price Adjustment." *Rev. Econ. Studies* 39 (January 1972): 17–26.

———. "Rational Expectations and the Role of Monetary Policy." *J. Monetary Econ.* 2 (January 1976): 1–32.

Gordon, D. F., and Hynes, A. "On the Theory of Price Dynamics." In *Microeconomic Foundations of Employment and Inflation Theory*, by E. S. Phelps et al. New York: Norton, 1970.

Gordon, R. J. "Recent Developments in the Theory of Inflation and Unemployment." *J. Monetary Econ.* 2 (April 1976): 185–219.

Lucas, R. E., Jr. "Econometric Testing of the Natural Rate Hypothesis." In *The Econometrics of Price Determination Conference*, edited by O. Eckstein. Washington: Board Governors Federal Reserve System, 1972.

———. "Some International Evidence on Output-Inflation Trade-offs." *A.E.R.* 63 (June 1973): 326–34.

———. "Econometric Policy Evaluation: A Critique." In *The Phillips Curve and Labor Markets*, edited by K. Brunner and A. H. Meltzer. Amsterdam: North-Holland, 1976.

Nordhaus, W. D. "Inflation Theory and Policy." *A.E.R.* 66 (May 1976): 59–64.

Phelps, E. S., and Taylor, J. B. "Stabilizing Powers of Monetary Policy under Rational Expectations." *J.P.E.* 85, no. 1 (February 1977): 163–90.

Sargent, T. J. "Rational Expectations, the Real Rate of Interest, and the Natural Rate of Unemployment." *Brookings Papers Econ. Activity*, no. 2 (1973), pp. 429–72.

Sargent, T. J., and Wallace, N. "'Rational' Expectations, the Optimal Monetary Instrument, and the Optimal Money Supply Rule." *J.P.E.* 83, no. 2 (April 1975): 241–54.

———. "Rational Expectations and the Theory of Economic Policy." *J. Monetary Econ.* 2 (April 1976): 169–83.

[20] Of course a rule relating (say) tax collections to *current* conditions would have real output effects. Thus the analysis provides no reason for doubting the existence of beneficial effects of "built-in stabilizers."

[21] Which would then have to be treated as predetermined rather than exogenous.

15

The Current State of the Policy-Ineffectiveness Debate

Bennett T. McCallum

The debate in question is, of course, over the applicability to the U.S. economy of the famous and controversial "neutrality" proposition—due primarily to Robert Lucas, Thomas Sargent, and Neil Wallace—according to which the choice among monetary policy feedback rules is irrelevant for the stochastic behavior of the unemployment rate in a neoclassical economy with rational expectations. Since the basic logic of this proposition has become well-known, I will not devote space to a formal statement or proof. It will be necessary, however, to inject some interpretive comments. This need arises because formal proofs of the proposition refer to effects of alternative policy rules on the stochastic *steady-state* behavior of key macro-economic variables. Thus the alternative policy rules are treated as permanently maintained, with transitional effects ignored. Under this interpretation the proposition does not imply that *actions* of the Fed (the "monetary authority") have no impact on unemployment rates. Since expectations at any moment of time are given, the more expansionary are the Fed's actions "this month" the lower will be "this month's" unemployment rate, even if the proposition is valid. Evidently, what the latter does suggest is that the Fed's choice among alternative reaction patterns, sustained over many periods of time, will have negligible effects on the level and variability of unemployment rates averaged over these periods. The distinction between policy actions and policy rules is crucial.

The proposition is straightforwardly applicable, therefore, only to hypothetical, maintained situations. One might even say that the proposition is a "long-run" result, though such terminology hardly seems helpful. But it does not follow that the proposition is irrelevant for actual policy, as some commentators have suggested. Clearly, it bears upon the following question: Does it matter, on average, if the money stock is typically increased rapidly, slowly, or not at all when high unemployment rates are observed?

I am indebted to the National Science Foundation for financial support under grant no. SOC 76-81422.

[American Economic Review, Papers and Proceedings, 1979, vol. 69, no. 2]
© 1979 by The American Economic Association

The proposition may apply only to the systematic, nontransitory component of policy behavior, but presumably that is the portion of primary interest to economic scientists and public-spirited policymakers.[1]

A few more matters should be clarified before I begin with the main discussion. In particular, it should be mentioned that the neutrality proposition refers to real output rates, as well as unemployment rates, but with the relevant concept in both cases measured relative to some "capacity," or "full employment," or "natural rate" benchmark. There are many models in which the proposition is valid for such measures even though capacity levels are themselves affected by the choice among policy rules. By taking these relative concepts as the ones under discussion, I will be focusing on "stabilization policy" and abstracting from issues of "economic growth." Notationally, the same symbol, y_t, will be used to refer to both concepts— unemployment and (the log of) output relative to natural-rate levels. Finally, it will be presumed that information on period t values of all relevant variables becomes available in period $t + 1$, both to the Fed and to individual agents.[2] Thus the theoretical discussion presumes that the Fed has no informational advantage. It is generally agreed that such an advantage would invalidate the neutrality proposition without providing a strong basis for policy activism (see Barro 1976).

I. Objections to the Neutrality Proposition

Let us now proceed by considering some of the main objections that have been raised by activist critics to the application of the proposition to the U.S. economy. For a while there was resistance to the notion that expectations are formed rationally, especially in the sense that all agents act as if they knew the true structure of the economy including the policy feedback rule.[3] More recently, however, macroeconomic researchers seem to have

[1]That most "policymakers" are not, in their day-to-day activities, concerned with the choice among sustained feedback rules hardly diminishes the importance of the proposition under discussion. With respect to economists, my position has received implicit support from the practice of leading activist critics of the proposition: the analyses of Fischer (1977), Phelps and Taylor (1977), and Taylor (in press) all focus upon stochastic steady-state behavior. (These examples also illustrate that the desirability of conducting policy by means of feedback rules is not at issue.) This sort of analysis abstracts from effects of two kinds: those due to initial conditions and those that occur while agents are in the process of learning about newly adopted policy rules. With respect to the latter, it is important to keep in mind that it is doubtful whether output or employment effects obtained by policy deception would be welfare enhancing.

[2]For simplicity, the discussion in this paper will be restricted to aggregate relationships. Aggregate supply functions like equation (1) below are typically rationalized by means of the analysis of Lucas (1973), in which agents in separate markets carry out transactions knowing values of aggregate variables for previous periods but only "local" absolute prices for the current period.

[3]Actually, the proposition permits the somewhat weaker assumption that expectations differ from the fully rational values by a random term uncorrelated with available data.

moved toward a sort of implicit agreement that this extreme rational expectations assumption is appropriate for analysis of stabilization policy. There are, I believe, two main justifications for this view. First, there is no reason to believe that the assumption is terribly inaccurate, empirically, at the macroeconomic level.[4] Of course it is literally untrue, but so is every behavioral relation in every formal economic model. Second, every alternative assumption has an extremely unattractive property: it requires the assumed existence of some particular pattern of *systematic* expectational error. One would not expect any systematic pattern of errors to persist, however, since each would imply the existence of unexploited opportunities for enormous entrepreneurial gain. The relevant issue is not whether expectations are "actually" formed rationally, but whether it would be fruitful to conduct stabilization analysis under any other assumption.

One of the most prominent activist arguments for the inapplicability of the proposition has to do with "persistence" of positive or negative values of y_t (output or unemployment). According to this viewpoint, the proposition implies that y_t values are serially uncorrelated, so the fact that measured U.S. unemployment and output values exhibit strong serial dependence immediately provides an empirical refutation. But, as several writers have noted, while the rationality assumption implies that expectational errors are serially uncorrelated, there is no such implication regarding values of y_t. To emphasize this, Sargent (1979) has developed an agent-maximizing, market-clearing model in which adjustment costs lead to an aggregate supply function of the form

$$y_t = a_o(p_t - E_{t-1}p_t) + \sum_{i=1}^{n} b_i y_{t-i} + \varepsilon_t \qquad (1)$$

where p_t is the log of an aggregate price index, $E_{t-1}p_t$ is its conditional expectation, and ε_t is a disturbance uncorrelated with past values of all variables. In the example explicitly worked out, Sargent takes $n = 1$, but the analysis could in principle be extended to the more general case. Now (1) is clearly a supply function consistent with standard proofs of the proposition. And for many parameter values (1) will imply positive serial correlation of y_t values.[5] Furthermore, Lucas (1975b) has developed a model, quite different from Sargent's, in which neutrality prevails yet persistence results from certain restrictions on the information available to individual agents. And very recently Blinder and Fischer (1978) have shown that persistence can be generated, without violation of the proposition, by in-

---

[4]Arguments based on expectational differences across individual consumers or firms amount to objections to macroeconomics, not rational expectations. Any readers who are *fundamentally* unsympathetic to the rationality assumption are urged to consider the position expressed in Lucas (1975a).

[5]Sargent (1979) also shows that the neutrality proposition is, in a two-shift model, consistent with the apparent failure of real wages to move countercyclically.

ventory behavior of a plausible type. Thus the persistence objection is not well founded.

The other main line of argument on the activist side has to do with "sticky prices." One version begins with the observation that many models yielding the neutrality result—most notably, the model of Sargent and Neil Wallace (1975)—assume that prices are "perfectly flexible" in the sense that the price level adjusts in each period so as to equate aggregate supply and demand. But actual prices are sticky—the price level seems to adjust very slowly to eliminate conditions of excess supply or demand. Accordingly, the argument goes, the neutrality proposition is inapplicable to the U.S. economy. There are, however, two flaws with this argument. First, it is not entirely clear that the Sargent-Wallace model rules out price level stickiness of the type that has been documented: the model permits a many-period, distributed-lag response of the price level to changes in the money stock. Second, it is possible to construct models in which prices are sticky in a stronger sense and yet the neutrality proposition prevails. For these reasons, discussed more fully in my 1978 paper, the proposition cannot be disposed of by simply noting that actual prices move sluggishly.[6]

There is, however, a more persuasive version of the sticky-price argument, one that involves the notion of "long-term contracting." In particular, it has been shown, most notably by Fischer (1977), that scope for activist monetary policy will exist—the neutrality proposition will fail—in an economy in which typical labor contracts fix nominal wages for two or more periods in advance. In such an economy, the choice of a policy rule will not affect the mean value of y_t—so unemployment cannot be kept permanently low—but will influence the variability of y_t. This is possible, even if monetary policy is fully anticipated, because the policy rule can take account of shocks that occur after a contract has set the wage for a (fixed) portion of the workforce. A similar result obtains, furthermore, for multiperiod price-setting arrangements (see Taylor, in press) and such arrangements may be formal or implicit.

In my opinion, this line of argument constitutes the most telling objection to the neutrality proposition that has been advanced to date. Nevertheless, it is not entirely compelling. As Barro (1977b) has emphasized, the procedure by which employment is determined in Fischer's contracting scheme is Pareto suboptimal: other contracts could conceivably be written that would improve the welfare of both firms and households. Thus there is no solid economic rationale for the presumption that Fischer-type contracts are written.[7] And it seems unlikely that any such contracts would

---

[6]A related argument invokes the concept of "disequilibrium." For a discussion of disequilibrium models, see the papers on "Macroeconomics: An Appraisal of the Non-Market-Clearing Paradigm": Barro (1979), Grossman (1979), and Howitt (1979).

[7]Indeed, Barro's analysis leads him to suggest that "sticky wages, layoffs versus quits, and the failure of real wages to move countercyclically" may be merely "a facade with respect to employment fluctuations" (1977b, p. 316).

remain in force if the policy authorities were to try to exploit them to a great extent. Fischer recognizes both of these points but argues that contracts of the form used in his model are, in fact, of the type that exist in actual economies.

II. Formal Empirical Evidence

Given the considerations discussed in the previous section, it appears unlikely that the ineffectiveness debate can be resolved by means of purely theoretical arguments or casual empiricism. Recourse to formal econometric evidence would seem to be necessary.

Unfortunately, however, it has become apparent that it is extremely difficult to bring such evidence to bear on the issue in an effective way. In part, this is because the neutrality proposition is compatible with supply functions more general than (1)—in particular, with functions that include *lagged* one-period expectational errors (lagged "innovations"), such as

$$y_t = \sum_{i=0}^{k} a_i [p_{t-i} - E_{t-i-1}(p_{t-i})] + \sum_{j=1}^{n} b_j y_{t-j} + \varepsilon_t. \tag{2}$$

The proposition is not, on the other hand, consistent with a formulation that includes multiperiod expectational errors, such as

$$y_t = \sum_{i=0}^{k} a_i [p_t - E_{t-i-1}(p_t)] + \sum_{j=1}^{n} b_j y_{t-j} + \varepsilon_t. \tag{3}$$

Simple inspection suggests that it could be difficult to distinguish empirically between formulations like (2) and (3).

Indeed, Sargent (1976b) has shown that, without the use of additional a priori information of *some* type, it is logically impossible to distinguish between (2) and (3) or, more generally, between models in which the neutrality proposition is valid and invalid. In other words, the neutrality property alone places no restrictions on time-series data taken from a single policy regime. This does not imply that attempts to test the proposition are hopeless, but it does emphasize the importance of giving careful consideration to the type of a priori information used in any test attempt.

At present, the two most well-known empirical studies are those of Sargent (1976a) and Barro (1977a). In the first of these, identifying restrictions are imposed by the adoption of a supply function of type (1): since (2) is more general, this amounts to the assumption that the parameters a_1, $a_2, \ldots, a_k$ are all equal to zero. (Actually, Sargent emphasizes innovations in policy variables, such as the log of the money stock, m_t, rather than p_t. Also, he notes that it may be appropriate to interpret y_t and m_t as *vectors* of variables.) While this specialization is not implied by the proposition, it seems plausible—why should past errors affect today's supply decision? In any event, with the additional assumption that the equation's disturbance term is free of serial correlation, this exclusion of lagged expectational errors permits Sargent to obtain the implication that y_t is, given the effect of lagged y's, uncorrelated with past values of policy variables. Accordingly, evidence consistent with this implication would seem to provide genuine empirical support for the neutrality proposition, even though inconsistent evidence could result either from the proposition's invalidity *or* from the presence of lagged innovations in the aggregate supply function. As it happens, Sargent's results are mixed, but reasonably consistent with the implication. It has been noted, however, that Sargent's auxiliary assumption regarding serial correlation is crucial to this procedure (see Sims 1977; Shiller 1978) and Sims has argued that the assumption is arbitrary. So, while Sargent's results may not be totally uninformative, they should probably be regarded as shedding little light on the validity of the proposition.

Barro's (1977a) test approach is quite different. It involves explicit estimation of an equation analogous to (2) but with monetary innovations appearing in place of expectational errors in p_t and with additional "real" labor market variables in place of lagged values of y_t. Testable implications are obtained under the neutrality hypothesis by the exclusion from the unemployment rate (y_t) equation of certain exogenous variables that appear significantly in the equation used to explain monetary policy. This exclusion permits Barro to distinguish between the effects of monetary innovations and anticipated values of the money stock (Barro, 1977a, pp. 109–10). His results for 1946–73 (annual data) are strikingly favorable to the neutrality proposition: current and lagged monetary innovations are highly significant while anticipated components of m_t provide no incremental explanatory power.

On the surface, it might appear that Barro's results are open to criticism on the grounds of implausibility: strong effects on y_t are found for expectational errors made one and two years earlier. The estimated equation can be interpreted, however, as resulting from the elimination of other real endogenous variables from an aggregate supply function in which only the current monetary innovation is present (see McCallum 1979). Thus this apparent objection is not telling. A more reasonable source of uneasiness over Barro's results is, I believe, their reliance on an accurate decomposition of money growth rates into anticipated and unanticipated components; analysis of policy behavior rules is not something with which macroeconomists have a great deal of experience. Also open to skepticism is Barro's explanatory variable (in the y_t equation) designed to reflect effects of the military draft. Still, Barro's results—recently augmented (1978) by evidence on price level behavior—are quite impressive.

A third empirical approach, as yet less well-known, has been suggested by Sargent (1976b) and implemented by Neftci and Sargent (1978). If the monetary authority's policy feedback rule *changes* at some point of time, there should be a shift in the distributed-lag relationship of y_t on actual m_t values if the neutrality proposition is true but not if it is false, with this implication reversed for a relationship between y_t and innovations in m_t. Using quarterly U.S. data for 1949–74, Neftci and Sargent located a policy break at the start of 1964 and then obtained Chow-type test statistics that are reasonably supportive of the neutrality proposition. The main weaknesses of this procedure are the absence of any formal statistical basis for reaching conclusions and (again) the difficulty of characterizing policy behavior. The approach would seem, nevertheless, to warrant additional attention.

III. Conclusions

For the most part, the formal econometric evidence developed to date is not inconsistent with the neutrality proposition. But the power of existing tests is probably not high and, in any event, the evidence is not entirely clearcut. Thus many economists may tend, at least for the present, to maintain adherence to their favorite theoretical model—whichever one offers the combination of features that seems essential. There is room for hope that future research will offer new insights, but it is hard to imagine that any conclusive breakthrough will occur. Thus it may be best to conclude by noting the extent to which the current brand of policy activism has been affected by the analysis and findings of the Lucas-Sargent-Barro school. Just over a decade ago, Milton Friedman's suggestion that unemployment could be kept low only by accelerating inflation seemed radical; now even many activists doubt that it can be kept low by *any* monetary policy stance.

References

Barro, R. J. "Rational Expectations and the Role of Monetary Policy." *J. Monetary Econ.* 2, (January 1976): 1–32.
———. "Unanticipated Money Growth and Unemployment in the United States." *A.E.R.* 67 (March 1977): 101–15.(*a*)
———. "Long-term Contracting, Sticky Prices, and Monetary Policy." *J. Monetary Econ.* 3 (July 1977): 305–16.(*b*)
———. "Unanticipated Money, Output, and the Price Level in the United States." *J.P.E.* 86 (August 1978): 549–80.
———. "Second Thoughts on Keynesian Economics." *A.E.R., Papers and Proceedings* 69, no. 2 (May 1979): 54–59.
Blinder, A. S., and Fischer, S. "Inventories, Rational Expectations and the Business Cycle." M.I.T. working paper no. 220, June 1978.
Fischer, S. "Long-Term Contracts, Rational Expectations, and the Optimal Money Supply Rule." *J.P.E.* 85 (February 1977): 191–205.

Grossman, H. I. "Why Does Aggregate Employment Fluctuate?" *A.E.R., Papers and Proceedings* 69, no. 2 (May 1979): 64–69.

Howitt, P. "Evaluating the Non-Market Clearing Approach." *A.E.R., Papers and Proceedings* 69, no. 2 (May 1979): 60–63.

Lucas, R. E. Jr. "Expectations and the Neutrality of Money." *J. Econ. Theory*, 4, (April 1972): 103–24.

———. "Some International Evidence on Output-Inflation Tradeoffs." *A.E.R.* 63 (June 1973): 326–34.

———. "Review of *A Model of Macroeconomic Activity*, Vol. 1, by R. C. Fair." *J. Econ. Literature* 8 (September 1975): 889–90. (*a*)

———. "An Equilibrium Model of the Business Cycle." *J.P.E.* 83 (December 1975): 1113–14. (*b*)

McCallum, B. T. "Price Level Adjustments and the Rational Expectations Approach to Macroeconomic Stabilization Policy," *J. Money, Credit, and Banking* 10 (November 1978): 418–36.

———. "On the Observational Inequivalence of Classical and Keynesian Models." *J.P.E.* 87 (April 1979): forthcoming.

Neftci, S., and Sargent, T. J. "A Little Bit of Evidence on the Natural Rate Hypothesis from the U.S.," *J. Monetary Econ.* 4 (April 1978): 315–19.

Phelps, E. S., and Taylor, J. B. "Stabilizing Powers of Monetary Policy under Rational Expectations." *J.P.E.* 85 (February 1977): 163–90.

Sargent, T. J. "A Classical Macroeconometric Model for the United States." *J.P.E.* 84 (April 1976): 207–37. (*a*)

———. "The Observational Equivalence of Natural and Unnatural Rate Theories of Macroeconomics." *J.P.E.* 84 (June 1976): 631–40. (*b*)

———. *Macroeconomic Theory*. New York: Academic Press, 1979.

Sargent, T. J., and Wallace, N. " 'Rational' Expectations, the Optimal Monetary Instrument, and the Optimal Money Supply Rule." *J.P.E.* 83 (April 1975): 241–54.

Shiller, R. J. "Rational Expectations and the Dynamic Structure of Macroeconomic Models: A Critical Review." *J. Monetary Econ.* 4 (January 1978): 1–44.

Sims, C. A. "Exogeneity and Causal Ordering in Macroeconomic Models." In *New Methods in Business Cycle Research: Proceedings from a Conference*. Minneapolis: Federal Reserve Bank, 1977.

Taylor, J. B. "Estimation and Control of a Macroeconomic Model with Rational Expectations." *Econometrica* (in press).

16

After Keynesian Macroeconomics

Robert E. Lucas, Jr., and Thomas J. Sargent

For the applied economist, the confident and apparently successful application of Keynesian principles to economic policy which occurred in the United States in the 1960s was an event of incomparable significance and satisfaction. These principles led to a set of simple, quantitative relationships between fiscal policy and economic activity generally, the basic logic of which could be (and was) explained to the general public and which could be applied to yield improvements in economic performance benefitting everyone. It seemed an economics as free of ideological difficulties as, say, applied chemistry or physics, promising a straightforward expansion in economic possibilities. One might argue as to how this windfall should be distributed, but it seemed a simple lapse of logic to oppose the windfall itself. Understandably and correctly, noneconomists met this promise with skepticism at first; the smoothly growing prosperity of the Kennedy-Johnson years did much to diminish these doubts.

We dwell on these halcyon days of Keynesian economics because without conscious effort they are difficult to recall today. In the present decade, the U.S. economy has undergone its first major depression since the 1930's, to the accompaniment of inflation rates in excess of 10 percent per annum. These events have been transmitted (by consent of the governments involved) to other advanced countries and in many cases have been amplified. These events did not arise from a reactionary reversion to outmoded, "classical" principles of tight money and balanced budgets. On the contrary, they were accompanied by massive government budget deficits and high rates of monetary expansion, policies which, although bearing an admitted risk of inflation, promised according to modern Keynesian doctrine rapid real growth and low rates of unemployment.

That these predictions were wildly incorrect and that the doctrine on which they were based is fundamentally flawed are now simple matters of

A paper presented at a June 1978 conference sponsored by the Federal Reserve Bank of Boston and published in its *After the Phillips Curve: Persistence of High Inflation and High Unemployment*, Conference Series No. 19. The authors acknowledge helpful criticism from William Poole and Benjamin Friedman.

[*Federal Reserve Bank of Minneapolis Quarterly Review*, 1979, vol. 3, no. 2]

fact, involving no novelties in economic theory. The task now facing contemporary students of the business cycle is to sort through the wreckage,
determining which features of that remarkable intellectual event called
the Keynesian Revolution can be salvaged and put to good use and which
others must be discarded. Though it is far from clear what the outcome of
this process will be, it is already evident that it will necessarily involve the
reopening of basic issues in monetary economics which have been viewed
since the thirties as "closed" and the reevaluation of every aspect of the
institutional framework within which monetary and fiscal policy is formulated in the advanced countries.

   This paper is an early progress report on this process of reevaluation and
reconstruction. We begin by reviewing the econometric framework by
means of which Keynesian theory evolved from disconnected, qualitative
talk about economic activity into a system of equations which can be
compared to data in a systematic way and which provide an operational
guide in the necessarily quantitative task of formulating monetary and
fiscal policy. Next, we identify those aspects of this framework which were
central to its failure in the seventies. In so doing, our intent is to establish
that the difficulties are *fatal:* that modern macroeconomic models are of *no*
value in guiding policy and that this condition will not be remedied by
modifications along any line which is currently being pursued. This diag-
nosis suggests certain principles which a useful theory of business cycles
must have. We conclude by reviewing some recent research consistent with
these principles.

Macroeconometric Models

The Keynesian Revolution was, in the form in which it succeeded in the
United States, a revolution in method. This was not Keynes' (1936) intent,
nor is it the view of all of his most eminent followers. Yet if one does not
view the revolution in this way, it is impossible to account for some of its
most important features: the evolution of macroeconomics into a quantitative, *scientific* discipline, the development of explicit statistical descriptions of economic behavior, the increasing reliance of government officials
on technical economic expertise, and the introduction of the use of mathematical control theory to manage an economy. It is the fact that Keynesian theory lent itself so readily to the formulation of explicit econometric
models which accounts for the dominant scientific position it attained by
the 1960s.

   Because of this, neither the success of the Keynesian Revolution nor its
eventual failure can be understood at the purely verbal level at which
Keynes himself wrote. It is necessary to know something of the way
macroeconometric models are constructed and the features they must have
in order to "work" as aids in forecasting and policy evaluation. To discuss
these issues, we introduce some notation.

An econometric model is a system of equations involving a number of endogenous variables (variables determined by the model), exogenous variables (variables which affect the system but are not affected by it), and stochastic or random shocks. The idea is to use historical data to estimate the model and then to utilize the estimated version to obtain estimates of the consequences of alternative policies. For practical reasons, it is usual to use a standard linear model, taking the structural form[1]

$$A_0 y_t + A_1 y_{t-1} + \cdots + A_m y_{t-m} = B_0 x_t + B_1 x_{t-1}$$
$$+ \cdots + B_n x_{t-n} + \varepsilon_t \tag{1}$$

$$R_0 \varepsilon_t + R_1 \varepsilon_{t-1} + \cdots + R_r \varepsilon_{t-r} = u_t, \; R_0 \equiv I. \tag{2}$$

Here y_t is an $(L \times 1)$ vector of endogenous variables, x_t is a $(K \times 1)$ vector of exogenous variables, and ε_t and u_t are each $(L \times 1)$ vectors of random disturbances. The matrices A_j are each $(L \times L)$; the B_j's are $(L \times K)$, and the R_j's are each $(L \times L)$. The $(L \times L)$ disturbance process u_t is assumed to be a serially uncorrelated process with $Eu_t = 0$ and with contemporaneous covariance matrix $Eu_t u_t' = \Sigma$ and $Eu_t u_s' = 0$ for all $t \neq s$. The defining characteristics of the exogenous variables x_t is that they are uncorrelated with the ε's at all lags so that $Eu_t x_s'$ is an $(L \times K)$ matrix of zeroes for all t and s.

Equations (1) are L equations in the L current values y_t of the endogenous variables. Each of these structural equations is a behavioral relationship, identity, or market clearing condition, and each in principle can involve a number of endogenous variables. The structural equations are usually not regression equations[2] because the ε_t's are in general, by the logic of the model, supposed to be correlated with more than one component of the vector y_t and very possibly one or more components of the vectors $y_{t-1}, \ldots y_{t-m}$.

The structural model (1) and (2) can be solved for y_t in terms of past y's and x's and past shocks. This reduced form system is

$$y_t = -P_1 y_{t-1} - \cdots - P_{r+m} y_{t-r-m} + Q_0 x_t + \cdots$$
$$+ Q_{r+n} x_{t-n-r} + A_0^{-1} u_t \tag{3}$$

where[3]

$$P_s = A_0^{-1} \sum_{j=-\infty}^{\infty} R_j A_{s-j}$$

$$Q_s = A_0^{-1} \sum_{j=-\infty}^{\infty} R_j B_{s-j}.$$

[1]Linearity is a matter of convenience, not principle. See *Linearity* section below.
[2]A regression equation is an equation to which the application of ordinary least squares will yield consistent estimates.
[3]In these expressions for P_s and Q_s, take matrices not previously defined (e.g., any with negative subscripts) to be zero.

The reduced form equations are regression equations, that is, the disturbance vector $A_0^{-1}u_t$ is orthogonal to $y_{t-1}, \ldots, y_{t-r-m}, x_t, \ldots, x_{t-n-r}$. This follows from the assumptions that the x's are exogenous and that the u's are serially uncorrelated. Therefore, under general conditions the reduced form can be estimated consistently by the method of least squares. The population parameters of the reduced form (3) together with the parameters of a vector autoregression for x_t

$$x_t = C_1 x_{t-1} + \cdots + C_p x_{t-p} + a_t \qquad (4)$$

where $Ea_t = 0$ and $Ea_t \cdot x_{t-j} = 0$ for $j \geq 1$ completely describe all of the first and second moments of the (y_t, x_t) process. Given long enough time series, good estimates of the reduced form parameters—the P_j's and Q_j's—can be obtained by the method of least squares. All that examination of the data by themselves can deliver is reliable estimates of those parameters.

It is not generally possible to work backward from estimates of the P's and Q's alone to derive unique estimates of the structural parameters, the A_j's, B_j's, and R_j's. In general, infinite numbers of A's, B's, and R's are compatible with a single set of P's and Q's. This is the identification problem of econometrics. In order to derive a set of estimated structural parameters, it is necessary to know a great deal about them in advance. If enough prior information is imposed, it is possible to extract estimates of the A_j's, B_j's, and R_j's implied by the data in combination with the prior information.

For purposes of *ex ante* forecasting, or the unconditional prediction of the vector $y_{t+1}, y_{t+2}, \ldots$ given observation of y_s and x_s, $s \leq t$, the estimated reduced form (3), together with (4), is sufficient. This is simply an exercise in a sophisticated kind of extrapolation, requiring no understanding of the structural parameters, that is, the *economics* of the model.

For purposes of *conditional* forecasting, or the prediction of the future behavior of some components of y_t and x_t *conditional* on particular values of other components, selected by policy, one needs to know the structural parameters. This is so because a change in policy necessarily alters some of the structural parameters (for example, those describing the past behavior of the policy variables themselves) and therefore affects the reduced form parameters in a highly complex way (see the equations defining P_s and Q_s above). Unless one knows which structural parameters remain invariant as policy changes and which change (and how), an econometric model is of no value in assessing alternative policies. It should be clear that this is true regardless of how well (3) and (4) fit historical data or how well they perform in unconditional forecasting.

Our discussion to this point has been highly general, and the formal considerations we have reviewed are not in any way specific to *Keynesian* models. The problem of identifying a structural model from a collection of economic time series is one that must be solved by anyone who claims the ability to give quantitative economic advice. The simplest Keynesian models are attempted solutions to this problem, as are the large-scale versions currently in use. So, too, are the monetarist models which imply the desirability of fixed monetary growth rules. So, for that matter, is the armchair advice given by economists who claim to be outside the econometric tradition, though in this case the implicit, underlying structure is not exposed to professional criticism. Any procedure which leads from the study of observed economic behavior to the quantitative assessment of alternative economic policies involves the steps, executed poorly or well, explicitly or implicitly, which we have outlined.

Keynesian Macroeconometrics

In Keynesian macroeconometric models structural parameters are identified by the imposition of several types of a priori restrictions on the A_j's, B_j's, and R_j's. These restrictions usually fall into one of the following three categories:[4] (a) a priori setting of many of the elements of the A_j's and B_j's to zero; (b) restrictions on the orders of serial correlation and the extent of cross-serial correlation of the disturbance vector ε_t, restrictions which amount to a priori setting of many elements of the R_j's to zero; and (c) a priori classifying of variables as exogenous and endogenous; a relative abundance of exogenous variables aids identification. Existing large Keynesian macroeconometric models are open to serious challenge for the way they have introduced each type of restriction.

Keynes' *General Theory* was rich in suggestions for restrictions of type (a). In it he proposed a theory of national income determination built up from several simple relationships, each involving a few variables only. One of these, for example, was the "fundamental law" relating consumption expenditures to income. This suggested one "row" in equations (1) involving current consumption, current income, and *no other* variables, thereby imposing many zero-restrictions on the A_j's and B_j's. Similarly, the liquidity preference relation expressed the demand for money as a function of only income and an interest rate. By translating the building blocks of the Keynesian theoretical system into explicit equations, models of the form (1) and (2) were constructed with many theoretical restrictions of type (a).

Restrictions on the coefficients R_j governing the behavior of the error terms in (1) are harder to motivate theoretically because the errors are by definition movements in the variables which the *economic* theory cannot

---

[4]These three categories certainly do not exhaust the set of possible identifying restrictions, but they're the ones most identifying restrictions in Keynesian macroeconometric models fall into. Other possible sorts of identifying restrictions include, for example, a priori knowledge about components of Σ and cross-equation restrictions across elements of the A_j's, B_j's, and C_j's, neither of which is extensively used in Keynesian macroeconometrics.

account for. The early econometricians took standard assumptions from statistical textbooks, restrictions which had proven useful in the agricultural experimenting which provided the main impetus to the development of modern statistics. Again, these restrictions, well-motivated or not, involve setting many elements in the R_j's equal to zero, thus aiding identification of the model's structure.

The classification of variables into exogenous and endogenous was also done on the basis of prior considerations. In general, variables were classed as endogenous which were, as a matter of institutional fact, determined largely by the actions of private agents (like consumption or private investment expenditures). Exogenous variables were those under governmental control (like tax rates or the supply of money). This division was intended to reflect the ordinary meanings of the words endogenous— "determined by the [economic] system"—and exogenous—"affecting the [economic] system but not affected by it."

By the mid-1950s, econometric models had been constructed which fit time series data well, in the sense that their reduced forms (3) tracked past data closely and proved useful in short-term forecasting. Moreover, by means of restrictions of the three types reviewed above, their structural parameters A_i, B_j, R_k could be identified. Using this estimated structure, the models could be simulated to obtain estimates of the consequences of different government economic policies, such as tax rates, expenditures, or monetary policy.

This Keynesian solution to the problem of identifying a structural model has become increasingly suspect as a result of both theoretical and statistical developments. Many of these developments are due to efforts of researchers sympathetic to the Keynesian tradition, and many were advanced well before the spectacular failure of the Keynesian models in the 1970s.[5]

Since its inception, macroeconomics has been criticized for its lack of foundations in microeconomic and general equilibrium theory. As was recognized early on by astute commentators like Leontief (1965, disapprovingly) and Tobin (1965, approvingly), the creation of a distinct branch of theory with its own distinct postulates was Keynes' conscious aim. Yet a main theme of theoretical work since the *General Theory* has been the attempt to use microeconomic theory based on the classical postulate that agents act in their own interests to suggest a list of variables that belong on the right side of a given behavioral schedule, say, a demand schedule for a factor of production or a consumption schedule.[6] But from

---

[5]Criticisms of the Keynesian solutions of the identification problem along much the following lines have been made in Lucas (1976), Sims (in press), and Sargent and Sims (1977).

[6]Much of this work was done by economists operating well within the Keynesian tradition, often within the context of some Keynesian macroeconometric model. Sometimes a theory with optimizing agents was resorted to in order to resolve empirical paradoxes by finding variables omitted from some of the earlier Keynesian econometric formulations. The works of Modigliani and Friedman on consumption are good examples of this line of work: its econo-

the point of view of identification of a given structural equation by means of restrictions of type (*a*), one needs reliable prior information that certain variables should be excluded from the right-hand side. Modern probabilistic microeconomic theory almost never implies either the exclusion restrictions suggested by Keynes or those imposed by macroeconometric models.

Let us consider one example with extremely dire implications for the identification of existing macro models. Expectations about the future prices, tax rates, and income levels play a critical role in many demand and supply schedules. In the best models, for example, investment demand typically is supposed to respond to businesses' expectations of future tax credits, tax rates, and factor costs, and the supply of labor typically is supposed to depend on the rate of inflation that workers expect in the future. Such structural equations are usually identified by the assumption that the expectation about, say, factor prices or the rate of inflation attribute to agents is a function only of a few lagged values of the variable which the agent is supposed to be forecasting. However, the macro models themselves contain complicated dynamic interactions among endogenous variables, including factor prices and the rate of inflation, and they generally imply that a wise agent would use current and many lagged values of many and usually most endogenous and exogenous variables in the model in order to form expectations about any one variable. Thus, virtually any version of the hypothesis that agents act in their own interests will contradict the identification restrictions imposed on expectations formation. Further, the restrictions on expectations that have been used to achieve identification are entirely arbitrary and have not been derived from any deeper assumption reflecting first principles about economic behavior. No general first principle has ever been set down which would imply that, say, the expected rate of inflation should be modeled as a linear function of lagged rates of inflation alone with weights that add up to unity, yet this hypothesis is used as an identifying restriction in almost all existing models. The casual treatment of expectations is not a peripheral problem in these models, for the role of expectations is pervasive in them and exerts a massive

metric implications have been extended in important work by Robert Merton. The works of Tobin and Baumol on portfolio balance and of Jorgenson on investment are also in the tradition of applying optimizing microeconomic theories for generating macroeconomic behavior relations. In the last 30 years, Keynesian econometric models have to a large extent developed along the line of trying to model agents' behavior as stemming from more and more sophisticated optimum problems.

Our point here is certainly not to assert that Keynesian economists have completely foregone any use of optimizing microeconomic theory as a guide. Rather, it is that, especially when explicitly stochastic and dynamic problems have been studied, it has become increasingly apparent that microeconomic theory has very damaging implications for the restrictions conventionally used to identify Keynesian macroeconometric models. Furthermore, as emphasized long ago by Tobin (1965), there is a point beyond which Keynesian models must suspend the hypothesis either of cleared markets or of optimizing agents if they are to possess the operating characteristics and policy implications that are the hallmarks of Keynesian economics.

influence on their dynamic properties (a point Keynes himself insisted on). The failure of existing models to derive restrictions on expectations from any first principles grounded in economic theory is a symptom of a deeper and more general failure to derive behavioral relationships from any consistently posed dynamic optimization problems.

As for the second category, restrictions of type (b), existing Keynesian macro models make severe a priori restrictions on the R_j's. Typically, the R_j's are supposed to be diagonal so that cross-equation lagged serial correlation is ignored, and also the order of the ε_t process is assumed to be short so that only low-order serial correlation is allowed. There are at present no theoretical grounds for introducing these restrictions, and for good reasons there is little prospect that economic theory will soon provide any such grounds. In principle, identification can be achieved without imposing any such restrictions. Foregoing the use of category (b) restrictions would increase the category (a) and (c) restrictions needed. In any event, existing macro models do heavily restrict the R_j's.

Turning to the third category, all existing large models adopt an a priori classification of variables as either strictly endogenous variables, the y_t's, or strictly exogenous variables, the x_t's. Increasingly it is being recognized that the classification of a variable as exogenous on the basis of the observation that it could be set without reference to the current and past values of other variables has nothing to do with the econometrically relevant question of how this variable has *in fact* been related to others over a given historical period. Moreover, in light of recent developments in time series econometrics, we know that this arbitrary classification procedure is not necessary. Christopher Sims (1972) has shown that in a time series context the hypothesis of econometric exogeneity can be tested. That is, Sims showed that the hypothesis that x_t is strictly econometrically exogenous in (1) necessarily implies certain restrictions that can be tested given time series on the y's and x's. Tests along the lines of Sims' ought to be used routinely to check classifications into exogenous and endogenous sets of variables. To date they have not been. Prominent builders of large econometric models have even denied the usefulness of such tests (see, e.g., Ando 1977, pp. 209–10; and L. R. Klein in Okun and Perry 1973, p. 644).

Failure of Keynesian Macroeconometrics

There are, therefore, a number of theoretical reasons for believing that the parameters identified as structural by current macroeconomic methods are not in fact structural. That is, we see no reason to believe that these models have isolated structures which will remain invariant across the class of interventions that figure in contemporary discussions of economic policy. Yet the question of whether a particular model is structural is an empirical, not a theoretical, one. If the macroeconometric models had compiled a record of parameter stability, particularly in the face of breaks in the stochastic behavior of the exogenous variables and disturbances, one would be skeptical as to the importance of prior theoretical objections of the sort we have raised.

In fact, however, the track record of the major econometric models is, on any dimension other than very short-term unconditional forecasting, very poor. Formal statistical tests for parameter instability, conducted by subdividing past series into periods and checking for parameter stability across time, invariably reveal major shifts. (For one example, see Muench et al. 1974.) Moreover, this difficulty is implicitly acknowledged by model builders themselves, who routinely employ an elaborate system of add-factors in forecasting, in an attempt to offset the continuing drift of the model away from the actual series.

Though not, of course, designed as such by anyone, macroeconometric models were subjected to a decisive test in the 1970s. A key element in all Keynesian models is a trade-off between inflation and real output: the higher is the inflation rate, the higher is output (or equivalently, the lower is the rate of unemployment). For example, the models of the late 1960s predicted a sustained U.S. unemployment rate of 4 percent as consistent with a 4 percent annual rate of inflation. Based on this prediction, many economists at that time urged a deliberate policy of inflation. Certainly the erratic "fits and starts" character of actual U.S. policy in the 1970s cannot be attributed to recommendations based on Keynesian models, but the inflationary bias on average of monetary and fiscal policy in this period should, according to all of these models, have produced the lowest average unemployment rates for any decade since the 1940s. In fact, as we know, they produced the highest unemployment rates since the 1930s. This was econometric failure on a grand scale.

This failure has not led to widespread conversions of Keynesian economists to other faiths, nor should it have been expected to. In economics as in other sciences, a theoretical framework is always broader and more flexible than any particular set of equations, and there is always the hope that if a particular specific model fails one can find a more successful model based on roughly the same ideas. The failure has, however, already had some important consequences, with serious implications for both economic policymaking and the practice of economic science.

For policy, the central fact is that Keynesian policy recommendations have no sounder basis, in a scientific sense, than recommendations of non-Keynesian economists or, for that matter, noneconomists. To note one consequence of the wide recognition of this, the current wave of protectionist sentiment directed at "saving jobs" would have been answered 10 years ago with the Keynesian counterargument that fiscal policy can achieve the same end, but more efficiently. Today, of course, no one would take this response seriously, so it is not offered. Indeed, economists who 10

years ago championed Keynesian fiscal policy as an alternative to ineffi-
cient direct controls increasingly favor such controls as supplements to
Keynesian policy. The idea seems to be that if people refuse to obey the
equations we have fit to their past behavior, we can pass laws to make
them do so.

Scientifically, the Keynesian failure of the 1970s has resulted in a new
openness. Fewer and fewer economists are involved in monitoring and
refining the major econometric models; more and more are developing
alternative theories of the business cycle, based on different theoretical
principles. In addition, more attention and respect is accorded to the theoretical casualties of the Keynesian Revolution, to the ideas of Keynes'
contemporaries and of earlier economists whose thinking has been regarded for years as outmoded.

No one can foresee where these developments will lead. Some, of course,
continue to believe that the problems of existing Keynesian models can be
resolved within the existing framework, that these models can be adequately refined by changing a few structural equations, by adding or subtracting a few variables here and there, or perhaps by disaggregating various blocks of equations. We have couched our criticisms in such general
terms precisely to emphasize their generic character and hence the futility
of pursuing minor variations within this general framework. A second
response to the failure of Keynesian analytical methods is to renounce
analytical methods entirely, returning to judgmental methods.

The first of these responses identifies the quantitative, scientific goals of
the Keynesian Revolution with the details of the particular models developed so far. The second renounces both these models and the objectives
they were designed to attain. There is, we believe, an intermediate course,
to which we now turn.

Equilibrium Business Cycle Theory

Before the 1930s, economists did not recognize a need for a special branch
of economics, with its own special postulates, designed to explain the business cycle. Keynes founded that subdiscipline, called "macroeconomics,"
because he thought explaining the characteristics of business cycles was
impossible within the discipline imposed by classical economic theory, a
discipline imposed by its insistence on adherence to the two postulates
(a) that markets clear and (b) that agents act in their own self-interest. The
outstanding facts that seemed impossible to reconcile with these two postulates were the length and severity of business depressions and the large-
scale unemployment they entailed. A related observation was that measures of aggregate demand and prices were positively correlated with
measures of real output and employment, in apparent contradiction
to the classical result that changes in a purely nominal magnitude like

the general price level were pure unit changes which should not alter real behavior.

After freeing himself of the straightjacket (or discipline) imposed by the classical postulates, Keynes described a model in which rules of thumb, such as the consumption function and liquidity preference schedule, took the place of decision functions that a classical economist would insist be derived from the theory of choice. And rather than require that wages and prices be determined by the postulate that markets clear—which for the labor market seemed patently contradicted by the severity of business depressions—Keynes took as an unexamined postulate that money wages are sticky, meaning that they are set at a level or by a process that could be taken as uninfluenced by the macroeconomic forces he proposed to analyze.

When Keynes wrote, the terms "equilibrium" and "classical" carried certain positive and normative connotations which seemed to rule out either modifier being applied to business cycle theory. The term *equilibrium* was thought to refer to a system at rest, and some used both *equilibrium* and *classical* interchangeably with "ideal." Thus an economy in classical equilibrium would be both unchanging and unimprovable by policy interventions. With terms used in this way, it is no wonder that few economists regarded equilibrium theory as a promising starting point to understand business cycles and design policies to mitigate or eliminate them.

In recent years, the meaning of the term *equilibrium* has changed so dramatically that a theorist of the 1930s would not recognize it. An economy following a multivariate stochastic process is now routinely described as being in equilibrium, by which is meant nothing more than that at each point in time, postulates (*a*) and (*b*) above are satisfied. This development, which stemmed mainly from work by Arrow (1964) and Debreu (1959), implies that simply to look at any economic time series and conclude that it is a disequilibrium phenomenon is a meaningless observation. Indeed, a more likely conjecture, on the basis of recent work by Sonnenschein (1973), is that the general hypothesis that a collection of time series describes an economy in competitive equilibrium is *without content*.[7]

[7] For an example that illustrates the emptiness at a general level of the statement that employers are always operating along dynamic stochastic demands for factors, see the remarks on econometric identification in Sargent 1978. In applied problems that involve modeling agents' optimum decision rules, one is impressed at how generalizing the specification of agents' objective functions in plausible ways quickly leads to econometric underidentification.

A somewhat different class of examples comes from the difficulties in using time series observations to refute the view that agents only respond to unexpected changes in the money supply. In the equilibrium macroeconometric models we will describe, predictable changes in the money supply do not affect real GNP or total employment. In Keynesian models, they do. At a general level, it is impossible to discriminate between these two views by observing time series drawn from an economy described by a stationary vector random process (Sargent 1976b).

The research line being pursued by some of us involves the attempt to discover a particular, econometrically testable equilibrium theory of the business cycle, one that can serve as the foundation for quantitative analysis of macroeconomic policy. There is no denying that this approach is counterrevolutionary, for it presupposes that Keynes and his followers were wrong to give up on the possibility that an equilibrium theory could account for the business cycle. As of now, no successful equilibrium macroeconometric model at the level of detail of, say, the Federal Reserve-MIT-Penn model has been constructed. But small theoretical equilibrium models have been constructed that show potential for explaining some key features of the business cycle long thought inexplicable within the confines of classical postulates. The equilibrium models also provide reasons for understanding why estimated Keynesian models fail to hold up outside the sample over which they have been estimated. We now turn to describing some of the key facts about business cycles and the way the *new classical* models confront them.

For a long time most of the economics profession has, with some reason, followed Keynes in rejecting classical macroeconomic models because they seemed incapable of explaining some important characteristics of time series measuring important economic aggregates. Perhaps the most important failure of the classical model was its apparent inability to explain the positive correlation in the time series between prices and/or wages, on the one hand, and measures of aggregate output or employment, on the other. A second and related failure was its inability to explain the positive correlations between measures of aggregate demand, like the money stock, and aggregate output or employment. Static analysis of classical macroeconomic models typically implied that the levels of output and employment were determined independently of both the absolute level of prices and of aggregate demand. But the pervasive presence of positive correlations in the time series seems consistent with causal connections flowing from aggregate demand and inflation to output and employment, contrary to the classical neutrality propositions. Keynesian macroeconometric models do imply such causal connections.

We now have rigorous theoretical models which illustrate how these correlations can emerge while retaining the classical postulates that markets clear and agents optimize (Phelps 1970; and Lucas 1972, 1975). The key step in obtaining such models has been to relax the ancillary postulate used in much classical economic analysis that agents have perfect information. The new classical models still assume that markets clear and that agents optimize; agents make their supply and demand decisions based on real variables, including perceived relative prices. However, each agent is assumed to have limited information and to receive information about some prices more often than other prices. On the basis of their limited information—the lists that they have of current and past absolute prices of various goods—agents are assumed to make the best possible estimate of all of the relative prices that influence their supply and demand decisions.

Because they do not have all of the information necessary to compute perfectly the relative prices they care about, agents make errors in estimating the pertinent relative prices, errors that are unavoidable given their limited information. In particular, under certain conditions, agents tend temporarily to mistake a general increase in all absolute prices as an increase in the relative price of the good they are selling, leading them to increase their supply of that good over what they had previously planned. Since on average everyone is making the same mistake, aggregate output rises above what it would have been. This increase of output above what it would have been occurs whenever this period's average economywide price level is above what agents had expected it to be on the basis of previous information. Symmetrically, aggregate output decreases whenever the aggregate price turns out to be lower than agents had expected. The hypothesis of *rational expectations* is being imposed here: agents are assumed to make the best possible use of the limited information they have and to know the pertinent objective probability distributions. This hypothesis is imposed by way of adhering to the tenets of equilibrium theory.

In the new classical theory, disturbances to aggregate demand lead to a positive correlation between unexpected changes in the aggregate price level and revisions in aggregate output from its previously planned level. Further, it is easy to show that the theory implies correlations between revisions in aggregate output and unexpected changes in any variables that help determine aggregate demand. In most macroeconomic models, the money supply is one determinant of aggregate demand. The new theory can easily account for positive correlations between revisions to aggregate output and unexpected increases in the money supply.

While such a theory predicts positive correlations between the inflation rate or money supply, on the one hand, and the level of output, on the other, it also asserts that those correlations do not depict tradeoffs that can be exploited by a policy authority. That is, the theory predicts that there is no way that the monetary authority can follow a systematic activist policy and achieve a rate of output that is on average higher over the business cycle than what would occur if it simply adopted a no-feedback, X-percent rule of the kind Friedman (1948) and Simons (1936) recommended. For the theory predicts that aggregate output is a function of current and past unexpected changes in the money supply. Output will be high only when the money supply is and has been higher than it had been expected to be, that is, higher than average. There is simply no way that on average over the whole business cycle the money supply can be higher than average. Thus, while the theory can explain some of the correlations long thought to invalidate classical macroeconomic theory, it is classical both in its adherence to the classical theoretical postulates and in the nonactivist flavor of its implications for monetary policy.

Small-scale econometric models in the standard sense have been constructed which capture some of the main features of the new classical theory (see, e.g., Sargent 1976a).[8] In particular, these models incorporate the hypothesis that expectations are rational or that agents use all available information. To some degree, these models achieve econometric identification by invoking restrictions in each of the three categories (a), (b), and (c). However, a distinguishing feature of these "classical" models is that they also rely heavily on an important fourth category of identifying restrictions. This category (d) consists of a set of restrictions that is derived from probabilistic economic theory but plays no role in the Keynesian framework. These restrictions in general do not take the form of zero restrictions of the type (a). Instead they typically take the form of cross-equation restrictions among the A_j, B_j, C_j parameters. The source of these restrictions is the implication from economic theory that current decisions depend on agents' forecasts of future variables, combined with the implication that these forecasts are formed optimally, given the behavior of past variables. The restrictions do not have as simple a mathematical expression as simply setting a number of parameters equal to zero, but their economic motivation is easy to understand. Ways of utilizing these restrictions in econometric estimation and testing are rapidly being developed.

Another key characteristic of recent work on equilibrium macroeconometric models is that the reliance on entirely a priori categorizations (c) of variables as strictly exogenous and endogenous has been markedly reduced, although not entirely eliminated. This development stems jointly from the fact that the models assign important roles to agents' optimal forecasts of future variables and from Sims' (1972) demonstration that there is a close connection between the concept of strict econometric exogeneity and the forms of the optimal predictors for a vector of time series. Building a model with rational expectations necessarily forces one to consider which set of other variables helps forecast a given variable, say, income or the inflation rate. If variable y helps predict variable x, the Sims'

---

[8]Dissatisfaction with the Keynesian methods of achieving identification has also led to other lines of macroeconometric work. One line is the index models described by Sargent and Sims (1977) and Geweke (1977). These models amount to a statistically precise way of implementing Wesley Mitchell's notion that a small number of common influences explain the covariation of a large number of economic aggregates over the business cycle. This low dimensionality hypothesis is a potential device for restricting the number of parameters to be estimated in vector time series models. This line of work is not entirely atheoretical (but see the comments of Ando and Klein in Sims [1977]), though it is distinctly un-Keynesian. As it happens, certain equilibrium models of the business cycle do seem to lead to low dimensional index models with an interesting pattern of variables' loadings on indexes. In general, modern Keynesian models do not so easily assume a low-index form. See the discussion in Sargent and Sims (1977).

theorems imply that x cannot be regarded as exogenous with respect to y. The result of this connection between predictability and exogeneity has been that in equilibrium macroeconometric models the distinction between endogenous and exogenous variables has not been drawn on an entirely a priori basis. Furthermore, special cases of the theoretical models, which often involve side restrictions on the R_j's not themselves drawn from economic theory, have strong testable predictions as to exogeneity relations among variables.

A key characteristic of equilibrium macroeconometric models is that as a result of the restrictions across the A_j's, B_j's, and C_j's, the models predict that in general the parameters in many of the equations will change if there is a policy intervention that takes the form of a change in one equation that describes how some policy variable is being set. Since they ignore these cross-equation restrictions, Keynesian models in general assume that all other equations remain unchanged when an equation describing a policy variable is changed. We think this is one important reason Keynesian models have broken down when the equations governing policy variables or exogenous variables have changed significantly. We hope that the new methods we have described will give us the capability to predict the consequences for all of the equations of changes in the rules governing policy variables. Having that capability is necessary before we can claim to have a scientific basis for making quantitative statements about macroeconomic policy.

So far, these new theoretical and econometric developments have not been fully integrated, although clearly they are very close, both conceptually and operationally. We consider the best currently existing equilibrium models as prototypes of better, future models which will, we hope, prove of practical use in the formulation of policy.

But we should not understate the econometric success already attained by equilibrium models. Early versions of these models have been estimated and subjected to some stringent econometric tests by McCallum (1976), Barro (1977, in press), and Sargent (1976a), with the result that they do seem able to explain some broad features of the business cycle. New and more sophisticated models involving more complicated cross-equation restrictions are in the works (Sargent 1978). Work to date has already shown that equilibrium models can attain within-sample fits about as good as those obtained by Keynesian models, thereby making concrete the point that the good fits of the Keynesian models provide no good reason for trusting policy recommendations derived from them.

Criticism of Equilibrium Theory

The central idea of the equilibrium explanations of business cycles sketched above is that economic fluctuations arise as agents react to unanticipated changes in variables which impinge on their decisions. Clearly, any explanation of this general type must imply severe limitations on the ability of government policy to offset these initiating changes. First, governments must somehow be able to foresee shocks invisible to private agents but at the same time be unable to reveal this advance information (hence, defusing the shocks). Though it is not hard to design theoretical models in which these two conditions are assumed to hold, it is difficult to imagine actual situations in which such models would apply. Second, the governmental countercyclical policy must itself be unforeseeable by private agents (certainly a frequently realized condition historically) while at the same time be systematically related to the state of the economy. Effectiveness, then, rests on the inability of private agents to recognize systematic patterns in monetary and fiscal policy.

To a large extent, criticism of equilibrium models is simply a reaction to these implications for policy. So wide is (or was) the consensus that *the* task of macroeconomics is the discovery of the particular monetary and fiscal policies which can eliminate fluctuations by reacting to private sector instability that the assertion that this task either should not or cannot be performed is regarded as frivolous, regardless of whatever reasoning and evidence may support it. Certainly one must have some sympathy with this reaction: an unfounded faith in the curability of a particular ill has served often enough as a stimulus to the finding of genuine cures. Yet to confuse a possibly functional faith in the existence of efficacious, reactive monetary and fiscal policies with scientific evidence that such policies are known is clearly dangerous, and to use such faith as a criterion for judging the extent to which particular theories fit the facts is worse still.

There are, of course, legitimate questions about how well equilibrium theories can fit the facts of the business cycle. Indeed, this is the reason for our insistence on the preliminary and tentative character of the particular models we now have. Yet these tentative models share certain features which can be regarded as essential, so it is not unreasonable to speculate as to the likelihood that *any* model of this type can be successful or to ask what equilibrium business cycle theorists will have in 10 years if we get lucky.

Four general reasons for pessimism have been prominently advanced: (*a*) Equilibrium models unrealistically postulate cleared markets. (*b*) These models cannot account for "persistence" (serial correlation) of cyclical movements. (*c*) Econometrically implemented models are linear (in logarithms). (*d*) Learning behavior has not been incorporated in these models.

Cleared Markets

One essential feature of equilibrium models is that all markets clear, or that all observed prices and quantities are viewed as outcomes of decisions taken by individual firms and households. In practice, this has meant a conventional, competitive supply-equals-demand assumption, though other kinds of equilibria can easily be imagined (if not so easily analyzed). If, therefore, one takes as a basic "fact" that labor markets do not clear, one arrives immediately at a contradiction between theory and fact. The facts we actually have, however, are simply the available time series on employment and wage rates plus the responses to our unemployment surveys. Cleared markets is simply a principle, not verifiable by direct observation, which may or may not be useful in constructing successful hypotheses about the behavior of these series. Alternative principles, such as the postulate of the existence of a third-party auctioneer inducing wage rigidity and uncleared markets, are similarly "unrealistic," in the not especially important sense of not offering a good description of observed labor market institutions.

A refinement of the unexplained postulate of an uncleared labor market has been suggested by the indisputable fact that long-term labor contracts with horizons of 2 or 3 years exist. Yet the length per se over which contracts run does not bear on the issue, for we know from Arrow and Debreu that if *infinitely* long-term contracts are determined so that prices and wages are contingent on the same information that is available under the assumption of period-by-period market clearing, then precisely the same price-quantity process will result with the long-term contract as would occur under period-by-period market clearing. Thus equilibrium theorizing provides a way, probably the only way we have, to construct a *model* of a long-term contract. The fact that long-term contracts exist, then, has *no* implications about the applicability of equilibrium theorizing.

Rather, the real issue here is whether actual contracts can be adequately accounted for within an equilibrium model, that is, a model in which agents are proceeding in their own best interests. Fischer (1977), Phelps and Taylor (1977), and Hall (1978) have shown that some of the nonactivist conclusions of the equilibrium models are modified if one substitutes for period-by-period market clearing the imposition of long-term contracts drawn contingent on restricted information sets that are exogenously imposed and that are assumed to be independent of monetary and fiscal regimes. Economic theory leads us to predict that the costs of collecting and processing information will make it optimal for contracts to be made contingent on a small subset of the information that could possibly be collected at any date. But theory also suggests that the particular set of information upon which contracts will be made contingent is not immutable but depends on the structure of costs and benefits of collecting various kinds of information. This structure of costs and benefits will change with every change in the exogenous stochastic processes facing agents. This theoretical presumption is supported by an examination of the way labor contracts differ across high-inflation and low-inflation countries and the way they have evolved in the U.S. over the last 25 years.

So the issue here is really the same fundamental one involved in the dispute between Keynes and the classical economists: Should we regard certain superficial characteristics of existing wage contracts as given when analyzing the consequences of alternative monetary and fiscal regimes? Classical economic theory says no. To understand the implications of long-term contracts for monetary policy, we need a model of the way those contracts are likely to respond to alternative monetary policy regimes. An extension of existing equilibrium models in this direction might well lead to interesting variations, but it seems to us unlikely that major modifications of the implications of these models for monetary and fiscal policy will follow from this.

Persistence

A second line of criticism stems from the correct observation that if agents' expectations are rational and if their information sets include lagged values of the variable being forecast, then agents' forecast errors must be a serially uncorrelated random process. That is, on average there must be no detectable relationships between a period's forecast error and any previous period's. This feature has led several critics to conclude that equilibrium models cannot account for more than an insignificant part of the highly serially correlated movements we observe in real output, employment, unemployment, and other series. Tobin (1977, p. 461) has put the argument succinctly:

> One currently popular explanation of variations in employment is temporary confusion of relative and absolute prices. Employers and workers are fooled into too many jobs by unexpected inflation, but only until they learn it affects other prices, not just the prices of what they sell. The reverse happens temporarily when inflation falls short of expectation. This model can scarcely explain more than transient disequilibrium in labor markets.
>
> So how can the faithful explain the slow cycles of unemployment we actually observe? Only by arguing that the natural rate itself fluctuates, that variations in unemployment rates are substantially changes in voluntary, frictional, or structural unemployment rather than in involuntary joblessness due to generally deficient demand.

The critics typically conclude that the theory only attributes a very minor role to aggregate demand fluctuations and necessarily depends on disturbances to aggregate supply to account for most of the fluctuations in real output over the business cycle. "In other words," as Modigliani (1977) has said, "what happened to the United States in the 1930's was a severe attack of contagious laziness."

This criticism is fallacious because it fails to distinguish properly between *sources of impulses* and *propagation mechanisms,* a distinction stressed by Frisch (1933) in a classic paper that provided many of the technical foundations for Keynesian macroeconometric models. Even though the new classical theory implies that the forecast errors which are the aggregate demand impulses are serially uncorrelated, it is certainly logically possible that propagation mechanisms are at work that convert these impulses into serially correlated movements in real variables like output and employment. Indeed, detailed theoretical work has already shown that two concrete propagation mechanisms do precisely that.

One mechanism stems from the presence of costs to firms of adjusting their stocks of capital and labor rapidly. The presence of these costs is known to make it optimal for firms to spread out over time their response to the relative price signals they receive. That is, such a mechanism causes a firm to convert the serially uncorrelated forecast errors in predicting relative prices into serially correlated movements in factor demands and output.

A second propagation mechanism is already present in the most classical of economic growth models. Households' optimal accumulation plans for claims on physical capital and other assets convert serially uncorrelated impulses into serially correlated demands for the accumulation of real assets. This happens because agents typically want to divide any unexpected changes in income partly between consuming and accumulating assets. Thus, the demand for assets next period depends on initial stocks and on unexpected changes in the prices or income facing agents. This dependence makes serially uncorrelated surprises lead to serially correlated movements in demands for physical assets. Lucas (1975) showed how this propagation mechanism readily accepts errors in forecasting aggregate demand as an impulse source.

A third likely propagation mechanism has been identified by recent work in search theory (see, e.g., McCall 1965; Mortensen 1970; Lucas and Prescott 1974). Search theory tries to explain why workers who for some reason are without jobs find it rational not necessarily to take the first job offer that comes along but instead to remain unemployed for awhile until a better offer materializes. Similarly, the theory explains why a firm may find it optimal to wait until a more suitable job applicant appears so that vacancies persist for some time. Mainly for technical reasons, consistent theoretical models that permit this propagation mechanism to accept errors in forecasting aggregate demand as an impulse have not yet been worked out, but the mechanism seems likely eventually to play an important role in a successful model of the time series behavior of the unemployment rate.

In models where agents have imperfect information, either of the first two mechanisms and probably the third can make serially correlated movements in real variables stem from the introduction of a serially un-correlated sequence of forecasting errors. Thus theoretical and economet-ric models have been constructed in which in principle the serially uncor-related process of forecasting errors can account for any proportion between zero and one of the steady-state variance of real output or em-ployment. The argument that such models must necessarily attribute most of the variance in real output and employment to variations in aggregate supply is simply wrong logically.

Linearity

Most of the econometric work implementing equilibrium models has in-volved fitting statistical models that are linear in the variables (but often highly nonlinear in the parameters). This feature is subject to criticism on the basis of the indisputable principle that there generally exist nonlinear models that provide better approximations than linear models. More spe-cifically, models that are linear in the variables provide no way to detect and analyze systematic effects of higher than first-order moments of the shocks and the exogenous variables on the first-order moments of the en-dogenous variables. Such systematic effects are generally present where the endogenous variables are set by risk-averse agents.

There are no *theoretical* reasons that most applied work has used linear models, only compelling technical reasons given today's computer tech-nology. The predominant technical requirement of econometric work which imposes rational expectations is the ability to write down analytical expressions giving agents' decision rules as functions of the parameters of their objective functions and as functions of the parameters governing the exogenous random processes they face. Dynamic stochastic maximum problems with quadratic objectives, which produce linear decision rules, do meet this essential requirement—that is their virtue. Only a few other functional forms for agents' objective functions in dynamic stochastic opti-mum problems have this same necessary analytical tractability. Computer technology in the foreseeable future seems to require working with such a class of functions, and the class of linear decision rules has just seemed most convenient for most purposes. No issue of principle is involved in selecting one out of the very restricted class of functions available. Theo-retically, we know how to calculate, with expensive recursive methods, the nonlinear decision rules that would stem from a very wide class of objec-tive functions; no new econometric principles would be involved in esti-mating their parameters, only a much higher computer bill. Further, as Frisch and Slutsky emphasized, linear stochastic difference equations are a very flexible device for studying business cycles. It is an open question whether for explaining the central features of the business cycle there will be a big reward to fitting nonlinear models.

Stationary Models and the Neglect of Learning

Benjamin Friedman and others have criticized rational expectations models apparently on the grounds that much theoretical and almost all empirical work has assumed that agents have been operating for a long time in a stochastically stationary environment. Therefore, agents are typically assumed to have discovered the probability laws of the variables they want to forecast. Modigliani (1977, p. 6) put the argument this way:

> At the logical level, Benjamin Friedman has called attention to the omission from [equilibrium macroeconomic models] of an explicit learning model, and has suggested that, as a result, it can only be interpreted as a description not of short-run but of long-run equilibrium in which no agent would wish to recontract. But then the implications of [equilibrium macroeconomic models] are clearly far from startling, and their policy relevance is almost nil.

But it has been only a matter of analytical convenience and not of necessity that equilibrium models have used the assumption of stochastically stationary shocks and the assumption that agents have already learned the probability distributions they face. Both of these assumptions can be abandoned, albeit at a cost in terms of the simplicity of the model (e.g., see Crawford 1971; Grossman 1975). In fact, within the framework of quadratic objective functions, in which the "separation principle" applies, one can apply the Kalman filtering formula to derive optimum linear decision rules with time-dependent coefficients. In this framework, the Kalman filter permits a neat application of Bayesian learning to updating optimal forecasting rules from period to period as new information becomes available. The Kalman filter also permits the derivation of optimum decision rules for an interesting class of nonstationary exogenous processes assumed to face agents. Equilibrium theorizing in this context thus readily leads to a *model* of how process nonstationarity and Bayesian learning applied by agents to the exogenous variables leads to time-dependent coefficients in agents' decision rules.

While models incorporating Bayesian learning and stochastic nonstationarity are both technically feasible and consistent with the equilibrium modeling strategy, we know of almost no successful applied work along these lines. One probable reason for this is that nonstationary time series models are cumbersome and come in so many varieties. Another is that the hypothesis of Bayesian learning is vacuous until one either arbitrarily imputes a prior distribution to agents or develops a method of estimating parameters of the prior from time series data. Determining a prior distribution from the data would involve estimating initial conditions and would proliferate nuisance parameters in a very unpleasant way. Whether these techniques will pay off in terms of explaining macroeconomic time series is an empirical matter: it is not a matter distinguishing equilibrium from Keynesian macroeconometric models. In fact, no existing Keynesian macroeconometric model incorporates either an economic model of learning or an economic model in any way restricting the pattern of coefficient nonstationarities across equations.

The macroeconometric models criticized by Friedman and Modigliani (1977), which assume agents have caught on to the stationary random processes they face, give rise to systems of linear stochastic difference equations of the form (1), (2), and (4). As has been known for a long time, such stochastic difference equations generate series that "look like" economic time series. Further, if viewed as structural (that is, invariant with respect to policy interventions), the models have some of the implications for countercyclical policy that we have described above. Whether or not these policy implications are correct depends on whether or not the models are structural and not at all on whether the models can successfully be caricatured by terms such as "long-run" or "short-run."

It is worth reemphasizing that we do not wish our responses to these criticisms to be mistaken for a claim that existing equilibrium models can satisfactorily account for all the main features of the observed business cycle. Rather, we have simply argued that no sound reasons have yet been advanced which even suggest that these models are, as a class, *incapable* of providing a satisfactory business cycle theory.

Summary and Conclusions

Let us attempt to set out in compact form the main arguments advanced in this paper. We will then comment briefly on the main implications of these arguments for the way we can usefully think about economic policy.

Our first and most important point is that existing Keynesian macroeconometric models cannot provide reliable guidance in the formulation of monetary, fiscal, or other types of policy. This conclusion is based in part on the spectacular recent failures of these models and in part on their lack of a sound theoretical or econometric basis. Second, on the latter ground, there is no hope that minor or even major modification of these models will lead to significant improvement in their reliability.

Third, *equilibrium* models can be formulated which are free of these difficulties and which offer a different set of principles to identify structural econometric models. The key elements of these models are that agents are rational, reacting to policy changes in a way which is in their best interests privately, and that the impulses which trigger business fluctuations are mainly unanticipated shocks.

Fourth, equilibrium models already developed account for the main qualitative features of the business cycle. These models are being subjected to continued criticism, especially by those engaged in developing them, but arguments to the effect that equilibrium theories are in principle unable to account for a substantial part of observed fluctuations appear due mainly to simple misunderstandings.

The policy implications of equilibrium theories are sometimes caricatured, by friendly as well as unfriendly commentators, as the assertion that "economic policy does not matter" or "has no effect."[9] This implication would certainly startle neoclassical economists who have successfully applied equilibrium theory to the study of innumerable problems involving important effects of fiscal policies on resource allocation and income distribution. Our intent is not to reject these accomplishments but rather to try to *imitate* them or to extend the equilibrium methods which have been applied to many economic problems to cover a phenomenon which has so far resisted their application: the business cycle.

Should this intellectual arbitrage prove successful, it will suggest important changes in the way we think about policy. Most fundamentally, it will focus attention on the need to think of policy as the choice of stable rules of the game, well understood by economic agents. Only in such a setting will economic theory help predict the actions agents will choose to take. This approach will also suggest that policies which affect behavior mainly because their consequences cannot be correctly diagnosed, such as monetary instability and deficit financing, have the capacity only to disrupt. The deliberate provision of misinformation cannot be used in a systematic way to improve the economic environment.

The *objectives* of equilibrium business cycle theory are taken, without modification, from the goal which motivated the construction of the Keynesian macroeconometric models: to provide a scientifically based means of assessing, quantitatively, the likely effects of alternative economic policies. Without the econometric successes achieved by the Keynesian models, this goal would be simply inconceivable. However, unless the now evident limits of these models are also frankly acknowledged and radically different new directions taken, the real accomplishments of the Keynesian Revolution will be lost as surely as those we now know to be illusory.

References

Aigner, D., and Goldberger, A., eds. *Latent Variables in Socio-Economic Models.* Amsterdam: North Holland, 1977.

[9]A main source of this belief is probably Sargent and Wallace (1975), which showed that in the context of a fairly standard macroeconomic model, but with agents' expectations assumed rational, the choice of a reactive monetary rule is of no consequence for the behavior of real variables. The point of this example was to show that within precisely that model used to rationalize reactive monetary policies, such policies could be shown to be of no value. It hardly follows that all policy is ineffective in all contexts.

Ando, Albert. "A Comment." In *New Methods in Business Cycle Research: Proceedings from a Conference,* edited by C. A. Sims. Minneapolis: Federal Reserve Bank of Minneapolis, 1977.

Arrow, Kenneth J. "The Role of Securities in the Optimal Allocation of Risk-bearing." *Rev. Econ. Studies* 31 (April 1964): 91–96.

Barro, Robert J. "Unanticipated Money Growth and Unemployment in the United States." *A.E.R.* 67 (March 1977): 101–15.

———. "Unanticipated Money, Output, and the Price Level in the United States." *J.P.E.,* in press.

Brunner, K., and Meltzer, A. H., eds. *The Phillips Curve and Labor Markets.* Carnegie-Rochester Conference Series on Public Policy, vol. 1. Amsterdam: North Holland, 1976.

Crawford, Robert. "Implications of Learning for Economic Models of Uncertainty." Manuscript, Carnegie-Mellon University, 1971.

Debreu, Gerard. *The Theory of Value.* New York: Wiley, 1959.

Fischer, Stanley. 1977. "Long-Term Contracts, Rational Expectations, and the Optimal Money Supply Rule." *J.P.E.* 85 (February 1977): 191–205.

Friedman, Milton. "A Monetary and Fiscal Framework for Economic Stability." *A.E.R.* 38 (June 1948): 245–64.

Frisch, Ragnar. "Propagation Problems and Impulse Problems in Dynamic Economics." [1933.] Reprinted in *Readings in Business Cycles,* edited by R. A. Gordon and L. R. Klein. American Economic Association, vol. 10. Homewood, Ill.: Irwin, 1965.

Geweke, John. "The Dynamic Factor Analysis of Economic Time Series." In *Latent Variables in Socio-Economic Models,* edited by D. Aigner and A. Goldberger, Amsterdam: North Holland, 1977.

Gordon, R. A., and Klein, L. R., eds. *Readings in Business Cycles.* American Economic Association, vol. 10. Homewood, Ill.: Irwin, 1965.

Grossman, Sanford. "Rational Expectations and the Econometric Modeling of Markets Subject to Uncertainty: A Bayesian Approach." *J. Econometrics* 3 (August 1975): 255–72.

Hall, Robert E. "The Macroeconomic Impact of Changes in Income Taxes in the Short and Medium Runs." *J.P.E.* 86 (April 1978): S71–S85.

Harris, S., ed. *The New Economics: Keynes' Influence on Theory and Public Policy.* Clifton, N.J.: Kelley, 1965.

Keynes, J. M. *The General Theory of Employment, Interest, and Money.* London: Macmillan, 1936.

Leontief, W. "Postulates: Keynes' General Theory and the Classicists." In *The New Economics: Keynes' Influence on Theory and Public Policy,* edited by S. Harris. Clifton, N.J.: Kelley, 1965.

Lucas, R. E., Jr. "Expectations and the Neutrality of Money." *J. Econ. Theory* 4 (April 1972): 103–24.

———. "An Equilibrium Model of the Business Cycle." *J.P.E.* 83 (December 1975): 1113–44.

———. "Econometric Policy Evaluation: A Critique." In *The Phillips Curve and Labor Markets,* edited by K. Brunner and A. H. Meltzer. Carnegie-Rochester Conference Series on Public Policy, vol. 1. Amsterdam: North Holland, 1976.

Lucas, R. E., Jr., and Prescott, Edward C. "Equilibrium Search and Unemployment." *J. Econ. Theory* 7 (February 1974): 188–209.

McCall, John J. "The Economics of Information and Optimal Stopping Rules." *J. Bus.* 38 (July 1965): 300–317.

McCallum, B. T. "Rational Expectations and the Natural Rate Hypothesis: Some Consistent Estimates." *Econometrica* 44 (January 1976): 43–52.

Modigliani, Franco. "The Monetarist Controversy, or Should We Forsake Stabilization Policies?" *A.E.R.* 67 (March 1977): 1–19.

Mortensen, Dale T. "A Theory of Wage and Employment Dynamics." In *Microeconomic Foundations of Employment and Inflation Theory,* edited by E. S. Phelps. New York: Norton, 1970.

Muench, T.; Rolnick, A.; Wallace, N.; and Weiler, W. "Tests for Structural Change and Prediction Intervals for the Reduced Forms of Two Structural Models of the U.S.: The FRB-MIT and Michigan Quarterly Models." *Ann. Econ. and Soc. Measurement* 3 (July 1974): 491–519.

Okun, Arthur, and Perry, George L., eds. *Brookings Papers on Economic Activity,* vol. 3. Washington: Brookings Inst., 1973.

Phelps, E. S., ed. *Microeconomic Foundations of Employment and Inflation Theory.* New York: Norton, 1970.

Phelps, E. S., and Taylor, John B. "Stabilizing Powers of Monetary Policy under Rational Expectations." *J.P.E.* 85 (February 1977): 163–90.

Sargent, T. J. "A Classical Macroeconometric Model for the United States." *J.P.E.* 84 (April 1976): 207–37. (*a*)

——. "The Observational Equivalence of Natural and Unnatural Rate Theories of Macroeconomics." *J.P.E.* 84 (June 1976): 631–40. (*b*)

——. "Estimation of Dynamic Labor Demand Schedules under Rational Expectations." *J.P.E.* 86 (December 1978): 1009–44.

Sargent, T. J., and Sims, C. A. "Business Cycle Modeling without Pretending to Have Too Much A Priori Economic Theory." In *New Methods in Business Cycle Research: Proceedings from a Conference,* ed. C. A. Sims. Minneapolis: Federal Reserve Bank of Minneapolis, 1977.

Sargent, T. J., and Wallace, Neil. "'Rational' Expectations, the Optimal Monetary Instrument, and the Optimal Money Supply Rule." *J.P.E.* 83 (April 1975): 241–54.

Simons, Henry C. "Rules Versus Authorities in Monetary Policy." *J.P.E.* 44 (February 1936): 1–30.

Sims, C. A. "Money, Income, and Causality." *A.E.R.* 62 (September 1972): 540–52.

——, ed. *New Methods in Business Cycle Research: Proceedings from a Conference.* Minneapolis: Federal Reserve Bank of Minneapolis, 1977.

——. "Macroeconomics and Reality." *Econometrica,* in press.

Sonnenschein, Hugo. "Do Walras' Identity and Continuity Characterize the Class of Community Excess Demand Functions?" *J. Econ. Theory* 6 (August 1973): 345–54.

Tobin, James. "Money Wage Rates and Employment." In *The New Economics: Keynes' Influence on Theory and Public Policy,* edited by S. Harris. Clifton, N.J.: Kelley, 1965.

——. "How Dead is Keynes?" *Economic Inquiry* 15 (October 1977): 459–68.

17

Estimation of Economic Relationships Containing Latent Expectations Variables

John F. Muth

It usually happens that behavioral relations in a simultaneous equation system contain expectations variables which are themselves not observed. Current practice favors representing expectations by some function of the past history of the series to be predicted. However, if expectations are reasonably well-informed, then all the variables of the system are relevant. Maximum likelihood, limited information, and two-stage least squares give consistent estimators when the distinction between rational expectations and realizations of endogenous variables is ignored. This fact is an additional reason to doubt the relevance of recursive systems in estimation from time series data.

Econometric studies are plagued by the fact that available statistics bear no close relationship to the variables appearing in the conceptual model. Data must usually be adjusted for spurious scale factors (inflation and population growth in partial equilibrium models), for extraneous variables or inappropriate weights in aggregated series, and so on. A further problem arises from the fact that expectations of events (income, prices, sales) are fully as important in economic models as the realizations themselves—and good expectations data are hard to come by.[1]

Using lagged variables as a substitute for expectations has become almost automatic in econometric studies (e.g., Klein and Goldberger 1955; Cromarty 1959). Although this assumption helps make the equations identifiable and the parameter estimates easy to compute, there is little evidence that it is economically meaningful. Exponentially weighted moving averages have recently been used with good results (Cagan 1956; Nerlove 1958), and a generalization of the model has already been suggested (Solow 1960).

This paper was written in 1960. References have not been updated.

[1] Available expectations data, mostly from survey questionnaires, are spotty in their coverage and are of doubtful quality. See Ferber (in press).

I have suggested elsewhere (Muth 1959) some reasons to believe that expectations are just as rational as other aspects of individual behavior. If expectations are not much different from the prediction of the model itself, as rationality would imply, how can the parameters be estimated from observable data? We shall show in the following sections that the answer is rather simple.

I. Rational Expectations of Endogenous Variables

The model we will examine first is composed of the following system of equations:

$$B_0 y_t + B_1 y_t^e + \Gamma z_t = u_t' \tag{1}$$

where y_t is the vector of endogenous variables associated with time t and y_t^e the vector of endogenous variables expected to prevail at that time on the basis of information contained in z_t, the vector of exogenous variables. The error term, u_t', is assumed to have a zero mean, a constant covariance matrix, no serial correlation, and no correlation with the exogenous variables.

Rationality implies that y_t^e be essentially the same as the prediction of the model, given the same set of information. That is:

$$y_t^e = E(y_t | z_t) + v_t'. \tag{2}$$

Although the error term v_t' allows divergences between expectations and the prediction of the model itself, we assume that the errors are not systematically related to the explanatory variables of the system. We also assume that v_t' has a zero mean, a constant covariance matrix, and no serial correlation.

We may find y_t^e explicitly in terms of the other variables of the system as follows. Take conditional expectations of equation (1) and substitute from equation (2) to obtain:

$$B y_t^e + \Gamma z_t = B_0 v_t' \tag{3}$$

where $B = B_0 + B_1$. Assuming B is nonsingular, the solution to equation (3) may be written as:[2]

$$y_t^e = -B^{-1} \Gamma z_t + B^{-1} B_0 v_t'. \tag{4}$$

Substituting from equation (4) into equation (1), we obtain a system expressed solely in terms of observable variables:

$$B_0 y_t + \Gamma_1 z_t = u_t \tag{5}$$

where $\Gamma_1 = (I - B_1 B^{-1})\Gamma = B_0 B^{-1}\Gamma$ and $u_t = u_t' - B_1 B^{-1} B_0 v_t'$.

---

[2]If the latent variables are serially dependent, the analysis is considerably more complicated. See Muth (1959, 1960).

Assume that u_t is distributed normally with a constant covariance matrix $\Sigma = E u_t u_t^T$ not subject to any identifying restrictions.[3] After maximizing the logarithm of the likelihood function with respect to Σ, we obtain the concentrated form (see Koopmans and Hood 1953):

$$L = \ln |B_0| - \frac{1}{2} \ln |(B_0, \Gamma_1) M (B_0, \Gamma_1)^T| \qquad (6)$$

except for irrelevant multiplicative and additive constants. M is the moment matrix of y and z.

Since, by assumption, B is nonsingular:

$$(B_0, \Gamma_1) = B_0 B^{-1}(B, \Gamma). \qquad (7)$$

The second term of L in equation (6) may then be written as:

$$-\frac{1}{2} \ln |B_0 B^{-1}| \, |(B, \Gamma) M (B, \Gamma)^T| \, |(B_0 B^{-1})^T|$$

$$= -\ln |B_0| + \ln |B| - \frac{1}{2} \ln |(B, \Gamma) M (B, \Gamma)^T|. \qquad (8)$$

Substituting into equation (9) the likelihood function becomes:

$$L = \ln|B| - \frac{1}{2} \ln|(B, \Gamma) M (B, \Gamma)^T|. \qquad (9)$$

This is the same likelihood function as would be obtained by ignoring the distinction between y_t and y_t^e in equation (1). Maximum-likelihood, limited information, and two-stage least squares (Theil 1958) all give consistent and asymptotically efficient estimates of B and Γ.

Ordinary least squares does not, even if $B_0 = I$. (Two-stage least squares intuitively seems best because it distinguishes the dependent variable from the expectations variables.)

The results above are obtained because this is essentially a problem of errors in endogenous variables.[4] The connection may be seen as follows. Subtracting equation (3) from equation (1),

$$B_0(y_t - y_t^e) = u_t' - B_0 v_t'. \qquad (10)$$

If B_0 is nonsingular,

$$y_t = y_t^e + v_t \qquad (11)$$

where $v_t = B_0^{-1} u_t' - v_t'$. The difference between the models, which evidently turns out to be immaterial, is that v_t is correlated both with y_t^e and u_t'.

---

[3] Of course, we cannot distinguish the variance of u' from that of v'.

[4] Properties of estimates with errors in variables have been known for some time. See Chernoff and Rubin (1953).

If relevant expectations data were available, they would of course be treated as separate (endogenous) variables. The extra information would allow B_0 to be distinguished from B_1, which is not possible with latent variables.

II. Estimation under More General Conditions

To include the possibility that exogenous variables are unknown but predicted in the behavioral relations, we augment equation (1) to read as follows:

$$B_0 y_t + B_1 y_t^e + A_0 x_t + A_1 x_t^e + \Gamma z_t = u_t' \qquad (12)$$

where x_t^e is the vector of exogenous variables predicted on the basis of the others z_t, and x_t is the vector of realizations of the variables. If there is some way to predict the variables x_t, exogenous in the original system, then we might as well assume the set of regression equations:

$$x_t = H z_t + u_t'' \qquad (13)$$

where u_t'' has a zero mean, a constant covariance matrix, no serial correlation, and no correlation with the independent variables. (z_t may, of course, include variables having zero coefficients everywhere in Γ. It is not obvious, however, why one would wish this.)

Equations (12) and (13) jointly define a system having the same properties as equation (1) if x_t is regarded as an endogenous variable. The results obtained earlier hold, including the analogy with the errors in variables model.

The assumption about the predictability of exogenous variables in equation (12) is a little disquieting, however. For certain variables, e.g., weather, there might be enough experience for predictions with reasonable statistical properties to be made. It makes much less sense, however, to regard as approximately normal the distribution of the prediction error of such important exogenous variables as war and other governmental action. The rational model is better than naive predictors in one respect. Any advance information about certain legislation, for example, might be represented by a dummy exogenous variable.

The model is also applicable if expectations for a longer horizon than one period are relevant. Future data may be included as additional endogenous variables. Of course there are severe practical limits to the extent to which such extensions may be carried out, not the least of which is a possible lack of identification of the equation. Two examples of the relevance of long expectations spans are as follows: (i) For certain theories of the consumption function (Friedman 1957; Modigliani and Brumberg 1954), the relevant income variable is not current income or expected current income, but either expected permanent or expected lifetime income. (*ii*) Speculative demand for a commodity by the end of period t depends on the difference between the price expected to prevail during period $t + 1$ and the actual price in period t (Mills 1959; Muth 1959). Such effects should be allowed for if strong time interdependence is an essential ingredient of the phenomena to be explained.

III. Improved Estimates with Forecasted Exogenous Variables

The coefficients of the model consisting of equations (12) and (13) may be estimated more efficiently if the restrictions of equation (13) are taken into account. We shall show that the information may be used in estimating A, B, and Γ with only a moderate increase in computational difficulty.

The maximum-likelihood estimate of H is the least-squares estimate:

$$H = M_{xz} M_{zz}^{-1}. \tag{14}$$

Substituting into the likelihood function for the system composed of equations (12) and (13), the expression reduces to:

$$L = \ln |B| - \frac{1}{2} \ln \left| (B, AH + \Gamma) \begin{pmatrix} M_{yy}^* & M_{yz} \\ M_{zy} & M_{zz} \end{pmatrix} (B, AH + \Gamma)^T \right| \tag{15}$$

where $A = A_0 + A_1$ and $B = B_0 + B_1$.

$$\begin{aligned}
M_{yy}^* &= M_{yy} - M_{yx}^* M_{xx}^{*-1} M_{xy}^* \\
M_{yx}^* &= M_{yx} - M_{yz} M_{zz}^{-1} M_{zx} \\
M_{xx}^* &= M_{xx} - M_{xz} M_{zz}^{-1} M_{zx}
\end{aligned} \tag{16}$$

Equation (15) can be modified in order to incorporate the usual form of identifying restrictions (the presence or absence of a certain variable of the relevant equation).

Suppose we are interested in the first equation of the system, whose coefficients are the row vectors:

$$\begin{aligned}
\beta &= (\beta^*, 0) \\
\alpha &= (\alpha^*, 0) \\
\gamma &= (\gamma^*, 0)
\end{aligned} \tag{17}$$

(The asterisked coefficients refer to the variables appearing in the first equation.) Corresponding to the partitioning of α, and γ, respectively, we define

$$H = \begin{pmatrix} H^* \\ H^{**} \end{pmatrix} \qquad I = \begin{pmatrix} I^* & 0^{**} \\ 0^* & I^{**} \end{pmatrix}. \tag{18}$$

Also define a new vector of coefficients as follows:

$$\theta = (\alpha^*, \gamma^*, 0) \tag{19}$$

with the dimensionality of the null subvector large enough that the number of components of θ is the same as that of z (exogenous variables which are not predicted).

Consider the following matrix of basis vectors of the space spanned by the rows of H and I:

$$T = \begin{pmatrix} T^* \\ T^{**} \end{pmatrix} \tag{20}$$

where

$$T^* = \begin{pmatrix} H^* \\ I^* & 0^{**} \end{pmatrix} \tag{21}$$

and T^{**} is composed of the remaining vectors for a basis of the row space of I. [We assume that H^* is linearly independent of $(I^*, 0^{**})$.] One way to construct T^{**} is to find

$$I - T^{*T}(T^*T^{*T})^{-1}T^*. \tag{22}$$

The appropriate number of rows of (22) constitute a basis for the space orthogonal to the row space of T^*; hence these are the desired rows of T^{**}.

The identity

$$\alpha H + \gamma = \theta T \tag{23}$$

may be augmented so that

$$AH + \Gamma = \Theta T \tag{24}$$

where Θ is a variable matrix whose first row is θ.

Substituting from equation (24) into equation (15), we obtain the likelihood function:

$$L = \ln |B| - \frac{1}{2} \ln |(B, \Theta)\bar{M}(B, \Theta)^T| \tag{25}$$

where

$$\bar{M} = \begin{pmatrix} M^*_{yy} & M_{yz} T^T \\ TM_{zy} & TM_{zz} T^T \end{pmatrix}. \tag{26}$$

Equation (25) is in the form suitable for estimation by either limited information maximum-likelihood or two-stage least squares. The following additional matrices are computed: (1) H, the matrix of regression coefficients of x on z; (2) M^*_{yy} from equation (16); (3) T^{**}, with rows linearly independent of those of T^*; (4) $\bar{M}$ according to equation (26). These additional steps lengthen the computational procedure, but not by nearly so much as full information methods.

IV. Some Implications of the Results

It was observed in Section I that even if only one endogenous variable appears in each equation (i.e., $B_0 = I$) rational expectations behavior introduces the problems of simultaneous equation estimation. As long as the rationality assumption is justified, therefore, our results cast doubt on the applicability of recursive systems as an estimation model.[5]

Three kinds of expectations variables have mainly been used in estimation from time-series data. All are based on the past history of the series: (1) lagged variables, (2) extrapolations of the last (two) observations, and (3) weighted averages of several prior observations.[6]

Variations on these have been used to explain certain expectations data, and tentative steps have recently been taken to use other variables as measures of expectations.[7]

Testing the alternative hypotheses is at best rough and qualitative, however. The main criteria are worth listing here, even at the risk of stating the obvious:

1. Consistency of the models with (more or less) direct evidence about expectations, and subject to limitations as to the quality of the data. The main properties seem to be the following: (i) fair accuracy, (ii) somewhat different characteristics during up- and down-swings, and (iii) apparent regressiveness.

2. Consistency of parameter estimates using the expectations variables with other information. Two items: (i) agreement of time-series estimates with cost, budget, or other cross-sectional studies and (ii) reasonableness of the implied long- and short-run behavior.

3. Effectiveness of the expectations variable in the estimated equation. Three items: (i) how well the expectations variable "interacts" with other variables of the system, (ii) serial correlation of the residuals, and (iii) correlation of the residuals with trend and cyclical variables.

References

Anderson, T. W., and Hurwicz, L. "Errors and Shocks in Economic Relationships" (abstract). *Econometrica* 16 (1948): 36–37.

Cagan, P. "The Monetary Dynamics of Hyperinflation." In *Studies in the Quantity Theory of Money*, edited by M. Friedman. Chicago: Univ. Chicago Press, 1956.

Chernoff, H., and Rubin, H. "Asymptotic Properties of Limited-Information Estimates under Generalized Conditions." In *Studies in Econometric Method*, edited by W. C. Hood and T. C. Koopmans. New York: Wiley, 1953.

Cromarty, W. A. "An Economic Model for United States Agriculture." *J. Amer. Statis. Assoc.* 54 (1959): 556–74.

---

[5] Aggregation of variables over time is another reason (cf. Strotz and Wold 1960).

[6] The most successful seems to be the exponentially weighted moving average. See Klein (1958) for a description of estimation methods and for further references.

[7] E.g., Darling (1959) used new orders as a measure of expected future sales (shipments).

Darling, P. G. "Manufacturers' Inventory Investment, 1947–1958." *A.E.R.* 49 (1959): 950–62.

Ferber, R. Paper to appear in *The Quality and Economic Significance of Anticipatory Data*. Princeton, N.J.: Princeton Univ. Press, in press.

Friedman, M. *A Theory of the Consumption Function*. Princeton, N.J.: Princeton Univ. Press, 1957.

Klein, L. R. "The Estimation of Distributed Lags." *Econometrica* 26 (1958): 553–61.

Klein, L. R., and Goldberger, A. S. *An Econometric Model of the United States, 1929–1953*. Amsterdam: North-Holland, 1955.

Koopmans, T. C., and Hood, W. C. "The Estimation of Simultaneous Linear Economic Relationships." In *Studies in Econometric Method*, edited by Hood and Koopmans. New York: Wiley, 1953.

Koyck, L. M. *Distributed Lags and Investment Analysis*. Amsterdam: North-Holland, 1954.

Mills, E. S. Paper presented at the meetings of the Econometric Society, December 1959.

Modigliani, F., and Brumberg, R. "Utility Analysis and the Consumption Function: An Interpretation of Cross-Section Data." In *Post-Keynesian Economics*, edited by K. K. Kurihara. New Brunswick, N.J.: Rutgers Univ. Press, 1954.

Muth, J. F. "Rational Expectations and the Theory of Price Movements." Paper presented at meetings of the Econometric Society, December 1959 (to appear in *Econometrica*).

Muth, J. F. "Optimal Properties of Exponentially Weighted Forecasts." *J. Amer. Statis. Assoc.* 55 (1960): 299–306.

Nerlove, M. *The Dynamics of Supply: Estimation of Farmers' Response to Price*. Baltimore: Johns Hopkins Press, 1958.

Solow, R. M. "On a Family of Lag Distributions." *Econometrica* 28 (1960): 393–406.

Strotz, R. H., and Wold, H. O. A. "A Triptych on Causal Systems: I. Recursive versus Nonrecursive Systems. II. Interdependence as a Specification Error (Strotz). III. A Generalization of Causal Chain Models (Wold)." *Econometrica* 28 (1960): 417–63.

Theil, H. *Economic Forecasts and Policy*. Amsterdam: North-Holland, 1958.

18

Econometric Implications of the Rational Expectations Hypothesis

Kenneth F. Wallis

The implications for applied econometrics of the assumption that unobservable expectations are formed rationally in Muth's sense are examined. The statistical properties of the resulting models and their distributed lag and time series representations are described. Purely extrapolative forecasts of endogenous variables can be constructed, as alternatives to rational expectations, but are less efficient. Identification and estimation are considered: an order condition is that no more expectations variables than exogenous variables enter the model. Estimation is based on algorithms for nonlinear-in-parameters systems; other approaches are surveyed. Implications for economic policy and econometric policy evaluation are described.

Expectations variables are widely used in applied econometrics, since the optimizing behavior of economic agents, which empirical research endeavors to capture, depends in part on their views of the future. Directly observed expectations or anticipations are relatively rare, hence implicit forecasting schemes are used. Most commonly expectations are taken to be extrapolations, that is, weighted averages of past values of the variable under consideration. However, these "are almost surely inaccurate gauges of expectations. Consumers, workers, and businessmen . . . do read newspapers and they do know better than to base price expectations on simple extrapolation of price series alone" (Tobin 1972, p. 14). An alternative approach is offered by the rational expectations hypothesis of Muth (1961), which assumes that in forming their expectations of endogenous variables, economic agents take account of the interrelationships among variables

The first version of this paper was written while I was spending a sabbatical term at the University of California, San Diego, whose kind hospitality is gratefully acknowledged. It was circulated as UCSD Department of Economics Discussion Paper no. 77–3, April 1977, and presented at, among other places, the Econometric Society European Meeting, Vienna, September 1977. The present version has benefitted from numerous comments, including those of two anonymous referees.
[*Econometrica*, 1980, vol. 48, no. 1]

described by the appropriate economic theory. "Price movements observed and experienced do not necessarily convey information on the basis of which a rational man should alter his view of the future. When a blight destroys half the midwestern corn crop and corn prices subsequently rise, the information conveyed is that blights raise prices. No trader or farmer under these circumstances would change his view of the future of corn prices, much less of their rate of change, unless he is led to reconsider his estimate of the likelihood of blights," again quoting Tobin.

This paper examines the implications of the rational expectations hypothesis for applied econometrics, and argues that its full force has yet to be appreciated in empirical work. The discussion is quite general, proceeding in terms of the standard linear simultaneous equation system, and pays little attention to specific applications of the hypothesis, such as the "efficient markets" literature and recent work in macroeconomic theory, both treated in the survey by Poole (1976). As noted by Barro and Fischer (1976, p. 156), "it is important to distinguish the rational expectations hypothesis per se . . . from the models known as rational expectations models that have usually been constructed so that money is neutral aside from possible expectations phenomena," and the statistical implications of the former are our concern. We therefore set aside a number of topics that have arisen in theoretical models incorporating rational expectations (or "perfect foresight" in a nonstochastic context) discussed, for example, by Shiller (1978). Thus in the face of a model yielding multiple solutions the econometric student of recent history assumes that the system did make a choice and the data-generation process did follow a particular path. Likewise the assumptions of time invariance and an infinite past conventional in practical time series analysis leave on one side questions of learning mechanisms and the transition to rational expectations. The question of the informational requirements of rational expectations has led some to doubt the empirical applicability of these models, but this seems to be as yet unresolved: there may be specific situations in which these requirements are approximately met, but until sound empirical investigations have been carried out, this remains an open question.

Section I describes the statistical properties of models which incorporate the rational expectations hypothesis, showing the source and nature of the various distributed lag formulations, and comparing the predictive efficiency of rational expectations and purely extrapolative forecasts. Section II is concerned with the identification and estimation of such models, and fresh approaches to the estimation of complete systems and single equations are presented. The rational expectations framework is useful for considering various aspects of economic policy, as in Section III, since it provides a model for the not uncommon sight of economic agents, having observed certain economic phenomena, anticipating the impact on the system of the government policy which they believe will be introduced in response to those phenomena. The framework used in the paper allows the force of Lucas's (1976) criticism of conventional econometric policy evaluation to be appreciated, yet it permits a practical response to be devised, by retaining the notion of an economic structure (incorporating the rational expectations hypothesis) that is invariant to the "structure" of exogenous processes.

I. Rational Expectations Models

A. Some Basic Properties

Our starting point is a "classical" static model in which expected or anticipated values of certain endogenous variables are included among the inputs:

$$By_t + A_1 y^*_{1t} + \Gamma x_t = u_t. \tag{1}$$

The parameter matrices B, A_1, and Γ are of dimension $g \times g$, $g \times h$, and $g \times k$, respectively, and the vectors y_t, y^*_{1t}, x_t, and u_t have g, h ($\leqslant g$), k, and g elements, respectively. The endogenous variables y_t and exogenous variables x_t are observable, whereas y^*_{1t} represents unobservable anticipations, formed in period $t - 1$, about the values of h of the endogenous variables, which without loss of generality we take to be the first h elements of y_t.[1] All adjustments are assumed to be completed within a single period; further dynamic complications such as lagged endogenous variables or the formation of expectations about *future* values of y_{1t} are held over for the moment.

In order to proceed to empirical implementation of the model, it is necessary to add a statement concerning the formation of expectations. A common assumption in applied econometrics has been that expectations are formed purely extrapolatively, that is, based solely on the past history of the variable under consideration. The simplest example is the "adaptive expectations" hypothesis,

$$y^*_{it} - y^*_{i,t-1} = (1 - \lambda)(y_{i,t-1} - y^*_{i,t-1}),$$

which implies that the current expectation is a geometrically weighted moving average of past observations,

$$y^*_{it} = (1 - \lambda) \sum_{j=0}^{\infty} \lambda^j y_{i,t-1-j}, \tag{2}$$

although more general forms have come to be used as a result of the growing influence of the methods of time series analysis popularized by Box and Jenkins (1970). In contrast, the rational expectations hypothesis

---

[1] Observable anticipations variables, such as those based on survey data, may be entered as endogenous or exogenous variables as appropriate.

assumes that "expectations, since they are informed predictions of future events, are essentially the same as the predictions of the relevant economic theory" and hence depend "specifically on the structure of the relevant system describing the economy" (Muth 1961, p. 316). Thus the variable y^*_{1t} is given as the expectation of y_{1t} implied by the model, conditional on information Ω_{t-1} available at time $t-1$, i.e., $y^*_{1t} = E(y_{1t}|\Omega_{t-1})$. The usual reduced form of the model (1) is

$$y_t = -B^{-1}A_1 y^*_{1t} - B^{-1}\Gamma x_t + B^{-1}u_t,$$

which we partition and rewrite as

$$
\begin{aligned}
y_{1t} &= \Pi_{11} y^*_{1t} + \Pi_{12} x_t + v_{1t}, \\
y_{2t} &= \Pi_{21} y^*_{1t} + \Pi_{22} x_t + v_{2t}.
\end{aligned}
\tag{3}
$$

Taking conditional expectations in the first matrix equation gives

$$E(y_{1t}|\Omega_{t-1}) = \Pi_{11}E(y_{1t}|\Omega_{t-1}) + \Pi_{12}E(x_t|\Omega_{t-1}) + E(v_{1t}|\Omega_{t-1}).$$

Assuming that the disturbances are nonautocorrelated and that the $h \times h$ matrix $(I - \Pi_{11})$ is nonsingular, and writing $\hat{x}_t$ for $E(x_t|\Omega_{t-1})$, we obtain

$$y^*_{1t} = (I - \Pi_{11})^{-1}\Pi_{12}\hat{x}_t.
\tag{4}$$

Thus the rational expectations are given as linear combinations of the predictions of the exogenous variables, and the relevant information on which to base these is the set of past values $x_{t-1}, x_{t-2}, \ldots$, assuming that the list of exogenous variables in the model is correct and complete. On substituting into (3) we obtain the "observable" reduced form as

$$
\begin{aligned}
y_{1t} &= P_{11}\hat{x}_t + P_{12}x_t + v_{1t}, \\
y_{2t} &= P_{21}\hat{x}_t + P_{22}x_t + v_{2t},
\end{aligned}
\tag{5}
$$

where

$$P = \begin{bmatrix} P_{11} & P_{12} \\ P_{21} & P_{22} \end{bmatrix} = \begin{bmatrix} \Pi_{11}(I - \Pi_{11})^{-1}\Pi_{12} & \Pi_{12} \\ \Pi_{21}(I - \Pi_{11})^{-1}\Pi_{12} & \Pi_{22} \end{bmatrix}.$$

Subtracting (4) from (5) gives the error in the rational expectation as

$$y_{1t} - y^*_{1t} = \Pi_{12}(x_t - \hat{x}_t) + v_{1t},
\tag{6}$$

which thus depends simply on the exogenous variable forecast error and the current-period disturbances.

For certain purposes it is convenient to write the model in an alternative way, by augmenting the matrix A_1 by a $g \times (g - h)$ block of zeroes and defining $A = [A_1 \vdots 0]$. Then (1) becomes

$$By_t + Ay^*_t + \Gamma x_t = u_t
\tag{7}$$

and the rational expectation is given as

$$y^*_t = -(B + A)^{-1}\Gamma\hat{x}_t.
\tag{8}$$

There is no difficult in defining the rational expectation of any endogenous variable, even though that expectation does not appear in the model, provided that $(B + A)$ is nonsingular, an assumption analogous to that made in deriving (4). The matrix P of observable reduced form coefficients is then given in terms of structural parameters as

$$P = [B^{-1}A(B + A)^{-1}\Gamma : -B^{-1}\Gamma]$$

and the counterpart to (6) is

$$y_t - y_t^* = -B^{-1}\Gamma(x_t - \hat{x}_t) + B^{-1}u_t. \tag{9}$$

To complete the stochastic specification of the model, we postulate the following vector autoregressive moving average (ARMA) model for x_t:

$$\Phi(L)x_t = \Theta(L)\varepsilon_t \tag{10}$$

where ε_t is a white noise process independent of u_t, and $\Phi(L)$ and $\Theta(L)$ are polynomials in the lag operator L of degree p and q, respectively, viz.,

$$\Phi(L) = I + \Phi_1 L + \cdots + \Phi_p L^p, \qquad \Theta(L) = \Theta_0 + \Theta_1 L + \cdots + \Theta_q L^q.$$

It is assumed that there is no "structural" information available regarding the generation of the exogenous variables, hence (10) is written in reduced form, with $\Phi_0 = I$.[2] With respect to the moving average side, normalization can be achieved in many ways, and two possibilities used below are (a) $\Theta_0 = I$, $E(\varepsilon_t \varepsilon_t') = \Sigma$ unrestricted, (b) $E(\varepsilon_t \varepsilon_t') = \text{diag}\{\sigma_{ii}\}$, Θ_0 lower triangular with unit diagonal; transfer from (a) to (b) is effected by the Choleski decomposition of Σ. We take the "invertible" or "minimum-delay" representation in which all roots of $|\Theta(z)| = 0$ lie outside the unit circle. The optimal[3] one-step forecasts are given by

$$\hat{x}_t = -\Phi_1 x_{t-1} - \cdots - \Phi_p x_{t-p} + \Theta_1 \varepsilon_{t-1} + \cdots + \Theta_q \varepsilon_{t-q} \tag{11}$$

(Granger and Newbold 1977, sec. 7.5). Alternatively, using the infinite autoregressive representation based on the expansion

$$\Theta(L)^{-1}\Phi(L) = I - \Psi_0 L - \Psi_1 L^2 - \cdots,$$

say (taking the normalization $\Theta_0 = I$), we have

$$\hat{x}_t = \sum_{j=1}^{\infty} \Psi_{j-1} x_{t-j} = \Psi(L)x_{t-1}, \tag{12}$$

[2]As an alternative to (10) we could specify a univariate ARMA representation for each x variable, but such a specification is obtainable as a form of solution of (10) (see Chan and Wallis [1978] for examples). However separate univariate analyses might be more convenient in practice, and ignoring the various restrictions and cross-correlations might not lead to much inefficiency if the exogenous variables are only weakly interconnected.

[3]Assuming that there is not a third group of variables outside the model and independent of u that nevertheless contains information useful in forecasting x.

where

$$\Psi(L) = \Psi_0 + \Psi_1 L + \Psi_2 L^2 + \cdots = \frac{1}{L}\Theta(L)^{-1}\{\Theta(L) - \Phi(L)\}.$$

Substitution of (12) into the observable reduced form (5) yields the "final form" relations, in which each endogenous variable is given as a distributed lag function of the exogenous variables:

$$y_t = P._2 x_t + P._1 \Psi(L)x_{t-1} + v_t. \tag{13}$$

First note that for a given exogenous variable the shape of the lag distribution is the same in every equation, with the exception of the leading coefficient, this shape being given by the optimal forecasting weights. In practice this implication of the rational expectations hypothesis might be tested; more generally one might check the agreement between the distributed lags and the estimated time series models for the exogenous variables as an aid to the empirical specification of distributed lag functions. In any event, note that such data-based distributed lag functions give the final form equations (13), and not the rational expectations themselves.

Secondly it is clear that the lag distribution depends on and changes with the stochastic structure of the exogenous variables, described by Sims (1974, p. 294) as a "negative result" of the rational expectations hypothesis: "what is called the structure in textbook treatments of simultaneous equation models can change under policy changes which affect only the time path of exogenous variables," although we see in Section IIIB that it is helpful to refine the notion of structure. If the exogenous variables have a finite-order autoregressive representation, then the distributed lag functions are similarly of finite extent. Any moving average element (i.e., $q > 0$ in [10]) implies that the autoregressive representation and hence the distributed lag functions are of infinite extent, but if p and q are finite the lag functions can be written as a ratio of two finite lag polynomials, whereupon (13) has the standard transfer function or "rational" distributed lag form. Nevertheless interpretations of such lags in terms of speeds of adjustment, rates of learning, and so forth are entirely out of place in the present context.

Finally, a univariate time series model for each endogenous variable can be deduced. Consider the ith equation of the observable reduced form (5): $y_{it} = \rho_1' \hat{x}_t + \rho_2' x_t + v_{it}$, where ρ_1' and ρ_2' are the ith rows of the coefficient matrices of $\hat{x}_t$ and x_t, respectively. The model (10) for x_t has the infinite moving average representation

$$x_t = \Phi(L)^{-1}\Theta(L)\varepsilon_t = |\Phi(L)|^{-1} \text{adj } \Phi(L)\Theta(L)\varepsilon_t,$$

and we take the normalization $E(\varepsilon_t \varepsilon_t') = \text{diag } \{\sigma_{ii}\}$. The forecast $\hat{x}_t$ can similarly be written $\hat{x}_t = \Upsilon(L)\varepsilon_{t-1}$ where

$$\Upsilon(L) = \Upsilon_0 + \Upsilon_1 L + \Upsilon_2 L^2 + \cdots = \frac{1}{L}\{\Phi(L)^{-1}\Theta(L) - \Theta_0\}.$$

Then on substituting and multiplying through by the scalar $|\Phi(L)|$ we obtain

$$|\Phi(L)|y_{it} = |\Phi(L)|\rho_1'\Upsilon(L)\varepsilon_{t-1} + \rho_2' \text{ adj } \Phi(L)\Theta(L)\varepsilon_t + |\Phi(L)|v_{it}$$
$$= \xi'(L)\varepsilon_t + |\Phi(L)|v_{it},$$

say, where the (finite-order) moving average operators $\xi'(L)$ have leading coefficients $\xi_0' = \rho_2'\Theta_0$. The right-hand side is a sum of $k + 1$ independent moving average processes, and hence has a moving average representation in terms of a single innovation η_{it} (Granger and Morris 1976). The resulting ARMA model (taking the invertible moving average representation) can be written $|\Phi(L)|y_{it} = \theta_i(L)\eta_{it}$. This could then form the basis of a purely extrapolative predictor y_{it}^{**}, say, whose one-step forecast error η_{it} is white noise, but the associated forecast error variance is greater than that of the rational expectation, as we now show.

The ith equation of (6) or (9) gives $y_{it} - y_{it}^* = \rho_2'\Theta_0\varepsilon_t + v_{it} = \xi_0'\varepsilon_t + v_{it}$; thus the error in the rational expectation is serially uncorrelated and uncorrelated with past values of exogenous variables, and has mean square

$$\sum_{j=1}^{k} \xi_{0j}^2 \sigma_{jj} + \sigma_{v_i}^2.$$

To compare this with the mean squared error of the extrapolative predictor y_{it}^{**}, we generalize the approach of Pierce (1975). We have

$$\eta_{it} = \frac{|\Phi(L)|}{\theta_i(L)}y_{it} = \frac{\xi'(L)}{\theta_i(L)}\varepsilon_t + \frac{|\Phi(L)|}{\theta_i(L)}v_{it}$$
$$= \sum_{j=1}^{k}\sum_{l=0}^{\infty} w_{jl}\varepsilon_{j,t-l} + \sum_{l=0}^{\infty} w_{k+1,l}v_{i,t-l}, \qquad (14)$$

where the expansions have leading coefficients $w_{j,0}, j = 1, \ldots, k$, given by ξ_0', and $w_{k+1,0} = 1$. Since the $\varepsilon_{jt}, j = 1, \ldots, k$, and v_{it} are mutually uncorrelated white noise processes, we have

$$\text{var}(\eta_{it}) = \sum_{j=1}^{k}\sum_{l=0}^{\infty} w_{jl}^2\sigma_{jj} + \sum_{l=0}^{\infty} w_{k+1,l}^2\sigma_{v_i}^2$$
$$> \sum_{j=1}^{k} w_{j,0}^2\sigma_{jj} + w_{k+1,0}^2\sigma_{v_i}^2$$
$$= \sum_{j=1}^{k} \xi_{0j}^2\sigma_{jj} + \sigma_{v_i}^2 = \text{var}(y_{it} - y_{it}^*);$$

hence the error variance of the optimal extrapolative predictor is greater than that of the rational expectation.

This is discussed in the context of two simple examples by Nelson (1969, 1975a), who remarks that Muth's initial example "was perhaps an unfortunate choice" since it was such a special case that the rational expectation and optimal extrapolative predictor coincided. That example was a two-equation market model, with no exogenous variables and a single auto-correlated disturbance. Muth further specialized this by taking the disturbance term to be a random walk, whereupon the rational expectation obeys the adaptive expectation model (2); perhaps this choice was also unfortunate, lending unwarranted support to the adaptive expectations approach. In general the prediction error in both the rational expectation and the optimal extrapolative predictor is free of autocorrelation, although the extrapolative prediction error, unlike the error in the rational expectation, is correlated with past values of the exogenous variables.

B. A Simple Example

Choosing $g = 2$, $h = k = 1$, and imposing two zero-valued parameters a priori, we have the just-identified model

$$\begin{bmatrix} 1 & \beta_{12} \\ \beta_{21} & 1 \end{bmatrix}\begin{bmatrix} y_{1t} \\ y_{2t} \end{bmatrix} + \begin{bmatrix} \alpha & 0 \\ 0 & \gamma \end{bmatrix}\begin{bmatrix} y_{1t}^* \\ x_t \end{bmatrix} = \begin{bmatrix} u_{1t} \\ u_{2t} \end{bmatrix}.$$

The usual reduced form, which cannot be implemented without an assumption about the formation of expectations, is

$$\begin{bmatrix} y_{1t} \\ y_{2t} \end{bmatrix} = \frac{1}{1 - \beta_{12}\beta_{21}}\begin{bmatrix} -\alpha & \gamma\beta_{12} \\ \alpha\beta_{21} & -\gamma \end{bmatrix}\begin{bmatrix} y_{1t}^* \\ x_t \end{bmatrix} + \begin{bmatrix} v_{1t} \\ v_{2t} \end{bmatrix}$$

$$= \begin{bmatrix} \pi_{11} & \pi_{12} \\ \pi_{21} & \pi_{22} \end{bmatrix}\begin{bmatrix} y_{1t}^* \\ x_t \end{bmatrix} + \begin{bmatrix} v_{1t} \\ v_{2t} \end{bmatrix}.$$

Taking expectations in the first equation conditional on Ω_{t-1}, and assuming that the errors are free of autocorrelation, we obtain the rational expectation of y_{1t} as

$$y_{1t}^* = E(y_{1t} | \Omega_{t-1}) = \frac{\pi_{12}}{1 - \pi_{11}}E(x_t | \Omega_{t-1}) = \frac{\pi_{12}}{1 - \pi_{11}}\hat{x}_t,$$

where $\hat{x}_t$ is the optimal predictor of x_t based on $x_{t-1}, x_{t-2}, \ldots$. This expression can be substituted into the structural or reduced form for empirical implementation, given an appropriate specification for x_t. (Note that the effect of a "fixed regressor" assumption, in which x_t is treated as known, is to remove the identifiability of the model.)

   Case (i):

$$x_t = \phi x_{t-1} + \varepsilon_t.$$

In this case the optimal predictor is $\hat{x}_t = \phi x_{t-1}$, hence the rational expectation is

$$y_{1t}^* = \frac{\pi_{12}}{1 - \pi_{11}}\phi x_{t-1}$$

and the final form distributed lag relations are

$$y_{1t} = \frac{\pi_{11}\pi_{12}\phi}{1 - \pi_{11}}x_{t-1} + \pi_{12}x_t + v_{1t},$$

$$y_{2t} = \frac{\pi_{21}\pi_{12}\phi}{1 - \pi_{11}}x_{t-1} + \pi_{22}x_t + v_{2t}. \tag{15}$$

Since the model is just-identified and the rational expectation depends on a single past x value, these relations are free of restrictions.

The optimal extrapolative predictor for y_{1t} under the rational expectations hypothesis can be readily deduced. The first final form equation (15) is

$$y_{1t} = \pi_{12}(1 + \psi L)x_t + v_{1t}, \qquad \psi = \frac{\pi_{11}\phi}{1 - \pi_{11}},$$

and on substituting $x_t = \{1/(1 - \phi L)\}\varepsilon_t$ and rearranging, we obtain

$$(1 - \phi L)y_{1t} = \pi_{12}(1 + \psi L)\varepsilon_t + (1 - \phi L)v_{1t}.$$

The right-hand side is a sum of two independent first-order moving average processes, and hence has itself a first-order moving average representation, giving an ARMA(1, 1) model for y_{1t},

$$(1 - \phi L)y_{1t} = (1 - \theta L)\eta_t,$$

where $\theta(|\theta| < 1)$ and var $(\eta_t) = \sigma_\eta^2$ are obtained in terms of π_{11}, π_{12}, ϕ, σ_ε^2, and $\sigma_{v_1}^2$. (Note that the "coincidental situation" in which $\phi = -\psi$, giving a lower order ARMA model, cannot arise unless $\phi = 0$.) Thus the optimal extrapolative predictor of y_{1t}, say y_{1t}^{**}, is $y_{1t}^{**} = \phi y_{1,t-1} - \theta\eta_{t-1}$, with mean square error σ_η^2. The rational expectation has error $y_{1t} - y_{1t}^* = \pi_{12}\varepsilon_t + v_{1t}$ with mean square $\pi_{12}^2\sigma_\varepsilon^2 + \sigma_{v_1}^2$, which is smaller than σ_η^2 by the analysis of the previous section.

Case (ii):

$$x_t - x_{t-1} = \varepsilon_t - \theta\varepsilon_{t-1}, \qquad |\theta| < 1.$$

This is the ARIMA (0, 1, 1) model, in which the optimal predictor is given as an exponentially weighted moving average of past observations, that is,

$$\hat{x}_t = (1 - \theta)\sum_{j=0}^{\infty}\theta^j x_{t-1-j},$$

and

$$y_{1t}^* - \theta y_{1,t-1}^* = \frac{\pi_{12}(1 - \theta)}{1 - \pi_{11}}x_{t-1}.$$

The resulting distributed lag equations are of the standard Koyck form,

$$y_{1t} = \frac{\pi_{12}}{1 - \theta L} \left\{ x_t - \frac{\theta - \pi_{11}}{1 - \pi_{11}} x_{t-1} \right\} + v_{1t},$$

$$y_{2t} = \frac{\pi_{22}}{1 - \theta L} \left[x_t - \left\{ \theta - \frac{\pi_{21}\pi_{12}(1 - \theta)}{\pi_{22}(1 - \pi_{11})} \right\} x_{t-1} \right] + v_{2t}. \tag{16}$$

The denominator lag polynomials are the same in the two equations, and this restriction might be imposed in estimation.

If $\theta > 0$ and $0 < \pi_{11} < 1$ so that the distributed lag coefficients in (16) are positive, a "mean lag" could be calculated as $\pi_{11}/(1 - \theta)$. Again, however, interpretations of this quantity in terms of a distributed lag adjustment mechanism are quite out of place—"adjustment" appears more or less "sluggish" simply as the stochastic specification of the exogenous variable (with respect to the parameter θ) changes.

In this case the pure time series model for y_1 is also ARIMA $(0, 1, 1)$ so that the optimal extrapolative predictor is of the adaptive expectations form, but again the prediction error variance is greater than that of the rational expectation.

If in this simple model it is postulated that y_{1t}^* is generated by an adaptive expectations mechanism, as an alternative to the rational expectations hypothesis, then the distributed lag functions relating y_1 and y_2 to x are the same as (16), in that the same lagged variables appear with the same cross-equation restriction (but the error specification is a little different). In effect the same final form is relevant to two different models, which is always possible. Of course this correspondence does not hold for the autoregressive x of case (i), and the difference between the lag distributions (15) and (16) results simply from the different autocorrelation properties of the exogenous variable in the rational expectations context.

C. Dynamic Complications: Future Expectations

We first consider how the above results are modified if the relevant expectations variables relate to a future period (or periods) as of time t. Then (1) becomes

$$By_t + \sum_{j=0}^{\tau} A_{1j} y_{1,t+j}^* + \Gamma x_t = u_t \tag{17}$$

where τ is an "expectations horizon," and the reduced form is

$$y_t = -\sum_{j=0}^{\tau} B^{-1} A_{1j} y_{1,t+j}^* - B^{-1}\Gamma x_t + B^{-1} u_t,$$

of which the block relating to the determination of y_1 can be written

$$y_{1t} = \sum_{j=0}^{\tau} \Pi_{11,j} y^*_{1,t+j} + \Pi_{12} x_t + v_{1t}.$$

Taking conditional expectations, again assuming nonautocorrelated disturbances, we see that the rational expectations $y^*_{1,t+j} = E(y_{1,t+j} | \Omega_{t-1})$ satisfy

$$(I - \Pi_{11,0}) y^*_{1t} = \sum_{j=1}^{\tau} \Pi_{11,j} y^*_{1,t+j} + \Pi_{12} E(x_t | \Omega_{t-1}).$$

This is a multivariate τ-order difference equation which, if stable, yields a solution for y^*_{1t} in terms of $\widehat{x}_{t+j} = E(x_{t+j} | \Omega_{t-1})$, $j = 0, 1, 2, \ldots$. Writing $C_{1j} = (I - \Pi_{11,0})^{-1} \Pi_{11,j}$, the difference equation in companion form is

$$\begin{bmatrix} y^*_{1t} \\ y^*_{1,t+1} \\ \vdots \\ y^*_{1,t+\tau-1} \end{bmatrix} = \begin{bmatrix} C_{11} & C_{12} & \cdots & C_{1,\tau-1} & C_{1\tau} \\ I & 0 & \cdots & 0 & 0 \\ \vdots & & & \vdots & \vdots \\ 0 & 0 & & I & 0 \end{bmatrix} \begin{bmatrix} y^*_{1,t+1} \\ y^*_{1,t+2} \\ \vdots \\ y^*_{1,t+\tau} \end{bmatrix}$$

$$+ \begin{bmatrix} (I - \Pi_{11,0})^{-1} \Pi_{12} \\ 0 \\ \vdots \\ 0 \end{bmatrix} \widehat{x}_t$$

or $y^{\dagger}_{1,t} = C y^{\dagger}_{1,t+1} + \chi_t$. The stability condition is that the eigenvalues of C have modulus less than 1, or equivalently that the characteristic equation

$$|(I - \Pi_{11,0}) z^{\tau} - \Pi_{11,1} z^{\tau-1} - \cdots - \Pi_{11,\tau}| = 0$$

has roots with modulus less than 1, and if this is satisfied the solution is

$$y^{\dagger}_{1,t} = \sum_{j=0}^{\infty} C^j \chi_{t+j}.$$

The first block gives the solution for y^*_{1t} in terms of the predictions of *all* future values of the exogenous variables, given their past values. The remaining blocks give the same expression for $y^*_{1,t+j}$, $j = 1, \ldots, \tau - 1$, except that the time subscript on the x forecasts is advanced j periods; the solution for $y^*_{1,t+\tau}$ is obtained in the same manner. The error in the immediate rational expectation has the same form as in the model of Section IA,

$$y_{1t} - y^*_{1t} = (\Pi_{11,0} - I) y^*_{1t} + \sum_{j=1}^{\tau} \Pi_{11,j} y^*_{1,t+j} + \Pi_{12} x_t + v_{1t}$$

$$= \Pi_{12}(x_t - \widehat{x}_t) + v_{1t},$$

and so is free of autocorrelation, while the future expectations variable $y^*_{1,t+j}$ (based on Ω_{t-1}) has an error which depends on $\varepsilon_t, \varepsilon_{t+1}, \ldots, \varepsilon_{t+j}$ together with $v_{1,t+j}$ and so exhibits autocorrelation.

The generalization of the observable reduced form (5) now involves all future x forecasts, and the general expression is not informative, but the final form equations are still of the same type. Using the autoregressive representation for x_t, the sequence of forecasts can be calculated recursively from the expression

$$\widehat{x}_{t+l} = \sum_{j=1}^{l} \Psi_{j-1}\widehat{x}_{t+l-j} + \sum_{j=0}^{\infty} \Psi_{j+l}x_{t-1-j}$$

which generalizes (12). If x_t has a finite autoregressive representation of order p, then each forecast $\widehat{x}_{t+l}$ is a linear combination of $x_{t-1}, \ldots, x_{t-p}$ and so are the rational expectations $y^*_{1,t+j}, j = 0, \ldots, \tau$. Then the same lagged exogenous variables appear in the final form distributed lag equations as in the case in which only contemporaneous expectations variables enter the model; all that changes is their relative weights.

An illustration is obtained by advancing the expectations variable of the example of Section IB by one period; thus the first reduced form equation becomes $y_{1t} = \pi_{11}y^*_{1,t+1} + \pi_{12}x_t + v_{1t}$. Assuming that $|\pi_{11}| < 1$ the solution for the rational expectations variable is

$$y^*_{1,t+1} = \pi_{12}\sum_{j=0}^{\infty}\pi_{11}^j\widehat{x}_{t+1+j}. \tag{18}$$

In case (i), where x_t obeys a first-order autoregression, we have $\widehat{x}_{t+j} = \phi^{j+1}x_{t-1}$; hence the rational expectation is

$$y^*_{1,t+1} = \frac{\pi_{12}\phi^2}{1 - \phi\pi_{11}}x_{t-1}$$

and the distributed lag relation is

$$y_{1t} = \pi_{12}x_t + \frac{\pi_{12}\pi_{11}\phi^2}{1 - \phi\pi_{11}}x_{t-1} + v_{1t}.$$

This contains the same variables as (15); only the interpretation of the coefficient of x_{t-1} has changed.

In case (ii), x_t is ARIMA (0, 1, 1) and the optimal predictor based on $x_{t-1}, x_{t-2}, \ldots$ is the same for any forecast horizon. Thus

$$y^*_{1,t+1} = \pi_{12}\sum_{j=0}^{\infty}\pi_{11}^j\left\{(1 - \theta)\sum_{i=0}^{\infty}\theta^ix_{t-1-i}\right\},$$

giving the same expression as previously, and the final form equations are identical to (16).

In this example, to assume that the rational expectation as of time $t + 1$, rather than t, is relevant to the particular behavioral equation causes no change at all in the distributed lag relations in case (ii); in case (i) the form of the relation is unaltered. In general one would not expect data to be particularly informative on this question. The specification of different timing relationships amounts to the specification of different models, which may nevertheless have the same reduced or final form, and so be observationally indistinguishable. Such specification should be based on a priori institutional and information flow considerations relevant to the given context.

Different assumptions about the amount of information available when expectations are formed are clearly possible, but result in only minor modifications to the foregoing material. For example, one might include the expectational variable $y^*_{1,t+1}$ as in the above illustration, but assume that the values of the exogenous variables at time t are known when expectations are formed. Then in computing the rational expectation (18), the forecasts are given by $\widehat{x}_{t+j} = \phi^j x_t$ in case (i), so that $y^*_{1,t+1}$ depends only on x_t, and x_{t-1} drops out of the final form. However in case (ii) the form of equation (15) remains unaltered, but the coefficients of x_t and x_{t-1} change. While McCallum (1976) begins with such an assumption about what is known when forecasts are made, some of his empirical results lead him to suggest "that current values of exogenous variables should perhaps be excluded . . . as market participants may not possess information on such values when forming expectations."

D. *Dynamic Complications: Lagged Variables*

The second modification to the basic model is to allow lagged values of the various endogenous to enter, as a result of dynamic adjustment problems, timing considerations, and so forth. We use the formulation (7), appropriately extended, and so write

$$B(L)y_t + Ay^*_t + \Gamma(L)x_t = u_t, \qquad (19)$$

where

$$B(L) = B_0 + B_1 L + \cdots + B_r L^r, \qquad \Gamma(L) = \Gamma_0 + \Gamma_1 L + \cdots + \Gamma_s L^s.$$

Taking conditional expectations and assuming nonautocorrelated disturbances as before, we obtain

$$y^*_t = -(B_0 + A)^{-1} E[\{\Gamma(L)x_t + B_1 y_{t-1} + \cdots + B_r y_{t-r}\} | \Omega_{t-1}].$$

The relevant information set now includes the past values of the endogenous variables; thus the only variable in the braces which needs to be forecast is x_t, and we have

$$y^*_t = -(B_0 + A)^{-1}\{\Gamma_0 \widehat{x}_t + \Gamma_1 x_{t-1} \\ + \cdots + \Gamma_s x_{t-s} + B_1 y_{t-1} + \cdots + B_r y_{t-r}\}. \qquad (20)$$

This modifies equation (8) by adding to the previous expression for y_t^* all predetermined variables in the model, appropriately weighted. Note that (20) is quite specific about the variables that appear; the maximum lags of variables are the same as in the structural form (19) and if a particular endogenous variable does not appear lagged in (19) then it does not appear at all in (20). Similarly the observable reduced form (5) is augmented by the same lagged variables that are introduced in (19). Again the error in the rational expectation depends solely on the unanticipated part of the current exogenous variables, together with the current disturbances:

$$y_t - y_t^* = -B_0^{-1}\Gamma_0(x_t - \hat{x}_t) + B_0^{-1}u_t.$$

To examine the impact of the rational expectations hypothesis on the stability of the model, we substitute the expression (20) for y_t^* into (19) and collect together the terms involving the endogenous variables. These are

$$B(L)y_t - A(B_0 + A)^{-1}\{B_1 y_{t-1} + \cdots + B_r y_{t-r}\}$$
$$= B_0 y_t + B_0(B_0 + A)^{-1}\{B_1 y_{t-1} + \cdots + B_r y_{t-r}\};$$

hence the model is stable provided that all roots of

$$|(B_0 + A) + B_1 z + \cdots + B_r z^r| = 0$$

lie outside the unit circle. The stability condition for the model without rational expectations depends on the roots of $|B(z)|$, so the only change is in the constant term of the matrix polynomial. While a general description of the impact of the introduction of rational expectations on the roots of the determinantal polynomial is not possible, it is clear that for A sufficiently close to $-B_0$, a model which appears stable if expectation formation is assumed to be exogenous can in fact be unstable.[4] On the other hand it is quite possible for a model that appears unstable according to the conventional condition to be stable under rational expectations.

II. Identification and Estimation

A. Identification

We first consider the basic model of Section IA, with structural form

$$By_t + A_1 y_{1t}^* + \Gamma x_t = u_t$$

and reduced form

$$y_{1t} = \Pi_{11} y_{1t}^* + \Pi_{12} x_t + v_{1t},$$
$$y_{2t} = \Pi_{21} y_{1t}^* + \Pi_{22} x_t + v_{2t}.$$

[4]A simple illustration is obtained by modifying our example of Section IB so that the lagged value of y_1, instead of the current value, appears in the second structural equation. Then the conventional stability condition, ignoring the expectations process, is $|\beta_{12}\beta_{21}| < 1$, but even if this is true the model will be unstable under rational expectations if $|1 + \alpha| < |\beta_{12}\beta_{21}|$, i.e., if α is sufficiently close to -1.

The nonobservability of y_{1t}^* is overcome by the rational expectations hypothesis

$$y_{1t}^* = (I - \Pi_{11})^{-1}\Pi_{12}\widehat{x}_t,$$

and equation (5) again gives the observable reduced form:

$$y_t = P(\widehat{x}_t' : x_t')' + v_t \tag{21}$$

where

$$P = \begin{bmatrix} P_{11} & P_{12} \\ P_{21} & P_{22} \end{bmatrix} = \begin{bmatrix} \Pi_{11}(I - \Pi_{11})^{-1}\Pi_{12} & \Pi_{12} \\ \Pi_{21}(I - \Pi_{11})^{-1}\Pi_{12} & \Pi_{22} \end{bmatrix}. \tag{22}$$

By treating $\widehat{x}_t$ as observable, this formulation incorporates the implication of the rational expectations hypothesis that lagged x values enter in a way dictated by the optimal forecasting equations corresponding to the given x structure. Other possibilities are discussed below.

It is assumed that interest lies in estimating the parameters of the structural form, and we consider the case in which the identification restrictions take the form of knowing specific elements of B, A_1, and Γ. Let δ be a column vector consisting of those elements of B, A_1, and Γ that are *not* known a priori, assumed to be r in number, and let ρ be the $2gk$-dimensional vector of the elements of P. Then the condition for at least local identifiability of the structural parameters is that the matrix of first partial derivatives $H = \partial\rho/\partial\delta$ has rank r (see, e.g., Rothenberg 1973). Using the matrix differentiation conventions and theorems given by Neudecker (1969), and defining $\pi = \text{vec}(\Pi')$, we have

$$H = \frac{\partial\rho}{\partial\delta} = \frac{\partial\pi}{\partial\delta} \cdot \frac{\partial\rho}{\partial\pi}.$$

The $r \times g(h + k)$ matrix appearing as the first factor on the right-hand side arises in the usual consideration of the identification of structural parameters given Π (it is the transpose of Rothenberg's H_{11}) and has rank r if the conventional rank and order conditions for structure identification are satisfied. To evaluate the second factor it is convenient to form π by taking vec (Π_{11}'), vec (Π_{12}'), . . . in turn (and ρ likewise), then by differentiating the relations (22) we find that the $g(h + k) \times 2gk$ matrix $\partial\rho/\partial\pi$ is given as

$$\begin{bmatrix} (I - \Pi_{11}')^{-1} \otimes (I - \Pi_{11})^{-1}\Pi_{12} & 0 & (I - \Pi_{11}')^{-1}\Pi_{21}' \otimes (I - \Pi_{11})^{-1}\Pi_{12} & 0 \\ (I - \Pi_{11}')^{-1}\Pi_{11}' \otimes I_k & I_{hk} & (I - \Pi_{11}')^{-1}\Pi_{21}' \otimes I_k & 0 \\ 0 & 0 & I_{g-h} \otimes (I - \Pi_{11})^{-1}\Pi_{12} & 0 \\ 0 & 0 & 0 & I_{(g-h)k} \end{bmatrix}.$$

The condition that this matrix be of rank $g(h + k)$ is in effect a condition for the identification of the elements of Π given no other information but P. A necessary condition is that the matrix must have at least $g(h + k)$ columns, that is $k \geqslant h$, so that there are no more expectations variables than exogenous variables in the model. To derive a rank condition for identifiability we first note that a simple permutation yields a block-triangular matrix; hence the rank of the matrix is equal to the sum of the ranks of the diagonal blocks. Recalling also that the rank of a Kronecker product is equal to the product of the ranks of the two factors, and retaining the assumption that the $h \times h$ matrix $(I - \Pi_{11})$ is of full rank, we obtain

$$\text{rank} \, (\partial \rho / \partial \pi) = gk + g \, \text{rank} \, (\Pi_{12}).$$

Thus the rank condition for the identification of Π given P is rank $(P_{12}) = h$,[5] which of course implies $h \leqslant k$.

With respect to the identification of the structural parameters given P, consider first the possibility that the structure is just-identified in the usual sense. Then $r = g(h + k)$, Π is unrestricted, and the requirement is again rank $(P_{12}) = h$: if $h = k$ we have an indirect least-squares type of situation while if $h < k$, P is subject to restrictions. We can also consider the extent to which a "shortage" of exogenous variables (an "excess" of expectational variables, $h > k$) can be traded off against overidentifying restrictions on the structure. Suppose that there are m of these, so that $r = g(h + k) - m$. Then a necessary condition for rank $(H) = r$ is

$$\text{rank} \, (\partial \rho / \partial \pi) = gk + g \, \text{rank} \, (P_{12}) = 2gk$$
$$\geqslant g(h + k) - m = r,$$

that is, $m \geqslant g(h - k)$, or each expectational variable over and above the number of exogenous variables should be matched by at least g overidentifying restrictions.

These results carry over to the model with lagged variables of Section ID in the same way that the standard identification results carry over to dynamic models,[6] with one additional complication. This concerns the possibility that a linear identity connects the predetermined variables in the observable reduced form, which would arise, if, for example, x_t obeys a p-order autoregression with $p \leqslant s$ so that $\hat{x}_t$ is a linear combination of lagged exogenous variables already in the model. To overcome this problem the forecast $\hat{x}_t$ should be a function of past x values not present in the model. The approach does not carry over to the model with future expectations of Section IC, since the observable reduced form is no longer a good starting point; nevertheless an order condition of the form $h \leqslant k$, counting in h each separate future value of an expected variable, remains relevant.

[5]For "almost all" matrices P_{12} in the usual sense (compare Malinvaud 1970, Sec. 18.3). However note that in the case of an overidentified structure and $h > k$, discussed below, it is not difficult to construct examples in which elements of P_{12} are identically zero.

[6]By which is meant that if the maximum lags of variables are known, each lagged value may be treated as a separate predetermined variable when rank and order conditions are applied, and if they are not known then extensions of the standard conditions such as those given by Hatanaka (1975) are needed.

B. System Estimation

We retain the specification for the exogenous variables given in (10), namely $\Phi(L)x_t = \Theta(L)\varepsilon_t$, and assume that the time series model is first estimated by an appropriate maximum likelihood procedure and that sufficient starting values are available to permit the calculation of the one-step forecasts $\widehat{x}_t$, $t = 1, \ldots, T$ (or that the sample period relevant to the basic model has been appropriately truncated). The estimation of the observable reduced form coefficients P is then a standard multivariate least-squares problem. Alternatives to the treatment of the constructed x forecasts as data are discussed below.

To estimate the reduced form coefficients Π in the case $h \leqslant k$, we form a vector π of the $n = g(h + k)$ elements and write the observable reduced form as

$$y_t = P(\pi)\overline{x}_t + v_t \qquad (t = 1, \ldots, T),$$

where $\overline{x}_t' = [\widehat{x}_t' \vdots x_t']$. This is an example of the multi-equation linear model in which elements of the coefficient matrix are continuous functions of a set of parameters π, considered by Sargan (1972).[7] If $h < k$, a test of the restrictions implicit in the construction of $P(\pi)$ amounts to a test of the rational expectations hypothesis in which the maintained hypothesis simply specifies a menu of variables and not a complete structural form. Assuming that the vectors v_t, $t = 1, \ldots, T$, are serially independent and normally distributed $N(0, \Omega_v)$, the first-order conditions for the concentrated likelihood function can be written

$$f_i(\pi) = -\text{tr}\left\{\Omega_v^{-1}(\pi)\left[\frac{Y'\overline{X}}{T} - P(\pi)\frac{\overline{X}'\overline{X}}{T}\right]\frac{\partial P'}{\partial \pi_i}\right\} = 0 \qquad (i = 1, \ldots, n),$$

where $\Omega_v(\pi) = [Y' - P(\pi)\overline{X}'][Y - \overline{X}P'(\pi)]/T$ and the $T \times g$ and $T \times 2k$ data matrices Y, $\overline{X}$ are given by $Y' = [y_1 \vdots \cdots \vdots y_T]$, $\overline{X}' = [\overline{x}_1 \vdots \cdots \vdots \overline{x}_T]$. Sargan describes the following gradient maximization procedure, which has been found to work well in practice. Writing π_κ for the value of π at the κth iteration and $\Delta \pi_i = \pi_{i,\kappa+1} - \pi_{i,\kappa}$, the iteration is

$$\sum_{j=1}^{n} L_{ij}(\pi_\kappa)\Delta \pi_j + \lambda f_i(\pi_\kappa) = 0 \qquad (i = 1, \ldots, n),$$

where

$$L_{ij}(\pi) = \text{tr}\left[\Omega_v^{-1}(\pi)\frac{\partial P}{\partial \pi_j}\left(\frac{\overline{X}'\overline{X}}{T}\right)\frac{\partial P'}{\partial \pi_i}\right].$$

---

[7]A simple example is the "unobservable independent variables" model of Zellner (1970). Maximum likelihood estimation of such models is considered by Goldberger (1972), whose procedure amounts to a slightly different iteration than that presented below. What distinguishes the present model from "multiple-indicator, multiple-cause" models is the particular structure for the unobserved (expectations) variables implied by the rational expectations hypothesis, involving nonlinear, cross-equation parameter restrictions.

For structural estimation it is convenient notationally to use the square matrix A and write the model as in (7), viz., $By_t + Ay_t^* + \Gamma x_t = u_t$. It is assumed that this structural form satisfies the identification conditions discussed above. The rational expectation of y_t is given by (8) and the system in terms of observable variables is

$$By_t - A(B + A)^{-1}\Gamma\widehat{x_t} + \Gamma x_t = u_t \qquad (t = 1, \ldots, T). \quad (23)$$

Placing the unknown elements of the matrices B, A, and Γ into a vector δ the model can be written compactly as $\Lambda(\delta)z_t = u_t$ where $z_t' = [y_t' \vdots \widehat{x_t'} \vdots x_t']$ and $\Lambda(\delta) = [B \vdots -A(B + A)^{-1}\Gamma \vdots \Gamma]$. This is again a form considered by Sargan (1972), although slightly simpler than his general case since our endogenous variable coefficient matrix involves no nonlinearities. Assuming that the vectors u_t, $t = 1, \ldots, T$, are serially independent and normally distributed $N(0, \Omega_u)$, the log-likelihood function concentrated with respect to Ω_u is

$$T \log|\det B| - \tfrac{1}{2}T \log \det [\Lambda(\delta)Z'Z\Lambda'(\delta)],$$

where $Z = [Y \vdots \overline{X}]$ is the $T \times (g + 2k)$ data matrix. Differentiating with respect to δ_i gives the first-order condition

$$T \operatorname{tr}\left[(B')^{-1}\frac{\partial B}{\partial \delta_i}\right] - T \operatorname{tr}\left[\Omega_u^{-1}(\delta)\Lambda(\delta)\left(\frac{Z'Z}{T}\right)\frac{\partial \Lambda'}{\partial \delta_i}\right] = 0$$

where $\Omega_u(\delta) = \Lambda(\delta)(Z'Z/T)\Lambda'(\delta)$. This can also be written

$$-T \operatorname{tr}\left[\Omega_u^{-1}(\delta)\Lambda(\delta)\left(\frac{Z'\widehat{Z}}{T}\right)\frac{\partial \Lambda'}{\partial \delta_i}\right] = 0$$

where $\widehat{Z} = [\widehat{Y} \vdots \overline{X}]$ and $B\widehat{Y}' = A(B + A)^{-1}\Gamma\widehat{X}' - \Gamma X'$.

Experience in solving FIML problems of this kind through a variety of numerical optimization procedures is described by Sargan and Sylwestrowicz (1976). The computer program includes a subroutine which differentiates analytically rational functions $\lambda_{ij}(\delta)$ of any order; alternatively in the present context the elements of $\partial \Lambda'/\partial \delta_i$ can be obtained from matrix derivatives given, for example, by Dwyer (1967).

The use of the constructed $\widehat{x}$ series as data treats the parameters of the exogenous process as given, but if this is not correct the estimated variance-covariance matrix of the model's parameter estimates obtained at the final iteration will be subject to a common error in two-step-type procedures, namely that of treating as known in the second step a parameter that has in fact been estimated in the first step. To avoid this the parameters of the model and the exogenous process may be estimated jointly, by substituting in (21) or (23) the expression (11) for $\widehat{x}_t$ and adjoining the vector ARMA model (10), then estimating the $(g + k)$-equation system by an appropriate algorithm as already discussed. (Separate estimates of the x process and the model as described above would provide convenient start-

ing values for this joint estimation.) This also achieves fully efficient estimates, since exploiting the parameter restrictions between the x process
and the y process gives an improvement despite the independence of ε_t
and u_t (or v_t).

The methods of this section are applicable to models containing lagged
variables, while the method of the previous paragraph is applicable to
models containing future expectations variables provided that the parameter restrictions resulting from the dependence of the rational expectations on the predictions of all future values of the exogenous variables and
the dependence in turn of such predictions on past values can be conveniently expressed. For example, to estimate the parameters of our simple
example as amended in section IC, with rational expectation given by (18)
and autoregressive x, the following three-equation system would be estimated:

$$y_{1t} + \beta_{12}y_{2t} - \frac{\alpha\gamma\beta_{12}\phi^2}{1 - \beta_{12}\beta_{21} - \alpha\phi}x_{t-1} = u_{1t},$$

$$\beta_{21}y_{1t} + y_{2t} + \gamma x_t = u_{2t},$$

$$x_t = \phi x_{t-1} + \varepsilon_t.$$

C. Limited-Information Methods

Under the limited-information heading we include single-equation estimation methods and other procedures that make less than the maximum
possible use of the restrictions implied by the rational expectations hypothesis: some of these procedures will be seen to be applicable to complete systems.

First, we assume that interest centers on estimating the parameters of
the first equation of the structural form, namely

$$\beta_1 y_t + \alpha_1 y_t^* + \gamma_1 x_t = u_{1t}, \tag{24}$$

where β_1, α_1, and γ_1 are the first rows of B, A, and Γ, respectively, and
together contain no more than $h + k$ unknown elements. The rational
expectations variables are given by

$$y_t^* = -(B + A)^{-1}\Gamma\widehat{x_t} \quad \text{or} \quad y_{1t}^* = (I - \Pi_{11})^{-1}\Pi_{12}\widehat{x_t}, \tag{25}$$

but in the absence of knowledge of the remainder of the system it is not
possible to specify the weights with which the elements of $\widehat{x_t}$ appear. However, substituting $x_t = \widehat{x_t} + \varepsilon_t$ into the observable reduced form gives

$$\begin{aligned}
y_{1t} &= \Pi_{11}(I - \Pi_{11})^{-1}\Pi_{12}\widehat{x_t} + \Pi_{12}(\widehat{x_t} + \varepsilon_t) + v_{1t} \\
&= (I - \Pi_{11})^{-1}\Pi_{12}\widehat{x_t} + (\Pi_{12}\varepsilon_t + v_{1t}),
\end{aligned} \tag{26}$$

hence a set of h least-squares regressions of the elements of y_{1t} on $\widehat{x_t}$ yields
consistent estimates of the coefficients in (25). Again, if it is unrealistic to

treat the $\hat{x}$ series as given, the expression (11) may be substituted for $\hat{x}_t$ in (26), which may then be estimated jointly with the vector ARMA model (10). The resulting regression estimates $\hat{y}^*_{1t}$ can then be substituted into (24), and treated as predetermined variables. If (24) is to be estimated by two-stage least squares, then the first stage comprises estimation of certain equations of the reduced form (3), where once more $\hat{y}^*_{1t}$ replaces y^*_{1t}. The error $y^*_{1t} - \hat{y}^*_{1t}$ comprises coefficient estimation error, which in turn involves the disturbances ε_t and v_{1t}, but this does not deny the consistency of the final parameter estimates, by an argument analogous to the standard proof of consistency of 2SLS.

Although this procedure is based on consistent estimates of the rational expectation coefficients, it does not provide a test of the rational expectations hypothesis, since having estimated but a single structural equation or reduced form equation the restrictions on the rational expectations coefficients cannot be checked. A restriction that has been imposed so far is that past information on the exogenous variables is used optimally. This can be relaxed by replacing $\hat{x}_t$ in (26) by past values of x_t, and no longer estimating jointly with the x process.[8] If the correct distributed lag formulations are employed, as given by the forecasting equations, then estimation using past x values will provide a better fit than that based on calculated $\hat{x}$ values or subject to restrictions, though the difference will not be significant if the optimality hypothesis is correct. In practice one would expect the distributed lag specifications to be determined empirically, nevertheless the agreement (or lack thereof) with the forecasting equations determined by separate time series analyses of the exogenous variables could then be checked. Although such regression-based proxies incorporate neither the rational expectations coefficient restrictions nor those implied by optimal forecasting of exogenous variables, they are consistent with the model to the extent that the correct (and complete) set of exogenous variables is employed.

Possibly as a result of Muth's initial special case, one might consider the use of extrapolative forecasts of endogenous variables. It is then necessary to heed Nelson's (1975b) warning that a purely extrapolative predictor is an inadequate proxy for a rational expectations variable. As shown in Section IA, a univariate ARMA representation for each endogenous variable can always be derived, providing a purely extrapolative predictor y^{**}_{it}, and the one-step forecast error $\eta_{it} = y_{it} - y^{**}_{it}$ can be written, from (14) as

$$\eta_{it} = \left\{ \sum_{j=1}^{k} \xi_{0j}\varepsilon_{jt} + v_{it} \right\} + \left\{ \sum_{j=1}^{k}\sum_{l=1}^{\infty} w_{jl}\varepsilon_{j,t-1} + \sum_{l=1}^{\infty} w_{k+1,l}v_{i,t-l} \right\}. \quad (27)$$

[8] Such regression-based proxies for the expectations variables are employed by Sargent (1973, 1976).

The first expression in braces is equal to $y_{it} - y_{it}^*$, hence the second expression in braces represents the difference between the rational expectation and extrapolative prediction of y_{it}. This term is added to the disturbance term in (24) when y_{it}^{**} is substituted for y_{it}^*, and through its correlation with the exogenous variables removes the consistency of conventional estimators applied to (24). This argument applies equally to a reduced form equation. In the event that (24) contains more than one endogenous variable, fewer than $g - 1$ zero restrictions being imposed on β_1, instrumental variable or 2SLS procedures are further invalidated by the replacement of y_{it}^* by y_{it}^{**}, as Nelson points out, since the potential instruments (exogenous variables) are now correlated with the composite disturbance term.

McCallum's (1976b) answer to these difficulties is to use as a proxy for the expectations variable y_{it}^* not y_{it}^{**} but the actual value y_{it}, and then to use y_{it}^{**} as the associated instrumental variable. Substituting y_{it} for y_{it}^* augments the disturbance term by the first expression in braces in (27), but this is not correlated with y_{it}^{**}, which is thereby a valid instrument. It is correlated with x_t, however, so further instruments are required and McCallum proposes the use of lagged exogenous variables x_{t-1}. Note, however, that the applicability of this procedure is limited to equations which do not simultaneously contain an endogenous variable and its own rational expectation. This difficulty does not arise in McCallum's discussion of Nelson's example, in which y_{2t}^* but not y_{2t} appears in the equation for y_{1t}. However, the substitution might still cause loss of identification, as when the Nelson-McCallum example is regarded as the first equation of the following just-identified two-equation system:

$$\begin{bmatrix} 1 & 0 \\ \beta & 1 \end{bmatrix} \begin{bmatrix} y_{1t} \\ y_{2t} \end{bmatrix} + \begin{bmatrix} \alpha & \gamma_1 \\ 0 & \gamma_2 \end{bmatrix} \begin{bmatrix} y_{2t}^* \\ x_t \end{bmatrix} = \begin{bmatrix} u_{1t} \\ u_{2t} \end{bmatrix}.$$

Clearly the use of actual values as proxies for rational expectations is not restricted to single equations (but may be subject to further identifiability problems in larger systems), and can also be applied when future expectations enter the model, as in McCallum's (1976a) empirical work. In effect the only information about the rational expectation now being employed is that it is unbiased, but its further properties clearly influence the choice of instrumental variables. As a consequence of the result on comparative forecast variance given in Section IA, the rational expectation is a more efficient instrumental variable than the extrapolative predictor, and although it cannot be fully implemented in this limited information context, taking account of its dependence on the past values of specific variables (and possibly with those past values entering in a specific way) when constructing instruments could be expected to lead to an improvement.

III. Economic Policy

A. The Effects of Policy Variables

We now extend the exogenous variable specification to include the possibility that certain variables are policy instruments under the control of economic policy makers. Writing

$$x_t = G(\Omega_{t-1}) + \varepsilon_t, \tag{28}$$

where Ω_{t-1} denotes information about the values of *all* variables available as of time $t - 1$, allows such policy instruments to be determined by feedback control rules, possibly with a superimposed random element. The relation

$$y_t - y_t^* = -B^{-1}\Gamma(x_t - \widehat{x}_t) + B^{-1}u_t \tag{29}$$

holds for the basic model of Section IA and its subsequent extensions, and states that only unanticipated movements in exogenous variables (or disturbances) cause endogenous variables to diverge from their previously expected values. Thus if the public has the same information as the policymaker including knowledge of $G(\cdot)$, so that $\widehat{x}_t = G(\Omega_{t-1})$, then there is no choice of $G(\cdot)$, i.e., no feedback rule, that permits the policymaker to offset expected movements in endogenous ("target") variables. Of course the policy in general affects the actual realized values of the endogenous variables, but the effect is fully anticipated unless the policy contains surprise or random elements, ε_t. From (8) and (9) we have

$$y_t = -(B + A)^{-1}\Gamma G(\Omega_{t-1}) - B^{-1}\Gamma\varepsilon_t + v_t. \tag{30}$$

The conventional view that, for example, under fixed exchange rates a devaluation must be sprung as a surprise, and that perfect foresight would frustrate the policy, is then presumably based on the relative signs and magnitudes of coefficients of ε_t and $G(\Omega_{t-1})$ in (30).

Special cases arise when for key endogenous variables the coefficients of certain policy variables $G(\cdot)$ are zero, as in macroeconomic models constructed so that output is independent of the particular deterministic money supply rule in effect, such as that of Sargent and Wallace (1975). A feature of such models is behavioral relations giving one endogenous variable (output, employment) in terms of the forecast errors in another (prices, wages); compare also the aggregate supply function of Lucas (1972), and note that the restriction that the variables y_{jt} and y_{jt}^* enter a given equation with coefficients that are equal but opposite in sign can clearly be tested following estimation as in Section II. In the present framework suppose that we can rearrange equations and variables so that in the first g_1 structural equations the last g_2 variables y_{2t} and y_{2t}^* either appear with equal and opposite coefficients or do not appear at all $(g_1 + g_2 = g)$. Then $(B + A)$ is block-lower-triangular and so is its inverse. If given policy instruments do not appear in these g_1 equations, the corresponding elements of Γ being zero (as is true of the Lucas–Sargent–Wallace models), then the systematic part of policy has no effect on the first g_1 endogenous variables, since the relevant elements of $(B + A)^{-1}\Gamma$ in (30) are zero.[9]

B. Econometric Policy Evaluation

The conventional approach to the quantitative evaluation of alternative economic policies is to take an estimated macroeconometric model and examine the implied behavior of the endogenous variables under alternative specifications of the future values of policy instruments (exogenous variables.)[10] Lucas (1976) criticizes such comparisons of alternative policy rules on the grounds that the "structure" of econometric models is not invariant to changes in policy. The elements of such models are behavioral relationships derived from optimal decision rules of economic agents, which are based in part on the agents' views of the future movements of relevant variables. Changes in the nature of these movements cause changes in the optimal decision rules, hence "any change in policy will systematically alter the structure of econometric models" (Lucas 1976, p. 41). This criticism also applies to ex post analysis of the effectiveness of an actual policy, where the procedure is first to estimate a model using data for periods when the policy was not in operation and then to compare its predictions for the periods when the policy was applied with either the actual outcomes or the predictions of a model estimated for the policy period. For such comparisons to be meaningful, it is necessary to assume that the nature of the economic system's response is unaltered when substantially different movements in key variables occur, movements which are such as to cause the policymakers to act.[11]

In the linear model context used throughout this paper, the force of the Lucas criticism and the nature of a practical response can be seen by

[9]The reassertion of the potential of monetary policy to stabilize fluctuations in output and employment by Phelps and Taylor (1977) rests on a model in which firms "set their prices and wage rates *1 period in advance* of the period over which they will apply, hence before the central bank decides on the money supply for that (latter) period"; thus the policymakers have a larger information set available to them. Likewise, Fischer's (1977) model in which labor contracts are made for *two* periods at a time also admits monetary policy effects on the short-run behavior of output. As discussed in Section IC, data are unlikely to be informative about the details of such timing relationships, so that when these models are implemented empirically, it will be necessary to give careful prior consideration to the relevant institutional and informational arrangements and decision sequences.

[10]Descriptions of the general procedure and its applications are contained in my survey article and lecture course (Wallis 1969, 1973), but pay no attention to the criticism to be discussed below.

[11]Such endogenization of policy may invalidate tests of structural change across policy regimes, since a division of a sample period into policy regimes is not arbitrary but is related to the behavior of key variables (Wallis 1972).

comparing the approaches of Sections I and II. The basic model of Section IA demonstrates the source of the distributed lag function relating endogenous to exogenous variables and the fact that the stochastic structure of the exogenous variables determines the nature of the distributed lag. Any change in the behavior of the exogenous variables perceived by economic agents changes these distributed lags, hence "old" lag functions do not provide an appropriate description of behavior in response to "new" exogenous shocks. However the focus of attention in estimation is the system (1) (or [17] or [19]), which is taken to represent the optimal decision rules of economic agents prior to the insertion of specific forecasting procedures, and the structure incorporating the rational expectations hypothesis *is* invariant to changes in the behavior of exogenous variables, since the parameters of, say, (21) or (23) do not depend on such behavior. To carry out policy evaluation in this framework it is then necessary to postulate a new *x* process and associated forecasts, and evaluate its impact on the endogenous variables using the estimated structure.

The difficulty in the usual approach is that data-based distributed lags confuse two separate aspects, namely economic optimization procedures and forecasting procedures, and the effect of a required change in the latter on the lag function cannot be perceived without separating the two components. Distinguishing an underlying economic structure, albeit one incorporating the rational expectations hypothesis, from a forecasting scheme relevant for particular exogenous or policy processes and changing when they do, then permits policy evaluation to proceed. In effect, keeping the "structure" of exogenous processes separate from the economic structure allows the traditional view of econometric policy evaluation to be reasserted. Moreover the cases we have considered amount to those of prediction under unchanged structure, providing the simpler case in which knowledge of the reduced form but not the structural form is usually held to be sufficient.

References

Barro, R. J., and Fischer, S. "Recent Developments in Monetary Theory." *J. Monetary Econ.* 2 (1976): 133–67.
Box, G. E. P., and Jenkins, G. M. *Time Series Analysis, Forecasting, and Control.* San Francisco: Holden-Day, 1970.
Chan, W. Y. T., and Wallis, K. F. "Multiple Time Series Modelling: Another Look at the Mink-Muskrat Interaction." *Appl. Statis.* 27 (1978): 168–75.
Dwyer, P. S. "Some Applications of Matrix Derivatives in Multivariate Analysis." *J. American Statis. Assoc.* 62 (1967): 607–25.
Fischer, S. "Long-term Contracts, Rational Expectations, and the Optimal Money Supply Rule." *J.P.E.* 85 (1977): 191–205.
Goldberger, A. S. "Maximum-likelihood Estimation of Regressions Containing Unobservable Independent Variables." *Internat. Econ. Rev.* 13 (1972): 1–15.
Granger, C. W. J., and Morris, M. J. "Time Series Modelling and Interpretation." *J. Royal Statis. Soc.* A, 139 (1976): 246–57.

Granger, C. W. J., and Newbold, P. *Forecasting Economic Time Series.* New York: Academic Press, 1977.

Hatanaka, M. "On the Global Identification of the Dynamic Simultaneous Equations Model with Stationary Disturbances." *Internat. Econ. Rev.* 16 (1975): 545–54.

Lucas, R. E., Jr. "Econometric Testing of the Natural Rate Hypothesis." In *The Econometrics of Price Determination Conference,* edited by O. Eckstein. Washington: Federal Reserve System, 1972.

———. "Econometric Policy Evaluation: A Critique." In *The Phillips Curve and Labor Markets,* edited by K. Brunner and A. H. Meltzer. Amsterdam: North-Holland, 1976. Carnegie-Rochester Conference Series on Public Policy no. 1, suppl. to *J. Monetary Econ.* (January 1976).

Malinvaud, E. *Statistical Methods of Econometrics,* 2d ed. Amsterdam: North-Holland, 1970.

McCallum, B. T. "Rational Expectations and the Natural Rate Hypothesis: Some Consistent Estimates." *Econometrica* 44 (1976): 43–52 (a)

———. "Rational Expectations and the Estimation of Econometric Models: An Alternative Procedure." *Internat. Econ. Rev.* 17 (1976): 484–90. (b)

Muth, J. F. "Rational Expectations and the Theory of Price Movements." *Econometrica* 29 (1961): 315–35.

Nelson, C. R. "Time Series Forecasting and Economic Models." Manuscript, Univ. Chicago, 1969.

———. "Rational Expectations and the Estimation of Econometric Models." *Internat. Econ. Rev.* 16 (1975): 555–61. (b)

Neudecker, H. "Some Theorems on Matrix Differentiation with Special Reference to Kronecker Matrix Products." *J. American Statis. Assoc.* 64 (1969): 953–63.

Phelps, E. S., and Taylor, J. B. "Stabilizing Power of Monetary Policy under Rational Expectations." *J.P.E.* 85 (1977): 163–90.

Pierce, D. A. "Forecasting in Dynamic Models with Stochastic Regressors." *J. Econometrics* 3 (1975): 349–74.

Poole, W. "Rational Expectations in the Macro Model." *Brookings Papers on Econ. Activity* (1976), pp. 463–505.

Rothenberg, T. J. *Efficient Estimation with A Priori Information.* New Haven: Yale Univ. Press, 1973. (Cowles Foundation Monograph 23.)

Sargan, J. D. "The Identification and Estimation of Sets of Simultaneous Stochastic Equations." Manuscript, London School of Econ., 1972.

Sargan, J. D., and Sylwestrowicz, J. D. "A Comparison of Alternative Methods of Numerical Optimisation in Estimating Simultaneous Equation Econometric Models." Manuscript, London School of Econ., 1976.

Sargent, T. J. "Rational Expectations, the Real Rate of Interest, and the Natural Rate of Unemployment." *Brookings Papers on Econ. Activity* (1973), pp. 429–72.

———. "A Classical Macroeconometric Model for the United States." *J.P.E.* 84 (1976): 207–37.

Sargent, T. J., and Wallace, N. "'Rational' Expectations, the Optimal Monetary Instrument, and the Optimal Money Supply Rule." *J.P.E.* 83 (1975): 241–54.

Shiller, R. J. "Rational Expectations and the Dynamic Structure of Macroeconomic Models." *J. Monetary Econ.* 4 (1978): 1–44.

Sims, C. A. "Distributed Lags." In *Frontiers of Quantitative Economics,* vol. 2, edited by M. D. Intriligator and D. A. Kendrick. Amsterdam: North-Holland, 1974.

Tobin, J. "The Wage-Price Mechanism: Overview of the Conference." In *The Econometrics of Price Determination Conference,* edited by O. Eckstein. Washington: Federal Reserve System, 1972.

Wallis, K. F. "Some Recent Developments in Applied Econometrics: Dynamic Models and Simultaneous Equation Systems." *J. Econ. Literature* 7 (1969): 771–96.

———. "Wages, Prices, and Incomes Policies: Some Comments." *Economica* 38 (1971): 304–10. Reprinted in *Incomes Policy and Inflation,* edited by M. Parkin and M. T. Sumner. Manchester: Manchester Univ. Press, 1972.

———. *Topics in Applied Econometrics.* Oxford: Blackwell, 1973.

Zellner, A. "Estimation of Regression Relationships Containing Unobservable Independent Variables." *Internat. Econ. Rev.* 11 (1970): 441–54.

19

Estimation of Rational Expectations Models

Gregory C. Chow

This paper considers the estimation of linear rational expectations models when the objective function of the decision maker is quadratic. It presents methods for maximum likelihood estimation in the general case and in a special case when the decision maker's action is assumed to have no effect on the environment (as under perfect competition). It proposes a family of consistent estimators for the general case. It also comments on the assumptions of rational expectations models, and extends the above methods to estimating nonlinear models.

In an optimal control problem where the model is linear

$$y_t = Ay_{t-1} + Cx_t + b + u_t \tag{1}$$

and the objective function to be maximized is quadratic

$$-E_o \sum_{t=1}^{T} (y_t - a_t)'K_t(y_t - a_t), \tag{2}$$

the optimal feedback rule for the vector x_t of the control variables is linear in the state variables y_{t-1} (see Chow 1975),

$$x_t = G_t y_{t-1} + g_t. \tag{3}$$

In this paper, we assume $K_t = \beta^t K$ and $a_t = \phi^t a$, β being a discount factor and ϕ being a diagonal matrix, with some diagonal elements known to be unity if the targets in a_t are time-invariant. We will be concerned with the estimation of the parameters β, K, ϕ, and a in the objective function and the parameters A, C, and b of the model, using data on (y_t, x_t).

In the literature of macroeconomic policy analysis following the tradition of Theil (1958) and Friedlander (1973), this note would be entitled the estimation of government preference functions in policy optimization

I would like to acknowledge financial support from the National Science Foundation through grant no. SOC77-07677.

[*Journal of Economic Dynamics and Control*, 1980, vol. 2]

problems. Its present title is motivated by the more recent literature on macroeconomic modeling and analysis which has been stimulated by the works of Muth (1961) and Lucas (1976), and further extended by Sargent (1978, 1979), Hansen and Sargent (1980), and Taylor (1979), among others. Consider economic agents (firms, households) facing a stochastic environment described by (1) and having an objective function (2). They are assumed to derive their behavioral equations (the demand equations for inputs, the consumption functions, etc.) given by (3) through the maximization of (2) subject to the constraint (1). Under the assumption of rational expectations, the econometrician shares the same functions (1) and (2) with the economic agents. The econometrician's problem is to estimate (1) and (2) by observing the data on x_t and y_t. It is important to estimate the parameters of (2) because, as Lucas (1976) has pointed out, when the government's policy rule changes, the environment (1) facing the private economic agents will change. In order to predict the latter's behavior as given by their new optimal feedback control equation (3), knowledge of the parameters of (2) is required; equation (3) will be rederived by the maximization of (2) given the new environment (1).

This paper presents methods for the maximum likelihood estimation of linear rational expectations models just described, covering the general case and the special case when the agent's action x_t does not affect the economic environment as in the model of perfect competition. The special case is exemplified by the models used by Sargent (1978, 1979) and by Hansen and Sargent (1980). We obtain explicit expressions for the coefficients in the agent's behavioral equation (3) in terms of the parameters of (1) and (2) using the known results on stochastic control theory in Chow (1975). To ease the computations in the general case, we propose a family of consistent estimators which are analogous to the methods of limited-information maximum likelihood and two-stage least squares for the estimation of linear simultaneous equations. In this paper, we will frequently be interested in estimating the parameters when the coefficient matrix G_t in (3) reaches a steady state G. The results will be extended to estimating nonlinear models.

I. Maximum Likelihood Estimation in the General Case

Our problem is to estimate the parameters of (1) and (2) using observations on y_t and x_t. It is understood that a system involving high-order autoregressive and moving average processes can be written in the form (1) where u_t are serially uncorrelated and identically distributed, as is done in Chow (1975). If one is willing to add a random residual to (3) and assume a multivariate normal distribution for this residual and u_t, the likelihood function based on (1) and (3) is well-known. It has A, C, b, G_t, g_t, and the covariance matrix of the residuals as arguments. If (1) is a set of reduced-form equations derived from a system of linear simultaneous structural equations, the parameters A, C, b, and the covariance matrix of u_t will be replaced by the corresponding structural parameters as arguments in the likelihood function.

What makes our problem different from the standard problem of estimating the parameters of a system of linear structural equations is that we need to maximize the likelihood function with respect to the parameters, β, K, ϕ, and a of the objective function (with $K_t = \beta^t K$ and $a_t = \phi^t a$) instead of the coefficients G_t and g_t in the behavioral equation (3). To apply any gradient or conjugate gradient method for maximization (see Goldfeld and Quandt 1972), it is first required to evaluate the likelihood function in terms of the parameters A, C, b, β, K, ϕ, and a (after the covariance matrix of the residuals has been concentrated out), where A, C, and b will further be written as functions of the coefficients of the structural equations if necessary. The problem then boils down to the convenient expression of G_t and g_t as functions of A, C, b, β, K, ϕ, and a.

The coefficients of (3) as solution to the optimal control problem (1)–(2) are given in Chow (1975, pp. 178–79):

$$G_t = -(C'H_tC)^{-1}C'H_tA \tag{4}$$

$$H_t = K_t + (A + CG_{t+1})'H_{t+1}(A + CG_{t+1}) \tag{5}$$

$$g_t = -(C'H_tC)^{-1}C'(H_tb_t - h_t) \tag{6}$$

$$h_t = K_ta_t + (A + CG_{t+1})'(h_{t+1} - H_{t+1}b_{t+1}) \tag{7}$$

with conditions $H_{t+N} = K_{t+N} = \beta^N K_t$ for (5) and $h_{t+N} = K_{t+N}a_{t+N} = K_{t+N}\phi^N a_t$ for (7) if the planning horizon is N. To compute G_t, we evaluate the right-hand sides of (4) and (5) backward in time starting from $t + N$, using the initial condition $H_{t+N} = \beta^N K_t$. Having completed these calculations, we compute g_t by evaluating the right-hand sides of (6) and (7) backward in time starting from $t + N$, using the initial condition $h_{t+N} = K_{t+N}\phi^N a_t$.

Even for fairly large N, these computations are inexpensive provided that the (symmetric) matrix H_t is not too large—say, with order less than 100. Some computational experience is recorded in Chow and Megdal (1978). The computations consist mainly of matrix multiplications. The matrix $C'H_tC$ to be inverted is of the same order as the number of control variables, which is very small as judged by the cost of matrix inversion using a modern computer. Furthermore, even if N is very large, experience shows that a steady-state solution for G_t and H_t from (4) and (5) is often reached after 4 or 5 time periods backward from $t + N$, as illustrated in Chow (1975, pp. 208, 270). Thus only several evaluations of (4) and (5) are required. If (4) and (5) do converge slowly, the model of rational expectations adopted to derive a steady-state G in equation (3) should itself be questioned. The failure for (4) and (5) to converge would mean that a rational expectations equilibrium does not exist for the behavior of the economic agent. A slow convergence means that the economic agent needs to plan many periods ahead under the questionable assumption of a constant economic structure for all future periods (the same matrices A and C being used in the calculations of [4] and [5] for all future periods). We thus argue that in practice the coefficients G and g_t in (3) can frequently be computed inexpensively from the parameters A, C, b, β, K, ϕ, and a.

Since the computation of G and g_t is only a first step (the step of evaluating the likelihood function) in the method of maximum likelihood, the second step being to maximize numerically, it would be very desirable if G could be expressed explicitly as a function of the parameters without resorting to repeated calculations of (4) and (5). In the next section, we treat a special case where this can be done. In the Appendix, we provide a method to maximize the likelihood function when $K_t = K$ and $a_t = a$.

II. Estimation When Environment Is Unaffected by Agent's Action

Let the environment be described by

$$\tilde{y}_t = A_1 \tilde{y}_{t-1} + \tilde{u}_t \tag{8}$$

which is not affected by the agent's action x_t. This special case includes the examples given by Sargent (1978, 1979) and Hansen and Sargent (1980). These references use an example of a firm trying to determine its optimal employment of an input while facing a set of stochastic difference equations (8) which explain the price of the input and a technological coefficient. To allow for the costs of the control variables and their changes, we introduce x_t and Δx_t as state variables in the objective function and write the model as

$$\begin{bmatrix} \tilde{y}_t \\ x_t \\ \Delta x_t \end{bmatrix} = \begin{bmatrix} A_1 & 0 & 0 \\ 0 & 0 & 0 \\ 0 & -I & 0 \end{bmatrix} \begin{bmatrix} \tilde{y}_{t-1} \\ x_{t-1} \\ \Delta x_{t-1} \end{bmatrix} + \begin{bmatrix} 0 \\ I \\ I \end{bmatrix} x_t + \begin{bmatrix} \tilde{u}_t \\ 0 \\ 0 \end{bmatrix} \tag{9}$$

which is a special case of (1) with

$$A = \begin{bmatrix} A_1 & 0 & 0 \\ 0 & 0 & 0 \\ 0 & -I & 0 \end{bmatrix}; \quad C = \begin{bmatrix} 0 \\ I \\ I \end{bmatrix}.$$

Note the special feature of the matrix C allowing for no effect of x_t on $\tilde{y}_t$.

The objective function is given by (2) with

$$K_t = \beta^t K = \beta^t \begin{bmatrix} K_{11} & K_{12} & 0 \\ K'_{12} & K_{22} & 0 \\ 0 & 0 & K_{33} \end{bmatrix}$$

where K_{22} and K_{33} are assumed to be diagonal, the former capturing increasing marginal costs of using the inputs x_t in the example on the demand for inputs, and the latter measuring the adjustment costs of changes in the inputs. We are concerned with the steady-state solution of (4) and (5), namely

$$G = -(C'HC)^{-1}C'HA \tag{10}$$

$$\begin{aligned} H &= K + \beta(A + CG)'H(A + CG) \\ &= K + \beta A'H(A + CG) \end{aligned} \tag{11}$$

where the second equality sign of (11) is due to (10).

Using equation (10) and the definitions for A and C, with (symmetric) H partitioned into 3×3 blocks corresponding to K, we have

$$G = -(H_{22} + H_{23} + H'_{23} + H_{33})^{-1}[(H'_{12} + H'_{13})A_1 \\ - (H_{23} + H_{33})0]. \tag{12}$$

Since A' has all zeros in its last row, so does $\beta A'H(A + CG)$. By equation (11) the last row of H equals the last row of K, that is,

$$H'_{13} = K'_{13} = 0; \ H'_{23} = K'_{23} = 0; \ H_{33} = K_{33}. \tag{13}$$

Using (13), we write (12) as

$$G = -(H_{22} + K_{33})^{-1}(H'_{12}A_1 - K_{33}0). \tag{14}$$

We need to find only H_{22} and H_{12} to evaluate G. Using (14) and letting $\theta = (H_{22} + K_{33})^{-1}$, we have

$$A'H(A + CG) = \begin{bmatrix} A'_1(H_{11} - H_{12}\theta H'_{12})A_1 & A'_1 H_{12}\theta K_{33} & 0 \\ K_{33}\theta H'_{12}A_1 & K_{33} - K_{33}\theta K_{33} & 0 \\ 0 & 0 & 0 \end{bmatrix}. \tag{15}$$

Equations (15) and (11) imply

$$H_{22} = K_{22} + \beta K_{33} - \beta K_{33}(H_{22} + K_{33})^{-1}K_{33} \tag{16}$$

$$H_{12} = K_{12} + \beta A'_1 H_{12}(H_{22} + K_{33})^{-1}K_{33}. \tag{17}$$

Since K_{22} and K_{33} are diagonal by assumption, a diagonal H_{22} is a solution of (16), with its ith diagonal element satisfying

$$\begin{aligned} &h_{22,i} = k_{22,i} + \beta k_{33,i} - \beta(k^2_{33,i})/(h_{22,i} + k_{33,i}) \quad \text{or} \\ &h^2_{22,i} - (k_{22,i} + k_{33,i}\beta - k_{33,i})h_{22,i} - k_{22,i}k_{33,i} = 0 \end{aligned} \tag{18}$$

which can be solved for $h_{22,i}$. We take the smaller root of the quadratic equation (18), since we wish to make $h_{22,i}$ as small as possible. The dynamic programming solution to the linear-quadratic control problem (see Chow 1975) transforms a multiperiod maximization problem into many one-period problems. For each period t, one minimizes the expectation of a quadratic function in y_t involving $y_t' H_t y_t$, $H_t \geq 0$. Hence H_{22} should be diagonal with small elements. Having obtained H_{22}, we use (17) to compute $H_{12} = (h_{12,ij})$. Denoting the diagonal matrix $(H_{22} + K_{33})^{-1} K_{33}$ by $D = \text{Diag}\{d_i\}$, and the elements of A_1 by a_{ij}, we have

$$h_{12,ij} = k_{12,ij} + \beta \sum_l a_{li} d_l h_{12,lj}. \tag{19}$$

The elements $h_{12,ij}$ in the jth column of H_{12} satisfy a set of linear equations (19). We have thus provided an explicit expression for G as a function of A_1, β, and K by using formulas (14), (18), and (19).

As an illustration for a scalar x_t consider the example of Sargent (1979, p. 335) and Hansen and Sargent (1980) where x_t (our notation) denotes the demand for an input labor; y_{1t} is technology which satisfies a qth order univariate autoregression

$$y_{1t} = a_{11} y_{1,t-1} + \cdots + a_{1q} y_{1,t-q} + u_{1t};$$

$y_{2t} = y_{1,t-1}, \ldots, y_{qt} = y_{q-1,t-1}$ are introduced to make the model first-order; and $y_{q+1,t}$ is the wage rate which satisfies an rth-order multivariate autoregression. This model can certainly be written as our equation (1).

The objective function is, for the current period 0,

$$E_0 \sum_{t=1}^T \beta^t \left[(\gamma_0 + y_{1,t} - y_{q+1,t}) x_t - \frac{\gamma_1}{2} x_t^2 - \frac{\delta}{2} (\Delta x_t)^2 \right]$$

where $\gamma_1 = K_{22}$ and $\delta = K_{33}$ in our notation, both being scalars. Equations (16) and (18) are identical for a scalar x_t. They become $h_{22}^2 - (\gamma_1 + \delta\beta - \delta)h_{22} - \gamma_1\delta = 0$, implying $h_{22} = 1/2[(\gamma_1 + \delta\beta - \delta) - \sqrt{(\gamma_1 + \delta\beta - \delta)^2 + 4\gamma_1\delta}]$. The matrix K_{12} becomes a column vector consisting of the coefficients of the products of x_t and y_{it} in the objective function. Since $H_{22} + K_{33}$ in (17) is the scalar $h_{22} + \delta$, we can write the solution of (17) as $H_{12} = [I - \beta\delta(h_{22} + \delta)^{-1} A_1']^{-1} K_{12}$.

The coefficient of x_{t-1} in the optimal feedback control equation (or a demand for labor equation) is $(H_{22} + K_{33})^{-1} K_{33}$ according to equation (14), or $\delta/(h_{22} + \delta)$. This result agrees with the coefficient obtained by Sargent (1979, p. 336) and Hansen and Sargent (1980) using classic (pre-1970) control techniques. Their coefficient ρ_1 is the inverse of the (smaller) root of the quadratic equation $\delta\beta - (\gamma_1 + \delta + \delta\beta)z + \delta z^2 = 0$.

The explicit solution of this section breaks down when the matrix C does not have a submatrix of zeroes, for then $(C'HC)^{-1}$ can no longer be written as $(H_{22} + K_{33})^{-1}$ as in (14) and one cannot solve an equation corresponding to (16) explicitly for the elements of H_{22} even if K_{22} is diagonal.

III. A Family of Consistent Estimators for the General Case

A family of consistent estimators is proposed for the general case. It is based on the observations that the least-squares estimator $\hat{G}$ of the coefficients G in the regression of x_t on y_{t-1} (which includes x_{t-1} as a subvector) is consistent, and that, if the rational expectations model is correct, G should satisfy equations (10) and (11). The situation is analogous to the estimation of structural parameters $(B\Gamma)$ in linear simultaneous equations by the use of the least-squares estimates $\widehat{\Pi}$ of the reduced-form coefficients Π. The latter are consistent, and, if the model is correct, Π satisfies $B\Pi = \Gamma$ which corresponds to (10) and (11) in the present problem. Therefore, if we solve (10) and (11) for H, K, and β (the structural parameters) using the least-squares estimate $\widehat{G}$ for G and consistent estimates $\widehat{A}$ and $\widehat{C}$ for A and C, we will obtain consistent estimates of the former, as we will obtain consistent estimates of B and Γ by solving $B\widehat{\Pi} = \Gamma$.

As the first step of this method, we obtain least-squares estimates $\widehat{G}$ of the coefficients in the multivariate regression of x_t on y_{t-1}. If the target vector a_t and the intercept b_t in the model are constant through time, h_t is also a constant satisfying equation (7) with the subscript $t + 1$ replaced by t. We have $g_t = g$. Otherwise, the coefficients $\widehat{G}$ will be estimated by adding some smooth trends in the regression equations.

Having obtained $\widehat{G}$, we will find H, K, and β to satisfy equations (10) and (11), but as in the case of overidentified structural equations, there may be more equations than unknowns. Defining $R = (r_{ij}) = \widehat{A} + \widehat{C}\widehat{G}$, we write these equations as

$$C'HR = 0 \tag{20}$$

$$K = H - \beta R'HR. \tag{21}$$

Let H be a symmetric $p \times p$ matrix with elements h_{ij}, and let C be a $p \times q$ matrix with elements c_{ij}. These two equations imply, respectively,

$$\sum_{i,j}^{p} c_{im} r_{jl} h_{ij} = 0 \quad (m = 1, \ldots, q; \; l = 1, \ldots, p) \tag{22}$$

$$h_{ml} - \beta \sum_{i,j}^{p} r_{im} r_{jl} h_{ij} = 0 \quad \text{if } k_{ml} = 0. \tag{23}$$

Both (22) and (23) are linear equations in $h_{ij} = h_{ji}$. Let h be the column vector consisting of the $p(p + 1)/2$ elements $h_{ij}(i = 1, \ldots, p; j \geqq i)$. Write (22) and (23) as

$$\underset{\sim}{Q}h = 0. \tag{24}$$

Exact, over-, or underidentification occurs according as the rank of Q is equal to, larger than, or smaller than $p(p + 1)/2 - 1$. In the overidentified case, there will be more equations than unknowns in (24); the elements on its right-hand side cannot all vanish. Corresponding to the method of indirect least squares, one can suggest discarding extra equations in (24) and solving the remaining $p(p + 1)/2$ homogeneous linear equations which are made nonhomogeneous by a normalization $h_{pp} = 1$. This method is still consistent but it discards useful information. Corresponding to the method of two-stage least squares, according to the interpretation of Chow (1964), we normalize by setting $h_{pp} = 1$ (or any $h_{ii} = 1$), partition Q and h', respectively, as $(Q_1 \, q_2)$ and $(h'_1 \, 1)$ to write (24) as

$$Q_1 h_1 + q_2 = 0 \qquad (25)$$

and estimate h_1 by $\widehat{h}_1 = -(Q'_1 Q_1)^{-1} Q'_1 q_2$ using the method of least squares.

Corresponding to the method of limited-information maximum likelihood, according to the interpretation of Chow (1964), we normalize symmetrically by setting $h'h = $ constant and find h to minimize $h'Q'Qh$ subject to this normalization constraint. The minimizing h is the characteristic vector associated with the smallest characteristic root of $Q'Q$. Unlike the method of two-stage least squares, this method yields a vector estimate of h which is invariant with respect to the choice of the variable for normalization. However, if the order of Q is very large, the symmetric normalization is not recommended because it is computationally expensive. If β is unknown, one has to find a scalar to minimize the appropriate sum of squares, be it $h'_1 Q'_1 Q_1 h_1$ or $h'Q'Qh$, but this is an easy problem. Having obtained h and β, we use the remaining equations of (21), other than (23), to compute the nonzero elements of K. Having estimated G, g, A, C, b, and H consistently, we can use (46) in the Appendix to estimate a. Given $H, \widehat{A}$, and $\widehat{C}$, we can obtain a new estimate $\widehat{G}_{(2)}$ of G by using (10).

If the estimates of H, β, and K by the method of this section are not accepted as final, they can serve as initial estimates to be used in the (more expensive) maximization of the likelihood function by the method of Section I. The consistent estimates of this section can be recommended if the numerical maximization of the likelihood function is too expensive.

IV. The Assumptions of Rational Expectations Models

Besides providing practical methods, the above discussion has pinpointed the problems involved in the estimation of linear rational expectations models. It should be pointed out that even when the problems are overcome, the estimates by the method of Section I will still not satisfy the assumptions of rational expectations.

If the economic agents and the econometrician share the same model (1) and (1) indeed is the true model of the economic environment (two strong assumptions), the optimal policy for maximizing the expectation of the objective function (2), correctly specified by the econometrician (another assumption), is *not* equation (3) with coefficients given by (4)–(7) because the economic agents do not know (and are not assumed to know) the numerical values of the parameters A, C, and b exactly. Given uncertainty concerning A, C, and b, equations (4)–(7) no longer specify the parameters of the optimal behavioral equation for the agents to maximize the expectation of (2). In fact, no one knows how to compute the truly optimal behavioral equation. Some perhaps nearly optimal solutions are given in chapters 10 and 11 of Chow (1975), for example. Equations (4)–(7) only specify the certainty-equivalent solution which is not optimal when A, C, and b are uncertain. Strictly speaking, a true believer in rational expectations models should use the optimal behavioral equation which no one knows, or at least the more complicated, but more nearly optimal behavioral equation as referenced above. Economists who build models other than rational expectations models have been criticized for their failure to take optimizing behavior into account. The question is how far one should push optimizing behavior in building economic models for multiperiod decision under uncertainty and where one should stop.

As it has been recognized, current practitioners of rational expectations models often ignore, or fail to model explicitly, the process of learning by the economic agents about the economic environment (1) and assume, as in the method of Section II, that a steady state is always observed for the optimal behavioral equation (3). The modeling of learning will automatically be incorporated if one uses a behavioral equation which is more nearly optimal than the certainty-equivalent strategy by taking into account the uncertainty in the model parameters. Such behavioral equation incorporates the process of learning, is strictly speaking nonlinear in y_{t-1}, and is time-dependent. The estimation of such models is much more difficult. Again, how far should one push the assumption of optimal behavior? How useful are the models based on approximate solutions (how approximate?) to optimal behavior as exemplified by the methods of this paper?

V. Estimating Nonlinear Rational Expectations Models

It is well recognized that the assumption of rational expectations makes the construction of nonlinear models difficult (because the expectation of a nonlinear function is not the nonlinear function of the expectation). Insofar as the world is nonlinear, it becomes an unattractive assumption to use. Since this assumption is not strictly followed by its practitioners even for linear models with uncertain coefficients, one may boldly apply the certainty-equivalent strategy to nonlinear stochastic models by first linearizing the models as suggested in Chow (1975, chap. 12). The methods of this paper will then be applicable to the estimation of nonlinear models by introducing the following modifications.

For the methods of Sections I and II: (a) Starting with some estimates of the parameter vector θ of a nonlinear model (1) and the parameters β, K, ϕ, and a of the objective function (2) linearize the model (1) to yield $y_t = \widehat{A}_t y_{t-1} + \widehat{C}_t x_t + \widehat{b}_t + \widehat{u}_t$. (b) Compute the coefficients G_t and g_t of the optimal linear feedback control equation (3) using the linear model and the parameters of (2). Note that equations (4)–(7) will have time subscripts for A and C. (c) Evaluate the likelihood function for models (1) and (3). (d) Take one step in a numerical maximization algorithm and return to (a).

For the method of Section III: (a') Using a consistent estimate $\widehat{\theta}$ of the parameter vector of a nonlinear model (1), linearize the model as in (a) above. (b') Compute least-squares estimates $\widehat{G}$ and $\widehat{g}_t$ of the coefficients in a regression of x_t on y_{t-1} and appropriate trends. (c') Define $R_t = (\widehat{A}_t + \widehat{C}_t \widehat{G})$. For each t, follow the methods of Section III to form $Q_t h = 0$, as in (24). Combine these equations by using $(1/n \sum_t^n Q_t)h = Qh = 0$ for (24) and proceed as before.

Appendix: Maximum Likelihood Estimation for $K_t = K$ and $a_t = a$

In this appendix, we provide a numerical method to maximize the likelihood function for the models (1) and (3), where (3) results from the maximization of (2) subject to the constraint (1), under the assumptions that $K_t = K$, $a_t = a$, that the system reaches a covariance stationary state, that the residual u_t in (1) is normal and serially uncorrelated, having a covariance matrix Σ, and that (3) contains an additive normal, serially uncorrelated residual which has a covariance matrix V and is uncorrelated with u_t.

Under the stated assumptions, the coefficients G and g in (3) are related to the parameters of (1) and (2) by the following four equations, as a specialization of (4)–(7).

$$(C'HC)G + C'HA = 0 \tag{26}$$

$$H - K - (A + CG)'H(A + CG) = 0 \tag{27}$$

$$(C'HC)g + C'(Hb - h) = 0 \tag{28}$$

$$(I - A - CG)'h - Ka - (A + CG)'Hb = 0. \tag{29}$$

The problem is the maximization of the likelihood function subject to the constraints (26)–(29). We form a Lagrangian expression which combines the log-likelihood with these constraints

$$L = \text{constant} - \frac{n}{2}\log|\Sigma| - \frac{n}{2}\log|V|$$

$$- \frac{1}{2}\text{tr}[\Sigma^{-1}(Y' - AY'_{-1} - CX' - bz')(Y - Y_{-1}A' - XC' - zb')]$$

$$- \frac{1}{2}\text{tr}[V^{-1}(X' - GY'_{-1} - gz')(X - Y_{-1}G' - zg')] - \text{tr}[\Omega(26)]$$

$$- \frac{1}{2}\text{tr}[\Phi(27)] - \omega'[(28)] - \phi'[(29)] - \frac{1}{2}\theta[\text{tr}(KK) - r]$$

where Y is an $n \times p$ matrix of observations on the endogenous variables; Y_{-1} is an $n \times p$ matrix of observations on the lagged endogenous variables; X is an $n \times q$ matrix of observations on the control variables; z represents a dummy variable being a vector consisting of n ones; Ω $(p \times q)$ and $\Phi = \Phi'$ $(p \times p)$ are matrices of Langrangian multipliers; ω $(q \times 1)$ and ϕ $(p \times 1)$ are vectors of Lagrangian multipliers; the numbers 26–29 in parentheses denote the corresponding constraints; and the last constraint $\text{tr}(KK) = r$ serves to normalize the matrix K, r being the number of target variables, or the number of nonzero diagonal elements in K. The unknowns in this problem consist of Σ, V, A, C, b, G, H, g, h, K, and a.

Using the differentiation rules $\partial \log |A|/\partial A = A^{-1\prime}$ and $\partial \text{tr}(AB)/\partial A = B'$, we differentiate L to obtain

$$\frac{\partial L}{\partial \Sigma^{-1}} = n\Sigma - (Y' - AY'_{-1} - CX' - bz')(Y - Y_{-1}A' - XC' - zb') = 0 \quad (30)$$

$$\frac{\partial L}{\partial V^{-1}} = nV - (X' - GY'_{-1} - gz')(X - Y_{-1}G' - zg') = 0 \quad (31)$$

$$\frac{\partial L}{\partial A'} = Y'_{-1}(Y - Y_{-1}A' - XC' - zb')\Sigma^{-1} - \Omega C'H + \Phi(A + CG)'H$$
$$- \Phi(Hb - h)' = 0 \quad (32)$$

$$\frac{\partial L}{\partial C'} = X'(Y - Y_{-1}A' - XC' - zb')\Sigma^{-1} - \Omega'(A + CG)'H - G\Omega C'H$$
$$+ G\Phi(A + CG)'H - g\omega'C'H - \omega g'C'H \quad (33)$$
$$- \omega(Hb - h)' - G\phi(Hb - h)' = 0$$

$$\frac{\partial L}{\partial b'} = z'(Y - Y_{-1}A' - XC' - zb')\Sigma^{-1} - \omega'C'H + \phi'(A + CG)'H = 0 \quad (34)$$

$$\frac{\partial L}{\partial G'} = Y'_{-1}(X - Y_{-1}G' - zg')V^{-1} - \Omega C'HC + \Phi(A + CG)'HC$$
$$- \phi(Hb - h)'C \quad (35)$$

$$\frac{\partial L}{\partial H} = -(A + CG)\Omega C' - C\Omega'(A + CG)' - \Phi + (A + CG)\Phi(A + CG)'$$
$$- Cg\omega'C' - C\omega g'C' - b\omega'C' - C\omega b' - b\phi'(A + CG)' - (A + CG)\phi b' \quad (36)$$

$$\frac{\partial L}{\partial K} \overset{*}{=} \Phi + a\phi' + \phi a' - \theta K \overset{*}{=} 0 \quad (37)$$

$$\frac{\partial L}{\partial g'} = z'(X - Y_{-1}G' - zg')V^{-1} - \omega'C'HC = 0 \quad (38)$$

$$\frac{\partial L}{\partial h} = C\omega - (I - A - CG)\phi = 0 \quad (39)$$

$$\frac{\partial L}{\partial a} \overset{*}{=} K\phi \overset{*}{=} 0. \quad (40)$$

Although K is a symmetric $p \times p$ matrix and a is a column vector of p elements, many of the elements in K and a are known to be zero. If there are r target variables, only an $r \times r$ submatrix of K and r elements in a are nonzero. The symbol $\overset{*}{=}$ in equations (37) and (40) indicates that only the derivatives of L with respect to the unknown elements of K and a are set equal to zero. Equations (26)–(40) will be solved for the unknown parameters.

First, consider equations (39) and (40). They are $p + r$ linear equations in the $p + q$ unknowns in ϕ and ω. If the number r of target variables equals or exceeds the number q of instruments (as we will so assume to make eq. [3] a unique solution of the economic agent's optimization problem), both Lagrangian multipliers ϕ and ω will be zero provided that the $(p + r) \times (p + q)$ matrix, with K^* composed of the r rows of K corresponding to the nonzero elements of a,

$$\begin{bmatrix} C & -(I - A - CG) \\ 0 & K^* \end{bmatrix}$$

is of rank $p + q$. The solution $\phi = 0$ and $\omega = 0$ from (39) and (40) simplifies many of the remaining equations.

Second, observe that as usual consistent estimates of the covariance matrices Σ and V can be obtained from (30) and (31), respectively, where the coefficients $(A \; C \; b)$ and $(G \; g)$ are replaced by the least-squares estimates. We therefore will treat Σ and V as given for the solution of the remaining equations. A firm believer in the method of maximum likelihood could always revise these estimates of Σ and V after the remaining equations are solved, and iterate until convergence.

Third, given any estimates of $(A \; C \; b)$, $(G \; g)$, and K, we will revise them for the next iteration by solving the following equations. (The initial estimates of $[A \; C \; b]$ and $[G \; g]$ are obtained by least squares; the initial K may be a diagonal matrix with r nonzero elements.) Equations (26) and (27) are used to solve for G and H. On account of (26) and $\phi = 0$, the last two terms of (35) vanish, and (35) can be used to solve for Ω. Equation (36) is used to obtain Φ by iteration,

$$\Phi = (A + CG)\Phi(A + CG)' - (A + CG)\Omega C' - C\Omega'(A + CG)'.$$

Equation (37) gives $K \overset{\pm}{=} \theta^{-1}\Phi$ for the unknown elements of K, where the Lagrangian multiplier θ is found by taking the trace of both sides of $\Phi^*\Phi^* = \theta^2 KK$ to yield $\theta^2 = \text{tr}(\Phi^*\Phi^*)/r$ where Φ^* is composed of nonzero elements from Φ and zero elements corresponding to the zero elements of K. Equations (32) and (33) are solved for A and C; they are modified "normal equations" for these coefficients. Equations (34) and (38) then give, respectively,

$$b = n^{-1}(Y' - AY'_{-1} - CX')z$$
$$g = n^{-1}(X' - GY'_{-1})z.$$

Now $(A \; C \; b)$, $(G \; g)$, and K are revised, and the iterations continue until convergence.

Fourth, there are only two remaining equations (33) and (34) to be used to solve for h and a. Solving (34) for h and substituting the result in (33), we obtain, denoting $A + CG$ by R,

$$C'[I - R']Ka = C'HCg + C'H[I - (I - R')^{-1}R']Hb.$$

Since C' is $q \times p$, this is a system of q linear equations for the r unknowns in a. If the number r of target variables equals the number q of control variables, the solution for a is unique. If $r > q$, the solution for a is not unique. This result is reasonable because the observable behavior of the economic agents which is relevant for the estimation of a consists of a $q \times 1$ vector g in the optimal feedback control equation. If a has more elements than g, it cannot be estimated uniquely.

References

Chow, G. C. "A Comparison of Alternative Estimators for Simultaneous Equations." *Econometrica* 32 (1964):532–53.
———. *Analysis and Control of Dynamic Economic Systems.* New York: Wiley, 1975.
Chow, G. C., and Megdal, S. B. "The Control of Large-Scale Nonlinear Econometric Systems." *IEEE Transactions on Automatic Control* AC-23 (1978): 344–49.
Friedlander, A. F. "Macro Policy Goals in the Postwar Period: A Study in Revealed Preference." *Q.J.E.* 87 (1973): 25–43.
Goldfeld, S. M., and Quandt, R. E. *Nonlinear Methods in Econometrics.* Amsterdam: North-Holland, 1972.

Hansen, L. P., and Sargent, T. J. "Formulating and Estimating Dynamic Linear Rational Expectations Models." *J. Econ. Dynamics and Control*, vol. 2 (1980), in press.

Lucas, R. E., Jr. "Econometric Policy Evaluation: A Critique." *J. Monetary Econ.* 1, suppl. (1976): 19–46.

Muth, J. F. "Rational Expectations and the Theory of Price Movements." *Econometrica* 29 (1961): 315–35.

Sargent, T. J. "Estimation of Dynamic Labor Demand Schedules under Rational Expectations. *J.P.E.* 86 (1978): 1009–44.

————. *Macroeconomic Theory.* New York: Academic Press, 1979.

Taylor, J. B. "Estimation and Control of a Macroeconomic Model with Rational Expectations." *Econometrica* 47 (1979): 1267–86.

Theil, H. *Economic Forecasts and Policy.* Amsterdam: North-Holland, 1958.

Robert E. Lucas, Jr., is John Dewey Distinguished Service Professor of Economics at the University of Chicago and author of *Studies in Business-Cycle Theory*.

Thomas J. Sargent is professor of economics at the University of Minnesota and advisor to the Federal Reserve Bank of Minneapolis. He is the author of *Macroeconomic Theory*.